CHRISTIAN
MISSION
TO
MUSLIMS

CHRISTIAN MISSION TO MUSLIMS

The Record

Anglican and Reformed Approaches
in India and the Near East, 1800 - 1938

Lyle. L. Vander Werff

William Carey Library

533 HERMOSA STREET • SOUTH PASADENA, CALIF. 91030

Library of Congress Cataloging in Publication Data

Vander Werff, Lyle L   1934–
   Christian mission to Muslims.

   (The William Carey Library series on Islamic studies)
   Bibliography: p.
   1. Missions to Muslims--History. I. Title.
BV2625.V36   266'.3'5   77-24027
ISBN 087808-320-0

In accord with some of the most recent thinking in the academic press, the William Carey Library is pleased to present this scholarly book which has been prepared from an author-edited and author-prepared camera-ready manuscript.

Published by the William Carey Library
533 Hermosa Street
South Pasadena, Calif. 91030

PRINTED IN THE UNITED STATES OF AMERICA

Contents

v

Contents

Preface

Th⸀ᵕ endeavor represents research growing out of the author's mission service in the Near East and doctoral work completed at the University of Edinburgh. The aim is to offer the reader access to the treasury of experience and literature resulting from nineteenth and twentieth century missions to Muslims. The author desires to acknowledge his deep indebtedness to the Rev. Dr. W. Montgomery Watt, Professor of Arabic and Islamic Studies, University of Edinburgh and the Rev. A. C. Cheyne, Professor of Ecclesiastical History, New College, University of Edinburgh, for their guidance and penetrating comments. Thanks are extended to the librarians and staffs of the University of Edinburgh, New College, the National Library of Scotland, Western Theological Seminary of Holland, Michigan, Princeton Theological Seminary, and numerous correspondents in India, the Near East and North America. The inspiration and support granted through the Arabian Mission of the Reformed Church in America, the Church of Christ in Kuwait, the Jerusalem School of Islamics under Dr. A. K. Cragg, the World Council of Churches and the Church of Scotland are likewise acknowledged with gratitude.

It is hoped that in some measure these labors will prove of good encouragement to the host of Christ's disciples living and witnessing among their Muslim neighbors. Hopefully this work is consistent with the larger biblical vision granted by God through prophet, Messiah, and apostle. This vision is voiced in the Abrahamic prayer and the motto of the Arabian Mission: "O that Ishmael might live in thy sight!" (Gen. 17:18); in Jesus' words: ". . . I lay down my life for the sheep. And I have other sheep that are not of this fold; I must bring them also, and they will heed my voice. So there shall be one flock, one shepherd." (Jn. 10:15-16); and the abiding hope of Rev. 11:15: "The kingdom of the world has become the kingdom of our Lord and of his Christ, and he shall reign for ever and ever."

Introduction

"What constitutes an adequate Christian approach to non-Christian religious and secular man?" This contemporary question elicits lively discussion among Christians in many lands. The urgency of the question appears to be intensified by rapid world change. Technological advance, revolutionary social and political ferment, and the growing inter-dependence of nations means that the religions of man are to be in unavoidable contact. This situation of proximity and plurality could be described as the new era of inter-religion.

Christian-Muslim relationships and attitudes are no small part of this world scene. The Islamic community of about 700 million and the Christian community of over one billion, roughly half of the world's population, will have increasing contact. What shall be the end result of it? Their past record of trial and error, tension and enlightenment, hope and fear is all too descriptive of our universe and its humanity. Yet man desires something more than fragmentation and continual chaotic conflict. He longs for the experience of community, a realization of the true family of man. He realizes that he does not fulfill the true destiny for which he was created simply by co-existing in time and space with other inhabitants of this planet. Conflicting or even parallel existence will not suffice. In his deep interior, man is aware that his problem is theological. The solution of wholeness (peace, shalom, salaam) is to be found in his Creator.

The Christian's relationship with his fellow-man has been revolutionized by God's revelation and action in Jesus Christ. While mission is older than Christianity inasmuch as the redemption of the universe is rooted in the eternal will and

historical activity of the Creator (Eph. 1, 3:1-12), it was only
with the coming of Christ that the offer of salvation to all
nations and the sending forth of messengers became fully manifest
(Matt. 28:18-20; Mk. 16:15; Luke 24:46-48; Jn. 20:21; Acts 1:8,
9:15, 26:16-18, etc.). Thus from its inception, the Christian
faith had been a call to mission; God requiring the disciple to
share in the work Christ initiated. Christ's mission becomes
the Christian's commission. Yet under the Spirit's direction,
each age of disciples must think out and work out the implications behind the ongoing energetic discussion.

The twentieth century has especially become the scene of debate
as to the interpretation and implementation of mission. World
War I and its aftermath concluded a great century of missions
from West to East and ushered in the spirit of re-evaluation.
This debate regarding the theory and practice of mission reached
a climax at Tambaram (Madras) in 1938. It had continued, however,
and with each new conference the participants increase, numer-
ically and vocally. The question as to what is the correct
strategy or approach, in this case towards Muslims, goes on.

In the post-Tambaram conversations, many stressed the uniqueness of God's revelation in Christ, i.e. the Christian message.
Some felt this implies a contrast, a discontinuity, with all
other religions of man. Most of those holding to this point of
view agree however that this unique message from God can be
presented in a sympathetic way to all men. This view finds various
expressions and emphases, but agrees as to the biblical fundamentals concerning the proclamation of a Christocentric message and
the requirements of discipleship, i.e. conversion and the new
life in the Christian community.[1] Another position holds that the
Christian faith in some measure is the corrective or fulfillment
of non-Christian religions in their efforts to express and meet
the religious needs of man.[2] Yet others contend that Christianity
must become the partner of the great, especially monotheistic,
religions over against naturalistic monistic religions and
secularization. Proponents of this view, while rejecting or re-
interpreting the idea of syncretistic religion, do hold to a
policy of co-operation, complementary religion, or reconception.
Often this view implies that behind all religions there is one
religion or that one religion will emerge from the inter-religion
scene.[3] Still others, while retaining their claim to being
Christian, would completely disassociate themselves from mission
except in the sense of pure service. They try to work out the
question of relationships in cultural or sociological, not
theological, terms.[4] Again others while agreeing that the Christian approach must be sympathetic, reject any compromise of the
uniqueness and theological essence of the Christian faith. They
hold fast to the content of the Christian message, but feel that
proclamation of a transcendental message and a stress on discontinuity is inadequate. They stress instead witness via Christian
presence and dialogue which reaches for the latent, partial

truths of Christ (the Logos) in the heart of the listener.[5]
Another group observes that Christianity is in an age of revolution, a world that is undergoing secularization. This process,
they note, is sweeping the world clear of religion, perhaps even
Christianity in its present form. This is not to be feared for
it will permit the kingly rule of Christ to be realized in fuller
measure. Some would go so far as to say that the Christian faith
and secularization stand over against all religions and pseudo-
religions, i.e. secularism, humanism, etc.[6] Finally others have
critically and cautiously re-emphasized the biblical basis of
mission, the motive and spirit of love, and the ambassador-
servant role of the church. Perhaps the healthiest approaches
to Muslims that have recently evolved are those which have made
critical use of the Gairdner-Cragg and Zwemer-Kraemer trends.
Such views have emerged at Asmara (1959), New Delhi (1961) and
since. There is usually emphasis on the nature of witness, the
value of personal friendship in communication, the necessity of
discipleship and church-building, and the missionary[7](as well as
ecumenical and eschatological) nature of the church.
    It is the author's view that any attempt to understand or
participate in, much less evaluate, this present on-going debate
regarding mission demands certain prerequisites. First, the
biblical-theological basis for Christian mission as given in
God's revelation in Christ (recorded in the Bible) and received
within the community of faith (the church) must be examined.[8]
Second, one must grasp something of the theological development
in the Western church from the Reformation to present. Certain
aspects of these developments had repercussions in both mission
theory and practice.[9] Third, one must become acquainted with
the actual history of Christian missions. The expansion of
Christianity (i.e. the encounter with many cultures and religions,
the birth of younger churches and the renewal of ancient ones)
has brought a fuller realization of the nature of the church-
kingdom of Christ and its role in world history.[10]
    This study will examine the historical development of various
Anglican and Reformed missions to Muslims as an answer to the
vital question: What consitutes a Christian approach or approaches
to Muslims? It is written in the conviction that history contains lessons that man can learn in the light of Christ. As
McGavran says:

    The Church can develop right strategy in mission. All she
    has to do is to observe what has taken place in the hundreds
    of matchless laboratories which a hundred and sixty years of
    modern missions have provided. By amassing knowledge, by
    pooling the common experience of missions and churches, by
    assembling the evidences of instances where the Church was
    planted, where it grew, where it stopped growing, and where
    it never even started, she can discern which processes in
    which specific circumstances receive God's blessing and
    which do not. Right strategy will spend large sums of money

and the lives of some of its best men and women in intensive
research into the most effective ways and means of reconciling
men to God and of multiplying churches. [11]

The inquiry into what actually occurred in-the-field during the
nineteenth and early twentieth centuries has but begun. This
history of the church-in-mission demands serious consideration.
In a missiological study, one finds two levels requiring attention. First, there is the actual activity of a person or group
as they labor on the field to communicate their message, build
the church and achieve other objectives in the given situation.
Their interpretation of their message greatly affects their
course of action. Second, there is the reflection of a person
or group upon their activity, the formulation of what may be
called, an approach. In such they describe their motives, methods, means, and objectives. They may also struggle with such
crucial issues as the meaning of mission, the content of their
message, their relation to non-Christian religions, their relation to the culture of the land, the eschatological understanding
of the church-kingdom, etc. Some scholars attempt to keep these
two levels of activity and approach separate, but this seems
neither possible nor desirable. [12] This is especially true when
examining the nineteenth century where one finds the best source
materials for Christian approaches interwoven into the very life,
work and writings of men serving in the field. Occasionally the
life and work of individuals or groups discloses an approach
which may not agree with their written statements.

The quantity of primary materials for Anglican and Reformed
contributions to the Christian mission to Muslims in India and
the Near East from Henry Martyn to Samuel Zwemer, 1800-1938, is
almost overwhelming. There are surveys, appeals, and reports of
individual missionaries and mission societies; studies of lands,
peoples, their history and religion; tracts, booklets, and literature used in evangelism on the mission field; autobiographical
accounts and frequently articles and monographs by missionaries
themselves. Of more secondary nature, yet valuable, are the
official histories and numerous biographies. Wherever possible,
the author will show preference for primary monographs, correspondence, and writings of personnel engaged in the actual work.
The reports of the various missionary conferences also contain
a wealth of material.

Of necessity, a study such as this must contain certain self-
imposed restrictions. First, this study has been confined to the
time-span from the advent of modern Protestant missions to the
crisis at Tambaram, 1800-1938. While this may appear unwieldy
in itself, it proves a needful overview revealing important
development in both theory and practice. For those who would
fully realize the strides achieved, the preceding twelve centuries
of Muslim-Christian relationships and attitudes must also be
examined briefly. Second, this research has been limited geographically to endeavours in northern India (present-day Pakistan

and North India) and the Near East (sometimes called the Middle
East or Western Asia, but defined in this case as running from
Egypt to Iran, from Turkey to the Arabian Peninsula). This is
not to minimize the vital mission work carried on in Indonesia
and the Far East, or Africa, or in southern Europe. Thirdly,
this study concentrates on the work of the churches of the
Reformation. Roman Catholic ventures preceded, paralleled and
sometimes surpassed Protestant efforts. More limited, and not
yet given their due credit, are the Russian Orthodox missions.
In the process of this research, it was discovered that the bulk
of mission work for Muslims in the above lands was initiated by
various Anglican and Reformed (includes Presbyterian and Congregational) groups. By confining this study to them, it is not to
be forgotten that many other dedicated individuals and bands
sacrificially labored and labor still in the name of Christ.
Fourthly, wherever possible representative figures of Anglican
and Reformed efforts have been selected as focal points. Where
available, monographs of these representatives have been examined
in addition to their life and work. In those areas or situations
where the work lacked distinct leaders or the emphasis was placed
upon a team-effort, the broader activity and approach of the
group have been treated. Other details have been extracted from
thousands of pages of surveys, reports and histories to describe
the milieu and flow of this unfolding drama of mission.
    A quick preusal of the table of contents reveals the author's
arrangement of the materials. In chapter one, a brief examination
is made of the development of the concept of mission and the
growth of various attitudes towards Islam in Protestant circles
from the Reformation to 1800. Chapter two, a study in methods,
presents the development of the rather direct approaches made to
Muslims by Anglican and Reformed workers in northern India from
1800 to 1910 and the emergence of churches conscious of their
unity and mission to Islam. Chapter three describes the activities and approaches of Reformed and Anglican workers in the Near
East from 1800-1910. One discovers the Near Eastern situation
was complicated by ecclesiastical relations, governmental restrictions, social pressures, and communal tensions. In order to
grasp what was intended and what actually happened, the student
of history must devote more attention to the activity of the
mission societies and churches and thus less to individuals.
The concluding chapter discloses the emergence of maturing ecumenical Anglican and Reformed approaches to Muslims in the persons
and writings of W. H. T. Gairdner and Samuel M. Zwemer. These
two outstanding figures give honorable representation to developments in their traditions over the preceding century. It is the
author's belief that they deserve fuller attention than they
have been given inasmuch as they serve as hinges between the best
of their traditions in two centuries. They give expression to
the culmination of nineteenth century efforts to reach Muslims
for Christ and introduce the twentieth century's concern for
sympathetic communication of the Gospel to the people of Islam.

It is hoped that this study may contribute in some measure to
an appreciation of the great achievement made in thought and
action between 1800 and 1938; to an understanding of the significance of the debate regarding theology and mission since World
War I; and to the strengthening of the church in her present
resolve and effort of mission to Muslims in the name of Jesus
Christ.

1

The Formation of a
Protestant Concept of Mission
1500 - 1800

THE STATE OF AFFAIRS AT THE BEGINNING OF THE SIXTEENTH CENTURY

The prospects for a successful Christian mission to Muslims
were far from promising at the start of the sixteenth century.
The Roman Catholic Church itself was suffering from internal
decay and stagnation. Forces within and without its borders
threatened its fragmentation. Numerous ills resulted from its
close identification with empire. Still it is reasonable to
believe that lack of vitality was not the most serious obstacle
to the evangelization of those peoples living under the banner
of Islam. The real barriers were deeply embedded in the past.
These were the inheritance of Protestantism.

First, there was the legacy of Christian-Muslim frictions and
resultant attitudes. Even the rise of Islam had stemmed from
past difficulties. The political struggles of Rome and Persia,
the controversies of the ancient churches and the failure to
convey the Christian faith to the Arabs had left a situation ripe
for an alternative religion.[1] Muhammad's milieu (A.D. 570-632),
his contacts with dynamic and distorted Christianity and his
disturbing experiences with the Jews not only shaped his understanding of the Christian faith, but future relationships with
Christians.[2] Military clash soon had generated hatred. The
amazing success of the Arab conquests under the four caliphs
(Rashidun, A.D. 632-661) brought many Muslims and Christians
face-to-face in unequal relationship.[3] Under the Umayyad Dynasty
(A.D. 661-750), Christian teachers, translators and office
bearers (e.g. John of Damascus) made direct contributions to
Muslim life and began to shape apologies patterned after earlier

7

controversies with Judaism.[4] While the process of exchange and
assimilation (esp. philosophy and theology) continued under the
'Abbasids and Saljuqs (A.D. 750-1258), Christian and Muslim communal life and opinion further polarized.[5] As the dhimmis (subject peoples) felt increased pressures to convert, Christian-
Muslim apologetics/polemics intensified. Although favorable
encounters did occur in such provinces as Spain and Sicily,
Christian-Muslim relationships under the Saljuqs (A.D. 1055-1258)
broke down. In the medieval period, life retreated into feudal
isolation. Then the rise of the Italian city-states, the crusades
and the Latin states signaled new stirrings in Europe. While the
crusades produced certain benefits (e.g. commercial, cultural,
religious intercourse), they also manufactured the acids of
bitterness long remembered.[6] They almost obscured the brighter
opportunities, then tragedy, that surrounded the entrance of the
Mongols into Near Eastern life.[7] Certainly they nurtured the
rancor and polemics of the thirteenth and fourteenth centuries.[8]
These were active ingredients still shaping both Christian and
Muslim attitudes in the sixteenth century.

Second, there was frequent military conflict with only limited
contacts for conversation. The Turkish forces continued to press
northwards through the Balkans deep into Hungary, at times
threatening all of Europe. One of the few benefits accruing
from this struggle was the returning prisoners of war who brought
with them a new awareness of Islam. Ottoman advances resulted
in many captive Christians being carried deep into Muslim territory. The eyewitness accounts of those who did return would
serve to remove many illusions about Islam and the East.[9] For
example, Johannes Schiltberger, who was captured at the Battle
of Nicopolis (1396), wrote of his experience in Bondage and Travels
upon release (1427).[10] Another, Fr. George of Hungary (ca.1422-
1502), recorded his years in Ottoman domains (1436-1458) in
Tractus de Moribus Condicionibus et Nequicia Turcorum. This
document which saw many editions (Latin edition of 1530-31 included a preface by Luther) was marked by a lack of polemics. Its
simple narration must have provided fascinating reading for an
information-hungry Europe.[11] Europe borrowed and benefited from
her Mediterranean, especially Spanish, contacts with Muslims.[12]

Thirdly, it must be admitted that Europe's knowledge of Islam
was rather restricted. Attitude rather than lack of opportunity
produced this situation. Much literature was created simply for
polemic or propaganda purposes. Fragments of fact and ornate
fiction were blended to defeat the opponents and to defend
Europe's alleged superiority. Many prejudicial distortions of
Islam continued to flourish in medieval Europe.[13]

Fourthly, the sixteenth century was heir to the attempts and
failure of Roman Catholic missions to Muslims. The twelfth century of learning had witnessed the efforts of the monks of Cluny
under Peter the Venerable to gain knowledge of and access to
Islam via Spain.[14] The thirteenth century saw increased missionary activity and writing under St. Francis (who served in Egypt)

and his order; such Dominicans as Humbert of Romans, San Ramon, and Raymond Martini; the Redemptionist Fathers in North Africa; the embassies of William of Rubroek and others to the Mongols, and such leading figures in missions and learning as William of Tripolis, Thomas Aquinas and Roger Bacon.[15] Darkness and despair, indifference and defiance of Islam again troubled fourteenth century Europe. Christian missions were in difficult straits in spite of the realism of Ricoldus de Monte Crucis (d. 1320) and the vision and courage of Raymond Lull (1235-1314), whom many consider the first great missionary to Muslims.[16] While Jerome Xavier bravely engaged in controversy at Akbar's Court (1580) in North India and others continued writing to Muslims, no one could erase the fact that mission to Islam had largely failed.[17]

While the record of missions to Muslims looked unpromising, there were certain glimmers of hope, moments of vision. Forces and figures were at work, in fact the very ones influencing the Reformation, shaped improved attitudes and activity concerning Islam. Europe was experiencing intellectual and religious "combustion". A middle class or bourgeois arose to give new vitality to society and church. Contacts with the world outside Christendom gave added impetus to linguistics, military science, manual crafts, commerce, philosophy, etc. During the Renaissance, advances were made in translating Greek and Arabic works and in the development of science. Roger Bacon helped form a new methodology by replacing the metaphysical question of "Why things happen" with "How they happen". Robert Grosseteste added to this experimental approach to subjects.[18] This helped clear the way for a more scholarly approach to Islam, e.g. Richard Fitzralph.[19] At the same time Eastern mysticism became the subject of the Florentine poets and the German Mystics. All Europe was being transformed as the frozen concept of Holy Roman Empire gave way to new national states. Europe abounded with new energy.

Even more remarkable were the religious stirrings. Although the Roman Catholic Church claimed to be the sole channel of salvation and at times exhibited a calloused exclusiveness to those outside her borders, there were notable exceptions. Brave individuals attempting a more accurate presentation of the Christian faith, began uprooting the misconceptions obstructing the mission of Christ to extend the grace of God to men of all realms, races and religions. Several examples may suffice. Uthred of Boldon, a Benedictine monk at the University of Oxford during the 1360s, had declared that at the moment of death all human beings, Christian, Muslim and others were given a direct vision of God. Their response to this determined their eternal destiny. Although this view was condemned, it discloses a man trying to relax Rome's restrictive grip and to recover the concept of God's mercy in Christ. His compassion for non-Christians breathes the spirit of Christian mission.[20] The pre-reformer, John Wyclif (ca.1328-1384) attained an understanding of Islam far in advance of his age. He acknowledged that the

ills of the church had separated Latin and Orthodox Christians,
promoting the rise of Islam and that pride, worldly power and
self-will afflicted both Rome and Islam. Only a return to the
poverty and spirit of Christ could meet the "problem" of Islam.
Wyclif mocked the appeals to war and the claims of either religion
to "given realms", i.e. Christendom or Dar-al-Islam. Salvation is
offered to the whole world and the sole condition is "belief in
the Lord Jesus Christ". His views and works were seen as dangerous and condemned, yet his ideas continued to percolate in the
West long after his bones were burnt.[21] Similar concern for
those outside the Christian community was expressed by John Hus
of Bohemia (1313-1415), Peter Waldo and his Poor Men of Lyons,
the German mystics (Theologia Germanica), the Brethren of the
Common Life and Girolamo Savonarola of Italy (1452-1498).

    Some Roman Catholic leadership also expressed concern for bet-
ter Christian-Muslim relationships. The ventures of four bishops
of different nationalities and experience in the period (1450-
1460), have been described as a moment of vision.[22] Spaniard
John of Segovia (ca. 1400-1458) directed a translation of the
Quran (Qur'ān) from the Arabic and proposed a conference of the
two religions. Even if the assembly failed to win Muslims to the
Christian faith, he argued, it would produce thirty other
religious and practical benefits. Nicholas of Cusa (1401-1464),
a German textual scholar of note, compares the Quranic and Christian portrayals of God in a hypothetical dialogue of representatives of the world's religions who are seeking the good and the
true. Free from polemical narrowness, he advised studying the
ideas and practices of Islam via the "lay-opinion" of merchants
of the Near East and then to discuss the issues with Muslim
delegates in a great conference. By use of literary, historical
and philological criticism in The Sieving of the Koran (Cribratio
Alchoran, 1460), he reveals that the Quran has three strands:
(1) basic Nestorian Christianity, (2) anti-Christian sentiments
urged upon Muhammad by Jewish advisors, and (3) corruptions added
after Muhammad's death by correctors. His ability to limit the
area of discussion, his treatment of the Quran as a historical
document (hence eliminating the need for vicious polemics), and
his realization that Christian-Muslim tension reflected Western-
Nestorian discussion regarding the nature of God's manifestation
in Christ, identifies Nicholas of Cusa as a distinguished
Christian scholar. In a more polemic spirit, the tracts, Adversus
Mahometanos et infideles and Adversus Alcoranum by Jean.Germain
(ca. 1400-1461) a Frenchman of Cluny concluded that there must be
a revival of martial and spiritual Christianity to improve Christian-Muslim relationships. Aeneas Silvius (1405-1464; Pope:
1458-1464) reflected the rational humanism of the Renaissance.
His letter to Muhammad II, the conqueror of Constantinople (1460),
is simply a polemical show of strength. While neglecting the
finer Christian spirit, it represents a humanisitc attempt to
find a solution other than the sword. These four men, as Southern has shown, have mastered the new knowledge of the thirteenth

century, gained the capacity of self-criticism of the fourteenth
century, and admit the complexity of the Muslim problem while
differing in their solutions.[23] This then was the setting for
the Reformation, the legacy of attitudes and activity that Protestants were to inherit.

THE REFORMATION: FORCES OF FERMENTATION

To the surprise of many, the Reformation did not bring a sudden
unleashing of Protestant mission activity. A number of writers,
including several Roman Catholics, charge the Reformers with
neglect of the subject.[24] Others, more fairly it seems, find the
missionary ideal latent in their teachings.[25]
The Reformers disrupted as well as renewed the affairs of the
church. They plowed up the establishment to make way for new life:
recovering the Word, unshackling the doctrine of grace and liber-
ating a sector of the church of Christ. Although preoccupied
with the Scriptures, popes and politics, they took a preparatory
step towards modern missions.
Admittedly, Martin Luther (1483-1546) did not explicitly devise
a mission program, but he did have much to say about Islam and
the preaching of the Word. It is a mistake to test him by the
standard of nineteenth century missions, but fair to expect a
biblical understanding of mission.[26] Again it is wrong to hold
that Luther's eschatology and doctrine of election curtailed the
development of his concept of mission. Frequently eschatology
works as an incentive. In Luther's case, it may have promoted
his pessimism (He saw the church surrounded by devils in an era
of darkness) and his belief in the vocation of every Christian
to witness (against the Roman idea of apostolic succession). He
stands closer to the twentieth century theologians of the Word
than to the nineteenth century confidence in man's ability and
progress. Luther never allowed his belief that the Turks were
God's instruments of judgment on the sins of Christendom to rule
out their evangelization. Nor did the expectation of Christ's
return dispose this vigorous preacher to inactivity. He writes:

Before the last day comes, church rule and the Christian
faith must spread over all the world, as the Lord Christ fore-
told that there should not be a city in which the Gospel should
not be preached, and that the Gospel must go through all the
world, so that all should have the witness in their conscience,
whether they believe it or not....The Gospel has been in Egypt,
but is now away; then it has been in Greece and Italy, in
Spain, France and other lands. Now it is in Germany, for how
long who knows? In the eleventh chapter to the Romans, St.
Paul says also that the Gospel must be preached through all
the world, so that all the heathen may hear, that the fulness
of the heathen is thus to be brought to heaven.[27]

While Luther does not prepare a program of missions _per se_, he
was keen on preaching the Gospel to all lands. He certainly was
aware that the task was unfinished.

All the world does not mean one or two parts; but everywhere where people are, thither the Gospel must speed and
still ever speeds, so that even if it does not remain always
in a place, it yet must come to, and sound forth in, all parts
and corners of the earth.[28]

There is of course, partial realization of the Kingdom.

The spiritual Jerusalem, which is the Kingdom of Christ,
must be extended by the Gospel throughout the whole world.
That has already come to pass. The Gospel has been preached,
and upon it the Kingdom of God has been firmly established
in all places under heaven, so that it now reaches and abides
to the end of the world, and in it we, by the mercy and compassion of God are citizens.[29]

But Luther was too pessimistic about man's ability and the
presence of evil to imagine victory without struggle.

What the Lord says of other sheep which He must also bring,
so that there shall be one fold and one shepherd, began immediately after Pentecost, when the Gospel was preached by the
Apostles through all the world, and will continue so to be
until the end of the world. Not so that all men shall turn
and accept the Gospel. That will never be. The Devil will
never let that come to pass. Therefore there will ever be in
the world many faiths and religions.[30]

An Ascension Sermon reveals Luther's awareness of the call to
evangelize.

Here there rises a question on this passage: 'Go ye into
all the world,' as to how it is to be understood and held
fast, since verily the Apostles have not come into all the
world, for no Apostle has come to us, and also many islands
have been discovered in our day where the people are heathen
and no one has preached to them: yet the scripture saith
their voice has sounded forth into all lands. Answer; their
preaching has gone out into all the world, though it has not
yet come into all the world. That out-going has been begun
and gone on, though it has not yet been fulfilled and accomplished; but there will be further and wider preaching until
the last day. When the Gospel has been preached, heard, published and through the whole world, then the commission shall
have been fulfilled, and the last day shall come. [31]

Although he did not deputize messengers for the East, Luther
emphasized the universality of Christianity and its elevation
above the limits of place, time, rank, and nations. There is a
tremendous mission impulse latent in some of his teaching.

> When it is said in the 117th Psalm, 'Praise the Lord all
> ye heathen,' we are assured that we are heathen, and that we
> also shall certainly be heard by God in heaven.... If all the
> heathen shall praise God, it must first be that He shall be
> their God. Shall He be their God? Then they must know Him
> and believe in Him, and put away all idolatry since God cannot
> be praised with idolatrous lips or with unbelieving hearts.
> Shall they believe? Then they must first hear His Word and
> by it receive the Holy Ghost, Who cleanses and enlightens
> their hearts through faith. Are they to hear His Word? Then
> preachers must be sent who shall declare to them the Word of
> God. [32]

Luther lamented the difficulty of filling Protestant pulpits in
Germany, for alas he had no preachers to spare for foreign lands.
Yet the Gospel could be preached abroad, for witness was also the
activity of the laity! It must be concluded that Luther's limited
treatment of mission is due to external circumstances, not to
theological defect.

What was Luther's attitude towards and understanding of Islam?
The Turks were certainly a significant problem! They had overrun
Belgrade, destroyed the King and the prime young men of Hungary
in the battle of Mohacz (1526), besieged Vienna (1529) and
threatened the yet unorganized League of German States (1532).
Luther's response to the situation is related to his doctrine of
the two swords (re: the Christian's dual but separate obligations
to church and state). Temporal rulers must counter the political-
military threat but not in the name of Christianity (i.e. rejects
crusade idea). Something more is expected from the church.

> It does not belong to the Pope, in so far as he would be
> a Christian, yea, the chiefest and best preacher of Christ,
> to lead a church army or a Christian army, for the church must
> not fight with the sword. It has other weapons, another sword
> and other wars, with which it has enough to do, and must not
> mix itself up with the wars of the emperor and the princes. [33]

In his Bulla de Coena Domini (1522), he demanded that the Pope
send evangelists rather than warriors to the Turks. He hoped that
Christians in Muslim lands might have a radiating influence; even
urged captive Christians to witness.

> Where thou dost faithfully and diligently serve, there thou
> mayest adorn and honour the Gospel and the name of Christ, so
> that thy master, and perhaps many others, evil as they are,
> shall be constrained to say, 'These Christians are faithful,

dutiful, pious, humble, diligent people,' and thus thou mayest
confound the faith of the Turks, and mayhap convert many when
they see that Christians surpass the Turks in humility, patience,
diligence, fidelity, and such like virtues. [34]

Here is then a mission of the laity. Under the circumstances,
Luther's attitude towards Turks is quite moderate in comparison
to many medieval writers.[35]
    In an ill-informed Europe, Luther took a rather scholarly
approach to Islam. Familiar with Avicenna and Averroes, he urges
use of Islam's primary materials. He published: Libellus de vita
et moribus Turcarum (1529), a study of the life and customs of
the Turks;[36] a preface and appendix to the German edition of
Ricoldo's Confutatio Alcorani (1542); and a preface to Buchmann's
Latin translation of the Quran (1542-43) which he had encouraged.[37]
This was in line with his desire for a knowledgeable laity.
Historically, Luther saw Islam as God's judgement upon Roman
corruption, a "rod of correction for our sins". But Islam has
set aside revelation for rationalism. It is the religion of "the
natural man". This partly explains its appeal and success, even
though it, like Rome the Anti-Christ, must one day be judged
according to revelation. There are numerous parallels between
Rome and Islam: abuse of secular power, lax morality, tradition
bound, and the legalistic doctrine of "salvation by works".[38]
Luther's solution to the dilemma is two-fold: reform and evangelism. In light of man's sinfulness, only prayer and repentence
will suffice. This means a return to the Word, the only news of
God's grace for men in despair. Closely akin to this is the
necessity for the preaching of this Word! Man's joy and hope are
linked to this task.
    Much could be said about Huldreich Zwingli (1484-1531), A. H.
Bullinger, Theodore Buchmann (or Bibliander), Philip Melanchthon
(1497-1560) and Martin Bucer (1491-1551),[39] but this study must
be confined to the other great figure of the Reformation, John
Calvin (1509-1564). Calvin's correspondence with Farel after
1538 reveals his full awareness of the battles in Hungary, the
threatening Turkish advances, and the problem of dealing with
those who have gone over to Islam. Differing from Luther and
Melanchthon, he cannot find "turks" in the prophecy of Daniel.
For him, Islam is not to be compared to "True Religion" according
to the Word of God, but to the commentaries of the Pharisees or
to the papal doctrines appended to the Gospels. The distorted
biblical stories and rabbinical traditions in the Quran illustrate
how serious is a departure from the pure and simple Word of God.
Like Luther, Calvin was preoccupied with biblical studies, Rome's
threats, and political instability; hence he contributed more to
the understanding of the Word than to direct consideration of a
religious encounter of Christians and Muslims.[40] Yet in other
ways, he creates a foundation for modern missions, standing in a
class by himself. His renewed grasp on the core of the Christian
faith gave rise to a rich development of missionary activity,

i.e. his handling of <u>Soli</u> <u>Deo</u> <u>Gloria</u> (sovereign glory of God) and
<u>Sola</u> <u>Gratia</u> (salvation by the grace of God) provide incentive
which later cause Reformed church witnesses to fan out across the
globe. Zwemer has summarized some of Calvin's mission-related
ideas.

> The Call of the Gospel is for all men, says Calvin (Sermons
> on Deut., <u>Opera</u>, 28). God desires all men to be saved and to
> come to the knowledge of the truth--'all states and all peoples'
> (Sermons on I Tim., <u>Opera</u>, 53). Nor is the duty of evangelism
> to all the world hemmed in or contradicted by the doctrine of
> predestination (<u>Inst</u>. III, 23:12-14). 'We do not know,'
> writes Calvin, 'whom God has elected nor where his elect dwell.'
> Moreover we are in duty bound to pray for the heathen,
> 'for all people in the whole earth' (<u>Inst</u>. III, 20:36-40).
> This comes out clearly in his exposition of the second petition
> of the Lord's Prayer. The same thought is emphasized in a
> powerful sermon on Daniel (<u>Opera</u>, 41) where he exclaims, 'When
> we think and pray only about our own needs and do not remember
> those of our neighbors, we cut ourselves loose from the body
> of Christ Jesus our Lord and how can we then be joined to God.'
> Calvin also sees as the goal of all missions the Glory of
> God. To draw souls out of hell and put them on the way of
> salvation is to glorify God (Sermon on Deut., <u>Opera</u>, 33:18-19).
> The same thought occurs in a sermon on Isaiah 12:4-5. 'This
> is our duty, everywhere to make known among the nations the
> goodness of our God.' [41]

Calvin's understanding of the image of God in man and of common
grace (which leaves man ever longing for God) avoids an extreme
discontinuity between God and man (e.g. Barth)[42] which allows
no points of contact between Christianity and other religions
(cf. <u>Institutes</u> I, 3:1-3, II:8; II, 2:13-15). Calvin's views of
the sovereignty of God, the authority of revelation, faith as the
regulative principle for all of life, and Christianity's claim
to finality, universality, gave him a base for world wide missionary action. It is interesting to note that of the Reformers,
Calvin was the only one to correspond with a missionary venture
in a foreign land. Unfortunately his correspondence with the
three hundred Swiss-French Calvinists who settled in Brazil (and
sought to evangelize the Indians there) did not survive.[43] But
his far-flung interest and correspondence with Knox in Scotland,
the King of Poland, England, France and the Netherlands testify
to his zeal for evangelism abroad. He saw the whole world as the
setting for the struggle between Christ's kingdom and the Satanic
powers of darkness, but he was never hemmed in by despair as
Luther.

> God has created the entire world that it should be
> the theater of his glory by the spread of his Gospel. [44]

Warneck held that Calvin encouraged Christian magistracy to
spread the Christian faith to non-Christian lands (e.g. Dutch
theory of missions).[45] While this is doubtful, it is correct to
state that wherever Calvinism spread, it planted the latent
seeds of missionary zeal.[46] It was this that later motivated
churches of the Reformed faith to tackle the Muslim work
almost alone for a century (1800-1900). The best demonstration
of the missionary ideal latent in Calvin's thought is demonstrated
by Adrianus (Hadrian) Saravia (1531-1613), a Dutch Reformed pastor
who later became Dean of Westminster. He set forth the "present
missionary obligation" of the Church in a treatise in 1590.
Unfortunately by this time the Reformation was moving into its
scholastic-orthodox phase and many disputed the validity of missions.[47] Yet this does not obscure Calvin's own spirit of
expectation, prayers for the conversion of the heathen and desire
to draw all men to Christ. Vanden Berg captures the balance
found in Calvin.

> If we venture to draw a conclusion...we would say that
> Calvinistic missionary activity was at its height when there
> was perfect harmony and unity between the theological and
> soteriological line in Calvinism. Where the theological
> line is emphasised at the expense of the soteriological, there
> looms a secularised Calvinism, which in its desire to fight
> 'the wars of the Lord' on the broad front of life loses its
> passion for souls, but on the other hand a one-sided stress
> on soteriology leads to a sterile mysticism which is quite
> passive with regard to the missionary task. [48]

While Luther and Calvin stressed both the theocentric and soteriological, it is Calvin who had the stronger view of world renewal,
the more driving concern to save the perishing.[49] The undeveloped
concept of mission in the Reformers is thus due to outward circumstances, rather than to theological failings. As the Turkish-
Roman threats subsided; as means and entrance to other lands
presented itself to Protestants; Protestantism consolidated
itself, then passed through the adolescence of scholastic orthodoxy to rediscover its evangelical experience and motives for
mission.
Four positive elements in the Reformers' teaching stand out.
First, mission must have its starting point in what God has done
in Jesus Christ, for no human enterprise is adequate. Calvin
stresses grace.

> We are taught that the Kingdom of Christ is neither to be
> advanced nor maintained by the industry of men, but this is
> the work of God alone; for believers are taught to rest
> solely on His blessing. [50]

Second, both Calvin and Luther live in expectation regarding God's
unfinished work in creation. Luther makes lively use of the

future tense: "The gospel will be the preaching that illumines
all the world" and "the preachers will fly across the orb and
find out those who expect them and receive them with joy". Likewise Calvin lives in hope for the world out there.

> As our own salvation proceeds from the sheer unmerited
> mercy of God, why should he not do the same to those who are
> still on the road to ruin which we, too, have been treading. [51]

Third, man has a role in God's work. The awareness of sin, longing for the Second Coming and discussion of election never blunted
the Reformers' activity, for God's initiative of grace energizes
rather than paralyzes preaching. The idea of the priesthood of
believers provides the basis of a dynamic witness. Fourth, the
Reformers' limited understanding of mission would expand as the
supply of evangelists increased, contacts were re-established
with the East, and the explanation of uncharted lands filled
Europe with hope. As Europe broke out of its cocoon, the growing awareness of God's glory, salvation by grace, and the coming
kingdom would provide Protestants with the motives for mission.
The Reformation marks a step forward in that the church coupled
self-criticism to a rediscovery of the Word of God's grace in
Christ. Although providing no immediate answer to Islam, this
would generate a fresh sensitivity for Muslims and others. By
clarifying the role of the Word (over against tradition and
institution) and by stressing the church's independence from
empire, the Reformation shook an ingrown church and turned her
concern to the world beyond.

HELPS AND HINDRANCES IN THE UNDERSTANDING OF MISSION AND ISLAM

In the seventeenth and eighteenth centuries, a number of forces
were at work promoting or obstructing the emergence of a Protestant concept and program of missions. There were what can be
called external, perhaps geographic incentives. First, there
was the link between the Reformation and the Oriental Church which
had brought a new awareness of the needs of the East. Cyril
Lucaris, Patriarch of Constantinople (1621-1638), having studied
at Wittenberg and Geneva, continued to correspond with Reformation
leaders in Geneva, Holland, and England. The teachings of Calvin
encouraged him to attempt to reform the Greek Orthodox Church.
Antoine Leger, a Swiss Reformed minister was called to the Dutch
Embassy at Constantinople to assist in translating Reformed
writings and the New Testament, and in the preparation of Cyril's
significant Confessio Fidei.[52] Although this venture proved
fatal for Cyril, it did stimulate new life in the East (Jerusalem
Synod, 1672) and a new awareness in the West. Many other travelers in this period brought back reports of the trials of
Christians and Turks under the Ottomans.[53] Second, exploration
and colonization reflected a Europe on the move. Travel to the

West (Columbus, 1492) and to the East (Vasco da Gama, 1498) lifted many horizons. The Peace of Westphalia (1648) gave Protestants
a stable base for expansion. The rival embassies at Constantinople
symbolized the inroads made into the declining Ottoman Dynasty.[54]
The new Protestant nations of northern Europe were in the competition for territory. Protestants became conscious of the vast
realm of God's creation and its many peoples and began to feel
a responsibility towards them. As David Livingstone (1813-1873)
would later say; the end of the geographical enterprise is the
beginning of missionary activity. Cook's travels influenced
Carey. Zinzendorf became concerned even with Labrador and the
Nicobar Islands. Third, there was the stimulus that came from
Roman Catholic and Russian Orthodox missions. Pope Gregory XV
founded the Congregatio de propaganda fide(1622) and sent new waves
of French, Italian, and other missionaries out to claim the earth.
By decree (1700), Peter the Great urged Orthodox missions to
probe towards the Pacific and the Near East.[55] These manifestations of vitality in Christ's name stood in sharp contrast to
Protestant lethargy. With a sting, Robert Bellarmine noted that
missions are a mark of the true Church! These and other stimuli
prompted the first ventures in Protestant missions. At the
start there were only lone individuals such as the Reformed
preacher Wenzeslaus Budowitz who served in Constantinople (1577-
1581), the sacrificial labors of Presbyterians John Eliot (1604-
90) and David Brainerd (1718-47) among the American Indians,
and the early work of the Anglican S.P.G. (founded 1701). The
larger organizational ventures were closely identified with
commerce or nationality. The Dutch East India Company (1602)
established a seminary at Leiden and imitated Roman Catholic
methods in the East Indies, Ceylon, Formosa and the New World.
The only remarkable difference between Roman Catholic and
early Protestant enterprizes was the latter's emphasis on the
Scriptures (Malay New Testament, 1688). The powerful British
East India Company maintained a chaplaincy but restrained the
forming of an English mission program in the East. Fortunately
Anglicans were more active in the New World via the S.P.G..
Early Danish-Halle Missions exhibited a pietistic spirit under
the patronage of King Frederick IV. With the aid of August
Francke (1663-1727), Bartholomew Ziegenbalg (1683-1719) and
Henry Plütschau (1677-1746) were sent to Tranquebar, India
(1706) where they established principles which guided many later
Protestant endeavors. The English S.P.C.K. (founded 1699) aided
the Lutherans in these efforts. Yet it is apparent that these
early Dutch, English and Danish-German missions all operated
under severe handicaps.[56]

Equally significant was the church's internal debate regarding
mission which occurred between 1600 and 1800. Various ecclesiastical barriers and theological incentives are to be noted.
Not only were there exhausting inter-Protestant quarrels (e.g.
Lutherans v.s. Philippists, Calvinists v.s. Arminians, Anglicans
v.s. Puritans and Independents), but the growth of a Protestant

rationalism or scholasticism (sometimes called orthodoxy) which
was coldly indifferent or vocally opposed to missions. These
Post-reformation theologians frequently proof-texted their own
views regarding missions in elaborate fashion. Warneck and others
have documented this running debate. It began when figures such
as English Puritan Thomas Sibbs (d. 1635) and Dutchman Hadrian
Saravia (d. 1613) declared that the missionary obligation was
presently valid for the whole church. Surprisingly the bitterest
opposition came from the most orthodox leaders. Their argument
included: the great commission had been fulfilled by the Apostles;
the theory of mission was based on a faulty construction of the
apostolic office or precluded by the doctrine of election; the
task on mission belonged to civil rulers; or that while the
principle was valid, the time was not ripe for its practical
discharge. Such opinions were set forth by Theodore Beza (d.
1605) of Geneva and Johannes Gerhard (d. 1637). Yet at the same
time others were taking practical action. Hugo Grotius (1583-
1645) prepared his treatise, De veritate religionis Christianae
(1627), to help Christian workers in the Far and Near East and
"to awaken the lapsed churches of the East to new evangelical
life". Peter Heyling of Lubeck labored in Egypt and Abyssinia
(1634) until the day of his martyrdom. The next verbal round
came in 1651 when Count Erhardt Truchsess called the Theological
Faculty of Wittenberg to acknowledge that Matthew 28:19 still
required obedience. In true orthodox fashion, they rejected his
challenge. In 1664 Baron Justinian von Weltz (1621-1668) prepared
numerous treatises urging his fellow Lutherans to missionary
action. He set forth the biblical, historical and doxological
reasons for mission, refuting the oft repeated arguments for
inactivity. He taught these ideas in Holland and after conse-
cration at Zwoll, went to serve till death in Dutch Guiana.
Even Oliver Cromwell backed the idea of missions.57 Something
of a breakthrough came in 1700 as more voices arose to support
missions. Many causes for the success of the emergence of
missions at this time have been suggested; the Enlightenment
(Aufklärung, from Leibniz, d. 1716 to Kant, d. 1804); scientific
discovery (Copernicus, Kepler, Galileo, Harvey, Newton) and
parallel philosophies (Descartes, Hobbes, Spinoza); the penetration of Pietism into most sectors of Protestantism; and the
accumulative arguments of von Welzt and others. Amidst the complexity of the situation, August H. Francke and Count N.L. von
Zinzendorf (d. 1760) successfully launched mission schemes.58
    Eighteenth century Protestant missions extended from four
sources. In Holland, the Dutch East India Company became a
patron of "colonial missions" reflecting the pre-Reformation
idea that the civil authority is responsible for Christianizing
its territory. There were efforts in Brazil and North America
as well as in the East Indies. Begun with great enthusiasm
for the Scriptures and the conversion of the inhabitants of the
land, these ventures slowly wore down under the restrictive
hand of the patron. The Danish-Halle Mission received royal

approval and the support of the Pietists. This solid enterprise
established many principles in mission methods and ecumenical
cooperation, but it too began to taper off by the end of a century.
Perhaps the most zealous, sacrificial and warm-hearted missions
sprang forth from the pietistic Moravians of Herrnhut (Saxony)
under Zinzendorf. Their idea of the whole church as a missionary
church reintroduces the element of vitality into the church's
history.[59] British missions were prompted partly by the "religious tyranny" of the Crown and partly by volunteer action. The
emigration of Scottish and English Puritans (Pilgrim Fathers) in
1620 and the formation of the Massachusetts Bay Company transferred a work force to the New World with the stated purpose of
converting the natives. In this setting arose such pioneer
missionaries as John Eliot (d. 1690) and David Brainerd (d. 1748)
and mission advocates such as Cotton Mather (d. 1725) and Jonathan
Edwards (d. 1758). Indeed, a fifth base for missions
was evolving. Equally remarkable were those two free associations
outside the British churches dedicated to promoting the Christian
faith among colonists and natives abroad in both West and East,
namely the S.P.G. (1701) and the S.P.C.K. (1699).[60] Yet sad to
say, as the eighteenth century progressed, these missionary forces
waned. Missionary enthusiasm once more reached a valley, a nadir,
before rising (1792-1815) again to a new summit, the zenith of
the great century of modern missions (1815-1914).

Within the crucible of European thought, another parallel
struggle regarding Islam was in process. There were those insisting upon preserving traditional distortions or creating new
rational-romantic opinions of Islam as well as those who were
seeking new information or a scholarly understanding of this
religion. These four groups or strands demonstrate the diversity
of European views and warn against any statement as to a cohesive
European image of Islam. A study of these developments in attitude towards people of another religion run closely parallel to
the emerging Protestant concept of mission. First, there were
those "traditionalists" oft standing in the stream of Roman
Catholic and Protestant scholasticism who were content to reiterate
in uncritical fashion many of the existing prejudices about Islam.
Like medieval writers, they added little new data.[61] Readers in
the smugness of the early Elizabethan era wanted an entertaining
presentation of Islam's falsehood and her predicted doom. Lacking necessary details, many writers borrowed from medieval
legends, the acids of the polemicists, and the reports of travellers; and then freely filled the gaps with fiction and fantasy.
These conglomerations were usually prepared for reasons other
than to inform.[62] For example, Humphrey Prideaux's (Dean of
Norwich, d. 1724) famous work must not be understood as a polemic
against Islam. It is really an attack upon the Deists and a
defense of "revealed religion".[63] The topic of Islam often proved
to be merely the battleground for other struggles.[64] These traditional views were fortunately on the wane under the light of
new facts and a changing spirit.

A second strand composed of satirists, historians, romantics and humanists shows more interest in literature _per se_ than religion. Frequently they attack one form of prejudice only to replace it with another. Anonymous authors in the seventeenth century defended Islam by satirical literature.[65] Later the Count of Boulainvilliers lauded Muhammad:

> ...You will easily forgive an old Companion, who is fond of introducing to your Acquaintance a very extra ordinary Personage: One who from an able Merchant, became a wise politician, and a renowed Legislator. In a word, a great man, a great genius, and a great prince. Much has he been injured, by the false colours in which the zeal and ignorance of former ages has transmitted him down to us. But the Count of Boulainvilliers has done him justice; he has wiped off the aspersions that deform'd his character; let him in the fairest point of light; and described this Heroe, and this Orator, with an eloquence equal to his own.... [66]

He then uses Islam as a tool to attack what he considered superfluous Christisnity and to present his own religion of reason and naturalism. In a preface to his translation of the Quran, the humanist Savary gave Muhammad favorable treatment as a wise politican, praised Islam as a natural religion, and made the story of Zayd and Zaynab into a romantic narrative.[67] Voltaire's criticism of Islam is a thinly disguised attack on all religion. His play (1741) and essay (1756) caricature Muhammad and religion in general in order to promote his own philosophical natural religion. Unfortunately Voltaire's snobbish life and acid pen provided little comfort to those seeking God.[68] The skeptical historian Gibbon shows little originality as he acknowledges Islam's complex origin, nature and success; expounds the Prophet's love for women, ambition and subtle politics; and notes the break between the idealistic reformer of Mecca and the politician of Medina.[69] Thomas Carlyle (1795-1881) considered Muhammad "by no means the truest of Prophets, but I do esteem him a true one".[70] Frustrated by many sects and wearisome arguments, the Prophet sought the world's Maker and attuned himself to the "Law of Nature or the great Mystery of Existence". Muhammad thus became the advocate of Carlyle's brand of romantic naturalism (a reshaped Christianity), the model of individualism ("the minority of one"), and a hero of his people.[71] The Talisman by Sir Walter Scott and Lives of Mahomet and his Successors (ca. 1830) by Washington Irving also retain many legends. This literary effort discloses the West's growing interest in the Muslim world.

Thirdly, travellers bearing new information did much to correct misconceptions about Islam and the Muslim world. England's growing sea power brought new contact with the Mediterranean shores. Richard Hakluyt, the noted historian recorded this wider scope of adventure.[72] Visits to Persia by Jean Chardin

(1643-1713) and Welsh Protestant, Sir Thomas Herbert brought word
of the seemingly parallel denominational structures of Islam and
Christianity. Former captives Christopher Angell and Francis
Knight, and the English agent for the Barbary Coast, John Harrison,
found a ready market for their narratives.[73] Pere Nau, an outstanding French Jesuit serving in Syria, vividly described Muslim-
Christian encounters and urged Christians to "deal with Muslims
with a humble air full of gentleness as the Gospel commands".[74]
Reports by Joseph Pitts, Carsten Niebuhr, Thorkild Hansen and
Paul of Aleppo combine penetrating exploration and accurate observation of the secrets of Near Eastern geography, peoples and
religion.[75] The travel literature of the eighteenth century soon
warranted a separate section in many European libraries, inevitably affecting attitudes.[76]

Fourth and most noble was the growth of Islamic and Arabic
scholarship amidst concerned Christians. Raymond Lull had pressed
the Pope and councils prior to the Reformation to establish
schools of Arabic and oriental languages in Europe's universities
to facilitate the training of missionaries. Now in the seventeenth century with the rebirth of interest in the East and
missions, one finds biblical scholars producing Arabic grammars
and lexicons. A translator of the Authorized Version (1611),
William Bedwell, published the Epistles of St. John in Arabic
at Leiden and translated from Arabic several mathematical treatises and a dialogue (reportedly between two Muslims disclosing
the ills of Islam). In 1632, Sir Thomas Adams founded the first
chair of Arabic at Cambridge and in 1636 Archbishop Laud endowed
a chair at Oxford. Abraham Wheelock accepted the former chair
and William Bedwell, who had meanwhile served with the Levant
Company in Aleppo (1629-1636), the latter. Edward Pocock (the
Elder) also served as chaplain at Aleppo collecting Arabic manuscripts, translating Grotius' great work on natural theology into
Arabic (1660) and with his contemporary J. H. Hottinger greatly
furthering oriental studies.[77] Christian Raue of Berlin showed
zeal for semitic languages, displayed respect for Muslim piety
in his edition of Quranic extracts, collected manuscripts for
Archbishop Ussher in the Levant, and then established a missionary training college at Kiel.[78] Serious scholarship in this
period was often linked to mission plans and programs. The
excellent linguistics and careful scholarship regarding religions
as exemplified by Hugo Grotius, Thomas Erpenius (grammars),
Rapheleng (Lexicon Arabicum, Leiden, 1613), and Adrian Reland
were often linked to Dutch missions and colonies.[79] Many contributions centered about the translation of the Quran. André
du Ryer bypassed Latin versions to make a fresh translation from
the Arabic into vernacular French in 1647.[80] Ludovici Maracci
demonstrated his skill in a new Latin translation with introduction and refutation (1698).[81] But the peak of Quranic scholarship
for many years was the tempered English translation by George
Sale (1734).[82] German scholars, J. C. Schwartz and M. G.
Schroeder sought to show by textual-linguistic studies that the Qur

is dependent on the Bible, but Jacob Ehrhart rejected the theory.[83]
There appeared to be a ready market for these new studies and such
works as J. Morgan's <u>Mahometism</u> <u>Fully</u> <u>Explained</u> (1723). European
and British Islamic scholarship was on its way.[84]   What
is significant is that the best of this had its birth and nurture
in the midst of Christians concerned for peoples. Interest in
missions prompted many a scholarly work and that in turn became
impetus and instrument for the missionary.

EMERGENCE AND IMPLEMENTATION OF AN EVANGELICAL CONCEPT OF MISSION

     The concept of mission was inherent in Reformation teachings
inasmuch as they were true expressions of the biblical message.
Yet many factors were needed to stimulate the actual re-formation
and implementation of this idea. The labor pains already observed
led to the actual birth of the evangelical missionary movement.
First to be noted are the leaders and events prompting this
movement. While circumstances varied in Europe, Britain and the
New World, these simultaneous evangelical stirrings disclose that
Lutheran, Anglican and Reformed groups were equally influenced
by Christian piety and revival. In Germany, pietistic groups
formed for Bible study, fellowship and Christian experience (the
idea of the little church within the church, <u>ecclesiola</u> <u>in</u> <u>ecclesia</u>)
under P. J. Spener (d. 1705), the author of <u>Pia</u> <u>Desideria</u> (1675).
This influenced A.H. Francke, Leibniz and Zinzendorf and spawned
the moravian ideal of the missionary church. As state missions
began to suffer from spiritual-sclerosis, the Brethren and other
pietistic bands kept the task of mission alive. The religious
and moral decline in eighteenth century Britain has been oft described. Sermons were rational treatises on ethics little affecting
the morals and lives of the people. A. W. Boehme (pupil of Francke),
William Law (<u>A</u> <u>Serious</u> <u>Call</u> <u>to</u> <u>a</u> <u>Holy</u> <u>and</u> <u>Devout</u> <u>Life</u>, 1729), and
Northampton's Philip Doddridge (d. 1751) belonged to a minority
concerned for revival and missions. Then came the dawning of a
new day of personal experiences of salvation, powerful preaching
and moral transformation as epitomized in John Wesley (1702-1791),
his brother Charles, and George Whitefield (1714-1770). This
awakening resulted in an evangelical wing of the Anglican Church,
Methodism and new life for churches in Scotland and Wales. Charles
Simeon at Cambridge and Joseph White at Oxford were soon challenging young men to overt mission action. The outstanding leader of
the Great Awakening in America was Jonathan Edwards (d. 1758)
who reinterpreted Calvin (perhaps more accurately than the post-
reformers) and asserted the need of evangelical conversion. His
student, Samuel Hopkins (d. 1803), further modified New England
Theology appealing to Christians to act out of disinterested benevolence for the conversion of all men and for the greater glory
of God. The American Revolution (1776-1783) and the formation
of American church structures were followed by a Second Awakening
in 1790 which began in Reformed, Presbyterian and Congregational

bodies, but also provided great growth for Baptist, Methodist and
Disciples groups. These revivals resulted in missionary activity,
first to the Indians of the nation and then to lands abroad.
During these events, there was much interaction: Cotton Mather
(d. 1728) corresponded with Francke of Halle and missionaries in
South India; Whitefield and the Wesleys enthused the Americans;
and Moravian visits enlivened England. The whole field of Pro-
testanism was being prepared and seeded on the eve of the nineteenth century that it might produce that fruit known as the
Evangelical Missionary Movement.[85]
      The actual features or characteristics of the Evangelical
Movement are more dynamic than definable, better captioned by
spirit than by statement. The movement professed to emanate from
the conviction, spirit and activity of early biblical or evangelical Christianity. It claimed continuity with the New Testament
and the Reformation. Yet so did orthodoxy and later nineteenth
century liberalism! How then are they to be distinguished? Both
the evangelical and liberal movements in theology were reactions
against what they called orthodoxy, the mere preservation or con-
serving of tradition. This is distinguished from true orthodoxy
i.e. sound doctrine and practice of the Christian faith as
formulated in the great church creeds and confessions. The evangelicals blended the biblical-creedal aspect of orthodoxy with
the pietistic stress on the personal experience of salvation and
compassion for the lost.[86] Later the liberals drew upon the
rational-philosophical aspect of orthodoxy (and Kant) and upon
the pietistic emphasis upon human experience and human needs
(e.g. F. D. Schleiermacher, d. 1834). Later liberalism coupled
receptiveness to new scientific ideas with varied proposals for
social-religious reforms and willingness to discard large portions
of traditional belief as unessential.[87] While this brief description has its limitations, it may help explain the eventual clash
of these streams in theology and missions. For the moment, the
positive features of the evangelical movement are to be considered.
While it is difficult to cover all the strands of the revival
movements, certain common charactieristics stand out. There
arose a burning seriousness with regard to the ultimate issues
of life and the biblical message. There was the shattering awareness that the salvation of sinful man was solely by the grace of
God in Christ. There was a consciousness of the Holy Spirit, of
God's work in man's heart and the accompanying experience. While
the emphasis on feeling and enthusiasm stood in contrast to the
cold rationalism of the day, it was not unduly excessive. It
was joyfully affirmed that Christ died for all and that men
everywhere could respond in faith and experience new life in
him. The aim was soteriological; whether in Whitefield or
Edwards' description of judgement or Wesley's hymn, "Jesus, lover
of by soul". The Wesleys combined the universalism of grace with
the indispensability of faith, while Whitefield and Edwards were
more impressed by God's sovereignty and the grace which presses
in on man. There was also in these men and the European pietists,

a compassion for souls and an urgency to reach those still outside
the Gospel.[88] Eschatological hope stimulated all the leaders
of the movement and some of their followers held to beliefs
regarding establishing the millennium on earth. These features
were reflected in the motives for mission set forth by the leaders
of the revivals.[89]

The great breakthrough for evangelical missions came in the
period, 1792-1815. The figure who symbolizes the start of modern
Protestant mission is William Carey. Carey's challenge found
reception and growth in hearts which had been warmed by the evangelical awakenings. Carey in 1786 proposed that a conference of
Baptist ministers discuss: "Whether the commandment given to the
Apostles to teach all nations in all the world must not be recognized as binding on us also, since the great promise still follows
it?" His counsel was at first squelched! Nevertheless, his
thoughts found expression in what was to become the charter of
modern missions, An Enquiry into the Obligations of Christians
to Use Means for the Conversion of the Heathens. This document
was soon followed by the formation of an agency for the practical
implementation of the missionary ideal. At Carey's suggestion,
"The Particular Baptist Society for the Propagation of the Gospel
amongst the Heathen" formed in 1792. Carey's first letter from
India stimulated the interdenominational London Missionary Society
(L.M.S.) to take shape in 1795. This was followed by the Scottish
(Edinburgh) and Glasgow Missionary Societies (1796), the Anglican
oriented Church Missionary Society (1799), the Religious Tract
Society (1799), the British and Foreign Bible Society (1804), and
the Wesleyn Methodist Missionary Society (1817-18). The continent
witnessed the emergence of the Netherlands Missionary Society
(1797), the Basel School (1815) and Society (1822), and other
societies in Denmark (1821), France (1822), Berlin (1824), Sweden
(1835) and Norway (1842). In America, Congregational, Reformed
and Presbyterian Churches joined to form the American Board of
Commissioners for Foreign Missions (1812). Then American Baptists
(1814), Methodists and Episcopalians (1821) joined in the tremendous surge to send witnesses to the uttermost parts of the
earth. Dynamic cores in almost every church acted voluntarily
to provide funds and recruits until whole churches once again
assumed their role as agencies of Christ's mission.[90]

The motives and means for implementing the Protestant concept
of mission deserve attention for they introduce viable new elements
into church history. The complex subject of missionary motivation
has been given thorough investigation. The primary motives for
early nineteenth century missions included obedience to Christ's
command, proclamation of salvation to man in need (soteriological),
building the church (ecclesiological), preparing for the coming
King and his kingdom (eschatological), and serving to the glory
of God (theocentric). Of less importance were romantic, ascetic,
political motives; acting out of a sense of indebtedness or the
desire to share humanitiarian-cultural enlightenment. Evangelicals didn't spend much time analyzing their motives, for they

felt compelled towards action. Periodically these human motives
in their historical setting would need be re-confronted with the
Bible, made subservient to the one dominant "constraining love"
of God in Christ.[91] Secondly, Protestant missions found they
could be independent of the commercial and colonial interests of
their home lands. They often became the sharpest critics of
commercial exploitations. This is largely due to the credit of
the mission societies, voluntary societies of consecrated individuals, who could act where the institutional church could not
or would not. These societies became indeed the conscience of
the church, challenging the whole church to be concerned for the
world's redemption.

It has been observed how the churches of the Reformation underwent an amazing transformation in the three hundred years between
medieval and modern times, 1500-1800. Under the renewing power
of God's Spirit and the scholarly effort of dedicated Christians,
the church was shaking herself free from the old shackles of
prejudice and traditionalism. Again she was being filled with
the joyful news of salvation through Christ. First, there had
been a recovery of the Word of grace. Second, there had been a
rediscovery of the world. Third, many within her borders had
recaptured the motive and spirit of mission. Still the long
neglected Muslim world spread out before her largely unchartered
and untouched. It remained unknown how this vast realm of peoples
should be approached or when this great sector of humanity would
acknowledge the redemptive reign of God in Christ. This was the
challenge of faith before that great host who would go to India
and the Near East to witness in their Master's name. In the next
three chapters, it will be seen how this dynamic vitality in earthen
vessels was poured out in the mission of Christ. Attention will
be given to the methods applied, the factors encountered, and the
maturation that evolved with experience in the mission to Muslims.

2

Anglican and Reformed Missions to Muslims in India, 1800-1910: A Study in Methods

THE OPENING OF INDIA TO PROTESTANT MISSIONS

Removal of Political, Commercial and Ecclesiastical Barriers

India was destined to be the first country of the East open to the modern missionary movement. It was here that after centuries of isolation Islam and Christianity came into direct encounter again.[1] Three formidable barriers, however, faced those desiring to reach the Muslims of India: Indian Muslim rulers, the vested interests of the British East India Company and the anti-mission sentiments of many in the British state and churches.

In 1800, Islamic rule prevailed in much of North India. Entering with the Arab invasions of Sindh (A.D. 712), Muslim influence extended to the key centers of Lahore and Delhi by the twelfth century, attaining a peak under the Mughal emperors between Akbar and Aurangzeb (1556-1797). Other enclaves of Muslims settled in Hyderabad State, the United Provinces, Bengal and South India. Encroaching European power gradually weakened the authority of Muslim leaders. While the Portuguese of the sixteenth century had been confined to Goa and Ceylon, they daringly dispatched a delegation to Akbar's court in Lahore. The Dutch settled irregularly at Chinsure (nr. Calcutta) and later acquired Ceylon. Tranquebar and Serampore were occupied by Danes. French strength in the Southeast centered around Pondicherry. But it was the ascending British East India Company that attained the strategic ports of Madras, Bombay and Calcutta and after eliminating the only serious rival, France,

in the Battle of Plassy (1757), was poised to assume control over
the subcontinent. During a century of expansion, British rule
reached northwards. With the Mutiny of 1857, India's government
was transferred from the East India Company to the British Crown
(1858). Resisting military and cultural penetration, the fierce
independent Afghans in the Northwest yielded only to treaty relationships. It must be noted however that British control was far
from synonymous with Christian missions.

To protect its commercial interests, the British East India
Company catered to the religions of the lands. Not only did it
follow the pattern of former rulers by supporting native shrines
and festivals with tax money, but it curtailed Christian "prosel
ytism" lest the enmities of Hindus and Muslims be aroused. Such
restrictive practices kept mission work at a minimum. Concerned
English Christians (S.P.C.K.) of the eighteenth century circum-
vented the Company's obstructing neutrality via gifts to the
Danish-German Mission in South India. In spite of the respected
work of Ziegenbalg, Schultz, Schwartz and Kiernander, the Company
refused passage on its ships and entrance to its territories to
missionaries. Only after a heated contest, did evangelicals secure a renewed Company Charter (1813) which permitted mission
activity and the establishment of an Anglican bishopric. Greater
liberty in this direction came with the Charter of 1833. These
acts of Parliament were preceded by a chain of dramatic events:
challenges for missions by Charles Simeon and other evangelical
preachers; the scheme for a Bengal mission (1786) set forth by
Charles Grant, William Chambers, George Udny and other evangelicals within the Company;[2] the activity and speeches in Parliament of William Wilberforce; the initiative of the Baptist
Missionary Society and Carey; the stirring petitions of the
Scottish Societies and church; and the requests of mission-
minded chaplains such as David Brown and Henry Martyn.[3]

It must be remembered that resistance to missions was often
as fierce within British churches as in the state or Company.
Churches preoccupied with rationalism, deism, and morality
would be stimulated by the evangelical movement and mission
societies to renewed faith and action during the crucial years,
1786-1813.[4] The societies must be credited in large measure for
assisting the church in the development of a truly Christian
supported mission program and the pioneering of new fields.
The birth of the mission societies, voluntary groups of like-
minded Christians dedicated to the work and its support by
personal gifts, gave Protestant missions a new independence from
external controls.[5]

Role of the Serampore Trio

The famous Serampore Trio of the Baptist Missionary Society
play an important part in inaugurating mission work in British
ruled India. Aroused to his spiritual responsibilities by

Thomas Scott (later C.M.S. secretary) and by Cook's voyages to
the heathen world, William Carey (1761-1834) tried to interest
his brethren in the Lord's last command (1786). His sermons and
pamphlet prepared the way for the formation of the Baptist
Missionary Society (1792) and his own departure to Calcutta
(1793).[6] His trials with his surgeon-colleague John Thomas,
work in the indigo factory, opposition from the East India Company, and his pioneer mission ventures have oft been narrated.
The arrival of Ward, Marshman and other Baptists (1799 onwards)
bolstered the work even though Company prohibitions and pressures
were severe from 1806-1813. Carey along with the printer and
editor, William Ward (1764-1823) and the schoolmaster-author,
Joshua Marshman (1768-1837) set forth proposals influencing
many future missionaries.[7] The grand vision of this trio included the Muslims of North India as well as the peoples of Burma,
China and Japan. Their program called for:

> (1) the widespread preaching of the Gospel by every possible
> method; (2) the support of the preaching by the distribution
> of the Bible in the languages of the country; (3) the estab-
> lishment at the earliest possible moment of a Church; (4) a
> profound study of the background and thought of the non-Chris-
> tian peoples; (5) the training at the earliest possible moment
> of an indigenous ministry.[8]

Their achievements included these and more. Translations, schools
and college, stations and churches, an incredible program of
evangelism, all capture the imagination of the reader.[9] As will
be observed, many evangelical Anglicans also joined in this
crusade to create a conscience, a public opinion favorable to
missions within the British Isles.

Major Developments in Mission to Muslims

How is one to tackle the massive mission program in India?
Certain dominant strands in Anglican and Reformed missions to
India's Muslims suggest that workers were struggling to develop
an adequate methodology. These methods provide a useful device
for organizing materials covering Muslim work in India. The
following schema attempt to do justice both to the major developments and their historical context. First, one observes the
development of an apologetic approach from 1800 onwards.[10] At
first it appears to blend pietism, Protestant rationalism and
elements of medieval polemics, but after 1850 it modifies into
what can be called an evangelical apologetic for Muslims. This
is best examined under Anglican activity. Second, a new educational approach to Muslims and others is formulated by Alexander
Duff and his successors after 1830. Scottish Presbyterians
afford the choice data for this study. Third, an interdenominational service-centered approach gains prominence with

improved medical techniques in the 1860s. Fourth, while many
groups realized that an indigenous church-oriented approach was
most desirable, the American Presbyterians seem to have most
successfully directed their multi-phased program towards its
achievement. Fifth, the phenomenon of missionary conferences
united indigenous churches and mission bodies after 1860 to shape
what may be described as an embryonic ecumenical approach to Muslims

It is possible to chart the emergence and development of these
parallel approaches (or the combinations of such). Beginning at
various points in the nineteenth century, they continue into the
twentieth century where they sometimes clash because they unfortunately become associated exclusively with one type of theology
or mission theory. One must take caution however not to stereo-
type any denomination or its mission program. All missions participated in the various forms of activity (e.g. evangelism-
apologetics, education, medicine and service, and church building).
The author has selected the distinctive contributions of each to
a specific area (e.g. Anglicans to apologetics, Scots to education,
etc.) because these can be most clearly documented. While it is
legitimate to claim this party made the major contribution in this
area, it was by no means exclusive. Likewise one must not
surmise that because a distinctly service-centered approach did
not appear until the 1860s that therefore earlier missionaries
lacked concern for the physical needs of man. The humanitarian
efforts of Carey and Martyn disprove that. What can be ascertained
is that this now became a distinctive medium or channel by which
the objectives of mission were to be achieved. If one holds the
above warning in mind, then a focusing upon these major developments
in Anglican and Reformed missions to Muslims in India can prove
helpful.

THE ANGLICAN CONTRIBUTION: WITH REFERENCE TO THE DEVELOPMENT OF AN APOLOGETIC APPROACH TO MUSLIMS

Pioneer Anglican Missionary Work Among Muslims: From Medieval to Modern Apologetics

Henry Martyn and the Missionary Chaplains

In the dark days between 1786 and 1813, several chaplains manifested the dynamic of the Evangelical Awakening thus prompting a
concern for mission within the Church of England. Fuller provision for Protestant Company chaplains in the Charter of 1793
had been achieved by the intercession of Grant and Wilberforce.
Several of these men, strongly influenced by Charles Simeon of
Cambridge, e.g. Brown, Buchanan, Martyn, Corrie and Thomason, gave
distinguished service in India. Known as the "missionary chaplains", they stimulated missions and the establishment of the
church in that land. David Brown (Calcutta, 1787-1812) spurred
spiritual renewal in the European community and garrison;

supervised an orphanage, a school for Hindus and Fort William
College; and contributed to the birth of the Church Missionary
Society.[11] Claudius Buchanan (India, 1797-1809) contributed
to the founding of the Anglican episcopate for India (1814) by
his activity and noted Memoir.[12] Reaching India in 1808, Thomas
T. Thomason devoted his energies to the evangelization of its
peoples.[13] Daniel Corrie served India over thirty years becoming
the first bishop of Madras (1835).[14] Strengthened by fellowship
with the Baptist missionaries and their colleague, Henry Martyn,
these men helped to change attitudes in the Church of England
and in Parliament. Coupled with that influence radiating from
Cambridge and Oxford, this stimulated the church to break out of
its shell and spread abroad.

Henry Martyn (1781-1812), a famous evangelical chaplain, was
one of the first Protestant workers to direct his energies almost
entirely to Muslims. Reared in the midst of England's Evangelical
Awakening and well qualified for mission work, he accepted the
better-paid chaplaincy of the East India Company when family
obligations blocked his plan to serve under the C.M.S. Arriving
at Calcutta (1806) after a strenuous voyage, he wrote in his
diary: "now let me burn out for God". In the six years between
his arrival and his death at Tokat, Asia Minor (October 16, 1812),
he did just that. Although his life was snuffed out at thirty-
two by unceasing toil and exhaustion because of disease, climate
and travel, he is remembered as the first modern missionary to
Islam.[15] Contributions in five areas account for this high
estimate.

His vision concerning the needs of the Muslim world and the
coming kingdom of God constitutes a major contribution. His
attention almost immediately drawn to the Muslim community, he
perceived that missions to them would not be achieved merely by
knowledge and improved technique.[16] Reconciliation calls for
costly personal endeavor! His burden for Muslims never led to
despair because he believed that the new age of technology and
Western expansion, with all its difficulties, was somehow related
to a fuller realization of the kingdom. The lay opinion and
activity of Captain and Mrs. Sherwood and Sir James Machintosh
strengthened this conviction.[17] Human dedication, he felt, could
become the instrumentality of the Holy Spirit. Martyn's pietistic
consciousness of sin and uselessness was balanced by consecrated
exertion. His introspective sensitivity was linked to an
appreciation for fellowship and cooperation by all Christians in
mission. In the five months at Serampore with the Baptist Trio
and chaplains Brown and Corrie, he helped forge a team spirit
for evangelization.[18]

Second, Martyn claimed that effective preaching and education
among Muslims and others could be accomplished. As chaplain he
was responsible for the English military and civilian communities
of Dinapore, near Patna (1807-1809) and Cawnpore (1809-1810).
In spite of continual sickness, he re-established prayer and
worship in small witnessing circles amidst these largely

indifferent numbers. Preaching was not an end in itself, but the
means for arousing the existing Christian community to the duty
of mission: "The evangelization of India is a more important
object than preaching to the European inhabitants of Calcutta."[19]
In sermons at Calcutta in 1810, he calls for a consistent obedience to the biblical commission of Christ and urges all Christians
in India to launch a program of Scripture distribution in con-
junction with the British and Foreign Bible Society.[20] Although
Warren Hastings (1732-1818), governor-general, had once dismissed
a chaplain for distributing tracts (reportedly saying, "the man
who could be rash enough to speak of Christ to the natives would
let off a pistol in a powder magazine"), Martyn dared to advocate
missions to Muslims.[21]

While occasionally preaching to Indians, Martyn considered
education as a prime means to penetrate Hindu discontent and
Muslim separation. He set up schools at Dinapore, Bankipore,
Patna and Cawnpore under native schoolmasters, often Muslims, who
taught pupils to read and write. Selected Old Testament portions
and Christian books (e.g. Christian Book Society) were introduced.
Justifying his work among Indians by a clause in an old Company
charter (perhaps by William III), he saw elementary teaching as
a preliminary step towards the study of the Bible and possible
conversion.

Third, Martyn contributed to the translation and publication
of the Scriptures and Christian literature. The central role or
authority of the Bible was reasserted. Like the Dutch in Ceylon
and the Danes in South India, the Serampore trio initiated a
phenomenal program for the translation and publication of the
Scriptures. Anglican chaplains, Bible Societies and others joined
in. Martyn, the Cambridge scholar trained in philology, Hindustani
(Urdu), Sanskrit, Persian and Arabic, brought needed skills to
this work. He made critical translations of the New Testament
into Urdu, Persian and Arabic. The Urdu translation completed
with the assistance of Sabat a Muslim convert (1807-1810), saw
nearly a score of editions between 1810 and 1847. The Persian
version begun at Cawnpore (1809) and revised in Persia (1811-12)
was published at St. Petersburg (1815), Calcutta (1816), London
(Lee editions, 1827, 1837) and Edinburgh (1846). In addition
to a preliminary Arabic draft of the New Testament (superseded
by the Smith-Van Dyck version, Beirut, 1837-1865), Martyn translated the Book of Genesis and the Book of Common Prayer into
Urdu. He considered the press a vital instrument of mission and
expected an explosive reaction to the printed and preached Word
of God.[22] This anticipates his contributions in Christian
apologetics and personal evangelism.

Fourth, Martyn's involvement in public discussions with Islam
represents the beginning of a nineteenth century apologetic
approach. In spite of the sensitive personality of Martyn, he
was inevitably drawn into the so-called "controversy with Islam".
In present day terminology it might be called public debate,
but controversy remains the more accurate description. This

method often led to aggressive verbal attack, to the viewing of the other as the pundit or opponent to be defeated in the public arena with the audience acting as the judge and score-keeper . In Martyn's case, however, it must be noted that such bitterness was avoided. Nevertheless he inherited something from his predecessors, John of Damascus, Raymond Lull and Jerome Xavier. William Carey advised Corrie and Martyn in December 1808 "not to argue with the Mahomedan doctors."[23] Why then was Martyn drawn into these debates? The answer is that it was the accepted pattern for two who differed in religious conviction to engage in public discussion. Hindus and Muslims accepted this practice of rational debate. Martyn records how Brahmin Ram Mohan Roy disputed with him eloquently concerning the Gospel.[24] At Dinapore and Patna, both strongholds of Islam, Martyn was challenged to study the Quran and works such as Maracci's Refutation. Again at Cawnpore, he met the Shi'ahs of Lucknow. He had a natural revulsion to attacking another religion and criticized Marshman's polemical approach to Hinduism at the festivals. Nevertheless one could not avoid a defense of one's faith. For a Hindu or Muslim the failure to make an apology was tantamount to a denial of one's faith. Perhaps a sharp vocal confrontation was unavoidable after ages of separation. Constance Padwick writes:

As the first meeting after centuries...two gigantic spiritual forces all unguarded and unaware, coming together with a first rude clash, unsoftened by intercourse and interaction of thought....[25]

Because of Martyn's attractive personality and holy life, he was soon much sought after by Muslim scholars.

In Persia (1811-1812), especially in the city of Shiraz, he was incessantly pursued by Muslim visitors and there was an extraordinary stir about religion.[26] He welcomed these singly or in small groups and shared with each some knowledge of the Gospel in spite of his pressing translation work and sickness. Soon however, he was again drawn into "public discussions". The first was held in the house of the "Moojtahid of Shiraz" (July 15, 1811). This leader, who had direct access to the Shah and whose house was sanctuary, had been aroused by Martyn's teachings concerning the person and work of Jesus. The initial aim of the meeting was to discuss the evidences of God, but it resulted in an evening-long lecture by the host. The spirit of inquiry was halted ten days later as the Shi'ah authorities had Mirza Ibrahim, a leading mullah, prepare a written defense of Islam. Any future argumentation was to be "on paper".

Earlier at Dinapore, Martyn had questioned the validity of the controversial approach.

April 28, 1807...For myself, I never enter into a dispute with them without having reason to reflect that I mar the work for which I contend by the spirit in which I do it....

They mean to have down their leading man from Benares to
convince me of the truth of their religion. I wish a spirit
of inquiry may be excited, but I lay not much stress upon
clear arguments; the work of God is seldom wrought in this
way. To preach the Gospel, with the Holy Ghost sent down
from heaven, it is a better way to win souls.[27]

In the months following he could neither avoid nor completely
accept the apologetic approach. He prepared for an encounter
with a great Muslim Imam but with little hope "of doing him or
any of them good in this way". He spends hours with inquirers
Mirza and Morrad Ali presenting the unique role of Christ, His
eternal kingdom and the way of salvation and discussing objections
to Islam's laws and Muhammad's authority. He finds little joy
in seeing them painfully proceed from that religion to almost
unbelief.[28] He observed the dangers of this approach in Sabat,
who still preferred rational argument and clever logic to the
point of antagonism rather than the spirit of a new life in
Christ.[29] After these experiences, Martyn was assured of the
failings of rational controversy. "I have now lost all hope of
ever convincing Mohammdeans by argument....I know not what to
do but to pray for them."[30] Martyn's words reflect the dilemma
of a man who is considering how he can employ means which are
consistent with his message and goal.

> Sept. 8, 1811... I do use the means in a certain way, but
> frigid reasoning with men of perverse minds seldom brings men
> to Christ. However, as they require it, I reason and accord-
> ingly challenged them to prove the Divine mission of their
> prophet. In consequence of this, a learned Arabic treatise
> was written by one who was considered as the most able man,
> and put into my hands; copies of it were also given to the
> college and the learned. The writer of it said that if I
> could give satisfactory answer to it he would become a Christ-
> ian, and at all events would make my reply as public as I
> pleased. I did answer it and after some faint efforts on
> his part to defend himself, he acknowledged the force of my
> arguments, but was afraid to let them be generally known. He
> then began to inquire about the Gospel, but was not satisfied
> with my statement. He required me to prove from the very
> beginning the Divine mission of Moses, as well as of Christ;
> the truth of the Scriptures, etc. With very little hope that
> any good will come of it, I am now employed in drawing out the
> evidences of the truth; but oh! that I could converse and
> reason, and plead with power from on high. How powerless are
> the best-directed arguments till the Holy Ghost renders them
> effectual.[31]

Martyn could not however extricate himself from his human circumstances and so he seeks to shape an acceptable Christian
apologetic.

The best of Martyn's apologetics are set forth in three
Persian tracts. Although he considered Islam and Sufi mysticism
as burdened with man's sinfulness and its founder ensnared in the
web of delusion, these tracts show considerable improvement over
medieval apologetics. Their biblical content and sensitivity to
the Muslim would frequently reach levels superior to the more
rationalisitc spirit of Martyn's immediate successors: Abdul
Masih, S. Lee and K. Pfander. These tracts deserve special
attention.32

Fifth, Martyn's personal evangelism among Muslims is a new
feature of nineteenth century missions. Martyn was at his best
when quietly sharing his experiences in Christ with a small circle
of interested Muslims. These intimate talks produced mutually
responsive notes.

> A new impression was left on my mind; namely that these men
> are not fools and that all ingenuity and clearness of reason-
> ing are not confined to England and Europe....I find that
> seriousness in the declaration of the truths of the Gospel is
> likely to have more power than the clearest argument conveyed
> in a trifling spirit.33

He found that "A tender concern manifested for their souls is
certainly new to them, and seemingly produces corresponding
seriousness in their minds."34 It did leave a lasting mark on
Sheikh Salih (baptized Abdul Masih) and others in India. By a
careful study of these semi-private talks with Mirza Ibrahim, Aga
Baba (brother and disciple of Aga Akbar), Mirza Seyd Ali, and
Jaffir Ali Khan, one can gain several insights into Martyn's
personal approach. Seven observations can be made. (1) With the
serious inquirer, Martyn shared his own religious experience of
the forgiveness and peace attained through Christ.35 (2) Martyn's
sensitive nature permitted him to appreciate the best found in
his Muslim acquaintances and to ascribe such to the activity of
God.36 (3) His message centered upon the grace of God, the person
of Christ and progressive sanctification in the Holy Spirit.37
Whether talking with Sufi or Sunni, he spoke of Christ as the key
to the Creator-creature relationship. (4) Martyn would direct
the inquirer to the study of the Scriptures themselves.38 (5)
He saw the need for the Christian to remain a supporting friend
while the Muslim inquirer passed through the throes of critical
contemplation and decision.39 (6) He saw the value of creating
an atmosphere in society favorable to inquiry. Shiraz was
more hospitable than he had expected.40 (7) He realized that
one must leave room for the working of the Spirit of God and the
interaction between the inquirer and his own society, in the
transformation of individuals and societies: "Synthesis is the
work of God alone."

Martyn understood that the hidden dynamics of personality are
involved in the communication of the Christian message. Martyn's
own personality, speech and self-revealing journal made an impact
not only upon Sheikh Salih, the learned teacher of Luchnow but

upon Corrie, Thomason, Wilberforce, Grant and hundreds of others.
His intense devotion, intellectual and linguistic gifts, natural
enthusiasm and keen ability made him something of an ideal for
those dedicating themselves to work in the Muslim world. More
important, he pointed out that the problems of communication
are rooted in the communicator as well as in the receiver. He
raised the questions of language, culture, religious background,
when he sought to convey the idea of incarnation.

> March 22, 1812. These two days I have been thinking from
> morning to night about the Incarnation; considering if I could
> represent it in such a way as to obviate in any degree the pre-
> judices of the Mohammadans; not that I wish to make it appear
> altogether agreeable to reason, but I wanted to give a consis-
> tent account of the nature and uses of this doctrine, as they
> are found in the different parts of Holy Scriptures. One thing
> implied another to such an extent that I thought necessarily
> of the nature of life, death, spirit, soul, animal nature,
> state of separate spirits, personality, the person of Christ,
> etc., that I was quite worn out with fruitless thought....
> /Martyn then sought to help his questioner comprehend the mys-
> tery of the Incarnation by having the latter describe the
> "essence of deity"/...After an effort or two he found that every
> term he used implied our frightful doctrine, namely, personality,
> locality, etc. This is a thought that is now much in my mind--
> that it is so ordered that, since men speak of God but through
> the meduim of language, which is all material, nor think of
> God but through the meduim of material objects, they do
> unwillingly come to God through the Word, and think of God
> by means of an Incarnation.[41]

Thus, Martyn, by his questions and contributions to apologetics
and personal evangelism, set the pace for the missionary movement to Muslims.

Anglican Mission Activity before 1850.

    Anglican activity in India before 1850 centered about these
chaplains, the episcopate, and the mission work of the Church
Missionary Society. As a result of the overtures of Buchanan
and others, the first Anglican bishop, Thomas F. Middleton
(1769-1822) reached Calcutta in 1814. He was annoyed by his
limited jurisdiction over the missionaries (mostly Germans) and
some of the chaplains.[42] This three-cornered tension between
higher clergy, missionaries, and chaplains frequently plagued
Anglican work in India. Reginald Heber (1783-1828), second
Bishop of Calcutta and famous hymn writer, strongly supported
the mission societies and demonstrated an ecumenical spirit far
in advance of his age.[43] Further encouragement to evangelical
missions came from Daniel Wilson (1778-1858), fifth bishop of
Calcutta (1832-1858) and Metropolitan (1833-1858).[44] Administrators and laymen such as   Herbert   Edwardes,

Robert Montgomery and John Lawrence joined in their support.
Although the episcopate did not initiate missions to Muslims,
there was growing favor shown to such. This is seen especially
in the first bishops at Madras (Corrie), Bombay (Carr) and
Lahore (French). Clashes between evangelical missionaries and
higher clergy would however continue.

The Church Missionary Society was founded in 1799 by Simeon,
Grant, John Venn and others who were determined that it should
be both evangelical and "within" the church. It became a major
force in missions to Muslims in North India. The S.P.C.K.,
S.P.G. and other Anglican groups made more limited contributions.
Three C.M.S. Secretaries who greatly influenced this work were
Thomas Scott (1799-1802), Josiah Pratt (1802-1823) and Henry
Venn (1841-1873). Due to the shortage of candidates, C.M.S.
could send no missionaries to North India until 1815. The
missionary training school at Bledlow (1806) under Thomas Scott
did begin to teach Arabic however in anticipation of Muslim
work. The majority of the first C.M.S. missionaries were
German, only a few were ordained, and fewer still were university graduates.[45] This must be kept in mind when viewing the
diverse Anglican strands of pietism and rationalism, ecumenical-
ism and sectarianism, pragmatism and clericalism.

Unofficially C.M.S. began work via a "Corresponding Committee" in Calcutta (1807) composed of the "Five Chaplains" and
George Udny. By 1812 only Corrie and Thomason assisted by
Abdul Masih continued the work. The latter ministered from
the Word and his stock of medicines to the hundreds he met
during his travels. During the sixteen months Corrie and Abdul
Masih worked in Agra, they baptised over fifty adult Muslims
and Hindus. The arrival of four C.M.S. workers (1815) was
thus an occasion of joy. From 1814 to 1824, C.M.S. sent twenty-
six men to India of whom fourteen went to the North. These
were aided by Abdul Masih and William Bowley (an Eurasian).
Corrie meanwhile devised a system (1817) for raising part of
the growing budget from European Christians in India.

By 1824, there was conscientious examination of the methods
employed to spread the Gospel.[46] The Press of the Bible Society
in Calcutta (1810) drew the cooperation of almost all. Schools,
begun by Marshman and Martyn, now gained more attention.
Regional Anglo-Vernacular schools with "Christian subjects"
were successfully introduced at Burdwan by Captain Stewart and
John Perowne. By 1822 the gospels were being read in mission
schools at garrison towns and mission stations. These activities
came under the "mission station" with its ordained missionary.
The typical compound included dwellings, school, church, and
sometimes printing office and "seminary". Stations at Agra,
Benares, Chunar, Meerut, Cawnpore, and Krishnagur were main-
tained by Abdul Masih, Corrie, William Bowley, Greenwood,
Fisher, Anund Masih and the lay help of the Sherwoods and
Lieutenant Tomkyms. Among the first Eurasian, Muslim and
Brahmin converts ordained were Bowley, Abdul Masih and Anund

Masih. C.M.S. work at Allahabad, Lucknow and Delhi was later
overshadowed by the forces of the S.P.G. and Cambridge Mission.
In addition to the above, one observes the early forms of Christian service and women's work. Orphanages began at Calcutta
(1783), Cawnpore (1812), and Agra (1826). The Agra Relief
Society formed to help during the periodical famines. The wives
of missionaries (e.g. Mrs. Marshman), clergy (Mrs. Wilson) and
civil or military employees (Mrs. Sherwood) began work among the
women of India. The barrier to single women cracked when the
British and Foreign School Society sent Miss M. A. Cooke to
Calcutta to begin a girls' school (1822). Societies promoting
"female education" (1824) served as fore-runners of the Zenana
Societies.[47]

During the years, 1800-1840, a vicious pamphlet war was continuing in Britain. Major Scott-Waring, Sydney Smith, Abbe
Dubois, N. Wiseman and others attacked Indian Missions with the
objective of halting them! C. Buchanan, Wilberforce, J. W.
Cunningham and James Hough fought back brilliantly. Josiah
Pratt began the monthly C.M.S. paper "Missionary Register"
(1813), "provincial associations", and "deputations" to inform
the public, raise funds and stimulate interest. These efforts
proved most fruitful.[48]

The years of 1824-1841 were troubled ones for C.M.S. Although
a Missionary College began in England at Islington (1825), the
evangelical camp experienced internal tensions. On top of this,
the Tractarian or Oxford Movement, which began with John Keble
(ca. 1833) and gained fuller expression in John Henry Newman,
offered a revival of interest in liturgy, the Church Fathers and
relations with Rome as an alternative to evangelicalism. Fortunately with the accession of Henry Venn to the secretariat
(1841), C.M.S. regained its vigor. When Russia expelled the
Basel Mission from Persia, these German missionaries (e.g. Pfander)
shifted their energies to the C.M.S. work among Muslims in India.
By 1841, C.M.S. had fifty-six workers in India. The mission
press and preaching displayed a fresh burst of energy and "Christian Villages" emerge in some regions. In Bengal, mass movements
to Christianity with an increasing number of baptisms among the
Karta Bhoja sect (mixture of Hindu-Muslim beliefs) appear in the
1830s and 1840s, but C.M.S. was not ready to cope with the
opportunity.[49]

The mid-point of the century revealed the results of this
pioneer mission work. Many obstacles to missions (except for
the Mutiny, 1857 and Afghan Wars) had been overcome. The combined
efforts of missionaries, Indian Christians and enlightened civil
administrators such as Governor-General Lord William Bentinck
were able to effect tremendous social reforms curtailing several
inhumane Indian practices and British patronage of native
religions.[50] From its opportune position in North India, C.M.S.
was especially suited to develop its missionary methods among
Muslims.

Major Anglican Contributions to Apologetics before 1850

Anglican contributions to the apologetic-evangelistic 'approach to Muslims in India before 1850 can be traced from Martyn through Abdul Masih, S. Lee and K. G. Pfander. These representative figures reflect the larger effort.

Sheikh Salih (later baptized Abdul Masih, 1765-1827), scholar-teacher of Islam, Arabic, and Persian became disgusted by an assassination plot which involved swearing on the Quran. At Cawnpore, he was attracted by Martyn's sermon on the Ten Commandments which interpreted law in light of the Sermon on the Mount, noted the impossibility of salvation by obedience to the law, and observed that the law was a schoolmaster to bring us to Christ. His appetite whetted he sought work with Martyn, gained access to Persian and Urdu translations of the New Testament, and in his new faith requested baptism. After further instruction under David Brown in Calcutta, he was baptized (1813). The conversion of this Muslim teacher and former keeper of the king's jewels excited Lucknow. As lay-missionary of C.M.S., he won to Christ the chief physician (Taleb Massee'h) of the Rajah of Bhurtpore, prepared converts for baptism, toured with Corrie, and for twelve years ministered at Agra. He preached to poor and educated, shared his bread and medicine with those in need. He was the first of a long chain of Christian Indian apologists to Islam. When the Anglican bishop hesitated to ordain him, he became a Lutheran (1821) and only later rejoined the Anglican under Bishop Heber (1825). His gifted service convinced English and Indian, Anglican and Lutheran alike of the feasibility of an Indian ministry. He died shortly after beginning new work at Lucknow (1827). Abdul Masih's pioneer ministry blended the methods of Martyn with the rational methodology inherited from Islam to form a uniquely Indian Christian apologetics.[51] This work about Agra suffered a lull between his death and the arrival of Pfander (ca. 1841).

Samuel Lee (1783-1852) became the England based Islamic scholar and apologist for C.M.S. and the vital link between Martyn and Pfander. Self-educated like Carey, he studied Latin, Greek, Hebrew, Syriac, Arabic, Persian and Hindustani. Buchanan introduced him to Pratt and it was arranged that he should continue study at Cambridge. C.M.S. was anxious to gain a scholar to translate the Scriptures and Prayer Book into Near Eastern and Asiatic languages, (Urdu) and to put Martyn's Persian New Testament to print. As the Society's orientalist, Lee became Professor of Hebrew, Arabic, Sanskrit and Bengali at the College at Islington (1825) and later professor of Arabic then Hebrew at Cambridge (1819-1831). He helped develop two approaches to Islam: the controversial-apologetic and the academic.[52]

Samuel Lee had an excellent grasp of the development of Christian-Muslim controversy from Jerome Xavier (at Akbar's Court, 1580) to Martyn.[53] Two things prompted Lee to write his own apology. First, Martyn's reply, written in ill health and with

limited resources, needed improvement. Second, the rejoinder of
Muhammad Ruza of Hamadan following Martyn's death needed a reply.
After translating these recent Persian tracts into English, he
adds his own apology in <u>Controversial</u> <u>Tracts</u> <u>on</u> <u>Christianity</u> <u>and</u>
<u>Mohammedanism</u> (1824). Lee's rational argumentation proposes:
First, if there are to be fruitful results the criteria for
measuring truth must shift from miracles to the Scriptures, i.e.
trustworthy revelations from God.[54] Second, the key question is
that of the validity (authenticity) of the Scriptures and this
criticism. He traces the preservation of biblical manuscripts
from the time of Moses to the modern period. He fails to dif-
ferentiate between Christian revelation as centered in a Person
attested to by recorded historical witnesses (Bible), and Islamic
revelation as centered in a Book (miraculous, supra-historical).[55]
Third, Lee asserts that the scientific approach of Locke must
be applied to separate the historical from legend, tradition and
fiction.[56] Fourth, Lee applies the above criteria to Muhammad
and the Muslim community. The Prophet failed by contradicting
the prophets of the Old Testament and Jesus the Messiah. The
Muslim community mistakenly ascribed unproven authority to its
founder and book.[57] Fifth, Lee noted the many linguistic simi-
larities between the Quran and the Syriac versions of the Bible
and called for Muslims and Christians to research as to Islam's
debt to Syrian and Nestorian Christianity. In this year of 1824,
Lee sets the stage for a scholarly approach to the origins and
sources of the Quran and Islam.[58] Sixth, Lee's presentation of
the Christian faith and life is rooted in a philosophic-rational-
istic outlook that often lacks the warmth and personal appeal
of Martyn.

     We find in Scripture, that man is treated by his Maker as
a reasonable, accountable, and passible being. Precepts are
laid down to be observed by him, and rewards or punishments
are promised...also informs us all men are sinners....It will
be foreign to our purpose to enquire why God permitted this
state of things to exist; that must be left to his inscrut-
able wisdom;.../yet God gives a way of salvation. He then
lists Old Testament promises of salvation including the sacrifice and death of the Messiah./...In the N.T. the same thing
is declared; and, that, it is the exertion of faith alone, in
the merits of Him who hath thus suffered for mankind, that
man can be brought into a state of acceptance with his Maker...
this does by no means relax man's responsibility....Under the
first dispensation, certain precepts were laid down, and men
were commanded to obey them. Under the new dispensation,
additional precepts were laid down, which we are also commanded to observe...to practice holiness, and to follow every good
word and work....[59]

Revelation, reason, religious precepts and ethical obedience are
the prime elements in Lee's apology. Although Lee never served

abroad, he contributed substantially to scientific Islamic
scholarship and to the apologetics of Pfander, John Wilson, T.
French, and W. Muir.

Karl Gottlieb Pfander (1803-1865) is undoubtedly a central
figure in the development of the apologetic approach to Muslims
in the nineteenth century. Born in Würtemburg, educated at Korn-
thal (a Moravian school) and the Basel Missionary Seminary, he
was sent by the Basel Mission to Georgia or Transcaucasia. From
1825 to 1837, he travelled and preached in Persia and nearby
countries. During these demanding years he wrote Mizan-al-Haqq
(The Balance of Truth). Pfander had an exceptional gift for
languages as well as a sure grasp of indigenous thought patterns.
Russia's expulsion of the Basel Mission (1837) led to Pfander's
appointment to the C.M.S. in India. For sixteen years he served
at Agra and Peshawar (1841-1857). Although his life was frequently threatened, he continued to preach in public even during the
Mutiny. He felt he had work to do and he set about it in his own
systematic fashion. After the Mutiny, Pfander was considered
qualified to begin the strategic new C.M.S. work in Constantinople
(1858).[60] The open apologetic methods which had succeeded in
British India however brought down the heavy hand of Ottoman
authorities. Pfander retired to England and died there in 1865.

Those who knew Pfander considered him not only courageous, but
of warm disposition and well-balanced temperment. He was undoubtedly of keen intellect, a blend of European pietism and rationalism.[61] Pfander was drawn into several well-known controversial
debates. Much interest about Agra resulted from his work and he
agreed to meet the mullahs publicly. The two day discussion proved
inconclusive, each claiming the victory, but two of the subordinate
mullahs present were impressed with the validity of Christianity
and later became Christians. They are typical of the number of
outstanding converts Pfander won in each of his three fields.
Safdar Ali later became an official in the India Education Department and Imad-ud-Din of Amritsar, a noted missionary minister and
author.[62]

Although Pfander's writings do not convey his personal warmth
fully, they provide a basis for examining his mission methods.
The first and most influential of his writings was Mizan-al-Haqq
(The Balance of Truth). Written at the request and advice of his
colleagues, the German text saw many translations and publications.
The content of this widely circulated volume deserved special
attention.[63] The clear logic and the near-oriental style of
Pfander drew the attention and admiration of many Muslims.[64]

What criticism may be leveled at this document? Although
Pfander states that revelation is the key, the appeal is basically
to reason and conscience. Part I is an exercise in apologetics
justified by the application of modern research on the extant
manuscripts of the Scriptures. Part II is a positive statement
of the Christian faith appealing to "intellectual belief" at
times to a neglect of "the new life in the Spirit". His effort
at recovery of historical fact and his insistence that the

decision ultimately belongs to the reader remain acceptable even
by modern standards. Pfander's greatest weakness is in Part III.
His outright attack on the Quran, Muhammad and Islam was a tactical
mistake even if he was convinced that it could be historically
substantiated. Pfander wanted the Muslim to apply the methods of
his historical criticism to the origin and development of Islam.
But because that criticism came from without rather than from
within the Muslim community it often produced only an angry defensive reaction. The document relied too heavily on rational
argument, reflecting the outlook of the Ulema and nineteenth century Europe. It overlooked the fact that men are emotionally
tied to community and religious archetypes and hence consider such
attack as on themselves. Other weaknesses included a heavy
dependence on inadequate European sources for Muslim history
(Islamics was yet an infant science), a terminology which sometimes
reflected the prejudices of medieval Europe, and a length (ca. 370
pages) which rather restricted its appeal to scholarly circles.
In spite of the above limitations it was honored as the classic
model of Christian apologetics by many.

Pfander's other works also deserve review. Miftah-ul-Asrar
(The Key of Mysteries) is a short treatise presenting Jesus as
the divine Saviour and the doctrine of the Trinity. His basic
premise was that these truths can be found only by faith in God's
revelation, not by human experience (reason or science). He
moves from careful biblical exposition to philosophical argument
e.g. "the possibility of a Plurality in Unity". He adds that
"A true knowledge of God and the Salvation of man are dependent
on the Doctrine of the Trinity" inasmuch as God's love and mercy
are extended to men through the eternal Son and the Holy Spirit.
He concludes:

> He who denies the Trinity is obliged to believe in an abso-
> lute Unity which excluded knowledge and will in God, as also
> His other moral attributes, leads to a denial of Revelation,
> and if followed up, plunges its advocates into Pantheism!
> -God's Holiness and Justice, as well as His love and Mercy
> can be rightly understood only in Christ, and right knowledge
> of these is necessary for salvation. -Christ is Mediator
> and Saviour only because he is God and man, whoever therefore
> disbelieves his Divinity excludes himself from Salvation.[65]

The treatise, Tariq-ul-Hayat (The Way of Life), which was published
in India before 1844, concentrates on sin and redemption. It
examines the account of the fall, the inwardness of sin, and various ideas of pardon. He finds the Muslim treatment of sin
legalistic and the idea that "millions are predestined for hell"
unacceptable. In contrast the Good-News of faith in Jesus not
only appeals to the human heart but results in restoration to
God's favor and a new inner life for the Christian. Some consider this his finest work.[66] The Tree of Life, a small Urdu
tract, describes Christian morality and life with the support of

biblical quotations. Pfander also engaged in correspondence
with the leading maulvis of North India. Only part of this was
published.[67]

Remarks on the Nature of Muhammadanism is a most valuable
personal statement giving insight into Pfander's concern for
honest scholarship.[68] The true nature of Islam cannot be grasped
by examining its literary documents. The Traditions, a mixture
of fiction and fact retold by mullahs, exert more influence on
the practice of the people than the Quran. Thus he urges Christian scholars to study the Hadiths and lists the recently published collections. Identifying popular Muslim misconceptions
regarding God, creation, sin, forgiveness, hell and paradise,
he explains how the Gospel speaks to each. The concluding
comments to Christian readers disclose Pfander's personal feelings.

> These extracts will, to every enlightened mind have fully
> justified the assertions we made at the beginning. They show
> clearly how foolish the Muhammadans have become, when, think-
> ing themselves wise, they rejected the wisdom and the power
> of God revealed in the cross of Christ, and how little their
> own system could save them from sinking into the most appalling
> errors and the grossest superstition. It is true that in the
> Qur'an, as well as in their traditions, many a truth and many
> a good moral precept is contained; but it will not be necessary
> to mention it again, that all that is good and true in their
> religion, has been either literally, or according to the sense
> borrowed from the Jews and Christians, that is, from the Holy
> Scriptures. But as they did not receive the whole of divine
> truth and rejected Christ, this part, thus separated from the
> stock, from the tree of life, could neither actually enlighten
> nor save them. We further allow that the extract we have made
> from their traditions, is a partial one; but this was just our
> object, for the fair side of Muhammadanism has been presented
> often enough....As the eye is created for the light, so man's
> spirit for truth....These wants the Muhammadans too have
> within their spirits, but the light of divine truth did not
> in former ages shine upon them in its original and heavenly
> slendor; it was badly reflected and greatly darkened by the
> ignorance and ungodly conduct of the Jews and Christians
> around them. What is now required is, that the light of the
> Gospel, reflected in the holy walk and conversation of true
> believers, may be made to shine upon them in its unadulterated
> heavenly splendor. This alone can break their bonds, con-
> vince them to accept the salvation offered in the Gospel.[69]

Regardless of one's evaluation of Pfander's controversial approach,
his intellectual abilities, literary skills and Christian dedication remain. He stands as a vital link in the formation of a
Christian apology to Muslims.

The development of a Christian apologetic from 1850 onwards
can be seen as admiration of, reaction to and modification of

the work of Pfander. Although no one again attempted his
strenuous rational procedure, many admired him as a master of
apologetics. His approach was slowly modified and incorporated
into a broader, ever maturing evangelistic effort. Bishop T. V.
French was proud to be Pfander's disciple and successor at Agra.[70]
He in turn willed a methodological legacy to Bishop Lefroy. A
still more matured apologetic would emerge in the Near East via
Tisball, Thornton, and Gairdner. Another scholarly strand stimulated by Pfander found expression in the Islamic scholar, William
Muir (civil servant of North India and later administrator at the
University of Edinburgh). Muir examined Muslim tradition, origins
and history and produced one of the first massive lives of Muhammad.[7]
Even more significant is the fact that Pfander was the model for
many Indian evangelists and catechists from Imad-ud-Din onwards
into the twentieth century.

Because of the liberal reaction to rationalism (Schleiermacher
to Schweitzer) and a growing appreciation of oriental culture and
religion, Pfander's works came under attack. By the end of the
nineteenth century most evangelicals (W. Tisdall, E.M. Wherry,
W.A. Rice) agreed that "argument and abuse" were out of place
while insisting that a Christian apology was still needed.[72]

The Second Era of Anglican Confrontation with Islam, 1850-1910: Further Modification of the Apologetic-Evangelistic Method

Anglican efforts among Muslims in North India were carried on
mainly by the C.M.S. with limited work being done by the S.P.G.,
Cambridge Mission, and Zenana Society. While the key developments
in the apologetic approach are visible in French and Lefroy,
parallel and slightly varying aspects will be seen in Robert Clark,
Rowland Bateman, and S. S. Allnutt.

T. V. French: Evangelist, Teacher and Churchman

Thomas Valpy French (1825-1891) was born into an evangelical
clerical home and educated at Rugby and Oxford.[73] Acquainted with
both Evangelicals and Tractarians, he remained surprisingly independent. His first task in India with C.M.S. was the founding
of St. John's College in Agra (1850), the new British center for
the Northwest Provinces. Its enrollment reached 300 before the
Mutiny (1857) even though most Muslims resisted western
education. French's continuing emphasis was "evangelism via
education".[74] After a furlough in England (1859-1862), French
began his second task of frontier evangelism in the Derajat, on
the border of Baluchistan. Administrators and retired officers
of Christian conviction had encouraged this expansion into the
Punjab and the Northwest. French travelled and preached in the
bazaars of Dera Ismail Khan and other villages until struck down
by fever and forced to return to an English parish (1863-1869).
Returning to India in 1869, the founding of St. John's Divinity

School at Lahore (capital of the Punjab) became his third major
task. In this period (1869-1874), he did extensive pioneer
preaching about Lahore and even into Kashmir. From 1874-1877,
he aroused interest in England for Muslim work and assisted in
the birth of the Cambridge- Delhi Mission. Fourthly, he was appointed as Bishop of the newly established diocese of Lahore
(included Punjab, Sindh, and Kashmir) and soon found himself
mediating between S.P.G. workers who were concerned with ecclesiastical orders, liturgies, etc., and C.M.S. personnel concerned
about indigenous forms of evangelism and church. As bishop
(1877-1887), French encouraged direct evangelism, schools for
youth, Zenana mission, literary production by nationals and the
Amritsar Medical Mission (1882). At times, this pioneer evangelist and capable churchman was troubled by "organizational burdens"
and "Anglican in-fighting". At the age of 62, he resigned his
office to tour the Near East and North Africa, to review the
Eastern Churches and establish cordial relationships, and to
issue a ringing call for missions to Muslims in Arabia. While
the C.M.S. debated the issue, French felt compelled to begin his
fifth and final project; he started work at Muscat, Oman where he
was to die within a few months (May 14, 1891). French can be
recognized as being first and foremost an evangelist to Muslims;
secondly, an evangelist who saw the validity of educational work;
and thirdly as a churchman who saw the establishment of an
indigenous church as the key to the evangelization of India.

Although French spent many years as a teacher at Agra (1850-58)
and the Divinity School in Lahore (1870-74) and as Bishop (1877-87),
he remained an evangelist. The proclamation of the Gospel to the
Muslims had priority. Every other method and means, especially
the church's indigenous ministry must serve that objective. Known
as the "seven-tongued" evangelist for his linguistic ability, this
scholar argued that the colloquial must be learned, that "to the
poor the gospel may be preached" for "till the language is known,
it is like digging with a broken spade".[75] At Agra, public or
bazaar preaching occupied much of his time. Preaching and teaching
had to be related if the school was to be a force in the community.[76]
French wrote secretary Henry Venn warning of the danger of neglecting evangelism for educational institutions (1852). He was also
critical of the haphazard itinerant evangelism being done. He
called for a strategy, "a preconcerted and well-digested scheme"
which was not content with spasmodic campaigns in key cities but
which fostered an on-going witness to distinctive social units.
This would call for experienced foreign and Indian workers engaged
in direct evangelism in situations which had been carefully
studied.[77]

During French's early years (1850-1858), he came under the
influence of Pfander and at times used controversial methods.
French saw such activity not so effective in winning converts
as gaining the attention, awakening the interest of an indifferent
society.[78] He admitted that public debates generally produced
little good. Nevertheless it was difficult to dodge the

challenge of two maulvis to a public debate in Agra (1854).
These men had studied the Bible and Pfander's writings for two
years and deserved to be heard. Pfander, with French as his
second, debated for two days to a growing audience on issues such
as the corruption of the Scriptures, the mission of Muhammad,
the role of the Quran, and the divinity of Christ. French discouraged such confrontations believing that Indian evangelists
equipped with oriental thought patterns could devise better
formats for evangelism.[79] While French continued to admire the
work of Pfander, he knew that such fiery clashes produced unnecessary hostile reactions while a sympathetic spirit was more
conducive to effective communication.[80] Discovering spontaneous
converts and Christian communities resulting from the reading of
the printed Word, French became convinced that Christian literature was more effective than noisy debate. As the Word of God
was seeded throughout the region, converts appeared in most
unexpected places.[81]

As a pioneer evangelist in the Derajat (1862) French applied
his knowledge of language and Islam in a most sacrificial manner.
By elementary preaching and warm friendship with Muslims, the
foundations for this new work were laid before he succumbed to
sunstroke.[82] Again in 1869, he returned to Lahore determined to
evangelize and to train evangelists. Whenever the Divinity School
was not in session, French toured and preached about Lahore,
Rawalpindi, Peshawar and even Kashmir. With Clark he began
"bazaar preaching" in Kashmir (1871) amidst great hostility.
Years later a native church, schools, hospital and leper asylum
would be rooted in this soil (1895). In spite of frequent abuse,
French "seldom let the day pass without going to the bazaar in
the evening and talking to the people about Christ."[83] With the
growth of organized resistance by the Wahhabis and others (1872-73),
the evangelists avoided public dispute and where possible built
special halls for public preaching.

The maturing evangelistic methods of Bishop French can be
observed as he retraced the footsteps of Martyn in Persia (1883).
His approach to the Persian Muslims was to hold small discussion
groups in which he quietly expounded the Bible. His diary for
April discloses that he found a great receptivity for such
themes as the kingdom of God, the death and burial of Christ, the
atonement, the second coming, the idea that trinity is rooted in
unity, and especially the new birth.

April 12, 1883. Thank God for some most interesting conversation with some askhoods....It is surprising to see how much
is admitted, and apparently in some assurance of faith. The
Lord does seem to have His own everywhere. They did not attempt
to set up Mohammed against Christ....The dying and rising with
Christ seemed marvellously to commend itself to them. The
Word and Son of God, His eternal oneness with the Father, seemed to present no difficulty. "How can we come thus," they
said, "to be dead and buried with Christ?" I dwelt on baptism

and the yielded heart and life as the true means of death to
sin in repentence....A general in the army and a sheikh called
....They said much about the "tauhid" or unity, and I showed
how the unity was the first principle of all religion and all
truth. So far we were all agreed; but there were idiomati,
which were the mysteries of faith. I must try to show how
barren, empty, and naked the idea of absolute deism is, and
how the Trinitas is out of the root of the unity....They
inquired particularly about "wiladat-i-sani" (new birth),
what it meant and how it was attained, which gave occasion
for bringing out the work of Christ and the Holy Spirit....A
long and pleasant evening with a Nicodemus-like moolah who
sat one and a half hours,..."Masih imroz aram" (Christ is
peace, today) and the teaching based upon it, struck him
much. "Being justified by faith" must follow this evening....[84]

Agreeing with Alexander Mackay of Calcutta (1849-90) and General
Haig, French saw Muscat as a strategic point.[85] In his last days,
this solitary figure inaugurated work there under most primitive
conditions. By personal conversations in the bazaar and coffee
shops he spoke to the outcaste poor and sheikhs alike on the
theme of "the death into sin and new birth into righteousness".[86]
Long after his death (May 14, 1891), French continued to inspire
such figures as Allnutt, Lefroy and Zwemer to the evangelization
of Muslims.[87]

Three aspects of French's apologetic-evangelistic approach
appear in an article published after his death.[88] First, one
begins with an element of the human predicament or Islamic
thought and then proceeds to demonstrate how the Gospel speaks
to this need. For example, the mystic devotion and desire for
fellowship with God expressed by Sheikh 'Adb-al-Qadir (leader
of the Qadiriyya) appealed to French. The Sheikh had once
prayed:

     O Lord there are two boons I ask Thee to grant me; if
     Thou grant me but these two, I will never ask of Thee any
     petition more. First, I ask Thee to give me the death in
     which there is no life; and second, to give me the life in
     which there is no death.

French used this as a point for introducing the idea of surrender
to Christ and the rebirth to eternal life. Second, reconciliation
must be proclaimed so as to meet man's great longing for brotherhood. Communion (with God in Christ and with other men undergoing
renewal in his church) is at the heart of the Christian message
and experience. Third, courageous converts from Islam must be
trained to serve as apostles to their own nations as soon as
possible.[89]
Elsewhere the insights of French were recorded. First, the
mission to Islam will be fulfilled only by personal contact and
sacrifice. "If we would win these Moslem lands for Christ, we

must die for them."[90] Second, this mission involves the whole
Christian community, lay and ordained, national and foreigner.
French saw the danger of overstressing episcopacy and admitted
laymen as co-ordinate members of church synods. Lay responsibility and lay testimony were essential to the church's life and
mission.[91] Third, mission transcended denomination and nationality. Although a convinced Anglican churchman, French cooperated
with and urged his own church to learn from Lutherans, Presbyterians and others. French's ministry to Muslims reflects the
maturation process beginning to occur in the church.

The potential of education as a means of mission gained French's
attention. He was sent to Agra to establish and direct an institution of higher education"as the true way of introducing the
Gospel to the upper classes of society".[92] Appropriating the
methods introduced by Duff in Bengal, St. John's College at Agra
(1850) succeeded reasonably well in terms of enrollment. French
sought to generate a spirit of mutual respect as well as free
discussion in his Bible studies. He hoped that "sustained and
steady influence" rather than violent shocking ideas would
elicit from the students an interest in Christianity.[93] The
Christian college was able to compete with the governmental college
only because of the attractive character of its faculty and its
superior program of English. Muslim and Hindu parents also
appreciated the religious-moral element of the curriculum (in
contrast to the frequently agnostic spirit of governmental
schools).[94] French became very critical however of the mono-
tonous teaching of elementary courses and "prestige" English.
He favored the use of the vernacular and urged that the church's
work in higher education should aim at recruiting and training
a Christian work force.

> Amid the colleges growing up around us shall no regard be
> had to India's Christian future?...We can nevertheless con-
> ceive it as very possible, to say the least, that there may
> hereafter gather within and around these walls a band of
> native evangelists, catechists, and teachers, towards whom
> the founders of native Churches may look for a supply of
> qualified instructors; and often does encouragement arise,
> in carrying on a seemingly insignificant theological class,
> consisting of three catechists and six or eight boys, from
> which the thought that this class may hereafter become the
> most important and strictly missionary branch of our college
> work....[95]

Because the immediate results at St. John's College were small
(only one Muslim convert, more Hindus), French turned more and
more attention to outside evangelism. Yet over the years as he
saw how many of these former pupils later entered the church and
served in Christian callings, his estimate of the educational
approach rose. Baptizing one of these at Agra, he wrote:

January 20, 1869. I see more and more that schools form
the very stamina of our mission efforts and that those daily
instilled lessons leave an impression which, though long and
determinately resisted, is never wholly lost. May this lead
me to fervent daily intercession for them.[96]

Out of these experiences two ideas were born: first, the Divinity
School at Lahore, and second, that seats of learning in Britain
should send the most dedicated and talented scholars to serve
similar institutes in the midst of Islam and Hinduism. French's
paper (Feb. 16, 1876) helped give shape to the Cambridge-Delhi
Mission (Cambridge Brotherhood) led by Edward Bickersteth, which
by 1879 had six of its number abroad including Allnutt and Lefroy.[97]
In a minor way, French contributed to the idea of "education as
the handmaiden of evangelism" as did Duff, Wilson, Forman, and
Ewing.

As a churchman, French made two distinctive contributions to
the changing pattern of mission. First he founded St. John's
Divinity School in Lahore for the training of an Indian ministry.
Second as Bishop of Lahore he sought to organize the church's life
that it might be more effective in mission. In a paper on the
proposed Divinity School (1866), French sets forth several of
his ideas:

(1) We need an improved system of theological training for
our more advanced converts with a special view...to their being
efficiently entrusted with the work of pastors and evangelists.
The remarks thus elicited have implied a secret conviction in
the minds of many that the materials in hand for constructing
and building up the native Church in India are not turned to
the best possible account....

(3) It is clear we must not compromise the future character
of the native church by attempting to trammel it with too
rigid adherence to our institutions....Its growth in the main
must be free and spontaneous....

(4)...the early churches...did fix upon convenient centres
which should form rallying points for the promotion and diffusion abroad of the light of the Gospel. In these a small
body of Christian teachers devoted themselves to the more
complete establishment, and firmer building up in the truth
and doctrine of Christianity, of a portion of the choicest
and ablest converts, with a view to their becoming in their
turn teachers and preachers of the Word....

(6)...Northwestern India. The ancient and well-earned
reputation for learning /of this area/...demand of us one or
more centres or headquarters of Christian literature; not
such merely as should count a theological department among
many devoted to literary and scientific acquirement, but an
institute, standing apart and alone, addicted to theology, and
to other sciences only so far as they are kindred and related
to it....

(10)...it should be as strictly as possible vernacular...
whenever an English course is going on, there should be a
corresponding and collateral course in the vernacular...the
college I propose should be dedicated to the purely native
church--to its building up, its strengthening and encouragement. A Mohammedan convert, brought up all his life in
distaste and prejudice of English, should here find his want
of English does not disentitle or incapacitate him for per-
fecting his curriculum of theology up to the full measure of
perfection which the college course reaches. Here Christianity
should be domesticated on the Indian soil, and be able to
reckon on a home and hearth of its own. Here, when it is
possible to obtain them, should be found men who, by a severe
and close attention bestowed on Mohammedan and Hindu literature, can express the delicate shades, the nice distinctions
of thought, which some, at least, of our standard works of
theology involve....⟨Needed is⟩ the power to expound them
freely and with confidence to the vast masses of India.

(14)...The Committee are not ignorant how rich a store of
wealth is embraced in the range of Hindu literature ⟨and Muslim,
which can be harnessed⟩...for the purpose of Gospel extension,
of its more forcible expression, of its deeper and firmer
engrafting in the national mind,...we should try to act upon
the principle enunciated in so many forms in Holy Scriptures,
---"I will consecrate their gain unto the Lord."...Is it not
hard to suppose that God has suffered that vast mass of eru-
dition and result of mental force to accumulate for so many
ages to be utterly purposeless towards setting up the Kingdom
of His dear Son?[98]

The above approach includes advanced ideas regarding evangelism,
the indigenous church and ministry, communication and culture
adaptation. In some measure these were put into action at the
Divinity School with the assistance of J. W. Knott, R. Clark, R.
Bateman and others. Situated in Lahore, the school enrolled
mainly converts from Islam. By 1872 two of the twenty students
were ordained. Modelled on the British curriculum with special
study in oriental religious systems, the program was certainly
not anti-intellectual. Priority was given to biblical studies
(in the original Hebrew and Greek texts) so that the student could
transfer these ideas into Indian thought patterns and terminology.[99]
In addition to other subjects, French personally instructed in
homiletics, pastoral care and practical theology. Teacher and
students gained fuller experience by touring, preaching and
baptizing converts.[100] This school with its disciplined but
devotional life, quarters for married students and required
native dress poured a valuable line of catechists, lay-evangel-
ists and clergy into the church's work.
    What kind of church did French visualize for India? First,
the national church must be indigenous yet not lose its catholic
nature. French could be described as an independent mediating

Anglican, at times fiercely resisting the importation of high
church rituals which would check the growth of Indian church
forms and yet firmly holding to the idea of episcopacy and
apostolic succession.[101] By the time he became bishop, his great
fear was that there would emerge two Anglican churches in India:
a native one under C.M.S. missionaries and Indian ministers, and
an English one under appointed chaplains. Such a tragedy would
have shattered the church's ministry of reconciliation. Resisting
all efforts to split the church, he labored to bring the two
extremes into harmonious co-operation and occasionally gained the
criticism of both![102] Coupled with this was the question of the
church's relation to the British government. French went to India
advocating government support for Christian missions.[103] By the
time of the Mutiny, he saw why the Indian church must be cut free
of such crippling entanglements. Yet he was never able to escape
the fact that he was appointed a bishop with governmental approval
and thus obliged to supervise the care of English civilians and
troops.[104] His creation of a representative government in the
Indian church was a major accomplishment. For the three synods
(1878, 1880, 1885) called by French, a system of lay representation
from the congregations was introduced which helped alleviate the
problem of foreign workers outnumbering nationals. The laity
became co-ordinate members of the church synods and not mere
assessors.[105] The responsibility of the Lahore bishopric were
most exhausting.[106] French persisted in his effort to shape a
truly indigenous yet catholic young church in spite of the
organizational machinery, fund-raising, cathedral building, and
party-in-fighting for ten years before passing the reins to another
and returning to his first love, evangelism.

    Second, the national church must give expression to her true
"united nature" as it is a vital part of witness. This unity
must begin among all Anglicans in India, but not remain there.
French established good relations with the Scottish and American
Presbyterians. In spite of his early caution and later restriction
by the Church of England, he managed to cross traditional lines
in many ways.[107] French was optimistic about the possibility of
"one common church for all India" provided truth and unity were
sought in the Holy Spirit's presence. Such a church must be
built on an early church (biblical) model which provided unity
without enforced uniformity. He was in favor of fuller use of
Oriental worship patterns "free from stiffness of our English
liturgical services" and introduced several reforms himself. He
also foresaw the drawing together of episcopal and presbyterian
forms of church government. The introduction of lay representatives in church synods was a step in this direction. Nearby
Presbyterian activity, internal "native church" pleas (cf. Robert
Clark), and the Missionary Conferences all strengthened this move
towards church-unity and a united Protestant witness to Islam
and others.[108]

Third, French stressed that the national church must fulfill
the mission for which she lives. In encouraging the development
of indigenous missionary methods, he was open to some very unor-
thodox methods, e.g. idea of the Christian "guru or fakir",
traveling poets, etc. While ever on the search for clerical
candidates, he felt that a lay movement was what India needed.
When the Presbyterians and Wesleyans built divinity schools, he
worried lest too high a proportion of Christian youth enter the
ministry and thus diminish the lay witness.[109] On the other hand,
French was at times too cautious. When distinctly Indian movements took shape, he feared lest they be cut adrift from links
with the past. At times he appears suspicious of the Native
Church Council in the Punjab under his friend Robert Clark. As
bishop he must "protect" the organization and traditions of the
Anglican Church in India.[110] In spite of this, French remains
a major contributor to an apologetic approach to Muslims. His
vision included the day when missionaries would travel from East
to West.[111]

> In ages to come what judgement is the Church likely to
> pass upon our missionary agencies?...I have a sorrowful con-
> viction that the Church of the future will, in some respects
> at least, profit rather from being warned by our mistakes
> than helped by the record of our wisdom, courage, abilities,
> and patient constancy and preseverance....I should say that
> it is our attempt to invent fresh models and courses of action
> instead of throwing ourselves with ventures of unfaltering
> faith into old missionary pathways, which must largely be
> credited with our failures and limited successes in the
> East....[112]

Robert Clark: the Indigenous Church

Robert Clark (1825-1900) spent a long career in direct evangelism (1852-1898) and provided good balance to French. By his service,
retirement and death in India, he represents one who completely
identifies himself with this land and its young church. Clark
was reared in an evangelical home, trained in commerce in Germany,
served with a Liverpool merchant firm before his call to the
ministry (1844), educated at Trinity College and offered a tutor-
ship at Cambridge prior to accepting the challenge of the Punjab
(1851). When the American Presbyterians at Ludhiana urged the
C.M.S. to join in the work, Clark founded a central station at
Amritsar where he served most of his life. He also pioneered in
Afghanistan, Kashmir, Tibet and other points in the Punjab and
served as Mission Secretary.[113]

As an evangelist, Clark left an impressive record. The program
and scattered mission stations in the city of Amritsar were
geared for outreach, instruction and discussion. His foremost
principle was that evangelism was best carried out by national
workers. Clark identified himself with the life and witness of

this small band. By 1854, there had been some twenty-three baptisms including notables such as a Maharajah, a Muslim doctor,
a Sikh priest and soon the first Muslim woman. A number of these
were soon in the field as evangelists. Amritsar's school (1852),
College (1862) and Christian Girl's Boarding School were also
graduating a number of qualified Christian workers. Clark's
ability to work with and through Indian evangelists is seen in
his relationships with Imad-ud-Din (a former Maulvie) and Pandit
Narain Dass Kharak Singh (former Sikh and Sanskrit scholar).
Clark knew how to train pastors and then to step back while
respectfully delegating responsibilities to them. Miyan Sadiq
became the elected pastor of the Amritsar Church after thirteen
years as catechist, two years training at the Lahore Divinity
School, and a tour with Clark to the Holy Land. Of the 555
adult converts baptized at Amristar between 1852 and 1883, 253
were from Islam.[114] No channel for evangelism was to be lost.
Literature work found a solid base in the Punjab Religious Book
Society, a cooperative venture of the C.M.S. and Presbyterians.
Clark began a series of commentaries on the Scriptures in 1874
to help train the native pastors, teachers, families, and inquirers.
He soon realized his limitations as an European and urged Imad-
ud-Din and others to take over this and other literary projects.
Imad-ud-Din, a respected author, acknowleges that the inspiration
and even much of the content of his works are to Clark's credit.[115]
Clark's adopted son began the monthly Punjab Mission News (1885).
Robert Clark was the first missionary to cross the Indus to the
Afghans (1853). He worked with Pfander at Peshawar the doorway
to Kabul and Central Asia, yet avoided controversy and preached
the Gospel in its "simplicity and fulness".[116] With the help
of Indian evangelists, first efforts were made in Kashmir and
Tibet as well (1854, 1863-4).[117] Space does not permit full
acknowledgement of Clark's work in education[118] or Christian
service and medical work. However, it must be noted that in
1863 he was the prime mover behind the C.M.S. medical program
associated with the Edinburgh Medical Missionary Society.[119]

Clark's most distinctive contribution was the role he gave to
the national church. The growing young churches about Amritsar
helped him to visualize the importance of accenting the missionary
structure of the church, and the Indian ministry. Clark considered the natural tendency of converts to congregate about mission
compounds and to depend on European missionaries as a retrograde
step sure to stunt the church's growth. Converts were urged to
live as citizens spread out among their countrymen, each radiating
light in the encircling night.[120] Since native Christians survived
India's climate better than the foreign missionaries, it was
apparent the future belonged to the national church.[121] Therefore he attacked missionary domination and stressed training
for independence.

It would seem to follow, then that we _must_ make them the
actors in missionary work, and must not let them be merely

the persons who are always <u>acted on</u>. We must throw responsibility on them, and throw on them difficulties too, as, they
occur; and, placing them in the arena, in the sight of God
and man, we must let them act,...Have we not, we may ask, made
duties, and especially mission duties, too easy for native
Christians....It would seem that they must begin to act for
themselves; to preach for themselves; to conduct schools...;
to go out on itinerations; to publish books...to raise sub-
scriptions...to live...leaning on no arm but their own and
God's. [122]

This somewhat forceful if common sense approach brought results.
Not only were congregations increasing their stewardship, but
learning the value of cooperation with other Christian bodies.
Clark and John Newton promoted the idea of a federal union of
Anglicans, Presbyterians and others. The Missionary Conferences
from 1861 onwards stimulated such hopes. [123]

Remaining at Amritsar after his appointment as Mission Secretary (1878), Clark began his hardest battles in behalf of the
young Indian Church. Its independent action was often blocked,
he felt, not only by the English majority of the organized church
but also by the institutionalized program of the C.M.S. [124] He
differed on several points with his respected friend, Bishop
French. For Clark, the episcopalian form of government was not
an ultimate. God's grace depends not upon nationality or forms. [125]
For twenty years, Clark battled that the Punjab Native Church
Council might gain more responsibility. He argued: "Our missionary policy should always be that we (the Europeans) must decrease,
they (the Indians) must increase." [126] This transference of authority, the termination of entangling alliances of the church with
the crown, and the incorporation of missionary planning into the
national church (rather than leaving it in a foreign mission
organization) were urgent requirements for the future health and
mission of the church in India according to Robert Clark. His
plan was that mission activity should be rooted in native congregations and regional church councils under Indian jurisdiction.
This was opposed or rivaled by entrenched mission stations, an
English dominated episcopacy, and a few foreign workers jealous
of their authority. [127] It is well to note that in South India
where his type of ideas were adopted the united church emerged
much earlier than in the North. Clark's confidence in Indian
Christians, congregations and councils nevertheless contributed
immensely to the growth of the church in Sindh and the Punjab
and to the formation of an indigenous evangelistic-apologetic
approach to Muslims. [128]

Rowland Bateman: Itinerant Evangelism

During thirty years of service in Northwest India, Rowland
Bateman (1840-1916) became an itinerant evangelist with a capacity
for communication few Europeans could match. After various

teaching assignments at Dera Ismail Khan (1868-9), Amritsar
(1869), and Lahore Divinity School (1869-72) in which this Oxford
graduate personally won his Muslim teachers and students to
Christ, he gained an affection for itinerant evangelism.[129]
Working as a free-lance evangelist with one or two Indian companions he demonstrated how the church must be built. First, he
gave personal attention to an inquirer no matter what might be
the time, distance, or risk involved.[130] Second, he took pains
to train capable converts to seek out and follow up other serious
inquirers. Thus were friends, class-mates and relatives of converts
drawn to Christ. While maintaining close contact with schools,
congregations, Christian industries and villages, he preferred
that Indian Christians should control these while the missionary
set the pace by pioneering new areas. Bateman's concern for the
poor and sick led him to tie medical work together with evangelism.
With Herbert U. Weitbrecht (-Stanton). he became involved in the
mass movement of outcaste peoples to Christianity in the Punjab
(esp. 1886-1897). The theme of "deliverance from bondage" in the
Gospel struck a responsive note in these groups. Their transformation in turn captured the attention of enlightened Muslims
who began to inquire for themselves as to the validity of this
faith. Bateman's travels and work about Narowal, Clarkabad and
the Jhang Bar plus the migratory nature of his converts produced
an amazing sphere of influence radiating out from this one
figure. His approach has been well summarized by his biographer:

> First, however, something must be said about his methods
> of doing his divinely commissioned work....One of his gifts
> was, so to speak, an insatiable sociability—a faculty which
> I have sometimes called Socratic, in that, as is said of
> Socrates, he "talked to all comers, questioning them about
> their affairs,"....His manner in doing this was so manly, and
> simple, and engaging, that offence was not easily taken, and
> his great-hearted optimism enabled him to meet non-Christians
> with cordiality....it was the humanness of his sympathy with
> and comprehension of men as men....His character drew young
> men to him like a magnet, and a goodly band became Christians
> under his influence, and have ever since been leaders in the
> Punjab Church.[131]

Samuel S. Allnutt: Education Evangelism

Samuel Scott Allnutt (1850-1917), along with French and Lefroy,
demonstrates how the higher education approach of Duff was adapted
for Anglican usage. Allnutt belonged to the **Cambridge**-Delhi
Mission which French had nurtured in 1876.[132] While G. A. Lefroy
became a leading evangelist to Muslims, Allnutt concentrated on
the educational work. Allnutt was reared in an evangelical home
and later influenced by the Tractarian movement. His high
church view laid great stress on devotional study and prayer.
A stickler for quality education, he founded St. Stephen's

School and College (1881) and served for 18 years as principal.
Both institutions attracted an increasing percentage of Muslims
over the years.[133] In an occasional paper, "Education as a
Missionay Agency" (1897), Allnutt expressed his approach.

> First of all it should be distinctly understood that by
> missionary education is meant, mainly and predominantly,
> seminaries of sound learning and religious education for
> non-Christians....Almost all the subjects are capable of
> having a religious bearing imparted to them, and the indirect-
> ness of the lesson often enhances its effectiveness. Still
> actual instruction in the Bible is, for all that, the part of
> the day's teaching which we endeavour to make the piece de
> resistance, so to say of our teaching. It is certainly the
> subject in which the men come to take as keen an interest as
> any of their course.[134]

The Cambridge Brotherhood was able to devote considerable time
to individual students and inquirers. Allnutt's extended effort
with one student exemplifies this:

> It is no intellectual process by which he is gradually feeling
> his way to Christ as his Saviour. I have felt lately how sig-
> nificant is the order in which we are taught to think of the
> three great functions, so to say, of our Lord--Prophet, Priest,
> and King. My friend has fully grasped the first...his sincere
> object now is to find in Him his Priest, his Saviour... /in a
> letter/...He has I am thankful to say, witnessed boldly for
> Christ his Master.[135]

Allnutt observed that his students were keenly aware of the con-
tradiction between their Western science and literature, and the
essential beliefs of their Indian religions. He encourages them
to discern what were the good elements in their religions and what
was fragmentary and worthless accretion. In this way he hoped
to pave the way to the Christian faith rather than produce a
critical spirit which rejects all religion. Allnutt's apology
was based largely upon natural theology, that is, reason indicates
that Christianity is the true religion.[136]

George A. Lefroy: Evangelist, Teacher and Churchman

Changing British attitudes greatly affected mission work. While
the government's policy was supposedly one of neutrality, many
Christians in civil and military service for a time (1850-1870)
supported mission work.[137] But in the last quarter of the century
the growth of liberal thought produced a reversal of this trend,
an attack on conservative theology and missions. Some found the
origin of religion in human experience or culture rather than
revelation. Others imbued with the new science of literary
criticism attacked the documents of Christianity. One asserted

that Muhammad had restored to Christianity what Paul had perverted.[138]
New awareness of Eastern religions, the growth of humanistic and
agnostic thought in Europe, and the changing relationship of
Britain and her colonies brought new pressures on the overseas
mission program.[139]

In this setting, George A. Lefroy (1854-1919) continued to
develop the Anglican apologetic-evangelistic approach to Islam
inherited from French. This distinguished member of the Cambridge
mission served with St. Stephen's College and the Delhi evangelistic program (1879-1989), as Bishop of Lahore (1899-1912),
and as Bishop of Calcutta and Metropolitan of all India (1913-
1919). A natural leader and diligent scholar, he was remembered
for his "big humanity" and Irish humour.[140] After gaining elo-
quence in Urdu for preaching to Muslims, Lefroy studied Arabic,
the Quran and Muslim theology. While others concentrated on
the schools, he was drawn to the rough give and take of bazaar
preaching. The changing social-religious climate in North India
was accompanied by increased vocal opposition to public preaching
and by 1890 Lefroy changed his strategy.[141] A Preaching Hall
(named after Bickersteth) provided an opportunity to preach with
less interference.

Lefroy's apologetic took shape in the "hammer and anvil"
setting of bazaar preaching. The persistence of Lefroy is
illustrated by his continuation in the bazaar in spite of being
constantly abused by a blind Muslim teacher whom he called his
"thorn in the flesh". After nearly eight years of opposition,
this Maulvi confessed his faith in Christ in the new Preaching
Hall (1892). Baptized as Ahmed Masih, he went on to proclaim
his new-found faith for over 20 years. Lefroy found his audiences
most receptive to the theme of "the Atonement as the supreme
manifestation of the love of God, i.e. of the one power adequate
to wean us from our habits of sin". He went on to say:

> It is extraordinary how one's experiences at Bazaar
> preaching differ. One night one comes away with an almost
> hopeless sense of having done nothing...and then one gets an
> experience like last night....If the lessons of our Lord's
> life are true for us, it is evident that it is rather through
> apparent defeat and failure than through conscious triumph
> that victory in the true sense of the word is won;...Every
> week I seem to be getting a little more into touch with
> these Mahommedans, and it may possibly please God to give one
> some real power amongst them during the coming years.[142]

In another venture, Lefroy sought to enter into direct discussion with Muslim leaders. An hour was appointed for this
dialogue in a local mosque (June 19, 1890). Lefroy was at
first hopeful.

> I have been meeting some Mahommedans in a much more
> intelligent and reasonable way than I ever did before in one

of their mosques, and really trying to get them to understand our creed. I must say they have been on the whole
wonderfully courteous and willing to understand, which is to
me a wholly new experience of them. I had a close set-to of
three hours last Friday morning with one of their leading
teachers here....I hope in this way I may keep it up, for it
is exactly the kind of work which I most long for, but which
only a short time since seemed so difficult, almost impossible
to attain. It is, however, as you may imagine, terrible work
arguing on the Trinity and such-like subjects in Hindostanee.
...Still I believe we must meet them on such ground and try
to draw them on....[143]

Gradually however the discussions became more controversial in
nature, momentarily returning to the debate pattern of Pfander.
Such was no longer desired by either Muslim or Christian representatives and the dialogue broke off. Recognizing the presence
of Muslim inquirers, Lefroy realized a more positive presentation
was necessary. Thus in later tent-sessions, he spoke gently about
"the position which Jesus Christ occupied in our respective systems."[144] Convinced that proclamation must replace polemic,
Lefroy's approach shows definite maturity. At a public discussion
near Delhi (May 12, 1892) with representatives of Islam, Hinduism
and Jainism, he was careful to avoid debate or attack on other
religions and simply to present the Gospel. Such discussions he
felt could help prepare listeners for their search for faith and
eventual turning to Christ. It is to be noted that by the turn
of the century much of the argumentative spirit in Christian-
Muslim relationships in India had disappeared.
    A maturing Lefroy sought to remove certain misconceptions
concerning Islam within the church which acted as barriers to
effective mission work. Extremes were to be avoided. Archbishop
Benson of Canterbury spoke uncritically of the glory of Muslim
ethics. These quotes were picked up by Muslim newspapers in
India to support their case. T. Williams of Rewari, upset by
this, wrote a pamphlet attacking the character of Muhammad and
this angered many in the Punjab. Lefroy took up the pen to offer
a more balanced reply countering both extremes.[145] In two later
papers on Islam (1894 and 1907), Lefroy revealed the results of
his studies and experiences. In the first "Occasional Paper",
he speaks sympathetically of the truths found in Islam regarding
one God, resurrection and revelation. Islam has however distorted
the true Revelation of the Bible.

    Nowhere have light and darkness been so interwoven the one
    with the other. Nowhere have high truths of God and man been
    so clearly stated, and yet at the same time so neutralized in
    their practical effect, if not perverted to evil results, by
    the admixture of falsehood in its system.[146]

In addition to the failure to give just treatment to the person
and work of Christ, Islam is weak in: its metaphysical treatment
of God; the arbitrary character of Quranic morality; the low estimate of paradise; and Muhammad's abuse of women and power. In
a second paper directed at those who were beginning to stress
ethical experience over revealed doctrine, Lefroy offers warning
in an appreciative note on Islam.

> ...a need of our own time is met when it is shown on a
> large scale of human life that a truth about God lies at the
> base of one of the strongest social and political structures
> which the world has ever seen, and that this strength and
> power is due rather to a religious truth than to any maxims
> of practical morality. It is the knowledge of God which lies
> at the base of human life and gives strength to human society.[147]

He then goes on to speak of the needs of Islam and of the essence
of the Christian message. Lefroy combines sympathetic study of
Islam with dedicated effort to communicate the Gospel. He presents Anglican efforts at the turn of the century at their best.
     While both Allnutt and Lefroy agreed that education could be
the handmaiden of evangelism, they differed in their methodology.
Allnutt stressed natural religion, "man's need",
eliciting the student's opinion and urging him to quest for the
truth. He combined the more liberal policies of education with
Pfander's emphasis on reason, e.g. "True Religion". Lefroy
emphasized the fact that the revealed knowledge of God must be
communicated via a solid curriculum and committed teacher.
While agreeing that there must be a free human response, he gave
attention to biblical history and the message regarding the person and work of Christ.[148]
     A church-oriented approach to Muslims increasingly occupied
Lefroy's mind. Working among the Chumars, a poor class of leather
workers near Delhi, he saw how a "vital community in Christ" was
needed for the transformation of converts. He took issue with
easy requirements for membership and helped set standards which
meant the eradication of caste and drug abuse, the observance of
Sunday and worship, and a new life of holiness. For him the
Christian community must be truly indigenous, a refuge for converts from Islam, and a force in every area of secular life.[149]
Two of the greatest barriers to the achievement of this, contended
Lefroy, were the burdensome mission machinery and the popular
association of the church with the British government.[150] By
the end of the nineteenth century, the organizational complexities
of the mission station system and the church frequently appear
to be more of a handicap to work among Muslims than those barriers
existing within India's environment!
     As third Bishop of Lahore (1899-1912), Lefroy became concerned
with the witness of the whole community of Christ. Having an
aversion to "one-man rule" he strengthened the Bishop's representative council. Aware of the impact made by European Christians

in India, he called for new levels of Christian purity, attitudes
and practice. He openly attacked the British racial prejudices,
gambling and the neglect of the Lord's Day. He urged the church
to take the lead in the young national movements of India.[151]
Something of Lefroy's concreteness may be seen in a letter he
sent to his fellow-bishops regarding the life of the young church
(1908). First, he calls for united action with Presbyterians,
Methodists, and others in every possible area of the church's
life and mission. Second, regarding present political unrest,
the church must admit it is "responsible for this awakening in
India", identify herself with these "national hopes and aspirations" and work for their sane realization. Third, the National
Missionary Society of India under its Secretary V. S. Azariah
(later an Anglican bishop) represents the secret to the evangelization of India's millions. Fourth, attacking Britain's half-
hearted efforts, he calls for Christian action to block the opium
trade. Fifth, an Indian church weekly paper and other literature
are needed for Muslim and Hindu inquirers.[152]

In an address at the Cairo Conference (1906), Lefroy lists
the qualifications of an evangelist to Muslims: a mastery of
Arabic, the Quran and Islam's theological classics; patience and
fairness in discussion; a sympathetic attitude able to lead the
Muslim from the truth he knows to Christ, the Truth; a readiness
to discard the controversial method of past centuries; and a
spirit of hope. Reflecting on the change in attitude and approach,
he notes:

> Most of the older controversial literature on the Christian
> side is...very hard indeed, as though intended to confute
> the enemy than to win the disguised friend. Similarly much
> of our preaching seems to me rather as though we were hoping
> to convert men by throwing brick-bats at them in the form
> of truth.[153]

Lefroy saw the dawning of a new day in Christian apologetics and
evangelism to Muslims. This would find fuller development in
W. H. T. Gairdner and his successors. For while it had long been
acknowledged that Christians must be ready to give answer for
their faith, the twentieth century brought with it an improved
spirit in Christian-Muslim relations. Apologetics would be
re-clothed in the terminology and spirit of that new age. Nevertheless Anglicans in India made a distinct contribution to the
transition from a medieval to a modern Christian apologetic to
Muslims.

THE SCOTTISH PRESBYTERIAN CONTRIBUTION:
AN EDUCATIONAL APPROACH

The Scots contributed significantly to the development of an
educational approach to Muslims. Developments in educational work

can be observed in the following stages and views. First, there
was the concept of the village school as a means for instructing
men to read the Word. It could be called the pre-Duff idea of
personal evangelism via education. Second, came the almost
revolutionary concept of Duff to use higher education to penetrate
and eventually overthrow the native religions and to transform
culture. This idea was borrowed and adapted by Anglicans, American Presbyterians, as well as continued by Scottish Presbyterians.
Third, this concept of education underwent considerable modification under some educators whereby it became simply a public
service or disinterested benevolence rendered for the enlightenment
of a people. Some educators optimistically held that education
was the means for hastening the arrival of the progressive new
world which must evolve. Increased government control over the
colleges via the university affiliation scheme pressured Christian
institutions to neutralize their emphasis on biblical instruction
and evangelism. Fourth, a major reaction to the above came (ca.
1854) within the ranks of the American Board of Commissioners
for Foreign Missions (A.B.C.F.M.) when Secretary Anderson stressed
that the church must become indigenous (three selves concept).
He insisted that all Christian schools should exist for the
nurture of the church! Sharp differences of opinion were soon
voiced. The Wesleyn Methodists became most critical of the
third view above and after a "controversy" (1890), restricted
their work to village schools and the Anderson-Venn idea of
training the native church. Another reaction was seen in J. N.
Farquhar a Scottish teacher who turned Y.M.C.A. secretary in
order to develop his own peculiar brand of evangelism. He in
turn was answered by A. G. Hogg, a Scotsman, who defended the
modified educational-evangelistic college approach of Duff.
This leads to the twentieth century crisis in theology and missions
when the above views all faced a reckoning. It must be noted
that independent colleges such as those founded by Christian
missionaries in Constantinople, Beirut, and Cairo are uniquely
Near Eastern phenomena and are not found in India. These
Indian developments deserve fuller treatment.

Pre-Duff Education in India

Efforts in education in India prior to Duff's arrival (1830)
were rather limited. British rulers before William Bentinck
often preferred to keep the ruled as they were. The pioneering
Serampore Baptists could not abide by such status quo mentality.
Marshman and his wife not only sketched a plan for evangelizing
India with Christian schools, but planted a number of boys' and
girls' schools near Calcutta. They convinced Henry Martyn and
C.M.S. workers of the validity of this method.[154] Carey was
awakened to this idea also and accepted appointment at the Fort
Williams College until the Baptists founded their own college
(1818). Marshman even helped Ram Mohan Roy and Dwarkanath Tagore
to produce several struggling vernacular schools about 1816. The
Hindu College, founded in Calcutta (1817) under the joint auspices

of individual Englishmen and Hindus, failed because its neutral
religious position soon became virtually anti-religious (influenced
by the works of Hume, Paine, etc.) which alarmed both Muslims and
Hindus.

As noted, the Anglican chaplains began a few schools in outlying areas in order to reach Eurasian and English offspring.
C.M.S. began to form elementary village schools, but the earliest
of these made no effort to be Christian lest it alarm the natives.
The reading of Christian Scriptures and English in a central
Anglo-Vernacular school was first introduced by Captain Stewart
and John Perowne at Burden. By 1822, C.M.S. reported "The Gospels
are now read in all the schools." By the entering of this thin
wedge, village education was acclaimed as a handmaiden of evangel-
ism.155 With the arrival of Miss M. A. Cooke at Calcutta (1820),
resistance to single women teachers declined and the application
of these principles to girls' schools also took effect. It would
remain however for Alexander Duff to make the mission school the
popular channel of missionary work, the agency for confronting
the best of India with the revolutionary Gospel of Christ. But
how was it that the Scots came to India?

Scottish Missionary work began only after overcoming great
opposition at home. The evangelicals in the Church of Scotland
influenced by the Wesleys, Whitefield and Carey, by the new interest in lands abroad (e.g. Cook's explorations, Adam Smith's
Wealth of Nations) and by renewed concern for the common man
(cf. Burn's poems, Scott's novels) became alert once again to the
church's mission. The proposal for a church mission was defeated
by the Moderates in 1796 and not passed until the Assembly of
1824. In the meanwhile, the Glasgow Missionary Society and the
Scottish (Edinburgh) Missionary Society formed (1796) in spite
of the charge of sedition.156 Missionaries were sent to West
Africa, to Karass near the Caspian Sea to work with Muslims and
Orthodox Christians (1800), to Concan in South India (1823-4),
Bombay (1829), and Poona. Most of these personnel transferred
to the Church of Scotland Mission Society in 1835. At the same
time, many courageous voices spoke out at home. James Bryce, the
first Scottish chaplain to India played a decisive role by his
writing and the scheme proposed to the Assembly of 1824.157 John
Inglis and Thomas Chalmers helped conceive the concept of evangelism through a system of Christian education which Duff would
develop. Earlier Scottish schools in Western India founded by
Robert Nesbit, J. Murray Mitchell and John Wilson had up to this
time followed the vernacular village school pattern.158

The Educational Ideas and Activity of Alexander Duff

Alexander Duff (1806-1878), the first official missionary of
the Church of Scotland to India (1829) and after the Disruption
(1843) a missionary of the Free Church of Scotland, exercised a
revolutionary influence on missions by his idea of evangelism
via education. Although his activity was more among Hindus than

Muslims in Bengal, he introduced the educational approach used
extensively among the Muslims of India. Duff considered himself
an evangelist in the fullest sense and exerted an immense influence
in India (1829-35, 1839-50, 1855-63) as well as in his homeland.[159]
Certain aspects of Duff's approach deserve acknowledgement.
First, Duff held that education and evangelism must go together.
Arriving in Calcutta, Duff surveyed the existing missionary methods
to find that vernacular preaching and village schools were drawing
converts (some score at the time) only from the lower classes
leaving the whole superstructure of Indian society untouched.
His plan was to establish an English School/College in Calcutta
which would shake the whole social structure. Duff later defended
this attempt to win the "more enlightened upper classes" in a
speech before the General Assembly of the Free Church (1850):

> Were our Church alone the Church of Christ in this land,
> were missionary operations confined to us, I would then desire
> to see our Church diverting some of her present strength from
> teaching to the more direct preaching of the Word. But in
> looking on all the various sections combined as forming the
> Church of Christ, and in seeing others engaged in preaching,
> is it not a sufficient answer to objectors to say that both
> means are necessary and that we by teaching are supplementing
> what is wanting in their system? But there is a reason of
> greater weight still, and that is what our young friend from
> Madras /Rajahgopal, visiting Scotland/ has well pointed out.
> The mere preaching of the Word would not have reached the
> vast majority of the people. The better classes will not
> attend the preaching of the missionary; the only way in
> which they can be reached is by the agency of such Institu-
> tions as those of the Free Church....[160]

Beyond that, education was needed lest converts be left to
degenerate into "mongrel" Christians as had those baptized by
Xavier and the Jesuits.[161] It was essential to the growth and
elevation of the indigenous church.
Second, Duff saw educational missionary work as the means for
penetrating, transforming Indian society with the Gospel and for
overthrowing the native religions. Education was never bait; but
a dynamic force, a _preparatio_ _evangelica._ A biographer captures
the presupposition behind Duff's vigorous activity.

> The whole world of reality, fact and idea, was God's;
> Christ was the centre of it and the key to its mysteries;
> and it was his privilege to introduce his pupils to the
> world that God had made and to help them to understand both
> the variety of its outer manifestation and the inner soul
> and meaning of it all. Education therefore was not a thing
> extraneous to the missionary's purpose, but of its essence.[162]

Duff's idea of an English school met opposition from the orientalists, the government and missionary educators who insisted on
the vernacular. Even James Bryce complained that English was
too attached to the tavern and rogue crowd of Calcutta. Duff
and other Anglicists argued that it was the only medium which
could transcend the several hundred Indian languages and dialects
to form a new society; that English literature was the reservoir
of much Christian teaching; and that the popular demand for
English would carry the day. Duff gained unexpected support from
Carey and Ram Mohun Roy.[163] Duff's educational program was to
be Christian in every phase. There was to be daily study and
expounding of the Bible and the teaching of every variety of
"useful knowledge" (history, literature, logic, philosophy,
natural and other sciences). The Christian religion was not
only to be the foundation of all knowledge but the animating
spirit pervading and hallowing all.[164]

Duff's target was nothing less than the penetration of the
culture of India with the truths and spirit of the Christian
faith. This faith was not to be compartmentalized either in the
curriculum or within the structures of society and life. The
explosive force of the Gospel must be unleashed. Duff wrote
(1840):

> In this way we thought not of individuals merely; we looked
> to the masses. Spurning the notion of a present day's success,
> and a present year's wonder, we directed our view not merely
> to the present but to future generations....While you engage
> in directly separating as many precious atoms from the mass
> as the stubborn resistance to ordinary appliances /preaching,
> etc./ can admit, we shall, with the blessing of God, devote
> our time and strength to the preparing of a mine, and the
> setting of a train which shall one day explode and tear up the
> whole from its lowest depths.[165]

Duff's method was to present "useful knowledge" so closely inte-
grated with the Christian faith as to undermine both native religions and the new agnosticism. He sensed that the educational
approach avoided unnecessary antagonism. His long-range goal was
that the adherents of Hinduism and Islam be readied to accept the
Christian faith. India, he felt, would be won for Christ through
the leadership of her own sons, highly educated and equipped to
appeal the masses. From the viewpoint of the twentieth century,
Duff's study of Hinduism, India and India Missions (1839) appears
unsympathetic to other religions.[166] Duff was equally concerned
that the new agnosticism should be thwarted. Education devoid
of spiritual direction was no panacea for the world's ills.

> From the circulation of European literature and science,
> but wholly exclusive of morality and religion, the young
> illuminati, too wise to continue the dupes and slaves of an
> irrational and monstrous superstition, do, it is admitted,

openly enlist themselves in the ranks of infidelity. Here,
then is a new power which threatens soon to become more formidable than idolatry itself. Already it has begun to display
some of its ghastly features....[167]

Duff prepared his curriculum to achieve his goals. He wrote his
own graduated school books entitled Instructors which blended
grammatical exercises, useful knowledge and religious-biblical
lessons. Believing that all truth was one in God, he could mix
science, literature and religion and apply the discoveries of
the West to the East. Enrollment in Duff's School surged into
the hundreds and his off-campus lectures on "Natural and Revealed
Religions" turned the city into an uproar. Yet the popularity
of his work did not cease. By 1835, his institution reached
college status with courses in Bible, natural and revealed religions, philosophy and the sciences. After the Disruption in
Scotland (1843), Duff founded a second college (Free Church) in
Calcutta. Fortunately the demand for higher education permitted
both Free and Established Church colleges to prosper.[168]
     Four results of Duff's work can be tabulated. First, the
limited number of converts won in his colleges became leaders of
church and mission in North India.[169] Duff was most anxious that
the Church of Scotland should train and ordain young men for the
ministry.[170] Yet when the young presbyterian church and its
ministry took shape (1841), the tendency was to retain authority
in a "Missionary Council" rather than to transfer it to presbytery.
The case of Lal Behari Day (ordained 1856) demonstrates the
unreadiness of both home church and its missionaries to grant the
young church power for decision-making. Duff's letter of 1877
argues that self-support be a prerequisite to transfer of authority.[171] In spite of this particular weakness, Duff lived to see
his graduates engaged in mission work in North India. They
served as teachers, ministers and catechists with C.M.S., American
and Scottish Presbyterians in the evangelization of Muslims in
Simla, Lahore, and Karachi.[172] Second, Duff made many indirect
contributions to India. Higher education in English gave India
a unifying common language, the benefits of Western science, an
awareness of nationhood, and a sprinkling of Christian ideas.
Duff urged that Sunday become a day of rest for Indian employees
in Calcutta's factories. He helped unleash an enlightenment
with mixed blessings.

     We rejoiced when we came in contact with a rising body of
     Indians who had learnt to think and to discuss all subjects
     with unshackled freedom, though that freedom was ever apt to
     degenerate into license in attempting to demolish the claims
     and pretensions of the Christian as well as of every other
     professedly revealed faith. We hailed the circumstance, as
     indicating the approach of a period for which we had waited
     and longed and prayed. We hailed it as heralding the dawn

of an auspicious era--an era that introduced something new
into the hitherto undisturbed reign of a horary, and tyran-
nous antiquity.[173]

Duff was later to observe that India's religious convulsion produces not only Christian congregations but also resurgent and
reform groups in other religions.[174] Some of these were hostile
to Christian endeavors, others sympathetic. Aware of this risk,
Duff and John Wilson fought hard to secure the right of free
conscience in religion and the retention of property for converts
in the Regulation of 1832.[175] By higher education, civil service
was opened to trained Indians (1854) and Duff's stress on useful
knowledge helped usher in the age of technology.[176] Third, Duff
initiated an educational method soon adopted by almost all the
missionary societies in India.[177]

Fourth, Duff stimulated increased government action in education.
The Charter of 1813 had a clause providing funds to revive and
improve literature and education in British-held India. But it
was the action of the mission societies which stirred fuller
governmental implementation. Duff's popular work resulted in the
resolution known as the Macaulay's Minute (1835) promoting modern
European education, literature and science via the English medium
in the government's schools.[178] Again Duff's testimony before
committees of Parliament helped bring about a new Educational
Charter for India (1854) which provided for governmental universities with which Christian colleges could affiliate and for
grants-in-aid to the latter. Strangely enough, this development
put pressure upon the very mission colleges Duff sought to help
and finally modified the theory of "evangelism via higher education" he initiated.[179] In spite of this unforeseen weakness,
Duff remains one of India's greatest Christian educators.

Fuller comprehension of Duff's approach may be gained by a
perusal of his literary output.[180] His contributions to his
home church, interdenominational cooperation, medical work and
"female education" unfortunately lie beyond the scope of this
study. Duff's willingness to try new methods to render more
effective witness to Christ gained the admiration of several
generations of missionaries.[181]

The Extension, Criticism and Modification of the Ideas of Duff

Adoption and Adaptation

The educational theory of Duff was adopted and adapted not
only by Anglicans (French, Lefroy, Allnutt) and the American
Presbyterians (Newton, Forman, Ewing) but continued and expanded
by the Free Church Mission in Calcutta, Madras, Bonbay, Poona,
Nagpur and the Punjab. At Bombay, John Wilson (1804-1875), a
graduate of Edinburgh University, worked with Christian schools
(1829). Wilson put more value on vernacular tongues than Duff
yet used English and every other means to communicate the Gospel.

In his forty years in India, he befriended Hindus, Muslims, Parsis, Jews and Negroes and led several hundred to Christ. In addition to organizing a Presbyterian Church in Bombay, he founded many schools and a college named after him. In the 1830s, even prior to Pfander, Wilson was engaged in public discussions with leaders of other religions.[182] Wilson's encounters with Muslims are of interest, especially his confrontation with Haji Muhammad Hashim.

> Hadjee Mahomed Hashim of Ispahan, who, as his name shows had performed the pilgrimage to Mecca, and was the most learned Moulvi in Bombay challenged me to the proof of the licentiousness and imposture of the author of the Koran, and I readily attempted to establish my position. After several letters had appeared in the native newspapers, the Hadjee came forward with a pamphlet of considerable size in Goojaratee and Persian, in which he evinces at once great sophistry and great ability.[183]

Wilson's response was a booklet: "Reply to Hadjee Mahomed Hashim's Defence of the Islamic Faith" (Persian, Bombay, 1836) with twenty-one brief chapters criticizing the moral irregularities and shortcomings in Muhammad's Quran and private life. Here is a blend of medieval polemics and scholarship (prior to Muir's biography of the Prophet). Inadequate as it was, it received wide distribution. Wilson managed to reach a number of Muslims: baptizing a fakir (Oct. 1833), touring extensively in the North to distribute Scriptures,[184] befriending dethroned Afghan ruler Dost Muhammad and heir-apparent Prince Haider-Khan, and defending Muslims following the Mutiny (1857-1872). Haji Ghulam Hyder (baptized Haji Ghulam Mashiah, July 25, 1852) of the Sindh was but one of the converts who would interest the Scots in a fuller work in the North. The baptism of Wazir Beg, teacher of the Poona School (Sept. 24, 1847) and of Mikhail Joseph of Bombay caused no small stir. The latter toured Arabia, Mokha and Sana (1862) selling several hundred Scriptures en route.[185] Wilson's educational principles were in basic agreement with Duff. In brief, it may be said that the prime difference was Wilson's more sympathetic attention to the languages, religions and culture of India in hopes that these concepts could be adapted rather than simply replaced.[186] Wilson maintained close contact with the government college (Elphinstone College) and drew a number of its students into his Catechumen School and the thriving young church (e.g. Syud Hussan Medinyeh, bapt. 1856).

The Free Church institution at Nagpur was founded by Stephen Hislop (1817-1863) in 1844. Hislop's varied talents contributed to education, governmental reform, scientific discovery, anthropology and linguistics. Hislop College (1883), affiliated with the University of Calcutta, would later be the scene for T. W. Gardiner's creative efforts to draw Muslims and Hindus into Christian worship.[187]

The Central Institution at Madras (1837), founded by the trio, Anderson, Johnston and Braidwood, had a long stormy passage

before it emerged as Madras Christian College. In 1853 the
schools about Madras included some 327 Muslims. The baptism of
the first Muslim converts (1853) aroused great opposition until
the Supreme Court affirmed the individual's right to change his
religion (August, 1854). Two of these converts, Abdool Ali and
Abdool Khader, became fiery evangelists attracting great crowds
at Madras, Nellore and Triplicane. Their courageous preaching
coupled with the work of the schools gradually opened the way
for other converts from Islam.[188] The Madras institution received
new vitality in 1862 with the arrival of William Miller (1838-1923),
again when Madras Christian College went interdenominational as
the C.M.S. and Wesleyns joined forces with the Scottish Free
Church (1887).[189]

Scots in North India: Modifications

All three Scottish churches: the Church of Scotland, the Free
Church and the United Presbyterians extended their work northwards after the Disruption (1843).[190] The effort of the Church
of Scotland around Sialkot is of special importance because of
its contribution to educational work in the midst of Muslims.[191]
The Punjab work was begun by Thomas Hunter (1827-1857) in 1856.
While serving in Bombay, Hunter baptized two Muslim converts:
Nasrullah (July 28, 1856) and Saiyid Mohamet Ismael (August 21,
1856). The latter was to help lead the way north (ordained
1869). It is important to note that Hunter was against simply
beginning another educational program at Sialkot. He reflects
the feeling of a group of evangelists (perhaps influenced by R.
Anderson of A.B.C.F.M.) who felt education was dominating too
much of Scottish work. Hunter wrote:

> April 2, 1856...Permit me...to give a sketch of a plan of
> operation...to further the cause of Christ in the Panjab. Of
> course the conversion of souls, not the education of the young,
> is the Church's design in sending her ministers to India. The
> time was when education was the only means open to our Church,
> and with praiseworthy zeal have we lavished large sums in
> preparing--simply preparing--ground for the reception of good
> seed, for educated men do listen to, and reason on, Bible
> truth....If you still propose entrusting me with the Church's
> work in the Panjab, I should propose that no educational
> institution be formed, but that I should be as one of the
> natives, never resting until I have thoroughly mastered the
> language and customs of the country,...to proclaim the great
> salvation directly, faithfully, fearlessly. Afterwards native
> Christians might quietly collect a small school; but never em-
> ploy heathen teachers. A small earnest machinery, then, will
> be sufficient in the establishment of this mission. I am
> perfectly willing to go alone, and commence the work.[192]

Arriving in Sialkot, Hunter gave proclamation priority before he
and his family were killed in the Mutiny (1857). When this work
was restarted, John Taylor, Robert Paterson, and Mohamet Ismael
modified Hunter's policy and began an Anglo-vernacular school
(1860). Other schools opened at Wazirabad, in Sialkot's suburbs
and in Gujrat. By 1896, there were 3 high schools, 6 middle
schools and 50 primary schools. Many of the converts from Muslim
and upper class background had mission school training.[193] In
1868, the Central Sialkot School enrolled 320 boys. By 1896, it
and Murray College (founded in 1889) listed 600 students. Murray
College continued to expand under its first principal, J. W.
Youngson, benefitting from the government grant-in-aid scheme
which Parliament passed in the 1850s at Duff's urging. Shams-
ul-Ulema Maulvi Mir Hassan served as professor of Arabic for 61
years and its graduates included Muhammad Iqbal, national poet
and philosopher of Pakistan. By the twentieth century, only a
minority of faculty and students were Christian[194] and the college
faced problems similar to those known at Edwardes College, Peshawar
(Anglican); Forman College, Lahore; Kinnaird College for Women,
Lahore; and Gordon College, Rawalpindi (United Presbyterian,
U.S.A. Colleges). These colleges discovered that the shortage
of Christian faculty, limited mission funds, increased curriculum
requirements and government control made it difficult to maintain
a Christian content and spirit on campus. Increased political
agitation would further limit campus evangelism and required Bible
courses. Murray College was thus forced to redefine her role in
a land desperately needing education.[195]

Proclamation was not neglected however. Tours by Taylor,
Youngson, Mohamet Ismael and numerous other Indian evangelists
soon led to the establishment of centers at Wazirabad (1860),
Gujrat (1865), Chamba (1863), and Jammu (1884). The dynamic
outreach of William Ferguson at Chamba and the Chamba Church under
Pastor Sohan Lah (1868) demonstrated the value of grassroots
evangelism.[196] As will be seen, the Scots also developed programs
of Christian medical work and service. The Hunter Memorial Church
at Sialkot (1865) with its core of Muslim converts included several
teachers and an assistant-surgeon. The beginning of a presbytery
emerged in 1869 at Jalandar.[197] The church's numbers began to
swell rapidly about 1885 due to the mass movements. By 1896,
5000 out of the 20,000 Christians in the Punjab were in the
Scottish Mission.[198] In 1904, the Scottish Presbyterian Church
would join with the other Presbyterian churches of the region to
select Youngson as its first moderator. In 1924, the United
Presbyterian Church of the Punjab was joined by the Congregationalists to form the United Church of Northern India (UCNI).[199]

Reaction: Exemplified by R. Anderson

Modifications in the educational approach begun by Duff soon
brought reactions and criticism. Certain factors prompted review.
First, success brought its own problems. Increasing enrollments

meant a shortage of personnel and funds. Mission schools began
to bring more non-Christian teachers onto their staffs and the
character of the schools could not but change. Second, Duff
unknowingly contributed to this change by encouraging Parliament
to pass the Educational Charter of 1854 which founded regional
government universities (with which Christian colleges could
affiliate) and "grants-in-aid". Both provisions aimed to help
Christian colleges but in fact resulted in increased control over
their curriculum and finances. Third, education and theology in
the West were both undergoing liberalization and this was felt
more quickly in educational institutions than in the churches.

The reaction of Thomas Hunter has already been noted. He
represented those who stressed evangelism. More radical reaction
took place in the work of the American Board of Commissioners
for Foreign Missions. The A.B.C.F.M. began work in India in
1812 and by 1851 had a growing church. Its schools enrolled some
1,700 pupils.[200] Its work at Kolhapur, begun in 1852 by R. G.
Wilder, made extensive use of the education. Secretary Rufus
Anderson became convinced that the main object of mission was
to form self-supporting, self-governing, self-propagating indigenous churches. He began to question educational work which
sought to elevate the whole of society and often ended in
providing jobs for non-Christian teachers on mission funds. In
1854, Anderson headed up a Deputation to India which radically
undercut such educational programs. Only those schools under
Christian teachers and for Christian children or adults would
henceforth warrant mission support! In short, mission schools
must exist solely for building up the indigenous church. R. G.
Wilder radically differed with Anderson and defended the operation
of schools for non-Christian children even when it necessitated
the use of non-Christian teachers. In Mission Schools in India
(1861), he confesses little sympathy for those who "would limit
our great commission to the oral proclamation of the Gospel, or
on the other hand, to teaching it technically and only in the
schoolroom". He argues that schools are necessary:

> to procure a stated audience;...to secure hearers from the
> more intelligent and better classes of the heathen community..;
> to remove ignorance and lay stable foundation...; to conciliate
> the favour of the heathen and convince them that the mission-
> ary seeks to benefit them.[201]

In short, they are the necessary opening wedge for reaching a
closed community. Nevertheless Anderson broke with the policy
espoused by Duff, Greene and as generally practiced by Protestant
societies in India. He hoped that a strictly Christian education
(curriculum, teachers and students) might result in a trained
Christian force which would in turn permeate society and win
growing numbers into the church. Wilder returned to Kolhapur
(1861) to make that field independent. Later he turned the properties and work over to the Presbyterians of Ludhiana (1873)

who continued a modified form of Duff's approach. The policy
of Anderson and Hunter discloses growing criticism of the traditional educational approach.

Later Criticism of Christian Higher Education

By the 1860s the criticism of evangelism via higher education
increased. Especially under consideration were: the limited
number of converts, the increasing number of non-Christian teachers,
the tremendous operational costs, and the increased government
control via the universities. Duff and others at home tried to
remedy this, e.g. by limiting the portion of the budget spent on
the colleges. Perhaps one of the most telling criticisms of how
Christian higher education had strayed from Duff's intent comes
from Lal Behari Day, a former student of Duff's, an ordained
minister who had served with the Free Church Mission and a professor of the government college of Hooghly. While pointing out
Duff's failings regarding the Indian Church, he admired Duff's
educational theory and practice. Day contended that the Free
Church Institutions under Duff had attained an advanced level in
both educational method and Christian spirit not yet acquired by
Bengal colleges some thirty-five years later.

> The system of teaching adopted by Duff was somewhat different
> from the systems in vogue at the time in India. It was called
> by some the _intellectual_ system, as its object from the begin-
> ning was the development of the intellectual powers of the
> pupil, however young, and not merely the communication of
> information. It was also sometimes called the Socratic or
> interrogatory system, as teaching was carried on chiefly by
> a series of questions....Education he contended, is...the
> development of all its powers and susceptibilities, intellectual,
> moral, social, and religious. In most systems of education
> knowledge is communicated to the pupils. Duff _did_ communicate
> knowledge; but before communicating, he brought out of his
> pupils whatever knowledge they had by a process of close
> questioning....[202]

What Day criticized most in later mission schools was their
neglect of the Christian content and objectives exhibited by Duff.

> As the chief object of the General Assembly's Institution
> was to convert the students to Christianity, the course of
> studies pursued in it was thoroughly saturated with the
> spirit of that religion from lowest to the highest class.
> The very first Primer that was put into the hands of a boy
> learning the English alphabet contained some of the facts and
> doctrines of the Christian religion; and the course of studies
> was so regulated that his knowledge of Christianity increased
> in the same ratio with his knowledge of English:....This was
> the case before the establishment of the Calcutta University,
> which institution, it must be confessed, has greatly affected

the religious character of the missionary colleges. As
missionaries prepare their students for the degrees of the
University, they adopt the curriculum of studies prescribed
by that learned body; they have, therefore, at present, less
time for the Christian and theological training of their pupils
than before; while the students themselves naturally pay little
or no attention to those studies which do not pay in the University examinations. The state of things was different,
however in the pre-university day of which I am now speaking.
The students were in those days thoroughly grounded in a
course of natural theology, a course in the evidences of Christianity, a course of systematic theology, a short course of
ecclesiastical history, besides a course of lectures on almost
the whole of the Holy Scriptures, from the Book of Genesis to
the Book of Revelation. In addition to these Christian
appliances in the classroom, public lectures were delivered
by the missionary professors to the students on Sunday even-
ings.[203]

Day also sharply criticized the use of non-Christian teachers,
many who used language, floggings, etc. quite contrary to the
Christian spirit. With Duff he agreed that everything depends
on dedicated and talented teachers.[204]

Those espousing the cause of Christian higher education found
further accommodation almost inevitable. William Miller (reached
Madras, 1862) is an example of one who sought to cope with the
problem. A brilliant innovator, he gave Christian colleges a
new raison d'être: to diffuse Christian thought throughout
Indian society rather than to win converts. His strategy of
spreading Christian ideas rather than preaching and pressing for
baptism, was defended at Allahabad (1872).[205] Whereas Duff had
hoped educated converts would go out to transform society, Miller
contends that the very principles of Christian thought would
leaven the whole mass of Hindu society.[206] While Madras Christian
College gained heightened respect, Miller's modified concept of
education was not unanimously accepted.[207] Miller was sympathetic to Hindu culture and urged that it be encouraged to assimilate
Christian ideas. Others contended that confrontation with God
in Christ called for more radical conversion, a turning from one
way of life to another. This debate as to substitution/displace-
ment or completion/fulfillment would extend to Christian Colleges
among the Muslims of North India too. It appears again in the
writings of Hendrik Kraemer and S. Radhakrishnan, a graduate of
Madras Christian College.[208] Scottish investigation committees
went to India in 1884 and 1889.[209] An example of how stinging
this criticism could be is seen in the controversy in the
Wesleyn Methodist Church in 1890. It was charged that Duff's
predecessors were closer to the truth when they sought to preach
the Gospel to the poor; that a high proportion of mission funds
were being used to educate a Hindu aristocracy, to promote an
anti-Christian Hindu renaissance; and that these schools divert

the energies of three-quarters of the ablest missionaries from evangelism and a national movement. The critics counseled a return to primary Christian schools for the masses, the development of democratic native agencies, and a renewed effort by missionaries at identification with the peoples of India (rather than aloofness, fraternizing with the upper classes, etc.).[210] The new policy stated that (1) educational agencies should be subordinate to the direct work of preaching the Gospel, (2) educators should if possible be laymen, hence freeing clergy for evangelism and pastoral work, and (3) the advantages of education should be given mainly to native converts.[211] These investigations gave several workers new determination to bridge the social, ethnic gulf between the Western missionary and the people of India.

One of these was J. N. Farquhar (1869-1929), a Scottish lay-missionary teaching at the L.M.S. Christian College at Bhowanipur. He observed that missionaries in the European enclave of an English-medium college often did not come into touch with Indian thought and religions, much less engage in evangelism. Even the respected William Miller while professing the superiority of Christianity was rather vague about its relation to India's religions. Farquhar wanted to develop a sympathetic yet distinctly evangelistic approach. He gave up his "joyless, hopeless work of college" to become a Y.M.C.A. secretary, responsible for literary and student work. Sensitive to the religious renaissance and national movements in India and to the evolutionary theories of the day, he developed the idea that Christianity was the fulfillment of other religions.[212] Since Christianity was not out to destroy but to fulfill, progressive Hindus and others could embrace it and Christians could be more sympathetic to other religions. Professor A. G. Hogg, another Scotsman in Madras criticized Farquhar, asking "What in Hinduism does Christianity fulfill?" Hogg was conscious of the distinctiveness of each religion and felt the conflict could not be so easily resolved. Influenced by the twentieth century revival of evangelical theology he stressed the sympathetic presentation of the Christian message. Hogg stood for continuing the educational approach of Duff as well as direct evangelism.[213] The survival of the Anglicans, American and Scottish Presbyterian colleges revealed that the vision of Duff and modified by many forces still had widespread support. It must be achnowledged that many Muslim converts had their first contact with the Christian faith in these colleges even if they did not come under conviction of its truth until later years. The various educational approaches would again come under closer scrutiny during the crisis in mission and theology, 1920-1938.

AN INTERDENOMINATIONAL CONTRIBUTION: MEDICAL
MISSIONS AND CHRISTIAN SERVICE

Christian service and medical missions have had a visible impact on India. Medicine was at first an auxiliary service of the evangelist and his wife. Missionaries took the lead in this field, sharing the meagre medicines and generous compassion they possessed, founding orphanages and relief centers for the unfortunate. Indian evangelists, e.g. Abdul Masih, treated patients in a style similar to that of the native Hakim. Missionaries gained what assistance they could from medical textbooks, British Army surgeons and the dispensaries in Calcutta and Bombay. As medicine came into its own, all this changed. Medical missions emerged as a distinct method, a phenomenon crossing denominational lines. In the last quarter of the century, this means gained prominence in work among Muslims in North India.

Americans in Medical Missions

Americans took the lead in medical missions. One of the early leaders was Dr. John Scudder who went to Ceylon in 1819 under the A.B.C.F.M. Later generations of his family served with the Reformed Church in America at Vellore and in Arabia. The Rev. Peter Parker, M.D., went to China (1835) and later inspired the founding of the Edinburgh Medical Missionary Society. The first professional medical work in North India began with the Presbyterians (U.S.A.) of the Ludhiana Mission. John Newton, Sr. had hoped to add medical training to his theological studies, but this was not granted. Nevertheless his amateur medicine practice was soon swamped with requests. So inspired, his son, John Newton, Jr., M.D. began successful work at Kapurthala in 1858. His leper work at Subathu and zealous evangelistic-medical tours convinced many including Robert Clark of the future of this approach. The Presbyterian Hospital and Medical Training Center that evolved at Ludhiana was to the North, what Vellore was to the South. Dr. William Wanless developed another esteemed center at Miraj, Kolhapur (1889).[214] Mary Reed of the American Methodist Episcopal Church and the international Mission to Lepers Society experienced that dreaded disease and yet carried on a long ministry of healing at an Asylum in the Himalayas.[215] Most of these programs began with a single missionary doctor who gradually gained Christian Indian assistants, then a dispensary, and sometimes a hospital. The touring doctor was both evangelist and healer. Medical institutions became points of contact for evangelists and colporteurs. Services rendered to the blind, deaf, diseased, handicapped and the destitute in the spirit of Christ made a deep imprint on many non-Christian. A prominent Indian Muslim in 1905 declared:

It is these medical missionaries who are winning the hearts
and the confidence of our people. If we do not do as they do,
we will soon lose our hold upon our own people. We must build
hospitals and care for the sick and dying if we wish to keep
our religion alive.[216]

Scottish Medical Missions

Peter Parker visited Edinburgh in 1841 to report to a group
of medical and mission-minded persons including John Abercrombie,
Thomas Chalmers and William Swan.[217] The Edinburgh Medical
Missionary Society was formed (November, 1841), with Abercrombie
as president, in order: (1) to circulate information encouraging
medical missions; (2) to aid medical work in as many stations as
possible; and (3) to help recruit and train medical personnel.
The concept of medical evangelism was hammered out by W. Burns
Thomson and other students at P. D. Handyside's Mission clinic
at 39 Cowgate. Thomson also served as agent of the Society
(1860-1870) and did much to promote medical missions and inspire
such as J. Hutchison of the Church of Scotland.[218] Dr. Hutchison
reached India (1870) to establish a dispensary and cottage hospital at Chamba and to make extensive medical-evangelistic tours
into Tibet. Other dispensary-hospitals opened at Sialkot (1889),
Gujrat and Jalalpur. The majority of the patients were Muslims.
Every effort was made to introduce the Gospel by public services
of Scripture and exposition at the beginning of each day. North
India suffered many outbreaks of disease, famine, and flood and
so when Christians ministered to those deserted by others it
made lasting impressions on the populace. In the twentieth
century scene of political-religious unrest, this ministry of
healing and reconciliation by the Christian community gained
even greater importance.[219]
The Edinburgh Medical Missionary Society (EMMS) had far
reaching influence. Its Training Institution in Edinburgh under
J. Lowe helped prepare forty students between 1872-1886 for
the Churches of Scotland, C.M.S., L.M.S., English Presbyterians,
Scottish Episcopalians, Baptists, Methodists, A.B.C.F.M., China
Inland Mission and its own hospital at Nazareth. Colin Valentine
became head of the Agra Medical Missionary Training Institution
which trained many Indian Christians. Dr. Lowe, a capable
spokesman for medical missions, reflects the new concern for the
whole man whose hungry, diseased, or broken body must be attended
even as he is given the Gospel. Medical missions offered a
"divine method" for pioneering and opening closed doors; for
changing wrong ideas about God; for gaining the confidence of
the populace and permeating whole districts with Christian
ideas; for manifesting the greatest love to the most needy men;
for demonstrating the nature of the kingdom, the creation of a
new social order; and for winning men to Christ. The Society's
literature drove home the fact that medical missions could serve
where others could not, e.g. among Muslims.[220]

Anglican-Associated Medical Missions

The successful medical-evangelism of John Newton, Jr. at
Srinagar, Kashmir (1863-64) was observed carefully by Robert Clark
and his active wife.[221] At the Punjab Missionary Conference
(1863), Clark advocated the formation of the Punjab Medical Missionary Society (formed at Lahore, January 24, 1864) to work in
cooperation with the Edinburgh Medical Missionary Society
especially in the Valley of Kashmir. Dr. William J. Elmslie
arrived at Amritsar in 1865 to reach out to Kashmir. His successor at Srinagar, Dr. T. Maxwell saw the erection of the hospital
there (1874). Medical work at Amritsar dates from 1872, but St.
Catherine's Hospital opened only in 1880. While many at the
Decennial Missionary Conference at Allahabad (1873) questioned
the idea of diverting "sacred funds" to medical work, Robert
Clark declared:

> Medical Missions are amongst the most important means of
> evangelising India; and the attention of all Societies should
> be more distinctly drawn than has hitherto been the case to
> the opportunities which they afford.[222]

Closer observation of several medical missionaries associated
with the C.M.S. provide insight into this field. Presbyterian
William Jackson Elmslie (1832-1872), a medical graduate of the
University of Edinburgh, responded to the C.M.S. call to establish
a mission station at Srinagar (where earlier efforts had failed).
After three summer seasons (1865-1867) and the treatment of several
thousand patients, the first converts came forward. In spite of
the opposition of the mullahs, the Maharajah permitted erection
of a small school (1868). The increase in clinic-patients and
inquirers (especially interested in the writings of Imad-ud-Din)
continued. Elmslie's method on tour was to seek out the village's
chief man and to identify himself. While offering his medical
services he shared the "Injil" of "Isa Masih". Catechist and
literature supplemented his work. He advocated that the Gospel
be presented prayerfully in the simplest language. Elmslie's
paper: "Scheme for Training Native Medical Missionary Evangelists"
(C.M.S. Conference at Amritsar, 1866) advocated the training of
gifted Indian Christians in both medicine and evangelism. Elmslie
himself travelled to Calcutta to consult with Sir John Lawrence
and Sir William Muir on this scheme. He also visited Scotsman
W. Ferguson at Chamba Mission and introduced the work that
Hutchinson was to develop. Elmslie's sudden death (1872) left
a great gap in this pioneer realm.[223] In his brief career,
however, he had sounded the theme: "Heal the sick, and say
unto them, the kingdom of God is come nigh unto you".
    Devout Anglicans Arthur (1859-1919) and Ernest Neve were top
ranking graduates of the University of Edinburgh and members of
the E.M.M.S. Serving in Kashmir, the Neve brothers built up the
Srinagar Hospital as a "practical manifestation of Christianity"

which affords "opportunities for witness and treatment". In this
predominantly Muslim land, they linked healing, touring and preaching together. The respect they earned was evidenced by a Muslim
publication of sorrow at Arthur's death (1919).[224] Arthur's
theology and methodology are best expressed in his own words:

> From the same Divine source, whence flowed miraculous gifts
> to the holy apostles and the early Church, does Western civil-
> ization owe its medical science and surgical art. Let these
> be consecrated to the use of their Creator...the preaching of
> a Saviour's love to them that are afar off and to them that
> are nigh. So long as sickness can soften the heart, so long
> as kindness can win gratitude,...so long "what God hath joined
> together let no man put asunder." Vital as are the ever inter-
> esting relations of body and soul, so are the relations between
> the science which deals with the one and the philosophy that
> ministers to the other, vital and imminent. Not upon the
> temporizing policy of human wisdom but upon the eternal and
> immutable decree of Omniscience was founded the Divine mandate,
> first uttered by the shore of the Sea of Galilee, "Preach,
> saying the Kingdom of Heaven is at hand. Heal the sick."
> Love is at once the inspiration of Medical Mission work and
> the chord it seeks to strike. It is a strain which can be
> awakened in most hearts but vibrates not in the creed of
> Islam....A creed whose object is a loveless deity attracts
> not love, for love-worshipping demands a loving God. "That
> the All-Great is the All-Loving too" is a faith that cannot
> find expression truer than the Cross of Calvary. The awakening
> of Mohammedans to the realization of love as an intuition of
> religion must involve a recoil from the loveless void of
> Islam, and with the first breathings of the love of humanity
> will come faith in One whose crucifixion testifies the love
> of Him who loved us and gave Himself for us.
> This we apprehend to be the scope of Medical Missions. The
> stern intellectual barriers of Mohammedanism are to be attacked
> through the heart....[225]

While opposed to controversy, the Neve brothers never allowed
opposition to halt the sympathetic proclamation of the Gospel.
Ernest Neve saw the Christian faith as the only reconcilor,
transformer, which could "give birth to the national unity which
is so conspicuously absent in these days of communal strife".[226]
His positive presentation of the news of the kingdom of God slowly
gained respect among Muslims, Hindus, and Sikhs and strengthened
St. Luke's Church.[227] He understood that all evangelism among
Muslims depends on personal sacrifice.

> Both the Hindu and Moslem religions are peculiarly resistant
> to the impact of Christianity....The great need in India is
> constructive friendship. Theological dialectics between op-
> posing religions are of little value. Religious controversy

is more apt to engender hatred than love. If men cannot be
attracted by the love and sympathy of Christ, history and
logic will not succeed.

For the continued presentation of Christianity to Hindus
and Moslems there is no more potent agency than the work of
Medical Missions.[228]

The Neve brothers personified in their lives an approach of
"constructive friendship" which both communicates and serves in
the name of Christ.

Theodore Leighton Pennell (1867-1912) served the Afghans in
a brilliant sacrificial ministry of healing for twenty years
(1892-1912). His work with C.M.S. at Dera Ismail Khan and at
Bannu demonstrated how difficult it was to establish the church
among the fierce Pathan Muslim tribes. Pennell's approach was
to identify himself with these people by adopting Pathan dress,
eating habits and customs, yet retaining a distinctly Christian
witness. On one occasion he and a convert traveled 1500 miles
to Bombay as Christian Sadhus without purse or script (1903-1904).
He did this not as an adventurous orientalist, but to achieve
entrance into the inner circle of the Afghans. He succeeded
remarkably well in gaining mullah, fakir and other Muslims as
friends. His favorite method was to take one or two Christian
converts, e.g. Jahan Khan (Lord of Life) and Taib Khan (Pleasant
Lord) on an evangelistic-medical tour instructing inquirers,
distributing Scriptures and preaching in the bazaar. Native
preachers gained his praise.

We say diamond cuts diamond, and so I have found that it
requires a converted Pathan to cope with a Pathan Bazaar
audience....It is seldom wise to attempt to answer objections
in the bazaar....I ask the objector to name a place and time,
and I shall be pleased to explain any difficulties....To my
mind much more good can be done with a bazaar audience by
a patient exposition of the spirituality of Christianity then
by a however brilliant a demonstration of the faults of Islam
or Hinduism.

Our Indian brethren are, as a rule, more resourceful in
illustration and orientally picturesque in description than
our more prosaic selves, and when touched by the Spirit form
spendid preachers....[229]

A new preaching hall at Bannu (1900) assisted this form of the
work. Not confining himself to medical work, Pennell started a
school with a hostel (1895), printed a local newspaper (1897), and
rendered many other services for the needy. The hospital at
Bannu and other substations such as Karad and Thal provided the
backbone of the mission served by the preacher-doctor Jahan Khan,
Dr. and Mrs. Barton, Dr. Bennett, and others. The rather unor-
thodox, experimental methods of Pennell did not always gain full
approval in the mission, but Pennell succeeded in forming the

nucleus of a small church. Under persecution and the pressures
of a hostile environment, Pennell held that the Christian communi-
ity must be something of an **Anjuman** or brotherhood with common
property, table, worship and "serving God in serving others".
The Bannu congregation rejoiced in being able to hold "public
services" for laying the foundation stone of "the Church of the
Holy Name" in 1912.[230]
Pennell's views on medical missions were set forth in a speech
in London (May, 1910).

> Medical Missions are the laboratories of practical mission-
> ary effort. Modern education differs from that of thirty years
> ago in the prominence it gives to practical teaching and
> experiment. Just as we have realized that we need something
> more than the mere verbal setting forth of the Gospel message
> to non-Christian nations, we need the practical exposition of
> it which is given by medical missions. India is surfeited
> with doctrine and dogma, and turns away from the preacher to
> her own philosophies and speculations, but when brought face
> to face with a practical exposition of the Christ life, she
> is captivated....[231]

Here then was a demonstration to balance declaration, a means
for penetrating closed communities.

> Afghanistan is closed....yet the influence of Medical Mis-
> sions has penetrated through and through. I suppose there are
> few, if any villages in East and South Afghanistan which have
> not sent their quota of patients to our Frontier hospitals.
> These patients have heard the Gospel preached in our out-
> patient departments; have, many of them, lain week after week
> in the wards, receiving the ministrations of the Christians,
> watching our lives and gauging the reality of our professions,
> and then they have gone back to their district homes and retail-
> ed their experiences...Often a Testament or other book, care-
> fully secreted from prying eyes, is smuggled back to their
> homes and studied in private, and passed on in secret to some
> friend, thus the people have become familiarized with the Gos-
> pel story....[232]

There were few who would dispute the fact that medical missions
were a prime means for entering predominantly Muslim areas. The
work at Bannu, Srinagar, Peshawar, Dera Ismail Khan and Quetta
testify to this.
This work was not confined to men. The interdenominational
Zenana Bible and Medical Mission (ZBMM) formed in 1852 and the
Church of England Zenana Missionary Society (CEZMS) in 1880. By
1900 the former had 154 women missionaries and 289 Indian workers,
and the latter 175 and 829 respectively, serving in schools,
medical work, and visitation ventures.[233] These spread over the
territories north of Bombay and Calcutta. Their numbers included

such as Dr. Maria Holst, later founder of the Danish Pathan Mission
at Mardan; Fanny Jane Butler, first woman doctor to Kashmir; and
Amy Carmichael whose sensitive pen has enriched the lives of
many.[234]

Medical missions among Muslims in India helped create a new
public spirit of compassion for the sick and afflicted as well
as drawing many into the sphere where the Gospel could be heard.
Serious minded medical workers considered their work as a living
demonstration of the nature of the kingdom of God and the redemptive power of Christ. Yet medical work was not to be divorced
from the proclamation of the Gospel, for only Christ can deliver
man from sin, sickness and ignorance. Prior to World War I,
medical work experienced rapid growth.[235] During the critical
1930s, it would become apparent however that the medical approach,
like educational work, could suffer from institutionalization,
the idea that humanitarian objectives were ends in themselves.
Until then the medical approach received almost unceasing praise.

THE PRESBYTERIAN (U.S.A.) CONTRIBUTION:
A CHURCH-ORIENTED APPROACH

Exactly what is meant by a church-oriented approach? Faced
by the millions of **India** did not every mission group realize that
the evangelization of that country ultimately depended upon the
creation of a native agency, an indigenous church? Was it not
apparent that evangelism, education and service must be directed
to this end? While this was admitted by all, the American
Presbyterians especially succeeded in cultivating an indigenous
Christian community. The exact cause for this success is difficult
to determine. Perhaps the free spirit of the American frontier
permitted greater liberty in baptizing Indian forms? Perhaps the
varied program of the Presbyterians maintained greater flexibility
than that of their European counterparts? Perhaps presbyterianism
with its representative government was peculiarly adaptable to the
situation? Most would confess that this idea of approaching
Muslims via national Christians and churches, was exemplary. To
comprehend the scope of this approach, one should look briefly
into the larger American scene, the actual endeavors of the American Presbyterians, and their concept of church and mission.

The American Scene

American efforts began early in India with the arrival of
A.B.C.F.M. workers (1812). Work in the predominantly Muslim
Northwest started with the relaxation of restrictions on missions
(1833) and the expansion of the pax Britannica. The American
churches like their British and European counterparts were not
appreciably involved in mission during the post-Reformation era
(1555-1691). At first, American energies were expended in
establishing a free church in a new land. Small mission circles

appeared in the century of evangelical revivals (1691-1789), but
it was after the Revolution that the idea of missions to the East
came into being (1789-1815). The new Calvinism of Edwards and
Hopkins with emphasis on disinterested benevolence and the desire
to win souls provided the needed dynamic. The American missionary movement in its pioneering days (1815-1884) expanded with
great rapidity and slackened little with the arrival of a more
liberal theological outlook late in the period. As the liberal
forces brought forth a strong emphasis on humanitarian service,
philanthropic benevolence, and social progress; the evangelicals
retained the concern for proclaiming and teaching the Word.
Before long, mission endeavors hit a new peak in terms of personnel
and expenditure (1884-1914). There was increased appreciation
for the cultures and societies as well as individuals of other
lands. Higher education, medical services, industrial training
and welfare work gained new prominence. These general characteristics describe American efforts prior to the Edinburgh Conference (1910).[236] American efforts in India, while starting later
than British circles, were nearly equal in scope by the beginning
of the twentieth century.[237]

While the Presbyterians (U.S.A.) maintained the largest concentrated effort in Muslim work in North India, mention must be
made of two other American bodies: The American Baptists and
the Methodist Episcopal Church. Organized under Adoniram
Judson (1814), the Baptists reached Assam in 1836. Later they
encountered Muslims in Bengal-Orissa. Known for their ecclesiastical flexibility and touch with the common man, they had greater
success among India's depressed peoples than among Muslims.[238]
Starting late in India (1856), the Methodist Episcopal Church
expanded rapidly to become the largest American force in India
by 1910. The United Provinces (Oudh and Rohilkhand), with
Bareilly as a center, became their northern territory. Under
William Butler, James M. Thoburn (1836-1922) and William Taylor,
a program of dynamic evangelism and the organization of self-
supporting congregations produced phenomenal results. Wherry
testifies that their effective pattern of village evangelization
influenced the Presbyterians.

The example of the American Methodist missionaries, who
authorized their evangelists to baptize any of the people,
who are ready to openly declare their faith in Jesus Christ
as their Saviour, led the Presbyterians to adopt the methods
at least in part. The influence of the evangelists, who were
given to the first Methodist missionaries, men like Joel
Janvier, who soon became a noted leader, could not but
inspire a similar holy zeal and enthusiasm among the Presbyterian workers. The fire of missionary zeal began to glow.
The writer well remembers an address made by request of a
Presbyterian, asking the Rev. Mr. Thoburn to give some account
of the village work then claiming the attention of missionaries
everywhere. We were urged to adopt the methods of wise

fishermen, who ever sought the places where the fish would
bite....The effect of that address was to arouse us to call
in question some of our ideals of fitness for service. The
practical lesson was to turn away from the jabbering crowds
in the market places of the city and go into the quiet villages
and seek a hearing from the sons of the soil and the children
of toil.[239]

Thoburn demonstrated the on-the-spot creativeness for which the
Methodist circuit rider of the American frontier was famous.
Evangelism, education, medicine, and service were all geared to
the erection of the church.[240]

The Presbyterian Program

The Presbyterians (U.S.A.) developed what may be called a
church-oriented approach to Muslims in North India. All phases
of their varied program sought to establish and invigorate an
Indian church for action in the field. After consultation with
Marshman, Duff and Corrie, John C. Lowrie laid the foundations
for the mission at Ludhiana in two busy years (1833-1836).[241]
Encountering the Punjabi, Kashmiri and Afghan elements of that
city, he anticipated the demanding nature of work among Muslims.

I find that actual observation has corrected and modified
by views of this field...(1) The way does not seem to be yet
open for direct efforts,...(3) The proportion of those, who
embrace the religion of Muhammad, is much larger than I had
supposed, and they constitute the better class of the people.
...There is less prospect of their conversion than of any
other class.[242]

He proposed an unobtrusive beginning which would take new
opportunities as they occurred. For him, education appeared to
be the key to the heart of India, to correct misconceptions of
God and to prepare the way for the Gospel.

The importance of Christian schools becomes still more
apparent when we recollect that the main hope of success in
our endeavours to convert any heathen people, so far as the
use of means is concerned, consists in preparing native agents
who shall preach the Gospel to their country men. These must
be found and qualified, in heathen as in Christian countries,
chiefly amongst the youth. Missionaries from foreign countries
are indispensable in the first instance. It is theirs to
sow the seed, to plant Christian institutions, to organize
and train the army of native soldiers of the cross,...But
they labour under great disadvantages: their numbers are small
...they are and ever must be regarded as foreigners, imper-
fectly acquainted with the language, the usages, and the
habits of the people....[243]

Education and other means were to aim for the early formation
of an indigenous community.

The Presbyterians were fortunate in having leaders of vision
and longevity to fulfil these objectives. They included John
Newton, Sr. (1810-1891), James Wilson, Joseph Warren (trained
printer), Charles W. Forman (leader in education reaching India,
1848), Elwood Morris Wherry (leader in literature work reaching
India, 1868), and many more. The expansion of the network of
stations was rapid.[244] By 1856-57, there stretched along the
foothills of the Himalayas for a thousand miles, a cordon of
mission stations of the Scottish and American Presbyterian and
Methodist Episcopal Churches.[245] Ludhiana, a key link in this
chain, started the first high school (1836), the first organized
church (1837) and the Christian Press of North India.

It is well to note how efficient use of grassroots evangelism,
literature, and education contributed to the budding Indian church
and work force. In the cities, American Presbyterian missionaries soon avoided open street or bazaar preaching (which gained
so much attention in English and Scottish circles) shifting
instead to the quieter setting of a hall or the erected church-
buildings. Those attending the latter were often advanced
inquirers who occasionally made spontaneous confessions of
faith.[246] Extensive touring, preaching, tract and Scripture
distribution in the villages became a main channel for reaching
the people. The mission soon delegated this responsibility to
Indian evangelists and ministers, e.g. Babu John Hari, K. C.
Chatterji. This was the key to the church's rapid growth after
1870. Chatterji for example was able to reach the Muslim village
of Ghorawah (Hoshyarpur district) via a dissatisfied fakir,
Gumu Shah, and his disciples. The time came when they accepted
the authority of the New Testament instead of the Quran (ca.
1869). When twelve of these disciples were baptized, a court
of fifty maulvies examined them. The converts fearlessly declared
their new faith, giving reason why they accepted the way of
Christ over the teachings of Muhammad. After a massive two day
assembly, the Fateh Muhammad, declared that henceforth Muslims
and Christians could have social intercourse. This helped
clear the way for future converts. Missionaries on tour such
as John Newton, Jr., often found pockets of secret inquirers
and led them through Bible study to become the nucleus of a
congregation. Indian pastors such as Jaimal Singh, Ashraf Ali,
Mattias and Ahmad Shah took over these congregations and
equipped them for a persuasive witness to the people of the land.
It is well to note that a high percentage of the evangelists were
converts from Islam.[247] The church meanwhile grew extensively
from the mass movements out of the depressed classes of the
Punjab, Kolhapur and elsewhere.[248]

Literary work was a mainstay of the Presbyterian program.
The Ludhiana Press (1836) and Allahabad Press supplied the eight
major societies in North India for many years. Preparation,
translation and publication centered on the Scriptures, books,

tracts and a newspaper, <u>Lodiana</u> <u>Akhbar</u>. John Newton, W. Rodgers,
Joseph Warren. J. R. Campbell, James Wilson, and Joseph Porter
contributed their skills to this prodigious output.[249] James
Wilson became the secretary of the North India Bible Society
(auxiliary of B.F.B.S.) in 1845. The Punjab Conference of 1862
gave new impetus to literature work. It encouraged the presses
(1) to orientalize writings in both language and style, (2)
to eliminate controversial attacks on Islam and Hinduism, and
(3) to introduce an oriental format and cover for books.[250]
E. M. Wherry soon took the lead in producing a more constructive
literary approach to Islam.[251] The Ludhiana Press became the
voice of the Indian church to Islam.

In prayer, Ludhiana also led. Its Annual Meeting (1858) called
the whole Protestant world to join in the first Week of Worldwide Prayer (January, 1860) beseeching God to pour out His Spirit
upon all nations. This annual season of prayer was to prove the
source of revival and united zeal for mission for many churches.[252]

From the start, education was a vital channel for communicating
the Gospel to Muslims and others.[253] As already seen, the very
success of the school program created problems.[254] Forman College
(begun by Charles W. Forman, 1848; reopened 1885) however retained
a Christian staff, curriculum and purpose when many schools were
submitting to secular influences. Under Principal James C. R.
Ewing, 1888-1918, it experienced growth and increased respect
from all groups in the Punjab. Ewing could report in 1899 that:

> The purpose of the College is two-fold. It aims to bring
> the knowledge of Christ to the non-Christian youth of the
> Province, who resort to us in great numbers; and to educate
> the young mem of the Christian Church that they may be fitted
> to take their places as leaders in the great task of evangel-
> izing this country. Young men come to us from all quarters
> of Northern India, and our daily opportunity for influencing
> them is a most enviable one. A fair number of non-Christian
> students are seriously studying their Bibles, and from
> amongst these some will, we trust, be led by the spirit to
> a fuller faith, and ultimately to a public profession of
> their personal allegiance to Jesus Christ.[255]

Many other institutes, colleges, and a theological school further
strengthened the Presbyterian program for training a Christian
leadership and laity.[256] The key to the success of the American
Presbyterians lies not simply in methods, however, for other
groups also applied these means. The key lies more in that the
program was flexible, even dispensable, so that it could be
altered or sacrificed to suit the young church. One remembers
that by the end of the century, the temptation in most mission
circles was to place such high premium upon the system so as
to cause the infant church to suffer. While certain tensions
in the Presbyterian camp between mission organization and young
church were visible, the latter fortunately gained top priority.

Church and Mission Among the Presbyterians

Developments within the Indian Presbyterian Church however best reveal the strength of the church-oriented approach. A strong sense of community, the early recognition of an Indian ministry, the encouragement of mission by Indians for Indians, the gradual transfer of authority, and the tangible realization of the ecumenical nature of the church provide salient points to be observed. The first baptism and the organization of the first congregation at Ludhiana occurred in 1837. Every effort was exerted that the convert might belong to a new family. Soon congregations were electing ruling elders and deacons. After a slow start the membership doubled between 1857 and 1861.[257] By 1900-1901 there were 2,584 communicants including some 418 Indian workers.[258] This means about one in six were active in some form of evangelism. By 1914 there were 4,543 communicants and the church was beginning to experience a tidal influx of converts via the mass movements to Christianity.[259] Muslims gained new respect for the transforming power of the Gospel as displayed by a truly Indian Presbyterian Church.

The Presbyteries of Ludhiana (1837), Allahabad (1841), and Farrukhabad (1841) formed quickly and met as the Synod of North India in 1845. The Presbyteries of Lahore (1868), Kolhapur (1872) and Saharanpur (1841, 1884) joined later. The fact that they were willing and able to ordain national Christians such as Gopinath Nandi (convert under Duff), as well as Europeans (e.g. Adolph Rudolph and Julius F. Ullmann), from the start gave Indians opportunity to demonstrate their gifts for ministry. The presbyterian system permitted Indian Christians a healthy voice in church affairs. At the Third Synod meeting at Ambala (November, 1865), 120 Indian ministers, teachers, and colporteurs represented twelve Indian congregations and other phases of the work.[260] From 1834 to 1870, prospective candidates for the ministry trained under individual missionaries and were examined, licensed and ordained by presbytery. The first Theological Seminary at Allahabad (1872-1875) even had a lecturer on Islam, J. H. Morrison. The Seminary at Saharanpur (1884) included two professors concerned with work for Muslims, E. M. Wherry and J. C. R. Ewing.[261] Many of the candidates for the ministry were converts from Islam intent on reaching their own people for Christ.

The young church early inaugurated missions by Indians for Indians. At first such outreach revolved around the local congregation. Gradually Indian workers alone or with missionaries established new stations, sub-stations or village congregations. Another major step forward came when the Ludhiana Presbytery developed its own program of district missions known as the Thenesar Home Mission Field. Evangelist Talibuddin, graduate of Forman Christian College and Saharanpur Theological Seminary, served as superintendent. By 1920, this work was completely financed by Presbytery and served as a model for programs of the other Presbyterians in North India.[262]

Cooperation in mission between the young Presbyterian Church
in India and the parent body, Presbyterian Church, U.S.A. and
the transfer of authority were also achieved, but not without
the expected struggles. At first, the mission organization had
full control. But as issues and cases arose in the young
church it became apparent they could not be resolved by the
General Assembly in the U.S.A., so the Synod of North India was
made the final court of appeal for all Indian members. This
indicated an inequality as American members still had a voice
in both Presbytery and Mission. Many policy decisions were
still made by the latter even though John Lowrie in 1834-36 had
urged that Presbytery be granted fuller responsibility. John
Newton Sr. in 1877 proposed "to draw up a definite plan for
conducting Mission business through the Presbyteries with a view
to dissolving the Mission and to present it at the next annual
meeting."[263] The Mission compromised (1880) by retaining
control of women's work, schools, medical work, inter-mission
schemes, government correspondence, Mission funds and personnel.
It offered to Presbytery control of the evangelistic sphere,
formation of churches, appointment of pastors and evangelists
and oversight of the church's life. Although approved by the
Board in America (1882), the Presbyteries lacked men and
finances to accept this offer. In the middle years (1885-1920),
there was an aloofness between parent and daughter bodies.
The Mission was stressing the ideas of self-support, self-
government, self-extension (advocated by Anderson, Venn, etc.)
to such a point that the church at times felt isolated. While
Indian leaders and members wanted independence, they often
resented the separateness of younger missionaries. It became
apparent that this boycott of each other hindered the growth of
the church.[264] The question was "How to reunite the Church and
its mission?" One suggestion (1891) was that Indian ministers
should become full members of the Mission but this would have
sapped the self-respect of the indigenous church. J. C. R.
Ewing became field secretary (1918) in order to iron out the new
church to church relationships. His work, the Union of 1904,
the war-time internationalization of India, improvements in
stewardship, and mounting ecumenical movement all helped parent
and daughter bodies to enter into an adult relationship, a new
partnership in mission.[265] By 1924, the Presbyterian Church in
North India was distinctly independent and an equal in the
mission to Muslims.

Movements toward union gained early attention among the
various Presbyterian bodies in India. Scottish and American
Presbyterians had cooperated in the support of David and John
Brainerd, missionaries in America (1744) and a similar scheme
for India appeared by 1863.[266] Scottish, Irish, and American
Presbyterians began conversations in 1871, but when it became
evident that they were not yet ready for a complete merger, a

confederation, the Presbyterian Alliance of India took shape
(1875). When the Scottish Presbyterians and Reformed Church in
America of Madras Presidency formed the South India Presbyterian
Church, those in the North gained new courage. After four years
of discussion, the General Assembly of the Presbyterian Church
in India met (December 19, 1904) drawing into union nine
Presbyterian bodies. Congregational churches later joined
them to form the South India United Church (1908) and the United
Church of North India (1924).[267]
    Mention also must be made of the United Presbyterian Church
Mission (North America) at Sialkot begun by Andrew Gordon in
1855. This work resulted in a church numbering 31,631 members
by 1913. Conservative in nature, it bypassed the union of 1904,
but later became part of the United Church in North India.
Its Gordon Christian College at Rawalpindi and its contribution
to the Theological Seminary at Gujranawala are highly
respected.[268] All told, it appears that the church-oriented
approach by Presbyterians emphasizing the democratic, indigenous
life and mission of the Christian community has been exception-
ally suited for the twentieth century nations of Pakistan and
India.

MISSION CONFERENCES BEFORE 1910:
TOWARDS AN ECUMENICAL APPROACH TO MUSLIMS

    In addition to references to apologetic, educational and
service-centered developments, the interdenominational mission
conferences in India before 1910 afford some indication of the
growth of an ecumenical consciousness in the confrontation with
Islam. Protestants in India shared not only one faith and life
but a tradition of church councils. They felt constrained to
assemble knowing that unity was essential to effective witness;
that contact with other religions in hostile environments posed
many unanswered questions; and that the answers must be found
together. In 1810, William Carey had proposed that a general
missionary conference be held at the Cape of Good Hope.[269] The
Conference at Edinburgh a century later far surpassed his
fondest dream. A new vitality was manifested in the conferences in India prior to that. These conferences can be seen
as indicators of the changing attitudes and activity concerning
Islam.
    The South India Missionary Conference (1858), although
preceded by lesser regional conferences at Calcutta (1855) and
Benares (1857), marks the real beginning of a chain of interdenominational gatherings. Among its resolutions was a
proposal by the Scudders that medical missions be employed to
reach the "great masses of Heathen and Mohammedan people."[270]
The Reformed Church in America and A.B.C.F.M. argued that
education must be used to raise up the national church while
Scots and Anglicans saw it as an avenue for penetrating non-
Christian communities. This Conference, with the Mutiny fresh

in mind, views Islam through eyes of fear. Islam is portrayed as a fortress, "artfully planned to destroy souls...."[271]
    The Punjab Missionary Conference held at Lahore (1862-1863) was attended by all Protestant societies except the S.P.G. This conference was significant in that it symbolizes the beginning of united Protestant efforts among Muslims in the North and introduces themes which continue on into the twentieth century. The papers presented and discussions recorded make fascinating reading and give insight into the moods and methods of workers among Muslims.
    "Preaching to the Heathen" by John Newton indicated this was still considered the prime method. Essays "On Hindoo and Mahomedan Controversy" surprisingly reveal that most missionaries had little regard for controversy as a method. The few who favored it did so only as a tool to awaken the men out of their apathy. Orbison (American Presbyterian) outspokenly criticized it as a type of verbal force used by one person over another which lacks biblical support. While men may debate in private or by letter, public debate should not be tolerated for it breeds hard hearts, bitterness, hate and that contrary to the goals of the Gospel. He openly opposed the techniques applied by Pfander. In the discussion that follows, Robert Bruce (C.M.S.) and Hauser (Methodist Episcopal) defend controversy as a method.[272] The report contains only one note of medieval abuse regarding Islam.[273]
    Education gained both support and criticism. C. W. Forman's essay: "Schools: How can they be made in the highest degree auxiliary to the work of evangelizing the country?" sets forth this advice:

> We must keep more steadily in view the conversion of our pupils, and the fitting of them for extending still further the work of conversion, as the great end at which we are to aim.... There should be no attempt to conceal the truth that our schools were established to make converts.... Let the education given in our schools be thoroughly, manifestly Christian, and let everything else be subordinate and contributory to this.[274]

The storm-clouds of government interference, grants-in-aid and the problem of non-Christian teachers were arising, however, and W. Ferguson (Church of Scotland) rejected the majority opinion that education was the key to reaching Muslim and other youth. R. Thackwell added:

> Most of the brethren who have spoken in favour of allowing Hindoos and Mahommedans to teach the Bible in our schools, seem to take it for granted, that such teachers will do their duty faithfully. But what guarantee have we, that they will not wrest the Scriptures from its natural and legitimate meaning in order to favour their own peculiar

systems? For instances: the Mahommedan in teaching the
fourteenth chapter of John's Gospel, may tell his pupils
that the Comforter there spoken of, is Mahomed, and so
teaching his own religion out of our Bibles.... I have
insisted that none other than a Christian should impart
Christian instructions.[275]

As noted, the Conference contributed to many other vital
areas.[276]

Before the Indian church could face Islam, many hard questions had to be faced. With searing honesty, Goloknath, an
Indian Presbyterian warned against the paternal system, i.e.
the missionary who sees his converts as "objects of his compassion and pity, but hardly worthy of his friendship, or
capable of communion with him, except on religious subjects".[277]
The shocked responses blended confession with self-defense!
Three topics pointed towards an ecumenical church-oriented
approach towards Muslims and others: "On a Native Pastorate;"
"Intermission Discipline;" and John Newton's essay, "An Indian
Catholic Church: Is the formation of such a Church desirable?
And, if so, what can be done at present in furtherance of the
subject?" This latter paper developed into what is called
comity, the cooperation not competition of societies in various
fields. The third paper by Newton was most visionary. It
set forth plans for mergers and confederations disclosing that
some workers in India were far in advance of their home
churches.[278] Many of the proposals of the Punjab Conference
were to be accomplished in the twentieth century.

The first Decennial Missionary Conference at Allahabad
(1872-1873) reflected the churches and societies growing closer
in fellowship through revival and prayer (parallel to developments in Britain and America). Five papers on preaching to
Muslims deserve special attention. Imad-ud-Din declared that
preaching must (1) remove the doctrinal barriers surrounding
the basic truths, e.g. the sonship-divinity of Christ, Trinity
and the Bible as the Word of God; (2) provide commentary to
the Bible; and (3) give a true account of biblical history to
those whose views were muddled. The preacher needed maturity
in reason and a winsome friendliness.[279] Maulvi Safdar Ali
held that effective preaching involved (1) focusing on the
main truths essential to man's salvation, e.g. Christ's death
in man's behalf; (2) avoiding the insignificant and fanciful
matters which distract; and(3) crossing denominational lines
so that observers may see love as the prime characteristic of
the Christian community.[280] T. V. French advised preachers to
avoid the recent wave of Muslim reaction and to probe to the
heart by using the Sufi writings to introduce listeners to an
awareness of sin, repentence, and the life of fellowship with
God. He hoped for the rise of a group of Christian fakirs.[281]

Scotsman Mitchell challenged the church to meet the opportunity
of presenting Christ to India's 21 million Muslims.[282] T. P.
Hughes criticized bazaar preaching and suggested a more attractive form of itinerant preaching.

> I do not attach very much importance to this method of
> bringing the Gospel to the people. The ordinary bazaar
> preaching provokes opposition. If there should be a
> Muhammadan Moulvie in the crowd, he must, if he values his
> reputation, oppose the Christian preacher. Besides this,
> the arguments brought forward by an ordinary bazaar
> opponent, are those which have to be answered over and over
> again.
> I prefer meeting Muhammadans _alone_, either in my tent or
> study, or at their homes, when I can calmly bring before
> _the_ individual the spiritual claims of Christ's religion
> as compared with the legality of the system of Islam....[283]

Higher education also came under increased attack but the
essays by S. Dyson (C.M.S.) and William Miller (Madras) and the
discussion by veterans Mitchell and Wilson seemingly sustained
its case.[284] Newer efforts in medical, zenana and literary
work gained extensive treatment. How to make the native church
a viable, united missionary force gained much attention.[285]
Self support was seen as the prerequisite to independence from
missionary control. Several speakers were concerned about the
crippling after-effects of the financial largesse of earlier
missionaries. Congregations in South India were apparently
making faster progress towards self-support than groups in the
Muslim Northwest. Papers concerned for a united church, church
to church relations, and the missionary nature of the church
showed promise. In the first, J. Barton (C.M.S.) noted that
unity was not simply "uniformity of ecclesiastical organization,
but oneness of spirit and doctrine". In the atmosphere of India,
Congregationalists, Presbyterians and Episcopalians were all
learning and borrowing from each other and there was no need to
mold the Indian church strictly after any one pattern. It
must be allowed to evolve its own form. This vision of 1872
was not accepted by all![286] Robert Clark surmised that the
growing pains of the young Indian church were healthy and
should be welcomed by the parent bodies as pointing to the day
when churches could walk hand in hand. He urged that the
native church be recognized as the "nucleus of all missionary
work in the country".[287] H. Stern (C.M.S.) while affirming the
idea of Christian community, rejected the concept of "Christian
villages" as creating ghettos which isolate Christians from
society and not in keeping with the church's mission in the
world.[288] The vision of these workers certainly went beyond
their trying day to day circumstances.
   The Second Decennial Missionary Conference at Calcutta
(1882-1883) drew 475 members of 27 societies to discuss 30

papers in seven days. Of the various mission methods discussed,
e.g. preaching, primary education, women's work, the press,
medical missions, only higher education found itself in the
defensive position. W. Miller, evangelical educator at Madras
Christian College, did not even attempt to answer the charges
that many colleges were succumbing to secular and government
influence but suggested how Biblical teaching and a Christian
atmosphere could be maintained. Miller stressed careful
selection of instructors, keen discipline and a winning presentation of Christian truths.[289] It was clear that college
work had lost the respect of many. A new method introduced
was that of Sunday Schools for Muslim children. Americans
were finding it helpful in reaching youth and revolutionizing
home-life. This experimental effort would harness the energies
of many dedicated laymen.[290] Under the heading of the Indian
Church, much attention is given to selecting and training the
"Native Agency", the church's spiritual life, self-support and
self-propagation.[291] Participants were again preferring the
vernaculars for training Indian workers and asking how to root
the Christian truth and life in Indian life. The nurture of
spiritual life was gaining attention proportionate to that of
direct evangelism. Temperance and ethics were vital topics for
a young church trying to avoid the pitfalls of Hindu, Muslim
and secular Western culture. Discussion of self-support
reveals poverty stricken Indian Christians practicing stewardship, often with a sacrificial handful of rice. Only one
paper by E. M. Wherry gives direct treatment to Islam. He
notes the growing influence of converts from Islam. Fifty men
such as Imad-ud-Din were penetrating Islam by preaching and
pen in a remarkable way. Still more missionaries trained for
Muslim work were needed.

> The present unpreparedness of missionaries for this work
> is simply marvellous. The success of their work testifies
> not to missionary wisdom, but to a Divine power graciously
> manifested in human weakness. But how much greater might
> be our successes were we better prepared, and were we to
> adopt the best means at our disposal! The Mahomedans of
> India are a hopeful class for missionary effort...so far as
> North India is concerned, and in proportion to the labour
> bestowed, five Muslims have been converted to Christianity
> for every Hindu convert. Let it be remembered that many
> nominal Muslims are dissatisfied with Islam, shall we lead
> these to Christ or leave them to seek comfort in the
> rational faith of Sayad Ahmad?[292]

Wherry concludes by pointing out measures ensuring greater
success in Muslim work.

> (1) Men must be specially set apart and educated for
> this work. The Arabic language should be studied immed-

> iately.... (2) The Missionary must not be a recluse. He
> must be able to mingle freely with the people. The people
> can best learn the Gospel by seeing it exemplified in the
> loving-kindness, probity and holiness of the preacher.
> (3)...the preacher must preach Christ and Him crucified.
> In my opinion controversy in public places and especially
> in the bazaar should be avoided. What is wanted there is
> not so much debate, or assault on Mahomed and Islam, as
> clear statements of Gospel truth, bearing on the practical
> side of religion.[293]

Workers among Muslims had learned many lessons over the decades
and were seeking the best vocabulary to convey the news of
Christ to India's 41 million Muslims.

The Third Decennial Missionary Conference at Bombay (1892-
1893) proved to be the largest ever with 620 members from
forty societies discussing 30 papers in a week. While the
methods of "Work Among the Educated Classes," education,
women's work and literature gain full treatment, reference to
preaching is missing.[294] One could say it was simply taken
for granted, but more likely it had fallen into disrepute
partly due to its earlier association with controversy and
partly due to the rise of liberal theology which stressed
human experience over divine revelation. At the next conference at Madras (1902), some delegates attempt to correct this
omission. A strong Christian humanism appears under headings
concerned with the depressed classes and masses, lepers, lower
classes, and Eurasians.[295] Concern for the poor, rejected
and diseased of humanity is clearly rooted in the Gospel but
has come to the fore with the rise of the liberal movement.
Unfortunately the liberal reaction against rationalism was
frequently linked to a reaction against revelation. Feeling,
religious experience and humanitarian concern were given new
priority. This surfaces under such rubrics as religious training, industry, economics, social and legal rights. It reveals
that the Indian church feels strong enough to challenge social
and cultural practices which are in conflict with the Gospel.

The most obvious omission at this conference was the treatment of missions to Islam! Only ten years before there had
been pleas for more concentrated effort. Now the subject was
neglected! What caused this? First, the mass movements of
low caste peoples into Christianity were absorbing a major
proportion of energies in most regions. Second, late nineteenth century liberalism was rather conciliatory towards
monotheistic non-Christian religions.[296] What was under
concern was the attainment of civil rights for Muslim converts.[297] Because of a more enlightened public opinion regarding religious liberty, thousands of Christians coming out of
Islam in Bengal, Punjab, Sindh and the Northwest were slowly
securing essential human rights.

The Fourth Decennial Indian Missionary Conference at Madras
(1902) was limited to 200 delegates and programmed on the basis
of eight working committees, each giving carefully weighed
reports. This system would be used at Edinburgh (1910).
While organizationally effective, one must confess the papers
lack something of the spontaneity and personal flavor of the
earlier conferences. Yet this too is significant. Mission
work in India is no longer the program of the individual missionary, but the team effort of the missions and the Indian
churches.

When one surveys the increase in the number of societies
and churches it is easy to see why cooperation was so urgent.
The first committee discussed the church's development (three
selves concept), training of the ministry and youth work. The
growth of the Protestant church in India was an inspiration to
all. In 1855 it could have hardly exceeded 100,000 yet by
1861 it numbered 213,000. In 1891 it rose to 671,000 and by
1900 it numbered about 1,012,000. The second committee on
evangelistic work covered educational work and proclamation.
Whereas preaching was slighted in 1892, such was not the case
in 1902. Education was admired as a valid agency and powerful
auxiliary to evangelism. The report urged: (1) the systematic
teaching of Christian truth in every class, (2) an increase in
the number of Christian teachers, and (3) careful selection of
qualified teachers.[298] A special plea was issued for increased effort to reach the world's 250 million Muslims (62
million in India alone). "Not one sixtieth of them have ever
been reached by a Christian missionary." Yet the success of
dedicated workers in India testifies to what can be done.[299]
Chairman Canon Sell (C.M.S. Madras) made certain that Islam
gained proper attention on this Conference's agenda. A report
on the Muslims in Bengal noted hopeful signs.

> A change certainly has come over many of the Muhammadans.
> There was a time when they would not admit the wisdom of
> reading the Christian Scriptures, believing as they did
> that the Scriptures had been repealed. But now many of
> them manifest a deep interest in the Bible....[300]

While rationalistic and aggressive Islamic movements had
arisen, Wherry noted that the Christian ideas and practices of
religious freedom had helped to generate more tolerant attitudes
among liberal minded Muslims. Islamic ecclesiasticism and
hierarchical dogma were losing their grip on many Muslims, he
claimed, and various Christian methods were making inroads into
Islam. He felt as did Goldsmith that the Christian worker had
no reason to be discouraged by the new era of Islamic
revival.[301]

This Conference marked the end of an era in India regarding
missions to Muslims. The next developments toward a more
advanced, internationalized (ecumenical) Christian approach to

Islam would be forthcoming in the Conferences held at Cairo
(1906), Lucknow (1911), and Edinburgh (1910).

SUMMARY COMMENTS ON CHURCH AND MISSION IN INDIA

India in the nineteenth century affords a remarkable picture
of the growth of Christianity. The determined Protestant church
that emerged from 1900 onwards was not simply the product of
missionary work. It was to be the twentieth century pattern for
the world church in terms of unity and mission. Various stages
are visible. First, there were efforts to unite within
denominational lines as evidenced in the Presbyterian Alliance
(1875) and the Presbyterian Church (1904). Next, the Societies
of different traditions agreed upon comity, the definition of
geographical fields of work for each, and the Board of Arbitra-
tion (1903) to advise on opening new territories. Third, Congregationalists and Presbyterians were able to cross traditional
lines to form the South India United Church (1908). This
was a milestone towards the day when Presbyterians, Congregationalists, Methodists and Anglicans would be one church (1948).
The Jubbulpore Conferences (1909 and 1911), the Edinburgh
Conference (1910), and the Continuation Committee (1912),
would give birth to the regional councils and the National
Christian Council of India (1914).

Equally important was that responsibility for mission was
shifting from the overseas agencies to the Indian church.
The Mukti Mission (1887) and the Keskari's Mission at Sholapur
(1899) had Indian leadership even though they were aided by
overseas finances and personnel. Interesting enough, the first
indigenous mission work found its expression in the Muslim
North. The Home Mission of the Ludhiana Church Council (1895)
stimulated similar projects among the Presbyteries of Allahabad,
Gujarat, and Sialkot. The National Missionary Society founded
at Serampore (1905) with V. Z. Azariah as its secretary would
have a staff of 97 in five areas of India backed by Indian
stewardship by 1925. Other Indian missions from Tinnevelly
(1903) and the Mar Thoma Syrian Christians also reflected the
growing concern for reaching their countrymen for Christ.
Christ, The Desire of India was the confession of more than
one convert.[302]

The transfer of authority produced a problem of its own. In
the churches of the North there were hundreds and thousands
of converts from Islam.[303] While the patriarchal system had
to go, these converts required disciplined training before
they were ready to assume leadership of the national church.
While the revolutionizing principles of self-support, self-
government, and self-extension as advocated by R. Anderson and
H. Venn seemed most rational, unexpected problems appeared
when these principles were pressed too fast and too far. In
making the national church the ultimate goal of mission rather

than the winning of the nations and the formation of the church
universal, the movement came dangerously near breaking contact
between parent and daughter bodies and the withdrawal of the
mission societies. Some failed to observe that gifts and per-
sonnal can pass from one church to another without imperialism.
While Roland Allen continued to press for radical application
of the "three selves" concept, others early in the twentieth
century saw that what was needed was cooperation, a partnership
in mission which acknowledged the interdependence of all the
brethren in the church worldwide. Fortunately the church in
India was able to attain a healthy blend of the indigenous and
ecumenical in both church and mission.[304]

    This had direct bearing on the approaches made to Muslims
and others. The Indian church took charge of the work of
proclamation very early. This meant that more Muslims encountered Indian evangelists and pastors (often themselves converts
from Islam). While Indians assumed the bulk of this work, many
missionaries continued to participate in itinerant evangelism
insisting that only by this down-to-earth labor could they
identify with their Indian colleagues and the spiritual needs
of the people. Evangelism, it has been noted, developed from
a medieval to a modified apologetic. While some Indian evangelists retained an aggressive approach to Muslims, most sought
a more attractive proclamation of the Gospel. Institutional
operations were the slowest to be transferred to the Indian
church. While much of the literature for Muslims was written
and distributed by nationals, overseas missions continued to
supervise and support most of the 40 presses and 100 periodicals which existed in 1914. Educational institutions were
slow to come under Indian jurisdiction. St. Stephen's College,
Delhi was one of the first to have an Indian president, S. K.
Rudra. This set the pattern other institutions would follow.
Gradually gaining higher positions on faculties, Christian
nationals projected an inspiring example in Indian life.
Medical institutions tended to remain under foreign control
even longer due to the technical nature of the work. It also
took considerable time for the servant image of medical work
and nursing to catch on in caste-minded India. Indian
Christian doctors and nurses were true pioneers in creating a
public conscience and program of welfare work for the masses.
The combined efforts of Indian and overseas Christians in
behalf of orphans, lepers, zenanas, the hungry, diseased and
depressed peoples of India gained the respect of many Muslims.
In many cases it was Christian service that prepared the way
for their consideration of the witness and worship of Christ[305]

    Two important lessons had been learned in working with
Muslims and others in India. First, a sympathetic, sensitive
approach to non-Christian religions and the culture of the land
was not contradictory to the objectives and efforts of Christ's
mission. While every tradition contributed to this awareness,
some of the best examples are found in the writings and work

of John Wilson, J. N. Farquahar and E. M. Wherry. Second, it
was learned that people are prone to move towards the Christian
faith as social units as well as individuals. It has been
said that about four-fifths of the Protestant church membership
came in this fashion. This observation applies to Muslims as
well as to the depressed classes.[306] These new findings would
yet need to be put into effective practice by those working
among Muslims. Maturer efforts in communicating the Gospel
and bridging the gulf in Christian-Muslim communal relationships
would be seen in men such as Thornton, Gairdner, Zwemer and in
the conferences of the twentieth century.

3

Reformed and Anglican Missions to Muslims in The Near East, 1800 - 1910: Ecclesiastical and Environmental Factors

OPENING THE NEAR EAST TO PROTESTANT MISSIONS

Factors in the Ottoman Recession and the Rise of Western Influence

The tremendous movement from West to East in the nineteenth century, like the earlier Arab-Islamic movement in the reverse direction, is one of the significant facts of history. As a tide flowing into a great basin, it represented the penetration of one civilization by another. There is no doubt that the Christian faith in its expansion harnessed the currents of this larger movement. Yet it is important to note that although Christian missionaries traveled the same road used by traders, warriors, and diplomats, their motives were far from identical. Not only did they frequently clash, but Christian workers were often the sharpest critics of Western policies and the advocates of indigenous-national interests. It is at this point that students of history, rightly proud of their own national heritage, occasionally fail to grasp the motives and objectives of Christian missions.[1] It is this growing disassociation from the political and commercial interests of home countries that differentiates nineteenth century Protestant missions from Christian endeavors in previous centuries.

Latourette's monumental studies have shown, in the nine-teenth century Protestant missions were less directly associated with governments, received less help from them,

and were more often in conflict (and effectively so) with
colonial policies vis-à-vis the welfare of the people among
whom they worked than any since the fourth...by 1914,
probably the majority of Protestant missionaries were working
overseas in countries where their homelands held no political
control. On so vast a scale this was a new feature of
Christian history.[2]

It is valid however to detect certain factors breaching aged
walls, opening gates and constructing roadways by which Protestant missionaries might enter the lands of the Near East.
While it is difficult to separate cause and effect, it is
possible to describe some of the forces at work in the recession of the Ottomans and the rise of European and national
influences.

Political-military factors in the Ottoman recession included:
internal breakdown, territorial losses and European inroads.
The centralized military nature of Ottoman bureaucratic government centering around the Sultan and his officials gradually
isolated Asia Minor from her far-reaching colonies. When
this bureaucracy became infested with corruption, favoritism,
then suppression and persecution, the normal channels of
government between the main office and the provinces were
disrupted. Lawlessness, unbearable taxation and rebellion
increased proportionately.[3] Although the first sultans were
most capable men, the later system of selection and training
candidates virtually precluded the emergence of an effective
ruler. The Ottoman state lost its inner purpose, its raison
d'être. After mid-eighteenth century the disintegrating
Ottoman system was challenged by Persians, Arabs, Russians and
Europeans.[4] Internal decline was paralleled by provincial
rebellions, struggles for independence, and in some colonies,
European control. Two disastrous wars (1767-1774, 1788-1792)
shattered the myth of Turkish invincibility. The Treaty of
Kutchuck (1774) citing Russia as the protector of Christian
minorities and granting her real or supposed extraterritorial
rights (capitulations) was a turning point.[5] From then on,
struggling Serbs, Bulgars, Greeks and others looked to Russia
as their champion and one observes the erosion of the empire
with territories continuously being lost to nationalist or
European powers.[6] While outlying regions could achieve independence, Armenians, Assyrians and Maronities within reach of
the capital pursued this policy only with disastrous consequences. They became the pawns, the massacre victims, of a
vile game of power politics. Equally important was the French
and British contest over the Near and Far East. Setting out
to destroy British power and seize India, Napoleon invaded
Egypt (1798) and promoted the establishment of French culture.
Britain reasserted herself at Waterloo. The Egypt that had
tasted of European learning was no longer content to be an Otto-

man pawn. Mohammed Ali in his bid for power might well have
extended his rule over all Turks and Arabs had he not been
stopped by a Britain in collusion with the Ottomans. Yet
strange enough it was the destruction of the Egyptian fleet at
the Battle of Navarino (1827) that gave European fleets control
of the Eastern Mediterranean and incidentally provided missionaries and others new freedom of travel. Politics remain a
cobweb spread over Near Eastern life. In this maze, missionaries would sometimes find themselves opposing both Turkish and
European policies and defending the people of the land.

Economic factors played a part too. From 1583 onwards,
France and Britain became the great commercial rivals of the
Eastern Mediterranean.[7] The new factor was the industrial revolution which made Britain a manufacturer needing raw materials
and in turn outlets for the finished goods. Egypt and Syria
were drawn into the Anglo-European market and their economics
became more dependent. The agrarian system of the Ottomans
broke down as Egypt entered into cotton production and
lucrative commerce with Europe. This brought on benefits and
ills, changes and reactions, felt by missionaries and nationals
alike. The construction and control of the Suez Canal symbolize
how economics not only helped open the Near East but brought
continual pressure upon it.

Intellectual, moral and religious forces were also at work.
Demonstrating an amazing ability for assimilation, the Ottomans rapidly reached a golden age. By the eighteenth century,
they unfortunately shifted to a defensive maintenance of the
status quo. This led to mental and moral stagnation, the
preservation of a delicate balance of power between provinces,
millets and bureaus which saw every ambition or move for progress as a threat.[8] During the second period (1451/1517-1622),
the dhimmis, especially the ancient Christian millets, found
their hopes for independence swamped by a stricter Muslim
majority. Because the Empire was a religious rather than
national, racial or linguistic structure, their spiritual
longings (at times identified with national hopes) were often
misinterpreted.· By the third period (1622-1800) and 1800-
1919), great tensions arose within and between the Greek
Orthodox, Armenians, Nestorians, Monophysite Jacobites, Copts,
Maronites, Melkites and Latin Catholics. This weakened their
witness to the Jews and the Muslim masses. These communal
jealousies upset the delicate balance necessary for survival.
This process of fragmentation was hastened as millets became
segregated ghettos within the empire, each seeking to advance
themselves independently. By the Peace of Carolvitz (1699),
the millets in the Balkans were making their own way.[9] Roman
Catholic and Protestant missionaries did not always appreciate
this delicate balance within the empire.

When they found Eastern Christian laymen reacting against
Turkish corruption, excessive taxation and repression and sometimes against their own clergy, (e.g. the Greek revolutionaries

v.s. the Phanariot Greeks of the capital), they lent their support. The cry for liberty and life by the Eastern brethren plus
the concern to evangelize all peoples including Jews and Muslims
aroused the interest of evangelical Christians in Europe, Great
Britain and America.

Early Protestant Missionary Efforts in the Near East

Early individual Protestant efforts in the Near East were
made by von Sonegg (among Muslims in the Balkans, 1540-1560)
and Lutheran Peter Heyling who served as a missionary in Egypt
(1632) and Abyssinia (1634) until death (1652).[10] The first
organized church mission is to the credit of the Moravians who
sent workers to Constantinople (1740), Rumania (1740), Persia
(1747-1750) and Egypt (1768-1783). Circumstances did not permit
these heroic missions to be continued.[11] Many overlook the fact
that the first sustained Protestant mission to the Near East of
the nineteenth century was Scottish (1800-1849). The Edinburgh
Society gained a charter from Czar Alexander (1802) to establish
a colony of converts from non-Christian peoples under Russian
rule.[12] They began work at Karass, half-way between the Caspian
and Black Seas, while the Glasgow Society began at nearby
Kaffraria (1822). Hostile Greek, Turkish and Russian authorities
forced the abandonment of these stations, but Astrakhan,
Caucasian capital on the Caspian Sea, continued for the time to
be a center for Bible distribution and itinerant preaching.[13]
A helpful description of the work is found in William Glen's
account of conversations, Muslim objections, and the baptism
of Muslim converts on tour.[14] His translation of the Old Testament into Persian and its revision (Tabriz and Teheran, 1838-
1842) was a lasting contribution. He personally supervised
its printing in Scotland and at the age of seventy (1847)
returned to Persia to ascertain its distribution before his
death at Teheran (1849). This edition combined with Martyn's
Persian New Testament was a mainstay for many decades.

The Basel Mission to the Caucasus (1822-1835) was one of
several German settlements in that region.[15] Emperor Alexander
granted them a charter to establish schools, seminary, press
and churches (1821). Under secretary, T. Blumhardt five workers
(incl. Karl G. Pfander) were sent to Tiflis and Shoosha. In
addition to their work in Armenian and Russian schools, extensive tours were made in Persia and Mesopotamia. A number of
mullahs and Muslim laymen became secret believers and several
including Alexander Kasim Beg, professor at Kazan, openly confessed the Christian faith. The missionaries became convinced,
however, that it was necessary to enlighten and reform the
Armenians that they might be co-workers in the mission to
Muslims. This opinion and effort undoubtedly influenced Smith,
Dwight and the policy of the American Board. The Bible Society
of Russia had cooperated with both Scottish and Basel missions
but unfortunately a decree of the Russian government closed the

Basel Mission in this region in 1835.[16]

The Pattern of Protestant Missions in the Near East

Protestant mission societies coming to the Near East found a
set of circumstances quite different from those in India. Three
factors contributed to this altered situation. First, politically the Near Eastern countries fell under Muslim rule, the
application of Islamic law. While this study is not primarily
concerned with political history, politics had unavoidable bearing on church life and mission activity. The religious liberty
found in India would for many decades stand in contrast to the
Near Eastern scene. Second, was the ecclesiastical factor.
Ancient Orthodox Churches existed in most Near Eastern lands
which had to be considered as hindrances (i.e. needing reform)
or helpmates in the mission to Muslims. No Protestant body
suggested that these brethren could be ignored. They shared a
life and faith which could be enriched as an end in itself, or
cultivated as a means to more effective mission to Muslims.
Third, the majority of the population was Muslim. There were
no large groups of depressed classes, Hindus, and others to whom
the missionary could turn when frustrated by the exhausting
nature of Muslim evangelization. Missionaries and national
Christians were caught in the continuing tension between their
commission in Christ to these masses and the circumstances
crippling their efforts to fulfill it. Environment, ecclesia,
and the ideals of evangelization pulled the concerned worker in
many directions at once!

Each Reformed and Anglican mission force responded to these
three basic factors in various ways reflecting their own background and immediate situation. All groups used in various ways
the methods discussed in chapter two, e.g. apologetic-evangelistic, educational, medical-service, etc. These will become
secondary headings in this chapter. What is of distinctive
interest is how each group responded to the above factors.
Briefly one might say that the American Board, working in the
Ottoman strongholds of Turkey, East Turkey, etc., found little
latitude for Muslim work.[17] The Eastern churches, viewed as
obstacles to future Muslim work, soon absorbed the bulk of the
mission's energy. The background of those serving with the
Board shaped the direction their work took. Influenced by New
England enlightenment, education gained a prominent role. Influenced by the American individual-congregational pattern,
scattered evangelical congregations appeared. Influenced by
American pragmatism, workers tackled the "permitted" spheres
when Muslim work was opposed. The two Presbyterian bodies from
America were farther removed from the capital and in a more
heterodox Muslim society with strong pockets of ancient Christians (Persia, Syria-Lebanon, and Egypt). Their evangelistic
background was reflected in dealing with Muslims. Their indivi-

dualism was modified by their esteem for a presbyterian type of
government. They felt obliged to benefit Muslims as well as
the Eastern churches via education, literature and medical
service. The Anglicans were also farther from the capital and
in areas acquainted with British influence (esp. Palestine,
Persia and Egypt). The Orthodox churches in Palestine concentrated about the Holy Places, and while in need of reform, were
powerful enough to resist it. This called for more delicate
inter-church dealings. The mixed background of Anglicans (high
and low parties, rational orthodoxy, evangelical piety, liturgical revival, etc.) produced a varying, sometimes conflicting
opinion as to the correct relation with Orthodox churches. The
Anglicans were not without utilitarians who contended that
everything must be directed towards evangelizing Muslims. By
the turn of the century, their number had increased. Reformed
churches (Reformed Church in America and the churches of Scotland) who turned to Arabia found themselves in the ultra-
conservative heart of Islam. In the absence of ancient churches,
their sole objective was to evangelize the Muslim populace and
to form an indigenous evangelical church. Only the background
of their strong evangelical conviction and zeal could have
directed them to this near impossible task. The presbyterianism of the founders of these missions was bolstered by strong
individualism. They were practical people and realized that
medicine, schools and literature were required means for getting
a toehold in the obdurate soil. It will be observed that the
environment of the Near East made both individual missioner
and Muslim convert more dependent upon the mission organization
than in India.

Creating adequate titles to describe the minute differences
of policy or approach is most difficult. The captions selected
have been based on the group's response to three objectives.
This might be diagramed thus:

Body	Objectives and Their Priority:		
	To encourage reform within the Orthodox churches	To reform Orthodox churches by estab- lishing evangelical churches	To evangelize Muslims and form evangelical churches
American Board:	First intent	Became immediate goal	Ultimate goal
	(hence entitled the "via Eastern churches" approach)		
Presbyterians from America:			
	Secondary	Primary	Primary
	(hence entitled the "two-pronged approach")		

Anglicans:
Stages:
1st (1815-1840)

	Primary	Disavowed	Ultimate goal

2nd (1841-1890)

	Still stated as primary goal	Undeclared goal	Emerged as an immediate goal

3rd (1890-1910)

	Sought maturing church to church relations	Rejected	Immediate goal

        (hence entitled "Varying relations with Orthodox
        churches and an emerging mission to Muslims")

Reformed-Presbyterian
Action in Arabia:

	------------	------------	Primary goal

        (hence entitled "Pioneer missions to Muslims
        in Arabia")

The task of examining and evaluating these Reformed and Anglican approaches and activities is an immense undertaking. Resources for Near Eastern history are certainly not wanting.[18]
This study will concentrate upon the first hand documents of the
missionaries and societies actually engaged in field work.

THE AMERICAN BOARD:
DEVELOPMENT OF A VIA THE EASTERN CHURCH APPROACH

Initial Policy, Explorations and Establishment: 1818 -ca. 1840

The American Board of Commissioners for Foreign Missions
(A.B.C.F.M.) operated the most comprehensive and stable mission
program in the Near East in the nineteenth century. This Board,
composed largely of Congregational Churches of New England,
included a number of other Reformed bodies on the Eastern sea-
board, e.g. Old School Presbyterians until the split of 1837,
the Reformed Church in America until the 1850s, and the New
School Presbyterians until their reunion with the Old School in
1870. Rufus Anderson, the outstanding secretary of this early
era was personally acquainted with all the missionaries except
Parsons and Fisk.
The Board's ultimate objective in the Near East and elsewhere was nothing less than the winning of all peoples to the
kingdom of God.[19] The basic policy regarding how the Muslims
of the Near East should be approached was soon forthcoming.
Representing the Board, Anderson wrote:

    We may not hope for the conversion of the Mohammedans
    unless true Christianity be exemplified before them by the
    Oriental Churches....Hence a wise plan for the conversion

of the Mohammedans of Western Asia necessarily involved, first a mission to the Oriental Churches.[20]

In the Report of 1819, the Prudential Committee was not too optimistic about the state of the Eastern churches.

> In Palestine, Syria, the provinces of Asia Minor, Armenia, Georgia, and Persia, though Mohammedan countries, there are many thousands of Jews, and many thousands of Christians, at least in name. But the whole mingled population is in a state of deplorable ignorance and degradation,--destitute of the means of divine knowledge, and bewildered with vain imaginations and strong delusions.[21]

This critical opinion was confirmed rather than changed by extensive travels and surveys on the field. To their Protestant eyes the ills were deep-rooted and doctrinal.

> Their views of the Trinity, and of the divine and human natures of Christ, are not unscriptural; but their views of the way of salvation through the Son, and of the work of the Holy Spirit, are sadly perverted. The efficacy of Christ's death for the pardon of sin, is secured to the sinner, they supposed, by baptism and penance. The belief is universal, that baptism cancels guilt, and is regeneration....Being thus freed from the condemning power of original sin, and regenerated by baptism, men were expected to work their way to heaven by observing the laws of God and the rites of the Church.[22]

It was concluded that if Muslims and other non-Christian peoples in the Near East were to be won to Christ, it must be by a mission to the Eastern churches. The first missionaries were, however, in no way restricted. Secretary Worcester instructed Fisk and Parsons destined for Jerusalem thus:

> You will survey with earnest attention the various tribes and classes who dwell in that land and in the surrounding countries. The two grand inquiries ever present in your minds will be, What good can be done? and By what means? What can be done for Jews? What for Pagans? What for Mohammedans? What for Christians? What for the people of Palestine? What for those in Egypt, in Syria, in Persia, in Armenia, in other countries to which your inquiries may be extended?[23]

Parsons' farewell sermon in Boston was on "The Dereliction and Restoration of the Jews", but he was soon to focus more intently upon the oriental churches.

The years 1818-1831 were years of exploration and survey.

The American Board was determined to gain first hand information
before launching into a major program. Accurate reports regarding the religious conditions of Near Eastern lands were still
wanting in America. Two major explorations were carried out
under Fisk and Parsons (1818-1820) and Dwight and Smith (1830-
1831). Pliny Fisk and Levi Parsons reached Malta (1819) and
after conversations with William Jewett (C.M.S.) and Wilson
(L.M.S.), settled at Smyrna, Turkey (1820). From this base they
visited the region of the seven churches of Asia Minor, Jerusalem and then Beirut (1821). In another effort to reach Jerusalem, ill health forced Parsons to Alexandria where he died
(1822).[24] Fisk was soon joined by two valuable recruits:
Daniel Temple and Jonas King (1792-1869).[25] Fisk, King and the
celebrated Joseph Wolff journeyed to Jerusalem via Alexandria,
Cairo and the desert (1823). Political unrest and climate soon
prompted them to move to the more secure city of Beirut. Here
their ranks were bolstered by the arrival of William Goodell
and Isaac Bird (1832), Eli Smith (1827), Harrison Gray Otis
Dwight (1830), George B. Whiting and Dr. Dodge (1835), John F.
Lanneau (1836), Charles S. Sherman (1839), Dr. Harves (1844) and
others.

A two month conference of the Board's missionaries and Secretary Anderson at Malta (1828) determined much of the future course
of action. Whiting and Bird returned to Syria to continue the
work begun in 1823. Goodell proceeded to Constantinople to inaugurate a program there. The exploration of the largely unknown
regions of Turkey-Armenia-Persia was committed to Smith and
Dwight. At the risk of life, they made the dangerous journey
along the "high road" from Constantinople via Armenia, Transcaucasia, Kurdistan to Tabriz and returned via Trebizond on the
Black Sea (total mileage, 2500) in 1830-1831. Their report not
only prompted the Board to begin extensive programs among
Armenians and Nestorians and limited direct work with Muslims
but was read in America and Europe as a valuable primary document
for nearly forty years!

This report, Researches in Armenia, deserves attention as a
policy shaper.[26] The Basel missionaries encountered apparently
were a fountain of information and opinion. In this document,
Smith and Dwight remark frequently about the haughtiness of the
Turkish Muslims, especially the nomadic Turks living by the law
of the survival of the strongest. Many of the Muslims living
in the larger villages and cities gave evidence of their Christian and non-Arab backgrounds. Some Greeks and Armenians about
Trebizond were "still secretly Christian" who "reduced to despair by the oppression of their Turkish masters...embraced the
Mohammedan faith".[27] The travelers found the Persian Muslims
refined and better educated than their Turkish counterparts.
While respecting the Persians' religious tolerance and cool
ability to discuss the merits of various religions, they frequently suspected their diplomacy was cover for deceitful enter-

prise, e.g. bribes for official papers. The authors noted the
various strands of Islam in Persia.

> Most of the higher class of the nobility and the learned
> profession, indeed pay little regard even to the external
> forms of religion, and are at heart infidels or sceptics. In
> fact, Soofy is known to be little better than another name for
> the sceptic....You must not understand that all Persians are
> inclined to free-thinking. The mass of the people are not
> only very sincere in their faith, but have decidedly an appear-
> ance of greater strictness in the observance of their rites
> than even the Turks....Even among the free-thinking part of
> the community a nearer view will discover hardly an easier
> access for the truth. They are either wrapt in a bewildering
> labyrinth of philosophical speculation or are utterly regard-
> less of all religion....[28]

They perceived that a convert to Christianity might gain the
Shah's official protection yet face the wrath of mullahs and
masses. Visiting the Nestorians at Urumia, they were warmly received and filled with hope.

> Permit me to add to this report of our visit to the Nestor-
> ians, some considerations respecting the expediency of estab-
> lishing a mission in this part of Persia.--We have little to
> say, in addition to the account already given of the Persian
> Moslems, to enable you to judge what would be the prospects
> of a mission established specially for them. Such a mission
> we are not prepared decidedly to recommend; though our per-
> suasion is strong, that a missionary, while directing his
> attention expressly and primarily to the Christian population,
> would find many occasions and means of doing good to the
> followers of Mohammed also, as a secondary branch of labour.[29]

Smith and Dwight came to the conclusion that the Eastern churches,
Greek, Armenian and Nestorian must be reached and revived before
any appreciable good could be done for non-Christians in the Near
East.

> In view of the extensive ground we have surveyed, a few
> thoughts arise with which you will permit us to close the
> report of our tour....It is the deeply affecting spiritual
> condition of the people we have visited, calling upon us to
> labour for their conversion to Christ.
> Of those people, the nominal Christians have engrossed the
> most of our attention.--To give them the same prominence in
> your own, we might mention the name they bear--the same holy
> name by which we are called....that the religion we hold so
> dear is made the hereditary scorn of Mohammedans?
> But, of the considerations which above all others deserve

to be named, the first is, <u>that</u> <u>they</u> <u>are</u> <u>in</u> <u>a</u> <u>perishing</u>
<u>state</u>. Though called Christians, they are all out of the way
and fatally so....The only apology that can be made for them
is the stale one....they are sincere in believing that their
superstitious rites and ceremonies will cancel their sins....
We would suggest respecting them is, that their reformation
is practicable....[30]

The team was not neglectful of the Muslims. The Muslims were
to remain an ultimate, if delayed, objective to be attained
through the reformation and witness of the Eastern churches.

    <u>Another</u> important consideration is <u>the</u> <u>relation</u> <u>in</u> <u>which</u>
<u>these</u> <u>nominal</u> <u>Christians</u> <u>stand</u> <u>toward</u> <u>Mohammedans</u>. Their
present influence is exceedingly to be deprecated. The
Moslem has hitherto known Christianity only as the religion
of the Christians around him. And in such a position are
they placed by his oppressive laws that in all the associations of his earlier and riper years, they occupy the rank
of despised inferiors. Such too, I am sorry to say, is their
conduct, that he has ever been able to look upon the comparative practical effects of their Christianity and of his
Mohammedanism with self-congratulation. Never in the course
of their history have Mohammedans been brought in contact
with any form of Christianity that was not too degenerate
in its rites, its doctrines, and its effects to be worthy of
their esteem. Preach to him Christianity, therefore, and the
Moslem understands you to invite him to embrace a religion
which he has always regarded as beneath him, and as less
beneficial than his own....Let every missionary station raise
up from the corrupt mass of nominal Christians round it, a
goodly number of true followers of the Lamb, and it will be
a city set on a hill which cannot be hid, a light to lighten
the Gentiles also....Restore to them their primitive purity,
therefore, and the prop upon which Mohammedanism has so long
stayed itself is gone, and it must fall.[31]

It may be commented that the team lacked appreciation for the
strengths of the Orthodox churches, nevertheless their analysis
would form the backbone of the Board's policy. While they
expected Islam's early collapse, they were not blind to its
fearful present powers and the long contest ahead.

    ...Mohammedan law denounces death without mercy upon
every apostate from Mohammedanism; and wherever that law is
in force, direct attempts to make proselytes may naturally
be regarded as highly objectionable. But by labouring among
Christians, we gain an easy entrance into the heart of our
enemy's territory....The bearing of our labours in Western
Asia upon Mohammedanism increased inconceivably their

importance; and we look with intense interest upon every new
station that is formed as an additional intrenchment thrown up
against the armies of the false prophet.[32]

In its first fifty years of work the American Board established eight Missions to Palestine, Syria, Greece, Armenians (Turkey-Armenia), Nestorians, Assyrians (Eastern Turkey-Iraq),
Jews and Muslims. The bulk of this energy was directed towards
the oriental churches. The early objective was to stimulate
Orthodox churches to reform, but gradually the idea that this
might mean forming evangelical churches emerged. By 1842,
Rufus Anderson reported to the Board and it responded with this
resolution:

  ...2. The great object of our missions to the Oriental
Christian communities, should be the revival of spiritual
religion, the conversion of souls to Christ, the wide diffusion of the great regenerative idea of justification by
faith alone, and not a controversy with the hierarchies of
these communities about particular institutions, forms, and
ceremonies.
  ...4. Whenever those Oriental churches, having had the
Gospel fairly proposed to them, shall reject it, exscinding
and casting out from their communion those who receive it,
--...then it will be necessary for our missionary brethren
to turn from them...and to call on all God's children to
come out from among them and not to be partakers.[33]

Time and space does not permit a full detailed examination of
the history of all eight missions but the following four have
been selected:

1. The Mission to the Armenians (Turkey-Armenia).
2. The Mission to the Nestorians-Assyrians prior to the
    transfer of 1870.
3. The Mission to Syria prior to 1870.
4. Limited direct efforts among Muslims before 1910.

In each case, the application of the above policies will be
examined.

Among the Armenians and Peoples of Turkey, 1831-1910.

Ecclesiastical Relationships

The American Board began work in Turkey-Armenia-Kurdistan in
1831 with the arrival of William Goodell at Constantinople.[34]
Their first objective was to stimulate reform among the Orthodox
churches of the area. Literary-evangelism and education became
the two prime channels for achieving this goal. Genius and longevity strengthened the work. William Goodell (1792-1867) served

in the capital (1831-1865) demonstrating qualities well suited
to his task.

> He was evidently just the man for the peculiar and multi-
> plied types of human character to be found among the Orient-
> als. His plan was to exert an influence over those with whom
> he came in contact, without having the appearance of in-
> fluencing them at all, and so to avoid exciting opposition.
> He aimed at securing a moral and religious reformation
> among the people, not by outside demonstrations so much as
> by leading the people to adopt by themselves those principles
> and measures that would secure the end....So, also in the
> work of evangelization. He had not come to do a work of
> proselyting. He did not feel called upon to make an open
> assault upon the Greek and Armenian churches....His aim was
> to cast the leaven into the existing church organizations...
> knowing that...the movement for a purer church would come
> from themselves.[35]

His major contribution was the translation of the Bible into
Armeno-Turkish (Turkish in Armenian script). Other contributions
to proclamation and publication came from H. G. O. Dwight (1803-
1862),[36] William Schauffler (1798-1883) a converted Jew, and
Jonas King (1792-1869). The outstanding linguist and professor
Elias Riggs (1810-1901) made four major translations of the Bible
and taught Greek and theology in mission schools in Argos
(Greece), Smyrna and Constantinople. This literary tradition
was carried on by his son, Edward Riggs, Henry O. Dwight (son
of H. G. O. Dwight), Henry S. Barnum, and George Herrick.[37]
Their Turkish-Armenian Press (shifted from Malta to Constantinople) poured out a torrent of Scriptures, Bible handbooks,
school texts, devotional books, and tracts to a region athirst
for learning.

Grammar schools were begun at Constantinople (1834) and each
new station by either missionaries or Armenian associates according to the Lancasterian Plan.[38] Mission boarding schools for
boys and girls at key centers afforded opportunity for more
intensive biblical instruction. The mission soon observed that
if revival was to come the Armenian clergy must be reached.
Thus a preparatory theological institution was begun at Bebek,
six miles from the capital, under the energetic Cyrus Hamlin.
While primarily for Armenians, a few Greeks, Bulgarians and
Muslims also enrolled.

The reformation of the whole Armenian or Gregorian Church
appeared most feasible at first. Armenian laymen were open to
European progress and education. The scholarly priest Gregory
Peshtimaljian, the Erasmus of the Armenian Reformation, founded
a seminary (1829) and many of his students became leaders of
the evangelical movement. Missionaries worked in most cordial
relations with the Armenian ecclesiastical structure and
Armenians began to demonstrate a hidden vitality retained during

the long years under Muslim rule. As new stations began at
Nicomedia, Brusa, Adabaza, Trebizond and Erzerum, priests and
people manifested a new spirit of prayer and bible study. An
Armenian Evangelical Union was formed (1839) but it too remained
within the church working for the mutual encouragement of all.

Suddenly a storm broke loose when Patriarch Matteos backed the
reactionary element for somewhat unknown reasons.[39] It may have
been the fear of loss of authority by the hierarchy, or that a
lively Christianity would invite Muslim persecution and destroy
the limited security of the millet. Whatever the cause, a
solemn anathema was issued against Vertanes, a known evangelical
priest (January 25, 1846) and another against all who shared
evangelical views. Because of the civil authority of the Patriarch over his millet, this resulted in total economic and
social boycott of the accursed. It was a reaffirmation of the
values of icons, relics, the honor of the Virgin and the seven
sacraments. Some thirty evangelicals were bastinadoed, imprisoned or exiled and over 100 ejected from their homes and
vocations.[40] While the mission would henceforth continue to en-
courage reform in the Armenian Orthodox Church, this turn of
affairs prompted more independent action.

The Armenian Evangelical (Protestant) Churches

Given no option but to recant, forty evangelicals in Constantinople met to form the first Armenian Evangelical Church,
drafting a "Declaration of Reason for Organizing", a confession
of faith, a covenant and rules of discipline. Within a week
the congregation chose their own pastor. Similar congregations
formed at Nicomedia, Adabazar, Aintab, Trebizond and Erzerum.
These six churches with 166 members (May, 1848) were destitute
of material means and for a time dependent upon gifts of Christians in Europe and America. Only slowly did their political-
social-economic status improve.[41] This reformation continued
by the preaching of the Gospel and the two powerful auxiliaries
of education and the press. While the evangelical ministry and
congregations were soon the primary agency for the expansion of
reformed ideas, the mission served as counselor, trainer, and
supporter with its schools, seminaries, finances and personnel.[42] While the full narrative of the American Board-
Armenian Evangelical Church cannot be described here, certain
stages may be mentioned. First, there was a period of expansion covering fifty years (1846-1895) in which both church and
mission experienced tremendous growth.[43] Second, there came the
years of crisis, 1895-1896, when the world was shocked by the
first tragic Armenian massacres.[44] Third, came the era of relief, recovery, and redirection, 1896-1910. The distinct characteristics of this American Board-Evangelical Church activity
will be examined below.

Political Factors Affecting the Evangelical Churches and Muslim
Work.

Political factors affected the Armenian Evangelical Churches
and Muslim work most radically. Western governments, especially Britain's Sir Stratford Canning, Ambassador at Constantinople, played a responsible role in the various intercessions
to improve the status of Christians, esp. Protestants in the Near
East. The various stages and documents aimed at this might be
listed thus:

1. The National Charter of equal rights for all peoples,
Muslims, Christians and others in the Ottoman Empire, 1840
and the Hatti Sherif of Gul Hane, November 3, 1839.
2. Alledged Abolition of the death penalty for religious
opinion of apostasy, 1843.
3. Release of Protestants (Evangelicals) from the Armenian
Patriarch's control over trade licenses, passports, marriage
and burial permits, December, 1846.
4. A Letter from the Turkish Minister of Foreign Affairs
to the British Ambassador establishing the ecclesiastical
independence of the Protestant Armenians, November 19, 1847.
5. An Imperial Decree (firman) by the Sultan recognizing
the Protestant Community as a distinct millet or religious-
civil community, sometimes called the Protestant Charter,
1850. (This Decree was communicated to all the pashas of the
Empire about 1853, hence giving fuller protection to Protestants outside the capital.)
6. Documents giving Christian evidence/testimony equal rank
with that of Muslims in Turkish Courts.
7. The famous Hatti Humayun (Imperial Decree or firman)
establishing religious liberty for all, February, 1856.
8. The Treaty of Paris (1856), especially the ninth
article.[45]

These developments were taken to mean two things. First, Protestants had gained an identity of their own and were independent of Orthodox interference. Second, many Christians and
Muslims too, saw the Hatti Humayun as ushering in a new era of
religious and other liberties not unlike those known in Europe!
Even missionaries were buoyant. In 1857, Jewett wrote:

Never within the same space of time, has there been as
much religious discussion with the Mussulmans as since the
issue of the late firman, and never before, I think, has
there been such a spirit of religious inquiry among Mohammedans and readiness to discuss the merits of the Christian
religion, as had been evident during the past year. It has
awakened hope of a good day even for the Moslems.[46]

After the Decree of 1850, the evangelical churches were free to

advance and that they did until the tragic massacres of 1895-
1896. Unfortunately the hot-cold waverings, interference and
indifference of Russia, Britain and other Western powers in the
last quarter of the nineteenth century and the first quarter of
the twentieth century in actuality appears to have made life
more difficult for the enlightened Armenian evangelical community. Their political life improved somewhat from the Turkish
revolution to the abolition of the Caliphate as some dared hope
for genuine religious liberty and representative government for
all. Later restrictions on Christian schools, evangelism and
literature would indicate the emergence of a secular-national-
istic state with strong Islamic overtones. The age-old encounter of church and environment had not yet ended. It is a testimony to the courageous faith of the Armenian Evangelical Church
that it was stronger in 1908 than in 1895.[47]

Characteristics of the Armenian Evangelical Churches and the
American Board

The first characteristic of these two bodies was a strong individualism and independence which gradually moved towards a
church maturity. The New England spirit of integrity and self-
reliance found early welcome among the industrious Armenians.
The congregational pattern aimed at democratic self-government
and self-support from the start. Self-sustaining stewardship
was attained only with pain however, as the destitute beginning
had led to a financial dependence.[48] While all congregations
had a similar Confession of Faith, Covenant and Rules of Discipline, each was an autonomous body. At times regulations were
as strict as any in New England. For example at Diarbekr, the
congregation founded by medical missionary Azariah Smith admitted only eleven of fifty Armenian and Jacobite applicants to the
Lord's Table (1851).[49] Congregations were expected to rear
their own pastors and to evangelize the surrounding districts as
soon as possible.[50] Because they were left on their own, congregations felt isolated and began to form unions such as those
of Kharput (1865), Bithynia (1864), Central Turkey (1868), and
Cilcia. After about 1860, the evangelical churches entered
into improved relations with the Orthodox churches and in many
places cooperated in schools, bible distribution and study,
prayer and even preaching services. The progressive-reform wing
of the mother church, while not Protestant considered itself
equally evangelical. Protestant Armenians (about 85% literate)
were stimulating a mental, moral, and social revolution by 1872.
Anderson wrote: "Protestant ideas of truth, of liberty, of
conscience, of progress, are spread far and wide, and are con-
vulsing these nations."[51] This leaven and its reactions are
certainly related to the sorrows of 1895-96 and the upheavals of
1908 and 1922. The Armenian Harpoot Evangelical Union in 1866
resolved to establish their own mission to the Armenians of
Kurdistan and to the Jacobites, Muslims, Kurds and Yezidis of

the area. In prayer and giving for this work, the churches experienced revivals (1867-1872) and the two seminaries at Harpoot
were full in 1868 with fifty students each. Here was emerging
a new people of faith with their own unique life and mission in
the midst of Islam.

The second characteristic (which some consider the greatest
contribution of the American Board in the Near East) was the
importance attached to education. Their curriculum reflected
the New England blend of Christian faith, action and democratic
ideas. While most of the students were evangelicals, other youth
including Muslims were soon drawn in. Some would later charge
that this training of able leaders (with high expectations for
a minority group) increased the fears of Turk and Kurd.[52] Certainly education was a vital revolutionary force transforming
social structures and disturbing the status quo.[53] After the
formation of the Evangelical churches (1846), education took on
a serious note. Rufus Anderson pursued his policy that education was to be by Christian teachers for Christian children.
Elementary schools for boys and girls were attached to almost
every congregation (some 300 schools by 1908). Boarding and high
schools at mission stations provided the next level. Soon several of these were developed into colleges for men and women.
Theological seminaries under the various Unions were established
and largely manned by Board personnel. In line with Anderson's
policy, the seminaries were shifted from the expensive distrac-
tions of the capital to regional centers at Harpoot, Marsovan,
Marash and Mardin "where pastors could learn to identify with
people". Vernacular courses reflected the desire not to "de-
orientalize" the student. This demand for higher education also
resulted in Central Turkey College at Aintab (1874), Anatolia
College at Marsovan (1886), Euphrates College at Kharput (1876),
International College at Smyrna plus women's colleges at
Kharput, Marash, and Scutari.[54].

A conflict regarding educational policy produced a new phenomenon, independent Christian higher education. Cyrus Hamlin
(much like Duff) took issue with Anderson, contending that English and higher education should be used to reach and evangelize non-Christians. He argued that Anderson's policy failed to
meet the actual needs and demands of the capital, made Protestant pastors inferior to bilingual Jesuits, disappointed the
Orthodox community and lost the prestige already gained.[55] By
his own sheer strength of personality, inventiveness, and a fund-
raising lecture tour, he founded what was to be known as Robert
College (Bebeck). This college was incorporated in the State of
New York with an independent Board of Trustees.[56] Hamlin believed this college would help "to irrigate the parched fields
of the ancient churches, and perhaps even the corrupt Turkish
society, with life-giving streams of English Christian culture."
As president (1863-1873), he used the college workshops, scientific displays and western technology both to benefit students

and to give the evangelical Christian men marketable skills.
During the Crimean War, a mill, bakery, laundry and other industry netted a substantial profit. This successful blend of
theology and industry was hard to beat![57] Under Hamlin the enrollment and facilities increased and the school's ability to
bridge the differences of race (17 nationalities) and religion
(6 religions) in some measure spoke of "Christ's reconciling
power". Even Rufus Anderson gave the college a salute of praise
in 1872.[58] Its graduates gained the highest positions and respect in theology, education, government, law and medicine. Under
Presidents C. F. Gates and George Washburn, it maintained a
Christian atmosphere until World War I.[59] Its parallel institution at Scutari (1871) under Mary M. Patrick experienced similar
growth (1883-1924) as the Constantinople College for Women.[60]
Both schools, known as The American Colleges in Istanbul, Bebek,
Istanbul have since drifted out of the Christian orbit.[61]

A third characteristic of American Board was the shift from
evangelistic to service efforts. The Board was a leader in
medical missions.[62] Many of the physicians were also ordained
ministers organizing and serving congregations. Medicine and
evangelism went hand in hand at first. Clinics were established
in Muslim centers in order that the Christian demonstration of
love and compassion might prepare the way for the Gospel. While
medical work did remove many prejudices, it was at times misun-
derstood (e.g. giving the doctor a chance for good works) or
misused (e.g. simply taking the foreigner for what he offers).
The massacres prompted a tremendous surge in relief-medical-
service work. Nearly one and a half million dollars were raised
for relief in the U.S.A. alone. The American Board also became
the administrator of European contributions. Protestant orphanages (6,000 orphans in 1898, 1,000 by 1907); emergency industries; reconstruction of homes, churches and shops; seed-grain,
breeding animals, food and clothing; and other gifts reflected
both the compassion and guilt of the West. By 1914 some ten
hospitals and numerous dispensaries with trained national assistants were treating 180,000 patients annually until after World
War I.[63] The sheer masses and quantities of materials handled
would in a sense alter the nature of the American Board's work.
But other factors too must be considered. New England theology
early knew a spirit of disinterested benevolence and with the
growth of liberal American theology the concept of service became
the preferred channel of mission for those stressing experience
over doctrine. Others hoped that the increased contact with
Muslims through the medical-service approach would provide
greater success in their evangelization.

Among the Nestorians of Persia, 1834-1870

The application of the Board's policy among the Nestorians of
Persia was most sympathetic and the resulting reformation was

for the most part contained within that Orthodox Church until
about 1870.[64] Geographically and politically, nineteenth century Persia was truly the "Land in Between".[65] Although the
Moravians had attempted to reach the Guebers (Zoroastrians) in
1747, Joseph Wolff had toured in the 1830s and Basel Mission
held a brief station at Tabriz (1833), the most sustained mission
in Persia from 1834 to 1870 came under the American Board. This
work centered among the Nestorian remnant in northwestern
Persia along the shores of Lake Urumia and in the mountains of
Kurdistan.[66] The Nestorians were at a low ebb with few Bibles
and fewer still who could read the ancient Syriac, the language
of worship. The missionaries considered this dearth and not
theological error as the main handicap of this people.[67] Justin
Perkins (1805-1869), founder and leader of the mission until his
death, carefully analyzed the situation.

> The Nestorians are numerous in the villages, on the plain
> of Oroomiah, in some cases occupying a village exclusively,
> and in others, living in the same villages with Muhammedans.
> Most of them are employed in the cultivation of the soil, of
> which they are, sometimes, though rarely, the proprietors. A
> few are mechanics as masons, and joiners. Their common
> relation to the Muhammedan nobility in the tenure of the soil
> is that of serfs and lords. The Muhammedan peasantry sustain
> nominally the same relation to the higher classes though
> their rights are better respected than those of Christians.
> The Nestorians often suffer lawless extortion and oppression
> from their Muhammedan masters. Their circumstances are how-
> ever, quite tolerable for a people in bondage, and their
> fertile country yields such an overflowing abundance....[68]

Perkins' instructions from the Committee had been very explicit.
Learning the language, he was to get first-hand knowledge and
establish cordial relationships, the purpose of which could not
be misconstrued.

> A primary object which you will have in view will be to
> convince the people, that you come among them with no design
> to take away their religious privileges, nor to subject them
> to any foreign ecclesiastical power....But your main object
> will be, to enable the Nestorian church through the grace of
> God to exert a commanding influence in the spiritual regenera-
> tion of Asia...The mission of the English Church Missionary
> Society among the Syrian Christians of Malabar will be, in
> some respects, a model for your own. Our object is the same
> with theirs, and the people are supposed not to be essen-
> tially different....It is proper to caution you to beware,
> in your personal intercourse with the people, of whatever
> may be construed as having a political bearing....
> With respect to the Muhammedans, and the adherents of the
> Papal Church, you will do them good as you have opportunity...

nor is it probable that you can make much impression upon
Mussulman, until they see more of the fruits of the gospel
among its professed believers among them....Concentrated
effort is effective effort.[69]

Accompanied by Mar Yohannan, Nestorian Patriarch, on his visit to
the United States (1841-43), Perkins could report the establishment of cordial church to church relations and a mission aimed at
restoring the Nestorian Church to its former role of a witness
to the surrounding peoples. In eight years, the four mission
families had developed a seminary of fifty pupils, a girls'
school, a printing establishment, a school for young Muslims, and
a medical dispensary. A survey trip by J. L. Merrick to Teheran,
Isfahan and Shiraz to determine whether it was expedient to
preach and work with Muslims there gave a negative reply and so
the work concentrated at Urumia in the hope that Muslims could
be reached via the Nestorians. The missionaries were soon
endeared to the Muslims there and by request Dr. A. Grant began
the school for Muslim youth so as not to give the impression they
were benefactors of Nestorians alone.
   Literature, preaching and education became the primary means
for encouraging the Nestorians. Scholarly Perkins translated
the New Testament (1846), a Nestorian hymnbook and the Old Testament into the modern spoken Syriac and David Stoddard con-
structed the first grammar in that tongue.[70] The press under
Edward Breath published 110,000 volumes of Bibles, portions,
Christian novels and tracts from 1839 to 1873. Evangelical
preaching became a feature of Nestorian life. Perkins wrote:

     But the most interesting department of our labors, is our
   preaching the gospel in the Nestorian Churches, as already
   noticed....Some of the native clergy, who had been a considerable time under the influence of the mission are becoming
   themselves very able and faithful preachers of the gospel.
   Often have I heard them address their people, with a solem-
   nity and power, which we associate with the preaching of the
   apostles.[71]

The schools became the key to the revivals that spread from
students to parents and villages. By 1837, three bishops and
four priests were helping in the seminaries (boarding schools)
and soon sending a stream of evangelical teachers and ministers
into the life of the community. Stoddard and Miss Fidelia Fiske
were the superintendents of the two seminaries and by their
example and encouragement largely responsible for the evangelical
revivals which led most students to be "born again".[72] Already
in 1841, Perkins attested:

     ...Our education efforts hold out the cheering prospect,
   in connexion with our other labors, of furnishing the Nestor-

ians with an intelligent and pious ministry; and with their
aid, of gradually raising the whole mass to an intelligent
and virtuous people.[73]

Medical work began in 1835 with the arrival of Asahel Grant
(1807-1844). While Rev. Austin Wright, M.D. developed the
plains dispensary (1840-1864), Grant began work among the scattered Nestorians, Kurds and Yezidis in the mountains. Trying
to remain politically neutral, he was deceived by the situation.
Even Perkins wrote:

> ...The savage Koords and the wild <u>independent</u> Nestorians
> are in little danger of injury, by being made to yield to
> the influence of a regular <u>Muhammedan</u> government /Ottoman
> Turke<u>y</u>7; especially a Muhammedan government, which is now
> rapidly passing through a series of mutations, that in their
> process will shake to pieces the whole existing fabric and
> distribute the fragments among <u>civilized</u>, <u>christian</u> <u>nat-</u>
> ions.[74]

But the presence of missionaries heightened the ancient Kurdish
suspicions of the Mountain Nestorians who maintained a precarious independence under their patriarch. Turkish authorities,
afraid of losing their minimal control, used the Kurdish fear
and desire for booty in a program of liquidation and subjection.
In 1843, some 800 Nestorians including part of the patriarchal
family were killed. By 1845, one-fifth of their number (10,000)
had died. After this the only successful work among the Mountain Nestorians was by the Plains Nestorians.[75]
The extent of the mission's success is seen in the dozen revivals between 1846 and 1863. These revivals started with
students and spread through Urumia and to outlying villages via
teachers, evangelists, priests and bishops, e.g. Bishop Elias
(d. 1863) and the Patriarch's brother, Deacon Isaac (d. 1864).
With the conviction of sin came a new awareness of Christ's
power to save, the joy of forgiveness, a hunger for the Word
and a willingness to serve. The important fact was that this
all took place within the traditional structure of the Nestorian Church. Perhaps it would have continued this way had it not
been for interference by Roman Catholics, High-Church Anglicans
and the State Church of Russia. The Lazarists backed by France
became more aggressive (1842-49) and urged the Nestorian Patriarch to throw out the Americans. While unsuccessful, they did
alienate a good number of Nestorians.[76] Political pressures increased also. Russia and England prodded the Shah to appoint
Dawood Khan of Tabriz, an Armenian from Georgia, to act as Governor of the Nestorians and as their protector from Muslim
nobles and Kurds. About 1843, the S.P.G. sent George P. Badger
with letters from Anglican dignitaries to the Patriarch. Ignor-
ing the American workers, he urged the Patriarch to turn from

the American dissenters to the episcopal and catholic S.P.G.
which could also provide schools. Although the venture failed,
it further damaged relationships.[77] Evangelical Nestorians torn
in many directions were beginning to feel need of the strength
and discipline of congregations. A second factor was the sacra-
ment of communion. At first missionaries celebrated the Lord's
Supper alone. But as some Nestorian priests desired a separate
evangelical movement, the agonizing question of whether to form
evangelical Nestorian "communions" arose.

> Can the 'evangelicals' further unite in the morning and
> evening services conducted by priests...reviving these super-
> stitions. Almost the whole church are surprisingly united in
> the decision to withdraw.[78]

Although the first Protestant congregation (158 communicants)
formed in 1855 and an annual convention of congregations elected
Mar Yohanan as Moderator in 1867, the separation was gradual and
with a minimum of estrangement. Only by 1870 did the Assyrian
Evangelical Church stand ecclesiastically independent.[79] That
year was a pivotal point for both mission and church. The
mission was transferred to the Presbyterian Board. The staff
decided to rename it, the Mission to Persia, and to expand its
objectives to the Armenians of Tabriz and Hamadan and Muslims
throughout Persia.[80]

At Work in Syria-Lebanon, 1823-1870

   Application of American Board policy in Syria-Lebanon (1823-
1870) took a different form. At an early date, it was concluded
that the goal and means of mission in Syria's diverse society
must be "an Independent Evangelical Church". Because of the
multiplicity of Christian and Muslim sects in the area, and
their fierce suspicion of one another or foreigners, it was decided that those who responded to the evangelical presentation
of the Christian Scriptures and faith would be gathered into a
new community. In addition to the fact of pluralism, there was
also greater freedom, due perhaps to the distance from Constantinople, the fierce independence of the mountain peoples, and
the longer contact with Europe. Syria, the home of Gentile
Christianity, still contained the most viable if varied Christianity in the Near East.[81]

Politics, Protestants and Missions to Muslims

   Politics made direct work with Muslims extremely difficult.
Due to the Greek War of Independence and the battle for Beirut,
missionaries had to retreat to Malta (1828-1830). The arrival
of Mohammed Ali's army (1831), the return of the region to Turkey by Britain (1840), plus the bloody civil wars between Maron-

ites and Druzes (1841-42, 1845, and 1860) kept the tension high.
While it was hoped to reach Muslims, in reality, there was only a
limited evangelism among the Druzes (1835-1842). Although hostile to their hereditary enemies the Maronites, the Druzes responded favorably to Protestant missionaries. Several of their
leaders attended Arabic services, and mission school, and so when
they requested instruction, they knew what it meant. While the
motives of some were mixed (perhaps the hope to gain exemption
from Ottoman military services), there was a genuine spiritual
ferment. Ultra-cautious about conversion en masse, the missionaries hesitated! The Turkish Army hastily subjected the Druze
Sheikhs and insisted on an oath that they would never become
Christian. While the Protestant and Druze continued to be fast
friends, such an opportunity for conversion did not reoccur
within the century.[82]

Several good results came from these stirrings. The Missionary Convention in Beirut (1844) concluded that all peoples in
Syria, Christian and Muslim alike, were to be considered Arabs
and the object of missionary work. They also resolved that congregations should be formed as soon as a small company professed
faith no matter how varied their background might be and that
they should be led by a native ministry.[83]

Ecclesiastical Resistance and Missionary Persistence

Almost from the beginning Protestant missions in the Levant
were resisted. Intense Roman Catholic opposition was seen in
the unsuccessful papal attempt (1824) to get Turkish authorities to ban Protestant distribution of the Scriptures. The
best documented case of persecution of native evangelicals is
that of Asaad Shidiak (1797-1839), a well educated Maronite
teacher and theologian under evangelical persuasion, who was
spirited away, imprisoned in a dungeon till death by the Maronite hierarchy.[84] Roman Catholic and Orthodox hostility continued long after the formation of the Protestant church.

In addition to the labors of Isaac Bird, Pliny Fisk, and
William Goodell, Jonas King made a brief (1822-25) but lasting
impression on Syria. His "Farewell Letter to his Friends in
Palestine and Syria" was an apology of the evangelical faith.
Following its criticism of the Roman Catholic Church and implied
suggestions for Eastern churches, it set forth the tenets of
Protestantism.[85] Other men making a deep impact in Syria in-
cluded Eli Smith (1801-1856), Cornelius V. A. Van Dyck (1818-
1895), Daniel Bliss (1823-1916), Henry H. Jessup (1832-1910),
Simeon H. Calhoun (1804-1876), and Wm. Thomson (1806-1894).

Literary evangelism, education, women's work and medical
missions all played a part. In the fourteen years after
shifting the Arabic press from Malta to Beirut (1834), the mission published seven million pages of tracts and books. A
system of colportage spread this from Aleppo to Jerusalem. The

greatest feat was the translation of the Bible into Arabic.
Smith worked eight years on this task and Van Dyck added nine
more years before the standard edition of the Bible for Arab
peoples was completed (1864). Van Dyck also prepared a New Testament in the style of the Quran especially for Muslims. The
first mission schools centered about Beirut drawing some 600
pupils. A landmark in Near Eastern history was the opening of
the first Girls' School in Beirut about 1834. Mrs. Smith, Dr.
and Mrs. DeForest, and Miss Temple set a pace in "female education" eventually followed by Greeks, Maronites, Jews and Muslims
alike.[86] As evangelical congregations formed, elementary schools
were generally attached. High schools opened in key centers,
e.g. Abeih Seminary (1850) which enrolled four Druzes, four
Maronites, nine Orthodox and two Protestants. These shared one
common table, study and prayer life and it was soon evident that
new ideas of Christianity and democracy were being implanted.
While the first ministers were instructed privately or in a
theological class at Abeih, e.g. John Wortabet and Suleeba Jer-
wan, a theological seminary was formed there in 1869 under Henry
Jessup, W. W. Eddy and S. H. Calhoun (This institution shifted
to Beirut in 1873.). Medical work, without benefit of dispensary
or hospital, was mainly a field service. During the tragic
civil wars, this channel gained greater attention and funds.
With the establishment of the medical school at Syrian Protestant College, it drew still more respect.

Several missionaries became concerned about providing a
Christian institution of higher education to meet the needs of
Protestants and others in the international port of Beirut.
The concept of the Syrian Protestant College was proposed by
the mission in 1861. Since the edict of Anderson had virtually
barred the door to such, it was decided that independent Christian action was needed.[87] The college was to offer a liberal
arts course including languages, literature, mathematics, natural
science, law, medicine as well as moral science and Biblical
studies. Incorporated and endowed in America, the local Board
of Directors was to be composed of American and British missionaries and residents in the Beirut area. Christian purpose was
at the heart of the proposal.

> The objects deemed essential, were to enable natives to
> obtain in their own country, in their own language, and at a
> moderate cost, a thorough literary, scientific, and profes-
> sional education; to found an institution, which should be
> conducted on principles strictly evangelical, but not sectar-
> ian; with doors open to youth of every Oriental sect and
> nationality, who would conform to its regulations, but so
> ordered that students, while elevated intellectually and
> spiritually, should not materially change their native cus-
> toms. The hope was entertained that much of the instruction
> might at once be entrusted to pious and competent natives
> and that ultimately the teaching could be left in the hands

of those who had been raised up by the college itself.[88]

Under Daniel Bliss, the College's first president (1866-1902),
educational evangelical (if not evangelistic) goals were seen
as co-ordinates. All students attended morning and evening
prayers, daily Bible lectures, and Sunday services. But under
the presidency of his son, Howard S. Bliss (1902-1920) and Bayard
Dodge, the college moved towards religious neutrality.

Formation of the Syrian Evangelical Churches, 1848-1870

After the intense opposition by Maronite, Greek and Armenian
clergy, the mission staff were barely prepared for the breakthrough experienced. An awakening among Greek Orthodox Christians began at Hasbeiya (fifty miles from Beirut) in 1845. One
hundred and fifty men and women seceded from the church and
declared themselves to be evangelicals. Persecutions by Greek
authorities and brutal attack by Turkish forces delayed their
actual organization and selection of a pastor for seven years.[89]
Soon reform parties at Aintab and Aleppo were sending letters
and delegations to Beirut pleading for missionaries and
teachers. The mission, short on personnel, sent an urgent request to the United States (1847), but the response was unequal
to the opportunity.[90] Ottoman recognition of Protestants (1847,
1850, 1853) nevertheless did fortify the right of evangelicals
to organize and assemble for worship.

The first purely Arab Protestant Church formed at Beirut
(1848). Its membership of twenty-seven testified to the reconciliation wrought by Christ.[91] Evangelical circles emerged at
many points in Syria and requests for teachers, schools, Bibles
and assistance in forming churches sent the missionaries fanning
out across the countryside. After 1848, congregations began at
Abeih, Hasbeiya, Sidon, Suk el Gharb, Bhamdun, Zahleh, Aleppo,
Aintab, and a dozen other places. Friendly relations with
Armenian and Jacobite clergy were cultivated, but Roman Catholic
and Greek Orthodox leaders opposed evangelical efforts all the
way. During the contest in Aleppo, Muslim Arab raiders swept in
to rob, wound and kill the Greek Orthodox and Greek Catholic
aristocracy of the town. In the caldron of suffering, many
evangelical and Orthodox Christians recovered the fellowship
that transcends denomination.[92] This healing and stablization
of relationships was a necessary preliminary to any witness to
their Muslim neighbors. The practice of self-support developed
slower than the other statistics of church life. The ravages
of war and American generosity undoubtedly contributed to this.[93]
In spite of all, it was later recognized that the formation of
Protestant congregations was the key to the strength of the work
of the American Board and their successors, the Presbyterians.
For while ventures by the English, Scottish and Germans gained
converts they could refer them to no sustaining body. Fortunately

many of these united with the evangelical congregations. A
report in 1870 noted that Islam had not been forgotten.

> ...The relative positions of the crescent and the cross
> are not what they were when the missionaries came to Syria.
> The Bible has gained ground, and the Koran has lost it, as a
> controlling influence in the land. Some Mohammedans are
> among the attendants upon our preaching and these would doubt-
> less be more numerous, but for the risk to property and life,
> which inquirers from among them incur.
> Not without results have the children of the Druzes been
> taught in our schools during all these years, and so many
> conversations been held with adults of that sect. The leaven
> of the Gospel has penetrated even to the secret inner sanc-
> tuaries of their religion; and the white turbans of the
> initiated Druzes seen in our Sabbath congregations, the
> inquirers who come to our houses, and the baptized converts
> from among them, show that not in vain to the Druzes has the
> light of the Gospel again dawned upon Syria.
> But principally among the nominally Christian sects have
> the indirect results of the missionary labor extended....[94]

The forthrightness of the American Board program in Syria-Lebanon was outstanding for this period.[95]

Limited Work Directly With Muslims and an Evaluation of the American Board Program

In a sense all the Near Eastern activity of the American
Board was in the midst of Islam. Its declared objective was to
stimulate Eastern Christians to join in the evangelization of
Muslims. Yet in many ways, this was a delaying action, a waiting for a more opportune hour. In reality it did not always
breed the spirit of mission to Muslims in evangelical congregations. They could always ask "Do you want us as residents to do
what you as missionaries will not attempt?" Courageous missionaries periodically attempted to break through this barrier. This
may be considered under three periods.
From 1820-1856, political circumstances made Muslim work
practically suicidal. Missionaries turned thus to the Eastern
churches and sought to restore them to earlier purity and
apostolic fervor. Brave souls, like James L. Merrick, William
G. Schauffler, and William Hutchinson, who tackled purely Muslim
work soon became frustrated and exhausted. While converts from
the Druzes offered a glimmer of hope, the hasty squelching of
this movement towards Christianity and the bloody application of
the death penalty for apostasy elsewhere curtailed all chances
of success.[96]
From 1856-1866, the Imperial Decrees assuring Christians and
others of their civil and religious rights ushered in a brief

era of religious liberty. Some Muslims took the Hatti Humayun at
face value and openly inquired into the Christian faith. The
American Board and C.M.S. intensified their Muslim work. Muslims
actually became Christians and were permitted to live on! Hamlin described the remarkable visit of government authorities to
a Muslim family recently baptized. After ascertaining their
freedom of choice, they were left unmolested. Many Muslims pur-
chased the Bible and others gained instruction. By late 1860
over a score of Muslim converts had been baptized including an
Imam, Abdi Effendi, who immediately became a fervent evangelist.
Between 1857 and 1877, at least fifty baptisms took place and
many leading Muslims intimated interest. George Herrick of the
Turkish Department at Bebek Seminary wrote (1869):

> Quite a number of Mohammedans have renounced Islam and
> become true Christians; many more are soberly inquiring
> after the truth; and many others are turning unsatisfied, from
> a religion which cannot save, or wavering in a merely nominal
> devotion to Islamism. That which is most striking is the
> clear evidence, often of the work of God's Spirit in indivi-
> dual cases, and in general movements.[97]

These experiences were most revealing! First, mission work among
Muslims can be successfully carried out and converts won, when
the social-political setting permits equality between Christians
and Muslims and freedom to transfer from one religious community
to another. Second, Muslim work is such an all-engrossing work
that if it is to be effective it must be carried on by those
totally dedicated to it. Those having other duties (e.g. among
Eastern Christians) were too often diverted. Third, Muslims were
best won by converts from Islam. Such were more effective than
either American or Armenian evangelists in gaining and sustaining the interest of inquirers. Yet in fact, the American Board
did not concentrate on training its own missionaries in Islamics
nor on procuring evangelists of Muslim background. As will be
seen, a storm of hostility (1864-66) wiped out this bold effort.
The reassertion of Turkish power (after the Crimean War), the
indecisive wavering of English and European powers, and the
aggressiveness of C.M.S. workers in Constantinople brought
violence to the Muslim converts of the city and extinguished
prospects of a direct approach to Muslims in Turkey.[98]
From 1866-1910, missionaries were ultra-cautious. The seiz-
ure of Bible depots, imprisonment and persecution of converts,
and threat to banish missionaries to Maronites, Armenians, and
Assyrians strengthened this alarm. Neither missionary nor national wished to court martyrdom. There was thus little interest
in re-opening direct Muslim work until the revolt of the Young
Turks (1908) and even then the situation remained delicate.
Under the Republic of Turkey, "non-proselytism" became a test
applied to recognized foreign organizations working within the

land. Thus the American Board consoled itself with educational
and medical work among Muslims and with a supportive role'was to the
evangelical churches. While the question of Muslim work'was
raised again in 1910 by enterprising individuals, the will to
pursue it appeared lacking.99 This may have been due as much to
the change in the theological climate of New England Congrega-
tionalism as to the circumstances in Turkey.

It is regretable that the views of George Herrick did not
receive fuller application. Herrick held that a lofty concept
of revelation was essential for those seeking to make an impact
on Islam.

> Any missionary who holds the positions or makes the assump-
> tions of the advanced German school, which treats all relig-
> ions as evolutions out of man's religious nature, ruling out
> any supernatural element in the origin of the religion of
> Israel, or doubts the personal existence of Moses or of
> Abraham would find his position untenable among Mohammed-
> ans....a missionary to Mohammedans must hold to a Bible which,
> in a true and defensible sense, contains a revelation from
> God....The missionary's great message is, indeed to proclaim
> Christ Himself, but he must trust to that Book whose very
> Purpose--testify of Christ, to hold that wonderful Person
> before Mussulman eyes. Theological discussion will be barren
> of good results. But a loving and confident presentation of
> Christ Himself just as the Gospels reveal Him to us is ever
> effective beyond all argument.100

Herrick contended that it was not "evangelization in this generation" but a "Christianization" over many generations that
would reach Muslims.

> The leading and controlling purpose of missionary endeav-
> our in our day is not, as it was in the inception of foreign
> missions a century ago, to snatch a soul here and there as
> a brand from the burning. It is the enlightenment, and educa-
> tion, the uplifting of entire races of men, of all races of
> men, by the power of Chritian civilization, of Christian
> education, by the persistent use of all the forces and acces-
> sories of Christian philanthropy. The impetus and motive is
> found in our Lord's summing up the second table of the law,
> 'Thou shalt love thy neighbor as thyself.'101

Herrick tries to hold in balance the emphasis of service-ethics
and the emphasis on revelation-proclamation which were soon to
clash so violently in the crisis in theology and mission. The
missionary is ever the herald.

> The duty is twofold. The missionary places in the hands
> of the people to whom he goes God's written message to man-

kind in their own vernacular, and he proclaims that message,
viva voce, all his life long....He is a prophet in the true
meaning of the word. He is God's messenger: he is Christ's
apostle. The very heart and core of his mission is here. It
is this and this alone which constitutes the uniqueness of
the service he is called to render....he goes...at the call
of Him who bade His disciples preach His Gospel everywhere,
teach men what He has taught them, make men His disciples,
and that till all men shall know and follow Him....But first
and last and all time...the missionary is God's herald of
hope, of paternal love.[102]

He envisaged the time when the adherents of Islam would at least
in part acknowledge the Lordship of Christ.

And then, not in a receding or distant, but in an approaching and near future, there will come...acceptance by Mussulman peoples of Jesus Christ as their Redeemer and Reconciler
with God.
The chasm between Christian and Mussulman will be closed
when devotees of Islam shall discard the name Mohammedan,
but retain the excellent name Muslim, and when their muezzins
shall, in the call to worship, couple with that of the one
God the name and office of the one Saviour of men: and in
life shall be conformed to the teachings and the example of
Jesus the Christ. May God hasten the day.[103]

Herrick represents perhaps the best of American Board thought
and action regarding Muslims.
How successful was the program of the American Board? A
judgement depends almost entirely on what place is given to the
Eastern churches. If one holds that reformation of the Eastern
churches was a prerequisite to Muslim evangelization in the Near
East, then they were reasonably successful. For in spite of
political restriction, ecclesiastical opposition, and interference by foreign powers, they accomplished amazing things.
Churches, evangelical and Orthodox, were reformed and given a
new vitality. The Eastern churches became a viable force once
more in their environment.[104] Not only did they become a more
acceptable witness but they became the stimulant producing a
renaissance of Near Eastern peoples, a leading cause in the elevation of the whole intellectual, social and spiritual life of
the Near East.[105] This achievement was marred only by the failure to create within either young evangelical churches or older
Orthodox churches a missionary zeal for Muslims. Exceptions were
the Harpoot missionaries and the Urumia evangelists among the
Kurds and Syrian Protestants among the Druzes. In charity,per-
haps one must say, circumstances did not permit such visible
zeal among either overseas or national workers. The work of the
American Board may best be described as a first step, a prepara-

tory work among Muslims. By word and deed it demonstrated the
meaning of Christian love, yearning, and service. In fresh form,
it was manifesting the vitality inherent in the faith and life
dedicated to God in Christ. The second step may yet appear
with a realization of religious liberty. As the Christian community and its leaders in the Near East concentrate on their
theology and mission anew, there appear signs of promise.[106]
Near Eastern churches today hold a more strategic position for
the evangelization of Muslims than ever before.

AMERICAN PRESBYTERIANS:
DEVELOPMENT OF A TWO-PRONGED APPROACH

In 1870, the Old School and New School Presbyterians in America reunited to form the Northern Presbyterian Church (U.S.A.).
Inasmuch as New School personnel and finances were to be withdrawn from the American Board, that Board wisely and graciously
transferred her responsibilities in Syria, Persia and later
Iraq (1892) to the new body and concentrated upon Turkey. The
Northern Presbyterian Church was able to mount a considerable
mission operation. Its approach in the Near East may be called
two-pronged. It retained the via the Eastern churches approach
inherited from the American Board, but also gave increased attention to direct evangelization of Muslims, especially in Persia.
It will be noted that the separate work of the United Presbyterian Church in Egypt applied a similar approach.

Northern Presbyterians in Syria-Lebanon, 1870-1910

Historical Development in the Syrian Mission

In the first two decades after the transfer (1870-1890), the
Syrian Mission still faced political bars to Muslim work.[107]
The mission benefited from long terms of service by such able
figures as H. H. Jessup, Daniel Bliss (both celebrating their
jubilee as missionaries in 1906), but conditions were by no means
favorable. The massacres of 1860 had been followed by French-
British intervention and a Christian governor for the Lebanon,
yet Ottoman authorities became increasingly stringent regarding
Christian activity. The Muslim majority often harassed the
minorities at will. Illiteracy, lack of Christian and educational literature, the tyranny and jealousies of the Orthodox
ecclesiastics, the intrigues of papal emissaries plus cholera
epidemics further complicated matters. Some Protestant missionaries in the 1870s hoped that Britain would help bring about reforms in the corrupt tax system, curb the wild Bedouin and Kurd
tribes, and stimulate religious and literary freedom, but H. H.
Jessup and others soon admitted that few benefits would accrue
from the influence of Western governments.[108] Direct Muslim
work was still blocked. When the Nusairiyeh, a Muslim sect,

began to convert as result of American Reformed Presbyterian
Mission schools, Turkey closed the schools (1874). When M.
Arnold formed a Muslim Missionary Society (1861) to work with
the Arab Bedouin tribes, it was halted by the Turks. C.M.S.
schools for the Druzes near Damascus were likewise closed (1885).
The Syrian Mission frequently found its schools and churches
sealed, construction delayed, and applications pigeonholed.
About 1888, some seventy-one missionaries and teachers of Protestant bodies petitioned the Turkish government via foreign
ambassadors to suspend this official persecution. This produced
a brief respite, but the Turkish system was so honey-combed by
graft and espionage that reform by enlightened officials seemed
virtually impossible.[109]

From 1890 to 1900, the Syrian Mission made limited advance in
spite of hardships. Various attempts to reach the Bedouin Arabs
of Northern Arabia were frustrated. Yet two outstanding Muslim
converts, Jedaan Owad (bapt. Feb. 21, 1889) and Kamil Aietany
(bapt. Jan. 1890) received training at Suk el Gharb and returned
to proclaim Christ among the Arab tribes near Hums and Hamath.
Kamil became a full-fledged apostle to the Muslims. With Cantine
and Zwemer, he explored southern Arabia, the Gulf and pioneered
at Basrah before his early death.[110] These were by no means the
only converts. H. H. Jessup in his fifty-five years in Syria
personally baptized some thirty Muslim converts and was acquainted with nearly fifty. In his later years, he baptized about
two per year. Many of these had to flee the country for their
own safety and others had to resist all types of persecution
and temptations to revert to Islam.[111] Three other factors
affected this decade. First, the overflow of Armenian refugees
(resulting from the Massacres) and turkish hostilities towards
missionaries put strain on the Syrian Mission. Second, the re-
duction in the Presbyterian Syrian budget (1897) forced missionaries to curtail their gratis work and to advance self-support
in the evangelical churches. Third, emigrations (1896-1897)
sent not less than 75,000 Syrian Christians to Egypt, Australia,
and the Americas to seek security and employment. Although many
of these were Protestants, the local churches held their own.[112]

From 1900 to 1910, growth in the Syrian Mission and its
churches continued. The energies, evangelical aims and deputations of Presbyterian Board Secretary A. J. Brown gave new
impetus to the work. Political changes filled all with cautious
hope. After the revolt of the Young Turks (1908), new freedoms
of press, speech and education were gained. Experienced leaders
like Jessup however observed the sullen mood of mullahs and
sheikhs and anticipated a struggle between Pan-Islamism and this
new republicanism. Three small missionary conferences in Brum-
mana, Lebanon (1898, 1901, 1904) not only provided opportunity
for prayer, devotion and fellowship but a foundation for the
maturer ecumenical approach to Muslims which would soon appear
(1906-1911).

The Quest for a Means

Since public preaching was not permitted in Syria, the mission continued to develop its literary evangelism. In spite of the Imperial Press and School Laws (1869) and censorship, the press continued to be a disseminator of Christian truth. The Beirut Press became the center of Arabic work throughout the world, producing some fifty editions of the Smith-Van Dyck Arabic Bible by 1910, a weekly Arabic paper (Neshrah, The Herald, 1865-), a popular four volume New Testament commentary (W. D. Eddy), plus many educational and devotional materials. Because Arabic was the language of Muslim and Christian, this was truly a two-pronged endeavor.[113]

In 1898, Secretary Brown mildly rebuked missionaries for clinging to literary and educational centers and urged more itinerant work as done by Samuel Jessup. Henry Jessup had a ready reply:

> ...The real evangelistic work of the future is to be done by native evangelists and these can only be fitted for their work by large and systematic Bible study....Dr. Eddy was giving six hours a day to the preparation of a commentary of the New Testament for which the native preachers and people of Syria have been waiting for years....
>
> Teaching the Bible is evangelistic work. Translating, editing, and training theological students are only different forms of evangelistic work. And as the missions grow older one thing after the other is handed over to the natives, the foreign missionaries, with their long experience and more thorough training, will more and more confine themselves to the training of a native ministry and preparing helps for their work....Let us not say 'institutional versus evangelistic work' but, 'the institutional for the sake of the evangelistic work'.[114]

Nevertheless, Brown had a point. Far too few nationals were being trained as evangelists to Muslims and missionaries were not always setting an example in this trying activity.

In education, the Presbyterians in Syria took the lead for the Near East. Protestants (as did Roman Catholics) built a full system of education reaching from village school to college. Syrian Protestants soon became leaders in many fields, e.g. journalism, medicine, etc. The Protestant system had 100 common schools at its base, advanced secondary schools for girls and boys at five centers, and the Syrian Protestant College at the top of the pyramid. This reached over 8,000 students.[115] Up to 1910, schools were certainly wedges by which the Bible and evangelical instruction penetrated areas closed to other types of work. Since only one-quarter of the students were Protestant, many Orthodox and Roman Catholic students were also influenced. Turkish regulations prohibited Muslims from attending these

schools, yet nearly 100 managed to do so. While Syrians continued to call for Christian schools, both national governments
and conservative missionaries began to criticize them after
1910. Eventually all but the advanced institutions were
nationalized.[116]

The mission was rather halting in its program of theological
education. A Presbyterian Theological Seminary under James S.
Dennis struggled for a few years (1881) only to cease.[117] Secular trades and emigration were drawing away the most talented
youth. In actual fact, it appears that the Mission neglected
the training of the Syrian ministry until the formation of the
union venture, the Near East School of Theology (1932). Only
after this period of crisis did church-related colleges like
Aleppo College, Beirut College for Women and Hagazian College
(actually under the Armenian Evangelical Church) gain adequate
attention. What in actuality happened was that the independent
liberal arts Syrian Protestant College siphoned off top mission
personnel, attention, and qualitied Syrian youth. While there
is no doubt that this institution in its early years permeated
the Near East with revolutionary evangelical and democratic
ideas, it did not necessarily nurture a Christian ministry or a
missionary force willing to reach to Muslims and others. The
historical development of this independent Christian institution which by 1920 became the near secular American University
of Beirut deserves separate attention.[118]

Medical work under the Syrian Mission did not gain the pro-
portions it did elsewhere. The Presbyterians maintained a hospital at Tripoli and dispensaries at Hamath and Hums. Presbyterian medical men at the Beirut college cooperated with the
German St. John's Hospital as did the Kaiserswerth nurses to
make it the largest and finest in the land. Mary P. Eddy was
the first woman doctor to gain the Ottoman Empire diploma in
medicine (1893). Her itinerant camp work and clinic reached as
many Muslims as any single effort. Scottish, Irish, English
and American Reformed Presbyterians and Anglicans also carried
on medical programs in Syria. National and overseas Christians cooperated in founding the Asfuriyeh Hospital for the In-
sane (1896) with Rev. John Wortabet, M.D. as president and H.
H. Jessup as secretary. The fruit of such Christian public
service gave Muslims in the Near East new understanding of
Christian life.[119]

What evaluation can be made of this Presbyterian approach in
Syria? Simply this, the prong of the program directed towards
Muslims was far weaker than the one pointed towards Eastern
Christians. If this was true, then the important question is:
"What role was the developing Syrian Evangelical Church to
play in the evangelization of Muslims?"

The Development of the Syrian Evangelical Churches and Muslim
Evangelization

The Syrian Evangelical churches gradually felt the need for
stronger union and accepted the plan for forming a Synod and
Presbyteries (1881). The Presbyteries of Sidon (1883), Tripoli
(1890) and Mount Lebanon (1896) included missionaries as corresponding members as well as Syrian ministers and elders. In
spite of war, disease, and emigration, the church experienced
healthy growth so that by 1910, there were 34 Presbyterian congregations with over 2,600 communicants and nearly 10,000 souls.
The lack of self-support noted in 1876 was being remedied by
1908. Mission schools and Sunday schools were also flourishing.[120]

The most serious defect was the failure to attract and train
young men for the Christian ministry and evangelism. While the
loss of talent through emigration explains this in part, the
failure to provide a stable and enduring theological seminary
cannot be overlooked. In view of the fact that Western sciences and new technical skills afforded a chance for personal advancement to a people long subdued, it is not difficult to
understand why students turned to these alluring marketable
trades. To understand how serious this problem was, it must be
noted that although 95 had been taught in theological classes
only 14 had been ordained by 1908.[121] While the mission made
considerable talk about a native ministry, it failed to give it
the attention and the quality training-center deserved. Its
projection of the ministry could not compete with the profes-
sions advertized at the Syrian Protestant College. The occupation of key pulpits by ordained missionaries, e.g. H. Jessup in
Beirut, while qualified nationals such as John Wortabet turned
to medical education may indicate an unwillingness of missionaries to stp down.[122] Whatever the causes, this severely handicapped the Syrian churches and work among Muslims.

Although emigration drained off nearly one half of the evangelical membership in centers such as Tripoli and Beirut, one
must not minimize the quality of lay and ordained leadership
remaining. Protestant Syrians were some of the finest educated men in the Near East. For example, Butrus Bistany (d.1883),
a charter member of the Beirut church and elder for 35 years,
rendered scholarly assistance to the Arabic translation of the
Bible, founded a National School (1862), and edited a news-
sheet, periodical and Arabic encyclopedia.[123] Others went to
Egypt to found newspapers, periodicals and to give impulse to
the educational-literary awakening among the Arabs. Some
traveled to the Americas, Africa and Australia. Settling there
or returning, they produced a creative exchange of ideas.[124]
Every Christian tradition in the Levant felt this stimulus. A
Syrian leader once remarked, "You Protestants are a small sect,
yet you have changed us all."

What bearing did this have on Muslim evangelization? First, the ultimate objective had not been forgotten by either Syrian church or the mission. Jessup understood the spiritual and political issues well.

> God has been preparing Christianity for Islam; He is now preparing Islam for Christianity....It is a work of surprising difficulty which will require a new baptism of apostolic wisdom and energy, faith and love.[125]

The whole design awaited the arrival of religious liberty in his opinion. Yet the simple fact remained that even in 1910 the more nominal groups of the Druzes, Metawileh and Nusairiyeh (much less the Sunni and Shi'a) remained largely untouched. Some reasons are obvious. First, neither the Ottoman government, nor succeeding Turkish and Syrian governments, permitted open work among Muslims. Religious freedom was really theoretic and an inquirer's or convert's existence most precarious. Even so, one Muslim sheikh admitted the existence of secret believers: "Many Christians will rise from Moslem graves in Syria".[126] Second, while transfer from one religious community to another is always difficult, actual provision for re-registering (upon conversion) was non-existent in many places. Third, the competitive spirit of Christian groups in Syria-Lebanon made them jealous of growth in another, e.g. in the past Maronites might attempt to block any widespread Muslim movement to Protestantism. Fourth, evangelical churches were often reluctant to receive and assimilate a convert from Islam. They were suspicious of him as an individual and fearful of possible consequences for their community. They inherited many of the prejudices of the Orthodox or Roman Catholic bodies from which they had come. Fifth, missions also had problems with vested interests. Addison detects this problem and the hope of the future.

> The Evangelical Church and the missionary institutions have become vested interests, whose welfare must not be jeopardized by the persecution which would arise if Moslems deserted their religion in appreciable numbers. There are moments then, when the workers wonder if perhaps they are not almost more afraid of success than of failure. But we may assume with confidence that these are only their weaker moments. The coming years will prove them equal to a beckoning opportunity.[127]

What favorable signs were appearing? First, this region, especially the Lebanon, was leading the Near East in moving towards a pluralistic society in which religious freedom was permitted. As Christian communities dropped their foreign backing (French, Russia, Anglo-American), they became better

oriented to their own lands. Access to one another and to Muslims improved with the emphasis on nationality. Second, all
were learning that Muslim evangelization must be sustained by
the support and activity of a corporate group. Private theories and individual experiments soon terminate. As Jessup
stated "the Moslem citidel is not to be taken by theories but
by faithful instruction, personal acquaintance and persevering
effort".[128] As the evangelical churches slowly gained vision
and determination to evangelize their Muslim neighbors, all
were assured they would find the strength for this labor of
love. Third, the twentieth century brought with it new channels for communicating Christian truth, e.g. radio and tele-
vision, and a new awareness of the vast resources of lay-wit-
ness. The growing influence of world opinion supporting religious liberty would undoubtedly help open these channels. Even
the World Mission Conference at Edinburgh (1910) acknowledged
the great strides made in evangelistic work among Muslims in
the Levant and the promise of things to come.[129] Presbyterians
in Syria were encouraged to strengthen the arm of their two-
pronged approach which was extended towards their Muslim neighbors. They did so in the hope inscribed upon the Great Mosque
in Damascus which had survived the terrible fire of 1893: "Thy
Kingdom, O Christ, is a Kingdom of all ages, and Thy dominion
from generation to generation."

Northern Presbyterians in Persia (Iran), 1870-1910

With the transfer of 1870, Presbyterians took charge of what
was now the Mission to Persia. Regretably, the extensive and
in a sense successful work among the Nestorians about Urumia
(Western Persia), must be passed over so that attention may be
given to work among Muslims and others at Hamadan, Tabriz, Teheran, etc. Suffice it to mention that the revivals among the
Nestorians did contribute a number of outstanding evangelists
who reached out to Muslims, Kurds, as well as to their own
people. Mission rivalry (1880-1914) between the Presbyterian
Mission, the Anglican "Assyrian Mission", and the Russian Orthodox Church did however lead to what appeared to be unnecessary fragmentation. What proved to be most disastrous for this
ascending Assyrian people were regional and international politics. World War I would usher in a chain of tragic events
which would destroy and scatter this people caught in the midst
of reformation and renaissance.[130]

The Presbyterian program for Muslims was to become much
stronger in Persia than Syria, but at first it was seriously
hampered by limited manpower. In 1871, there were only three
male American missionaries and Robert Bruce (C.M.S.), nevertheless, they tenaciously clung to the hope that all might be
privileged to hear God's news in Christ. Gradually it emerged
that the Presbyterians would expand north of the 34th parallel

and the Anglicans would strive to cover the southern region
(e.g. Ispahan, Kerman, Yezd, etc.).

Within the context of the larger history of Persia, it is
very apparent, perhaps more than the missionaries realized at
the time, that politics had an immense bearing on their work.
Persian Christians were frequently caught in the middle of international intrigues, invasions and withdrawals, each with
their own consequences. While it is impossible to scrutinize
this whole political question, it will continue to intrude into
any portrayal of work among Muslims. Two things needing examination, however, are the mission's geographic expansion to
centers of Muslim population and experimentation in means for
their evangelization.

Geographical Expansion to Muslim Centers in Persia

The Persian mission gradually opened up new centers at Teheran (1872), Tabriz (1873), Hamadan (1881), Resht (1902), Kermanshah (1905) and Meshed (1911) in addition to Urumia (1834).
The procedure at the first three centers was to begin with the
Armenians and Nestorians of the city and then to reach the
Jews and Muslims as fast as possible. In other stations, Muslims were among the first contacted. The station at Teheran
established by James Bassett gives insight into the difficulties
encountered and overcome. Except for a Nestorian colporteur,
this capital of growing international importance had been without a Protestant witness since William Glen's death.[131] In
addition to linguistic and political issues, the basic questions
were "How to root the church?" and "How to prepare the Muslim
for the Gospel?" The selection of the linguistic medium was
most vital to the future of Muslim work:

> It was a serious question in the opening of the mission
> in Teheran, whether efforts should be directed especially
> and exclusively to the Armenians, following the example of
> the Mission to the Nestorians, or whether the missionary
> should seek to reach all classes, and make use of the Per-
> sian language for this purpose....The Persian tongue is
> known by all classes of the people, but there was the pos-
> sibility that the authorities of the State would forbid the
> use of Persian language, owing to the fact that it is not
> the tongue of the non-Mohammedan races, and the use of it
> might be thought one evidence of an attempt to proselyte
> the Mohammedans to the Christian faith. It was determined,
> however to make the Persian tongue the medium of missionary
> work in teaching and especially in preaching....The first
> evangelical efforts consisted chiefly in preaching and in
> the sale of the Scriptures.[132]

Bassett was soon drawing Armenians, Jews and Muslims to services at a chapel. A wave of interest among the city's Jews

(1875) produced results when a court ruled their right to become Christians (1878). A school for Jewish children under a
converted Hebrew principal drew 125 students within its first
week (1879). By 1890 the Shah favored both the Teheran Boys'
and Girls' schools with a visit. Many of the students were
at that time Muslim! The church in Teheran organized (1876)
with twelve Persian charter members including one Muslim convert, Husain. By 1883, two congregations with fifty members
included four converts from Islam and three from Judaism. L. F.
Esselstyn began English services (1887) for the foreigners of
the city.[133] Although some evangelical members returned to the
Armenian Orthodox Church in 1896, the Evangelical Church by the
turn of the century had an average attendance of over one hundred including numerous Muslims.

Political obstructions to work with Muslims continued. In
1879-1880, there was a new wave of interest in Christianity
among Muslims. Joseph L. Potter reported that "so numerous
and so prolonged were the calls upon the missionary that it was
sometimes difficult for him to find time for his meals."[134]
An alarmed Persian government, via the British minister, ordered the Mission to prevent Muslims from attending Christian services or religious instruction. Failing to have the order
modified, the Mission painfully resolved (1881) to close the
chapel until such time as the Gospel could be shared with all.
Obedience to God rather than man, they observed, made it impossible to discriminate![135] It appeared for a time that the
missionaries might be expelled. In 1882, the government relaxed its stand somewhat by transferring responsibility to the
Persian police and while not prosecuting such attendance,
warned against apostasy. In Tabriz, Muslims attending services
were arrested and flogged. In this same period, schools were
twice closed and reopened. The arrival of S. G. W. Benjamin,
first American resident diplomat (1883), supplied the mission
with a regularized channel for communication and appeals. By
1884, Muslims were attending services in even greater numbers.
By next year Muslims were receiving public baptism and some
score of converts were scattered throughout the land. Work in
Teheran was handicapped by the close scrutiny of the Shah and
Muslim authorities, high costs, foreign intrigue, and time-
consuming lobbying, yet it is certain this confrontation in
Persia's capital cleared the way for the future. Barrett was
especially concerned that preparatory work among Muslims might
open the way for future acceptance of the Gospel. He argued
that Muslims had:

> ...no intellectual and religious preparation inclining
> them to accept the distinguishing doctrines of the gospel.
> Whatever of Christian faith has reached them has come in the
> distorted and perverted form presented in the Koran, and is
> intended to prejudice their minds against the Christian

statement of the gospel. In every people which has been
brought under the power of the gospel there has been a long
period of preparation before any great reformation has been
effected.[136]

Similar concerns were voiced in other stations. In Tabriz
(1873), Peter Easton and Mary Jewett found opposition from both
Armenian priests and the mujtahids. Still Muslim attendance
persisted in spite of beatings and the death of one inquirer.
In 1892, the government without notification locked the church
and school charging:

> lack of proper permission to build the church, having the
> ten commandments written in the interior of the church in a
> Mohammedan language and in the sacred blue color, having a
> water tank under the church in which to baptize converts,
> having a tower in which we intended to put a bell, baptizing
> Mussulmans of whom Mirza Ibrahim was now in prison, receiv-
> ing Mussulman boys into our school and women to the church,
> having Dr. Bradford's dispensary near the church.[137]

Reopened after delays, the school and church were composed mainly of those of Muslim background until the city was overrun by
armies and Christian refugees during W.W.I.
     At Hamadan (the Ecbatana of Ezra 4:2) and surrounding vil-
lages, James W. Hawkes, Mullah Mohammad Rasooli (known as Kaka)
and others established a full medical, educational, literary-
evangelism program. At least fifty percent of the enrollment
at the Boys' School was Muslim by World War I. More than half
of the 255 members received into St. Stephens Church before
1915 had attended the Faith Hubbard School. Jews and Muslims
were likewise attracted to the congregation (1875) by the appealing preaching of Pastor Shimoon. A second congregation composed entirely of converts from Judaism and Islam was named the
Peniel Church in 1894. A Christian village was proposed to
escape the persecution and hardship inflicted upon converts,
but its failure was probably a blessing in disguise for it
meant that this witness was kept within society.[138] Work at
the Resht station (1902) saw a small church (1883) undergirded
by schools and medicine. The evangelical church at Kermanshah
organized with seven nationals, two converts from Judaism and
five from Islam. Following World War I, an influx of Assyrian
Christians bolstered the membership to two hundred. One of the
most interesting developments took place at Meshed in Northwestern Persia (chief city of Khorasan and gateway to Afghanistan). Bassett ventured to this holy city of conservative Muslims in 1878 to sell many bibles and books there. Translating
the Gospel of Matthew into Gaghatta (the region's Turkish dia-
lect), he later struck a response among several prominent
Muslims who were disgusted by the conditions about them. In

another attempt, Esselstyn was forced to leave the city after
one month (1895), but by 1900 he had won the friendship of Haji
Mullah Ali, the mujtahid of Semnan (on the Teheran-Meshed road).
Esselstyn eventually resided in Meshed alone for four years
(1911-1915) and by quietly setting books and persuasively sharing the Gospel, gained a following. Joined by D. M. Donaldson
and others (1915), they cared for thousands strickened by star-
vation and typhus during the war. While Esselstyn baptized
only a few converts before his death by typhus (1918), but
Donaldson was to baptize fourteen on Christmas, 1920, thus to
usher an all-convert church into existence.[139]

Extension and Experimentation in the Means of Muslim Evangelization

What methods lie behind the successful work in Persia? It
appears that in the nineteenth century, literature and education were the choice tools of evangelism. Early in the twentieth century, medicine and education gained a slight edge in
priority. Yet even during this time, Secretaries Brown and
Speer promoted direct evangelism among Muslims and missionaries
J. Christy Wilson and William Miller were determined to implement the same. After the government's takeover of the educational system (1918-1940), the crisis in theology and mission
(1928-1938), and the formation of the Evangelical Church in Iran
(1933-1934), attention was certainly refocused on the proclamation of the Christian message.
    Literary evangelism expanded as Persian works from the Urumia
Press filtered across the land. The total Persian Christian
library before 1875 included only a positive tract presenting
Christianity (without criticizing Islam) by Merrick, his translation of Keith's Evidences (Edinburgh, 1846), and Pfander's
Balance of Truth (1835) plus the newer portable edition of the
Glen-Martyn Persian Bible being distributed by William Wright.
About that time, the presses in Teheran and Hamadan began a
program of publication for Christian and Muslim Persians.
Bassett helped with the Persian Hymnbook (1876-1898), translated a Primer (1876) and the Westminster Shorter Catechism
(1884) while Potter tackled Pilgrim's Progress (1884) and Hawkes
produced a Bible handbook (1897). Later the Inter-Church
Literature Program under J. D. Frame, W. N. Wysham (1924-1938)
and John Elder (1938-1960) would tap many talents in producing
materials.
    Preaching found greater response among the Muslims of the
land than in most Near Eastern countries. Bassett found isolated communities in Khorasan as well as citizens of Teheran
willing to hear the Gospel.

    There is apparent everywhere a deep seated dissatisfaction
with the prevalent form of religion. We have all we can do,

and more, to merely meet the demands now made for religious instruction and for the Bible. The disposition of the government is known to be favorable to religious liberty, and its establishment cannot long be delayed.[140]

This ferment was evidenced by the rapid growth of the Babi (Bahai) movement. The mission avoided controversy, however, and never attempted to distribute Pfander's works (it appears some C.M.S. workers felt differently) but only used them in training sessions with workers. Bassett felt that "the conversion of the people must be effected, if at all, by the teaching of the Bible by the missionary".[141] The balanced talented personality and work of Esselstyn makes a good study in effective evangelism among Muslims. Here was a man who never failed to give verbal expression to God's plan as disclosed in Christ. Traveling over wide areas, distributing Scriptures and preaching, he won the confidence of leaders and laymen alike. An example of his approach is seen at Semnan (1900). Calling privately upon Haji Mullah Ali, a chief mujtahid whom he had earlier befriended, he spent three hours explaining the path of salvation and Christ as the crowning expression of God's love (esp. I Cor. 13 and John 3:16). Requesting a Bible, the Haji confessed, "You have the way of salvation, be faithful". Esselstyn was invited to attend prayers at the mosque and following worship requested to speak to the 1,000 assembled. His message on the Prodigal Son and repentence was so well received that again he gained the Haji's praise. During the rest of his stay, Esselstyn spoke with a constant stream of visitors. It was this same spirit of work by Esselstyn at Meshed that prepared the way for an all convert church. Later itinerant evangelism would increase under William M. Miller, J. Christy Wilson and John Elder. Grass-roots evangelism met friendly response in the populous province of Khorasan as well as about Tabriz and Hamadan. It was found that converts in rural areas generally gravitated towards the towns where they could unite in fellowship with other Christians.[142] Persian converts made a growing contribution to literary work as Iran developed a nationalism of her own. Mansur Sang, a Christian dervish, was a unique example of adaptation to Persian modes of life. He earned his living pulling teeth and giving vaccinations as he distributed great quantities of literature across Iran.[143]

Educational institutions started for Nestorians, Armenians or Jews and then gradually attracted increasing numbers of Muslims. From 1870 to the first World War, this expansion continued in nearly every city. After visiting Europe, Shah Nasr-ad-Din gave western type education greater freedom in spite of complaints from mullahs and mujtahids. Persian nobles and the royal family quietly sent their children to mission schools so that by 1910, one-third of the enrollment was Muslim. After the Cairo Conference (1906), S. G. Wilson (d. 1916) tried to

instill the idea of educational evangelism for Muslims among all
Armenian and Persian Christians. Later at Teheran, Iran Bethel
for girls would become Sage College for Women and the Boys'
school under S. M. Jordon would expand into Alborz College. As
in Turkey and Syria, a national movement in post-war Iran would
lead to the nationalization of the Mission's educational work.
At first, primary (1932) and then high schools and colleges
(1940) were taken over. Earlier transfer to the national church
might have saved them, but some felt the young church was better
off unfettered by an expensive educational system. Nevertheless
these schools produced many national leaders and created a
public opinion much more favorable to the Christian faith.[144]

Medical work among Muslims received a fairer test in Persia
than in either Turkey or Syria. No activity experienced such
growth as that of medical work. Early missionary doctors confined their practice to dispensary-clinic work and itinerating,
but as western medicine came into its own and demands for sur-
gery increased, hospitals became a necessity. This required
larger staffs, complex equipment, and increasing budgets. Quality treatment for growing numbers soon exhausted the time and
energies of missionary doctors and nurses. They found less
time to converse with patients of their faith in Christ. While
creating favorable impressions, they paradoxically were often
unable to follow up the opportunity. Thus as the twentieth
century progressed, medical missionary work became a subject of
much debate.

The statistics concerning the number of Persian Muslims
reached by medical work is almost unbelievable. Joseph P.
Cochran,(d. 1905) son of J. P. Cochran, returned to Persia
(1878) and adeptly put his medical and linguistic skills to
work. Westminster Hospital at Urumia (1882) became the first
Mission hospital in Persia.[145] W. W. Torrence, pioneer physician in central Persia, was so respected that he served on the
official Persian Envoy to Washington, D. C. (1888) and G. W.
Holmes of Tabriz acted as physician to the crown prince. Mary
Bradford of Tabriz brought compassion and care to women and
children (1888-1905) while Mary Smith and J. G. Wishard saw the
famed Teheran Hospital come into being. There is no gauge for
measuring the influence this program had upon Persian Muslims
and others. In time Persian Christians entered into medical
evangelism, e.g. Dr. Saeed Kurdistani (d. 1942), a former Muslim
mullah and brother of Kaka, became a beloved shepherd of healing
and witness in Teheran.[146] During and after World War I, the
Mission became heavily involved in relief and refugee work, industrial and farm schools, recreation centers, clubs, clinics
and leper work. These reflected both the crying needs of the
land and the theological-mission outlook in America. This consuming sacrificial work, compassion and courage, won the lasting
respect and confidence of many in Persia.

Both Presbyterians and Anglicans were increasing their medi-

cal programs at the turn of the century, but these were still in
need of fuller evaluation. Certain assets were obvious, First,
they opened doorways to the Persian people, i.e. the first avenue reaching great numbers of Muslims. When properly carried
out, the hospital became a dynamic evangelistic center and the
doctor, an effective evangelist whose words were readily received. He proclaimed and demonstrated the healing that Christ
offers to the whole man. Second, medical work proved effective
in breaking down prejudices based on ignorance, fear or suspicion. It eliminated the idea that Christians were ceremonial-
ly unclean. Thus it paved the way for good human relationships
between Christians and all classes, royalty, ulema and peasant
alike. Third, the saving of life and the alleviation of suffering were a justifiable expression of Christian compassion. Regretably circumstances gradually made medical work more of a
case of charity than communication. The government gradually
curtailed the itinerant evangelistic medical work and restricted
the mission to institutionalized centers.

While medical work and medical education multiplied, it became obvious again that certain factors easily became liabili-
ties. First, improving medical technology and facilities, while
a blessing, made the budget a bottomless pit which could soon
swallow other phases of mission or stifle their growth. Only
one-eighth of the medical budget came from abroad yet this was
still a major share of the Mission's total resources. Charges
to patients had to increase. This was good in that it made
patients more discerning as to the worth of labors and medicines
rendered, but it did make the work look more like a business.
Increasing government controls further complicated matters.
Second, and perhaps more serious, was the query: "What was the
relationship between this service and Christian witness?" In
some humanitarian circles it was held that medical work needed
no word for the deed was valid in itself. In practice however
the patient could construe the deed to mean many things, e.g.
earning merit, etc. Even when there was the will to preach as
well as heal, the multiplication of physical chores could soon
reach a point where the worker was too exhausted to convey the
idea it was done in Christ's name. Often verbal witness was re-
legated to chaplains and others. When this happened, it could
be asked, why not let secular institutions take over the medical
phase? Such were the questions fired about in mission circles
from the First World War onwards.[147]

An Evangelical Church and Evaluation

The Evangelical (Presbyterian)Church in Iran included scores
of converts from Islam by 1910. Work among Muslims met with
greater success here than in most Arab-Turkish lands, being surpassed only by efforts in North India and the East Indies. The
Persians were receptive to ideas of religious liberty and while

these were not incorporated into a constitution, they were practiced as an unwritten code. The fact that Islam had been forced
on the Persians, that Persian Muslims were divided by many sects,
and that they felt a kinship to Aryan peoples may have contributed to this openness. Yet fanaticism was not unknown in the
early days. Mirza Ibrahim, a convert baptized at Khoi and
arrested while preaching at Urumia, died of injuries received in
prison (1893). Yet his bold testimony at his trial and before
the governor marked a step towards the day when Muslim and Jewish converts could live without fear of physical molestation
in Iran. Talented Persian converts like Dr. Saeed of Teheran
and his brother, Kaka gained the respect and hearing of many
Muslims.[148] The congregations at Teheran (1878), Hamadan (1876),
Tabriz and Resht included Muslim converts and those at Kermanshah and Meshed were composed almost entirely of such. Jews,
Armenians, Nestorians, Muslims, Kurds, Parsis and Europeans
knit together as a worshipping family made a fine demonstration
of God's reconciling work in Christ. The personal sacrifice
experienced kept the churches mindful that reconciliation is a
costly present activity rather than a guaranteed status.

The Evangelical Church continued to grow in spite of political and social pressures and by 1910 numbered over 3,000 communicants. During World War I, the Nestorian sector of the
church was almost wiped out. Nevertheless the Evangelical
Church of Iran would organize into three presbyteries and select
its own Persian moderator (1934) while receiving full recognition as an independent church by the parent body, the Presbyterian Church, U.S.A. (1935). At this time, it consisted of 26
organized churches and 45 unorganized groups with about 2,272
communicants. Relationships between this young Evangelical
Church and the Anglican Church in the South were most cordial
and found expression in the All Persian Inter-Church Conferences held at Hamadan (1925), Isfahan (1927) and Teheran (1931).
The continuation of these conferences have provided opportunity
for inspirational fellowship, discussion of problems facing
Persian Christians and possible church union, and a growing
ecumenical concern for the fuller evangelization of Iran. The
churches of Iran continue to exhibit every prospect of a rich
future in a country of equal promise.[149]

What evaluation can be made of the Presbyterian work in Iran?
First, it was successful in terms both of church-renewal and
direct conversions (two-pronged). Although the Nestorian and
Armenian churches had become ingrown, defensive and lacking
evangelistic zeal, they gradually experienced degrees of revival even at the cost of life. This progress at a price,
according to John Joseph, broke the spiritual stalemate which
had gripped Persia.[150] The conversion of so many Jews to
Christianity was remarkable, but the conversion of so many Muslims in a land under Islamic law still more noteworthy. It
revealed the power of Christ to draw men from all corners of

the earth when even minimal liberty is allowed. The Presbyterian Annual Mission Reports listed converts from Islam every
year although specific names, places and details were discreetly
omitted. The turn of the century was described as "The Beginning of the Harvest" in the centennial volume as workers found
Muslims "surprisingly accessible".[151] Second, the work successfully permeated society, improved various human relationships
and advanced the spirit of religious liberty. Besides the contributions in literature, education, public health, the Mission
did its part in shaping a new public opinion. John Elder
rightly tells how the Mission:

> came to a country so fanatical that any work with Moslems
> was pronounced impossible, and by loving service and friendly
> relations helped to build mutual understanding and respect
> and to bring nearer the era of complete religious freedom.[152]

Missionaries and Persian Christians threw themselves wholehear-
tedly into the work of nation-building and have gained the public's respect. Thirdly, the work succeeded in finding points of
contact in Persian thought through which the communication of
the Gospel could be channeled. Missionaries found in Shiʻite
Islam some understanding of sacrificial death and atonement
(Muharram and Husain's martyr death), of messanic hope (the
hidden Iman), and of religious liberty which rejected rigid
Sunni structures and enforcement. These points opened the way
to discussion of revelation and incarnation, the Messiah, the
cross, suffering, atonement, repentance and conversion. The
speculative outlook of the older Mutazilite school lived on
among Persian sufis in spite of mujtahid controls. This segment
of the population often was disgusted with Islam. While some of
these took the full step to Christianity, others went halfway
to Bahaism or took on a secular, agnostic or nationalistic outlook which excluded religious content. A number of missionaries paid close attention to effective communication of the Gospel to Muslims, e.g. Pitman, J. Christy Wilson, William Miller,
etc. Pitman's approach was to make a simple positive presenta-
stressing (1) our need of a mediator, (2) our need of an example,
(3) our need of divine power to follow this example and (4) how
all these are met in Christ. His avoidance of verbal comparison
gained a convert's approval.

> From my experience I believe that comparison creates anta-
> gonism. I believe that we should show the love of God
> positively. This is the principle I follow, just to preach
> Christ. If we make comparisons, then people must defend
> themselves.[153]

Miller held that as soon as persons received this proclamation
and declared their allegiance to Christ, they should be given
the privilege of baptism. This stood in contrast to the long

probation period practiced by some. J. Christy Wilson stressed
a flexible evangelistic program. The main effort must be to
found churches not mission stations.

> No David who may be sent to Zenjan or to Maragha should
> be encumbered with the Saul's armour of any institution.
> When churches have been found that will stand upon their own
> resources and propagate the Gospel in their districts, the
> mission force should be ready to leave.

Wilson would help in a series of evangelistic services at Tabriz
in the post-war period which resulted in 116 confessions of
faith (including five Muslims). Appreciating the value of group
movements, he noted:

> It is probably true that many of these people came first
> within the influence of the Gospel hoping to receive loaves
> and fishes, (but) people came to Christ in the same spirit
> and whatever their first motives they offer a stirring
> challenge...

Secretary Robert Speer backed the opinion that all institutions
and agencies must be geared to the primary task of evangelization. The Mission must remain mobile, engaged in proclamation,
in order to stimulate an indigenous Christian movement which
would have the spontaneity and adaptability to spread over the
whole country.[154] The two-pronged Presbyterian approach in
Persia was worthy of commendation and circumstances allowed
that it should be truly doxological.

United Presbyterians in Egypt, 1854-1910

Ecclesiastical and Environmental Elements

The Coptic Orthodox Church had an illustrious history dating
back possibly to St. Mark. The Alexandrian school of theology
under Origen and Athanasius was most influential and the monas-
ticism of Upper Egypt reached west via Benedict of Nursia.
Holding to the monophysite position in tension with the Greek
church, this great church was overrun by Arab invaders (A.D.
639) and soon isolated from other Christians for centuries of
Islamic rule. Enduring numerous political, social and economic
restrictions and persecution for faith's sake, the church survived in a land that eventually became about 90% Muslim. Commendable as this was, the church suffered from stagnation and
was reluctant to be either the agent or object of mission.[155]

Egyptian politics influenced the shape of Protestant missions. Nearly three centuries of Turkish rule were shattered
by French designs. Napoleon Bonaparte's invasion (1798) shook

confidence in Ottoman might and only by British force was Egypt
theoretically restored to Turkey (1801). Muhammad Ali, an Alba-
nian officer with a modernized army, became the real power
(sometimes called the Father of modern Egypt). At first he defeated the British and executed the Mameluk line before pressing
north into Syria. Recognized as Pasha by the Sultan (1811), his
realm at one time spread from Khartoum to Anatolia (1833). It
was the British who forced him back within Egypt's borders and
under Turkish suzerainty (cf. Treaty of London, 1841). Yet
before his death (1849), Egypt had borrowed extensively from
European science, military techniques, cotton production, etc.
Ali's son, Abbas earned a name as a harsh reactionary (1849-
1854) but his successor Said Pasha (1854-1863) was a progressive
leader anxious to establish greater religious liberty. During
his rule, the United Presbyterian Mission (sometimes called the
American Mission) formed and became the largest Protestant
endeavor in the land.[156]

United Presbyterian workers in Damascus conceived of the program for Egypt.[157] Two veterans of Damascus, James Barnett
(1817-1884) and Gulian Lansing (1815-1892) joined with recruit
Thomas McCague to begin work in 1854.[158] Scottish missionary
John Hogg (1833-1836) accepted appointment with their board
(1859)[159] and Andrew Watson arrived (1861)[160] to make up the
early leadership. Other active figures included Ebenezer Currie,
S. C. Ewing, W. Harvey, Dr. D. R. Johnston, J. R. Alexander,
the troublesome B. F. Pinkerton, and Miss M. J. Mcknown.[161]
Charles R. Watson and Earl Elder appeared later.[162] Their
policy from the start was to proclaim the Gospel to the whole
population of Egypt. Continual effort was exerted that Muslims
might hear, however, it was soon agreed that two things must
precede any widespread response from Muslims. First, the Coptic
Church and other Christians in Egypt must be revived. Second,
political upheaval or ferment must shatter the political, social
and economic grip of Islam upon the land.

Response to the Environmental Factors

Egypt's intense heat, disease and overwork snuffed out the
lives of many missionaries and forced others into sick leave or
retirement. The Crimean War and the American Civil War brought
added hardships, yet these were not as depressing as the lack of
religious liberty. Missionaries, especially Lansing, spent
much time battling to gain equal rights for Christians and to
secure the rights of scattered converts from Islam (1858-1864).
For a time it was feared that open Muslim hostility might take
the same form as India's mutiny, but the impartial and firm
rule of Said Pasha saved the day. A case at Assiut (1861) demonstrates the pressure placed on Christians. A formerly Coptic woman married to a Muslim wished to return to the Christian

faith and took refuge in the Bishop's residence. Faris, an
educated Syrian, was requested to defend her in court. He suffered both physical and verbal abuse from those who refused to
take seriously the Sultan's new decrees on liberty. With the
aid of W. S. Thayer, Consul-General of the U.S.A., the case was
won and the air finally cleared. Relations with Muslims improved and the Christian faith gained new respect.[163] Abraham
Lincoln sent a letter of congratulation to the Khedive for his
just dealings with the Assiut situation.[164] The next major case
was that of Ahmed Fahmi, the Muslim student and teacher who was
baptized November 26, 1877. This difficult test case helped
prepare the way for Muslim consideration of the option of Christianity.[165] Once the Evangelical Coptic Church became a viable
social unit, it sought to curb the drunkedness, theft and im-
morality so rampant in the land. One major accomplishment was
the changing of Market Day from Sunday to Saturday in Assiut
and neighboring towns. Christianity in Upper Egypt was once
again a faith to be respected, an agent of social reform. Perhaps one of the hardest problems faced by the Evangelical Church
was the rise of Plymouthism under B. F. Pinkerton. His "Brethren" following among Egyptian Protestants created tension for
several years (1869-1883) even after his resignation from the
mission. Through this experience the whole church gained new
appreciation of the price of religious liberty and the need for
sound comprehensive teaching in theology.[166]

> Inherent in the Protestant way of life is freedom of
> thought and tolerance, allowing a diversity of opinions.
> That might be at times detrimental to its own cause, but the
> conviction that truth by its own valour will be victorious
> without the help of enforcing laws and restrictions is such
> a lofty conception that it never should be abandoned, even
> if we have to go through dark periods during which the law-
> less forces take advantage of misunderstood liberty.[167]

The Evangelical Church in Egypt was challenged to demonstrate
Christian love and reconciliation in its new-found liberty.
    Under Khedive Ismail (1863-1879), Egypt sought greater inde-
pendence but ultimately ended in economic dependence. Ismail
built the Suez Canal, railways, telegraphs, irrigation works;
sponsored the Cairo opera house and Verdi's "Aida"; and encouraged Syrians to publish newspapers, periodicals and translated
works. In the midst of much promise, he indebted his country
for several hundred million dollars. Indiscreet spending,
governmental corruption and bankruptcy caused his creditors
(France, Germany, Russia, Austria, Italy and Great Britain) to
be alarmed. Ismail was deposed and his son Tewfik placed under
the guidance of French and British financial controllers.
Pressures on Egyptian Christians again increased. The military
rebellion led by Colonel Arabi (1881) disclosed the land's in-

stability. Tewfik caught between Arabi and the Europeans was
practically helpless. The massacre of Europeans in Alexandria
(June, 1882) brought prompt British action. With the battle of
Tel al-Kabir, Britain inaugurated a period of varying influence
over Egypt (1882-1952). There has been much debate over the
merit of British rule in Egypt. While it sought to treat individuals with justice and equality, Coptic Christians felt they
were handicapped by the British administration. Perhaps they
had expected too much consideration? However, many missionaries
also charged that British interests were served first. This
often meant catering to the sentiments of the Muslim leaders,
patronizing existing systems, and maintaining the status quo
rather than advancing reform and education. Nevertheless, there
was some improvement in human rights and the economy. Egyptian
nationalism eventually led to recognition of the country's independence (1922) and the Revolution (1952). Progress towards
religious liberty in these years of ferment (1882-1922) were
advanced most by liberal Muslims and evangelical Christians.
Foreigners increasingly bore a stigma which curtailed their contribution to the cause. In spite of the new spirit of freedom,
it is questionable, however, if the populace would have tolerated a massive movement of Muslims to Christianity.[168]

Response to Ecclesiastical Factors

The mission's response to ecclesiastical issues was expressed
by John Hogg.

> The great stumbling-block in the way of doing much for
> them /Muslims7 is the Coptic Church. Mohammedans have not
> the means at present of knowing what true Christianity is.[169]

His biographer could rightly add:

> In the light of this fact, all effort for the regeneration
> of the Copts acquired a unique value. He saw in it the forg-
> ing of a Key that must eventually unlock the closed portal of
> Islam, and prepare the way for a more direct and concen-
> trated effort to secure the entrance he coveted amongst
> Egypt's millions....The Copts seemed to him to bear the same
> relation to the salvation of the Moslems that the Jews of
> Christ's day bore to the salvation of the Gentiles....[170]

United Presbyterian policy differed from that of the Anglicans
who for decades worked with the Coptic clergy hoping to effect
reform without disrupting the existing structure of the Coptic
Church. The American Mission began work directly with the Coptic laity as well. When enlightened laymen, priests and monks
desired to form evangelical congregations, support was given.
Strangely enough this was not necessarily detrimental to the

ancient church. The Coptic Church experienced its greatest revival in the very regions where evangelical churches sprang up.
The Mission continued to visualize this work among Copts as a
part of its larger mission to the Muslim populace.

How did this policy manifest itself in practice? At Cairo,
Scripture-literature distribution, schools, and Sunday afternoon
preaching in Arabic and English drew many inquirers. Gradually
there emerged evangelical leaders such as Saleh Awad of Cairo,
Makhiel, a monk, Wasif Khayat and Hanna Buktor of Assiut, Butrus
of Manfalut, and Fam of Kus. When these men could not achieve
reform within their own churches, they created evangelical congregations. This sparked discussions among Copts all along the
Nile.[171] At Alexandria (1857) a similar process ensued. There
Hogg and Lansing set forth the basic principle that all mission
work must aim at attracting and training a native agency.[172]

By 1858, a vision of potential work at Assiut, Girga, Luxor
and Upper Egypt caught the Mission's eye. The river was a
natural highway in this great valley where hundreds of villages
dotted the 750 miles between Alexandria and Aswan. By winter
tours, missionaries could avoid the intense heat yet reach this
people humbled by poverty and depotism. The first Nile River
Boat was outfitted with living quarters, conference room and
book-store (1860). The MacCagues, Lansings, and Hoggs, accompanied by national Christians, began the annual system of tours
which would continue for several decades. These boats became
the vital link between stations, itinerant evangelists, book
depots, colporteurs and young congregations in Upper Egypt. The
procedure was to travel by sail or by tow to Aswan and then
float downstream halting at key villages to sell Bibles and
books, hold discussions and short tours, conduct services in
schools and churches. Muslims as well as Copts were drawn to
these refreshingly simple presentations of the Gospel. It was
the spade work which would help fulfill the prophecy that
"Princes shall come out of Egypt....[173] For nineteen years,
Hogg provided leadership for the Assiut Station (1865) as teacher of the Boys' School (later Academy, then College), professor
to a theological class, leader of an evangelical congregation,
and as patriarchal shepherd to outlying churches, Egyptian pastors and evangelists. His ministry of biblical preaching and
teaching helped make Assiut a center of revived Christianity.
At first, Hogg tried to avoid head-on collision with the Coptic
Church by attending its worship and conducting evangelical services in the afternoon. Once reactionary Copts and Muslims
joined forces against these Protestant intruders by a <u>haram</u>
(interdict), public book burning and an effort to close the
schools, he had little choice but to form a separate church.
Evangelical adults and students soon became a target of the
levies for canal work and army. Mob attacks struck Protestant
homes in Kus and Fam Stephanos, a leading evangelist, was ban-
ished. His release and return was a significant chapter in the

annals of the young church.[174] Many Copts reacted against their
Patriarch's unholy alliance and began to probe the Scriptures
for themselves. Error was not all on the side of Patriarch
however. Several zealous but injudicious Protestant youths,
after reading of Gideon's throwing down the altar of Baal, un-
wisely destroyed pictures in a Coptic Church. These iconoclasts
were duly punished, yet strangely enough this sparked the interest of a number of Muslims in evangelical Christianity. Purchasing Bibles, they desired to learn of this Christianity
"without idolatry".[175] Perhaps this disruption of evangelical-
Orthodox relations was a necessary step in shaking off the spiritual stagnation that had long prevailed.

The formation and nurture of the Evangelical Church soon
absorbed a major proportion of the Mission's time and talent.
Once an Evangelical Church began to emerge, the mission be-
grudged it no good thing. As in North India, a Presbytery formed in Cairo (1860) to ordain John Hogg. This constituted a
unique advantage in terms of mission methods, i.e., keeping
assignments of **mission personnel** as the activity of the
church. Only in 1870, did an official Mission organization take
shape. This tactical error was prompted by the arrival of lay
missionaries (doctors, educators, single women) who called for
an organization in which they could have a voice and
demand that the Mission must manage its own properties, personnel and finances. It obscured the fact that the responsible
Presbytery, with a growing number of Egyptian clergy and laity
teamed together with missionaries, was becoming a truly democratic agency for discussion and action "in mission". This divor-
cing of church and mission in the popular mind would only be
remedied in the twentieth century. One cannot but wish that
this authority for mission to Muslims had been kept within the
Evangelical Church instead of delegated to a foreign agency!

The growth and vitality of the evangelical churches is nevertheless noteworthy. The growing congregations at Cairo and
Alexandria survived a first wave of Coptic persecution and firmly but courteously sought to improve inter-church relationships.
Notoriety and bible study both contributed to the tripling of
attendance and the organization of official evangelical congregations (1863). By that year, Presbytery also had six candidates for the ministry (including three former Coptic priests)
studying under Lansing in Cairo. Spontaneous growth of evanel-
ical circles continued as many Copts, from peasant to the Patriarch's brother, studied the Bible and prayed for a return to
a biblical Christianity. At Assiut, a group under Athanasius,
Girgis and Shenooda encouraged their bishop to hold Bible sessions for all the clergy. Amba Butros, metropolitan bishop of
Cairo on visit to Assiut, encouraged Bible study and increased
training for the clergy in hopeful anticipation of the coming
reformation.[176] Several factors contributed to this ferment:
(1) the existing Coptic reverence for the Bible was now rein-

forced by the Mission; (2) this evangelistic spirit was being
transmitted by laymen in their everyday channels; (3) Egypt's
encounter with western culture and science bolstered a spirit
of inquiry; and (4) the dedicated sacrificial work of missionaries and Egyptian evangelicals prompted a like response in
others.[177]

Steady growth in the Evangelical Church from 1870 to 1897,
resulted in a Presbytery of 21 ordained Arab ministers, 42
other Presbyterial workers, 39 organized churches and 197
stations, 5,355 communicants, 127 Sunday Schools with nearly
7,000 scholars, 34 colporteurs working from seven depots, plus
all the mission's personnel and projects.[178] The vitality of
the young church was demonstrated in more ways than statistics.
In the struggle of national and international politics, evangelical Egyptians gained respect for being above selfish intrigues. Meanwhile evangelicals gained their rights in matters of
marriage, estates, and guardianships by 1878. While missionaries such as Hogg (d. 1885) and Lansing (d. 1892) did their
best, the bulk of the credit for an improved social status for
Christians lies with Egyptian evangelicals. Men of the high
caliber of Pastor Tadros Yusef and Elder Athanasius soon were
taking the lead in evangelistic work and "night meetings".
Relationships with the Coptic Orthodox Church improved for the
mutual revitalization of all.

> The building up of the Evangelical Church and the reaction
> caused thereby, did more to revive the Coptic Church than
> all the previous efforts directed to this end. The present
> movement toward reform is strongest just where the Evangel-
> ical Church and its influence are the greatest. Experience
> has abundantly proved, therefore, that the revival of the
> Coptic Church from within, and the formation of evangelical
> congregations without, are not opposed to each other, but
> rather lend each other mutual support.[179]

While retaining its organic links with its parent body, the
Evangelical Church was entirely self-governing, self-supporting
and growing in its concern for self-propagation by 1926. The
qualification, "self-supporting" was possible because "unorganized groups" remained attached to the Mission until they could
go independent. The dual structure of church and mission lent
itself however to the misunderstanding that one was to exist
and the other to evangelize. Even J. R. Alexander's Sketch of
the Evangelical Church (1930) doesn't get down to the topic of
evangelizing Muslims until "An Afterword" of two pages! Some
of the blame for the Evangelical Church's neglect to assimilate
Muslim converts and to evangelize Muslim neighbors must rest
with the Mission.[180] Be that as it may, revitalized Evangelical and Coptic Orthodox Churches offer the most apparent hope
for the future evangelization of Muslims in Egypt.

The Muslim Masses and Mission Methods in Egypt.

It may be well to examine what missionary methods were used
to reach the Muslim masses of Egypt. Literature distribution
followed by private or small group discussion was a favored
means. This medium could circumvent governmental-public pressure opposing public display or preaching aimed directly at Muslims. A well laid network of thirty colporteurs working out
from eight shops was able to reach most towns in the Nile valley
several times per year. By the end of the century, thousands of
Bibles and religious books were sold annually. In addition to
translations of Christian classics, there were controversial
works on Islam, Roman Catholicism and the Coptic Church. An
examination of some 39 Arabic manuscripts of John Hogg reveals
that the bulk were solid biblical studies or helps on discipleship and Christian nurture. The founding of the interdenominational Nile Mission Press (1905) for publishing Arabic literature for Muslims and Christians was a great boon to this program.
By the twentieth century, mass rallies and evangelistic meetings, especially in Upper Egypt were attracting Muslims.

Education was woven into the very fabric of the Mission with
no station or congregation far from a school. There were five
types of institutions. Parochial schools under evangelical
congregations often had the Bible as the main textbook and a
church member as teacher. A higher quality education was found
at the central stations where mission day schools had qualified
Egyptian, Syrian and missionary teachers. Many of their graduates entered railway, telegraph and government offices. Mission
boarding schools especially for girls at Cairo (1866) and
Assiut (1874) became as it were teacher training colleges. The
Assiut Training College and the Theological Seminary deserve
special attention (cf. below). One must not underestimate the
scope of this work. These schools enrolled 15,000 scholars in
1899, only slightly less than all government schools. Protestants gained the highest literacy rate in the land. By 1900,
50% of the men and 20% of the women could read compared to the
national average of 10% and 1%. Muslims too were being reached.
Of the 16,771 students in 1908, 3,644 were Protestants, 3,495
Muslims, and 8,547 Copts and others.[181]

Theological classes began at Cairo (1864) and Assiut (ca.
1867) under Lansing, Hogg, and A. Watson. Students moved with
missionaries even to vacation centers and field assignments.
Instruction included the rudiments of arithmetic and grammar as
well as biblical and systematic theology. The advent of Plymouthism caused the church to realize the need of a permanent
seminary and a full curriculum. The Theological Seminary at
Cairo now concentrated on a training course which included
Islamics and apologetics. By 1896, the Seminary listed 26 graduates in the ministry and 23 licentiates.[182]

This same desire to train intelligent and dedicated Christian

workers prompted the formation of the Assiut Training College.
John Hogg held that the most effective way to evangelize the
whole country was to train an Egyptian Christian work force,
thus multiplying the limited mission personnel and finances. He
felt the Evangelical Church needed such a college to fulfill
her mission in the land. His determination was voiced in five
fiery articles in the home-church periodical calling for college facilities, means and workers so that the "legitimate results" of missionary labor could be harvested. In the heartland of the indigenous church, the number of evangelical students seeking advanced training increased fourfold in two years,
soon climbing to enrollments of 400, then 600. Hogg presented a
detailed resolution to the Mission (1874) speaking to the question; "What will prove the most speedy and effective means of
creating in this country a native evangelistic force adequate to
the task of bringing the Gospel within the reach of every inhab-
itant?"[183] This then was to be no ordinary college.[184] It
would seek to solve the dilemma in which the Presbyterians in
Syria found themselves (an independent soon secular college and
a haphazard theological program). Here was to be a college in,
of, and for the church. And to an amazing degree this was
achieved. Its graduates sent teachers, ministers, and skilled
laymen of marked Christian spirit into most spheres of the
nation's life. John R. Mott could declare:

> After visiting nearly all the missionary colleges and
> schools of importance in the non-Christian world, and study-
> ing their work and opportunities, I have no hesitation in
> saying that the Assiut Training College, of Egypt, is one of
> the most strategic in the world. In fact, I know of no other
> college which has yielded larger practical results for the
> amount of money expended than this particular institution.[185]

These schools under Presbyterian mission or church auspices continued to make a tremendous contribution to the cause of Christ
in the land of the pharaohs.[186]

Presbyterian medical work began with the arrival of D. R.
Johnston (1868) who reached many Muslims as well as Copts about
Assiut. The well-equipped hospitals and training centers there
and at Tanta were reaching over 35,000 patients annually before
1914.[187] This provided another direct contact with Muslims.
Coupled with the Egypt General Mission Hospital at Shebin and
the C.M.S. hospitals at Menouf and Old Cairo, they provided a
channel for conveying the spirit of Christ and a model for the
nation's public health-social welfare program.

Increased Work Among Muslims, 1880-1912

From its origin, the mission set out to evangelize Muslims
but this was no simple task. The greatest need at first was to

prepare a climate of religious liberty which at least made conversion to Christianity a live option. Scattered converts
slowly came forth such as Ibrahim Moosa of Faiyum (1868); Saeed
Abdullah, a Sudanese convert who remained a faithful member at
Alexandria until his death in 1871; and Ahmed Fahmi, the scholar-teacher of Cairo whose conversion (1877) served as a test
case. Ahmed later fled to Edinburgh where he studied medicine
before rendering distinguished service as a medical missionary
in Amoy, China.188 This in itself symbolizes the hostility a
convert faced. Even the missionaries were at pains as how to
approach Muslims. Lansing's encounters with muftis, sheikhs
and qadis in Upper Egypt indicate he used a socratic method
which at best questioned rather than communicated.189 By 1880,
Hogg was giving much attention to Muslim evangelization in his
theological classes and prepared a booklet under the title,
"Neither is there salvation in any other". He contended that
the answer to Islam must be demonstrated in the church's life.
In a pastoral letter he wrote:

> The work for which the Church exists is that for which
> the Son of God became incarnate. 'As Thou has sent me into
> the world so have I sent them into the world.' Christ's
> work was not completed by his incarnation, but was only then
> begun. Your work is not completed when you take to your-
> selves a bodily form as an organised congregation, it is
> only begun....190

In another letter he wrote that it was not so much the number
as the nature of the churches that would determine success or
failure of the mission to Muslims. He urged the Evangelical
Church to activate itself in reaching out to its Muslim neighbors and prayed for a baptism of the Spirit on the church.
  About 1881-1882, something of a movement among Muslims took
place. Arabi Pasha's rebellion, its sensational propaganda,
and its utter defeat at Tel-al-Kabir shattered any illusion of
Muslim impeccability. This led to numerous inquiries by those
disgusted with Islam. Up to 1881, the American Mission had
baptized about twenty-six Muslim converts. In the next two
years, twenty-two more professed their faith. The increase of
Muslim students in mission schools was most noticeable. At
Ekhmim, a score of Muslims attended the village church regularly. Hogg wrote: "If Egypt is given religious liberty worthy of
the name our success amongst Mohammedans will soon surpass that
amongst Copts.191 That "if" was never quite fulfilled. British
administrators were trying to satisfy all parties and ended up
by patronizing the old political structure rather than establishing a foundation for a democratic government. This inde-
finiteness frequently made it more difficult for converts under
the British than under the Khedives. Nevertheless, the American
Mission had baptized nearly 100 converts from Islam by 1895.192

The Mission set out to make good its declaration that it came
to serve the entire nation by establishing new work among Muslims in the Delta with stations at Tanta (1893), Benha (1894),
Zagazig (1894) and along the Red Sea. Mission schools, by the
turn of the century, enrolled roughly one-fifth Muslims. Other
experimental and ecumenical efforts were soon to begin.

The major project was to create a sense of mission to Muslims
within the Evangelical Church. John Hogg had warned that this
must be accomplished or that young church would do no more for
Muslims than did the Coptic Church.[193] Again in 1908, C. R.
Watson pointed to the enduring problem.

> There is also danger lest prejudice against Islam and
> against converts from Islam, should hinder this Church from
> exercising her widest influence among Moslems....Against
> this, missionaries and Church leaders must set their faces
> as flint, or the Evangelical Church will miss her true call-
> ing to become a National Church for Egypt.[194]

There were hopeful signs. A British observer, Robert Young in
1883, felt that the young church was recognizing its true
Scriptural function, "that it exists not simply or chiefly for
its own edification, but as a witness to the truth".[195] The
Evangelical Church joined the Mission in 1903 to request America
to send 280 additional workers to help them reach the non-Christian masses of Egypt. By 1908, the Evangelical Church was sending workers to the Sudan field. Its simpler form of evangelical
worship was more commendable to Muslims than Coptic Orthodoxy
and some were heard to remark, "If we become Christians, we will
become Protestants". But by the twentieth century, the new
factors of nationalism (at times both anti-foreign and anti-
Christian), resurgent Islamic forces (e.g. the Muslim Brotherhood), and a broader Egyptian renaissance added to the challenge.
The first Conference of Missionaries held at Cairo in 1906
symbolized something of a fresh beginning. The call extended
to Samuel Zwemer by the United Presbyterian Mission would bring
to this intellectual capital of Islam -- a leader in Muslim
work (1912). He and W. H. T. Gairdner would help usher in a
new era. The development of the Cairo School of Oriental Studies, the Nile Mission Press, the Inter-Mission Council (1920),
the Near East Christian Council, the Fellowship of Unity
(founded by Bishop Gwynne, 1921), and numerous conferences provided stepping-stones for advance. The Evangelical Church and
the United Presbyterian Mission were partners in a land knowing
the ills of poverty, disease and ignorance. As they faced the
massed Muslim millions of Egypt in the year 1910, they could but
humbly confess that the task of Christ was unfinished. Herein
lay the ever fresh call to mission.

ANGLICANS IN THE NEAR EAST: VARYING RELATIONS
WITH ORTHODOX CHURCHES AND EMERGING MISSIONS TO MUSLIMS

The various objectives and their priority among Anglicans in
the Near East have already been briefly noted. More detailed
examination will now be made of the chronological development
of Anglican missions under the headings: The Era of Cooperation
(1815-1840); The Era of Tensions (1841-ca. 1890); and the Era of
Consolidation (ca. 1890-1910). Following that, special attention will be given to Anglican effort in Constantinople, Persia
and Egypt.

An Era of Cooperation: "Mediterranean Missions", 1815-1840

Political events and Jewish missions attracted British concern for the Near East. Britain had largely by-passed the Near
East in her expansion to the Orient, but Napoleon's action in-
cited interest once again. Following Waterloo (1815), Englishmen were free to enter the Eastern Mediterranean. This co-
incided with a growing religious interest in the Holy Land and
its peoples. The London Society for Promoting Christianity
Amongst the Jews (London Jews Society, L.J.S.) developed from
the L.M.S. (1809) and became strictly Anglican by 1815. Joseph
Wolff, a converted German Jew, aroused much fanfare for mission
work in the Near East by his travels and published journals.[196]
L.J.S. work in Palestine under George Dalton, John Nicolayson
and others reported the need of an English church with episcopal
authority which could serve as a base for reaching Jews and
others. Malta, the stepping stone to the Levant, was soon
reached by the L.M.S. (1809), C.M.S. (1815) and the Bible
Society (1817) in this wave of interest.

About 1812, C.M.S. decided to extend its efforts to Christians and Muslims in this area due to a Roman Catholic challenge.[197] Since C.M.S. was founded "to propagate the knowledge
of the Gospel among the Heathen", it was debated whether it
was legitimate to enter lands inhabited by ancient Christians.
It was decided however that world mission included "assisting
in the recovery from their long sleep of the ancient Syrian and
Greek Churches".[198] William Jowett, the first C.M.S. missionary with a university diploma, set out for Malta (1815) to
collect information on the state of religion and the best methods for spreading Christian knowledge in the Eastern Mediterranean. While concerned mainly for the winning of non-Christians, C.M.S. contended that renewed Eastern churches could aid
in this work.

As these Churches shall reflect the clear light of the
Gospel on Mohammedans and Heathens around, they will doubt-
less become efficient instruments of rescuing them from
delusion and death....[199]

Jowett was cautioned to deal with the churches in a conciliatory spirit and not to proselytize. The tours or researches of Jowett helped crystalize C.M.S. policy. As he traveled through Egypt, Syria, Turkey and the Greek Islands, Eastern Patriarchs and clergy gave him warm welcome, gladly supported the idea of new editions of the Bible and appeared apprehensive only that Ottoman authorities might curtail their religious liberty. When Jowett returned to England (1820), he intimated in the C.M.S. Annual Sermon that the Eastern churches were not yet qualified to be evangelists to the Muslim world. In Christian Researches ...1815 to 1820, Jowett notes that Eastern clergy and laity were afflicted with superstition and ignorance and suggests education as an avenue of evangelism. This could begin with Eastern Christians (permitted under Turkish law) and gradually move into Muslim circles. Two important requirements would be to secure religious liberty under the Ottomans for missionaries and converts and for the establishment of some ecclesiastical authority.[200] In Christian Researches...1823 and 1824, Jowett surveys Syria and Palestine. While speaking relatively well of the Jews, he notes that Christians in the East are dominated by "darkness and discord" and "erring human nature". European businessmen and diplomats were viewed as nominal. He reports cordial relations with Fisk and other American missionaries and that Arabic Schools as used by Rome provide one of the best means to stimulate a pure form of Christianity which Muslims will respect.[201] He warns that any mission should not seek to win Eastern Christians to the English nation or Anglican communion.

> How studiously should missionaries aim at impressing on the minds of all around them, that they come, not to make a party, but solely to promote the good of those among whom they exercise their office.[202]

C.M.S. policy was that of cooperation with Eastern churches for their revival and the ultimate winning of the "heathen". There was to be no formation of Anglican congregations in this period (1815-1840). Jowett set up the C.M.S. Arabic Press in Malta (1815). With the help of Faris (a Lebanese), an Arab Greek Orthodox priest, and later C. Schlienz and S. Gobat (Germans), Scriptures and tracts were translated and published in Maltese, Italian, Modern Greek, Arabic and Abyssinian. Limited evangelistic-educational work stretched to Egypt (1816), Abyssinia (1829), Smyrna and Syria (1830), in addition to the Protestant College in Malta. Much of the work was done by German and Swiss missionaries trained at Basel. Limited personnel and political instability permitted little visible success for this policy of cooperation (1815-1840).

An Era of Tensions, 1841-ca. 1890

The establishment of the Anglo-Prussian bishopric (1841) was an attempt to cope with the thorny ecclesiastical and political problems. This is apparent when you consider that there was a bishop before there were church members! It was an episcopal answer to the Near Eastern dilemma. Yet it is questionable if this really cut through the webs of British church-state, Otto-man-Eastern church relationships.

Taking advantage of the unrest created by Mohammad Ali's aggressive moves against Turkey, Britain secured a firman to establish a British Consulate in Jerusalem (1838). Some argued that this would help stabilize local government and hence aid Christian work, biblical explorations of Palestine, and British commerce. Consul Young who had been instructed to assist the Jews in Palestine backed the case for an Anglican bishopric in Jerusalem.[203] This need was highlighted when L.J.S. desired to erect "Christ Church" but found Muslim authorities prohibited constructing new churches and barred foreigners from purchasing property. When the Porte refused a permit, Nicolayson bought the site through an intermediary and laid the foundations (1839). The authorities halted construction, frustrating it until 1849, thus forcing Protestants to clarify their course of action.

King Frederick William IV of Prussia, the Earl of Shaftsbury and others now formulated the concept of a united non-denomina-tional Protestant church in Jerusalem. The proposed Anglo-Prussian bishopric, while opposed by Tractarians Newman, Pusey and Keble, was accepted by British authorities. Literally an Anglican bishopric approved by the Porte and Archbishop of Canterbury, it permitted all desiring (e.g. Germans) to come under the bishop. While the King of Prussia had right to name alternate bishops, the Archbishop retained the sole right of veto. A few details reveal how entangling was this scheme. The first bishop, Michael Solomon Alexander (1841-1845), a convert from Judaism and professor of Hebrew at King's College (London), was given an official ship of the Royal Navy to convey him to the Holy Land. Arriving there, he found himself bishop of a handful of Jewish converts, unrecognized by the local authori-ties, and unprotected by the government that had appointed him.[204] Soon he was in conflict with Consul Young, attacked by high church leaders (as an experiment which failed), the subject of debate in British Parliament (1843), and frustrated by Turk-ish and local authorities. Exasperated, he sought the help of diplomats Rose (Beirut) and Canning (Constantinople) threatening to "go and rouse England" (1843). He continued to face the cold neutrality of Eastern churches fearing proselytism and Lutheran and Anglican clergy guarding their independence from his epis-copal control. All these bewildering barriers must have con-tributed to his early death at forty-five (d. 1845). The only active mission program in these years was among the Jews.

Christ Church gradually gained about 60 members (30 converts
from Judaism, remainder were Europeans). But this could hardly
be considered an impact on the Near East.

The first significant Anglican effort came under Samuel
Gobat, second bishop of Jerusalem (1846-1879), and the reorgan-
ized C.M.S. Mission to Palestine (1851-). Swiss-born, Basel-
trained, C.M.S. missionary Gobat, while a controversial figure
for Anglo-Catholics, was a most dynamic, ecumenical bishop
intent on reaching all peoples of the land.[205] Gobat's strategy was to carry on an expanding literature and educational
program until an evangelical church would spring forth on its
own accord. The land had already been "seeded" with thousands
of Bibles by American workers and the demand for the Word was
growing. Allowing the L.J.S. under the capable leadership of
Nicholayson (d. 1856) to carry on the work among the Jews,
Gobat set out to stimulate and if possible win the Arabic speaking peoples of the land.

Gobat tackled the ecclesiastical issues with a bold determination that gained the anger of some and the appreciation of
others. His policy towards the Orthodox churches was one of
"qualified cooperation". He aimed to stimulate reform within
these churches and not to proselytize, but when these bodies
expelled evangelical members, he was not one to sit back simply
to maintain peaceful church-to-church relations. Evangelical
churches must be formed to sustain this revived form of Arab
Christianity. He sent forth Bible Readers to read the Gospel to
any who would listen, creating a desire among the common people
for the Bible and for education. Schools were started at
Nablus, Nazareth, Jaffa, Ramleh, Bethlehem, Ramallah, etc. which
created strong nuclei of evangelical belief within Eastern
communions. These schools, he felt should present:

> the positive, historical, doctrinal, and moral truths of
> the Word of God, proceeding from a living conviction on the
> part of the teacher and interwoven as much as possible with
> other branches of education....Religion ought to be the salt
> of education.[206]

By 1848, Gobat faced the thorniest problem of his life. Evangelicals were pleading to be admitted to the Anglican Church.
He urged them to remain within their own traditions until the
Greek Patriarch began excommunicating them for their Protestant
leanings (1850). Then conferring with Archbishop Sumner and
Baron Bunsen (Nov. 1850), he established a new policy which was
expressed in a letter to King Frederick.

> ...What am I to do? I have never wished to make converts
> from the old Churches, but only to lead to the Lord and to
> the Knowledge of His truth as many as possible. From hence-
> forth, however, I shall be obliged to receive into our com-

munion such as are excluded for Bible-truth's sake from
other churches; and I trust that in doing so, even though
men should blame me for it, the Lord will grant His blessing
upon the proceeding....[207]

The King would later reply:

> I trust that you will not allow your courage to sink.
> Your idea of building up small national Churches out of
> those communions, in place of compelling the awakened
> Greeks, Syrians, Copts, etc. to become Anglican, Lutheran,
> or Swiss-Reformed, is a glorious, heaven-inspired, and truly
> Catholic one. You _must_ _not_ let it go.[208]

While Gobat remained very cautious about whom he admitted, even
turning some away, his new qualified relation with the Orthodox
churches was offensive to the high church party.[209] Gobat's
aggressive missionary approach to Jews, Muslims and others also
offended certain British diplomats who offered humanitarian
schemes for raising the standard of Jewish life but preferred
to rule out conversion.[210]

The formation of the C.M.S. Palestine Mission (1851) in
answer to Gobat's appeal (1849) greatly strengthened the Anglican arm in the Near East.[211] Henceforth C.M.S. under Henry Venn
would back Gobat's policy of evangelizing Muslims even if this
meant drawing some Eastern Christians into evangelical churches.

> It has appeared to the Society to be a legitimate and
> Christian object to endeavour to raise these lapsed Churches,
> by circulating amongst them the Word of God and Scriptural
> truth, and promoting the education of their children...
> /this/ has an important bearing upon the conversion of the
> Heathen....The Mohammedan population, comprising throughout
> the world a hundred millions of people, present everywhere
> the greatest obstacles to the advance of Christianity amongst
> the Heathen, and are themselves the most manifest objects
> of missionary labours....There is no country so favourable
> for presenting Christian truth to the Turks as those pro-
> vinces of their empire in which the Arabic language is
> spoken, and no locality so advantageous as Syria and Jerus-
> alem.[212]

Increased mission personnel and work resulted in the formation
of Anglican congregations composed of those drawn from Orthodox,
Jewish, Samaritan and Muslim backgrounds at Nazareth, Salt and
Nabulus and outbreaks of Greek Orthodox opposition in each of
these towns (1851-53).[213] The first converts from Islam, e.g.
Muhammad Amin Al-Qasim of Nabulus,[214] the new position of Protestants according to the Firmans (1850), and increased Protestant mission activity following the Crimean War (1854-1857)

brought forth a wave of Muslim hostility and violence. There were threats to exterminate the Christians of Nabulus (1857) and the massacres in Syria (1860). In his Circular Letter (1860), Gobat writes:

> Of the working of the C.M.S. here there is not much to be told. Their chief object, that of converting the Mohammed-ans, is at present unattainable, as all Mohammedans are in a very excited state, and filled with fanatical hatred against the Christians.[215]

Gobat's firm hand won respect from many in the hard years from 1861 to 1871 when short finances, crop failures and Turkish taxation were felt by all. Bishop Gobat served as a spiritual arbitrator acknowledged by Arab, Greek, and European. In addi-tion to benevolent institutions (hospitals and orphanages), Gobat had 25 schools attended by 1,000 Jewish, Protestant, Orth-odox, Samaritan and Muslim children, plus the Diocesan Boarding School at Jerusalem (1872). The church also grew. English and Hebrew Christians worshipped at Christ Church. A German con-gregation and pastor developed its own program (Church of the Redeemer, opened 1898). Some ninety Arab Protestants from Jeru-salem-Bethlehem founded St. Paul's In Jerusalem. Other Arab Protestant congregations formed at Nabulus, Nazareth, and Jaffa. The Arab church-buildings of C.M.S. were not consecrated, hence free of episcopal control. Nevertheless Gobat enjoyed good re-lations with all these groups which he described as "our mixed but united community".[216]

Muslims gained increased attention. Whereas the Mediterran-ean Mission had restricted itself to reviving the Eastern church and the L.J.S. to the Jews, the C.M.S. Palestine Mission gave prime attention to Muslims and other non-Christians. If this involved the reformation of Eastern churches and the secession of some of their members to evangelical churches, then so be it, but C.M.S. definitely was not out to proselytize. Reading the C.M.S. Annual Reports from 1851 onwards, one finds that the pre-fatory statements declare the prime aim is to "enlighten" and "evangelize" Muslims. Gobat left this imprinted upon those serving under him, e.g. J. T. Wolters (d. 1882), T. F. Wolters, R. H. Weakley, Christian Fallscheer, Johannes Zeller (d. 1902), and A. F. Klein (discoverer of the Moabite Stone, d. 1903), so that they never gave up their concern for Muslims. Although the results were limited to scattered individual conversions (who often had to flee for their lives), C.M.S. was not lacking in motivation. The Anglican Conference for Missions to Muslims (London, 1875) called by General Lake and attended by Bishop Gobat, Canon Tristram, Koelle, Zeller, T. F. Wolters, Bellamy, three workers from West Africa, Robert Bruce (Persia), Bishop French and Bateman (India) boosted this neglected work. It was agreed that Islam must be confronted at its center in Palestine and the Arab countries. This prompted the C.M.S. to re-enter

Egypt (1882) and to strengthen its Palestine program. By 1880-
81, Tristram could report:

> Our work in Palestine is a real and vast one. I have
> visited thirty-five stations and outstations; and I say with-
> out hesitation that the C.M.S. is saturating the villages
> with Gospel knowledge; and the result, under God's blessing,
> must one day be vast.[217]

For all its weaknesses, the Anglo-Prussian bishopric as recognized by the Porte and at times supported by British diplomats,
provided a workable approach to the political hurdles of the
nineteenth century. Likewise it provided a regularized means
for dealing with the Orthodox churches on a church-to-church
basis without minimizing evangelical convictions. As long as
this official seat was occupied by one who would welcome and
cooperate with C.M.S. workers, progress could be made towards
the evangelization of Muslims. But this was not long to be.
New conflicts, then consolidation were in sight.

High-low church controversy and Anglican-Lutheran tensions
(1879-1887) began to dominate the scene and caused great damage
to Anglican efforts among Muslims. Raging high-low church battles also hurt the finances of the mission societies. Such
made it almost impossible to find a successor to Gobat (d.
1879). Although Joseph Barclay was appointed bishop, he found
himself helpless to control L.J.S. or C.M.S. or to keep the
German, Arab and English-Hebrew congregations from going their
separate ways.[218] His death (d. 1881) left a vacancy impossible to fill. Germans were neither willing to submit to the
Archbishop of Canterbury's veto nor to the re-ordination of
Lutheran clergy into Anglican orders. While Anglican evangelicals supported the bishopric, high churchmen wanted it abolish-
ed. Archbishop Benson in correspondence with the Germans
finally gained the latter's word to dissolve this arrangement
(1886-87).[219] It marked the end of an era.

An Era of Consolidation, ca. 1890-1910

Archbishop Benson sought to establish a new basis for the
Anglican bishopric in Jerusalem. Bowing to high church pressure, he corresponded with the Greek Orthodox Patriarch who
ruled that this office should no longer be called "Bishop of
Jerusalem". The bishop was to become somewhat the ambassador
of the Church of England to the Orthodox churches, hence dependent on their favor. This meant a discontinuation of receiving
Orthodox members into the Anglican Church (unless mutually
acceptable to both ecclesiastical heads). Second, the bishop
was to have episcopal control primarily over the English congregation and school. When he would later try to extend this
control and "church order" to the L.J.S. and C.M.S. and their
congregations, there were severe repercussions. Third, the

bishop would guide the evangelization of the Jews, Muslims and other non-Christians of the land. When this led to a clash with the mission societies, he would form his own mission centering about St. George's Cathedral. All told it was hardly an improvement.

This unenviable chair was given to George Francis Popham Blyth who served as bishop from 1887 to 1914. Blyth, considered a moderate, appeared to swing to a high church position.[220] Hostility between the bishop and C.M.S. workers soon reached a high pitch. Blyth then proceeded to publish several Charges against the C.M.S. (i.e., purposeful proselytism among Oriental churches, failing to submit to his jurisdiction, etc.) and the C.M.S. replied.[221] Sensational newspaper articles did not help this tense relationship. In a trial of the two parties by Archbishop Benson and four Bishops (1891), Blyth was advised that he did not have direct jurisdiction over the missionary conference; that he should not refuse to confirm those baptized in Eastern churches who "intelligently and conscientiously" sought membership in the Anglican Church; and that C.M.S. was cleared of the charge of aggressive proselytism. It was, however, not the end of the feuding pamphlet war. There can be little doubt that this drained away energy which could well have been turned to Muslims. Only after each agreed to go their separate ways, did the bishop and C.M.S. consolidate their gains.

Bishop Blyth's achievements include the erection of St. George's Cathedral and training center in Jerusalem and a similar complex at Haifa; increased English work among merchants and troops in the Near East; and the start of conversations with the ancient churches of the East. He hoped to bring enlightenment to Eastern churches without internal rupture and to enlighten those non-Christians who attended his schools.[222]

Mission work under the C.M.S. also was advanced. Aided by the voice of General Haig, interest in missions to Muslim Arabs grew. Something of an evangelical Anglican approach to Muslims began to appear--a combination of scholarship, seeking to understand Islam, and an open declaration of the Gospel among Muslims.[223] By 1910, Julius Richter could write.

> The Church Missionary Society is the foremost society in Palestine in mission work among Muhammadans, both in the extent of the work and the thoroughness of its organization.[224]

C.M.S. sustained its program only by costly effort. It took 58 new recruits in fifteen years (1899-1914) to maintain the staff at the same level.[225] Yet it expanded its work wherever the political situation permitted with the greatest gains achieved in educational work. In 1880 it had 31 schools with 1,762 students, and by 1910, the respective figures increased to 54 and 3,000.[226] This continued in spite of a rival and commendable school system backed by the Russian Orthodox.[227] The British-Syrian schools founded by Mrs. James Bowen-Thompson were also in close cooperation with the C.M.S. program.[228] Only by pious doggedness did these schools, often under women teachers, hold out against Turkish interference. They survived, however, to win wide respect and to send numerous future leaders through their Teachers' College (at Kefr Yasif), the Bishop Gobat School and the English College in Jerusalem.

Anglican women workers began to pour into the Near East after 1882 to staff girls' schools, hospitals, orphanages, and home visitation schemes. About that same time, medical work increased with dispensaries and hospitals being erected at Salt, Gaza, Nabulus, Jaffa and throughout the Levant under Dr. Ibrahim Zurub, Rev. Sterling, M.D., and others.[229]C.M.S. workers cooperated with the fine programs of medicine and Christian service rendered by Father Spittler's group, Pastor Ludwig Schneller, the Kaiserswerth Deaconesses, and the Scots at Tiberias and Nazareth.[230] These service programs gave many Muslims their first contact with Protestant Christianity. In 1905, T. F. Wolters reported:

> It is true that the medical missionaries are breaking down the fence of social separation between Muhammedans and Christians and that medical men and nurses have precious opportunities of pressing the claims of Christ upon Moslems of all classes....But all this is as yet strictly confined to medical work....Whether the 'day of visitation' for the Moslem has come or not the hard fact...is that the Moslem is still very far from being accessible to direct effort, except when he is under medical care.[231]

The Anglican Church in Palestine doubled in size between 1879 and 1910 to reach a total of 2,323 members.[232] The majority of these came from Greek background, but a good many were Hebrew Christians and former Muslims (the records discreetly omit names and statistics for the latter often had to flee to British-supervised Egypt to avoid prison or death). Relationships between the bishop, missionaries and congregations fortunately improved from 1900 to 1914. As in North India, a Native Church Council arose (1905), but there were still signs that native pastors longed for more independence.[233] With the first C.M.S. Conference at Hebron (1894), Anglicans found new strength for their labors through broader fellowship and growing intermission cooperation. Palestine remained locked in a religious-political stalemate which called for sacrificial faithfulness. C. T. Wilson expressed it this way:

> As to the work among the Muhammedans, it would seem as if the day of grace were about to break....There is, therefore, no lack of blessing or encouragement. But the red of dawn must not be mistaken for the full light of day. Our exper-

ience can again point to the fact that before the day can
come, many social and political limitations have to be removed which hinder Moslems from making an open confession of
faith. How and when this will come to pass, no one can
say...we are waiting patiently until God reveals His purpose
of grace.[234]

For the more radical action, achievements and preparations of
Anglicans among Muslims, one must turn to the areas of Constantinople, Persia, and Egypt.

An Area of Disappointment: Constantinople, Turkey

Episcopal Missions in Turkey proper were to meet with keen
disappointment. First, an outgoing direct effort to evangelize
Muslims in the capital by C.M.S. workers met sharp reaction
(1858-1877). C.M.S. had been working for many years in Greece
and Turkey at such cities as Syra, Smyrna, Constantinople and
touring Asia Minor and Morea intent upon reviving the Greek Orthodox Church.[235] With the Hatti Humayun (February 18, 1856)
and prospects of equal religious rights for all Ottoman citizens, missionary optimism flourished. Launching a direct effort
for Muslims, C.M.S. called two of her most experienced workers
to Constantinople, Karl G. Pfander and S. W. Koelle; plus two
Turkish scholars, R. H. Weakley and Philip O'Flaherty. Work
began with a mixture of caution and bravo. There was no street
preaching or obtrusive book hawking, but one tactical error was
made: Balance of Truth was sold in the precincts of the Mosque
of St. Sophia.[236] Otherwise Turkish Scriptures were distributed and discussed privately. Results were forthcoming. On
Easter, 1862, C.M.S. baptized their first Turkish convert, an
inquirer from Smyrna who had been twice arrested by the authorities, but liberated by the British Consul. By 1864, there was
a wave of Muslim inquirers and converts. Hamlin (American
Board) estimated that more than 50 Turkish men, women and children were baptized (1857-1877). S.P.G. work under C. G. Curtis
and two Turkish converts trained in Canterbury, Rev. Mahmoud
Effendi and Rev. E. (Effendi Selim) Williams, also made progress. On one occasion, ten adults were baptized and prospects of a convert church seemed hopeful. Then Ottoman authorities, in typical form, struck with force that which they had
left unchecked.[237] On July 17, 1864, the High Porte had twelve
Turkish Christians seized and imprisoned, C.M.S. and S.P.G.
assembly halls closed, the Bibles and books of the Bible Society
confiscated and several missionaries put out of their dwellings.
Other Turkish converts disappeared. The Turkish government
demonstrated that, regardless of its firmans, conversions from
Islam must not be permitted. It sent a memorandum to Sir Henry
Bulwer (a more compliant ambassador than Canning) stating that
it would not tolerate any attempts to assail Islam, to prose-

lyte Muslims, or to distribute controversial works. The C.M.S.
virtually closed down the station as Pfander went to England
where he soon died, Weakley went to Smyrna, and Koelle hung on
for ten years under close police scrutiny. In 1875, Koelle
wrote:

> Proselyting efforts offend both the religious and the
> political susceptibilities of the Mussulmans....An European
> missionary could not visit in Muhammadan houses without rous-
> ing suspicion. No church for the public Christian service of
> Turks would have any chance of being authorized by the gover-
> nment. No missionary school for Muhammadan youths would be
> tolerated.[238]

This violent reaction revealed that Muslim authorities were not
actually ready for religious liberty and that Pfander's approach was inadequate for the situation. Successful communication of the Gospel and the response of faith by Muslims would
require a different spirit on the part of both missionaries and
Turkish rulers. Yet this experience shattered the myth that
Muslims would not be attracted to the Messiah if given freedom
of choice.

Another disappointment in Turkey resulted from Anglican contacts with Eastern churches. These were generally prompted by
high churchmen who felt the C.M.S. was not giving adequate attention to episcopal and other principles they held dear. George
Tomlinson visited Athens and Constantinople with letters from
the Archbishop of Canterbury and the Bishop of London to the
Patriarchs and Bishops of the East (1831). This resulted in
sending George P. Badger, sympathetic to the Oxford movement
and now under S.P.G., to Persia to produce a rival mission there.
His visits and those of William F. Ainsworth drew the affection
of the Nestorian Patriarch away from the American Board.[239] This
sporadic project was resumed for several years in 1876 when E.
L. Cutts and his successor Wahl worked in Kurdistan. The archbishops of Canterbury and York organized the Assyrian Mission
(1886) for the aim of reforming the Nestorian Church from within. This sympathetic approach revived the ancient Syrian
tongue, produced some fine literature, and developed a system
of schools.[240] Unfortunately, they settled at Urumia and
directly competed with the American Board. Their work was virtually wiped out by the inroads of the Russian Orthodox Church
in 1898. This Anglican approach was not unrelated to the high
church-evangelical contest which ensued under bishops Gobat and
Blyth.[241]

The Protestant Episcopal Church, U.S.A. experienced a similar
affair. Their Mission to Constantinople (1839-1850) under
Horatio Southgate (1812-1894) accepted the Anglican high-church
outlook which engaged in conflict with evangelical missionaries
in the area, ostensibly in a defense of the Orthodox churches.

The failure of these ventures and the damage they caused to
mission work drove home several hard lessons. First, while
episcopal churches had elements akin to Eastern churches, they
were still of the reformed Western wing of the church universal.
They would need to settle their issues at home before they could
clarify their relation to the Orthodox churches. Second, these
events highlighted how desirable harmonious relations between
Orthodox and Protestant churches were. It was, in a degree, a
step towards the ecumenical expression of a common life and
mission, e.g. the World Council of Churches. Third, it provided
impetus to Protestants to intensify their study of Eastern
Christianity, lest the same mistakes be repeated.[242] Thus in
Turkey, Anglicans hit head-on the ecclesiastical and environmental factors which made missions to Muslims in the Near East so
difficult.

An Era of Achievement: Persia, 1869-1910

The significant Anglican effort in Persia was begun by Robert
Bruce in 1869. On leave from the Punjab (1858-1868), Bruce
spent a year at Julfa, the Armenian Quarter of Ispahan, to re-
vise Martyn's Persian New Testament. By the time for his departure, some nine Persians asked for instruction in the Christian faith and baptism prompting his decision to stay on. By
gifts from England, Germany and India, he was able to offer food,
medicine and help during the famine of 1871-72. While laying
foundations for a full program before the Mission was adopted
by the C.M.S. (1875), Bruce had no illusion about the difficulty
of the work. He wrote of his efforts:

> I am not yet reaping; I am not yet sowing;
> I can hardly be said to be plowing,
> but I am gathering the stones from the field.[243]

Bruce wisely set for himself modest goals: to continue his
literary work, to establish personal relationships with Muslims,
to enlighten the Armenian community by education, and to make no
apologies when Armenians, Muslims or others sought admission to
the Anglican Church. It was 1879 before C.M.S. sent out a
second missionary, the Rev. E. F. Hoernle, an Edinburgh medical
man. By then, the Julfa congregation had 150 members (56 communicants). Bishop French arrived in 1883 to confirm 67 Armenian Anglicans and to ordain Minatzakan George.[244]

The Persia Mission opened a second station at Baghdad (1882)
hoping to reach Persian Muslim pilgrims traveling to Shiʿah
holy places. It was a difficult field, sustained mainly by determined medical workers, e.g. Henry M. Sutton, A. H. Hume-
Griffith, Stanley and Miss S. E. Hill.[245] Inquirers faced imprisonment for merely desiring Christian instruction. Other
stations at Kerman (1897), Yezd (1898) and Shiraz (1899) drew

patients and inquirers from even Afghanistan and Baluchistan.[246]
The central station at Julfa gradually shifted to the city of
Ispahan. The medical ministrations of Mary Bird, Emmeline
Stuart, Donald Carr and others did much to attract Muslims. The
strong leadership of Henry Carless, W. A. Rice, Edward C. Stuart
(retired bishop of New Zealand), W. St. Clair-Tisdall and C. H.
Stileman made this station the anchor of the Mission.

The breakthrough among Muslims came just before the end of
the century. Scripture sales tripled from 1891 to 1896 as some
mullahs publicly praised the Bible and recommended it be pur-
chased and read. Although the Babi movement had been severely
repressed, great numbers dissatisfied with Islam looked towards
Christianity. Stileman's tour in the districts of Ispahan, Yezd
and Kerman found a wide receptivity to the Gospel (1899). Sunday Services at Julfa found Muslims attending in such large
numbers so as to overflow the gallery reserved for them. Local
persecution made them cautious, however, until political reforms
(1905-1914) such as the formation of a constitution (1906) and
parliament, the settlement of Russian-British differences
(1907), and public demonstrations for reform improved the atmosphere for mission work. After the disruption of World War I,
the process of change in Iran would quicken once more.[247] While
the Anglican mission and church was never as large as the Presbyterian, its staff by 1910 numbered 48 (6 ordained, 8 laymen,
11 wives, and 22 single women). A friendly spirit of cooperation prevailed between the two missions and churches.

The prime methods applied by the Anglicans might be described as apologetic-evangelistic and medical-service. Their
schools never enrolled many more than one thousand, of which
about one-half were Muslim or Parsi. Literature work occupied
a major position in the program. Bruce revised the Persian N.T.,
then prepared a simple catechism, a Bible history Nur-ol-Anvar
(The Light of Lights, 3 vols., 1881-1886), and a Persian edition
of the Prayer Book. Some have suggested that the C.M.S. had a
hand in the Persian version of Apology of Al Kindy (litho-
graphed in India, 1888).

Increased distribution of the Scriptures by Persian workers
showed promise. Benjamin Badal (1844-1919), a Nestorian converted under Perkins and trained for C.M.S. and the Bible
Society by Bruce (1869-1872), became a dynamic colporteur and
personal evangelist reaching to Baghdad and Basrah. Between
1883 and 1919, he travelled the length and breadth of Persia
and even into Baluchistan and Bahrain enduring untold hardships
to sell over 30,000 Bibles. His life and work reads like a
modern version of the Acts of the Apostles and J. C. Wilson
rightly calls him "a radiant witness".[248]

Equally interesting is the development of an Anglican apologetic to Islam. William St. Clair Tisdall settled at Julfa
(1892) to develop the Henry Martyn Press and to publish literature geared especially to win Muslims and nurture Christians.

Tisdall benefited from the experience of Anglican apologists in India and developed an improved program on which W. H. T. Gairdner and others would build. His works deserve special examination.[249] This was only part of a quantity of tracts written, translated or supervised by Tisdall. By 1907, a catalogue by W. A. Rice of Persian Literature for Muslims listed 65 books and tracts in print. Rice himself prepared a handbook for missionaries to Muslims entitled, <u>Crusaders</u> <u>of</u> <u>the</u> <u>Twentieth</u> <u>Century</u> (1910). While this C.M.S. literature is somewhat handicapped by a mild controversial tone, it represents a tremendous advance in both scholarship and Christian spirit over most nineteenth century documents. It was an apologetic companion to be used to introduce and interpret the Gospel to Muslims.

Medical work proved to be one of the most successful means for combatting prejudice and superstition. Hospitals and dispensaries became centers for preaching, visitation, Bible distribution and quiet discussion. Reports indicate that about one half of the converts were first influenced through medical work. Mary Bird (1859-1914), though not a qualified doctor, was the first to demonstrate the drawing power and influence of medical work. Reaching Julfa (1891), she was determined to reach the Muslim women of Persia. Offering medicines and compassion, her fame soon spread beyond her capacity. Braving threats, she opened a clinic in Ispahan to dispense medicine, Gospel, prayer and hymn in equal measure. She so won the hearts of the Muslims and the wrath of jealous mullahs that the British Embassy was given notice (February, 1894) that missionaries were to be permitted to remain only if they "did not proselyte Moslems". Secretary Tisdall replied:

> We came to Persia to obey our Lord's command to preach the Gospel to all, and we are bound to do our duty, while trying not to be unnecessarily aggravating.[250]

Mary Bird prepared the way for the instruction and baptism of the first Jewish woman (1893) and the first Muslim woman and her son (1895). Qualified doctors, nurses and hospitals went on to win the respect of the multitudes for the care rendered in . Christ's name. Effective witness must identify itself with the needs of the people.

> It is not impossible to work as a simple evangelist, but it needs certain qualifications and abilities. Generally speaking, the ordinary missionary must be prepared to use both hands and both feet, and to enter in whatever way seems most expedient into the life of the town.[251]

Achievements and the Anglican Church in Iran

Muslims, Parsis, Bahais, Jews and others responded positively

to the C.M.S. presentation of the Gospel in Persia. Between
1900 and 1907, over 100 adult Muslims had the courage to face
opposition and receive baptism. One must remember that although
Persia was known for its openness, there was no law guaranteeing
religious liberty or prohibiting the "death penalty for apostasy". Yet about one quarter of the church membership of 400
had converted from Islam (1910). The number of inquirers increased and in 1911 alone, C.M.S. baptized over 100 converts
from Islam. This brought to the surface the problem faced in
every land where Islam is attached to the whole scheme of life,
"How to create a fully Christian life and community?" Converts
could not be sent out like sheep into hostile environment nor
should they be endangered by a social-economic dependency on the
mission.[252] A balanced emphasis was attempted which would instruct the Persian church in the distinctive way of life in
Christ, yet not destroy its identification with the customs of
the land. The future was after all with the life and witness of
this young community. The means to erect new church buildings
and to cultivate the groups of believers springing up independently out of their Iranian Muslim descent (e.g. Qalat near
Shiraz) strengthened the work.[253] So did the strong links with
the Presbyterian Church in northern Iran via cooperation in
literature, evangelism and Inter-Church Conferences. Stileman
was consecrated the first Anglican bishop of Persia on July 26,
1912, but even more significant was the day when an Iranian convert from Islam, Hassan Dehqani-Tafti would fill that office and
go forth to interpret the Gospel to his Muslim neighbors.[254]

An Area of Preparation: Egypt, 1882-1910

Anglican work in Egypt ground to a halt with the departure of
Lieder, last member of the "Mediterranean Mission" (1862).
Bishop Gobat analysed the mission's failure thus:

> The missionaries seem to follow almost too strictly the
> plan on which the mission was begun twenty-four years ago --
> to seek friendship of the clergy, especially of the high
> clergy of the Eastern Churches....But this system has failed,
> and I am convinced that it will ever fail with the several
> Eastern Churches, as well as with the Church of Rome. Indi-
> vidual conversion must be the aim, as it is the only means
> of promoting reformation.[255]

A fine independent work was carried on by Mary Louisa Whately,
daughter of the Anglican Archbishop of Dublin, who came to Egypt
for her health in 1856. Grieved to find no school for Muslim
girls, she gained the help of a Syrian matron, and Mansoor and
Joseph Shakoor, Protestants trained under the American Mission
in Syria. The Boys' School at times had 300 in attendance and
the Girls' School about 200, including many Muslims. Distribu-

tion of Scriptures, home visitation, coffee-house evangelism and
light medical work by these four workers made this a visionary
venture. Miss Whately wrote:

> The school opened doors which might never have been opened
> for the gospel without it, for Egyptians are shy of receiving
> total strangers without some reason, and having their girls
> under our care was of course the best reason. That curtain
> which in Muhammedan families of the better class hangs
> before the entrances to the women's apartments is not so
> easily raised for foreign visitors as might be supposed;
> even ladies do not gain admission into many of them, We are
> let in, however at once,...256

Before her death (1899), Miss Whately suggested that C.M.S. take
charge of her work, but when no action was taken, it was transferred to the American Mission (1901).

Advocates of missions to Muslims agreed that it was a basic
error to neglect Egypt, the religious-intellectual center of the
Arab world. Al-Azhar mosque-university alone enrolled over ten
thousand students. Since the completion of the Suez Canal,
Egypt had become a commercial crossroads and the home of a budding Arab nationalism. British occupation (1882) and the death
of General Gordon at Kartoum (1885) would also draw worldwide
attention. These cinched the re-establishment of a C.M.S. Mission to Egypt (1882) and the intensification of preparations for
reaching Muslims. F. A. Klein of Palestine arrived to make
translations into Arabic and to distribute literature. F. J.
Harpur made Old Cairo a base for mobile medical evangelism to
the Sinaitic Peninsula, Hodeida, Suakim, the Delta and along the
Nile.257 Women missionaries established girls' schools at Old
Cairo, Cairo and Helwan, a training course for Bible-women, and
a home visitation scheme. W. W. Cash and F. F. Adeney (Mission
secretary, 1893) initiated a limited evangelistic program, but
very few Muslims were baptized before 1895. Many British missionaries and Coptic Christians were perturbed by the policies
of British rulers. It appeared to them that British "neutrality" was in actuality a catering to a Muslim majority. Their
charges were not groundless. Copts were kept from high offices
they once held, not allowed representation on provincial councils; and were taxed to support schools in which Islam was
taught. As Friday was made the legal holiday, they were obliged
to work on Sunday. Missionaries found themselves restricted
from the Sudan and the Memorial Fund for Gordon College, given
by many who expected the Christian ideals of Gordon to be observed, was used for a college in which the Bible was excluded
and the Quran included. Many British administrators had little
sympathy for either missions or the Christians of the land.258

With the arrival of Douglas Thorton and William H. Temple
Gairdner, C.M.S. launched into a specialized work among Muslims.

W. W. Cash, Rennie MacInnes (Mission Secretary, 1903; Anglican
Bishop in Jerusalem, 1914), R. F. McNeile and others helped in
this vital work.[259] The vigor, initiative, and openheartedness
of Thornton was cut short by his early death (1907). Gairdner
was to become an acknowledged authority on Arabic and Islam.
His report on the Edinburgh Conference and his counsel at Jerusalem (1928) were given serious consideration. His life's work
and numerous writings will be examined in the next chapter.
Thornton and Gairdner sought to convey the Christian message to
the educated Muslims and students of Cairo. Gairdner wrote:

> 'Educated Mohammedans' is a term embracing very divergent
> types. These divergences, however, reduce themselves to two
> main classes, between which there is a great gulf fixed:
> those who have had a traditional Islamic education ending
> with the Azhar University, and those who have had a Western
> education with the Government Secondary School or Higher
> College. In dress the same divergence is for the most part
> marked; the former (the 'Sheikh' class) wearing orthodox
> Oriental costume, and the latter (the 'Effendi' class) wear-
> ing Western dress with 'tarboosh' (or fez).[260]

Thornton and Gairdner explored a variety of methods and approaches. First, open public lectures in English or Arabic on
topics of general interest, with a Christian theme interwoven,
attracted good audiences. In a society learning to give open
expression to its opinions, the discussions that followed were
at times even stormy. These well-advertized lectures often led
to personal interviews, Bible groups and instruction for inquirers. Second, a tour of evangelistic meetings by Thornton
in Upper Egypt gained the cooperation of Coptic priests and
bishops. Thornton, Gairdner and MacInnes were on very good
terms with the Coptic Orthodox Church and sought to stimulate
it by meetings, Bible instruction, literature, and assistance
to seminary students. Also on tour, W. Wilson Cash reached out
to Muslims in the villages.[261] Third, a bookstore served the
double purpose of attracting both sheikh and effendi classes to
Christian literature and to personal conferences with this dynamic duet. Fourth, Gairdner turned to the production of apologetical literature. In addition to tracts and booklets, the
Arabic paper, Orient and Occident (1905-) disseminated Christian ideas and induced intellectual ferment among several
thousand readers. Literature secretary Constance Padwick would
continue this good work. Fifth, Thornton and Gairdner demonstrated a willingness to combine experimentation and dedication.
Accepting invitations to speak to student groups, they maintained the spirit of openness and the sense of conviction that
attracts students seeking answers to life's basic questions.
Sixth, they cooperated in many ecumenical ventures such as the
training center for Protestant missionaries to Muslims and the

Nile Mission Press founded by Annie Van Sommer. Miss Van Sommer
also founded the mission quarterly, <u>Blessed</u> <u>be</u> <u>Egypt</u> (Isa. 19:
25) and the "Fellowship of Faith for Moslems" under the leader-
ship of S. M. Zwemer and Bishop Stileman. There was ample
evidence of catholic spirit among Christians in Egypt.

These efforts were not without results. Despite handicaps
imposed by British rulers, converts came forward. Mahmud, the
son of a sheikh in southern Palestine and graduate of al-Azhar,
began Christian instruction (Oct. 1905) and soon confessed his
faith in Christ before Lord Cromer and high Egyptian officials
(Feb. 1906). Sheikh Skandar Abd-al-Masih, the first Muslim
convert baptized by Thornton, read the prayers at the graveside
of the latter in 1907. A number of Muslims from Asia Minor
and Syria came to declare their Christian faith in the relative
security of Egypt. Some efforts to induce converts to return
to Islam succeeded, but most stood fast and served with strong
purpose. While the mission delayed in forming congregations,
so as not to unnecessarily draw from the Coptic Church, it did
form a "Church Committee" (1908) with a goal "to preach the
Gospel of Christ among those in Egypt who know Him not". The
several hundred strong "Episcopal Church in Egypt" (officially
founded, 1925) would later come under Bishop MacInnes of Jerusalem. C.M.S. work is not to be measured simply in numbers.
Cooperating with the Presbyterians and Samuel Zwemer it helped
prepare the way for the development of a maturer ecumenical
Protestant approach to Muslims. The first international Conference of Missionaries to Muslims in Cairo (April 4-9, 1906)
was a turning point in this development. Latourette would write
of the period: "In the age-old struggle against Islam results
which could be measured in statistics might be small. Yet momentum was being gathered."[262] This momentum and maturation
will be examined more closely in the next chapter.

PIONEER REFORMED MISSIONS TO MUSLIMS IN ARABIA, 1885-1910

Background

The set of circumstances faced by Protestant missions to the
Arabian Peninsula were quite different from that in lands pre-
viously described. Since the church once inhabiting sectors
of Arabia had ceased to exist, there was no question of ecclesiastical relations. Missionaries were thus to concentrate on
environmental problems and the evangelization of Muslims. The
peninsula, homeland of the Arab, had earned the respect of
many. A forbidding land to the outsider, it was fortified by
surrounding seas of water and sand.[263] For a millennium, this
veil protected the sanctuaries of Islam and the Tribal Arab.
. Even Turkish-Egyptian encroachment, however, did not prevent
the peninsula's radical religious puritanism (the Wahhabis) and
growing prestige (Ibn Saud, 1901). Few were the Europeans who

dared tread upon its sacred and inhospitable soil before the end
of the nineteenth century.[264] Even missionaries were at the
mercy of Muslim populaces which classed them as _kafirs_, infidels. The British presence had been established at Aden
(1839) and in the Persian/Arabian Gulf by agreements with the
sheikhs of Bahrain, Kuwait, and the Sultan of Muscat,but Brit-
i-sh residences were far from a guarantee of security.[265]
Missionaries in most cases purposely avoided seeking protection
under the flag lest it alienate them from the people of the
land.[266]

Up to 1880, Arabia and its coastal waters had known only a
few Roman Catholic workers at Jidda and Aden (1840-); the ex-
cursions of Sabat (later assistant of Martyn), Anthony Graves,
Joseph Wolff, Henry A. Stern; and the colporteurs sent by John
Wilson of Bombay and the Bible Societies.[267] About this time,
F. T. Haig, a dedicated Christian British officer, began to
make extensive journeys around the coasts of Arabia and to publish pleas for missions to Arabs.[268] His request to the C.M.S.
(1885) was met in part by the Scottish Mission to Aden. Haig's
written and verbal counsel proved helpful to the Cantine-Zwemer
team as well.

> There is no difficulty about preaching the Gospel in
> Arabia if men can be found to face the consequences. The
> real difficulty would be the protection of the converts.
> Most probably they would be exposed to violence and death.
> The infant church might be a martyr church at first like
> that of Uganda but that would not prevent the spread of the
> the truth in its ultimate triumph.[268]

The courage, death and prophetic words of Bishop Thomas Valpy
French also rallied Cantine and Zwemer to their calling.

> I understand that you also are intending to visit Muscat
> and the Persian Gulf coast of Arabia. Do not let the fact
> that I am preceding you change your plans. I am an old man,
> and it may be God's will that I can only view the promised
> land, while it is for you to enter in.[270]

Buried in a small cove near Muscat, French left a challenge
captured by A. E. Moule in poem.

> Where Muscat fronts the Orient sun
> 'Twixt heaving sea and rock steep,
> His work of mercy scarce begun,
> A saintly soul has fallen asleep:
> Who comes to lift the Cross instead?
> Who takes the standard from the dead?[271]

It remains now to see how those in the Scottish Mission and the

Arabian Mission accepted this pioneer work for Muslims in Arabia.

Ion Keith Falconer and the Scottish Mission to Aden, 1885-1910

Aden, strategic British link with India, was considered by
some a gate to Arabia's interior.[272] Just north of the harbor
and "Crater" lay Sheikh Othman, a town on the caravan route. It
was here that Ion Grant Neville Keith-Falconer (1856-1887) would
plant a mission.[273] Educated at Harrow (1869-1873) and Cambridge (Trinity College), he had earned honor in mathematics,
theology, Greek and Hebrew. Under Professor Wright of Cambridge, he intensified his study of Semitic languages, including
Arabic. In 1881-82, he traveled to Leipzig and Egypt to acquire
more Arabic before being forced home by fever. His concern for
mission was evidenced by his work for the Moody visit to Cambridge (1875), the Barnwell Mission, and the Tower Hamlets
Mission (East London). Here in the midst of humanity, he observed that man's temporal and spiritual needs were interwoven
and both needed attention if a whole man was to emerge in
Christ. Correspondence with General Gordon (1881) discloses
Keith-Falconer's consideration of the fields of Syria and Istanbul.[274] Meanwhile he continued to develop his linguistic skills.
His critical emendation and translation of the old Syriac version of Kalilah and Dimnah, Fable of Bidpai (published 1885)
reveals careful scholarship.[275] In 1883, he also participated
in the Congress of Orientalists at Leiden. Yet he felt he was
leading a double life: an examiner, tutor and lecturer at Cambridge and as secretary of Tower Hamlets Mission. What he
sought, however, was opportunity to unite his love for scholarship and mission service. The biographer of this missionary-
orientalist expressed it thus:

> ...still it seemed as if some scheme ought to present
> itself in which Christian zeal and linguistic power might
> work hand in hand or rather, shall I say, in which his intel-
> lectual attainments and his learning might be to him some-
> thing more than a mere parallel interest, existing side by
> side with, but having no connection with, work for Christ.[276]

After reading George Smith's Life of John Wilson of Bombay (also
a skilled linguist), seeing his intimate friend C. T. Studd
depart as a missionary to China, and conversing with Haig,
Keith-Falconer turned his thoughts towards Aden.[277] In spite of
the hazard of climate, here was an international port and crossroads for caravans with reasonable political stability.
Keith-Falconer surveyed Aden from October 28, 1885 to March
6, 1886. He found the Roman Catholic Mission and the Resident
British Chaplain doing no effective work for the Arabs. The
Arabs soon respected him as one who knew the Quran and literary
Arabic (nahwi). During this time, he decided that he must take

the risk and set up a mission at Sheikh Othman. His thoughts
on mission are reflected in his correspondence. First, mission
must be the witness extended from the church and not just an
individual. While financing this station from his own personal
funds, he offered it in the name of the Free Church of Scotland.
Second, the station must be identified with the Arabs. Sheikh
Othman fit this qualification better than Steamer Point. Third,
the work must minister to the visible needs of the people.
Hence he called for an educational-medical program to win the
hearts and minds of the people; a physician, especially a surgeon to reach the people and create new opportunities; and a
school to give students a regular base of knowledge and the
ability to read the Arabic Bible and Christian books. Fourth,
a straight forward presentation of the Gospel was necessary to
remove from the Arab mind misconceptions derived from "the evil
example set by so many Europeans who live in or pass through
Aden" and the Roman Catholics whom some Arabs classed with
Hindus for their use of icons and pictures. Keith-Falconer reflected that such a presentation of Isa and the Injil conveyed
with prudence and self-denial might be "welcomed as a message
from God."[278] Back in Scotland before the General Assembly of
the Free Church (May 26, 1886), he spoke of the Muslim Haji who
urged "If you want the people to walk in your way, then set up
schools". Keith-Falconer's confidence in the power of God's
Word was confirmed by this same Haji who refused a copy of St.
John because its message (esp. "If thou knewest the gift of
God, and who it is that saith to thee, Give me to drink, thou
wouldest have asked of Him, and He would have given thee living
water.") made him fearful. "That verse," said the Muslim,
"makes my heart tremble, lest I be made to follow in the way of
the Messiah."[279] Here in a nutshell was the problem of Arabia.
The social-political environment did not permit Muslims of such
sensitive perception to respond positively to the Gospel of
Christ.

    Before returning to Aden, Keith-Falconer began research for
his lecture, "Pilgrimage to Mecca";[280] spoke to churches in
Glasgow and Edinburgh; and enlisted Stewart Cowen, a qualified
surgeon of Glasgow to serve with him. Keith-Falconer's messages
indicate a sympathetic approach which considered that Islam was
to the Arabs as the Torah to the Jews, a schoolmaster to bring
them to Christ.[281] Reaching Aden in December, 1886, this one
who could speak fluent Arabic was soon gathering small groups
for Bible reading and visiting homes, coffee shops and outside
villages. Then suddenly the well-laid plans were disrupted by
malarial fever (Feb. 10th) and death (May 11, 1887).

    The Scottish Mission, bereft of her founder, continued by
the sheer dedication of a few determined workers. Of the thirteen students at New College who offered themselves for this
work, only William R. W. Gardner, a promising Semitic scholar,
was ordained for Aden.[282] Gardner conducted a school until

1904 when this responsibility was taken over by the Danish Mission. Educational work, an integral part of Keith-Falconer's
vision was recovered only in 1920 under James Robson and W.
Idris Jones. Medical work centering about the hospital became
the mainstay of the program under Alexander Paterson, John C.
Young (served 1892-1926), Alexander MacRae (served 1906-1917),
P. W. R. Petrie and others. Young, as both physician and evangelist in the fullest sense, became a beloved household name
among the people. In the hard soil and climate of Aden, the
mission has sought to weave Christian teaching into all its
activities. Its presence has demonstrated no ambition to
worldly power but a quiet effort to testify to the spirit and
love of Christ. One worker stated their aim thus:

> It is quite simply, to preach Christ to Arabia by word
> and deed and life, and by every means within our power. It
> is not an easy task or one likely to produce quick returns...
> The real hope of winning Arabia lies in the creation of an
> indigenous native church.[283]

The church has emerged and by faith seeks to demonstrate what it
is to be in Christ. In 1902, a sheikh was baptized; in 1908,
six more were admitted to the church; and others followed. One
of these, Ahmed Sa'eed Affara, baptized at the age of 19,
studied medicine in Edinburgh, and returned to witness as a
dedicated Christian physician in his home country.[284] For him,
it was the attraction of Christ and the true liberty found in
Him that prompted faith and obedience. Thus the minute Church
of South Arabia (officially formed January 8, 1961) maintains
its precarious existence patiently, prayerfully witnessing of
God's love for the people of Arabia. Who is to say the vision
and sacrifice of Keith-Falconer was in vain?[285]
What lessons exist here? Just this! Although the church in
mission to Muslims does not find instant success and solution
to environmental and religious problems, she is still called to
witness even if that be by her presence as the suffering
servant.

The Arabian Mission in Eastern Arabia and the Gulf, 1889-1910

The Arabian Mission, by far the most extensive endeavor in
Arabia, was founded largely by two men, James Cantine and
Samuel H. Zwemer, both who were privileged to celebrate its
Golden Jubilee.[286] The plan for the mission originated in the
heart of John G. Lansing, professor of Arabic and Hebrew at New
Brunswick Theological Seminary (Reformed Church in America),
the oldest seminary in the United States. Reared in Damascus
and Egypt, he shared his father's affection for the Arab
peoples who lacked the Good News of God in Christ.[287] Three
students, Samuel M. Zwemer, James Cantine and Philip T. Phelps

joined with him to draft their first plan (1889).[288] When the
Board of Foreign Missions, already heavily indebted, could offer
no support, the Arabian Mission went independent. Later the Reformed Church in America officially adopted this mission (1894)
which in reality was being supplied by its finances and personnel. The mission's aim was to reach the heartlands of Islam,
namely Arabia. Abraham's prayer and its fulfillment became
their motto: "Oh that Ishmael might live before Thee" (Gen.
17:18).

Cantine and Zwemer benefited by study of Arabic and Islam
under Presbyterian auspices in Beirut (1889-90) and the help of
H. H. Jessup, C. Van Dyck, James Dennis and others. Taking with
them a Syrian Muslim convert, Kamil Abdul Messiah, they surveyed the Arabian coast, e.g. Jidda, Hodeida, Aden, Makallah
and Bahrain before selecting Basrah (August, 1891) as a base
from which to "occupy the interior of Arabia". Basrah, a
thriving port of 60,000 inhabitants, sixty miles up the Shatt-
al-Arab (merged Tigris-Euphrates rivers) was a strategic crossroads. While Turkish and local authorities prohibited public
preaching, they did not halt the sales of Scriptures, private
conversation and tours. A major blow was the sudden death of
Kamil (1892), whose teaching and speaking was too effective to
be tolerated.[289] Assisted by two Eastern Christians, Salome
Anton and Elias Gergis, Zwemer and Cantine began a scheme of
colportage at Basrah and along the twin rivers to Baghdad.
After faltering starts with Charles E. Riggs and James T.
Wyckoff, Dr. H. R. Worrall (1895-) put medical work for Muslims on a permanent basis.[290] The strategic islands of Bahrain,
once the home of a Christian bishopric, were chosen for the
second station.[291] Purposely missing his ship, Samuel Zwemer
took up residence with a stock of Bibles (1892) and soon rented
a shop from which he entered the lively interchange of conversation and adventure that so marked his life. Taking the name
Dhaif Allah (guest of God), he was at times labelled Dhaif
Iblis (guest of the devil) but years later local citizens
called him, Fatih al-Bahrain, the pioneer of progress in the
Islands. His binding friendship with Arabs, his readiness to
serve the need of any and to converse of Christ with all attracted wide fame.[292] His adventurous tours by river steamer
and foot to Baghdad (1892); to the Arabian interior Province of
Hassa (city of Hofhoof, 1893); and to Sanaa, Yemen (1891 and
1894) gave him both the widest knowledge of Arabia of any
European in his day and the opportunity to distribute many
Scriptures.[293] Peter J. Zwemer, Samuel's brother, opened the
third station at Muscat, Oman (1893), a land of variety and
possibility.[294] While beginning with a school for freed African slaves, Peter Zwemer and James Cantine hoped this gateway
for caravans going into Arabia's interior would become an
entrance for missionaries.[295]

By the sacrifice of life, labour and resources in Christ's

name, the Mission rooted itself in these Arab lands and
hearts.[296] Fortunately the Mission was not lacking in qualified
recruits so that by 1909, there were 26 regular missionaries.
The Arabian Mission maintained an ecumenical flavour by drawing
its personnel from five denominations and several nationalities.
So strengthened the Mission could establish new stations at
Amarah on the Tigris River (1895), Nasirya on the Euphrates
(1897) and at Kuwait (1910).[297] The first modern hospital in
Eastern Arabia was dedicated at Bahrain in 1903, followed by
others at Basrah, Kuwait and Oman. Small schools, chapels or
house-churches also appeared. Syrian and Armenian Christians
from Baghdad, Mosul, Mardin and Turkey arrived (esp. 1900-1910)
to help as evangelists, colporteurs and hospital workers.
Friendly relations with the sheikhs of the Eastern Amirates and
King Ibn Sa'ud facilitated the purchase of properties and the
extension of tours. Even during the various Arab uprisings,
the Armenian and Assyrian massacres, and World War I, the Arabian Mission was permitted to continue its work. It had gained
the respect and appreciation of the Arab people prior to the
discovery of petroleum and its accompanying material progress.
This identification with the Arab people -- the diffusion of
biblical truth, and the demonstration of Christian love via
medicine and education -- lent itself to improved Christian-
Muslim relationships. Nevertheless, converts from Islam still
faced physical violence, economic boycott, social ostracism and
disinheritance by both family and government. The twentieth
century found many Arab lands still longing for basic human
rights.

An Examination of the Efforts of the Arabian Mission

    How was a Protestant mission to implement its program in
strictly Muslim lands? Faced by this question, the Arabian
Mission adapted traditional means to her environment. Litera-
ture-evangelism became one of the boldest direct efforts to
reach Muslims. Cantine and Zwemer refused to accept defeat.
During the first decade, bookshops, colportage, and personal
evangelism reached surprisingly large numbers. By 1912, over
8,000 Scriptures and several thousand religious books were sold
annually. This was remarkable when one considers that over
80% of these sales were to Muslims.[298] Samuel Zwemer was concerned that the volume and quality of Christian literature for
Muslims might increase. Thus he helped found the American
Christian Literature Society for Moslems which stimulated publication in Beirut, Cairo and India. The workers of the Arabian Mission lived under a compulsion to reach inland. Touring
received considerable attention as pioneer medical-evangelist
teams accepted the invitation of King Ibn Sa'ud. Paul Harrison
and others visited Riaydh (1917 and 1919); L. P. Dame also
reached into the interior on extensive tours (1921-22, 1923 and

1932); and Harold Storm toured the Hadramaut (1935). These ventures were a unique type of work in the annals of missions.[299]
While "to occupy the interior" was interpreted geographically
in the early days of the Mission, no evangelist would quarrel
with the reinterpretation that it implied bringing the Gospel to
bear upon the "interior" of Islam, upon the heart and mind of
all Muslims. This was to remain the awesome task of the twentieth century.

Medical work gained an approval in the Mission's program as a
legitimate means for contact and communication. Samuel Zwemer
appreciated this means more after an inquirer came to him
wrapped in a pseudo-bandage. The inquirer explained it convinced his Muslim neighbors that he had a legitimate reason for
talking with the Christian. This only highlighted the conviction that the Gospel is best conveyed through normal channels
of human activity. Storm wrote:

> Medical work has so far been the most helpful approach.
> It has disarmed opposition and paved the way for other forms
> of work. Through hospital, friendships are made which inf-
> luence regions far beyond the geographical boundaries of the
> mission....[300]

By 1914, three well equipped hospitals and a number of dispensaries were treating nearly 24,000 new cases and a total patient
load nearly double that.[301] Medical workers were not only highly qualified but most articulate Christians.[302] Two serious
technical and theological questions would become more acute, however, as the twentieth century progressed. How does one control
the snowballing effect that specialization, new techniques, new
public consciousness of health-needs produces in terms of staff,
facilities and finances? Most medical missionaries gradually
saw the need to limit the program to opening new doors, supporting mass movements, reaching resistant classes, and alleviating
the most needy cases of suffering. Yet who was to draw this
impossible line? As national governments began their own public
health programs, circumstances changed very radically (e.g.
the welfare state of Kuwait). This meant missionaries must concentrate on making a witness within the medical field or opt
out of the medical field altogether and select other channels
of witness. The training centers for Christian medical workers
in Edinburgh, London, Battle Creek (Michigan), Tübingen, Assiut,
Vellore, and the Medical Missionary Associations in India and
the Near East helped tackle these tremendous problems.[303] More
serious perhaps was the question of how to relate medical and
evangelistic functions? The doctor at times appears torn between the demands of the sheer quantity of physical work and the
call to witness. Some contended that the deed in itself was
adequate. But this point of view came under attack by those who
held that man's dilemma and health are really understood only in

the Word of God in Christ.[304]   Paul Harrison asserted clearly
that the doctor must also be an evangelist.

> It will require a good deal of knowledge of the language
> and it will require organization of the whole work with this
> end in view, but there is surely nothing unreasonable in
> this. The medical missionary came out here for this precise
> purpose. It will make severe demands on the doctor's physi-
> cal strength, but this is a matter of the very greatest
> importance, and a little medical work might even be sacri-
> ficed if necessary.[305]

Harrison tried to avoid both the pitfalls of institutionalization and a liberal theology which exalted experience at the
expense of the Word. His winning personality was a genuine
asset in communicating the Gospel to Muslim Arabs. While treating up to 125 patients per day and performing 15 to 20 operations a week in his years in Kuwait, Bahrain and Muscat-Mutrah,
he managed to convey something of the spirit and Word of Christ
to each. This life-long student of the Bible expressed his
approach thus:

> The approach, on the basis of simple, unaffected, demo-
> cratic equality is ninety percent of missionary method.
> Associating with the Arabs in this way you may easily meet
> them and have them meet you as warm friends, and many details
> take care of themselves....The missionary has no weapons to
> force an entrance except prayer and friendly service. He is
> not able, nor does he wish, to enter a place until he is
> invited. So the method of procedure has been to work out
> from a base hospital and school and evangelistic station on
> the coast and gradually so to commend ourselves to the people
> that our presence inland is desired. This has been to gain
> the good will of the people by steady, thorough medical work,
> by educational institutions and by a quiet uncompromising
> evangelistic campaign....Even the evangelistic missionary is
> eventually made welcome because of his obvious good inten-
> tions and practical benevolence....This is a task of years.
> In accomplishing it our most powerful instrument is the ex-
> ample of the Christian family life lived in full view of the
> people....Next...the most effective means of getting acquain-
> ted is the work of the mission hospitals....If the doctor can
> add to his professional skill an unfailing human sympathy and
> personal interest...he becomes almost irresistible....He can
> present and explain Christ's teachings to every one of his
> hospital patients. He can associate on terms of friendly
> equality even with the fanatical Akhwan (the Wahhabis). In
> twelve years' experience I have never met a patient with
> whom it was impossible to do this sort of personal work.[306]

This graduate of John Hopkins University and intimate friend of

Samuel Zwemer certainly represents one of the finest personable, Christ-centered approaches to the Muslim. Harrison was persuaded that the dynamic Word and spirit of Christ was able to transform every human relationship.

With the exception of the schools in Basrah which developed under John Van Ess, educational work appeared to be the weakest link in the Mission's program. Schools in Muscat and Bahrain remained at primary level. E. E. Calverly's school for young men in Kuwait made only a brief impact before being closed due to short finances.[307] In 1910, Van Ess gained the Sultan's Irade permitting mission schools for boys and girls including permission to teach Bible courses in all grades. After the customary delays, the primary, grammar and high schools at Basrah began drawing students from all ranks of society into a student-body that was more than 50% Muslim.[308] Respected by Arab governments, this excellent school became a model for numerous Arab educators. Van Ess understood that his task was not simply the conveyance of a set of ideals, truths, or ethics, but the leading of students into an encounter, a relationship, a life of faith with God in Christ.

> Now, of discipleship the crux is not knowledge but obedience, surrender. To be a disciple implies a conflict of wills, and when I have led the Arab to surrender his will to that of Christ, I have made him a disciple. Does this method work? In my experience it is the only method that does work. It eliminates from the Arab's mind the idea I am in conflict with him. It represents a constructive purpose rather than a destructive process....The missionary should capitalize (on) that in which government and secular schools, by their own confession, cannot compete with them, namely, the personal influence which he can exert, the lofty motives which inspire him and the development of high character....Christ must be at the very heart of the curriculum. I personally would not care to spend five minutes of my life in the East teaching in a school where Christ is not made such. I should leave the task to any philanthropic agency which cares to treat the sympton rather than the disease....A Christian missionary is contributing nothing whatsoever to the alleviation of the world's woe unless he brings to bear that which he possesses in unique measure.[309]

It is regretted that the Reformed Church in America did not apply these principles more widely. Unfortunately the shortage of men and means during World War I and the depression of the 1930s led to a neglect of the schools in Kuwait, Bahrain and Oman. Perhaps the fault was partly due to the American mentality which at the time gave such predominance to medical and philanthropic work with their visible statistics. Van Ess was assured, however, that once a maturer social-political climate developed in the Near East, his work would bear wider fruits.

Roughly two thousand boys and men have met Christ face to
face for from two to eight years each, every school day of
the year. Many of these now hold posts of responsibility
and trust in state and society. I know definitely of only a
dozen who have gone wrong. The sons of many of them are now
in school profiting by their fathers' newer outlook and by
the home environment of at least friendly attitude toward the
Gospel, and with the promise of an arrival of the time when
the convert's enemies shall not be those of his own household.[310]

The young church emerging in Eastern Arabia and the Gulf
faced some of the most severe environmental problems in the
world. No inquirer escaped some form of persecution. Often
those baptized disappeared, presumably to their death. While
neither numbers nor social circumstances warranted the official
organization of the church, it was there! The small congregations that eventually formed in Muscat and Mutrah were comprised
of nearly all converts from Islam. The congregations in Bahrain, Kuwait and Basrah included Arab converts, Assyrian and
Armenian Christians, plus Indian and European expatriate Christians. Following the discovery of petroleum and World War II,
these lands experienced phenomenal population and technological
growth. Kuwait town for example became an international city,
a full participant in the modern world. Faced with this challenge the church was called to demonstrate how the power of
Christ unites and reconciles men of many tongues, races and
nationalities. The united Church of Christ in Kuwait with its
tri-congregational pattern presented a multi-lingual Protestant
witness to this modern Arab city. It also welcomed and cooperated with late-arriving Orthodox and Roman Catholic groups.
By reconciling and uniting men of diverse backgrounds, it could
testify as to what God is effecting in Christ as well as provide worship and fellowship for all who would come. This ecumenical effort was not to hinder the development of a Presbytery
of Arab National Congregations in Eastern Arabia and the forming
of bonds with national evangelical churches in Egypt, Syria-
Lebanon and Iran. The Arabian Mission retained the spirit which
initiated such ecumenical ventures as the Conferences at Cairo
(1906) and Lucknow (1911).[311]
The Arabian Mission's vigorous encounter with a rigorous
Muslim environment produced several noteworthy lessons. The
Christian worker among Muslims must acknowledge certain fundamentals: (1) the hostile environment of many Near Eastern lands
is only slowly being modified. Only as a pluralistic society
evolves, will individuals be truly free to choose their faith,
Christian or otherwise.[312] Hence any effort among Muslim
peoples calls for a sustained, long-range program which identi-

fies itself with the people and land. Such a program calls for
the support of the corporate on-going church of Christ. Free-
lance sporadic endeavors are of little value. (2) The Christian
witness needs the best available training both in his given profession and the linguistic skills of the area. (3) But more
than qualifications and training, the witness needs the enthusiasm and friendly disposition towards others that comes from a
passionate devotion to Christ. Storm counsels thus:

> ...we must be quite certain that we are called to preach
> Christ. The desire to make men better followers of Mohammed
> can have no place in our programme. We seek to make men
> followers of Christ. That will make us unpopular and some-
> times put us in real danger, and maybe the honour roll of the
> Church will be filled with martyrs from Arabia; but 'it is
> enough for the disciple that he be as his Master and the
> servant of his Lord.'
> The subtle and semi-conscious effort to escape from under
> this burden of unpopularity, which is part of the reproach of
> the Cross, manifests itself in two directions both of which
> are to be avoided if we want God's blessing on our work and
> to be guided by His Word....[313]

The church must avoid both the pitfalls of simply being another
humanitarian agency and of escaping into pious isolationism if
she is to fulfill her mission to her Muslim neighbors. Certain
prerequisites are necessary. First, churches, Near East, West
and East, must experience renewed vitality and vision before the
Evangel shall be fully effected in Muslim Lands. Second, the
church must be sure of her message of the transcendent God who
has revealed Himself through Christ in time and space. The
serious Muslim is a deeply religious man who will not be satisfied by ethical or idealistic superficialities or the religio-
philosophical jargon so popular in contemporary Europe and
America. Only a dynamic presentation of the Gospel, of the
transcendent God who redeems and rules in the incarnate, crucified and victoriously risen Christ, will suffice. Theology is
at the heart of Christian-Muslim discussion. Third, the church
in mission is compelled to take seriously the world as it is.
This of necessity means, man in his religions (e.g. Islam,
etc.).[314] Still learning many difficult lessons, the Arabian
Mission persists in the hope that the Gospel and church of
Christ might be established in the midst of the Arab peoples.
This striving towards a maturer Reformed approach will be examined in the next chapter under the work of Samuel M. Zwemer.

DEVELOPMENTS IN THE NEAR EAST, 1800-1910: A RETROSPECT

Distinctive ecclesiastical and environmental factors plus an
overwhelming Muslim majority had tremendous influence on the
development of Protestant missions in the Near East (1800-1910).

The situation differed radically from that in India where there
was a relatively stable government, the absence of any ancient
church (except for Malabar), and the ameliorating effect of a
heterodox society. In India workers could concentrate on
methods and the resultant young church, but in the Near East
missionaries immediately had to define their relationships with
existing churches, sometimes hostile governments, and a population holding to a post-Christian monotheistic faith. It is not
surprising that this should have produced considerable tensions.
Yet even these struggles were productive.

New ecclesiastical relationships eventually brought mutual
blessing. No one acquainted with the religious history of the
Near East can help but be amazed at the spiritual renaissance of
the nineteenth century. Christians who had been restricted over
the centuries suddenly exhibited new vitality, becoming once
more the dynamic ingredient of the environment. The resulting
division and variety did not necessarily symbolize weakness.
Here was new wine seeking new bottles. The very fact that Christians were willing to leave protected circles of family, ancient
millet and perhaps profession for an unrecognized, marked-for-
persecution evangelical faith indicates unleashed conviction and
energy. These struggles helped churches, East and West, to
better comprehend the meaning of holy, catholic, apostolic
Church. "Holiness" (the church's relationship to God and the
resulting quality of life), missionaries rightly perceived, was
a pre-requisite to the evangelization of Muslims. Concerned
that the ancient churches might be revived to a holy life they
soon comprehended this applied equally to their own lives and
evangelical churches. The adjective catholic (the relationship
of Christians as individuals and as corporate communities) highlighted the failings of all! Orthodox and Roman churches had
made their traditions and hierarchies a law unto themselves. In
their pursuit of souls, pietistic Protestants had often ignored
the Christ-life as community. High-churchmen professed their
affinity with Eastern churches while remaining alienated from
their evangelical colleagues. Evangelicals frequently allowed
their terminology to isolate them into cliques apart from other
brethren in Christ. Nowhere more than in the Near East did the
ecumenical movement appear so urgent. Churches were also rudely
reawakened to the meaning of apostolic (the church's relation to
the world, surrounding peoples and religions). While the modern
missionary movement had started in small societies, it was to
lead all churches to seriously reconsider their relation to
particular cultures, governments and religions. The principle
of separation of church and state cast modern missions in a
light differing from its medieval predecessors.[315] Protestant
missionaries became the vocal patrons of indigenous interests
and protesters against colonial exploitation. They stimulated
the rise of nationalism and cultural renaissance as well as indigenous Christianity. Such national Christians exerted an

influence upon the Muslim community much greater than would be
indicated simply by statistics.[316] Multitudes who would not
consider the idea of conversion, perhaps vociferously resisting
it, unconsciously adopted Christian ideals and ethics. Prejudices and ignorance were modified by Christian education, medicine and service. Even those hardened by century old antagon-
isms gained a new compassionate understanding of humanity under
the radiating influence of Jesus. A historian standing next to
the nineteenth century mission program for Muslims might well
have been a bit despondent.[317] But from the broader view of
history, it was certainly a milestone of advancement for the
Christian faith in the lands of the Near East.[318]

Many questions however remained unanswered. Perhaps it was
only in the twentieth century that Protestant missions were
equipped to tackle the thorny issues of Muslim evangelization.
In the early years, most missions to the Near East were preoccupied with the Eastern churches. This was followed by preliminary probings in direct Muslim work (1850-1870s) and finally
in the development of substantial programs for Muslims (1880-
1910). By 1910 both Anglican and Reformed forces had the experience and personnel to realistically face these religious and
environmental obstacles. This maturer confrontation would be
supported by the new ecumenical concern for Muslims which rose
above denomination and nationality. The time was ripe for
Protestants to begin a reformulation of their theology of
mission.[319] The grindstone of the Near East forced workers to
ask hard questions. First, what is the Word given by God in
Christ and how is it to be communicated? Second, what is the
nature of this world and the church's relation to it? This
involved not only understanding the creation, the man who is the
object of God's gracious mission, but also man's prevailing religions. Third, What is the church and how is her life related
to her mission (Jn. 17:21)? W. H. T. Gairdner and Samuel M.
Zwemer were two representative figures who attempted to answer
these questions with regard to Islam. In the next chapter,
these maturing Anglican and Reformed approaches to Muslims will
be examined.

4

Maturing Anglican and Reformed Approaches Before 1938: W.H.T. Gairdner and S.M. Zwemer

FACTORS STIMULATING THE REFORMULATION OF A THEOLOGY OF MISSION

The accumulative experience and maturing approaches of Anglican and Reformed missions to Muslims are faithfully represented in the figures of W. H. T. Gairdner and Samuel M. Zwemer. In this chapter, it will be seen how they give expression to the best of nineteenth century developments and yet speak to the new challenges of the twentieth century. Living in a time when powerful forces were impinging upon the evangelical theological basis and program of missions, these men were convinced that mission was nothing less than the outgoing gracious love of God in Christ destined for the benefit of all peoples of the earth. This central motivation would continue to energize the missionary movement in the crises of the twentieth century. Certain factors would be calling for a reformulation of the theology of mission. While consciously avoiding the ascription of too much credit to these factors, they do deserve brief acknowledgement.

First, it is observed that a resurgence of ancient religions and the rise of nationalism or combinations of the two were occurring in most mission fields. If this was true in India, it was also apparent in Turkey, Syria, Egypt and Persia. The stimuli of western education, politics and technology, and Christian missions prompted these indigenous cultures to experience a renaissance. By 1890 these lands contained a new educated elite, often the product of Christian educators. Although the majority were not Christian, they actively worked for social reform, religious purification, and the modernization of society. Some of this promotion of national culture and ancient religion could be characterized as anti-foreign, possibly anti-Christian.

Yet the bulk of students and educated classes were critically
receptive to new ideas and hence a genuine challenge to missionary evangelists. Many missionaries, themselves strongly influenced by Christian student movements in Britain or America,
were keen that this opportunity not be missed.

Next, the rise of the liberal schools of theology following
such figures as F. Schleiermacher (1768-1834), David F. Strauss
(1808-1874), and Albrecht Ritschl (1822-1889) certainly posed a
threat to the very premises of evangelical theology. While this
shaking of the foundations was a healthy corrective to Protestant scholasticism, it still left many questions unanswered.
Evangelicals were convinced that appeals to experience, ethical
values, and rational ideals were not adequate substitutes for
the biblical record of God's revelation and the necessary metaphysical description of faith. But to make their case convincing in the twentieth century, they would need to recast their
theology, especially with regard to mission and the Word.[1]

Closely coupled to this was a third factor, the growth of
historical and literary criticism. The famous Tübingen school
of radical New Testament criticism under Baur had widespread
influence by mid-century. While Strauss' Life of Jesus (1835)
would suggest the historical unreliability of the Gospel accounts, Ritschl accepted the New Testament as a valid starting
point for examining God's self-attestation in history. Harnack
and Herrmann carried on his work, while the Bible's historicity
became a battleground for many. The concepts of biblical criticism were greeted with various responses in Britain where Professor Robertson Smith was dismissed from his chair in Aberdeen
(1881) and Congregationalist A. M. Fairbairn argued that he
could affirm evangelical truth by this historical method. It is
only necessary to point out here that this prodded evangelicals
to develop an apologetic that spoke both to critics in the West
and to non-Christians on the mission field.[2]

Fourthly, increased interest in non-western religions and the
application of the principles of historical criticism produced
what Max Miller titled the scientific study of religion. In
the Origin of Species (1859) and The Descent of Man (1871),
Charles Darwin had rocked the world with his ideas of development, evolution or progress. By 1900 his principles were being
applied to all branches of science, religion and ethics by
Herbert Spencer (1820-1903), T. H. Huxley (1825-1895), H. G.
Wells and others. Religion was viewed as a common human experience or function which could be categorized according to origin
and stages of development. Under these new surgical tools,
Christian and non-Christian scriptures differed only in degree,
not in kind. The idea of direct revelation from God was ruled
out or reinterpreted by many scholars. By undercutting the idea
of the uniqueness of the Word of God, Christianity was seen on
a par with other religions or as only the advanced product of
the same human aspirations. Scholars found parallels and

materials for comparative religion in all religions. The leading exponent of this new science, Friedrich Max Müller (1823-
1900), attacked the missionary idea of Christianity and proposed
instead the sympathetic encouragement of adherents of other religions that they might attain new heights. His solution was
the peaceful co-existence of all religions until the true
religion of the future would provide the fulfillment of all the
religions of the past.[3] While this point of view was partially
accepted by M. Monier-Williams and F. N. Farquhar, most evangelicals felt it was a challenge to battle.[4] The benefits of this
challenge are to be observed in the scholarly examination of
other religions by figures much as W. H. T. Gairdner, S. M.
Zwemer, and Duncan B. Macdonald.

Finally to be taken into account are the movements among
Christian students and the missionary conferences which nurtured
the phenomenon soon known as the ecumenical movement. This new
spirit, catholic Christianity, gained its first full demonstration at Edinburgh, 1910. Beginning with evangelical principles,
this movement became a creative discussion chamber responding
to the above forces and formulating new apologetical and other
missionary approaches. Since both Zwemer and Gairdner actively
participated in these student movements, mission conferences
and ecumenical enterprises, careful attention must be paid to
such developments. For here too was a force transcending existing denominational lines, requiring re-evaluation of traditional
statements, subjecting all to review and revision.[5]

It was soon apparent that nineteenth century traditional
theology and ecclesiastical practice would not satisfy the questions of the twentieth century situation. Heavy dependence upon
rational evidences and orthodox doctrines was not only under
attack from many quarters but no longer doing justice to the
uniqueness of Christ, the sui generis of Christianity. Evangelicals who had been content to share in the spirit and activity
of evangelization in the eighteenth and nineteenth centuries,
now faced the unavoidable task of restating the truths of Christianity. They were forced to delve deep into their own denominational beliefs and the Bible itself to rediscover three essential interplaying areas of Christian truth. First, they must
redefine the essence of Christianity. For many this meant re-
discovering the Christian message, the Word given by God in
Christ. Second, they had to come to a new understanding of a
changing world. They had to grapple with both biblical and
contemporary ideas of man and his religions and the relation of
Christianity to world religions and cultures. Third, this
meant rethinking the whole task of the church in mission in
light of changing circumstance. This would be in short, a reformulation of the evangelical theology of mission, a reshaping
which began at about the turn of the century and reached a
climax in the crisis in theology and mission at Tambaram, 1938.
Up to the turn of the century the evangelical premises for mis-

sion had been widely accepted. This had permitted workers in
India to concentrate on mission methods and the emerging church.
In the more complicated Near Eastern scene, they directed their
energies towards the iron triangle of environmental barriers,
ecclesiastical relations and the Muslim populace. But at this
transitional point in history, radical rethinking of the theological basis for mission was in order. One of the interesting
ways to observe this process in action is to examine the life
and thought of key participants. Temple Gairdner and Samuel
Zwemer provide vivid representation of maturing Anglican and
Reformed approaches with reference to Islam in this era of
change. Careful examination of their activity and thought will
disclose that they preserve the best of nineteenth century
effort and yet portray the positive elements of the twentieth
century evangelical understanding of evangelism, the relation
of Christianity to Islam, and the church as object and agent of
God's solution.

WILLIAM HENRY TEMPLE GAIRDNER (1873-1928):
AN ANGLICAN CONTRIBUTION

The Life and Work of Gairdner, A Biographical Sketch

The best of evangelical Anglican concern for the Muslim world
came to reside in the person of Temple Gairdner. In him, one
finds reflected the personal compassion of Henry Martyn; the
apologetics flowing from Pfander to Lefroy, the concern for the
indigenous church evidenced by French and Clark; the scholarly
literary labours of Tisdall; and more. His life's activities
highlight his right to serve as a representative of Anglican
effort among Muslims. Like the majority of his predecessors,
he was nurtured in the evangelical sector of the Church of
England and student circles. Other factors warranting attention
are: his choice of the strategic intellectual center of Islam
(Cairo) and his experimental work in evangelism and apologetic
literature; his participation in the ecumenical movement; his
research in Islam; and his combination of sympathetic scholarship and realistic churchmanship which strove towards the goal
of a reconciled and reconciling community of faith, a church
which would witness to the work of God in Christ amidst the
world of Islam. These elements stand out in an examination of
his life.

The Formative Years

Born in Ardrossan, Ayrshire, Scotland in 1873, William Henry
Temple Gairdner inherited two traditions.[6] He gained a breadth
of thought and a love of music from his father, William Gairdner, F.R.C.S., professor of medicine at Glasgow University, who
though reared a Unitarian had chosen to be associated with the

Church of Scotland. His father had a humanist bent, admired
Charles Darwin, and was proud of his broad ethical-religious
outlook. But it was the influence of his English mother that
appears most dominant in Temple's life. Their correspondence
reveals that she conveyed to him a love for the evangelical sector of the Anglican Church. After schooling at St. Ninians,
Moffat (1882), she arranged for his traditional English education at Rossall, undoubtedly encouraged his confirmation in the
Church of England while at school and his early communions at
Glasgow, and may have influenced the choice of a classical education at Trinity College, Oxford (1892).

While at Oxford, Gairdner found his own religious identity.
This discovery was made not among those continuing the traditions of the Oxford movement, but among the growing number of
evangelical students on the move in that city. Whereas at
Cambridge evangelical groups had gained early acceptance, at
Oxford they were not so well received. Their "hallelujahs" and
determined witness to the new life in Christ were considered
crude by Anglo-Catholics. Yet by 1892 these ardent evangelicals
had formed the Oxford Inter-Collegiate Christian Union (abbre-
viated O.I.C.C.U.) which became part of the British College
Christian Union (B.C.C.U., later renamed the Student Christian
Movement, S.C.M.), which in turn became linked to the World
Student Christian Federation (W.S.C.F.). The Oxford members
were indeed, pauperes Christi selling all in their concern to
win the souls of others. For a time, Gairdner remained on the
fringe of this circle with their uncalculating devotion, separateness from the world, and zealous evangelism. Sharing the
friendship of J. H. Oldham (future secretary of I.M.C.) at
Trinity, Gairdner became known as one who always talked for
truth, not for victory. Once he remarked, "Man, the only thing
in the world worth living for is to find out the will of God and
do it."[7]

It was following the fatal illness of his brother, Hugh, that
Gairdner underwent a spiritual crisis resulting in a deepened
faith. At the Congress of Unions at Oxford (March, 1893) he
experienced the overwhelming "embrace of Christ", and responded
in faith. He became a member of one of the Bible reading
unions and then gradually was drawn into the O.I.C.C.U. His
shyness gave way to enthusiastic witness and a "passionate
desire for service" as he experienced the meaning of his life-
long text, "Behold, I make all things new".[8] At the Keswick
Conference (July, 1893) of the newly formed S.V.M.U., he declared himself ready to serve as a missionary if God so willed
and established his friendship with Douglas M. Thornton of Cambridge. Complementing each other, these two produced a team
effort in missionary ideals until the latter's death, fifteen
years hence.

Although now marked as an O.I.C.C.U. man, Gairdner retained
his affection for the weekly communion and worship in the

college chapels. His evangelistic zeal, love for the church
and serious consideration of biblical criticism defied a party
label. He was one who saw the need to fuse evangelistic zeal
for the peoples of the earth with loyalty to the historic catholic heritage. Resisting the shibboleths of the ultra-evangel-
ical and Anglo-Catholic sectors of the church, Gairdner sought
to reconcil and relate his energizing experiences to the full
life within the church. Years later his appreciation for this
movement which set potential leaders on fire remained.

> On the whole, men who join these more definite and out-
> and-out bodies usually get somewhere, whereas so many
> attaches of broader societies get nowhere in particular. You
> see, these latter try hard to secure a very wide synthesis
> which is more naturally the fruit of maturity and experience.
> ...Societies like the O.I.C.C.U. make straight for fundamen-
> tal evangelical experimental Christianity, and make sure of
> that. Of course, if this crystalizes and nothing further
> happens, you are apt to get later on in life the hard, stiff,
> dogmatic shell-backs....But if only development goes on, then
> the warm evangelicalism of their origin expands, modifies,
> mellows, and the result is--power with maturity. The syn-
> thesis that such a man attempts later on will very likely
> have more in it than any precocious one.[9]

Like Thornton, Gairdner served as a traveling secretary of
the British College Christian Union, 1897-1899. Under the
friendly personalities of John R. Mott, Robert E. Speer and
others, Gairdner felt empowered for action. Even the oft mis-
understood watchword, "The evangelization of the world in this
generation" adopted at the Liverpool Conference (1896) gave a
healthy direction to student energies. Gairdner later wrote:

> The adopting of this watchword was not, of course, a
> prophecy that the world would be evangelized in the present
> generation but simply an affirmation that it might be and
> should be so evangelized (since every generation of Christ-
> ians is responsible for evangelizing the world of that gener-
> ation); and a self-dedication to a life consonant with that
> faith and that aspiration.[10]

Thornton and Gairdner with the help of Archbishop Frederick
Temple and others attempted three significant objectives in
these years: to confront the whole church, not just students,
with the call to mission; to inaugurate missionary and Bible
study groups for students and churches;[11] and to project the
missionary ideal into the theological colleges of both free and
established churches so that the remaining aloofness of the
clergy might be dissolved.[12] Both Thornton and Gairdner, however, felt drawn to Cairo, the intellectual capital of the

Muslim world. After Arabic study and ordination (St. Paul's, October, 1898), Thornton went there. Until his own ordination (St. Paul's, October, 1899) and departure for Cairo, Gairdner continued theological studies, and Arabic work under Professor Margoliouth.

The Years of Orientation (1899-1902) and Dynamic Teamwork (1902-1908)

Gairdner was accepted by C.M.S. (November 16, 1897) and assigned to work especially "among students and others of the educated classes of Moslems". Upon his departure he wrote these prophetic words to his father:

> Cairo is my destination for the present and perhaps for good. Though I am ready to go further, I have an idea that I shall not go. I believe that Cairo is the important centre: good work done there would certainly be felt in the Sudan. Cairo is the centre of Islam, par excellence. It is to Islam that I go--not to any particular phase of it. My ideal is to become a master of Arabic (an awful aim); and perhaps to help in creating a Christian literature in that tongue; and thus to get at the heart of the problem of Islam. Well, that might easily keep me at Cairo till the end of my days.[13]

These first years were enlivened by friendship with the Thorntons, Arabic study, ordination as priest by Bishop Blyth at Alexandria (1901), marriage at Nazareth to Margaret Mitchell, the daughter of a Glasgow physician, and the arrival of the first children. The stabilizing homelife of the Gairdners was filled with music. His collection of Syrian and Egyptian tunes, eventually numbering some 300, became a channel for worship and fellowship throughout his life. With his keen insight into the modes of Eastern music, he wanted the church to have the best of two worlds, the select music of Europe and the fine native airs of the East.[14] But life in Cairo was not all song. Observing how converts from Islam were tempted by threat and bribe to recant their faith in Christ, he was fully convinced of the demonic forces obstructing the kingdom of God.

> Some of the surface causes I know, but the psychological history of the whole matter I cannot even imagine. It is Satanic. I never felt as I have this week the fact of the hideous existence of a kingdom of darkness and of evil. It has come down on us like night.[15]

It was more than culture shock that he experienced as he saw the church as the suffering servant which must sacrifice self in the work of reconciliation. While this cost of discipleship

frightened off many potential disciples, it was a shaking that
would allow the eternal to stand.[16]

As they entered fully into their labors, Gairdner and Thornton became an inseparable team. A colleague, Maurice Richmond
recalled:

> Their close working friendship recalls historic combina-
> tions of men whose twin genius united extensive and inten-
> sive, prophecy and scholarship, the world of action and the
> world of ideas. We think of Luther and Melanchthon, of John
> and Charles Wesley....Thornton was the dauntless Cambridge
> evangelist, the man who 'thought in continents and arch-
> bishops' with prescient vision of opening years before they
> became visible to others.[17]

Gairdner by his intensive scholarly ability could give the prophetic strategy of Thornton the rational clothing necessary for
acceptance by others. This interpreter later wrote of his comrade:

> An ideal, a vision, was, then absolutely necessary to him.
> He could not work without it. And it is this that explains
> the largeness of his views and the magnitude of his schemes.
> ...His genius was, then, primarily synthetic rather than
> analytic, intuitive rather than logical.[18]

These two had a sense of the universality of Christ and of self-
abandonment which helped them to identify with Egyptians. Constance Padwick captures the tempo of their teamwork.

> And now Thornton envisaged a great Christian apologetic,
> saw the types of men to be met, saw the lines of action,
> secured premises, advertised fiercely, collected an audience,
> dreamed of a literature, bore down objections, toiled at
> estimates, wrote appeals, and Gairdner behind him all the
> time was thinking out the detailed content of that apolo-
> getic, pursuing an individual soul with prayer, mastering
> the niceties of Arabic style and courteous phrase, and above
> all interpreting his friend and his friend's plans to those
> who were annoyed or scared at the rush and sweep of their
> unceasing evolution.[19]

They laid the foundations for a dynamic ministry among Copts
and Muslims which would make Cairo an evangelistic center. At
once they spoke of: evangelistic services, Bible classes,
training classes for Arab Christian workers, literature for
Muslims and schools.[20] Their evangelistic efforts to reach
educated Muslims were often experimental.[21] In 1904, they
acquired Beit Arabi Pasha, the former dwelling of the revolutionary, a choice location in central Cairo near the colleges,

a prime area for reaching both sheikh and effendi classes. Here
they lived, sold books, led study groups and worshipped. The
discussions following the English-Arabic Bible courses were described as more than animated! The center which attracted
Muslims of high education and intelligence exhibited the drawing
power of these two men. Extensive use of handbills, the distribution of tracts to holiday makers, and weekend preaching services enlarged the audience. Such persistence, Thornton felt
must bear fruit.

> In this way Moslems are unconsciously absorbing principles
> that are in reality Christian, and often most un-Moslem, the
> result of which must be made manifest sooner or later.[22]

Gairdner believed this witness provided its own justification.

> If the efforts to evangelize Islam had not resulted in a
> single conversion, they would have been worth while; for they
> represented Christianity as a religion that is not afraid, a
> religion with a message of love and good will evinced in
> deeds of love and good will.[23]

Beit Arabi Pasha was more than a coffee-center, however, for
here sheikhs and effendis brought heart-searching questions. For
those entering the community of Christ, it was a center of
prayerful communion with God. The narrative of convert Sheikh
Bulus Fawzi (formerly Mahmud), the son of a Muslim leader and
editor in Jerusalem, conveys the meaning of cross bearing.[24]
Gairdner's evangelism was far too complex to be caricatured.
His preaching and personal work reveals one who was both a
patient shepherd and a stern disciplinarian.

> He was far too respectful to the human soul to bludgeon
> men, though his rapier thrusts at conscience could be keen
> enough....For whatever phrases men might miss from his
> preaching, none with ears could miss Christ and Him crucified.
> ...He could never be a demagogue, but the deeper a man's
> spiritual capacity the more did he find in Gairdner's preach-
> ing, which came from the depths of his own life and called to
> the deeps in other men.[25]

Yet he was under no illusions as to how long the work must continue.

> Do not think that moral transformation is quickly reached.
> I feel that if we can set up a new standard of integrity, of
> truth, in these men, that alone is a work of even national
> importance....The Eastern mind moves theologically much more
> quickly than it does ethically. Only gradually does the in-
> finitely high standard of Christian holiness make itself

felt, and if it is not seen in those Christians with whom the
catechumen has to deal, it will not be deeply felt at all.
And as the new ideals grapple with the old habits, through
what travail, what struggles, what anguish, what tears is the
Kingdom of God won![26]

The pen of Gairdner was soon an instrument of Christian apologetics. This was a natural channel for former student secretaries and appealed likewise to Egypt's intelligentsia. While
Thornton, the pragmatic experimenter, attempted to determine
what was appropriate, Gairdner tackled the writing and polishing
of such succinct articles and tracts. Leaflets were printed by
the thousands advertizing their lectures, answering routine Muslim objections, and simply presenting the Christian message.
While unashamedly writing in a apologetic vein, Gairdner aimed
to humanize his writings (hence the later use of drama, music,
poetry) so as to win men and not defeat antagonists. Travelling
to England (1904), the pair convinced the C.M.S. Committee to
approve their literary campaign for Christ in Cairo. They
received backing for their Anglo-Arabic magazine, Orient and
Occident which first appeared January 5th, 1905. Soon 3,000
subscribers, a large circulation for the time, became their
parishioners. Thornton describes their effort to present a
balanced diet.

> The scope of the magazine as we wish it to be and as it
> has already in some degree proved to be, is somewhat as
> follows: First and foremost, the promotion of the knowledge
> of the Word of God by means of short self-contained extracts,
> such as an Old Testament story or New Testament parable or
> miracle, or act of Christ, together with a short and simple
> study of the passage, adapted in thought and language to all
> readers....Secondly, articles of a definitely religious stamp,
> such as meditations on fundamental truths of the Christian
> faith, dialogues, apologetic of the faith....Thirdly,
> articles of a more general moral interest, such as such ac-
> counts of men who, anywhere and at any time have benefited
> their generation and stood for righteousness. Fourthly,
> articles of social interest, as the conditions of the time,
> national progress, the education and reverence for women....
> This section includes reports of addresses and debates held
> weekly at our house.[27]

Gairdner's considerable output reveals a writer probing to the
basic fundamentals of faith and life, ever seeking to be appealing and fair in his discussions.[28]

Gairdner and Thornton now became more involved with the
churches. As both friends and critics of the "ingrown" Coptic
Orthodox Church, they worked more directly with the laity than
earlier C.M.S. efforts, encouraging biblical exposition and

revived societies within the church. Thornton conducted three
tours in upper Egypt shortly before his death, holding rallies
in Coptic Churches which successfully drew large assemblies of
Copts, evangelicals and Muslims. The prevailing spirit of cooperation with Presbyterians is seen in that C.M.S. provided
hospitality for the Cairo Conference of Missionaries to Muslims
(1906) at Beit Arabi Pasha. This conference brought together 62
missionaries of 29 societies under the leadership of Samuel
Zwemer to stimulate not only the spirit of fellowship, but
greater concern for Islam, the formation of a central Literature
Committee, a specialized training program for missionaries to
Muslims in Cairo, and an educational scheme for qualified converts from Islam. This prompted the Pan-Anglican Conference
(1908) to add the topic of Islam to its revised agenda. Gairdner contended that the "Muslim Problem" (Unitarian Deism) should
force the whole church to rework her theology in terms both experiential and comprehensible for the Arab.[29] Although the
Anglican Church in Egypt was small in this decade, the number of
converts from Islam was increasing rapidly. Perhaps these years
of hard work, close friendship and family life were the happiest
in Gairdner's life. Although the death of Thornton (September 8,
1907) severely tested Gardner, he emerged as a scholar and
leader in his own right.

As Missionary Spokesman and Scholar-at-Large, 1908-1911

In the summer of 1908, Gairdner spoke at the Pan-Anglican
Congress held in England. He believed that the great denials of
Islam could produce a Christian apologetics giving an enriched
presentation of Christ and his kingdom.

> Christendom, as represented by some writers, scarcely
> realizes its heritage, scarcely realizes that Christ has once
> and for all differentiated between physical and moral power.
> Who can tell what moral results shall accrue; both in East
> and West, when we shall have allowed the Cross to dominate
> our philosophy and theology as well as our devotional life!
> Who shall gauge the debt we may yet have to confess if that
> great antagonist prove finally to have compelled us to ex-
> plore unknown depths of the riches of the revelation of the
> Triune God.[30]

Two of Gairdner's most significant books: D. M. Thornton and
The Reproach of Islam were speedily written in this summer. The
latter, developing the above theme, was widely read and appeared
in a revised edition as The Rebuke of Islam (1920). Returning
to Egypt in a time when both Muslims and Copts were equally
astir with the surging nationalism, he was soon lecturing to
audiences of students and others as large as one thousand. Meanwhile there were devotional meetings for Christian workers, the

Orient and Occident, inquirers' calls and classes, services in
Coptic and Anglican churches, inter-mission rallies and the revision of the hymnal. Significant was his participation in a
Cairo Debating Society (sometimes called the Anarchists), a
group of educated young men tackling the burning issues of the
hour. One of Gairdner's papers, "Queer Roads to Optimism in
Nineteenth and Twentieth-Century Thought" deals with H. G.
Wells' idea of social evolution. Gairdner rejected this way of
salvation on the ground that any philosophy which neglects the
fact of sin can hardly alleviate man's situation. His own reconciliation of scientific methodology and the Christian view
of the world received more conclusive treatment in his booklet,
"Science and Faith in Whom?" After five years of personal
struggle with this subject, Gairdner takes a provocative line of
thought which in some aspects (e.g. awareness of the burden of
evil) is an anticipation of the neo-evangelical development in
post war Europe. Certainly it is in contrast to the optimistic
views of man, society, progress, fulfillment so widespread at
the time.[31]

Commissioned to attend the World Missionary Conference in
Edinburgh (June 13-23, 1910) to prepare a popular report for the
church worldwide, Gairdner found himself amidst friends such as
Oldham and Zwemer. At Iona, he produced a reflective summary,
Edinburgh, 1910 which was published in September. The debate
that was beginning to broil at Edinburgh, especially between
such figures as J. N. Farquhar and the D. S. Cairns-A. G. Hogg
team under Commission IV, must have made a deep impression on
Gairdner. This will be given fuller treatment under the development of his own apologetic approach.

At Canon MacInnes' urging, C.M.S. granted Gairdner a year's
leave of absence to advance his study of Islamic and Arabic
literature. Gairdner first spent three months in Potsdam,
Germany examining the varied German literature on Islamic topics.
His contacts with two Turkish sheikhs there yielded a pamphlet,
The Way of a Mohammedan Mystic. Next he went to Hartford Theological Seminary (America) to study Arabic phonetics and Islamic
theology in consultation with Professor Duncan B. Macdonald. The
third part of his tour took him again to Europe (Leiden, Rotter-
dam, Hamburg, Berlin) where his acquaintances with Snouck Hurgronje and Ignaz Goldziher yielded rich rewards. They were
appreciative of his exactness and he of the unassuming nature of
these famour scholars. Then it was back to Aleppo, Cairo and
the crush of field work.[32]

The Mechanics of Missions (1911-1919)

Gairdner's hope to serve as a research missionary was partially eclipsed as he was caught up in three spheres of endeavor:
the Mission secretariat, the teaching of Arabic and Islamics,
and the affectionate shepherding of the Anglican church in

Egypt. The strength of his contribution would be that it was
made amidst, rather than aside from, his service in mission.
The vortex of mission life demanded his full energies. Already
in 1912, he suggested that R. McNeile might become the scholar
par excellence inasmuch as the young church required his own
time.

> Take the work of classes for catechumens and converts,
> and the whole work in general of building up what God has
> already given us. It is an enormously important, necessary,
> exacting, time-expensive branch of work. It is morally our
> first duty. It is, moreover, work that no novice can do....
> It is work, in short, that every week and every day falls on
> me....With all my heart I could have gone in for the research
> work, and I feel that I might have done some decent work in
> it. But I think it is not to be.[33]

Gairdner discovered in 1914 that reactionary Muslims had organized a heavily financed program for luring converts back to
Islam. In this critical hour only the application of discipline
saved the infant church. A pamphlet, The Anglican and Coptic
Communions in Egypt (1914) spells out Gairdner's plan for aiding
the latter, a policy officially addopted by bishops McInnes and
Gwynne. Research was not completely effaced as Gairdner concentrated his study on Al-Ghazali and produced his first critical
article in Der Islam (1914). Later at the suggestion of Professor Margoliouth of Oxford, Gairdner published his translation
of Mishkāt al-Anwār (A Niche for Lights, 1923).
      Stimulated by the Conferences of Cairo (1906) and Edinburgh
(1990), Zwemer and Gairdner jointly proceeded to develop the
Cairo Study Center (1912) for giving specialized training to
missionaries. This cooperative project of five missions later
became the School of Oriental Studies (1920) in the American
University of Cairo. Teaching here Gairdner earned respect for
a brilliant mind, a mastery of Arabic, a keen interpretation of
Islamic literature and a sense of the poetic. Arthur Jeffery,
a colleague at the school remarked:

> ...while reading the text with the class he would throw in
> a wealth of illustration. He excelled in discovering felici-
> tious translations. I remember reading Quran with him, and
> the joy it was to have him start up in excitement and bring
> forth a new rendering of some obscure phrase where Rodwell
> and Co. had made a hopeless mess. He was the one first-class
> mind we had.[34]

While not loving the technical work, Gairdner felt it a vital
task to be done. This talented figure revolutionized the teaching of Arabic by tackling the spoken colloquial before the literary classical form, setting forth his approach in two conver-

sation-grammars and a handbook on phonetics. H. A. R. Gibb, then a lecturer at the London School of Oriental Studies and later Professor of Arabic at Oxford and Harvard, wrote:

> The first edition of his "Conversation Grammar" of Egyptian Colloquial Arabic (1917) would have satisfied the ambition of most men, but it was like Gairdner to be dissatisfied until a second edition (1926), completely revised and rewritten perfected the work.[35]

His Phonetics of Arabic in use after 1912 was published only in 1925. Contact with Professor Louis Massignon of the College de France brought great joy to Gairdner as he observed that devotion to Christ lifted scholarship to new heights.[36]

One task which Gairdner did not relish and for which he was ill-suited was that of Mission secretary (1914-1919). While he was a scholar of note and a fine spiritual leader, he was not a natural administrator geared to the transactions and personnel problems of an organization. Yet as senior worker he bore this office until relieved, even producing a Scheme for the Policy of the Mission (1916), a sorely needed revision of the program.[37]

The Church and Her Mission, 1918-1928

Gairdner's experiments in the medium of drama reveal how he adapted poetic and musical talent to apologetic service.[38] While attending the Oberammergau Passion Play, he saw new possibilities. "The play is the self-expression of a Christian community representing in action that which is the subject of all their thinking and living."[39] In postwar Cairo he began to dramatize biblical narratives, capturing his inspiration in the picturesque and musical. Between 1921 and 1925, there came Joseph and His Brothers; Passover Night; The Last Passover Night; Saul and Stephen; The Good Samaritan; and King Hezekiah. In Egypt as in India, the people have a natural affinity for drama, a medium appealing to both illiterate villager and educated. Upon the counsel of Bishop Gwynne, the first play was presented "in the church" with prayers and hymns replacing applause. Five presentations of Joseph drew nearly two thousand Muslims and Christians and Gairdner gained new hopefulness that Egypt might see the Gospel. But this medium was in advance of C.M.S. supporters at home. The Committee fearful that gifts might be withheld, confined the use of drama to hospitals, schools, etc., thus nipping Gairdner's creative venture in the bud.

Realizing that the future depended upon an Egyptian Anglican Church equipped for her task in the midst of Islam, Gairdner's objective was to attain for it a well-balanced life, rich in worship, song, fellowship, healing and witness. Avoiding party labels, he aimed to create a liturgy which might express "the beauty of holiness and the holiness of beauty". His services were extremely devotional (with him prostrate before the communion in oriental fashion on occasion) and yet equally spontaneous. He borrowed freely from practices observed in America and Europe that the Arab church might know the drama of worship. Continuously rewriting the various liturgical services, he demonstrated a flexibility and freedom the worshipper immediately sensed. The Cairo congregation worshipped under Gairdner in the Church of the Saviour at Boulac, a semi-Byzantine building with simplified interior. Gairdner felt the sanctuary must be consistent with the poverty of the people (Boulac was a slum district) and the congregation's mission in the community. Painstaking preparation and a strong prayer life stood behind Gairdner's skill in leading men into the presence of Christ.[40]

To keep the young Arab church alive to its responsibility to Muslims, Gairdner helped them draft their "Working Principles" (1925) declaring their prime mission was to the Muslim world and to the sisterly care of other Christian communions. Approved by the Archbishop of Canterbury, this was a step towards the ordination of Arabs, e.g. Girgis Bishai, et al. C.M.S., having revised its policy in Egypt (ca. 1921), pressed now for the establishment of the Arabic Anglican Church. Gairdner noted:

> We now decided to have one real shot at getting on: to take stock of our members, quasi-members, adherents, see who was who, have a campaign of explaining what the Anglican Church is, what it stands for in Egypt, what is its order, liturgy, aim, spirit: regularize, take hold, take stock, rekindle, and finally ordain the first Egyptian pastor, as a first step towards building up a really indigenous non-foreign Church....the grand aim should be to raise up a truly militant, evangelical and therefore evangelistic Church, however small, a truly Catholic Church with power to absorb and unify the most diverse elements, and gifted with historical order and reverent, inspiring and liturgical services.[41]

Mission came first for Gairdner according to Ysef Effendi Tadros.

> No one else taught us as he did. Other teachers taught us how to refute Islam; he taught us how to love Muslims. He made us feel we understood them and felt with them. When he told us about the beginnings of Islam, we felt as if we were sons of that time and knew the first Muslims.[42]

As the years wore on, Gairdner realized that the redemption and the growth of the church was perhaps more important than his production of literature. For only as the church reached out and drew men in, demonstrating the new brotherhood in Christ, could Muslims be won. Only as it provided a warm spiritual home

for inquirers and converts could the work advance. His energies
were hence directed towards creating this sense of community of
reconciliation, a church continually learning of Christ. In a
time when personal and national interests dictated otherwise, it
was not easy to weld Egyptians, Syrians, and Europeans together
in faith and worship. Yet he sought this by his series of
Arabic leaflets on the Christian duties and lessons on baptism,
confirmation, communion, etc. In addition to emphasizing the
lowering of partitions, his Arabic Commentary on Galatians inaugurated a badly needed biblical literature for the young
church. Of one of his last papers, "The Egyptian Church as a
Home for Christ's Converts from Islam" he said to a friend: "If
I die before you, promise me that you will give what I said then
as my last message to the Egyptian Church. It is far the most
important thing I ever wrote."[43]

Gairdner had pressed very early for a wider fellowship of the
Egypt Inter-Mission Council in which each participant must positively contribute out of their strengths and not simply reduce
fellowship to the lowest common denominator. Fresh on the field
he had written:

> It takes faith, believing in Christ, His Church and minis-
> try, here in this Moslem city. But on my word, it takes more
> faith to believe in these when one thinks of the Church it-
> self as it exists here--sect upon sect, each more intolerant
> than its neighbor, each practically excommunicating the
> others in the name of the One Lord--and that in the face of
> an Islam which loathes all alike. It makes one feel passion-
> ately careless of ecclesiastical or doctrinal niceties and
> simply desirous to do something to promote spirituality and
> righteousness here in Egypt. 'The Church of Christ'--shades
> of Paul, of John, of Athanasius! O Lord, how long? And why
> is it that this grotesque travesty mocks these names and Thee
> and tempts us to feel that all is and has been empty?[44]

Before long he shared the hopeful expectation of Edinburgh,
1910.

> Unity when it comes must be something richer, grander,
> more comprehensive than anything which we can see at present.
> It is something into which and up to which we must grow,
> something of which and for which we must become worthy. We
> need to have sufficient faith in God to believe that He can
> bring us to something higher and more Christ like than any-
> thing to which we at present see a way.[45]

At a Scottish Missionary Conference in Glasgow (1922), he spoke
on "Brotherhood, Islam's or Christ's" driving home the theme
that only as Christian oneness is realized can the Muslim world
be won.

The brotherhood which Christ brought to earth is infinite and unlimited, <u>but</u> <u>Christians</u> <u>have</u> <u>limited</u> <u>and</u> <u>particularized</u> <u>it</u>. The brotherhood of Islam is finite and limited, but such as it is Mohammedans have universialized it. Not until the perfect thing is once more available and offered to Mohammedans can Islam's imperfect thing pass away.[46]

At the Conferences at Helwan (1924) and at the Mt. of Olives, Jerusalem (1924), Gairdner's stress was that the future depended more upon the church's life than upon any special method. J. R. Mott especially appreciated the depth of this devotional leader. In the summer of 1927, Gairdner was requested to prepare a paper for the World Missionary Council in Jerusalem (1928). Whether because of his slipping health or his distrust for the heavy emphasis being placed upon comparative religion and values, Gardner was curiously reluctant to take the job. Only when he was given a younger co-author, W. A. Eddy did he see fit to continue on. Even so, <u>The</u> <u>Values</u> <u>of</u> <u>Christianity</u> <u>and</u> <u>Islam</u> is not a creative work, but a summary of Gairdner's earlier writings. One suspects that the evangelistic-apologetic materials of Gairdner over the past nineteen years were reclothed to fit the schema of the meeting and simply signed by an "exhausted man". Indeed dental sepsis which later developed into fatal septic lung complications had been at its deadly work for some time before detected (about November, 1927). Gairdner faced a painful death (May 22, 1928). Thus was the exodus made from Egypt to the new Jerusalem by one who was optimistic about the church's life and mission to Islam.

It is sometimes said that little mission churches will be as islands in the sea of Islam—but let us not be enslaved by dreary metaphors. Let us rather say that such churches will be centres of life and heat and light, serving and saving the Islamic peoples round them.[47]

An Examination of the Thought and Contributions of Gairdner

The main contributions of Gairdner, as well as Zwemer, towards the formation of a maturer approach to Muslims revolves about three focal points: evangelism, Islam, and the church. By the turn of the century, the uniqueness of Christianity, hence the validity of evangelism, was being called into question in the West. This changing theological climate required clarification as to the essence of Christianity and its mission. Yet in the case of both Gairdner and Zwemer, a confident reliance upon God's revelation in Christ underlies their firm resolve in the realms of apologetics and proclamation. Next, these two men were able to make advances towards a sympathetic understanding of Islam and the crucial question of Christianity's relation to it without fear of compromising their mission and message. This

positive new attitude was due perhaps both to the lessons learned by their nineteenth century forerunners and to their own
awareness of the sovereignty and grace of God. Religious-
nationalistic stirrings among educated Arabs undoubtedly gave
added impetus to this sympathetic scholarship. A third point
concerned the relationship between the life and mission of the
church. Earlier missionaries had been able to avoid certain
thorny ecclesiastical issues, but the appearance of younger
churches not only progressively narrowed the gulf between mission
and theology but made the reshaping of a theology of mission
most urgent. Churches in the field had to be aware of their
ecumenical nature and apostolic task if they were to succeed.
For the purposes of this study, it is convenient to examine the
contributions of Gairdner in these three spheres.

Gairdner's Understanding of Evangelism

Gairdner had definite ideas as to the substance of the Evangel and the theory and practice of evangelism. For Gairdner the
content of the Gospel is Christ and evangelism the communication
of him. Although not opposed to the idea of general revelation
(hence one can be cognizant of something of worth in other religions), he was under no illusion as to the distinctiveness,
the uniqueness of God's work and word in his Messiah. During
his whole ministry, Gairdner held that it was only in Jesus
Christ that man can enter into a right relationship with God and
experience the full life for which he was created. "The Essentiality of the Cross" an article in the first issue of Orient
and Occident (1905) discloses Gairdner's position. It appears
that a Cairo newspaper had studied popular Western literature
and concluded that Christianity like Islam and Judaism was only
concerned with "monotheism, morality and ethics". While agreeing that Jesus set forth a personal and social morality which
has never been surpassed, Gairdner will not stop there.

> But all that was not the whole of the work of Jesus, nor
> the whole of the good news which He heralded....But in fact
> the real work of Jesus Christ was to introduce into the
> world--to make available for humanity--a fund of life capable
> of producing as fruit this 'morality and ethics' indefinite-
> ly, all down the ages, until the dawn of eternity. It seems
> incredible that it should be possible to say that anything is
> more wonderful or more precious or more necessary than what
> Jesus taught. And yet so it is. What He did was more won-
> derful or more precious or more necessary; and for this
> reason--that thereby the soul is enabled to penetrate to the
> heart of that 'One God,' and bring forth the fruit of that
> 'morality and ethics,' a nobler name for which is Holiness.[48]

Gairdner contends that Christianity is more than the highest

"ethical system" and that Jesus is more than the "ideal historical figure". The Christian faith centers on the inseparable
person and work of Christ and only by a personal faith-relationship with Christ does man come to know and live in communion
with God. It is important to keep this in mind when reading the
Gairdner-Eddy article in the Jerusalem Report (1928).[49] While
Gairdner did not deny the values in other religious systems, it
is only in Christ and not in some vague perception of truth that
man comes into a right relation with God. At this point he
would have agreed with Bonhoeffer that the ultimate question is
Who (personal encounter), not What (the attainment of right
knowledge) or How (the understanding of historical processes).[50]
Only in obedient faith in Christ as Lord and Saviour does man
experience the new life. Jesus disclosed that God is a reality
far different than religious man thought. The Creator is a
Father who requires of men a new law of love (stressing relationships). Christ is God's Wakeel, one with executive authority in
his very person.

> His teaching was not simply one of 'monotheism, ethics,
> and morals,' but proved the exact contrary, viz: that His
> own personality was of central importance in the religion of
> this complete revelation of God, which He came to unfold, and
> that His death was of central importance in regard to that
> personality. Let us go on....We shall show the relation be-
> tween the Kingdom of God and the death of the Anointed King--
> thus combining into one the two themes.[51]

The kingdom (an organization rooted in heaven and appearing on
earth as a body of renewed men and women) is entered only as men
experience re-birth through accepting and obeying "the Wakeel of
unseen Deity". Wisely avoiding such terms as ibn Allah (Son of
God) which blind Muslims to the truth being presented, Gairdner
proceeds to show how the sacrificial death of the Wakeel is consistent with God's plan. Although the crucifixion was an abhor-
rent idea for Jews (as for Muslims), the disciples gradually saw
it as the supreme "manifestation of divine energy" (Mk. 12:1-12)
resulting in "a glorified renewal of life and power; the vindication of that Messiah-King...victory, final and infinite; divine
power, released without limit, eternally available".[52] Thus the
cross is:

> the dynamo which created and made available a spiritual
> power that gave to 'monotheism' a new significance and trans-
> formed 'morality and ethics' from a teaching, a theory, a
> philosophy, into a life.[53]

Jesus is no mild teacher and prophet untouched by the world, but
the Saviour-King living on in the midst of the historical process. Following the resurrection, he is the glorified Lord who

sustains the church's life and commits to her the preaching of
"repentence and forgiveness of sins in His name" throughout the
world. History henceforth revolves about the cross and the
Christ who towers over all. He urges the reader to openly identify himself with the Christ assured that if he could transform
Saul of Tarsus, he can do the same for the talented graduate of
al-Azhar![54] Gairdner believed that man's understanding of God
is Christo-centric in content and must be so in presentation.
Thus when he looks at Islam, he often goes straight at its
"doctrine of God" (the heart of any religion, shaping its Welt-
anschauung). Personally, Gairdner never speaks of God except as
known in Christ.[55]

Mission strategy received serious attention by Gairdner in D.
M. Thornton: A Study of Missionary Ideals and Methods (1908).
This primary contribution to the science of mission was modified
only slightly as he later devoted more attention to research in
Islamics and the nurture of the Egyptian church. He was well
enough versed in missiology to challenge Roland Allen's hasty
charges that Islam was superior both in methods and results.[56]
Allen, uncritically accepting the premises of Dr. Blyden (1887)
and Professor Westermann (1912), had painted a glowing picture
of Muslim advances in Africa. Allen had written that:

> Islam is propagated spontaneously and voluntarily; it is
> maintained by self-support: it imposes no restrictions what-
> soever on those who become Moslems--all are welcomed; and
> thus it forms a true African Church....[57]

Gairdner knew both the Sudan and Islam better than Allen who had
spent his years in China. After an extensive survey, Gairdner
makes a critical response. He undercuts the myth that Islam is
indigenous by revealing how foreign its clothes, book, language,
and customs are for African tribes. Likewise its morality is
not superior simply because it accommodates itself to existing
patterns. Gairdner argues that Christianity is creating the
basis for a new mankind and not simply perpetuating the tribal
system. As in Allen's Missionary Methods: St. Paul's or Ours,
Gairdner believes in the goal of building African churches which
are self-supporting, self-governing and self-propagating. He
adds:

> sincere desire and the simplest faith should qualify for
> immediate baptism: and the Holy Spirit should be trusted,
> unreservedly and fearlessly trusted, to carry these immature
> converts forward into maturity; to preserve and stabilize the
> Church; and to bring it through the inevitable state of
> danger, of heresies and moral collapses, which were not evi-
> table in Corinth and will not be evitable in Africa, but
> which were dealt with in Corinth by quite a different method
> from that which seems to be the only possible method in

Africa today.[58]

While agreeing with Allen's ideas of admission and evangelization via national Christians, Gairdner takes issue with his
charges against "foreign" Christians. Gairdner stresses that
overseas workers have a continuing task of offering mutual encouragement to the national churches in mission. If the "Three
Selves" principle is pressed to the ultimate, it leaves the new
church in isolation, cut off from its truly catholic life. At
this point, Gairdner envisaged a church in which national and
foreigner work together in true brotherhood, in a spirit of genuine equality.[59] If one wants to attack the barriers to Christianity's advance in Africa, suggests Gairdner, one must strike
at that limited concept of mission which fails to involve the
laity, and at European administrators who disgustingly apply the
Roman policy of ruling via the established system (often Muslims
who have gained control over pagan regions). To maintain the
status quo, these administrators prefer aloof Muslims over African Christians who expect to be treated as equals and who desire
reform which might threaten the administrator's role. Nevertheless the Christian faith offers to Africans the greatest social
advancement, dignity and learning, a truly new way of life. The
church's role in Africa is not to be so underestimated!

How did Gairdner implement his methodology? Examination of
his effort in five areas should sufficiently illustrate this.
First, consider his contributions to apologetic literature. The
growth of apologetics can be traced in the student Christian
movements, especially the W.S.C.F.[60] These distinctly evangelical bodies (with their activistic rather than creedal emphasis)
entered into serious discussion as their work expanded overseas,
encountering resurgent religions, nationalism and the agnosticism stimulated by western education. Christian missionaries
were also struggling with their theology in light of the new
scientific approach to religion and the growth of biblical criticism. At the Tokyo Conference (W.S.C.F.) in 1907, the question
was raised: "Apologetics or Evangelism?" Some felt that the
older pattern of simply presenting Christ, leading men to him
was no longer adequate in light of the new circumstances. The
idea of apologetics as the removal of hindrances to the acceptance of the Christian faith by means of a reasoned intellectual
discussion of existing problems caught on in many circles.[61]
For most evangelicals, apologetics was not confined however to a
defense of the Gospel, it also meant communication of Christ.
While Gairdner was certainly alerted to these developments, he
remains heir to the long standing Anglican apologetics for Muslims developed by Martyn, French, Lefroy and Tisdall. Gairdner
went to Cairo committed to creating a Christian literature for
educated Muslims. He achieved his goal to a remarkable degree
by preparing over a score of Arabic works before his death. It
is interesting to note two stages in his writing. Up to about

1912, there were biographical presentations of Joseph, Abraham,
Isaac, O.T. prophets, the Messiah, and Paul in the eminent tradition of Alexander Whyte. After 1912, this continues in his
dramatic sketches. Parallel to this there were apologetic
writings which retained traces of the older controversial
methods of the past, e.g. the dialogue technique of Christian
apologetists to Judaism and Raymond Lull. This struggle to
prove Christianity as the superior system is seen in Ahmad and
Bulus (1906), The Gospel of Barnabas (1907), and What Happened
before the Hegira (1908). While agreeing that polemics must be
abandoned in Inspiration, A Dialogue (1909) and The Eucharist as
Historical Evidence (1910), Gairdner is still pitting Islamic
and Christian ideas against each other through comparison. It
is significant that Gairdner's more positive presentations begin
about 1912-1916. His new irenic approach reflects a fresh
awareness of Muslim attitudes and strives to communicate Christ
without offending. Even the titles reflect this advance in
method.

> Aspects of the Redemptive Act of Christ (1916)
> God as Triune, Incarnate, Atoner (1916)
> The Last Supper (1919)
> The Secret of Life (1924)
> The Divinity of Christ (1924)
> Who is the Founder of Christianity? (1927)

This remarkable development is evident in an article, "The Doctrine of the Unity in Trinity" (I.R.M.). In the first part
appearing in 1911, Gairdner is sweating to answer every Muslim
objection in a defensive battle. The second and third parts
(1916) however breathe with a reasonableness which would prove
attractive to anyone. One can conclude that Gairdner like the
church at large had to work his way through this tense adjustment period until he settled down to prepare a literature that
communicated Christ more effectively to Muslims.

Second, Gairdner was committed to preaching and dialogue.
There was no substitute for speech in working with the students
and educated Muslims of Cairo. While it is difficult to recover
Gairdner's efforts in this line, accounts of his lectures at
Beit Arabi Pasha, conversations in the bookshop, discussions in
the student societies and sermons indicate that Gairdner spoke
with a sustaining power.[62] Gairdner revealed ability to reach
the effendi class who were torn between traditional Islam and
the sceptical-naturalistic outlook of western type education.
He would begin with a non-religious address or topic and go on
to cultivate a rich acquaintance that gradually conquered suspicion. These young men frequently responded by attending the
services Gairdner led and evidencing affection for Christian
ideas.[63]

Drama was not simply a third channel for Gairdner, it was the

natural means by which the Christian community could convey the
basis of their faith and life. His biblical dramas are apologetic in the sense that they corrected Muslim misconceptions of
biblical accounts. In Joseph and His Brothers (4 acts, 72
pages, 1921), the speeches follow the Scriptural text without
change. Gairdner wrote in the preface:

> Though this play was written for acting, and with actual
> representation in mind all the time, it is hoped that it may
> also serve as sort of Bible-study on the Genesis narrative,
> and stimulate anew both the study and the teaching of the
> deathless tale.

Meticulous attention to staging and costumes helped establish
the historical atmosphere of ancient Egypt. The human characteristics of hatred, sin and greed are emphasized to show the
need for the reconciliation based on forgiveness. Only on this
basis does man know the peace and benediction of God. One can
sense the setting that reportedly led part of the audience to
"joyful tears". In The Passover Night (3 scenes, 24 pages,
1921), the impact of the ten plagues upon two ordinary Israelite
and Egyptian families encourages the audience to identify and
participate in this tragic-redemptive event clearly interpreted
as a symbolic prophecy of the cross of Christ. The reoccurring
theme is redemption "by the blood", "The Lamb of God! who redeemed me!" and concludes on the note of liberation and the
praise of God. Saul and Stephen (3 acts, 53 pages, 1921) sets
the news of the resurrection in the midst of the infant church.
Moving from the death of Stephen to the conversion of Saul, it
describes for the Muslim-Coptic audience how the power of the
risen Christ is able to sustain the church in spite of suffering
and persecution. This message so relevant to the Egyptian
church concludes again on forgiveness, peace and praise. The
preface reads:

> Persecution by inquisition is a dreadful business in any
> period or at any time. How smoothly we glide over the famil-
> iar texts which describe the first Inquisition when it forms
> part of 'the passage appointed for the Epistle' or 'the
> Second Lesson'! It is not until some occasion like a drama-
> tization forces us to interrogate those texts that they yield
> to us their terrible reality. But may we not for that very
> reason add that it is just thus that we may come more fully
> to realize the length, breadth, height and depth of the
> grace which purged such guilt away, and which made out of the
> fanatical and cruel Inquisitor the Apostle of Faith, Hope
> and Love?

The Last Passover Night (1921) and The Good Samaritan (1923)
also portray N.T. accounts. King Hezekiah (1923), a tragical

drama, is his most complex play and employs voices (a type of
Greek Chorus) which echo and interpret the unseen thoughts of
the characters and the deity. Driving home the consequences be-
falling a nation which continues to violate God's direction,
this play concludes with the dramatic deliverance by God of his
people ("remnant") as Isaiah prophecies the coming King, "Imman-
uel, God with us!" By 1923, religious drama was gaining a place
at the Old Vic in London. It is regretted that this medium did
not gain wider acceptance in the churches of Egypt. Nevertheless these dramatic biblical accounts reveal a skillful author
striving to allow God's Word to speak to a Near Eastern audience.
His objective was to stimulate the whole church to witness to
the great themes of redemptive history, events pointing to their
culmination in Christ. Later in the century, Miss Joyce Peel
would successfully develop this method of communication in the
villages of South India, appealing to illiterate and educated
alike.

Fourthly, Gairdner like Julius Richter, Robert Bruce and
others saw the need for a preparatory work which would create a
receptiveness for the Gospel within Islam. In many cases this
fostering of contacts, cultivation of friendship, must precede
presentation if the Gospel is to gain a hearing.[64] The White
Fathers (Roman Catholics) were making similar effort to overcome
age-old suspicions and fears by service prior to preaching.
With appreciation for this idea of Christian presence, he wrote
a friend:

> The name, work, mission and message of Charles du Foucauld
> is beginning to penetrate to these parts. It seems wrong
> that the fruits of the soul toil and mental travail, and men-
> tal toil and spiritual discipline of such a saint should not
> be as fully available as possible, especially among those who
> could receive light and instruction therefrom....I feel there
> is so much we have to learn and to unlearn. We stretch out
> our hands to these unseen and unknown Brothers, who have
> lived more celestially, and thought more profoundly, and
> loved more charitably than we.[65]

Following the Armenian massacres, service had gained widespread
popularity among Protestant workers in the Near East. Gairdner
however purposefully avoided becoming the pawn of the pressing
temporal needs about him (e.g. educational, medical, relief
work). This was prompted not by insensitivity but the desire to
hold presence and proclamation together. The church must not be
enslaved to the treatment of immediate symptoms but engaged in
conveying the long-range answer of God, the remedy for the human
dilemma found in Christ. Something of this concern for relating
presence and biblical presentation is also found in K. Cragg.[66]

Finally, Gairdner was equally concerned that Christians be
prepared. Following the suggestions of the conferences of

Cairo, Edinburgh and Lucknow, he and Zwemer established the
Cairo Study Center (1912) to train Christian workers to cope
with the growing complexities of Near Eastern life and Islamic
thought. Gairdner dedicated a good portion of his last sixteen
years to train missionary recruits and national workers in Arabic and Islamics. He revolutionized the teaching of Arabic so
that the student could gain surer and speedier acquisition of a
grammatical and idiomatic Arabic. Delving behind the scenes, he
gave the student new appreciation for the tongue to be mastered.[67] One could charge that Gairdner's fascination with Arabic
culture diverted him from his primary calling but this is not
justifiable inasmuch as he continuously related his scholarship
to the church's mission. The Islamics course examined the various factors contributing to the present outlook of the Muslim
community so that the Christian could present the Gospel in
terms most comprehensible and least offensive to his listeners.
The curriculum included:

> I. An historical sketch of the fundamentals of Islamic
> faith, including the life of the Prophet...the Koran...a
> survey of Moslem expansion, theologically, socially and poli-
> tically; and an examination of those other factors which have
> moulded the Moslem mind, individually and nationally, into
> its present form.
> II. An analysis, by study and experience, of the mind of
> the average Moslem...with an endeavour to comprehend his
> habits, his ideals, his mode of thought, his outlook, his
> environment, his literature, his hopes and his fears.
> III. The presentation in practice, after careful study
> and close observation, of the Gospel message to a Moslem
> audience, and with an adequate treatment of the current ob-
> jections to the Christian philosophy of life.[68]

Gairdner proposed a four-year course for each recruit with lectures, seminars, directed reading, and practice in making a
positive presentation of the Gospel. Of this apologetic-evan-
gelist, Duncan B. Macdonald wrote:

> As missionary, theologian, author, linguist, Arabist,
> poet, he has left a deep mark on our knowledge of Islam, of
> the technique of teaching the Arabic colloquial, and above
> all, on the method of interpreting Christianity to the Moslem
> mind. As a missionary he believed in evangelism by speech
> and in print and in thoroughly understanding the ideas of
> those whose minds and hearts he strove to reach. A great
> part of his later life was given to the training of younger
> missionaries in the same methods....[69]

Gairdner's Understanding of Islam

Gairdner took this world and its non-Christian religions

seriously acknowledging that they often shaped the environment
in which mission must be implemented. His early examination of
Islam took the form of The Reproach of Islam (1909), a study
volume for the home church which proved most popular.[70] Pouring
out his thoughts and feelings as fast as pen could move, he had:

> piled difficulty upon difficulty, discouragement upon dis-
> couragement, until faith almost reeled. I want it to reel,
> that it might reel back on to the arms of God in Christ.[71]

Through study of Islam's extent, origin, growth, nature, and
practice, Gairdner presents it as a challenge to the church, the
Christ occupied community.

> Throughout the book a very special emphasis has been
> placed on the Person and work of the Spirit of Jesus....The
> expression is pregnant to the very highest degree. It means
> all that God in Christ is; all that the heart of Him who was
> and is Jesus contained and contains; His whole character, His
> whole view of the world and God and religion and man and
> man's healing--His Spirit; all this, clothing itself in the
> lives of those who confess His name, taking flesh in the life
> of His Church.[72]

Yet the fact remains that in this world, Islam holds sway over
vast lands and populations, at times overwhelming Christians.
Its members are:

> tightly united by a belief in one God, and a common faith
> which carries with it a fraternity and a religious enthusiasm
> in its adherents without parallel; a people bound together by
> this Faith, and by a social system which insinuates itself by
> the privileges it offers, the penalties it can impose, and
> the easiness of the spiritual demands it makes;--such is the
> Islam which faces the Church of Jesus Christ in this twenti-
> eth century.[73]

How do you explain Islam's success and deal with it? Muir and
Margoliouth rightly drew attention to the failure of Byzantine-
Persian Christianity and the military and economic pressure
exerted upon subject peoples.[74]

> The explanation of Mohammed is the explanation of the
> Sacracens, as the Moslems used to be called. To understand
> why he triumphed in Arabia, is to understand why they tri-
> umphed in Europe, in Africa, and in Asia....The Kingdom of
> this world, of which he dreamed, was set up, and the methods
> which he sanctioned--with all their admirable, all their con-
> taminating features--were with enthusiasm adopted and em-
> ployed....as we trace the history of the spread of Islam...
> we shall get a tremendous lesson in missionary methods, those

which the Church might itch to use--yet must leave alone; and
that one which often seems very weakness; yet alone can
avail.[75]

Critically examining the Muslim idea of God, Gairdner finds that
"the conception of Will-Power is paramount, supreme". While one
may admire this belief in a God of pure power, it tragically
omits God's holiness and love (Father) revealed only in Christ.
This produces not a solid morality but only an arbitrary system
of permissions (halâl) and prohibitions (harâm). This "unconditioned Might" rules out atonement even though Muslim ideas of
sacrifice cry for it; produces an untouchable God and a man who
is neither free nor moral; and results in an agnosticism drain-
ing prayer of meaning. This latter negation is captured in
Egyptian rhyme: "Whatever idea your mind come at, I tell you
flat God is not that." Its physical paradise and eschatology
lack the perception of history and eternity, of the relation of
Creator and creation, found in the book of Revelation. In short,
Islam is an attempt by man to journey to God, to bridge the gulf
from the human side. Its pillars and duties provide the means,
the regulations which shape the whole social-political structure.[76] It lacks the link, the Christ, the incarnate Lord.

How colossal seems the sheer mass, how irresistible the
momentum of this league of nature, the world and the flesh!
...Why must we strive always up the hill, the wind and the
rain for ever driving in our faces; ever, ever conceding,
never never receiving the handicap and the odds!...If Islam's
forces are indeed nature, the world and the flesh, then Islam
has left us one weapon in taking away all the others--it has
abandoned to us the Sword of the Spirit--the Spirit of Jesus
is the only asset of the Church.[77]

During his wanderjahr (1910-1911), Gairdner began his sympathetic study of Islamic mysticism and Al-Ghazali. The Edinburgh
Conference, contact with orientalists, and absence from the
intense mission station encouraged this inquiry. Two Turkish
sheikhs (now Christians) at Potsdam were ideal interpreters of
their experiences in Islam. As former scholar and head of the
Sufi monastery of the Rifaʿite dervishes (an extreme type of
esoteric sufism), they described a 'Way' (tariqa) reminding one
of Freemasonry with its initiates, grades, and rites. These
fascinating interviews reveal elements akin to Christian movements: members are recruited not born; are conscious of sin and
the experience of human love but long for the love of God; begin
their training to recite the Dhikr (naming of God); and commit
themselves to a way of monastic life under a superior confessor
and disciplinarian. Gairdner diagrams their seven stage program
of the soul moving towards God.

But the whole purpose of Sufism, the way of the dervish,
is to give him an escape from this prison (in the body), an
apocalypse of the Seventy Thousand Veils (thick curtains sep-
arating him from God), a recovery of the original unity with
the One, while still in this body. The body is not to be put
off; it is to be refined, and made spiritual,--a help and not
a hindrance to the spirit (ruh). It is like a metal that has
to be refined by fire and transmuted. And the sheikh tells
the aspirant that he has the secret of this transmutation....
For every Stage transversed in this return journey to Allah,
then ten thousand of the Veils are apocalypted.[78]

While Sufism was dangerously near pantheism (The mystic in the
final stage claimed "All things are in him and he in all things.
There is no god but he.") and was probably saved only by al-
Qushairi and al-Ghazali who wedded it to Sunnite orthodoxy, it
did exhibit concern for the God-man gap. Gairdner hoped this
concern for sin and reconciliation, the transcendence and immanence of God, law and liberty might provide a gateway for presenting the Gospel. This compelled him to intensify his study
of Islam in Europe and America. He admired D. B. Macdonald for
his psychological insights into Islam and devout missionary
interest.[79] The Dutch Professor Hurgronje is taken to task however for implying that a missionary cannot be an objective
scholar.

Missionaries are supposed to be both inaccurate and unfair
in dealing with the life and character of Mohammed, though
they have (we believe) done more than anyone else to mediate
to the public moderate, fact-grounded views, and to destroy
the medieval-mythical one. This claim was strengthened by
reading Snouck Hurgronje's own result sketch (pp. 25-48). It
seems to us to differ little except in certain emphases from
the sketches given in recent missionary text-books.[80]

While appreciative of the orientalist's study of Islam, he rejects outright the idea that Christianity should abandon the
effort to draw converts from Islam.

Returning to Cairo, Gairdner centered his research about the
theologian-mystic, al-Ghazali. First, he tackled the critical
questions surrounding the Mishkāt Al-Anwār (The Niche for
Lights).[81] He published an introduction and translation of this
document which revealed considerable insight into Ghazali's life
and esoteric thought. In brief, Ghazali attempts to explain the
relation of creation (the soul) to God by examining the relation
of light to its ultimate source, the relation of symbol (language) to the 'thing' (visible and invisible worlds), and then to
apply these principles to the exegesis of the Quranic 'Light'
verse (Surah 24:35) and the 'Veils' hadith. Of the latter,
Gairdner remarks:

The origin of the tradition is, it is safe to hazard, Neo-
platonic, and it therefore lent itself completely to the
gnostic and theosophic mode of thought which so soon invaded
Muslim Sufism, after its less successful effort to capture
orthodox Christianity.[82]

Gairdner appreciated Ghazali's attempt to bridge the gap between
the transcendent God of Islam and the utter temporal creation,
but it highlighted the fact that Islam did not and could not
answer how God could have contact with this world. It leaves
the Muslim, even Ghazali, oscillating between mystic experiments
in extreme pantheism and cold rigid deism with its agnostic and
fatalistic effects. Perhaps this study of the Muslim giant convinced Gairdner anew that he must spend his time on the proclamation of God's bridging act in Christ and the resultant new
life of the church.
In a third step, Gairdner sought to help the Muslim community
to separate fiction from fact, myth from history. Because the
system of Islam is largely structured upon traditions, he encouraged Muslims to use historical criticism to get at the truth
about Muhammad and his teachings. His purpose was not to produce a reformed Islam but to help Muslims see their real dilemma
and to become receptive to God's news in Christ.[83] Two articles
illustrate Gairdner's approach. In the first, Gairdner points
out the questionable nature of many hadiths when submitted to
the historical tests usually applied to the Gospels.[84]

It is strange, therefore, that with these a priori resem-
blances, the two sets of records should present such immense
and striking differences. The most important of them are
(1) the much more modest dimension of the Christian records
as compared with the Moslem; (2) the lateness with which the
Moslem records were collected into book form as compared
with the Christian; (3) the absence in the Gospels of isnad
(i.e. the citation of the pedigree of each report, whether
of incident or saying), and the all-pervading and all-impor-
tant part played by isnad in the Traditions.[85]

The hadiths are suspect because they have no internal criticism
(often accepting absurd contradictory claims); the list of
transmitters break down under close scrutiny; and the companions
of Muhammad who could have offered the clearest witness give us
practically nothing.[86] In contrast the Gospels show strength by
requiring no isnad and by proving reliable even under the modern
criticism of Harnack.[87] What was Gairdner trying to prove?
Simply that the gigantic superstructure of Islam, even the
Shari'a lacked historical support and was not built on a law
given by God to Muhammad.

...the whole orthodox system of Koran exegesis and the

whole orthodox system of canon-law rest (as system) upon the
traditions even more than on the Koran itself. If the unreliability of these, then, is established, those systems ought
logically to be doubted and discarded. And modern intellectual Moslems do indeed attempt to go 'back to the Koran' and
to find in it alone (as far as possible) their data for constructive systematisation; thereby showing that they are
aware that the use of <u>traditions</u> as data cannot be justa-
fied.[88]

While this critical process continues today within Islam, perhaps Gairdner placed too much hope in scientific objectivity for
the emotive Muslim community could also use it to produce a
streamlined virile Islam. Gairdner's other objective was to
stress that the Gospel provides a trustworthy account of Jesus.

What does all this mean? It means that these Gospels were
simply the committal to writing of the Acts and Words of
Christ, as they had been taught and preached from the very
outset....Thus Islam conducts us to a Book which truly was
given forth by its founder. Christianity conducts us to a
Christ who truly lived, wrought, died, rose again on the
third day and passed alive into the unseen.[89]

In the second article, "Mohammad without Camouflage," Gairdner
attacks the so-called objectivity of Western scholars and the
<u>Islamic Review</u> (Woking) which ignores certain elements in Muham-
mad's life, Islamic history and literature in order to appear
unprejudiced to the English public.[90] This lack of historical
responsibility sometimes portrays Muhammad as "the perfect human
exemplar and final ethical standard" while glossing over such
plain but uncongenial facts as his violations of the morals of
war and conventions of life accepted by the Arabs, his role in
executions and enslavement and the element of desire in his mar-
riages. Gairdner counsels the consultation of such reliable
Muslim sources as al-Bukhari (traditionalist), Ibn-Hisham (historian) and al-Halabi (biographer) to unveil Muhammad without
camouflage. Thus he conclues:

...if admirers of Mohammed are content to regard him historically as a great Arabian, who had a real and strange
sense of prophetical call, and through this and his immense
natural genius, singular gifts, and many virtues, accomplished a stupendous life-work, then we join with the admirers
....The worst enemies of Mohammed are not his opponents, but
his friends, who will have it that the character of this
Arabian giant is the very type of perfected humanity;...that
no great wrong can be attributed to him; that his moral
splendour throws that of Jesus completely in the shade; and
that his example and precept make the best foundation not

only for codes of conduct but for national and international
law!...All we know is that these men one and all, are doing
a disservice both to truth and to their idol. For they as
little give the world the whole truth as did the old-time
wholesale obloquists; and they simply force those who see in
these assertions a gross offence against fact, and a definite
attack on the perfection and universality of the Man Jesus
Christ, to rise up and show from the sources that the real
Mohammed, the Mohammed of the sources and of the Agreement of
Islam, the only Mohammed who counts...will not fit the role
in virtue of which the human race is invited to travel from
Bethlehem to Mekka, from the Mount of the Beatitudes to the
Mount of ʿArafāt.[91]

Finally it is noted that as a scholar of Islam, Gairdner was
very alert to contemporary developments in the Muslim world.
His consciousness of the influence of politics and other forces
on missions is observed in his article for the first issue of
The Moslem World.[92] As an Anglican acquainted with the tension
which church-state relationships could generate, he was most
critical of British policy in Egypt, Sudan and throughout Africa.

> It is cowardly and unchristian; it is not even neutral. It
> ought to be wholly changed. The British official may one day
> see that all this subservience to the Moslem and neglect of
> his own faith gains him neither the respect, gratitude, nor
> affection of the people, but the very reverse of all three.[93]

He saw the Pan-Islamic movement mainly as a reaction to European
interference, but positively anticipated a bright future for the
national movements and urged Coptic Christians to participate in
their formation. He wanted to stamp out the idea that being or
becoming a Christian made one less a nationalist.

> I believe that any attempt to denationalize oneself is
> rather like unsexing oneself. It generally leads to becoming
> acidly anti one's own nation, and that defeats itself, for
> ultimately that sort of thing though it at first flatters the
> adopted nation, alienates and disgusts even it, while by the
> other it is rightly judged as a form of matricide.[94]

He would contend that even as he could be truly ecumenical only
by being a true Anglican so must Egyptian Christians be both
nationalists and internationalists. Thus Gairdner is to be respected as a scholar acquainted with theological, historical and
contemporary Islam.
    There remains the significant question: What is the Christ-
ian answer to the theology and practice of Islam according to
Gairdner? One discovers an apologetic approach that becomes
sympathetic to Muslims without compromising evangelical convic-

tions. At first, he frequently pitted Christian doctrine
against Islamic doctrine, system against system. About 1912
(after the conferences of Cairo, Edinburgh, Lucknow and the wanderjahr), a second stage in his approach appears which (a)
applies serious research to Islam to discover what is valid and
reliable, (b) acknowledges that Islam may be to the Arabs as
Judaism was to the Hebrews, a preparatio evangelica, and (c)
aims for a positive presentation of Christ. A slightly modified
version of this second stage appears in 1928 (perhaps due to the
structure of the Jerusalem Conference) in which Gairdner (a) is
aware of the values in Islam, (b) is convinced that Christianity
is the corrective and fulfillment of Islam, i.e. of the dilemma
and needs of the Muslim as a man; and (c) concentrates upon the
church as the present expression of new life in Christ and as
agent of Christ's work in the world. This evaluation can be substantiated by examining several of Gairdner's writings.

The final chapters of The Reproach of Islam (1909) depict
Gairdner's earlier attitude and approach. The House of Islam is
too ill to reform itself, salvation must come from outside.
Although he sees the two systems standing against each other, he
tries to direct men beyond to the Spirit of Christ.

> We therefore close with one observation...Islam and Chris-
> tianity are incompatible; they are different in ethos, in
> aim, in scope, in sympathy. Islam is the later born....If,
> in its very constitution, it is unfitted to be the universal
> religion, because only a religion in which Spirit is supreme
> and fundamental, and rite definitely subordinate to Spirit,
> can be universal, then the religion of Christ is the univer-
> sal religion. But if so, then that religion, as preached to
> the Mohammedan, must indeed be a religion of Spirit, of the
> Spirit of Jesus....Most futile, most disappointing, and most
> foolish of all quests would be that which were only to seek
> to substitute for one ritual another, for one system another
> system,....Nothing but the Spirit can bind and free Islam.
> Let the Church that does not believe in the Holy Ghost save
> herself the trouble of attempting the conversion of Islam.[95]

Gairdner then queries, "How is that Cross to be given the victory? How is He to be lifted up and draw all these unto Him?
Islam—How save it?"[96] His answer is that the church must obey
her great commission. Too long she has repudiated and shirked
the problem of Islam. He considers the Cairo Conference (1906)
something of a turning point in history. In spite of the armour
of Islam, Muslims can and are being reached. While the problem
of tackling a half-truth, a denial of a given truth, a post-his-
torical development is always more complex, it is not impossible
in the Spirit of Christ. As he examines the work of John
Damascene, Lull, Martyn, Pfander, French, it is apparent that
Gairdner's interest lies in an apologetic method. Mission is

however never just a job, for the "Church's understanding of
herself" is tied up with "world redemption".

What then will it not be when the Church as a whole has
realized that she exists to evangelise the World?...of
'making Jesus King' over all....Islam is the greatest call
the Church ever has had, or will have, to look to Him who is
invisible--to come to an understanding and realisation of the
meaning of CHRIST. In a score of ways the reproach of Islam
that lies upon us day by day, calls us to explore His forgotten secrets, and to realise what He in Himself is. Most
of all it calls us to a closer association with Christ Him-
self--to that continuance with Him in His temptations,--to
learn what is the Kingdom of God, Who is the Spirit of Jesus
....And if the Church is brought truly to learn this lesson,
she will face the reproach of Islam, with shame and sorrow
indeed, but without dismay, for she will, in so learning,
learn also the secret of Christ's Victory, and prove in herself the power of His Risen Life.[97]

From 1912 onwards, Gairdner's appreciative if critical research in Islam is paralleled by a more positive presentation of
Christ. This maturing is again seen in the lapse in time bet-
ween the parts of "The Doctrine of the Unity in Trinity".[98] "A
Reply to Mohammedan Objections and an Essay in Philosophic
Apology" (Part I, 1911) is a simulated conversation of a "Dis-
cussion Society" intended to show the scriptural and rational
foundations of the Trinity and to answer five Muslim objections.
For the moment Gairdner stands squarely in the lineage of
Martyn-Pfander-Tisdall. He follows the advice of the Edinburgh
Conference and prepares an apologetic literature touching the
primary issue of the concept of God. By 1916 (Parts II and III)
Gairdner has advanced. No longer the nineteenth century de-
fender, he has probed deep into Islam and knows how its Deism
(a "self-contained Monad") leaves an unbridgeable chasm between
Creator and creation.

How real this difficulty is all students of Islam know.
The Philosophers with their theories of Emanation and the
Eternity of the World; and the Sufis with their Tradition
are enough to prove that this difficulty is a real one; and,
as a matter of fact, most agnosticism is owing to the seriousness of this very difficulty to many minds. We say that
the doctrine of a Trinity makes the position easier, not more
difficult....(1) The doctrine of the Triune God reveals to us
a God with eternal activities, not latent, but patent in
eternal actions....(2)...shows that creation did not mean for
God the beginning of relations: for God in Himself is eternally related in the highest possible way--in a way that in-
finitely transcends the most highly organised and related

being on earth....(3)...removes the difficulty of ascribing
reaction, limitation, passivity, and emotion to God, which is
so fatal to pure transcendence, and which is nevertheless,
inevitable as soon as you have ascribed to Him creation.[99]

Christianity is well equipped to explain God's relation to man
("in His image") while Islam is disturbed to discover that the
attributes (names) applied to God can also apply to man. Although Muhammad and Muslims have been conscious of the presence
and "a mysterious self-relation of God to space and sense",
their theology prevented them from understanding or expressing
it, hence resulting in a denial of ongoing communication. Gairdner urges the Muslim reader to consider the incarnation again,
the Christ who gives man an understanding of his experience of
God, a mystery which baffles our boastful reason.
    Another example of Gairdner's maturing is "The Vital Forces
of Christianity and Islam" wherein he proposes that Islam may be
a dim preparatio evangelica which will find its correction in
the Christian faith.[100] Islam's vitality is found in four areas.

> (1)...its doctrine of God...that He is a personal force,
> and that He has a definite relation to the world--which in-
> cludes a real, though quite inscrutable and also passionless
> favour towards themselves....It may not always produce a
> particularly ethical fruit, but it...gives them a steady if
> stiff, Weltanschauung; it very often enables them to face
> loss, trouble, and adversity with complete stoicism....(2)...
> The Moslem's devotion to his Prophet, his admiration and
> enthusiasm, nay, his personal love for him, are intense
> realities. He believes that the Prophet suffered and sacri-
> ficed in loyalty to his mission....(3) Another reality of the
> Moslem's life is his pride in Islam, its position as latest
> and last of the religions, its triumphs, its literature and
> its learning, its saints and its doctors. It is this and...
> his sense of fraternity....(4)...what is really significant
> in the Moslem's spiritual life,...is the highly elaborate,
> ornate chanting of the Koran--an art of the delight of which
> is born half of music and half of word--that gives him that
> element of aesthetic uplift.[101]

Gairdner suggests that the Muslim must be approached as Aquila
and Priscilla approached Apollos (cf. Acts 18:26).

> The doctrines in question must be presented by us, not as
> hard, formulated lumps of creed, but as organic tissue of
> faith, warm with life and perpetually giving rise to new
> life.[102]

The Muslim must be led from admiration for Ecce Homo to faith
and obedience in Ecce Rex. Only the living Christ can really

unfold the cross.

> It is only when for one cause or other a Moslem's faith in
> Islam is shaken, and he finds a home in Christianity, that
> very gradually his thoughts about God expand and demand to
> find in Him what only Christ has ever revealed.[103]

This remedial presentation of the Gospel can begin with the
unity of God (stressing that incarnation and atonement begin in
the heart of God), the Christ as Logos (a concept Muslims acknowledge), and the Holy Spirit as the Presence of God (a concept given limited reference in the Quran). In this dynamic
experience both church and Muslim can discover anew how the fulness of God and the joys of man are realized en Christo.[104]

Gairdner's final paper, "Christianity and Islam", prepared
for the Jerusalem Conference (1928) with the aid of W. A. Eddy
and at the urging of J. H. Oldham, raises several significant
questions. Did Gairdner in his last years modify his views to
accept the comparative religions approach?[105] Did Gairdner
adopt the fulfillment concept popularized by J. N. Farquhar?[106]
The answer to both must be, No! Although it has been hinted
that Gairdner leaned in this direction and one must admit that
the outward appearance of the paper (with its structure of comparison, reference to values and fulfillment, etc.) suggests
such, a probing behind the scenes reveals otherwise. The content of this paper is but a resume of the evangelistic-apologetic writings of Gairdner over the last nineteen years. One
must remember that only reluctantly did Gairdner accept this
task. The Conference's structure for the comparison of values
in Christianity and other religions undoubtedly made Gairdner
uncomfortable.

This clarification of Gairdner's position dates back to Edinburgh, 1910. Commission IV under Chairman D. S. Cairns had been
searching for a correct apologetic approach for conveying the
Gospel to adherents of non-Christian religions. Gairdner himself calls this report, "one of the most remarkable, perhaps the
most remarkable, of a great series".[107] It was here that the
idea of Christianity as the fulfillment of other religions came
under the fire of the D. S. Cairns-A. G. Hogg team. This team
influenced by the neo-evangelical stirrings on the continent
rejected the application of the evolutionary principle to all
religions including Christianity. While supporting a sympathetic approach to other religions, they insisted that the Christian faith was unique, final, supernaturally revealed by God in
Christ and stood in contrast to, rather than as the fulfillment
of other religions.[108] Gairdner, coming out of a solid evangelical Anglican background, appears to have a closer affinity to
his friend D. S. Cairns than to Farquhar.[109] Sharpe rightly
detects that Farquhar uses fulfillment on two levels.

(1) The religious phenomena of Christianity are universal
religious phenomena on the highest level of their development. The corresponding Hindu phenomena, of which there are
many, are lower on the evolutionary scale, and are therefore
'fulfilled' by the former in the course of the process of
evolution....
     (2) Man's basic religious instincts are satisfied, i.e.
they reach fulfillment, only in Christianity, although all
religions provide partial answers to the questions raised by
the unsatisfied.[110]

Now Gairdner, along with Zwemer and A. G. Hogg, could give qualified acceptance to the second idea, but they rejected the first.
Christianity fulfills the spiritual longing of the Muslim (any
man), but it in no way fulfills Islam.[111] Thus it appears to be
a mistake to ascribe to Gairdner the characteristics of the comparative religion school of thought found at Jerusalem (1928).[112]
In fact his fatal sickness robbed him of the chair at this Conference which young Kraemer came to occupy. Kraemer was to play
the intermediary in the debate between the critical Germans
(insisting on the sui generis of Christianity and the grace of
the transcendent God), the Americans (varying from Hocking to
Speer and Mackay), and the mediating British.[113] Closer scrutiny of the paper "Christianity and Islam" reveals that the framework of comparison, values, and fulfillment has been largely
superimposed upon Gairdner's solid life-time contributions. The
content is composed of concise, practically irreducible blocks
of Gairdner's earlier writings placed under new headings and
leads. It is a compact statement of the Christian answer to
Islam as found in Christ and as expressed in the church.[114] It
is a final restatement of Gairdner's apology in the packaging of
Jerusalem, 1928. It represents no significant change in content,
only the matured convictions of Temple Gairdner.

Gairdner's Understanding of the Church

     At this point, one must review Gairdner's early experiences
in the ecumenical movement and his realistic criticism of the
church to appreciate his vision of the church. He hoped that
gradually her life as mission, community and as a center of
learning and worship might be realized.
     Closely associated with the student movements, missionary
conferences and such eminent friends as J. H. Oldham, J. R.
Mott, R. E. Speer and S. M. Zwemer, Gairdner grew with the ecumenical movement. While ever conscious of the gap between the
ideal concerning the church's life and mission (Jn. 17:21) and
the present reality, he was confident in his hope. His early
analysis of the situation of the church, worldwide, is found in
Edinburgh, 1910. It was written to:

give to many thousands of readers a new vision of the
central place of Christian missions in the current history of
the world, and of what God would have them now to do for the
coming of the Kingdom of God.[115]

The Conference made a lasting impact upon Gairdner and in the
next eighteen years he made contributions in the areas of all
eight commissions.[116] The awareness of the changing world made
one world mission and world church more urgent.

Humanity was awakening to self-consciousness: it became
tenfold more urgent to say to humanity Ecce Homo! The world
was realising that it was a unity;--was that unity to be or
not to be in One Lord and One Faith.[117]

Yet "Carrying the Gospel to all the Non-Christian World" (Commission I) required the best scientific study of the problems of
geographical expansion. Formed at Richter's suggestion, the
Continuation Committee became a vital tool for research and for
unifying those areas of the church isolated by Islam.[118] "The
Church on the Mission-Field" (Commission II) viewed the appearance of infant national churches and the growth of their corporate life as "the pledge of final victory". Yet in reality,
power in 1910 still rested with the mission boards and the young
churches were poorly represented. Commission III insisted that
Christian education could offer a nation a basis for unity,
brotherhood and freedom.[119] As already seen, Gairdner considered the Report of Commission IV under D. S. Cairns as one of
the greatest. The "Relation to Non-Christian religions" was
going to become the big issue at Jerusalem (1928) and Madras
(1938). Gairdner describes the attitude which held other religions to be "specimens of absolute error" which must be uproot-
ed and destroyed (e.g. Duff). Others, he noted, considered
other religions as "attempted solutions of Life's problems"
hence to be approached with sympathy, respect and study (e.g.
Zwemer). Still others as "broken lights" containing some truth
to be fulfilled in Christ the Light of the world. Gairdner
stands somewhere between the last two.[120] He went on to
wrestle with the question of unity, "the need of One Body to
give outward and visible expression to the inward and spiritual
grace of the One Spirit". He advocated not a "tame homogeneous
uniformity" but a "definite coherent heterogeneity," a "unity
amidst diversity and distinction".[121]

To restore to the whole Church this sense of proper function amounts to nothing short of the re-creation of the
Church--a work which only God Himself can work, yet a work
in which man can join by the almost forgotten secret of
prayer.[122]

The "Moravian Ideal" implies a church aware of "the Reality of God and the Sufficiency of His Grace for a World in Crisis".

The lessons of Edinburgh, 1910 were rigorously applied to the church in the years to follow by Gairdner. He alerts the Church of England and Christians in British circles to their duty to the people of Egypt.

> The National Mission was not merely a call to England to recognise certain internal diseases and to seek their cure; it was a call to a self-surrender to God of the whole universe and to the knowing and doing of His Will in all its length and breadth.[123]

He applies the pressure equally to Oriental Christian communities in 1925. Both evangelical and Orthodox bodies in the Near East are neglecting the evangelization of Muslims, failing to assimilate converts when they do appear. Why? Three factors create and sustain this non-evangelistic tradition. First, Eastern Christians have been filled with fear by living under:

> the age-long pressure of a conquering, a domineering, and an unsparing state-religion: a religion which has made 'proselytism' and even preaching criminal offences; a religion which has barely conceded to the depressed members of other faiths the right to exist, and then only on the express conditions that they kept themselves to themselves.[124]

Likewise the environment of the Near East has distorted the church:

> the historic development of religious communities in the East has tended to turn them all into something resembling nations, the governing bodies of which are charged with a multitude of duties concerning the personal and social and political status of their members: the direct result is the disinclination to admit outsiders, and the denial of the desirability or even possibility of conversion, along with a strong development of those feelings of antipathy and antagonism which are associated with national community-feeling.[125]

Again the fact that some converts from Islam have lapsed does not help, but this may possibly reflect the unreceptive atmosphere of the church. To combat and change this, Gairdner suggested three activities: to replace this negative mentality with one of Christian hope and courage, to recapture the concept of the church as "a spiritual brotherhood", and to restore the church as a home for the convert (implying all members share in pastoral care).

At this point, it is advisable to consider Gairdner's vision of the church: a reality to be realized. He saw the church as

the holy, temporal manifestation of the "Spirit of Jesus" in the
world, the ministry of the Incarnate Christ. Because Christ
died for the world, nothing less than the whole world can be the
objective of the church's apostolic mission.

> There is only one possible objective for those who 'take
> the cross' today--the Kingdom of God as inaugurated by Jesus
> Christ for the whole of humanity. No exceptions can be made,
> for to make an exception would be both the betrayal of the
> Kingdom and a slight upon the thing excepted. To offer
> Mohammedans Christ's Kingdom of God puts us right with truth
> and with ourselves.[126]

The conversion of thousands of Muslims to Christ in Africa, East
Indies and the Near East bear witness to God's activity. Yet
only as the whole laity of the church are effective, the "witness of Christ shall again regain the universality and direct-
ness that it had in apostolic times".[127] The church as catholic community reconciling all men is the theme found in nearly
every article written by Gairdner in his last decade. The basic
presuppositions are set down in "The Christian Church as a Home
for Christ's Converts from Islam",[128] a paper which he considered the crowning epitaph of his life.

> We are agreed that when Jesus Christ founded His Church
> He purposed to spread His message of Salvation everywhere by
> means of that Church.
> We are agreed that this work is the main duty of the
> Church as a whole:--that Christ's congregation in this world
> is not intended to live to itself--not even to build up it-
> self in holiness, only--but to live for its evangelizing
> task....
> We are agreed that the responsibility for the evangeli-
> zation of any country is and must be mainly, almost entirely,
> upon the local Christian community, denominations, congrega-
> tions, families and church members in that country....If
> these things be true, we are then agreed that the abiding
> test of the success of missionary work in those lands will
> be how far the Christian community which has been influenced
> or raised up through missionary effort takes up and prose-
> cutes the evangelization of the Moslem people.[129]

The realization of the new brotherhood, the new fraternity of
love found in Christ, is a pre-requisite to evangelization of
Muslims. He nurtured a "warm internal love, friendliness and
all-embracing benevolence" in the congregations he served.

> The brotherhood preached by our Lord in the Parable of the
> Good Samaritan is wholly unknown to the Moslem to whom
> 'neighbor' and 'brother' do precisely mean--consciously,
> officially, and admittedly--his co-religionist and him alone.

...The Christian fraternity, so magnificently realized in the first centuries, is to-day broken to bits, but the ideal is still with absolute faith and confidence....Before we can win our Moslem brother to the fellowship of the Twelve with their Master, we must issue to Christians and to Christian mission the call 'Back to Christ'....Back to the limitless brother-liness of the Spirit of Jesus.[130]

Gairdner stressed the theme of the missionary nature of the con-gregation that was to gain such attention at New Delhi (1961).

For the Church or congregation which desires to be, sets out to be, and succeeds in being a home for those converted to Christ from Islam, is in itself a gospel...let alone the fact that precisely such a church will certainly be the one most forward in preaching to non-Christians in the ordinary sense of the word.

Therefore, to see our congregations and communities as homes for those who are not yet Christ's, but for whom Christ is seeking, is our supreme task, our highest ideal, our fairest dream.[131]

Gairdner sees the church as a center of learning (discipleship) and worship (doxology). To mobilize the church for the twin work of witness and worship, he created a program of learning. First, he set out to build a handbook to guide the young church in equipping its membership. By death, he had not only com-pleted much of this curriculum, but was preparing his first com-mentaries in Arabic, perhaps one of the most needed tools in the church. Second, he sought to train teacher-friends (didaskaloi) who would welcome and instruct inquirers, catechumens and new members. Gairdner underplayed clerical control in order to arouse all members to their responsibility in winning and up-building others in the faith. Third, he was concerned with the bodily needs of converts frequently cut off from social and economic resources. He advised finding or making employment for them in order that they could retain a sense of self-respect.

Problems in no way diminished Gairdner's confident hope in the church's mission. Having experienced the power and pre-sence of the Christ who declared, "Behold, I make all things new", he anticipated the transformation of the whole world. Thus he could participate without fear of failure in the dynam-ic mission of God in Christ.

The man who really believes is always and without any hesitation commending his religion to others. This is the essence of 'mission'--an outgoing towards others based on complete confidence....[132]

Gairdner's love for the Muslim was rooted in the assurance of God's love and work within history for all men. Living in anti-

cipation of the King and his coming kingdom, he frequently
quoted the inscription on the church-mosque in Damascus.

> Thy Kingdom, O Christ, is a Kingdom of all ages,
> And Thy Dominion endureth throughout all generations.[133]

The radiating influence of Temple Gairdner would reach to Tambaram and beyond.[134] In the person and gifts of Gairdner, one
great branch of the church made the transition to a maturer
twentieth century approach to Muslims. It remains to be seen
what advances were taking place in Reformed ranks.

SAMUEL MARINUS ZWEMER (1867-1952): A REFORMED CONTRIBUTION

The Reformed faith radiating outwards from Geneva clearly
manifested itself in the life and work of the Dutch-American,
Samuel M. Zwemer. This keen student of the history of missions
benefited from earlier Reformed-Presbyterian enterprises (already observed in North India, Persia, Syria and Egypt) and
reflected their zeal for disseminating the written and spoken
Word, for pragmatic use of every means to raise up an indigenous
church, and for research literature which in turn could inform
and invigorate God's people for their task. Something of John
Newton, Charles Forman, John Wilson, Alexander Duff, Daniel
Bliss, Henry Jessup and Ion Keith-Falconer resided in Zwemer!
On the other hand, he belonged to the twentieth century, to the
ecumenical-missionary movement and the heightened emphasis on
evangelism as proclamation.

Our final objective in this study is to consider S. M. Zwemer
as a faithful representative of the pioneering and maturing
process of Reformed missions to Muslims. To accomplish this,
three periods/realms of his life's activities will be surveyed
briefly. Then will follow a closer examination of the substance
of his contributions to three vital themes: the church, Islam
and evangelism. In each case attention will be given to the
growth in his thought and attitudes. Finally, the focus will
be on his role in the debate on mission and theology (1920-
1938), a debate which sharpened his views on evangelism. Zwemer,
the author is convinced, is worthy of serious consideration as
the consummation of the nineteenth century of Reformed missions
and as a commencer of the rediscovery of the Word with reference
to Islam.

The Life and Work of S. M. Zwemer, A Biographical Sketch

Samuel Marinus Zwemer was born April 12, 1867 at Vriesland,
Michigan, the thirteenth of fifteen children.[135] From his
Huguenot-Dutch parents, he inherited a strong Calvinistic con-

viction and from his frontier experiences, stamina and a sense
of independence. Emigrating to the United States to settle at
Rochester, New York, then Holland, Michigan, his father studied
theology under local ministers before serving various pastor-
ates. Samuel took his academy work (1879-1883) then undergrad-
uate studies at Hope College, Holland, Michigan (1883-1887).
During his senior year he responded to an appeal to mission
service when Robert Wilder visited the campus on behalf of the
Student Volunteer Movement. Already active in the campus
mission band, a member of the Reformed Church in America (March
9, 1884), and an experienced colporteur of the American Bible
Society (summer, 1886), Samuel trained for the ministry at New
Brunswick Theological Seminary (New Jersey), the oldest seminary
in the nation. While a student there, he assisted in the medical clinic of Dr. William Wanless, later well-known missionary
doctor to India.

First Milestone: Founder and Pioneer in the Arabian Mission,
1888-1912

The idea of a mission to Arabia, the heartland of Islam, was
conceived by Zwemer and his fellow students, James Cantine and
Philip T. Phelps under the inspiration of Professor J. G. Lansing in 1888. Active in the S.V.M. and acquainted with Robert
Wilder, John R. Mott and Robert E. Speer, Zwemer selected the
most difficult field available for his part in "The evangelization of the world in this generation". Twenty-three years were
spent in Arabia in a sacrificial venture equal to the creative
venture of the White Fathers in the Sahara. The Arabian Mission's work at Basrah, Bahrain, Muscat and Kuwait bore a sustained witness to the life and light given in Christ.[136] Endowed with both literary and vocal gifts of expression, Zwemer became the Reformed authority on Islam and Arabia. Though plagued
with eye troubles for a time, he organized and led the Cairo
Conference (1906), served as field secretary of the Reformed
Mission Board (1907), became the first candidate secretary of
S.V.M. (1908), recruiting missionaries of the caliber of Paul W.
Harrison, and spoke at many conventions at the request of J. R.
Mott and his home church. After the S.V.M. Convention at Rochester (January, 1910), this representative to Edinburgh (1910)
was stimulated to found and edit the periodical, The Moslem
World. Back in Bahrain, he prepared for the Lucknow Conference,
a tour of India and Y.M.C.A. conferences in Bombay and Calcutta
(1911). Although resembling a jig-saw puzzle, every piece of
Zwemer's life had a part in his single purpose: the evangelization of the Muslim world.
     A call was extended to Zwemer in 1912 by the United Presby-
terian Mission in Egypt and supported by the C.M.S. (esp. Temple
Gairdner), Nile Mission Press, Egypt General Mission, and the
Y.M.C.A., to come to Cairo and make it a study center for

Islamics, a production point for Christian Literature for Muslims, and other inter-denominational activity. Released from the Arabian Mission, personally financed by a member of the Southern Presbyterian Church, encouraged by the Reformed Church in America and the Presbyterian Church (U.S.A.), and provided with travel expenses by the American Christian Literature Society for Moslems (A.C.L.S.M., which he served as volunteer field secretary), Zwemer became a missionary-at-large, the personification of ecumenical cooperation in missions to Muslims.

Second Milestone: Literary Evangelist and Ecumenical Leader-at-Large, 1912-1928

Of these intense and creative years (1912-1928), Zwemer calculated he spent thirteen in Cairo and hence about three on the road. Besides earning respect as an author and editor, Zwemer taught at the Presbyterian Theological Seminary and the Center for Oriental Studies in Cairo.[137] Literature gained prime place in his evangelistic concern. He never forgot a telegram from his colleague, Charles R. Watson.

> No agency can penetrate Islam so deeply, abide so persistently, witness so daringly and influence so irresistibly as the printed page.[138]

For thirty-six years, Zwemer was editor of The Moslem World, a periodical which remains a gold mine of information, a source book on a half a century of mission work among Muslims.[139] The opening editorial states that the periodical's aim was to present a scientific study of Islam in English (as did Revue du Monde Musulman and Der Islam.

> The existence of all this literature, however, and the revival of interest in the great problem of Islam shown by the publication of these reviews, and the issue of a new 'Encyclopedia of Islam' simultaneously in three languages, only emphasize the opportunity and the place for an English quarterly review of current events, literature, and thought among Mohammedans as they affect the Church of Christ and its missionary programme, if the Churches of Christendom are to reach the Moslem world with the Gospel. The Cairo Conference (1906) marked a new era in the attitude of Christian missions toward the subject. This Conference, through its reports and other missionary literature resulting from it, made clear the unity, the opportunity, and the importunity of the task of evangelizing Moslems everywhere. Missionary leaders felt that the Church was called to a deeper study of the problem, as well as to a more thorough preparation of its missionaries and a bolder faith in God, in order to solve it. To this end there is need for a common platform,

a common forum of thought; a common organ for investigation
and study.[140]

This was a commentary on his own life-long aims. Breathing the
spirit of Edinburgh, 1910, this quarterly aimed:

> to represent no faction or fraction of the Church, but to
> be broad in the best sense of the word. Its columns are open
> to all contributors who hold the 'unity of the faith in the
> bond of peace and righteousness of life.' It is not a maga-
> zine of controversy, much less compromise. In essentials it
> seeks unity, in non-essentials liberty, in all things charity.
> We hope to interpret Islam as a world-wide religion in all
> its varied aspects and its deep needs, ethical and spiritual,
> to Christians; to point out and press home the true solution
> of the Moslem problem, namely, the evangelization of Moslems;
> to be of practical help to all who toil for this end; and to
> awaken sympathy, love and prayer on behalf of the Moslem
> world until its bonds are burst, its wounds are healed; its
> sorrows removed, and its desires satisfied in Jesus
> Christ.[141]

Zwemer wisely created an editorial staff and a list of contribu-
tors which included the most eminent Islamic scholars and experienced workers available.[142] In addition to setting a scholarly
standard in content and style, the first issue established a
realistic if visionary missionary approach to Islam. With Charles R. Watson, Zwemer founded the A.C.L.S.M. (1910) which spent
a quarter of a million dollars promoting literature for Muslims
over thirty years.[143] Zwemer's own pen never seemed to stop its
flow of ink. His prodigious output included articles, editorials, surveys, pamphlets and some fifty books over the years
causing him later to reflect.

> The Moslem World Quarterly Review took a great deal of my
> spare time, and bound our mission by many ties of correspon-
> dence and friendship with scattered workers throughout the
> world of Islam....When I look back also to the six books in
> Arabic and the twenty-four tracts for Moslems...I can only
> thank God for the strength given me for so varied and exten-
> sive a literary effort.[144]

One must not forget that Zwemer was always involved in personal evangelism whether among the Arabs of Basrah, Bahrain or
Cairo or the citizens of Africa, Europe, and the Americas.
Books were a passion with him, but people, especially Muslims
were his first love. His personableness was probably even more
powerful than his pen. Inasmuch as personality is a bridge used
of God, Zwemer was convinced that the Gospel is best communicated in person to person situations. While all efforts depend on
the bridge, the incarnation, God uses disciples, the church, in

the horizontal task of linking men to Christ. Zwemer personally
extended himself to the students and professors of Al-Azhar and
encouraged convert Mikhail Mansoor in university work.[145] Zwemer
describes his work during the war years in Neglected Arabia
(publication of the Arabian Mission).

> ...Schools, hospitals, the Mission Press and public meet-
> ings have been conducted as usual....Under the able direction
> of men like Mr. Wm. Jessup and Mr. H. W. White, a special
> evangelistic campaign was conducted for two weeks and hund-
> reds of men made decisions for Christ.
> My special work this year, as heretofore, has been along
> literary lines in connection with the Nile Mission Press,
> teaching in the Theological Seminary and also at the Cairo
> Study Center. In the Theological Seminary this year we have
> sixteen students in the regular classes and fourteen in the
> evangelists' class, who are taking a special course. It is
> a rare privilege to read Al-Ghazali with these students from
> Assiut College who are preparing themselves for the ministry,
> and to study Islam with the future leaders of the Church in
> Egypt in order that they themselves may plan for the speedy
> evangelization of their own country.
> At the Cairo Study Center, Canon W. H. T. Gairdner has
> charge of language study and by his new method, through the
> use of phonetics and the colloquial, remarkable progress is
> being made. Mr. R. F. McNeile...and I have given lectures
> on Islam and methods of work. Twenty new missionaries of
> various societies are taking these courses....In the study
> of Islam one is more and more impressed how much Mohammed
> owed to Judaism and how much modern Jewish ritual is like
> that of Islam.[146]

Many other lasting associations with European and Arab scholars
(e.g. D. B. Macdonald, Arthur Jeffery) were established in these
years. In a circular letter (1924), Zwemer wrote:

> ...Almost as soon as I arrived in September the course of
> lectures at the School of Oriental Studies for new mission-
> aries began, and every week we have a group or groups number-
> ing all the way from thirty to fifty present. I have lec-
> tured on Methods of Evangelism, the Moslem Christ, Mohammedan
> Mysticism, and am just now beginning a new course on Christ-
> ian Literature for Moslems. In the Theological Seminary and
> the Evangelists' School we have similar courses, though more
> suitable to the Coptic students who attend. I have preached
> every Sunday since coming to Egypt, both in English and in
> Arabic. In addition to the churches in Cairo, it has been
> my privilege to visit Port Said, Benha, Zagazig, Assiut and
> other centers for conferences of the native church. At these
> conferences, it will interest you to know, we are using a new

study book in Arabic, entitled 'The Nearest Way to the Moslem
Heart.'...I was able to complete the manuscript of a new book
to be entitled 'The Law of Apostasy.' It deals with the difficulties Moslem converts have, and how they surmount them.
...We are greatly encouraged because of its (Orient and
Occident) increased circulation and the eagerness with which
the Christian message is welcomed everywhere.[147]

James Hunt's description of Zwemer as a leader and creator of
plans provides a clue to the magnetism of this man.

> He may be said to be a man of one idea. While his inter-
> ests and knowledge were wide, I never talked with him ten
> minutes that the conversation did not veer to Islam....He
> also had an inventive mind, fertile with fresh plans for the
> work. Almost too much so, in fact, for practical work. In a
> committee meeting, his mind would scintillate with new ideas
> that would commend themselves to the rest of us....I recall
> that he said once after leaving such a meeting that he could
> suggest plans but he needed someone else to carry them out.
> He was always a lovable character and had a keen sense of
> humor that made him a delightful companion. He was the
> center of any group in which he might be.[148]

These insights help one understand the strengths and weaknesses
of Zwemer, a man with the vision of a prophet and the diligence
of an evangelist. Yet he also stood in the larger company of
respected scholars of the time. The Cairo press referred to him
as "the leading authority on Islamics from the Christian standpoint".[149]

As a spokesman for the mission to Muslims and an ecumenical
leader, Zwemer stands in the ranks of Mott, Speer and others.
He was particularly equipped to arouse the church to fulfill her
God-given obligation to the Muslim world. His own Reformed
Church in America would elect him as President of General Synod
in 1923. In 1913 he addressed conferences in the Arab world and
in several European cities including Zurich. A lecture series
at Princeton and addresses across America and Europe followed in
1915.[150] He lectured at Robert College (Istanbul) (1921) and
later at a student conference at Smyrna. To the various mission
conferences, he made no small contribution. An honored platform
crusader in the Student Volunteer Movement, he spoke at conventions at Nashville (1906), Rochester (1910) and Kansas City
(1914). His Rochester words, "To His Kingdom there are no
frontiers" were oft repeated. Sherwood Eddy respected him as
"the blazing prophet of every platform summoning the Church to
its most difficult task,"...to convey the Gospel for the citizens of Arabia and Egypt.[151] After attending the Decennial at
Madras (1902), he set to work organizing a Conference at Cairo
especially dedicated to Muslim Work (1906). This was followed

by Y.M.C.A. conferences and the Lucknow Conference (1911), a
visit to India and China (1917), and extensive training tours in
India (1924, 1927-28). The latter sessions centered upon Christian Literature in Moslem Lands[152] and "How to Carry the Gospel
Message to the Moslem Heart".[153] Zwemer's travel as a roving
ambassador reached its peak between 1922 and 1927. In 1922, he
and J. R. Mott visited the various groups across North Africa.
With the same objectives of Christian unity and literature,
Zwemer traveled to the Dutch East Indies to cover 19,000 miles,
15 major conferences and make 99 addresses.[154] One can imagine
that this veteran made a considerable impact on young Hendrik
Kraemer and the other 400 missionaries of some 16 Protestant
Missions. Zwemer was himself impressed by the 45,000 converts
won from Islam in Java and nearby Islands. He reported:

> Missions in Java are remarkable; (1) in the large results
> secured among an almost wholly Moslem population, and these
> results were secured not by superficial methods, but by a
> most thorough requirement for baptism. (2) In the prepara-
> tion of Christian literature, including Bible translations,
> where the psychology of the people was taken into considera-
> tion, as perhaps on no other field. The Javanese mind was
> thoroughly understood in presenting the message, and there-
> fore it received acceptance. (3) In spite of the many socie-
> ties engaged in the work in one single field, the laws of
> comity have been strictly observed, and there is an increas-
> ing spirit of cooperation....[155]

This helps one to understand Zwemer's contribution to Kraemer's
thunderbolt volume at Tambaram. After full reports at the Jerusalem Session (1924), Zwemer chaired a special conference at
Bagdad for workers from Iraq, Iran and Arabia. In 1925, he participated in a deputation to South Africa to alert these
churches in their duties to Muslims. It is interesting that
this able Dutch speaker stressed the implications of the Gospel
on race relationships in the Johannesburg Conference. Again in
1926, he shared in a Conference at Tabriz, in a Persia with a
"future, bright as the promise of God". Between 1925-1927,
several trips were made West. This human dynamo ("a steam en-
gine in breeches" according to Gairdner) addressed 14 mission
organizations and 36 other groups (some 37,000 persons) during
23 days in Britain to establish something of a record. His
contacts also included Tor Andrae of Sweden, Alfred Neilsen of
Denmark and Julius Richter of Berlin. Such were the exploits of
this enthusiast for the cause of Christ.
    Two peaks of accomplishment, Cairo (1906) and Lucknow (1911),
stand out in Zwemer's career. The consensus of opinion is that
Cairo was "the beginning of a new era in the Christian Mission
to Muslims".[156] Organized and led by Zwemer, the Cairo Conference set the pace for Edinburgh (1910) and the Continuation

Committee. It inaugurated a more sympathetic, ecumenical Christian attitude and approach to Islam. Moreover it meant that for
the first time, Christian workers (62 delegates from 29 societies) assembled in a Muslim land to discuss their mission objectives regarding Muslims. Cairo represented a comprehensive
understanding of the whole Muslim world; set forth the issues;
united the participants in an evangelistic approach; examined
the lessons of past failures; saw the role of positive (not
polemical) literature; and challenged the whole church to fulfill its obligations to its Muslim neighbors. It set into
motion ventures in literature and evangelism still coming to
fruition fifty years later. At Lucknow (1911), Zwemer was again
the leading spirit. In a pre-conference sermon, he spoke of the
duties of the church as elder brother to the prodigal, Islam.
This application of the biblical themes of Jacob-Ishmael, elder-
prodigal, and our common need of the Father's mercy influenced
the whole conference.[157] The papers discussed the Pan-Islamic
movement, political changes and governmental attitudes towards
missions, Islamic advances among pagan peoples, missionary
training and literature, and Islamic reform movements.[158]
Zwemer was at his best--surveying the sweep of world movements,
providing factual data, and helping to set realistic goals in
light of both the situation and the Spirit's leading. He could
dramatically conclude that the victory belonged to Christ.

> As our eyes sweep the horizon of all these lands dominated
> or imperilled by this great rival faith, each seems to stand
> out as typical of the factors in the great problem....Each
> of these typical conditions in itself an appeal. The supreme
> need of the Moslem world is Jesus Christ. He alone can give
> light to Morocco, unity to Persia, life to Arabia, re-birth
> to Egypt,....[159]

Theologically, an evangelical by conviction (to some a conservative one), Zwemer would consider no compromise of the deity, incarnation and resurrection of Christ or the evangelistic nature
of the church's work. Yet he was always a most winsome figure
at these gatherings. Latourette says:

> Zwemer was a forceful speaker, pungent, and with an apt
> phrase to give point to his message. He had a robust sense
> of humor and an endless supply of stories. He was gifted
> with seemingly inexhaustible physical and nervous energy.
> Highly emotional, he never seemed to be fatigued by his out-
> pouring of himself in speech or conference.[160]

Third Milestone: Princeton and the Debate on Mission, 1929-1938

In 1928, Zwemer accepted the position of Professor of the
History of Religion and Christian Missions at Princeton Theological Seminary, a post he had been offered already in 1918. His

endeavors resulted in The Origin of Religion (1935) and seminars
on missions which were well-known among students and missionaries in residence for their blend of fact, wit and inspiration.
Even in his sixties he was the coveted guest speaker across
North America and Great Britain. As will be seen, he continued
to set forth the evangelical position amid the crisis of theology and mission. Even after his retirement (1938), the writings,
teachings, and travels of this tireless disciple breathed of the
deep personal faith in Christ which had set this dynamic life
into motion. Only in April 2, 1952, did Zwemer exchange this
active life for the fuller experience of "taking hold of God".

     The prolific pen of Samuel Zwemer produced works of varied
character and quality. A perusal of the appended bibliography
reveals how extensive were their scope.[161] Much of the material
is in a popular style yet without sacrifice of accuracy. A good
portion of his English works (a five foot shelf) were translated into Dutch, French, German, Danish, Spanish, Urdu and
Chinese. For Zwemer printed pages were the "leaves for the
healing of the nations". Several categories soon emerge in his
writings. First are those written to inform and challenge the
church in her mission to Islam. These volumes on missiology
were written mainly in the field and directed to the home-
churches, students, missionary recruits and workers.[162] During
the crisis in theology and mission (1920-1940), his evangelical
concepts were set forth with new clarity.[163] Second are his
scholarly studies in historical and popular Islam. Whereas
Gairdner delved into philosophical-theological Islam with a mind
to apologetics, Zwemer leaned towards the study of the phenomena
and theology of Muslims in order to achieve more effective proclamation. Some scholars consider his first hand observations
and discerning accounts of popular Islam his most exacting contribution to scholarship. Undoubtedly he was one of the better
informed Westerners of his day regarding contemporary Muslim
belief and practice. His "Factual Surveys" and statistics on
the Muslim World within each decade fall into this group.[164]
Third were his writings and tracts in Arabic for Muslims and the
Christians of the Near East.[165] Fourth are the biographical and
devotional works prepared for a wider audience.[166]

An Examination of the Thought and Contributions of Zwemer

     The major contributions of Zwemer were made before his re-
tirement from Princeton Seminary in 1938, with the peak of his
labors falling within the active Cairo years, 1912-1928. To
emphasize the strengths of Zwemer, his contributions will be
treated in reverse order of those of Gairdner. Gairdner began
by concentrating on evangelism (apologetics and student work),
enlarged his scholarly study of Islam and came to the matured
conclusion that mission in the Near East depended largely upon
the attitude and action of the national churches. While Zwemer

came from a solid church background and hoped to establish the
church in every land, he never engaged in the pastoral role that
Gairdner did. To the end he remained the prophet-evangelist
examining Islam primarily in its popular form to engage more
effectively in a precise proclamation of the Gospel of Jesus
Christ. Thus the reverse order of church-world-Word.

Zwemer's Understanding of the Church

First to be noted is Zwemer's deep love for the church. He
shared a loyalty to the Reformed Church in America and as a
Calvinist saw the church as the present manifestation of the
kingdom of God. As an evangelical churchman, he was not one to
be restricted by its organizational life or any narrow interpretation of its message. Traditions must ever be subservient to
the biblical message. In short he held that the church's form
must ever be shaped and reshaped by her message, mission and
Master. When the Reformed Church in America felt unable (fin-
ancially) to take up the work in Arabia, he helped establish an
independent "Arabian Mission" until such time as the church-at-
large rallied to the cause. Although a strong organizer himself, he saw the church as a community of believers, a people of
faith surmounting denominational borders. Thus without any
qualms of conscience he transferred his membership to the sister
Presbyterian Church, as required of the Princeton Seminary
faculty. The church for Zwemer was holy, catholic, apostolic
and doxological. The church beloved of Christ was supra-nation-
al, supra-denominational, supra-lingual, and supra-racial.
Secondly, one notes Zwemer's challenge to the church, a call
to mission. The church's life and mission are inseparably
linked. She only lives in Christ as she witnesses to Him. The
larger portion of his books and articles attempt to arouse the
church--student, laity and clergy to mission. Early in life, he
appears to have had a geographical concept of mission in mind.
It was the language of the day (Edinburgh, 1910) to speak of
the church's responsibility for the "unoccupied areas" of the
world.

> The unoccupied fields of the world have a claim of pecu-
> liar weight and urgency upon the attention and missionary
> effort of the Church. In this twentieth century of Christian
> history there should be no unoccupied fields. The Church is
> bound to remedy this lamentable condition with the least pos-
> sible delay...the closed doors are few compared with the open
> doors unentered. It is the neglected opportunities that are
> the reproach of the Church. A large proportion of the un-
> occupied fields are to be found within the Mohammedan world,
> not only in Northern Africa and in Western Asia, but also in
> China. Indeed, by far the greater part of the Mohammedan
> world is particularly unoccupied.[167]

Yet the church would be extended until she displaced the mosque
as she once displaced the synagogue. While the church might incidently benefit from European expansion, Zwemer was concerned
that the two should never be blurred into one. The church must
be established wherever Islam was disintegrating and in unoccupied Africa.[168] While conscious of the church's failings in her
dealings with Islam, he never placed the blame completely on her
shoulders. He was too conscious of the implications of mankind's revolt and the operation of evil-demonic powers in the
universe, to do that. Even the system of Islam, with its controls over a great culture, exercised a deadening influence
which could not be easily shaken off.[169] As time passed, Zwemer
saw the old geographical boundaries in a shrinking world crumble.
Christendom and Dar-al-Islam were neither accurate nor useful
titles with society everywhere becoming more pluralistic.
Zwemer increased his stress on person to person evangelism. For
although the Islamic system might lose some of its political
controls (disintegrate), the Muslim community would continue
long into the unforeseeable future. If such a world was to be
changed, it must be permeated by new persons in Christ. Only
ambassadors of Christ with a redemptive message could cope with
these changes. Zwemer thus applies his blend of individualism
and "moravian" motivation to the changing world of the twentieth
century. In a period when the church was under fire, he confessed that her theology and mission (motives, aims, and
methods), her organization and membership must be tested by
Christ alone.

Finally, Zwemer's concept of the church implied a call to
unity. Participating in the ecumenical movement from its stu-
dent-missionary genesis, he was active in its many conferences,
councils and committees and lived to see the emergence of the
World Council of Churches. His pragmatic emphasis was unity for
the sake of mission (Jn. 17:21), form as determined by function.
The central message "Be ye reconciled" applied to Christian
community as well as to non-Christian listener. As he pondered
over a map revealing how Christian forces in Muslim lands were
still vital if dormant and divided, he says:

> The time has come for securing a united front. Competi-
> tion is fatal over against Islam. Nor must we forget in this
> connection the debt we owe to the past....And did not the
> mantle of Raymond Lull fall on the 'White Fathers' as well as
> on Ion Keith Falconer and Thomas Valpy French? We can surely
> emphasize our unity in the words of the Apostle; 'One Lord,
> one faith, one baptism, one God and Father of all, Who is
> over all and through all and in all.'...In union will be our
> strength; none of us can do it alone, nor can any one Society
> in any one field.

Zwemer's awareness of the debt of the Reformed churches to their

brethren under Rome, his affection for Raymond Lull and St.
Francis of Assisi, and his cooperation with Roman Catholic scholars and clergy may come as a surprise for those unaware of his
magnanimity. No bare theorist, Zwemer proposed concrete action
in common scholarship,[171] in creating a catholic apologetics,[172]
and in strategic survey and expansion as begun by the Continuation Committee. Zwemer's dealings with the Orthodox churches
are marked by understanding.

> The history of the Armenian Church (faithful unto death dur-
> ing persecution), the present-day reforms in the Coptic
> Church, and the growing sense of responsibility among the
> younger leaders in some of the Oriental Churches for evangel-
> ization of the Moslems, are full of encouragement. We are
> too apt to underestimate the spiritual forces that remain
> alive throughout all the Moslem lands of the East. But the
> issues at stake are too vital and the urgency too great for
> anything but united effort.[173]

Zwemer visualized bringing all Protestant Christians into a uni-
fied program of world evangelism, then gradually drawing in
Orthodox and Roman Catholic bodies. Due to his preoccupation
with world evangelization, his concept of a world church went
undeveloped. Yet to the leaders of the ecumenical movement, he
left this advice:

> If there is to be a new global-strategy on the part of all of
> Christendom and if the World Council of Churches is to be
> more than a name and a dream, the Moslem world must have a
> primary place in such strategy.[174]

Aware of the need for a new baptism of apostolic wisdom and
energy, Zwemer urged the church to practice self-denial that the
Muslim world might be evangelized.[175]

Zwemer's Understanding of Islam

In Zwemer's growing understanding of Islam, one can detect
something of two stages. In the first quarter of a century of
his ministry (ca. 1890-1915/16), Zwemer reflects the legacy of
the nineteenth century which pits Christianity as a system over
against the various non-Christian religious systems. The ter-
minal point for this policy of "radical displacement" is found
in The Disintegration of Islam (1915) or Mohammed or Christ
(1916). In a second quarter (ca. 1915-1938 etc.), a second
approach gradually emerges and matures which can be described
as anthropological and Christocentric. Without compromising his
criticism of Islam as a system, he began a sympathetic study of
the Muslim as a man needing and seeking God. After study of
popular Islam (the practices of the man on the street), Al-

Ghazali and mysticism, Zwemer's terminology includes "our Muslim
brethren," etc. This sympathetic approach to the Muslim is
paralleled in his idea of evangelism as the proclamation of the
Christocentric message.

In his earlier aggressive approach to Islam, Zwemer saw Islam
as an overwhelming system controlling vast multitudes and portions of the earth. Although it was never as monolithic as
nineteenth century Europe imagined, yet for all practical purposes, Islamic law and rulers were in control. In fear or
wisdom, Europe had long bypassed the Near East. Although Zwemer
allowed his view of Islam as an animated system which stood or
fell as a single entity to long influence his vocabulary, it is
to his credit that he gradually changed his mind. His research
and writings revealed Islam to be far from impregnable. Nevertheless, his exposition of Islam as a system of belief and
practice (e.g. its origin, nature, prophet, book, history, view
of God and Christ) remained a challenge to the church.

According to Zwemer, the church must become a serious student
of Islam before it can effectively fulfill its mission.

> But if we are to reach that /Muslim/ world with the gospel of
> Christ we must first know of it and know it. There is no
> lack of literature on Mohammed and Islam, as is evident from
> the very extensive bibliography of the subject in all the
> languages of Europe not to speak of the literature written
> by Moslems themselves. But at the same time there is a great
> ignorance even among cultured people of the real character of
> Mohammed and the real doctrine and moral value of Islam, as
> well as of its widespread aggressive power as a missionary
> religion.[176]

Zwemer offered his studies from "the midst of Islam" as a balance to the historical-literary scholarship if Islam in the West.

> The spiritual burden of Arabia is the Mohammedan religion and
> it is in its cradle we can best see the fruits of Islam. We
> have sought to trace the spiritual as well as the physical
> geography of Arabia by showing Islam grew out of the earlier
> Judaism, Sabeanism and Christianity. The purpose of this
> book is especially to call attention to Arabia and the need
> of missionary work for the Arabs....We pray also that the
> number of those who love the Arabs and labor for their en-
> lightenment and redemption may increase.[177]

Agreeing with Rabbi Geiger and Tisdall on the origin and nature
of Islam, Zwemer held that Muhammad had drawn on the material of
older faiths to shape this new composite religion. While there
was a "time of ignorance" immediately before Muhammad, it was
incorrect to overstate this.

No part of Arabia has ever reached the high stage of civilization under the rule of Islam which Yemen enjoyed under
its Christian or even its Jewish dynasties of the Himyar-
ities.[178]

Feuding Roman, Abyssinian, Persian and Ghassan rulers plus internal breakdown in Arabia prompted Muhammad to lead the reform
and return to the monotheism of the Hanifs (the religion of
Abraham).

It is only a step from Hanifism to Islam. Primary Monotheism, Sabeanism, idolatry, fetishism, Hanifism, and then
the prophet with the sword to bring everything back to mono-
theism--monotheism, as modified by his own needs and character and compromise. The time of ignorance was a time of
chaos. Everything was ready for one who could take in the
whole situation, social, political and religious and form a
cosmos. That man was Mohammed....The result of a century of
critical study by European and American scholars of every
school of thought has certainly established the fact that
Islam is a composite religion....These heterogeneous elements
of Islam were gathered in Arabia at a time when many religions had penetrated the peninsula, and the Kaaba was a Pan-
theon. Unless one has a knowledge of these elements of 'the
time of ignorance,' Islam is a problem. Knowing, however,
these heathen, Christian and Jewish factors, Islam is seen as
a perfectly natural and understandable development.[179]

Islam's greatest danger lies in the Prophet's near-deification.

Islam denies the need of a mediator or of the incarnation,
but it is evident that, in popular thought and in Moslem
writings, Mohammed acts as a mediator, without an incarnation,
without an atonement, without demand for change of character
(e.g. the 'coronation hymn' of Islam, El Burda, the
Mantle).[180]

What really irks Zwemer is Western writers like Carlyle and Bos-
worth Smith who accept Muhammad as "a very Prophet of God" yet
ignore his obvious sins.[181] Turning to Arabic sources, Zwemer
cuts through this gloss:

It is possible to measure the prophet by three standards, of
which two at least would seem to be a fair test: the law of
the Pagan Arabs, the law he himself professed to reveal, and
the law of the Old and New Testaments, which he professed to
approve and supersede....Yet on basis of this and the Arab
accounts themselves Mohammed is revealed indeed as a very
finite man with many failings and deeds contrary to the above
codes. So the Koran also admits. Yet the Traditions and

practice of Muslims have made Mohammed almost sinless, divine, an intercessor, ever proclaiming his 'apotheosis'.[182]

While admiring the heights to which the Quran soars, Zwemer feels that it fails in its assessment of the human dilemma.

> The Koran is remarkable most of all not because of its contents, but because of its omissions. Not because of what it reveals but for what it conceals of 'former revelation.' ...It...seems to ignore the first and great barrier to such reconciliation, viz: SIN. Of this the Old and New Testaments are always speaking. Sin and Salvation are the subject of which the Torah and the Zaboor and the Injil are full. The Koran is silent or if not absolutely silent, keeps this great question ever in the background.[183]

If this is the case, how does one explain Islam's rapid spread?

> Many theories have been laid down and the true explanation is probably the sum of all of them. The weakness of Oriental Christianity and the corrupt state of the church; the condition of the Roman and Persian empires; the character of the new religion; the power of the sword and fanaticism; the genius of Mohammed; the partial truth of his teaching; the genius of Mohammed's successors; the hope of plunder and the love of conquest;--such are some of the causes given for the early and rapid success of Islam.[184]

What was Zwemer's method for understanding Islam over against Christianity, for claiming the latter's "superiority"? Like many evangelicals of the late nineteenth century, he used ethical-social arguments, the moderate forms of historical criticism, and the scientific-comparative study of religion.[185] He was not unmoved by the thought of Schleiermacher and Ritschl.

> The religion of Christ contains whole fields of morality and whole realms of thought which are but outside the religion of Mohammed....Its realized ideals in the various paths of human greatness have been more commanding, more many-sided, more holy....Finally, the ideal life of all, is far more elevating, far more majestic, far more inspiring, even as the life of the founder of Mohammedanism is below the life of the Founder of Christianity.[186]

Although he admitted ethics (fruit) as a test of religion, he held to the incarnation, the atonement (cross) and the Bible as objective realities. In the final analysis, a comparative study of Muslim and Christian ideas of God breaks down, and the only valid test for Zwemer is the revelation given by God in Christ.

In the comparative study of religious ideas there must be
a standard of judgment, and a Christian can only judge other
religions by the standard of the Gospel, Islam itself,
through its prophet and in its Book challenges comparison by
this standard. We are not dealing with the monotheism of
Greek philosophy which arose in the Court of the Gentiles
under Plato and Aristotle; but with a monotheism which arose
six centuries after Christ and professes to be an improvement
or at least a restatement of the Christian idea (cf. Surahs
42:1, 10:37, 93, 5:77, etc.). We accept therefore, Islam's
challenge. Jesus Christ proclaimed that no man knows the
Father save through the Son....that He came on a unique and
transcendent mission from the court of heaven--to show us the
Father. Instead of arriving at his theology through the mind
of Christ, as revealed in the gospels and developed through
the Holy Spirit's teaching in the epistles, Mohammed went
back to natural theology. He did not use, or would not use,
the channel of knowledge opened by the Incarnation. Instead
of learning from Him who descended from heaven, Mohammed
asserted that he himself ascended to heaven and there had
intercourse with God (Surah 17:2 and the commentaries).[187]

Already at this point one can see Zwemer is moving towards a
position which foreshadowed Karl Barth and Hendrik Kraemer.
Revelation given in Christ is not only the test of all religions
but the key to man's knowledge and experience of the redeemed
life. On this basis he set to work to examine the theology of
Islam in two valuable volumes: The Moslem Doctrine of God
(1905) and The Moslem Christ (1912).

Unless we know the Moslem's idea of God we cannot understand
his creed nor judge his philosophy, nor intelligently communicate our idea of God to him. The strength of Islam is
not in its ritual or in its ethics, but in its tremendous
and fanatical grasp on the one great truth--Monotheism.[188]

As a scholar, Zwemer insists on consulting the primary sources:
the Quran, the accepted Muslim commentaries and the Traditions
(edition of Mishkat-al-Masabih). For Zwemer, Muhammad's concept
of God stresses the oneness of God so exclusively that human
life is barren.

Mohammed's idea of God is out and out deistic. God and the
world are in exclusive, external and eternal opposition. On
an entrance of God into the world or of any sort of human
fellowship with God he knows nothing. This is the reason
Islam received the warm sympathies of English deists and
German rationalists; they found in its idea of God flesh of
their flesh and bone of their bone.[189]

God is known as "the name of the essence" (Ism-adh-Dhāt) or the
"being" that is absolute sovereignty and omnipotence. Other
than that he is defined mainly by negations (e.g. impersonal:
not body, nor spirit, does not beget). A study of the "Ninety
Nine Names of Allah" shows they describe his terrible and glorious attributes: unity, creatorship, mercy (24), powerful sovereignty (36), power to avenge and hurt, and moral or forensic
traits. Zwemer believes that Muhammad grasped the idea of God's
power as revealed in nature but failed to glimpse his holiness
and love. Palgrave rightly called Allah the pantheism of Force
or Act.

> God's will is absolute and alone; the predestination of every
> thing and everybody to good or ill according to the caprice
> of sovereignty. For there is no Fatherhood and no purpose of
> redemption to soften the doctrine of the decrees. Hell must
> be filled and so Allah creates infidels. The statements of
> the Koran on this doctrine are coarse and of tradition, blas-
> phemous. Islam reduces God to the category of the will; He
> is a despot, an Oriental despot, and as the moral-law is not
> emphasized, He is not bound by any standard of justice.[190]

This is quite different from Paul's or Calvin's understanding of
predestination as a grateful confidence in God's grace. Islam's
"one-sided truth" reduces men to pawns on a chess-board (cf.
Fitzgerald's Omar Khayyam), rules out human will, declares good
and evil come directly from God, and produces a fatalism which
breeds fear.[191] In light of Zwemer's critique, Islamic monotheism has serious omissions which may be summarized thus:
First, there is no Islamic Fatherhood of God and hence no true
brotherhood of man, only an exclusive brotherhood of believers.
Second, the Moslem idea of God is conspicuously lacking in the
attribute of love producing a being who is incapable of loving
or being loved, a figure from which even Muslim mysticism re-
volted. Third, Allah is not absolutely, unchangeably, and eternally just, sin and atonement are minimized and God's law is the
expression of arbitrary will not his moral nature.[192] For
Zwemer, "The Cross of Christ is the missing link in the Moslem's
Creed" for in it the justice and love of God, sin and salvation
come together, and men find reconciliation, true brotherhood.[193]

Relying on careful research in the Quran, the commentators
and Traditions, Zwemer portrays The Moslem Christ (1912). Herein he unveils that knowledge necessary if one hopes to lead
Muslims to the Christ disclosed in the New Testament. He re-
grets that Muslims depend more upon the Traditions and the
teachings of the mullahs than upon the Quran. For while the
Quranic account of Christ is piecemeal, lacks chronological or
logical sequence, it is at least somewhat open as to whether
Christ died or not (cf. Surah 3:47-50, 19:34, 4:155-156). But
the Traditions, according to Zwemer, are the "spoilers".

A study of the Koran commentaries on the texts given will
show how later tradition has taken the outlines of Mohammed's
revelation and made the picture more real, more full, but
also more fantastic. Whatever was unintelligible or contradictory in the words of Mohammed's revelation could only be
interpreted and made clear by means of tradition, and this
applied not only to the legislative portions of the Koran,
but also in its historical material....According to Goldziher,
tradition is the normative principle in Islam.[194]

The Tradition denies that Jesus is the Son of God, the pre-exis-
tent One, who died on the cross to achieve the way of salvation.
While admitting Jesus' dignity, sinlessness, miracles, and presence in heaven, he remains a human prophet. In the Traditions,
the content of Christ's teaching was slowly modified and ascribed to the Prophet.[195] Because "Jesus Christ has been supplanted
by Mohammed" in the mentality of the Muslim community, Islam
poses a problem different from any other religion.[196]

The sin and guilt of the Mohammedan world is that they give
Christ's glory to another, and that for all practical purposes Mohammed himself is the Moslem Christ....Jesus Christ
is supplanted by Mohammed not only in Moslem tradition and in
the hearts of the common people who are ignorant and illiterate. He is supplanted in the hearts of all Moslems by Mohammed. They are jealous for his glory and resist any attempt
to magnify the glory of Jesus Christ at the expense of
Mohammed.[197]

While Islam ignores or distorts the basic facts of Christ's
person and work, and gives him "a place" by "displacing Him",
there is still point of contact.

The very fact that Jesus Christ has a place in the literature
of Islam, and is acknowledged by all Moslems as one of their
prophets, in itself challenges comparison between Him and
Mohammed, and affords an opportunity for the Christian missionary to ask every sincere Moslem, 'What think ye of the
Christ?' This is still the question that decides the destiny
of men and nations.[198]

It is in the Muslim names for Christ that Zwemer finds the most
promising point of contact.[199] Of these, "the Word of God" and
"the Spirit from God" offer the greatest hope for leading
Muslims into the depths of faith. One wishes Zwemer would have
developed more fully the role of Christ as king and intercessor
inasmuch as Muslims admit Christ's presence in heaven and the
expected return. Thus for Zwemer these names provide clues to
"how to preach Christ to Moslems who know Jesus".
What is the relation of Christianity to Islam as a system?

Zwemer's early books speak of confrontation, clash and "radical
displacement". Yet in fairness to this view of "occupation", it
must be said that he did not call for any militant religious
imperialism, but only for the establishment of a Christian witness in Muslim lands until such time as the kingdom of Christ
would displace the religions of the world. Most interesting are
the motives for mission stated in The Unoccupied Mission Fields
of Africa and Asia (1911). They reflect the mood surrounding
"Edinburgh, 1910". Zwemer voices the various arguments for
nineteenth century missions: individual need (Pietism), reason
(Protestant Scholasticism), experience and feeling (Schleiermacher), moral values (Ritschl), social needs (James Dennis), as
well as the concern for the command and glory of Christ the Redeemer.[200] Before long, however, Zwemer clarifies his own
"Christological-anthropological" approach and sheds much of this
subjectivism and moral-social appeal.

The Disintegration of Islam (1915) marks something of a turning point in Zwemer's understanding of Islam and in his approach.
What did he mean by "disintegration"? Zwemer observed that
Islam was undergoing a transition (not necessarily disappearing).
Islam, as a political-social-economical-religious system was
"cracking", even though Islam as a "religion of the heart" might
continue for some time. There was some truth in his claim. For
with the dissolution of the caliphate in 1924, the formation of
secular Turkey, the rise of Arab national states, and the re-
jection of many Muslim traditions, Islam's iron grip relaxed in
most lands. The peoples of the Near East did undergo an emanci-
pation of sorts.

> Moslems have long realized that the dead weight of formality
> called tradition, the accumulation of many centuries, is an
> intolerable burden. Frantic efforts have been made in many
> quarters to save the ship by throwing overboard much of this
> cargo. Others in their despair have sought for a new pilot.
> Messiahs and mahdis have arisen and founded new sects or
> started new movements. The progress of western civilization
> and its impact has been felt everywhere in the economic and
> social life of Islam. We must add to all this the utter
> collapse of Moslem political power in Africa, Europe, and
> Asia....We, however, believe that when the crescent wanes the
> Cross will prove dominant, and that the disintegration of
> Islam is a divine preparation for the evangelization of
> Moslem lands and the winning of Moslem hearts to a new
> allegiance. Jesus Christ is sufficient for them as He is for
> us. 'When that which is perfect is come, that which is in
> part shall be done away.'[201]

Zwemer's interpretation of developments in the modern world is
not far removed from the opinion of missiologists who rejoice
that secularization is dissolving the grip of man's religions.

This crisis of Islam is thus interpreted as a sign of the coming of the kingdom of Christ.

In these five lectures given at Princeton, Zwemer sympathizes with young Muslims in revolt against traditional Sunni Islam.

> The revolt of Islam in its hard traditional form has generally been along one of three lines: attempts to spiritualize its doctrines /e.g. Al-Ghazali, Sufism/; attempts to rid it of excrescences, that is, to minimize the weight of traditions, as in the case of the Wahabis /or 'Back to the Quran' groups/; and finally, especially in recent years, syncretism by the establishment of new sects, such as Babism, Bahaism, and the Ahmadi movement. This might be called Moslem eclecticism.[203]

These latter resurgence groups benefit from Christ's leaven in society. Zwemer was confident that these new syncretic ventures would fail even though they might borrow the best of Christianity and Islam.

> Yet our review of the New Islam and its future may well conclude by reminding ourselves of the scientific fact that hybrids do not propagate and by pointing out in the words of Tertullian that men do not generally care to die for the compromise made between the faith of the Church and the philosophies of the heathen world.[204]

With A. G. Hogg and the new thought on the continent of Europe, Zwemer recognized the distinctive nature of each religion. One great religion cannot absorb the other, but its members could convert to the other. Islam like Judaism might well give her finest sons to Christianity, to Christ. Zwemer insisted that Islam's best (e.g. Al-Ghazali, Abdul-Wahab) fell short and could find redemption only in Christ.[205]

It is in the fifth lecture and a portion of Mohammed or Christ (1916) that Zwemer's anthropological-Christocentric approach begins to emerge. The attitude of some educated Muslims towards Christ provides hopeful signs. The great convulsions, tensions between the new and old orders in the Near East, are creating a "fullness of time". A decisive new hour is dawning in Cairo, Constantinople and Mecca. In the movement of history, God is working out his own will, ushering in his kingdom. It is almost as if Zwemer is a liberated man. No longer is it his duty to make battle against Islam as a system. He can now concentrate on the message which is Christocentric and eschatological, a message of Good News for the Muslim as a man.[206]

Zwemer's sympathetic anthropological-Christocentric approach springs from his devotion to Christ and his personal affection for many Muslim friends. His scholarship took him to primary

Arabic sources and first-hand research into Muslim beliefs and
actual practices. The work of this authority on "popular Islam"
did not go unnoticed in the Muslim community.[207] Agreeing with
Macdonald that "Islam must be taken as it is otherwise it is not
Islam," Zwemer revealed that the Islam described by some Western
orientalists is not the Islam that is practiced. Zwemer's life-
long study covers many areas of Muslim life: womanhood,[208]
childhood,[209] statistical-geographical surveys, [210] influence of
animism, popular practices, mysticism, Muslim Law and converts
from Islam, and the clergy-leadership of Islam. A wealth of
material is found in the Moslem World (1911-1947).[211]
     The Influence of Animism on Islam (1920) reflects twenty-five
years of keen observation, recording and evaluation of practices
in Arabia and Egypt.[212] This most original work reveals a mis-
sionary-anthropologist at work.

     From the standpoint both of religion and culture animism
     has been described as 'the tap-root that sinks deepest in
     racial human experience and continues its cellular and fib-
     rous structure in the tree-trunk of modern conviction.' All
     the great world religions show traces of animism in their sub-
     soil and none but Christianity (even that not completely) has
     uprooted the weed-growth of superstition. In this book it is
     our purpose to show how Islam sprang up in Pagan soil and re-
     tained many old Arabian beliefs in spite of its vigorous
     monotheism. Wherever Mohammedanism went, it introduced old
     or adopted new superstitions. The result has been that as
     background of the whole ritual and even in the creed of pop-
     ular Islam, animism has conquered. The religion of the com-
     mon people from Tangier to Teheran is mixed with hundreds of
     superstitions, many of which have lost their original signi-
     ficance but still bind mind and heart with constant fear of
     demons, with witchcraft and sorcery and the call to creature-
     worship....popular Islam is altogether different from the re-
     ligion recorded in its sacred Book. Our purpose in the chap-
     ters which follow is to show how this miry clay of animism
     mingles with the iron of Semitic theism....The rapid spread
     of Islam in Africa and Malayia is, we believe, largely due to
     its animistic character. The primitive religions had points
     of contact with Islam that were mutually attractive. It
     stooped to conquer them but fell in stooping. The reforma-
     tion of Islam if possible, must begin here. The student of
     Islam will never understand the common people unless he knows
     their curious beliefs and half-heathen practices. The mis-
     sionary should not only know but sympathize. Avoiding con-
     tempt or denunciation he will even find points of contact in
     Animistic Islam that may lead discussion straight to the
     Cross and the Atonement. In popular Islam we have to deal
     with men and women groping after light and struggling in the
     mire for a firm foothold on the Rock. This book may help us

to find their hand in the dark. As we read its pages we must
not forget that even in Egypt and India over ninety-four per
cent of the Moslem population is illiterate and therefore has
no other religion than popular Islam.[213]

This preface is a self-revealing commentary on Zwemer's growing
understanding of Islam in action. Islam's strength for him lies
in its versatile three-stranded nature: an animism able to en-
compass and adapt almost any practice of pagan religion, a Semitic deism which can wear a nationalistic cloak, and its claim
to supersede all that Jesus was, did and taught. In twelve
studies, Zwemer examines this"underground religion".[214] Practices which Muslim leaders have often sought to suppress still
persist. Little escaped Zwemer's experienced eye as he collected data and collaborated with scholars in Africa, India, China
and the East Indies. His accounts reveal that many Muslims live
in a spirit and demon-filled world.
Studies in Popular Islam (1939), a collection of papers prepared at Princeton, reveals additional research.[215] Zwemer's
museum in Princeton became a clearing house for artifacts and
data sent in by C. Padwick, L. Trotter and others. Alert to
recent reforms in the Muslim world, Zwemer warns of the emergence of a reactionary movement backed by traditionalists (e.g.
the Muslim Brotherhood).

The same has been true in the long history of Islam and
its relation to Christianity. At first there seemed to be a
glorious rising tide of monotheistic faith in Islam, and a
devotion to God--often sublime in its conception of Deity and
of duty. This has been followed by the undertow of reactionary Arabian paganism. That was true even in the case of the
Prophet Mohammed himself when he consecrated the Ka'aba-stone
and then, for a moment, lapsed to pay honour to Lat and
'Uzza...(Surah 53:19). Some Koran chapters that rise, like
'the verse of the Throne' (Surah 2:256ff) and 'the verse of
Light,' almost to the heights of Job and Isaiah, are followed
by puerile passages full of animistic superstitions such as
Solomon's jinn, Alexander's bellows-blowers, or Jewesses
blowing on Knots (Surah 113).
We note the same undertow in the history of Moslem theology and jurisprudence, as Dr. Duncan B. MacDonald has shown
in his interesting study of the subject. There have been
puritanic revivals and popular reactions, periods of enlightenment and culture, when Islam held aloft the torch of
civilization; these have been followed by dark centuries of
ignorance and superstition. Al-Ghazali's call to repentence
was forgotten for centuries while the mullahs pored over the
pages of Al-Bunī's encyclopaedia of magic and then the world
of Islam became illiterate to an extent hardly credible.[216]

If the Muslim world ever develops its own school of historical-
literary criticism, notes Zwemer, it would soon be cutting away
at the body of Islam.

During these years, Zwemer's affection for the Muslim seeking
after God finds fullest expression in his work on Al-Ghazali.[217]
The church's mission of love is described in the biblical
imagery of the Parable of the Prodigal and Elder sons in need of
the Father's mercy.

> Islam is the prodigal son, the Ishamel, among the non-Chris-
> tian religions; this is a fact we may not forget. Now we
> read in Christ's matchless parable of the prodigal how 'When
> he was yet a great way off his father saw him and ran out to
> meet him and fell on his neck and kissed him.' Have mission-
> aries always had this spirit? No one can read the story of
> Al-Ghazali's life, so near and yet so far from the Kingdom,
> so eager to enter and yet always groping for the doorway,
> without fervently wishing that Al-Ghazali could have met a
> true ambassador of Christ.[218]

The study of Al-Ghazali had helped Zwemer arrive at this point
of appreciation.[219] Zwemer's tributes to this man are start-
ling: "Such a rosary of pearls from Al-Ghazali's works might
well be used for devotion by Christians as well as by Muslims.[220] Zwemer evidently holds that fragments of God's earlier
revelation remain scattered among non-Christian religions, or
that the marred image of God still retains some capacity to reflect God's glory.

> It is noteworthy that when he rises to the highest ethical
> teaching he bases his remarks on the sayings (mostly apoc-
> ryphal) of Christ, which we collate in our final chapter.
> Al-Ghazali tried hard but failed to find in Mohammed the
> ideals of his own heart.[221]

Zwemer appreciates how the pious Muslim blended Sufism with Sun-
nism to save the former from deadly speculation ending in self-
deification or pantheism and the latter from cold scholasticism.
Al-Ghazali is viewed as producing a moral philosophy, an ethical
mysticism, which makes the happiness of the individual its highest good and the works of man the means for achieving this
righteousness and identity with God. The great mystic is not
free of superstition.[222] Zwemer shows empathy for Al-Ghazali's
understanding of Jesus Christ.

> Being a Moslem, Al-Ghazali was either too proud to search for
> the true historical facts of the Christian religion, or per-
> haps it would be more charitable to say that he had no ade-
> quate opportunity, in spite of his quotations and misquota-
> tions from the 'Gospels.' Otherwise he could have found

there what would have met his heart-hunger and satisfied his
soul--the manifestation of God not in some intangible principle, but in a living person, in Jesus Christ....Whenever
Al-Ghazali speaks of God's nearness to us and of the soul's
desire for human fellowship with the creator, he comes very
close to the Christian idea of the Incarnation, and yet
always stops short of it....Yet with all his efforts to explain the nature of the soul and of God, he still finds himself before a blank wall. He covets the vision of God but
cannot shake himself free from the Moslem conception that God
is unknowable and that nothing in creation resembles the
Creator.[223]

Al-Ghazali's lasting contribution was that he leavened Persian
thought with quotations of the Gospel, giving Jesus a larger
place, hence preparing a point of contact for Christian-Muslim
conversation. The best of this influence is seen in his pupil-
poet, Jal-al-ad-Din ar-Rumi who acknowledged Jesus as the Life-
Giver.

> Thyself reckon dead, and then thou shalt fly
> Free, free, from the prison of earth to the sky!
> Spring may come, but on granite will grow no green thing;
> It was barren in winter, 'tis barren in spring;
> And granite man's heart is, till grace intervene,
> And, crushing it, clothe the long barren with green.
> When the fresh breath of Jesus shall touch the heart's
>   core,
> It will live, it will breathe, it will blossom once more.[224]

This disciple of Al-Ghazali, suggests Zwemer, may yet serve the
coming kingdom of God. Standing near to the Gospel, he may
assist some Muslims as "a schoolmaster to lead them to Christ".[225]

The Law of Apostasy in Islam (1924) is Zwemer's most critical
and yet most compassionate work. While his affection for the
Muslim has increased, his estimate of the Islamic system has
not. The oppressive nature of Islamic law and society has not
only limited the number of converts, but deprived them of property, family and even life. In 1924, the law of death for apos-
tates had not been abrogated! In spite of intellectual awakening, western influence, economical development, constitutions
and parliaments, the "sword of Damocles" still hangs over the
head of every convert to Christ. This law must be modified before there will be liberty of conscience and the freedom to
confess Christ. Zwemer does not rate the holding power of
Islamic fraternity as high as Gairdner. He contends that its
power is a fear psychosis rooted in an awareness of the price of
treason (in contrast to the kinship experienced by those who
pray, "Our Father"). It is a group superiority which tolerates
outsiders as inferiors rather than a community of faith com-

mitted to serve mankind in God's name. Real change on the Near
East scene must be related to the development of a climate of
freedom.

> A truer freedom, a deeper religious experience, a higher life
> than the one supplied by their own faith, must come before
> Moslems can enter into the larger liberty which we enjoy.[226]

Zwemer is convinced of the existence of many hidden disciples in
the midst of the Muslim community. He praises the converts who
are publicly and often painfully pioneering in the Near East for
a new era of religious liberty.[227]

> The battle for religious liberty, freedom of conscience and
> worship has been age-long and world-wide. Christianity it-
> self has suffered during this struggle; witness the Inquisi-
> tion, the Crusades and the persecutions of the Middle Ages,
> as well as the conditions of those countries nominally Chris-
> tian where these great blessings do not yet obtain for all
> sorts and conditions of men...Christianity no less than Islam
> has sometimes failed to solve the difficulty. Religious
> liberty was purchased at so great a price in the Protestant
> lands of Europe and America that the principle of religious
> tolerance is one of our most cherished ideals.[228]

There is a cry for religious freedom in the Near East and unless
it comes, history's judgment upon Islam will be the more relent-
less. Christians can courageously work for "religious liberty
for All" knowing that behind history stands the Judge and Redeemer. In Heirs of the Prophets (1946), Zwemer hints at two
areas of activity which may well prepare the way for the kingdom.
The 'Ulema, the heirs of the prophets according to Muhammad, are
the authorized interpreters of the consensus. It is within
their power to re-interpret Islamic law and practice which could
result in greater political, social and religious liberty.[229]
Zwemer encouraged "personal friendship with their clergy, the
so-called imams, mullahs, and sheikhs" realizing what impact
these men could have on the future. He was amazed at the considerable numbers of converts who came from their ranks. As
such they were no longer:

> merely heirs of Islamic learning but 'heirs of God and joint-
> heirs with Christ' if so be that they fill up the measure of
> His suffering in the fearless proclamation of the eternal
> Gospel.[230]

Zwemer's life-long study of Islam was neither detached nor impersonal. It was rooted in the hope that Abraham's prayer:
"Oh that Ishmael might live before Thee!" might find fulfillment
in the Messiah of God. It was scholarship with a view to

evangelism.

Zwemer's Understanding of Evangelism

Parallel to the development seen in Zwemer's understanding of Islam is his understanding of the task of proclamation. In the early period (1890-1915) he is anxious to harness the best methods of the nineteenth century, but gradually he comprehends the church's dependency on revelation, the activity of God in Jesus Christ. Thus emerges the "Christocentric-anthropological" approach stressing personal commitment to Christ and a more empathetic understanding of his fellow human beings as persons needing the love of God in Christ. This awareness was sharpened by the crisis in theology and mission (1920-1940).

Reared in the Reformed Church in America, a body encompassing the comprehensive views of Abraham Kuyper (Dutch statesman and theologian) as well as the conservative views of Albertus Van Raalte (mid-nineteenth century founder of Holland, Michigan), Zwemer was a Calvinist committed to a continuing Reformation based on biblical scholarship. This breadth of mind finds him open to the whole spectrum of Protestant ideas regarding the evangelization of the Muslims. His first major work reveals his awareness of the history of mission from Raymond Lull (d. 1315) onwards, of the monolithic political-religious system of Islam, and of the traditional Protestant understanding of mission as the spreading of the written and spoken Word of God. Zwemer's finest thought at the time is rooted in his biblical exegesis of God's promises for the Arabs (theocratic covenants) and the assurances of the final victory of Christ and his kingdom.[231] "The Cross", in Zwemer's evangelical interpretation of the atonement, symbolizes the power which can transform the Near East.[232] Zwemer was critical of the church's hot-cold treatment of Islam and like Schleiermacher impressed by "moravian compassion". The Muslim was spiritually dead, but in Christ, potentially a new man.[233] Zwemer's mission-methods blend the best of evangelical, philosophical and humanitarian nineteenth century thought. In the year that the Tokyo Conference (W.S.C.F., 1907) was debating "Apologetics or Evangelism", Zwemer reflects the mellowing that was taking place.

Preaching must have for its subject the essentials of Christianity. Preach Christ crucified. Show the reasonableness of the mysteries of revelation, of the incarnation, and of the Holy Trinity; but never try to explain them by mere philosophy. The problem is to reach, not the intellect, but the heart and conscience, to arouse it from stupor, to show the grandeur of moral courage to the man who is intellectually convinced of the truth. In trying to convince the will-- that citadel of man's soul--we must follow the line of least resistance. Yet compromise must not take the place of tact.

The right angle for the presentation of truth can best be
learned by studying the strength and the weakness of Islam.
The history of Moslem theology, for example, shows that heterodoxy has nearly always been connected with a strong desire
for a mediator. This natural longing for an intercessor and
an atonement is fully supplied in Christ, our Saviour....
Preach to the Moslem, not as a Moslem, but as a man--as a
sinner in need of a Saviour.[234]

In these years, the language of "conflict" was slowly being displaced by that of the "challenge of faith" and the "love of
Jesus".[235] The conferences at Cairo, Edinburgh and Lucknow show
continual advance in this direction. At this time, Zwemer lists
his arguments for mission in this order: (1) The human need of
those destitute and neglected, (2) Christ's universal command
(3) the glory of God, and (4) the second coming of Christ (eschatological).[236] He toys with the Hegelian proposition of the
Edinburgh Report that because "Islam is the antithesis of Christianity, a synthesis is possible".[237] This idea he soon aband-
ons as he senses the judgment falling upon the world. Even before the shock of World War I and the cry of Barth, Zwemer insisted that only God's revelatory act in Christ could restore an
alienated world.

There is no stronger argument or plea for missions to Moslems than their concept of our Christ, and the fact that Mohammed has usurped the place of our Saviour in so many hearts.
...A passion for the glory of God, which is among the highest
missionary motives, will inspire us to preach the Christ in
all His fulness to those who are now following Mohammed.[238]

"The fact of Christ" is the primary contact point between Christians and Muslims and the central topic to be discussed. One's
relation to Christ, not simply affiliation to a community or
system, is the determinative factor regarding man's relation to
God and eternal destiny. The church must come to grips with incarnation, atonement, Trinity in an experiential theology which
neglects neither Christ's transcendent nature nor his humanity.

A loving and yet bold presentation of the distinctive truths
of our religion and of the surpassing grandeur and beauty of
the character of Jesus Christ will never alienate a Moslem
heart....We should ask Moslems to study the Gospel in any way
they like, but with only one object in view, 'namely, that
they may come face to face with Jesus Himself; that they may
learn to know Him, and see how He claimed to hold a supreme
position in the matter of the attitude of all men toward God,
a position which none other has ever claimed.' In other
words, we should press home the question which Jesus Himself
put to His disciples and to the world, 'What think ye of the

Christ?'[239]

By 1915, Zwemer's outlook is keenly Christocentric. Western
civilization, idealistic religious philosophies, and diluted
philanthropic programs of education are inadequate to meet the
needs of the Near East. Zwemer considers himself the friend and
mid-wife aiding educated Muslims who are eager to investigate
the claims of Jesus Christ and his place in history.

> We assert as strongly as do all Moslems that there is only
> one God, but because there is only one God there can be only
> one Gospel and one Christ....In no part of the world's battle-
> field for righteousness and truth does belief in the deity of
> Jesus Christ so naturally and almost spontaneously turn this
> mere theological dogma into a spiritual experience, a logical
> necessity, and a great passion, as when face to face with
> Mohammedan denials of the claims of our Saviour and their
> practical deification of Mohammed.
>   The utter helplessness and hopelessness of missionary work
> among Moslems on the part of anyone who wavers or is uncertain
> regarding this belief in the deity of Christ is self-evident.
> ...It is this anti-Christian character of the greatest of all
> the non-Christian religions which compels every worker among
> Moslems to look upon the doctrine of the Trinity or of the
> deity of Jesus Christ not as mere orthodox belief, but as the
> very life and heart of Christianity without which we have no
> message, no motive power, and no hope of success.[240]

Several factors stimulated the development of this maturing sympathetic Christocentric-anthropological approach to the Muslim:
first hand studies and experiences on the field, contact with
leading European and American mission-minded orientalists, and
the changing theological situation in the West.

Zwemer's affection for the Arabs was heightened by personal
contact with the citizens of Egypt. Studies in popular Islam
and discussion with educated Muslims unveiled their aspiration
for forgiveness, reconciliation and new life in God. He became
aware that the Gospel addresses itself primarily to "man in his
need" and is not addressed to other religions. The Christian
message to man regards God's love and action, past and present,
in behalf of the world. While the herald must study other religions to better understand the capacities and needs of man, he
does so to better communicate the Gospel and not to filter out
partial truths.[241] Zwemer's concern for communication was so
intense that he regularly reworked his materials until the expression forcefully captured the listener's interest.[242] There
were few who rivaled his persuasiveness on the street or platform. He was convinced that the coming of the kingdom was mys-
teriously related to proclamation. His desire was to treat the
disease not the symptoms of man's illness and thus he gave bib-

lical proclamation priority over philanthropic effort.

Exchange with mission-orientated scholars such as D. B. Macdonald undoubtedly helped Zwemer clarify his own position.   One
is amazed at the mutual influence and agreement between these
two men, as they focused on the question: "How can Christ be
best preached to Moslems?"[243]   Zwemer stood by Macdonald's contention that any Christianity which neglected the incarnation
would fail.   History has taught the church that:

> ...to the seeker in the great space that lies between Mater-
> ialism and Pantheism, the presentation that still expressed
> most adequately the mystery behind our lives, is that in the
> Christian Trinity and the words that come nearest are those
> of the Nicene Creed.[244]

While Zwemer admits, "There is some truth in all the non-Christian religions, and much good in many of them",[245] he is no
longer satisfied with the comparative religions approach.   He is
moving to a stronger emphasis on revelation and the Christ-
centered message.

> Christianity is the final religion, and its message--Christ
> incarnate, Crucified, Risen and Glorified--is the one thing
> needed to evangelize the world.[246]

Unless there is a calling of men to repentence and new life in
Christ, it is not mission.   Unless the messenger has experienced
Christ, he will simply be absorbed into his environment.   Opinions are no substitute for message, nor philanthropy for dynamic
proclamation.   "The real missionary spirit is the Holy Spirit.
He Himself gave us the message in the Scriptures, and in the
Christ enables us to interpret it to others.[247]   Reconciliation
is at the heart of the Christian experience and herein lies the
only real hope of men and nations.

> The yawning chasm between the devout Moslem and the devout
> Christian...is real and deep.   The chasm cannot be bridged by
> rickety planks of compromise.   Syncretism would be equivalent
> to surrender;...we must plan and sacrifice not to bombard the
> enemies position but to bridge the chasm...the missionary
> problem is how to bridge the chasm with courage and tact, by
> the manifestation of the truth in love....Islam is a spirit-
> ual problem and can only be solved in spiritual terms.   To
> the Moslem mind the unknown quantity is the exceeding great-
> ness of the love of God in Jesus Christ, His Son, our Saviour.
> This is the heart of the problem.   Prayer and pains will
> accomplish wonders in solving it....[248]

There is no by-passing the cross of Christ for Zwemer, for it
not only represents the mystery of God's love, but what the

church must experience in reaching Muslims with the news of reconciliation.[249] Oft reflecting upon Louis Massignon's words,
"The Cross cannot be defeated, because it itself was defeat",
Zwemer calls for a sacrificial but clear witness in behalf of
Muslims. Many of his editorials speak of this reconciling love
of God in Christ--"Behold the Lamb of God that takes away the
sins of the world".[250] Zwemer's labors never go limp in disappointment, for there is an eschatological note of triumph pervading his writings. While the social gospel and ethical Christianity have their appeal, it is the risen Christ alone who
shall fulfill mankind's deep hunger and the vision of the new
creation for which we all groan (Rom. 8).[251] These were a few
of the factors which made Zwemer's efforts in evangelism so
winsome.

Zwemer's Role in the Crisis of Theology and Mission (1920-1938)

Even as the development of Zwemer's thought concerning the
church, other religions, and evangelism foreshadows and parallels that of the continental theologians of the Word in many
ways, so Zwemer's criticism of the left wing of Protestant liberalism (esp. American) and restatement of evangelical tenets
provide a preview of the ideas expressed by Hendrik Kraemer and
others at Tambaram. This debate sharpened Zwemer's statements
regarding Christianity's relation to other religions and evangelism.

The Growing Tension of the 1920s

Protestants in the twentieth century were heirs of the past:
of the Reformers and scholastic orthodoxy, of the evangelical
awakenings and the growing humanitarian concern, of the new
emphases on religious experience and ethical-social needs, of
the new sciences of literary and historical criticism, and of a
world responding to global expansion and industrial revolution.
These forces and theologies influenced the missionary movement
and in turn were influenced by it. Even within that movement,
various competing views of mission were coming forth by the
twentieth century.

(1) It has been held that the attitude of Christian mission
should be that Christianity must supplant the other religions
because they are of purely human origin (Jn. 14:6). (2)--
Christianity is the fulfillment of other religions (Acts 17:
23). (3)--that there is in all religions the possibility of
'faith' between God and man (Luke 7:9). (4)--that in Jesus
all religions are brought to judgment, and that he remains
the judge of all religions including Christianity. (5)...that
the motive of Christian witness should be not one of seeking
to make Christians of adherents of other religions, but of so

presenting Jesus Christ to them that He Himself will become
for them the point of reconception with respect to their own
religion (Jn. 1:9). Thus it is held, in course of time there
will emerge a new religion in which all religions, including
Christianity, will be comprehended.[252]

Samuel Zwemer's role in this period can be understood only
against the background of this upheaval (1910-1928). The forces
noted at the beginning of this chapter plus the brutal shock of
World War I and ensuing depressions convinced a number of missionaries that traditional nineteenth century methods were inadequate. Roland Allen cried out for a return to the missionary
strategy of the New Testament.[253] J. N. Farquhar had extended
the application of Jesus' words "not to destroy but to fulfill"
to explain Christianity's relation to other religions.[254]
Others moved further afield. Albert Schweitzer left a brilliant
career in music and theology to engage in humanitarian work in
Africa on the motive of a reverence for life.[255] Historian
Arnold J. Toynbee, called for co-existence between various cultures and world religions.[256] Bernard Lucas advocated discon-
tinuing the effort to win converts and to simply permeate other
cultures with Christian ideas.[257] Others criticized the disrup-
tive nature of Protestant missions and urged a less disturbing
philanthropy as the ideal.[258] These ideas came under the fire
by those who were equally desirous of a sympathetic approach,
but conscious of the distinctiveness of each particular religion.
Continental voices and others such as A. G. Hogg and D. S.
Cairns held to the unique claims of the Christian message and
its enduring contrast to other religions. John R. Mott and Robert Speer attempted to steer a mediating position between those
who generously praised and those who sharply criticized all non-
Christian religions.[259]

These new ideas were soon appearing in Near Eastern educational institutions with Christian origins. President John E.
Merrill of Central Turkey College (Aintab, North Syria) spoke of
understanding "Islam and not Islam alone but Christianity itself
and the inner life of the human spirit of which both are expressions." What he found in the Saviour differed more in degree than in kind to that found in Islam. His message was "a
testimony to spiritual experience, not a teaching regarding religious doctrine and practice".[260] A more striking outlook was
found in the person of Howard S. Bliss, President of A.U.B.
(Beirut). His article on "The Modern Missionary" (1920) includes the liberal catchwords of the day in sharp contrast to
the evangelical convictions of his father, Daniel Bliss. Radically departing from the traditional concept of mission he
depicts the modern missionary as

trained in the scientific method...the broad aspects of Evolution, in Comparative Religion, in the history and philosophy

of religion, in the history of civilization, in the Lower and Higher Criticisms, convinced as never before that man's religious belief powerfully affects...man's happiness, usefulness, progress and salvation.[261]

Such a missionary would find truth re-echoed in his own heart, reason, and other religions.

He does not believe that Christianity is the sole channel through which divine and saving truth has been conveyed.... For it at once enlarges his spiritual fellowship. All men who are themselves seeking God and who are striving to lead others to God become his companions and his fellow workers... This widened conception of the work of God in the world has a profound effect upon the missionary method of presenting his own Christian message....He comes to supplement not solely to create....Coming into contact with men who are as convinced of the truth of their own faiths as the missionary is of his, his appeal to them must be upon the common basis of absolute fidelity to truth.[262]

"Religion" and the "Ideal" are tied to an optimistic view of man's progress.

Perfection, moreover, upon which Jesus insists as the goal of man's striving, will bring with it a due development of his intellectual and aesthetic nature....Faith in a loving, wise, righteous, and holy God; faith in self; faith in mankind; faith in truth, in love, in righteousness--this fulfills the conditions of the Catholic faith....[263]

The widespread approval of this type of thinking is seen in that this article was reprinted with the commendation of James L. Barton, a senior officer of the American Board. It was apparent that there were conflicting opinions as to the essence of Christianity. Arthur Jeffery, asserting that the solution to the Muslim's needs are found only in the person and message of the living Christ, speaks of the clash.

The problem of all problems to every Christian missionary is the problem of presentation--the problem, that is, of putting the Christian message in such a way as will appeal to and convince those to whom it is addressed. Obviously there are two sides to this problem, first, that of understanding the vital message of Christianity and being able to effectively set it forth; and second, that of understanding the mind of the one to whom the message is addressed so as to present it in a way that will most surely have the desired effect. Curiously enough it is on the first of these, that there is the greatest difference of opinion. Some have

insisted that the vital message of Christianity is one thing
and some another; some have emphasized one method of setting
it forth and some another.[264]

It was obvious that a crisis was in the making with regards to
the question: "What is the Christian message?" Meanwhile the
"understanding of Islam" would have to wait (until revived by
Levonian, Cragg, et al.).

In this tense situation, Zwemer's voice is heard in Christianity, the Final Religion (1920).[265] He criticizes the neutra-
listic attitude of Howard Bliss and others who negate the core
of the Christian faith by "thinking in gray".

On the contrary, we believe that the very nature of Christianity, its dynamic, its passion, its power of missionary
appeal, its esse as well as its bene esse consists in its
credo--its belief in Jesus Christ, the Son of God, born of
the Virgin Mary, who died on the Cross for our sins and arose
again, who gave us this message as our only commission and
sealed it with the promise of his presence.[266]

Aware of the solidarity of the human race, Zwemer remains convinced that the only hope for a reconciled humanity is found in
Jesus Christ. Long before Tambaram, he set forth ideas that
would triumph there.

Christianity and the non-Christian religions are two distinct
conceptions. Their real relation, therefore, when they come
into contact is that of impact, and not of compromise.
Christianity is distinct in its origin. Its revelation is
supernatural, and its Founder was the Lord from heaven....
The missionary character of Christianity, therefore, demands
impact with every non-Christian system.[267]

Criticizing the shift from deep theological doctrines to ethical
ideas, he called for a return to the "Apostolic Gospel"--
Christ's activity, death on the cross and resurrection for the
redemption of men. He was careful not to make Christianity (as
system or institution) itself final, but to subject all to
Christ, the Truth. In this sense Zwemer was a forerunner of the
theologians of crisis, judgement and the Word.[268] Following
World War I, a deep pessimism and despair gripped many intellec-
tuals as well as the masses (much in the spirit of Kierkegaard).
Optimism in man's progress and the illusive quest for a historical Jesus were inadequate for describing man's dilemma or God's
action in Christ. Karl Barth's Commentary on Romans (1919) fell
like a bombshell, ushering in a whole barrage of shots from
theologians of judgment and the Word of God.[269] This stress
upon the centrality of the incarnation, the uniqueness of the
revelation of the transcendental God in Christ, and the crisis-

judgment, as well as redemption, which accompanies Jesus Christ
in his confrontation with men, cultures and religion gave Protestant theology a new sense of direction. Latourette later described it thus:

> In Protestantism, the optimistic liberalism of the nineteenth
> century has been partly replaced by crisis theology, and the
> confidence in reason and the intellect as competent in mat-
> ters of religion had tended to be ushered out by a belief
> that God is utterly different from man and man is so corrup-
> ted by sin that knowledge of God can come only by God's re-
> velation of himself.[270]

Zwemer realized the serious implications this understanding of
the Word of God had for Christian missions, implications which
would come to light from 1930 onwards.[271]

The Crisis in Mission, 1930s

The conflict of opinions was raging so fiercely in the United
States by the nineteen thirties that a popular writer, Pearl
Buck, could ask, "Is there a Case for Foreign Missions?"[272] Unfortunately voices tended to polarize into two opposing camps
labelled as liberal and conservative-evangelical. Others tried
with little success to take a mediating position. This was unfortunate inasmuch as the church was reacting to a world undergoing rapid transition and needed to pool not divide her energies for the reorientation of mission. The glow of "Edinburgh,
1910", when the churches had been drawn together for a united
strategy for reconnoitering and occupying the non-Christian
world, had given way to the critical atmosphere of "Jerusalem,
1928". War and depressions had purified the church of some of
the dross and made her aware of her weaknesses. In this depressed setting, the questions "What is Christianity?" and "What
is mission?" were most relevant. What ignited this tinder into
a blazing conflict was the 1932 report entitled, Re-thinking
Missions by the independent group known as the Laymen's Inquiry.
The first part of this report was an exposition of the views of
William E. Hocking, professor of Philosophy at Harvard and
chairman of the inquiry group. As a spokesman of the left wing
of American liberalism, Hocking advised that a form of Western
Christian service to the emerging Eastern world should replace
the traditional program of missions. Since his statements
triggered the heated debate leading to and beyond Tambaram and
stand as a foil, an alternative to Zwemer and Kraemer, they deserve special attention.[273] Re-thinking Missions brought forth
a storm of protests and prompted a constructive restating of the
evangelical basis for Christian mission. While appreciating the
stimulus to think, the responses of K. S. Latourette (Professor
at Yale), John A. Mackay (President of Princeton Seminary), and

Julius Richter (Berlin) concentrate on Hocking's presuppositions
which they charge lack both biblical and historical support.[274]
Latourette is representative.

> The report calls for 'first of all a new kind of person as
> the unit of society if there is to be a new social order (p.
> 63) but fails to adequately discuss how such a new kind of
> person comes into being or how a new kind of society formed.
> ...It neglects the cardinal points of Christian message in
> the Cross, the Atonement, the Resurrection and the Holy Spir-
> it. The first four chapters speak of religion as though it
> were man's search for God, whereas multitudes of Christians
> have declared the Gospel to be the expression of God's
> search for man.[275]

After a very careful treatment of the report's recommendations,
Latourette counsels:

> What is most wanting in the missionary enterprise is not new
> machinery or new methods: first and foremost it is the nec-
> essity for what has always been most essential--a fresh out-
> burst of life in the Church. Without it the Church must go
> haltingly and half-heartedly about its great task. When it
> comes many of our problems will be solved or submerged by the
> fresh tide of the Spirit. That new life is to be found in no
> new or novel way. In the last analysis our dependence is
> upon the Living God. Our primary contribution must be to
> help prepare the way for Him by repentence, consecration,
> faith, prayer and love.[276]

Mackay felt that what was at stake was not mission methods but
theology. He accuses Hocking of failing to take stock of the
contemporary world, the new awareness of man's tragic state and
the issues raised by the theologians of the Word. Hocking has
not advanced beyond Harnack's essence of Christianity which results in a "religion of Jesus" which ignores the Christ as the
resurrected Lord. For Mackay, a former missionary in South
America, the objective is:

> To make Jesus Christ inescapable for men everywhere. Not
> acceptable but inescapable, the only possible solution, the
> only saviour of men who have become deadly in earnest about
> the problem of living. This will involve the closest and
> most sympathetic identification of missionaries with the
> people among whom they work....The missionary will devote
> himself to unfolding by word and deed the content of his
> message--'Jesus Christ'....The trouble is that we have so
> largely forgotten what Christianity means.[277]

Other thorough replies to the report were given by Robert

Speer[278] and by the principal of the United Theological College
of Poona, J. F. Edwards.[279]

Although in his sixties, Zwemer could not refrain from enter-
ing this crucial debate. In fact until the appearance of H.
Kraemer, he was the foremost Christian authority on missions to
Muslims in the exchange. For him, "the finality of Jesus
Christ" was indeed the issue.

> Any faith which challenges the finality of Christianity and
> professes to give a supplementary message, another gospel,
> higher ethics, a more adequate social program, must produce
> the equivalent of Jesus Christ. To call Christianity the
> absolute or final religion is, as Dr. Mackintosh asserts, 'to
> contend not merely that in Jesus Christ God is presented in a
> form higher and more spiritually satisfying than elsewhere,
> but that the relationship to the Father on which believers
> thus enter, is such that it cannot be transcended'(Cf. The
> Originality of the Christian Message, p. 175).[280]

Zwemer felt that Re-thinking Missions sought to undermine the
biblical conviction that the living Christ is the sole mediator
between God and all men. He offers his rejoinder in Thinking
Missions with Christ (1934). His readers are urged to look beyond the modernist-fundamentalist controversy and focus on the
basic problems of the universe and man. We, like the apostles,
must deal with the details of man's dilemma and God's answer in
Christ.

> God has divided the light from darkness, not only in the
> world of nature, but in the world of grace....The attitude of
> the apostles toward the non-Christian religions is not ex-
> pressed in gray or twilight shades.[281]

In contrast to the early church suggests Zwemer, the theoretical,
humanistic idealism of Hocking's report is filled with irrespon-
sible statements which only undercut mission work. For example
when confronted by Islam, one must think concisely about the incarnation and atonement as realities. Zwemer rejects Hocking's
basic idea that God-truth is discovered by subjective-experience,
holding instead that God is known only as he reveals himself.
Christians are not simply "stockholders sharing human thought
and experience" but ambassadors announcing a historical-eternal
fact, Jesus Christ. Zwemer appreciated Hartenstein's work on
this subject.

> Over against the eclipse of this message of faith by Amer-
> ican activismus, and against the minimizing of the truth of
> revelation by syncretism, and over against the worldly atmos-
> phere which threatens missionary service through secularism,
> we must hold fast the heritage of the Reformation and of Piet-

ism by a new emphasis on the Scriptures and the Scriptural
basis of the enterprise. Missions are nothing else than an
ambassadorship in Christ's stead to a lost world, and the
only source of authority, is the Holy Spirit.[282]

Zwemer's own revised list of motives takes this order: first,
obedience to Christ's great commission; second, the love of
Christ which constrains and sends forth Christians to meet the
world's need in his name; and third, the glory of God and his
coming kingdom.[283] Of the latter he writes:

> Some motives are ego-centric or cosmocentric. This is all
> theocentric and finds its source and goal beyond time and
> space in eternity. The chief end of missions is not the sal-
> vation of men but the glory of God. 'For of Him and through
> Him and unto Him are all things'--also missions--'to Him be
> the glory for ever.' Not only in Luther and Calvin but in
> our own day, Otto in 'Das Heilige' and Karl Barth in his Com-
> mentary on Romans have shown that the sovereignty and holi-
> ness of God are the basis of all theistic thought and that a
> Christian world-view is impossible without these numinious
> elements....The missionary motive and idea is proclaimed at
> the Incarnation....With it the Incarnate Word communicates
> His message and power, His mission and authority to His
> Church for all the ages.[284]

In his emphasis on the historical, eschatological nature of the
Christian message over against the religions of the world,
Zwemer was certainly in agreement with many theologians in
Europe. As a veteran missioner he likewise found little value
in the practical proposals of the report. What is needed is not
simply new methods, but new men and this happens only as men en-
counter Jesus Christ. Zwemer held in highest regard the state-
ment of the Scandinavian delegates to the I.M.C. meeting at
Herrnhut (1932) and quotes it at length as a corrective to the
Laymen's appraisal.

> If we have anything to bring in the name of God to a world in
> need, it is certainly not our own piety, our own way of life,
> our own modes of thought or our own human help. What the
> Church has to give in its world mission is the good news of
> a divine act in history, of the Word made flesh. Apart from
> a Word which is from God, and not from man, there is no Chris-
> tian mission.
>   We have considered afresh what is central in our mission-
> ary work and where the chief emphasis should be laid. We are
> convinced that our missionary task is to proclaim in word and
> life God's revelation and redemption in Jesus Christ. We
> have no other task; for while there is much that is useful
> and good, 'one thing is needful.' We need to ask ourselves

whether everything that forms part of present missionary activity serves the one dominant purpose of making clear the
message of Jesus Christ in all its fulness.[285]

The mature reflection of Zwemer is also set forth in The
Origin of Religion (1935).[286] He holds to the degeneration-de-
volution theory rather than to the evolutionary hypothesis regarding the origin of the world's religions, i.e. early monotheism degenerated after the fall into the plurality of religions. God, however, has continued to renew his covenant with
man through the Judeo-Christian stream of history.[287] Hence the
fragments of truth found in other religions are but fragments of
revelation. Zwemer's own historical method in anthropology had
convinced him that this applied equally to popular Islam. As an
anthropologist, Zwemer held to the "essential unity and solidarity of the human family", that is, man's physical, sociological, psychological, religious needs are basically one the world
around. But he rejected an overemphasis on natural theology for
one cannot understand the Christian faith by observing the phenomena of creation. At this point, Zwemer is much closer to
Brunner than Barth. He argues for the unique and final revelation of God in Christ without excluding general revelation. For
Zwemer, Jerusalem (1928) was but a blend of proclamation and
"sympathetic study of other religions". While the study of
other religions will not provide a solution, it will identify
"points of contact".[288] For Zwemer the only links between Christianity and Islam are the latter's borrowings from the former.

> The history of Islam, for example, is not the evolution of
> a people from animism to monotheism, but of a people, once
> monotheistic, under the influence of a new religion (which
> was nevertheless in part old), and which was borrowed from
> Christianity and Judaism as well as from Arabian paganism.[289]

If one takes seriously the study of other religions in contrast
to the message of Christ, he will be rewarded by a deeper understanding of the great concepts of revelation, incarnation,
atonement, and mediation; an appreciation of the need to communicate the Gospel in clear simple terminology; and a renewed conviction of the finality and sufficiency of Christ. For example:

> The central affirmation of Mohammedanism is the absolute
> unity of God and his sovereignty, the Pantheism of Force, an
> overemphasis on God's transcendence and a denial of his In-
> carnation....The central affirmation of the Christian reli-
> gion is that God, who is eternally both transcendent and
> immanent, became incarnate in Christ, taking sinful man back
> into his favor and that by his death and resurrection we have
> redemption through his blood and receive, by grace alone,
> forgiveness of sin and eternal life and joy,--and are trans-

lated from bondage into the glorious liberty of the sons of
God, to share with him the unspeakable privilege of extending
his Kingdom among men.[290]

At this point, Zwemer foreshadows Kraemer's volume for Madras.
The greatest need of the hour is to see how the Gospel is indeed
the final message of God in contrast to other religious messages
of the world.[291]

Zwemer's addresses on the "Glory and Uniqueness of the Christian Message" at the Keswick Convention (1937) would have provided encouragement to Hendrik Kraemer preparing for Madras.[292]
Zwemer states his convictions as the opposite of Mahatma Gandhi
who reportedly said, "I am unable to place Jesus Christ on a
solitary throne".[293] Christ for Zwemer is at the heart of the
church's message because He is King over all, the reconciler and
ruler of all. Zwemer rejoices in the comprehensiveness of
Pascal's Thoughts on Religion.

> Jesus Christ is the centre of everything and the object of
> everything; and he who does not know Him knows nothing of the
> order of the world and nothing of himself. In Him is all our
> felicity and virtue, our life, our hope; apart from Him there
> is nothing but vice, misery, darkness, despair, and we see
> only obscurity, and confusion in the nature of God and in our
> own.[294]

Indeed Zwemer stands as a signpost on the way to Tambaram (1938).

Tambaram, 1938, A Climax in the Crisis in Mission

The Missionary Conference at Tambaram (Madras, 1938) was a
climactic point in the history of church and mission. Some have
called the quarter of a century preceding Tambaram the second
Protestant reformation. Once again the "theology of the Word"
triumphed in the form of The Christian Message in a Non-Christian World. After enduring a tortuous struggle through scholasticism and revivalism, through a subjective emphasis on ethics
and experience, Protestantism found in its shattered world and
God's Word a new awareness of man's utter dependence upon the
grace of the transcendent God as given in Jesus Christ.
Equally important for this study is that the spotlight at Tambaram shifts from such veterans as Speer, Mott and Zwemer to
Hendrik Kraemer (1888-1965). One could rightly claim that
Kraemer and his book, the Christian Message, stand in the lineage of the Dutch-American, the evangelical missionary to
Muslims, Samuel Zwemer.[295]

The contest between competing approaches surrounding Tambaram
was in dead earnest. Henry H. Riggs and several workers in the
Near East were pressing for the acceptance of the views advocated by Hocking. As chairman of the Report of the Near East

Christian Council Inquiry on the Evangelization of Moslems
(Beirut, 1938), Riggs was able to set these views into print.
All agreed that the two major obstacles were: the Muslim dis-
tortion of biblical ideas (barrier to communication) and the
Muslim communal solidarity-loyalty (barrier to conversion).
Riggs' answer was that Muslims should be permitted to reconstruc-
a gospel about Jesus acceptable to them "remembering that
Christ's method left his own disciples to formulate the deepest
truths for themselves under God's guidance" and that followers
of Jesus should be permitted to remain hidden disciples (rather
than baptized converts) within the Muslim community. He advised against anything that "the inquirer or his neighbor may
interpret as clandestine efforts to alienate him from his own
people." One must strive to develop "groups of followers of
Jesus who are active in making Him known to others while remaining loyally a part of the social and political groups to which
they belong in Islam" in hope that ultimately these secret believers may become an indigenous church group.[296]
    In a Conference on Muslim Workers held at Delhi (December 6-
7, 1938) and at a pre-conference gathering of missionaries for
Muslim lands at Tambaram, the ideas held by Riggs and expressed
in the N.E.C.C. Report were openly rejected. A chorus of evangelical voices realized the dangers of confining mission to the
permeation of Muslim society with Christian teachings and
ideals; of postponing one's decision and the formation of the
church as a visible witnessing community; and of accommodating
the Gospel's call to repentence and discipleship. At Tambaram
(1938), this all came to a head. There it was that Riggs spoke
for the N.E.C.C. Inquiry.[297] There it was that the response
from Delhi and the pre-conference "Special Group 6" replied and
restated the evengelical basis and pattern for mission to Muslims.[298] The majority at Tambaram rejected the ideas set forth
by Hocking and Riggs because the basic presupposition that
"theological tenets are discovered by human experience" was no
longer acceptable! The disillusionment following World War I,
the renewed emphasis upon the "theology of the Word", and conviction that the church's mission involved proclamation had had
far-reaching consequences. The Christian Message verbalized
this majority viewpoint within the missionary movement even
though the debate might continue.
    The influences acting upon Kraemer are both visible and
hidden. It is obvious that he is strongly influenced by recent
developments in theology (Barth, Brunner, Hartenstein, Heim).[299]
However, there can be little doubt that he was also influenced
by his contacts with Zwemer, Speer and Mott. One must remember
that Zwemer helped awaken the missions in Indonesia to their
task regarding Islam. His visit in July-August, 1922 resulted
in the conference with the Netherlands Indies Missionary Union
in Djokjakarta. The veteran Zwemer was highly respected by the
Dutch missionaries. Kraemer himself testifies that Zwemer stim-

ulated the Dutch workers to increased Islamic studies, to create
a Christian literature for Muslims, to reorientate missionary
effort in light of the Islamic renaissance, and to attend to
Muslim concentrations in urban areas and to the youth of Java.
It is interesting to note that Kraemer became an accomplished
specialist exactly in these areas.[300] Kraemer, as chairman of
the East Indies Literature Committee and an authority on the indigenous church's work for Muslims, soon appeared as an ecumenical leader at Jerusalem (1928). At this time, Zwemer's Christocentric-anthropological approach to Muslims was closely akin
to that of Kraemer's, a remarkable point considering the well-
known Continental and Anglo-American tensions. Zwemer and
Kraemer stood in the mainstream of Reformed theology with a
binding respect for the authority of the Word. Hence they were
to find themselves as mediators between the sharp German critics
and the liberal sector of American Protestantism. "Jerusalem,
1928" appears to have stimulated both Zwemer and Kraemer to cast
off earlier references to the ethical and to concentrate on the
message in Christ. The refining fires of the 1930s would help
crystalize this process. As already seen the writings of Zwemer
in many ways foreshadow Kraemer's contribution at Tambaram. By
1938, the matured views of these two Reformed missionaries are
in close agreement.[301] Both are thoroughly theocentric-Christo-
centric stressing that the Christian message is rooted solely in
the revelation in Jesus Christ. Zwemer may at times put more
stress on act (the cross) and Kraemer upon Word, but both would
agree that Word and act, person and work of Christ are inseparable. Both saw Islam as a "totalitarian entity" and in light of
the resurging Islamic modernism agreed there would be no early
disappearance of Islam. Both called for intensified study of
Islam in its contemporary forms. Both agreed that the Muslim
must be approached not as a non-Christian ("religious man") but
as a fellow human being with like needs, problems and aspirations (what has been called an anthropological approach).[302]
Both agreed that evangelism, the proclamation of the Christian
message, was of the essence of mission. They were wary of novel
methods, insisting that the most effective means was personal
contact by evangelists (members of the missionary church).
Kraemer would go beyond Zwemer in terms of the younger churches
and indigenization but this was largely due to their different
locations and dates. Thus, between 1928 and 1938, the torch
(leadership in mission to Muslims) had passed from veteran to
younger hands.

Zwemer's contributions to the post-Tambaram scene confirm his
convictions as to the centrality of Christ and the proclamation
of the Word. He undoubtedly found new strength in what had
transpired at Madras especially the reaffirmation of evangelism
as the primary task. "Jesus knew the strategy of personal
contacts" and so must today's herald.[303] Dedicated to the students of Great Britain, Dynamic Christianity and the World Today

(1939) speaks of the reliability of the Christian message.

> That gospel which Paul preached has been the message of all
> who were in his apostolic succession, and is to-day, as in
> his day, 'the power of God unto salvation to every one that
> believeth.' Why should we be ashamed of its contents or its
> implications? In an age of doubt it is the only anchor of
> our hope; in the present chaos of international relations it
> alone can bring reconciliation.[304]

When W. E. Hocking and H. H. Riggs continued to press for the
acceptance of their views, Zwemer replied with penetrating realism and urged his readers to take serious the findings of
Madras.[305]

> The Cross is the one central message and method and power of
> Christianity. This evangel is startling news and good news
> to Moslems....But that is the very reason we should always
> present the heart of the Christian Gospel....There would have
> been no Apostolic missions, no medieval missions, no modern
> missions without the experience of redemption and the call to
> be ambassadors of the Cross....
>   It is time that a protest be made against the misuse of
> the word, evangelism. It has only one etymological, New Tes-
> tament, historical and theological connotation, namely, to
> tell the good news of One who came to earth to die on the
> Cross for us; who rose again and who ever lives to intercede
> for those who reprent and believe the Gospel. To evangelize
> is to win disciples, to become fishers of men, to preach the
> Gospel message to all the nations.[306]

Samuel M. Zwemer was recognized in neo-evangelical circles as
one who had helped keep the flame alive. One of his most popular books was The Cross Above the Crescent: the validity,
necessity and urgency of missions to Moslems (1941). Zwemer rejects both the harsh polemics of the nineteenth century and the
idea of a concilium of Christianity and Islam. He holds to the
uniqueness, finality, sufficiency and supremacy of the Christ of
the New Testament. While there is much that is good, there is
"no other name". There is cleavage between God's revelation in
Christ and the religions of the world.

> But between the earliest Revelation and God's last word is
> the Battle of the Books—the Word of God against the word of
> man. For there are many voices on religion, but only one Re-
> velation. There have been many prophets, but only one
> Savior.[307]

He rejoices that Islam is being permeated by Christian ideals
and spirit, but states there is no substitute for decisive

discipleship and the forming of visible Christian communities
(answer to Hocking, Toynbee and Riggs).

> After forty years' experience--sometimes heart-breaking ex-
> perience...I am convinced that the nearest way to the Moslem
> heart is the way of God's love, the way of the Cross. Paul
> in his great chapter on this Christian love, as the true and
> excellent way, used the Greek word <u>Agape</u>....[308]

The basis for mission was again set forth: <u>Into</u> <u>All</u> <u>the</u> <u>World</u>.
<u>The</u> <u>Great</u> <u>Commission</u>; <u>A</u> <u>Vindication</u> <u>and</u> <u>an</u> <u>Interpretation</u>
(1943). Zwemer's last volume on missions was <u>Evangelism</u> <u>Today</u>;
<u>Message</u> <u>not</u> <u>Method</u> (1944). In reviewing this volume which saw
five editions, Edward J. Jurji honored its author as one who
possessed a "penetrating theological acumen, the burning heart
of the pioneer, the charity and piety of the saint and the erud-
ition of the scholar." It finds Zwemer in the company of Emil
Brunner, Nels F. S. Ferre, C. H. Dodd, Karl Barth, C. S. Lewis
and H. Kraemer. For Zwemer "the message is of far more importance than the method or the messenger".[309]

> The Cross of Christ is the searchlight of man's sin and
> the revelation of His love for sinners; in carrying this good
> news we need the power of Christ's Resurrection, we need
> faith not only in the seed but in the soil, and we may use
> every possible method to drive the one message to the con-
> science of the hearer. He that would be thoroughly furnished
> for this good word and work needs to 'possess his possess-
> ions' and be a minister like unto 'a flame of fire'.[310]

Many are the tributes given to Samuel M. Zwemer, but among the
most fitting are those by Kenneth Scott Latourette.

> There was something of the Old Testament prophet about Dr.
> Zwemer. He had the prophet's fearlessness and forthright-
> ness, the burning conviction which would brook no compromise.
> That, indeed, must be true of any who would across the years
> present the message of Christ to adherents of so sturdy a
> faith as Islam. Yet there was in him much more than the Old
> Testament. It was the Old Testament fulfilled in the New.
> Dr. Zwemer was frankly a conservative Evangelical. In him
> there was no wavering or hesitation in the proclamation of
> the historic Evangelical faith. Yet he never forgot that
> Evangelical means Good News, and that the Good News of the
> Gospel is God's love. His zeal was always transfigured by
> love and it was not only for his simple unquestioning faith
> that those who were honored to be in the circle of his in-
> timate friends will best remember him, but it will be also
> and primarily for his loving heart that they will recall him,
> a loving heart which was the reflection of God's love in

Christ.[311]

Acknowledgement of his work as a missionary and scholar was
again to the point.

> Never in the history of the Church has any Christian covered
> the Moslem world as comprehensively, in study, travel, plan-
> ning and advocacy of Missions to it as Dr. Zwemer....Dr.
> Zwemer has no illusions about the resistance which Islam
> presents to Christianity....Yet he has no doubt as to the
> ultimate triumph of the Cross.[312]

Samuel M. Zwemer provides an appropriate conclusion to this
examination of Anglican and Reformed contributions to the Christian mission to Muslims, 1800-1938. He was a scholarly participant in the several strands of nineteenth and twentieth century
theology and mission. He was heir of the Protestantism which
had been motivated by pietism and the evangelical awakenings to
evangelize the world, to disciple for Christ the nations.
Zwemer, like Gairdner, represents the matured fruit of the
labors of Martyn, French and others. Again, he was captivated
with Duff's idea that education could be the handmaiden of
evangelism in the creation of a Christian society. Yet he became
alarmed when certain missiologists confined mission to the enlightenment of mankind. Again, he joined in the humanitarian
concern for the whole man and approved of harnessing the science
of medicine as a medium of mission. Yet when this handmaiden
also became an end in itself, a disinterested philanthropy, he
called it into question. Again, the new science of religion and
the historical-literary critical methods offered appealing solutions and promises. Yet in light of the harsh realities of a
world at war and the totalitarian claims of man's religions,
this too, soon appeared to be empty. Man's natural inclination
is to feel he must create handmaidens for the Christian Gospel,
only to discover that they, philosophy, education, philanthropy,
etc. become domineering. At one critical point in history,
Zwemer was among those who, like the Reformers, turned again to
the Word of God. There they found an apt description of and
answer to a world disillusioned with its optimism concerning
man's ability. "The triumph of God's grace" was an answer
needed by a world broken and gripped by the tragic reality of
sin. The Gospel alone provides a rebirth, a reformation, to
those caught in the crisis of theology and mission. It provides
a concrete basis for the church's work in a world in constant
transition. Thus it is fair to consider Zwemer a link, a
bridge, between conservative Protestant missions and theology in
the nineteenth century and the twentieth century's rebirth of
biblical theology and evangelical understanding of the mission
of Christ's church.
        This strenuous passage from Henry Martyn to Samuel M. Zwemer

was not in vain, for with it came growth and matured understanding.[313] Under the influence of pietism and evangelical stirrings, the church rediscovered the motive and methods of her mission. Later under the impact of introspective philosophy and the behavioral sciences, the church gained renewed appreciation of God's concern for man in society. As the world seemed shrouded in darkness, the grace and the glory of the transcendent God again broke through in Jesus Christ. Who is to say that these are not necessary steps in the unfolding of God's will and way in Christ—in our understanding of the Word, the world and the coming kingdom. Many questions remain unanswered and as open-ended as history itself. Discussion surely shall continue as long as the church's task remains unfinished. Yet once again God is to be praised for reviving his church for the mission of communicating Christ, the Word incarnate, to her Muslim neighbors.

Appendices

A SUMMARY EXAMINATION OF THE THREE PERSIAN TRACTS OF H. MARTYN

Two Muslim tracts prompted Martyn to take up the pen. The defensive tract of Mirza Ibrahim discloses an author with a keen mind and the ability to keep his work free of violent remarks. He declares that Islam's superiority is proven by the miracle of the Quran. The one great and lasting miracle of the Quran supports the divine mission of Muhammad and outclasses the imperfect miracles of Moses and Jesus. Muhammad's miracles are only mentioned in passing. Attached to Mirza's tract is an extract of the much inferior work of Aga Akbar on the miracles of Muhammad. This article, of a poorer style, is basically a catalogue of sensational, often strange miracle stories drawn from the hadiths (traditions). Henry Martyn responds in three tracts.

In the first tract, Martyn noted that he did not desire controversy. He begins as follows:

> The Christian minister thanks the celebrated Professor of Islamism for the favour he has done him in writing an answer to his inquiries, but confesses that, after reading it, a few doubts occurred to him, on account of which, and not for the mere purpose of dispute, he has taken upon himself to write the following pages....

Within the tract, Martyn stresses that a miracle must exceed more than the "common experience" of one ethnic group, e.g. of the Arabs. It must be submitted to (1) peoples of different places, (2) learned men who agree that it is not reproducible, and (3) comparison with secular world histories, not only the religious histories of the Arabs. The Quran, he declares, cannot measure up to these tests. Again the miracles recited by Akbar are rejected because these later hadiths were written for purpose of proselytism. Martyn contends that miracles to be acceptable must be (1) recorded by either the Prophet or his companions, i.e. first hand witnesses without a great time-lapse between the event and its recording, and (2) be recorded in an environment free from the use of force in religious matters. It is well known, he argues, that Muslims do not tolerate such religious freedom.

The second tract focuses on why faith should be placed not in Islam but in Christianity. The list of reasons include: the ancient prophecies do not mention Muhammad; his fallibility is seen in his relations with women, the use of the sword and rewards to make converts; and Islam's lack of a "means of salvation", i.e. a Person to make atonement. The point that "Mohammed was in a state of infidelity may be shewn from the Koran itself" was the only aggressive note in these three tracts and it caused a sharp reaction in Persia. Positively, Martyn shows why the Scriptures are authentic; notes how the Quran cancels the Law and Gospel whereas the Gospel fulfills not abrogates the Law; and presents Jesus as the Word and Spirit of God, the worthy means of atonement. Martyn wisely gives the bulk of his space to news of the Christ. The spread of the Christian faith, the transformation of men and society, is the greatest miracle and it was done by poor men without force. He closes with this appeal:

> It is now the prayer of the humble Henry Martyn that these things be considered with impartiality. If they become the means of procuring conviction, let not the fear of death or punishment operate for a moment to the contrary, but let this conviction have its legitimate effect; for the world, we know, passes away like the wind of the desert. But if what has been stated does not produce conviction, my prayer is that God Himself may instruct you; that as hitherto you have held what you believed to be the truth, you may now become teachers of that which is really so; and that He may grant you to be the means of bringing others to the knowledge of the same, through Jesus Christ, who has loved us and washed us in His own blood, to whom be the power and glory for ever and ever. Amen.

Martyn's third tract deals with the doctrines of Persian Sufism. This naturally touches on the questions of emanation, immanence and union with God. He agrees that there is no question concerning "the truth of the unity of Deity, or that union with him constitutes perfection, and is the greatest of human achievements". But he argues that neither (1) the contemplation of the Sufis nor (2) "the way of works" as adopted by some Jews, Muslims and Christians (e.g. Romanists) is an adequate means. These stress man's approach to God while the Christian faith teaches that God approaches man. God's goodness and holiness, in sharp contrast to man's sinfulness, is revealed not imagined. More than the fear of God's wrath (the basic motive in Islam, he claims) is needed if reconciliation is to be effected. "According to the Gospel, union is obtained with God when the Spirit of God dwells in man." "Wisdom of God", "Word of God", "Image of the invisible God" and other titles given to Jesus Christ indicate he is the manifestation of the God's manward movement. He then presents Jesus, his sacrifice, and miracles as verified by the testimony of the Apostles and secular historians. He emphasizes the "inward nature" (not outward observance) of the Christian faith in its obedience to God.

Except for the charges laid against Muhammad, these three tracts are very considerate of the Muslim reader. There is, however, a heavy strand of rationalism intertwined with Martyn's evangelicalism. He follows the eighteenth century pattern of evidences. In application this turns miracles into rational proofs. Martyn is at his best when positively presenting Christ and the new life. His ability to focus upon the person and work of Jesus and the "inward transforming" life in Christ draw justifiable credit.

Source: cf. Samuel Lee, Controversial Tracts on Christianity and Mohammedanism Translated and Explained (Cambridge, 1824).

APPENDIX B

A SUMMARY EXAMINATION OF <u>MIZAN-AL-HAQQ</u>, <u>THE BALANCE OF TRUTH</u>
BY K. G. PFANDER

Pfander states as his purpose the following:

Our object in writing this book is not controversy and strife; it is
only to enable those Mussulmans who are earnest seekers of the truth to
attain the object of their desires, by laying before them the state of
the case. Therefore, O thou who readest this book, thy friend who has
written these pages out of a desire for thy eternal happiness, and on
account of the love which he owes to his fellow-men, begs thee to bring
to their consideration a sincere heart and an undistracted mind; that,
laying bigotry aside, thou mayest read them through again and again.
And do thou pray for His grace who is the Dispenser of light, in order
that thou mayest find the truth; for until a man is illuminated by His
light, he cannot find the path of truth and happiness (Weakley edition).

The introductory argument might be summarized thus. After an acceptable
oriental tribute to God, Pfander acknowledges that God has revealed himself. God has made a way for man, sinful as he is, to seek and find the
truth: namely reason and revelation. True happiness is not to be found
in sensual pleasure or wealth but in fulfillment of the object of man's
creation: to know, serve, and please God. His major premise is that one
can gain a satisfying knowledge of God only through divine revelation. But
since there are two major monotheistic religions which claim to have this
revelation (Christianity and Islam), which is right? There are six criteria by which one can discover the "True Revelation": (i) It must satisfy
the yearnings of the human spirit to obtain eternal happiness, i.e. knowledge of truth, pardon, purification; (ii) must be in accordance with moral
law, conscience; (iii) must reveal God as just, holy, rewarding good,
punishing evil; (iv) must reveal God as One, eternal, almighty, unchanging
in purpose as He deals with the universe; (v) must make clear the way of
salvation, and in its teaching upon that subject there must be no contra-
diction in meaning; and (vi) since no book or prophet can possibly reveal
God fully to men, it must involve a personal manifestation of God so as to
call men to faith in all ages thereafter.
    The main body of the work contains three parts. Part I. In proof that
the Old Testament and the New Testament are the Word of God and that they
have been neither corrupted nor abrogated, Pfander offers this support:
(chapter 1) testimony of the Quran to the Bible; (2) the Bible has never
been abrogated in its facts, doctrines, and moral principles; (3) the Bible
now in circulation is the one existing in Muhammad's time; and (4) it has
not undergone corruption either before or after his time. In Part II,
Pfander aims to set forth the principle doctrines of the Holy Scriptures
and to show that they are in conformity with the criteria of the True Revelation as stated in the introduction. This includes: the attributes
of God, the condition of man in sin, the way of salvation, its achievement
in Christ, the triune manifestation of the One God, the life and conduct
of a true Christian, and the manner and history of the spread of early
Christianity. In Part III, Pfander makes a candid inquiry into the claim
of Islam to be God's final revelation. He attacks the claims that the
Bible prophesied Muhammad; that the language and style of the Quran prove
it is a miracle and inspired (points out certain contradictions); that
Muhammad worked miracles; that his life and conduct were as lofty as described by Muslim writers; and that Islam spread as a religion should, with-

out compulsion. In this sector, Pfander becomes polemical in dealing with
Muslim miracles, the Quran and Muhammad. A prophet must meet these tests:
his teaching must not oppose previous revelations; it must be supported by
evidence, e.g. miracles or prophecy; it must be supported by befitting conduct; and it must not be enforced by violence. Needless to say, Pfander
finds Muhammad wanting!

Within the text, Pfander has urged the reader to open "the door of thine
heart to the glad tidings of salvation so that Jesus Christ may enter in"
(Weakley edition, p. 68). In the conclusion, he expands his appeal:

> Now, respected reader, we have together examined all the asserted proofs
> of the truth of Islam, and we have inquired into Muhammad's claim to be
> the Lord of the Apostles and the Seal of the Prophets. It lies with you
> to decide for yourself, in the sight of God who knoweth men's hearts,
> whether this claim is true or false. May God Most Merciful guide you to
> a right decision!
>
> You have to choose between the Lord Jesus Christ, the Word of God,
> and Muhammad ibn "Abd-Allah; between Him who went about doing good and
> him who is called the Prophet with the Sword; between Him who said 'Love
> your enemies,' and him who said, 'Slay your enemies and the enemies of
> God'; between Him who prayed for His murderers, and him who caused those
> who lampooned him to be murdered. You are doubtless aware of what kind
> were Christ's life and character, and you know that these form one of
> the most decisive of the proofs of the truth of His claims.... Christ
> is alive, while Muhammad is dead. Which of the two is the better able
> to help you?...You believe that Christ will come again, and are now
> expecting His return with fear....For 'we must all be made manifest
> before the judgment seat of Christ.' To Him...every knee should bow....
> Some day you must kneel before Him; why not now?
>
> We bring you the good news of His love....Pray therefore, my brother
> that God may guide you aught and lead you to a right decision in this
> great matter ere it is too late....So shall you find the Truth in Him
> who is the Way, the Truth, and the Life....You shall receive from His
> pierced hand the crown of everlasting life (Tisdall edition).

APPENDIX C

THE SYRIAN PROTESTANT COLLEGE

Founded in 1866, Syrian Protestant College gained academic respect and
retained a Christian atmosphere under Daniel Bliss, its first president
(1866-1902). At his retirement there were five departments (preparatory,
collegiate, commercial, medicine and pharmacy), an enrollment of six hundred, and a faculty of forty (one-half American) on the beautiful campus
overlooking the Mediterranean Sea. Daniel Bliss held firmly to the principles stated in the Preamble:

> WHEREAS, It is deemed essential for the promotion of Protestant Mis-
> sions and Christian civilization in Syria to establish an institution
> where native youth may obtain in their own country and language, a lit-
> erary and scientific education; and ....
> WHEREAS, It is the distinct purpose of the founders of this College to
> have it conducted on principles, strictly Protestant and evangelical,
> but not sectarian or such as to exclude students of any sect or nation-
> ality who will conform to its laws; designing also so to identify the
> College with the interests of the people, as to make it thoroughly indi-

genous, and entertaining the hope that, in the course of years the instruction of the institution may be wholly committed to competent
evangelical natives....

By precept and example, Daniel Bliss fulfilled his dedicatory statement:
"It will be impossible for anyone to continue with us long without knowing
what we believe to be the truth and our reasons for that belief." In the
early years, the faculty included fellow ministers such as D. S. Dodge,
George Post, C. V. A. Van Dyck and John Wortabet. All courses stressed
Christian views and principles. Bible study, stimulating discussions, a
Sunday School, daily prayers and participation in the church in Beirut resulted in a revival (1885). John R. Mott, while leading campus evangelistic meetings (1895), noted that one fourth of the graduates to date had
entered Christian service as teachers and ministers. But this evangelical
program began to break down with an influx of younger faculty members not
sharing the founder's views. As long as Bliss was president and William
Booth headed up the Board of Trustees, the "Declaration of Principles" was
applied, however, and the storms of rebellion in 1888 and 1895 were put
down.

These safeguards were abandoned under the founder's son and the school's
second president, Howard Bliss (1902-1920). The Declaration became an
ideal instead of a test. Requirements of daily chapel and Bible classes
were modified. Student agitation and World War I hastened the process.
When the local Board of Managers (mainly missionaries and Syrian Christians) turned their responsibilities over to the faculty (1902), remaining
Christian controls were rapidly swept away. Professor D. S. Dodge, one of
the few retaining the original vision, fought a last ditch battle. For the
time, the Board of Trustees backed his statement.

First, the College was not established merely for higher secular education, or the inculcation of morality. One of its chief objects is to
teach the great truths of Scripture; to be a centre of Christian light
and influence; and to lead its students to understand and accept a pure
Christianity, and go out to profess and commend it in every walk of
life...Fifth, it has been suggested that the system of voluntary attendance might relieve the difficulty....Concessions such as these, if
granted, would go far to neutralize any positive witness for Christ and
evangelical Christianity which we might hope to maintain....

Howard S. Bliss, respected leader that he was, reflected the liberal
theological outlook popular at the turn of the century which accepted Christianity as ideals, ethics and experience rather than the revelation of God
in Christ in history. Jesus was the model of perfect character rather than
the Messiah of God. A new educational law by the government ruled that religious instruction could be given only to Protestants and that worship
services and Bible courses could be offered only on a voluntary basis.
While most students would continue to participate in these assemblies up to
World War II, the swing to a secular or simply religious outlook was apparent. The inaugural address of President Bayard Dodge (1923) could not have
offended anyone.

To us Protestantism means religious freedom....We feel that religion
is not an ulterior aim of education; it is not a quantity of tangible
facts to be taught, or a creed to be subscribed to; it is something much
more fundamental; it is consciousness of a spiritual power, controlling
life and seeking good....It is for the mosque, synagogue, or church, to
provide the practical formalities of organized religion, but the school
should join them in fostering a consciousness of God, and a desire to

live in accordance with God's moral purposes.

It is easy to observe the institution's drift from the Christian orbit into
the world of secular liberal education. Many institutions founded upon
Christian principles in the United States were undergoing this process at
the same time. Liberal theology, increased governmental controls, inadequate financial support from Christian sources, and the need to appeal to
a wider clientele were among the visible causes for this trend.

This institution was renamed the American University of Beirut (1920)
and continued to play a significant role in the regeneration of the people
of Syria and the great social, cultural and political Arab renaissance of
the twentieth century. Its ever growing enrollment contains a high percentage of Muslims as well as Protestant, Orthodox and Roman Catholic Christians. While no longer acknowledged as a Christian school, the University
still retains international fame for its academic excellence, its research,
and various social services. In a sense it remains the gift of its Christian founders to the peoples of the Near East.

Sources: Quotations from S.B.L. Penrose, That They May Have Life: the
Story of the American University of Beirut, 1866-1941 (New York, 1941), pp.
309, 139ff., 292. Also cf. F.J. Daniel, The Reminiscences of Daniel Bliss
(New York, 1920), esp. pp. 219ff.; Jessup, Fifty-Five Years, I, 303 II,
707ff.; Addison, Christian Approach to the Muslim, p. 130; George Antonius,
The Arab Awakening (London, 1939), pp. 35ff.; Time Magazine (July 8, 1966);
and personal interviews.

APPENDIX D

AN EXAMINATION OF THE APOLOGETICS OF W. ST. CLAIR TISDALL

The Sources of Islam (1900-1901) by Tisdall caused a stir almost equal
to his revised version of Pfander's Balance of Truth. Muslims did not
appreciate critical scholarship which found Islam's origins in pre-Islamic
customs, Sabaeanism, Judaism, heretical Christianity and Zoroastrianism.
Tisdall demonstrated his thesis by tracing the sources of certain stories
found in the Quran and the Hadiths.

Earlier lectures, The Religion of the Crescent (1895), reveal Tisdall's
scholarly understanding of Islam. In Lecture I, he sympathetically describes the great truths and strengths of Islam and credits Muhammad with
making real improvements over Arab heathenism. Lecture II covers the weaknesses of Islam; its errors regarding God's nature (a despot without love),
man's sinful nature, the atonement; prayer, eternity, history and Biblical
accounts. Islam has survived because its distortions are so interwoven
with the truth. It is contrary to God's fullest revelation, a substitute
for faith in Christ. Making use of recent research, lecture III points
out that Islam is a mixture of Abrahamic faith and later religious elements. There are five basic strands in Islam: (1) Pre-Islamic Arab religion, (2) Sabaeanism and Talmudic Judaism, (3)apocryphal and dissenting
forms of Christianity, (4) Zoroastrianism and (5) elements growing out of
Muhammad's personality and experience. Different combinations of these
explain the various Islamic sects and traditions. Lecture IV concentrates
on the practices and fruits of Islam. The writer discusses Muslim family
life, the identification of politics and religion, and an intellectual life
which is restricted by both tradition and the Quran. Tisdall reports on
the success of missions to Muslims in the Punjab. He warns that the carnal

methods of the crusaders must be replaced by a full reliance upon the spirit and way of Christ, upon love and sacrificial service to others. His vision of the future included the following:

> It is a rash thing to venture to predict the future of Islam, but it seems to me at least that the hopeful pictures which European enthusiasts have drawn of a reformed and purified Islam co-existing with Christianity are merely imaginary. We may well believe that the progress of education and the leavening influence of Christianity will lead to the formation in the Muhammadan world of more and more numerous reformed and non-orthodox sects. These, while still professing Islam, will strive more and more to get rid of the Traditions and to eliminate many of the manifest absurdities of the popular creed. Many statements of the Quran will be explained away and others mystically interpreted....The most earnest men will gradually draw nearer and nearer to Christianity, and the end will come gradually and almost imperceptibly, the darkness fading into twilight and the twilight vanishing in the full glory of the dawn of the Sun of Righteousness. Those Muslims who are unwilling to follow this path will find--as not a few even now do--that their Faith is opposed to their Reason, and will gradually lapse into unbelief and Atheism. But for all this the only cure lies, not in attempting to bolster up the decaying Faith of Islam, but in the full and free preaching of the Gospel of Christ (pp. 230f.).

In India: Its History, Darkness and Dawn (1901), Tisdall describes for university students the methods and results of evangelization in that great land. Incidently he discloses his own concept of mission. Much stress is given to the church.

> It is well understood that foreign missionaries, however high their attainments and however deep their spirituality may be, cannot do more than begin the work of the conversion of India. That grand and glorious task must, under God, be brought to a successful issue by the Indian Church itself (pp. 112ff.).

Tisdall emphasized the need of Christian unity, the imperative of lay witness and the danger of corrupting the simplicity of the Gospel with sacerdotalism. A chapter deals with misconceptions concerning a "proper attitude towards non-Christian religions". He deals with romantics, rationalists and orientalists who accuse missionaries of injuring the process of civilization by disturbing native religions and who advocate half-way houses or religio-philosophical systems which embrace all religions as valid (e.g. Carlyle, Davenport, Canon Taylor, Max Miller's Hibbert Lectures of 1878). Tisdall writes:

> Many people credit missionaries with a firm conviction that all religions but the Christian are simply and solely devices of the Evil One intended to destroy men's souls....owing to our increased acquaintances with the great religions and philosophies of the East, people are learning the fact that in every such faith or system there is to be found a certain modicum of truth and wisdom..../Yet/ A superficial student of Comparative Religion is only too apt to content himself with hasty generalizations, and to mistake for example, the Hindu Trimurtti for the Christian doctrine of the Trinity....It is the want of such thoroughly accurate and scientific study, coupled as it too frequently is with an eager desire for novelty and a false liberality of sentiment, that leads many otherwise logical minds to imagine that Christianity differs in

degree merely and not in kind from other great systems of religion. Of
course persons who assume the latter theory as an axiom ... will never
be able...to enter at all into the objects and aim of a Christian missionary, whether he belongs to the first or to the twentieth century
(pp. 120f.).

A scholarly missionary, says Tisdall, does not cull out a few gems from a
religion, but studies its total consequence for the life of a people.
Tisdall would agree with Tertullian and Calvin that the truth appearing in
these religions is the spark of God's image which remains in spite of the
fall, a witness to the Creator. This light of Socrates and Plato, however,
does not quench man's desire for the Light of God in the face of Jesus
Christ. Man's reconciliation with God can only be effected in Christ, not
by speculative philosophies. "History, ancient and modern, speaks with no
uncertain voice as to the possibility of forming a substitute for the
simple gospel of the historical Christ" (p. 139). Man's longings and needs
are best fulfilled in Christ. Tisdall holds that men should follow the
pattern of Justin Martyr, who although he continued to wear the philosopher's cloak long after he embraced the Gospel (cf. Dialogue with Try-
phone, ch. 8), yet never tried to amalgamate the Christian faith with
Platonism.

Tisdall's apologetic method is best set forth in the work he prepared
for missionaries, A Manual of the Leading Muhammadan Objections to Christianity (1904). He advises using the Quran where possible in reply and to
begin on such themes as "the unity of God". Tisdall cautioned that the
"difficulties" faced by the Muslim could spring from unregenerate human
nature (common to all men, Rom. 8:7) as well as from his Islamic background. Several excerpts disclose Tisdall's sympathetic spirit and approach.

(1) Remember that our aim is not to silence our opponent, nor to gain a
merely logical victory, but to win souls to Christ. Hence, in argument,
we should endeavour to remove misconceptions....We must not expect to
convert a soul. That is the work of the Holy Spirit,...urge the inquirer...prayerfully to read the Bible, especially the New Testament.
(2) Endeavour to limit the discussion on each occasion to one or two
definite points, which should be settled upon with your opponent before-
hand....(3) It is impossible to pay too much attention to fairness and
courtesy in your arguments....Regard him as a brother for whom Christ
died, and to whom you are sent with the message of reconciliation....
Never let an argument degenerate into a quarrel....(6) Never be beguiled
into answering such a question as, 'What do you think of Muhammad?'
or into making a direct attack upon him....(7) The missionary should be
careful to give some title of courtesy to Muhammad....(8) Be careful of
the theological terms you use. See that you thoroughly understand them
yourself in the first place, not merely the English terms but the words
used in the native languages....Whenever your opponent quotes and founds
an argument upon any passage in the Bible (or Quran) make a point of
turning to that passage and ascertaining from the context exactly what
is said and what is meant....(11) Readily accept, and make it plain that
you heartily accept, all the truth that is in any way common to Christianity and Islam....e.g. that Christ is Kalimtu'llah (the Word of God).
(12) Try to convince of sin and man's need of a Saviour....Endeavour
to reach men's hearts and not merely their intellects. Appeal to them
as men for whom Christ died,....(13) Put yourself as much as possible
in your opponent's place, so as to try to understand his difficulties.
...(15) Finally, let the servant of Christ remember and act on Bengal's

advice: "Never enter upon controversy without <u>knowledge</u>, without <u>love</u>, without <u>necessity</u>,' and, let us add, with <u>prayer</u> (pp. 13-12)!

Chapters two through eight proceded to answer questions regarding the Bible, various Christian teachings and Muhammad's role in history. They were to serve as helps for Christian workers rather than for Muslim readers. Tisdall's method was to strive to remove all obstacles so that the Gospel <u>itself</u>, not his book or method, could appeal to a man's heart and conscience. He fully realized the limits of rational argument and refused to abuse Islam or its Prophet for argument's sake. His aim was to sweep away barriers so that the Word and Spirit of God might enter and transform the listener's life. This stress on communication of the Gospel was a marked improvement over many earlier apologetic approaches.

APPENDIX E

AN EXAMINATION OF "THE VALUES OF CHRISTIANITY AND ISLAM"
PREPARED BY W.H.T. GAIRDNER AND W.A. EDDY FOR THE
JERUSALEM MEETING OF THE I. M. C. (1928)

The paper falls into three parts: (1) the question of spiritual values in Islam, (2) how Christianity transcends and answers Islamic theology, and (3) the problem of communication (the pouring of Christian content into "Islamic half-truths") and of community (making the church a spiritual home for converts from Islam). Gairdner cautiously prefixes the paper with a note on "kinetic" and "potential" values in Islam so that no one will misconstrue his use of this term, "values" into a synonym for truths. "Values" for him are those things of worth to the Muslim, "vital element(s) which contribute to the amelioration of individual or group life". He doesn't equate "values" with "universals" to be found in all religions inasmuch as every religion is unique.

Six main Islamic "values" are listed. These are not to be understood as something acquired by human reason, religious experience, natural theology, or separate Muslim revelation, but simply as "bad copies" of the Judaeo-Christian faith inadequately conveyed to Muhammad and his followers in the early milieu of Islam (p. 244). (1) The Muslim <u>doctrine</u> <u>of</u> <u>God</u> as power, absolute and irresistable, as "unconditioned Might", forces God's love and holiness into recession. Yet by beginning with the Islamic ideas of Holy Spirit and the Logos, the Christian can lead the Muslim to the biblical God who is present to communicate and act in the temporal world. (2) The Quranic <u>veneration</u> <u>for</u> <u>Jesus</u> can be a starting point in transferring Muslim affection and loyalty from Muhammad to Jesus as the living intercessor (<u>wagih</u>). Indeed the "Islamic teaching is not intentionally derogatory or antagonistic to the claims of Christ; it is an attempt to venerate and esteem him". (3) Muslim <u>devotional</u> <u>life</u> which reaches a peak in Quranic chanting, the emotional <u>Zikr</u> and the Sufi Way points to a desire for "the ideal of life in and for God". (4) <u>Personal</u> <u>attachment</u> to <u>Muhammad</u> makes possible the Islamic system of "minute legalism and casuistry". If Muslims would take historical criticism serious, they would turn from the adoration of this "wholly idealized leader" and find in the Christ, a new life. (5) Islamic <u>fraternity</u> does create a powerful force, gripping the individual Muslim, but one equally matched by the indigenous church. (6) Islam's <u>self-propagation</u> warrants some merit but its compromising adjustment to human nature leaves much to be desired.

In part two, "Values in Christianity", the Christian faith is seen as the corrective and fulfillment of Islam in the sense that it resolves the

human dilemma and brings man into a realization of that for which he was
created. The assignment given to Gairdner was:

> only to emphasize afresh those features of the Christian message and
> experience which are of first importance in the conflict with Islam.
> There is no element of Christianity which is not needed desperately in
> Moslem lands, as elsewhere. We can note here only those elements which
> specifically cure the maladies and fill the voids created by Islam.

The Christian Message then is the needed "corrective" and "enrichment of
Islamic half-truths" which are but "dimly perceived or distorted". The
holiness and love of God revealed in Christ must correct the hard deistic,
non-moral notions of will and force found in Islam. Only knowledge of God's
activity and human responsibility can correct the Muslim fatalism--quietism
which tolerates sin and social suffering.

> At the expense of appearing to obscure the proofs of divine omnipotence,
> Christianity must insist upon God's desire for man's cooperation in re-
> claiming the waste places of this world. The Sacrifice on the Cross,...
> nay, a hundred truths, have taught the Christian what his Moslem brother
> does not know: that God appeals to man, but does not compel his obedi-
> ence....God's providence does indeed control all, but it is a providence
> of love, not of imposed and irresistible power.

The New Testament concept of eternal life through a faith-relationship is
needed to correct the Muslim's mistaken idea that salvation comes by adherence to a creedal community and results in a sensual paradise. The biblical
concept of the Holy Spirit is essential to disclose how God can be both
transcendent and "in our hearts". This vital point resolves issues with
which many Muslim mystics have long struggled. Again the Muslim "hunger for
a mediator who shall be a high-priestly intercessor" can be satisfied only
with a transfer of allegiance from the Muhammad to the eternal Messiah.
Communication is the concern of part three. The Christian faith must be
understood as a living experience, not as an intellectual assent to orthodoxy. Thus the church confronted by Islam must work out its "theology experientially". (a) The doctrine of the Trinity affirms that God is not only
transcendent but that "He is here...is touched with the feeling of man's
infirmities". Islam's agnostic reply that "God is unknowable" or that
"Revelation is only a formal and mechanical link between incompatibles" represents a retrogression to Gairdner. Christians must continue to witness
to their experience of "God in Christ" because according to the New Testament "God's essential nature" has been revealed through the incarnate Messiah and the effusion of the Holy Spirit. (b) The incarnation and atonement
of Christ must not be neglected.

> In saying that the Christian message must ever center in Christ, and in
> Christ crucified, the center of gravity is not thereby made to fall out-
> side God;...for Jesus Christ, and in particular Christ crucified, is the
> definitive projection of God upon the world of space and time...All these
> differences of view culminate in the Cross, which (rather than the In-
> carnation) is the battleground between the two faiths. To the Moslem,
> as to the carnal Jew, the Cross is a blasphemy, the very embodiment of
> weakness and defeat; to the Christian it is the very symbol of moral
> strength and victory, and through it he has learned to say 'the weakness
> of God is stronger than men.'...The Incarnation says "God was in Christ':
> the Atonement adds, 'reconciling man unto Himself.'

Only the communication of this can lead Muslims to experience the "heart of

the Eternal God" who has projected himself into the world. (c) Workers
must get away from the "gentle Jesus", (of oriental Christianity and liberal Protestantism) to the triumphant "Living Intercessor" who is more than
a match for the late Prophet. (d) Christian worship too must be upgraded
to convey "the true riches of experience in God's glory" and to surpass the
best of Muslim mysticism in "the secret of freedom and spirituality, combined with reverence and order". (e) A Christian brotherhood like that of
the first centuries likewise will attract Muslims who know only the limited
Islamic fraternity. (f) Christian practices of chastity and family life
again can attract Muslims dissatisfied with Near Eastern practices of marriage and sex.

   In conclusion, we must learn the key lesson concerning method: there
are but **two agencies** for winning Muslims to the King, namely "the Spirit of
Jesus" and the church as a spiritual home for converts".

> The justification of missions to Islam is not to be found in the super-
> iority of Western culture or theology or even morals...but rather in
> the fact that Islam is predominantly a religion of the letter, Christ-
> ianity the religion of the spirit....The Spirit of God which was in Him,
> and which through Him is the divine Means of Grace today....Nothing
> but the Spirit can bind and free Islam....The Spirit of the Father in
> Jesus Christ....

The church remains both the object and agent of God's mission. Under "A
Spiritual Home for Converts" the best of Gairdner challenges the church to
be the full realization of life for and with God, hence the fulfillment of
the destiny for which man was created by God.

Sources: "Christianity and Islam" is found in the Jerusalem Report (1928),
I, 235-283. Parts II and III are also in the Moslem World, 18 (1928), 336-
355.

APPENDIX F

CLASSIFIED BIBLIOGRAPHY OF THE PUBLICATIONS OF W.H.T. GAIRDNER
BOOKS FOR THE CHURCH AT LARGE:

Studies in Prayer, London, 1897.
Helps to the Study of St. John's Gospel, Parts I and II, London, 1898-1899.
Helps to the Study of the Epistle to the Romans, London, 1899.
D.M. Thornton: A Study in Missionary Ideals and Methods, London, 1908.
The Reproach of Islam, London, 1909,
      fifth edition revised as The Rebuke of Islam, London, 1920.
Edinburgh, 1910: An Account and Interpretation of the World Missionary
      Conference, Edinburgh, 1910.

WORKS ON LINGUISTICS:

The Metres of Arabic Poetry, Cairo Study Center, 1917.
Egyptian Colloquial Arabic: a Conversation Grammar and Reader, Cambridge,
"A Modern Meter of Egyptian-Arabic Verse," American Journal of Semitic
      Languages and Literature, 37 (1920-21), 230-231.
A Class-book of Arabic Accidence (with Atallah Athanasius), Cairo, 1921.
The Phonetics of Arabic, London, 1925.
"The Arab Phoneticians on the Consonants and Vowels," M.W., 25 (1935),

242-257.

WORKS ON DRAMA AND MUSIC:

Egyptian Hymn-tunes and Notes, privately published, 1911.
Syrian Hymn-tunes, privately published, 1912.
"The Source and Character of Oriental Music," M.W., 6 (1916), 347-356.
Joseph and His Brothers (O.T. Play), English, London, 1921; Arabic, Cairo,
    1921.
Passover Night, English, London, 1921; Arabic, Cairo, 1921.
The Last Passover Night, English, London, 1922; Arabic, Cairo, 1922.
Saul and Stephen, A Sacred Drama, English, London, 1921; Arabic, Cairo, 1922
The Good Samaritan, London, 1923.
King Hezekiah, London, 1923.
Oriental Hymn-Tunes: Egyptian and Syrian, London, 1930.

LITERATURE FOR MUSLIM LANDS:

Life of Joseph, Cairo, 1906.
Ahmad and Bulus (Dialogue on Moslem objections to Christianity), Cairo,1906.
Life of the Messiah (4 parts), Cairo, 1906-1912.
Abraham, Isaac, and Ishmael, Cairo, 1907.
The Gospel of Barnabas (with Selim Abd el Ahad. A Refutation of the valid-
    ity of a pseudo-Gospel written by a medieval pervert to Islam),
    Cairo, 1907.
What Happened before the Hegira? (A Dialogue Refuting the Moslem Assertion
    that the Christian Scriptures now in use have been tampered with),
    Cairo, 1908.
Egyptian Studies (with Douglas Thornton, Studies for Egyptian Student Meet-
    ings), Cairo, 1908.
Life of St. Paul, Cairo, 1908.
Inspiration, a Dialogue (Comparison of Muslim and Christian Ideas),
    Cairo, 1909.
Life of Samuel, Ruth and David, Cairo 1909.
The Verse of Stoning (Quranic Controversy), Cairo, 1910.
The Eucharist as Historical Evidence (of the Death of Christ), Cairo, 1910.
Science and Faith in Whom? (Discussion Society), Cairo, 1910.
Life of Joshua, Cairo, 1912.
Inspiration, Christian and Islamic, Cairo, 1913.
The Moslem Doctrine of Tanzih (Transcendence), Cairo, 1914.
Aspects of the Redemptive Act of Christ, Cairo, 1916.
God as Triune, Incarnate, Atoner, Cairo, 1916.
Ecce Homo Arabicus, Cairo, 1918.
The Last Supper, Cairo, 1919.
The Secret of Life, (A Tract for the Times) Cairo, 1924.
The Divinity of Christ, Cairo, 1924.
Who is the Founder of Christianity? (Articles on the Cross), Cairo, 1927.

WORKS FOR THE EGYPTIAN CHURCH:

The Anglican and Coptic Communions in Egypt, privately printed, 1912.
Preparation for the Holy Communion, Cairo, 1916.
Instructions for Catechumens, Cairo, 1924.
A Harmony of the Passion Story from the Four Gospels, Cairo, 1925.
Preparation for Confirmation, Cairo, 1926.
Lessons on Membership in the Anglican Church, privately printed, 1926.
The Book of Comforts (Readings for Mourning Gatherings), Cairo, 1927.
The Message of the Fast, privately printed, 1928.

Commentary on Galatians with New Arabic Translation of the Epistle, Cairo,
     1928.
Commentary on Hebrews, Cairo, n.d.
Commentary on Philippians with Translation of the Epistle, Cairo, 1931.
Bible Rhymes for Children, Cairo, n.d.

ASSORTED ARTICLES AND PAPERS:

Orient and Occident (Anglo-Arabic Periodical), Cairo, January 5, 1905-1928,
     including various and numerous articles, editorials, etc.
"Work among Educated Moslems in Cairo: Western or Government School Men,"
     in Methods of Mission Work Among Moslems (Cairo Conference), New York,
     1906, pp. 59-70.
Strategic Problems. Some Important Moral Issues involved in the Conflict
     Between Trinitarian and Islamic Monotheism, London, 1908, 8 pages.
The Muslim Idea of God, London, 1909.
"Moslem and Christian Views of God: An Imaginary Dialogue," C.M. Review,
     March and May, 1909.
"Islam Under Christian Rule," in Islam and Missions (Lucknow Conference),
     New York, 1911, pp. 195-205.
"Notes on Present Day Movements in the Moslem World," M.W., 1 (1911),
     74-77, 187-191, 435-443.
"The Doctrine of the Unity in Trinity," (three parts) M.W., 1 (1911),
     381-407; M.W., 6 (1916), 28-41, 127-139.
"El-Azhar Collegiate Mosque and the Mohammedan Propaganda," E.W., July,
     1911, 256ff.
"Review of Professor D. B. Macdonald's Works on Islam," M.W., 2 (1912),
     312-17.
"The 'Way' of a Mohammedan Mystic," M.W., 2 (1912), 171-181, 245-257.
"Vital Forces of Christianity and Islam," I.R.M., 1 (1912), 44-61. Also
     published under separate cover with same title, London, 1915, pp.
     11-44.
"Review of Fatima et les Filles de Mahomet by Henri Lammens," M.W., 3
     (1913), 432-434.
"Al-Ghazali's 'Mishkāt al-Anwār' and the Ghazali Problem," Der Islam, 5
     (1914), 121-153.
"Editorial: Tempora Mutantur," M.W., 4 (1914), 1-2.
"Moslem Tradition and the Gospel Record. The Hadith and the Injil,"
     M.W., 5 (1915), 349-379.
"Review of Professor Snouck Hurgronje's Mohammedanism," M.W., 7 (1917),5-14.
"The National Mission and Mohammedanism," M.W., 7 (1917), 343-348.
"Christian Literature for Moslems" Blessed Be Egypt (Nile Press), October,
     1918.
"Mohammad without Camouflage. Ecce Homo Arabicus," M.W., 9 (1919), 25-57
"The Study of Islamics at Cairo" M.W., 12 (1922), 390-393.
Brotherhood, Islam's and Christ's (Speech made at the Scottish Missionary
     Congress, Glasgow), London, 1922.
"Introduction and Conclusion to the Missionary Significance of the Last
     Ten Years. A Survey," I.R.M., 12 (1923), 3-58.
"Islam in Africa: The Sequel to a Challenge (Reply to Roland Allen),"
     I.R.M., 13 (1924), 3-25.
Al-Ghazzāli's Mishkāt al-Anwār (The Niche for Lights, a translation with
     introduction), Royal Asiatic Society, London, 1924.
"The Christian Communities and the Evangelization of the Muslims," in The
     Moslem World Today edited by J.R. Mott, New York, 1925, pp. 279-287.
"Editorial: Signs of Progress--A Backward Look," M.W., 18 (1928), 1-5.
"The Values of Christianity and Islam". A Paper prepared for the Jerusalem

Meeting of the International Missionary Council with W.A. Eddy, in The
Christian Life and Message in Relation to Non-Christian Systems, Jerusa-
lem Reports, London, 1928, I, 235-283.
"Values in Christianity" (Jerusalem Report)," M.W., 18 (1928), 336-355.
W.H.T.G. to His Friends. Some Letters and Informal Writings, London, 1930.
"The Essentiality of the Cross" (Reprint from the Orient and Occident,
     Jan. 5, 1905), M.W., 23 (1933), 230-251.

APPENDIX G

A POSTSCRIPT TO TEMPLE GAIRDNER

The scholarly evangelistic approach of W.H.T. Gairdner, his sympathetic
understanding of Islam, and his great concern for the indigenous church
did not cease with Jerusalem, 1928. His concern that the church be enabled
to live amid the stresses of the Near East—amid this great "organized religious system", ever witnessing to the populace under its sway—is continued in such Anglicans as W. Wilson Cash, S. A. Morrison, Kenneth Cragg, et
al. Their emphasis upon the church as the witnessing body of Christ, the
Logos in active contact with the world and its religions (hence the need of
serious study of other religions in the shaping of an apologetic presentation of the Gospel) is a healthy balance to the continental emphasis upon
the Christian message as the unique revelation of the transcendent God of
grace and the utter "discontinuity" (hence the need to concentrate upon
proclamation). Much in the same way that Gairdner and Zwemer complemented
each other in the first quarter of the century, so have Cragg and Kraemer
served the church in more recent days.
Respected by Gairdner for his work in Egypt, William Wilson Cash's sympathetic understanding of Muslim mysticism and of the indigenous church
served him well as General Secretary of the C.M.S. Heading the British
delegation to Jerusalem (1928), his report firmly rooted the faith in revelation. Cash also had a role in selecting H. Kraemer for the preparation of the now famous Tambaram volume. Conscious of the change in the
Muslim world,[1] he called for presenting the "unadulterated message of
Christ" not some "diluted form of Western Christianity".[2] Mission policy
must be re-orientated to give the indigenous churches greater responsibility for evangelism.[3] Cash's approach however relies heavily upon
religious experience.

In my earlier days as a missionary I studied controversy and examined the Koran critically for the purpose of argument and debate. But
I came to realize the utter futility of it....For years I searched for
a key to the Moslem mind, a way of approach that would not alienate....
I asked myself, Is there anything similar in the two religions which
would enable Moslems and Christians alike to approach the subject of
their faith in a better spirit?...I became intrigued by the strength of
the Dervish orders....They were seekers after God. They sought a spiritual experience through meditation upon God that would help them in
their lives. This drove me to a further study of the influences of
mysticism upon Islam....I came to the conclusion that I could frankly
accept the reality of their experience without in any way detracting
from my own conviction that in and through Christ men find ultimate
reality...Christ can therefore be presented to all the world as the hope
of mankind without it being necessary to decry or vilify sages and
leaders of other ages. He is the revelation of God to mankind, and because of this He is the crown of all religions. He is as one has said,

'The express image of God's person'.[4]

This approach was criticized by his friend, Kraemer at Tambaram, who insisted that since faith rested on revelation rather than religious experience, it called for proclamation rather than fraternization.[5] Appreciative of Kraemer's contribution, Cash continued his biblical studies and work for the missionary church.[6]

After 1923, **S. A.** Morrison was a joyful comrade to Gairdner in the work of evangelism.[7] As Secretary of the C.M.S. in Egypt, Morrison became a prominent figure in Near Eastern missions and was highly respected, even consulted by H. Kraemer prior to Madras.[8] Morrison tackled the two great ecclesiastical and environmental problems. The Oriental churches were the "key to the problem of Moslem evangelism" and it was up to the Anglican Church to awaken "the immense powers which lie latent in them" for a witness in true partnership in mission.[9] Bishop MacInnes and Bishop Gwynne supported this program. Taking off from Zwemer's realistic report,[10] he went on to study the question of "religious liberty" in Near Eastern Lands. His sensible reports, especially at Madras, advocated (1) concrete effort to secure "religious liberty", (2) to detach the Gospel from foreign politics, (3) to allow the Gospel to be related to the indigenous culture, and (4) to realize the truly ecumenical character of the church which rises above national politics.[11] Already one finds Morrison stressing the need to "interpret" the Christian message via "Christian presence" and practice.

> The primary call to the Church of Christ in the Near East is to atone to the Moslem and Jewish peoples for the centuries of misrepresentation of the person of her master, and to reveal Him as Saviour and Lord, by life and by word. There is no other way to win the peoples of Palestine and Egypt to Christ than the way of the incarnate and crucified Lord, the way of love and the way of suffering. The Christian Church must 'out-think, out-live, and out-love' Islam. As the rigid Moslem doctrine of divine Unity compels the Christian theologian to reconsider the precise meaning and richness of content of the doctrine of the Trinity, so the moral and spiritual coldness of the Moslem peoples in response to the Christian message calls for still more lavish and joyous outpouring of the sacrifice and service in the Spirit of the Risen Christ.[12]

Certainly the labors of W.H.T. Gairdner have not been lost. They have been reflected on **and** enlarged on within the Anglican community by the probing scholarship of W. Montgomery Watt;[13] by the persisting awareness of the presence of the Incarnate Christ of E.C. Dewick;[14] by the surveys of John S. Trimingham; and by the evangelical concern and action in behalf of Muslims seen in Douglas Webster and Max Warren.[15] Undoubtedly the most respected Anglican authority on Christian mission with reference to Islam today is A. Kenneth Cragg. He best represents that blend of evangelical conviction, Islamic scholarship and concern to communicate biblical Christianity in terms comprehensible to Muslims—that which so occupied the life and thought of Temple Gairdner.[16] Developing the concept of "Christian presence", he provides a healthy complement to the stress upon proclamation in the ongoing discussion of the Christian mission to Muslims.

Notes to Appendix G:

1 W.W. Cash, The Moslem World in Revolution (London, 1925).

2 W.W. Cash, "The Missionary Outlook and the Moslem Problem," M.W., 11 (1921), 138-144 and "The Christian Approach to Moslems," M.R.W., Oct. 1926, 286ff.

3 W. W. Cash, "Missionary Policy: A New Orientation," The East and West
Review, 1 (1935), 14-21.

4 W. W. Cash, Christendom and Islam: Their Contacts and Cultures down
the Centuries (Haskell Lectures, Oberlin, 1936), Edinburgh, 1937, pp. 7-11,
78ff., 167ff.

5 H. Kraemer, The Christian Message, pp. 357f.

6. W. W. Cash, The Missionary Church (London, 1939) plus six commentaries.

7 S. A. Morrison, "A New Approach to the Moslem Student," M.W., 12
(1912), 373-85; "Modern Types of Moslem Thought," M.W., 15 (1925), 374-384;
"El Azhar, Today and Tomorrow," M.W., 16 (1926), 131-137; "The Church in
Egypt," C.M. Review, (June, 1927), 134-146; "New Tendencies in Islamic Re-
ligious Thought," I.R.M., 16 (1927), 199-215; "Theory and Practice of Evan-
gelism with Special Reference to Egypt," I.R.M., 19 (1930), 550-562; "The
Indigenous Churches and Muslim Evangelism," I.R.M., 25 (1936), 306-320; and
"Missions to Muslims," I.R.M., 27 (1938), 601-615.

8 Hallencreutz, Kraemer towards Tambaram, p. 273.

9 S. A. Morrison, The Way of Partnership: With the C.M.S. in Egypt and
Palestine (London, 1936), esp. pp. 28-31.

10 S. M. Zwemer, The Law of Apostasy in Islam (London, 1923).

11 S. A. Morrison, "The Church and the State," Madras Series, VI, 90ff.

12 Morrison, The Way of Partnership, pp. 79f.

13 E.G., cf. W. M. Watt, Muhammad at Mecca (Oxford, 1953), Muhammad at
Medina (Oxford, 1956), Muslim Intellectual: A Study of Al-Ghazali (London,
1963), Islamic Philosophy and Theology (Edinburgh, 1962). A perusal of
Professor Watt's numerous volumes and scholarly articles (cf. Index Islamicus) reveals the extent of his research.

14 While holding that Christ is the central revelation of God, Dewick
rejects Kraemer's claims as to the finality and absoluteness of that revelation. Cf. The Indwelling God (London, 1936); The Gospel and Other Faiths
(London, 1948); and The Christian Attitude to Other Religions (London, 1953)
pp. 93ff., 137ff. and esp. resume, p. 202. For a contrast read Bonhoeffer's
Christology, which asserts that truth is not simply propositional but
personal.

15 Cf. bibliography.

16 For a partial listing of the works of A. K. Cragg, cf. the bibliography, and the periodicals Muslim World and International Review of Missions. His scholarly sympathetic studies and instruction at the Jerusalem
School (summers) have been an inspiration and help to many.

APPENDIX H

A SUMMARY OF "THE THEOLOGY OF THE WORD AND MISSIONS" BY K. HARTENSTEIN

Karl Hartenstein, the director of the Basel Missionary Society, hammers
home the missionary implications of "the self-manifestation of God in Jesus
Christ"--the One who is not a religious idea, mere teacher of ethics or
religion, but the "incarnation of the eternal Word of God" and "Saviour of
the world". Such revelation can never be attained nor controlled by man
and stands in sharp contrast to the reason, cultures and religions of man.
The church's mission is to bear witness to this revelation in the world of
other religions. He writes:

We are told that missionary work must be nothing less than the Church
of God in actu confessions, nothing less than the proclaiming of God in
the world. A number of definitions of missionary work must then be

called in question. Missions cannot be 'the spreading of Christianity,'
the spreading that is, of western religions and ecclesiastical forms,
but a proclaiming of the word of God which is always calling afresh for
a decision for or against Christ. Missions, again, cannot be 'the
evangelization of the world in this generation,' but only a witness of
the word of God which is always being accepted by one and rejected by
another. Missions cannot be 'the sharing of the social and cultural
benefits of the West,' for the whole of Christian culture stands at a
period of terrible crisis, every section of it under the judgment of
God. Missions cannot be the "preaching the social gospel' in order to
bring in a new social and political world order. The Church knows that
the present age will pass away, and she 'looks for a new heaven and a
new earth wherein dwelleth righteousness.' The one thing needful is to
learn anew what is meant by preaching the word of God aright, and opening a road to the living God for the passage of His works and His word.
The special significance of this new theology for missions is that their
leaders should be led to examine themselves anew as to their preaching
and service.

The basic presuppositions of the "theology of the Word" are: (1) "Mission
is first and foremost an activity of God" standing in contrast with all of
mankind's attempts to be re-united with God since the fall without acknowledging the fall. (2) "The proclaiming must be done by members of the
Church, the Christian community which has been created by His word." (3)
"Missionary work is carried on with a view to the Kingdom of God" for it
too is provisional ('Between the Times'), subject to the Judge's last word.
     Certain points follow from these premises: (1) "God desires to speak to
the non-Christian through human messengers" but the latter are only "witnesses" who must continue to ask: Why we preach? How we preach? What we
preach? and To whom do we preach? The "What" is none other than God's
action in Christ. "To Whom" is never an audience in general but "Always
ad hominem, to individual actual men". He notes that:

> The Scriptures recognize only one man, who remains one and the same in
> spite of all differences of race, language, religion, and culture, and
> that is the Prodigal Son, bound in a world of stress and death, in bond-
> age to the power of sin....But this is not all: the message is not only
> proclaimed to the soul of men, but to the actual man standing before us
> at the moment, never again the same. Therefore the missionary has to
> do all he can to understand the spiritual and religious world of this
> man confronting him. He must take him as he actually is. The mission-
> ary cannot study too closely the religions of the world in order to find
> that needy spot through which the word of God can find entrance into
> this man.

(2) Mission means an invasion of man's world by the message which brings
both judgment and redemption--shattering illusions and requiring a decision
for or against God. (3) "The message goes to the religions of the earth"
as a judgment of all religions. He contends that religion:

> ...expresses on the one hand all the longing and the questioning which
> breaks from man's needy soul. Religion is the outstretched hand towards
> the One who alone can lead and uphold man. For the main thought under-
> lying the word 'religion' is a man, a pious, seeking human being. ...who
> is seeking along a thousand paths to fulfill that which is lacking in
> his life, to satisfy the longing of his soul, to become united again
> with God--and all this by his own effort. The 'religious' man believes
> he is able to find God and stand before Him, without needing at every

moment the revelation of God. 'Religion' therefore, will always be a
main attempt to still longing, and is in itself the answer which a man
conceives, experiences or achieves to his own questions. Therefore--
and this is the third point--all religions efface the irreducible gulf
between God and man. To speak rightly about God one must speak of His
grace.

Only God who gives truth and bestows life, can bridge the gulf and
unite men again with Himself. But in all religions there always exists
a belief in a postulated, ultimate, deep continuity between man and God.
...Therefore, in the conception of 'religion' there lies an ultimate
crossing of boundaries, which a man can accomplish by his own meditation, his own vision, his own activities, his own sacrifices....The
Message of Christ, therefore, spells sentence and judgment on all
'religions', first and last.

Hartenstein thus pointedly stresses the issue of "discontinuity" and the
sui generis of the Christian message which stands in sharp conflict with
the position that "all religions are uni generis; at bottom there is only
one religion and in that one all unite".

The aim of mission then must be not simply to divert men from one religion to another, but to bring man into a new relationship with God, into
a new life and realm (the kingdom) through Jesus Christ. While this involves personal decision and faith, it results in a communal relationship,
the church, a visible if temporal form of the kingdom.

Source: Located in I.R.M., 20 (1931), 210-217.

APPENDIX I

A GLIMPSE AT RE-THINKING MISSIONS: A LAYMAN'S INQUIRY (1932)

This independent commission was begun in 1930 by a group of self-
appointed laymen and clergy from the Northern Baptist and six other American denominations in response to a changing world and a public critical,
even questioning the validity of missions. First, a corp of research
workers (reflecting the new science of surveys) was sent to India, Burma,
China, Japan, etc. These "Fact Finders" then reported to the commission of
fifteen under Chairman Hocking. The final report consisted of three parts.
The first was an endorsement of the need of missions and a statement of the
theory of missions. While this reflected some of the commission's discussions, it was largely the work of Hocking. His presuppositions became the
bone of contention. He admitted that the report would stand or fall on
the theological premises of these chapters (cf. Proceedings, p. 8). The
last two sections, reviewing the methods and administration of missions
with recommendations, were more readily received. Convinced that the missionary program needed a drastic overhauling, Hocking set forth the theo-
logical-philosophical principles for a revised policy in the first four
chapters. The foreword of the report had reflected the various opinions of
the commission, but the chapters are dominated by Hocking's ideas. Chapter
one declares that a complete reconstruction of mission is necessitated by
three great changes: the altered theological outlook (liberal-minded men
have "progressed" to a point where they hold that "the function of religion
is to bring men into the presence of the everlasting and the real," p. 18);
the emergence of a world-culture; and the rise of nationalism in the East.

Yet for Hocking "the fundamental motive, the imperative of sharing whatever certainties we have in the field of religion, remains" (p. 23). But the temporary functions of "planting the Church" and "making disciples" must gradually be displaced by foreign service and ambassadorship (i.e. education, medical work, etc.) for the upbuilding of society (humanity) in general.

Chapter two on "Christianity, Other Religions and Non-Religion" reveals Hocking's feelings regarding the inevitable progress of human history and religion. The rise of materialism-secularism will likely realign all religions in an allied fraternity over against non-religion. Liberal-minded Christians reject the mistaken idea of making converts and see men of all religions as brothers in a common quest. This "creative relationship" emerging in missions will "make a positive effort first of all to know and understand the religions around it, then to recognize and associate itself with whatever kindred elements there are in them" (p. 33). Hocking rejects the traditional concept of mission.

> The original objective of the mission might be stated as the conquest of the world by Christianity: it was a world benevolence conceived in terms of a world campaign. There was one way of salvation and one only, one name, one atonement: this plan with its particular historical center in the career of Jesus must become the point of regard for every human soul....But particular facts cannot be proved: they must be recognized. Hence in respect to its central fact Christianity was necessarily dogmatic—it could only say Ecce Homo, Behold the Man; and it was committed to a certain intolerance, beneficent in purpose—in the interest of the soul it could allow no substitute for Christ. It came to proclaim truth, which is universal; but its truth was embodied in a particular person and work (pp. 15ff.).

Hocking's epistemology regarding the "growth" of man's religious knowledge/experience stood in opposition to the concept of a unique, particular "revelation". Knowledge of God was innate for Hocking and the task of mission is thus not to transmit a message or light but to elicit or liberate the Light 'which lightens every man". Hocking ignored the Barth-Brunner reemphasis upon the fall and sinful man's inability to comprehend God. For him, there was a "Figure" behind all religions and religious language, a Christ who bears many names and guises (p. 44 and Proceedings, pp. 15ff.). He sets aside the biblical concept of the "finality of God's revelation in Jesus Christ".

> Hence all fences and private properties in truth are futile: the final truth, whatever it may be, is the New Testament of every existing faith. ...The relation between religions must take increasingly the form of a common search of truth (pp. 44, 47).

Under "Christianity: Its Message for the Orient" (chapter 3), Hocking points out that the uniqueness of Christianity consists only in its peculiar combination of doctrines and ethics for these truths are rooted in "nature...the human mind everywhere". While allowing that there are sharply differing opinions as to "what is" or "who is" the message and person of Jesus Christ (pp. 49-59), he proceeds to extract from historical particulars, universal principles and morals. For him, the "Kingdom of God" is a new emerging world culture of many peoples sharing their varied quests and experiences of religious truth.

"The Scope of the Work of Missions" (chapter 4) is thus a broad humanitarianism—a philanthropic "new evangelism" of "human service" by which a

"new social order" is to be ushered in. Yet this must be done without
promoting the church, (not by individual conversions and discipleship pp.
60ff.). The report concludes on this same note. Missions must fulfill
the potentialities of humanity by drawing men everywhere "together in a
full and ennobling experience of God" (pp. 323ff.).

Sources: <u>Re-Thinking</u> <u>Missions</u>: <u>A</u> <u>Laymen's</u> <u>Inquiry</u> <u>After</u> <u>One</u> <u>Hundred</u> <u>Years</u>
By the Commission of Appraisal, W. E. Hocking, Chairman) New York, 1932.
<u>The</u> <u>Proceedings</u> <u>of</u> <u>the</u> <u>Meeting</u> <u>of</u> <u>the</u> <u>Directors</u> <u>and</u> <u>Sponsors</u> <u>of</u> <u>the</u> <u>Laymen's</u>
<u>Foreign</u> <u>Missions</u> <u>Inquiry</u> <u>and</u> <u>the</u> <u>Representatives</u> <u>of</u> <u>Foreign</u> <u>Mission</u> <u>Boards</u>
(Hotel Roosevelt, New York City, Nov. 18-19, 1932), New York, 1932.

Page references are to <u>Re-Thinking</u> <u>Missions</u> except where marked <u>Proceedings</u>.

APPENDIX J

HENDRIK KRAEMER AT TAMBARAM: THE CHRISTIAN MESSAGE

It was by no accident that Hendrik Kraemer prepared the volume, <u>The</u>
<u>Christian</u> <u>Message</u> <u>in</u> <u>a</u> <u>Non-Christian</u> <u>World</u> for the Madras Conference (1938).
He had been a scholar of Oriental languages and religions at Leiden (1911-
1921) before serving with the Dutch Reformed Church Mission in Java (1921-
1935). The work there, even among Muslims, had been most effective and
young Kraemer gained distinction for his literature work and understanding
of the indigenous church. By 1928, he was an active participant in the
international missionary discussions. The debate as to a correct evangelistic approach to non-Christian religions intensified following Jerusalem
(1928). The chain of meetings at Herrnhut-Salisbury-Northfield-Basel heightened the tension. Under the influence of W.W. Cash, J.H. Oldham, J.R.
Mott, and William Paton, the <u>Ad</u> <u>Interim</u> Committee of I.M.C. at Old Jordans,
England (June, 1936) decided that Kraemer was the man to prepare the volume
for Tambaram on the "evangelistic approach to adherents of different non-
Christian faiths". Kraemer was urged to visit America and there he came
into the midst of the crisis precipitated by <u>Re-Thinking</u> <u>Missions</u>. He
quickly sensed that the thought of Hocking ignored recent theological developments in Europe, the new biblical studies in Britain, the emerging
younger churches, and the evangelical basis of the ecumenical movement.
There also he found encouragement for his task from Speer, Zwemer, Latourette and others.

Preparing the <u>Christian</u> <u>Message</u> (Sept. 1936-end of 1937), Kraemer corresponded with missionaries around the world (e.g. Morrison, Padwick,
Nielsen, A. G. Hogg); renewed contacts with Emil Brunner and Karl Heim;
participated in conferences at Oxford and the Netherlands; and was appointed to the chair of comparative religions at Leiden (Dec. 3, 1937).

The <u>Christian</u> <u>Message</u> has become perhaps the most discussed missionary
volume of the century. It placed the whole issue of mission directly back
into the heart of theology. It shocked those side-tracked by anthropology,
philosophy and philanthropy and reorientated the whole critical discussion
to biblical theology. It did for mission circles what Barth and Brunner
were doing for continental theologians. Evangelism could not be treated
in isolation in this revolutionary era. It must be centered in theology.

...the problem of 'evangelistic approach to the great non-Christian religions' cannot remain confined to the field of the proclamation of the
Word or the preaching of the Gospel to the fundamental and concrete

realities of the different religious systems. The entire missionary
enterprise in all its manifestations, activities and obligations has to
envisage itself essentially as approach, as evangelistic approach, because all these manifestations can only legitimately be called Christian
and missionary when they issue directly from the apostolic urgency of
gladly witnessing to God and His saving and redeeming Power through
Christ (pp vi-vii).

To extract the essentials of Kraemer's comprehensive volume is no simple
task. Only a few details can be mentioned here. Kraemer saw the various
non-Christian religions as "totalitarian entities" which could not be ade-
quately described by comparative studies, phenomenological descriptions, or
arrangement in an evolutionary order. They were separate human attempts at
the "apprehension of totality of existence". They fail, however, to appre-
hend reality, for reality is theocentric and understood only as "God reveals". The self-communication of God reveals man is in revolt, blinded to
general revelation and often hardening himself against the revelation in
Christ. Yet he has no grasp of God nor reality apart from the revelation
in Christ. "Revelation in its proper sense is what is by its nature in-
accessible and remains so, even when it is revealed" (p. 69). This revelation or "Biblical realism" can never be reduced to a system of teachings.
It remains centered in the person of Jesus Christ, the Lord.
    Kraemer has two objectives in his study of non-Christian religions: (1)
to point out their totalitarian nature and (2) to evaluate their "appre-
hensions of reality" in "the light of Christ". Islam has a unique place
amid the "prophetic religions of revelation" because it contains fragments
of Judaism and Christianity. Most other primal and Asiatic religions are
described as "naturalistic religions of trans-empirical realization" basing
their totalitarian claims upon "naturalistic monistic thought-forms"
(pp. 142ff.). Islam is treated in three places in this volume. First, the
Islamic system is described as "a great syncretistic body wherein are weld-
ed in one system theocratic and legalistic Islam, mysticism and various
sorts of popular religions, in which the naturalistic vein of the primitive
apprehension of existence shines through". Although Islam has a "background of empirical Christianity and Judaism" it is a distinct, theocentric
religion binding man as a slave under the iron law of God and his Apostle.
"Islam in its cradle was already a specimen of religious imperialism, which
is another name for secularized theocracy" (pp. 215ff.). After examining
the present situation in Islam (pp. 268ff.), he set forth his approach to
Islam. He realizes that Islam is marked by a group solidarity that is
hard to penetrate (p. 353) and has incorporated antagonism to Christianity
into its creed, but this calls for an unusual degree of faith, love, hope
and patience from the church (pp. 354ff.). He rejects many known approaches to Islam: namely, the via mysticism approach (pp. 357f.); the comparative religions approach (p. 360); the presentation of Christian teachings about Jesus and the Holy Spirit as the enrichment of the half-truths
of the Quran (pp. 355f.); and the traditional nineteenth century presentation of Christianity as a set of doctrines (p. 356). For Kraemer, the best
method involves:

    direct personal contact and study of the Bible in a spirit of human
    sympathy and openness, the Moslem being treated not as a non-Christian
    but as a fellow-man with the same fundamental needs, aspirations, and
    frustrations, whose religious experience and insight are as worthwhile
    as the missionary's, simply because he is a living human being (p. 356).

For Kraemer it is the "Word of God", Biblical realism, that has recruiting power (p. 345). The missionary is the "point of contact" between the Word and the Muslim, therefore, he must have both "a direct and vital contact with Biblical realism and a real knowledge of the Moslem ways of thinking and living and of the religious vocabulary of Islam" (p. 357). Kraemer like Zwemer concentrates on evangelism and the missionary is the "point of contact" (pp. 130-141). This approach places great strain on the agent.

> In the first place, there is the obligation to strive for the presentation of the Christian truth in terms and modes of expression that make its challenge intelligible and related to the peculiar quality of reality in which they live. For the missionary or evangelist this means a constant process of self-denying training, for the love of Christ, and the love of souls, to find the ways in which to tune this presentation to the peculiar sound-waves of these peculiar human hearts....The preaching of the Gospel in a foreign world with a different spiritual climate and background is a translation of meanings and not of detached words. Openness and truthfulness and not antagonism are the natural implications of this attitude, because to win men for Christ is the dominant inspiration in this activity.
>
> In the second place, it includes the presentation of the Christian truth against the background of the universal human problems of aspiration, frustration, misery and sin, because these men and women must be for us in the first place human-beings, fellow-men, and not non-Christians (p. 303).

These demands apply to the whole missionary church. This "obedient society" receives life and fellowship only via God in Christ and is sent into the world for a threefold, inter-related task of witness, worship and ministry (pp. 405ff.). Kraemer perhaps because of his experiences in Indonesia, goes beyond many of his contemporaries in the adaptation of elements of indigenous culture for the work and life of the young church. Kraemer did not forget to insert his criticism of the Laymen's report (and Hocking's ideas) with its "very weak sense of apostolic consciousness" (cf. pp. 36, 45, 49, 313, 321f.). The Christian Message is not as critical of other points of view, however, as Kraemer's work of 1956. Kraemer concludes on a note reflecting the Reformation.

> ...The heartening lesson is that the Gospel can spread under any circumstances, provided a living and ardent faith burns in the hearts of men.
>
> The Christian mission in the non-Christian world must be accomplished in the present complicated world with all the means that human intelligence, ingenuity and devotion put at our disposal, because it is our plain duty to make the hearing and expression of God's revelation and Message as palpable as possible. Theology, history, psychology, anthropology must be exploited to achieve one aim and one aim only: to be a better instrument in conveying the conviction that God is speaking in Jesus Christ His decisive Word to individuals, nations, peoples, cultures and races, without any distinction. The undying fire, however, without which all our endeavours are nothing and all our missionary enthusiasm is powerless, is only kindled by the faith and prayer which are born from the vision of the triumphant Divine Love that burns in the heart of the Universe and which became incarnated in Jesus Christ, our Lord (p. 445).

It is a matter of historical record that Hendrik Kraemer went forth from Madras to become one of the great strategists in mission, a widely read author, and a leader in the ecumenical movement.

Sources:
Hendrik Kraemer, The Christian Message in a Non-Christian World, London, 1938.
Carl F. Hallencreutz, Kraemer Towards Tambaram. A Study in Hendrik Kraemer's Missionary Approach, Uppsala, 1966.

APPENDIX K

THE LITERARY CONTRIBUTION OF SAMUEL M. ZWEMER

PUBLISHED BOOKS:

Arabia: The Cradle of Islam, New York, 1900.
Raymond Lull: First Missionary to the Moslems, New York, 1902.
The Moslem Doctrine of God, New York, 1905.
Islam, A Challenge to Faith, New York, 1907. Abridged as The Moslem World, New York, 1908.
The Unoccupied Mission Fields of Africa and Asia, New York, 1911.
The Moslem Christ, London, 1915.
Childhood in the Moslem World, New York, 1915.
The Disintegration of Islam, New York, 1915.
Mohammed or Christ, London, 1916.
A Primer on Islam, Shanghai, 1919.
The Influence of Animism on Islam, New York, 1920.
Christianity the Final Religion, Grand Rapids, Michigan, 1920.
A Moslem Seeker After God, Life of Al-Ghazali, New York, 1921.
The Law of Apostasy in Islam, London, 1923.
Report of a Visit to Mesopotamia, the Persian Gulf and India, New York, 1924.
The Call to Prayer, London, 1923.
The Glory of the Cross, London, 1928.
Report of a Visit to India and Ceylon, New York, 1928.
Across the World of Islam, New York, 1929.
Thinking Missions with Christ, Grand Rapids, 1934.
The Origin of Religion, London, 1935.
Taking Hold of God, London, 1936.
It is Hard to be a Christian, London, 1937.
The Solitary Throne, London, 1937.
Studies in Popular Islam, New York, 1939.
Dynamic Christianity and the World Today, London, 1939.
The Glory of the Manger, New York, 1940.
The Art of Listening to God, Grand Rapids, 1940.
The Cross Above the Crescent, Grand Rapids, 1941.
Into All the World, Grand Rapids, 1943.
Evangelism Today: Message not Method, New York, 1944.
Heirs of the Prophets: An Account of the Clergy and Priests of Islam, Chicago, 1946.
A Factual Survey of the Moslem World, New York, 1946.
The Glory of the Empty Tomb, New York, 1947.
How Rich the Harvest, New York, 1948.
Sons of Adam, Grand Rapids, 1951.

WORKS OF JOINT AUTHORSHIP/EDITORSHIP:

Topsy Turvy Land, with Amy E. Zwemer, New York, 1902.
Methods of Mission Work Among Moslems, with E. M. Wherry, New York, 1906.

Mohammedan World Today, with E. M. Wherry, New York, 1906.
Our Moslem Sisters, with Annie Van Sommer, New York, 1907.
The Nearer and Farther East, with Arthur J. Brown, New York, 1908.
Zig-Zag Journeys in the Camel Country, with Amy E. Zwemer, New York, 1911.
Islam and Missions: Report of the Lucknow Conference, with E. M. Wherry,
    New York, 1911.
Daylight in the Harem, with Annie Van Sommer, New York, 1912.
Christian Literature in Moslem Lands, with a committee, New York, 1923.
Moslem Women, with Amy E. Zwemer, New York, 1926.
The Golden Milestone, with James Cantine, New York, 1939.

TRACTS AND BOOKS IN ARABIC: Printed by the Nile Mission Press (1913-1930)
    According to the Appendix of The Cross Above the Crescent.

Arabic Tracts:

The Ninety-nine Names of Allah.
The Ninety-nine Names of Christ.
Is There Progress in the Moral Law?
The Three Blind Men.
The Centre of the Circle.
Bir Zemzem and the Water of Life.
The Two Paradises.
The Truth of the 'Aqiqa Sacrifice.
Ya Fattah ("O Opener").
Peter's Gospel.
Pray without Ceasing.
Do You Pray?
Two Ways in the Quran.
Return to the Old Qibla.

Arabic Books:

Raymond Lull, First Missionary to Moslems.
Isa or Jesus (The Moslem Idea of Christ).
The Pearl-Diver: Life of Al-Ghazali.
Childhood in Moslem Lands.
The Greatest Personality in History.
The Glory of the Cross.
The Lover's Pathway to Moslem Hearts (3 editions).

THE MOSLEM WORLD (Muslim World after 1947): A Quarterly Review of Current
    Events, Literature and thought among Mohammedans and the Progress of
    Christian Missions in Moslem Lands.
    Vols. I-VI. published by Christian Literature Society for India, London.
    Vols. VII-XXVII. by Missionary Review Pub. Co., New York.
    Vols. XXVIII-Present. by Hartford Seminary Foundation, Hartford, Conn.
    Zwemer served as Editor, 1911-1938 and as co-editor with E. E. Calverly,
    1938-47.
    The following list does not include all the book reviews Zwemer prepared.

"Editorial," M.W., 1 (1911), 1-4.
"Book Reviews," M.W., 1 (1911), 78ff. (first of several hundred over the
    years).
"A General Survey of the Moslem World. Address at Lucknow," M.W., 1 (1911),
    408-30.
"A Working Library on Islam," M.W., 2 (1912), 32-36.
"Reviews of the works of Caetani," M.W., 2 (1912), 79f., 190-193.

"The True Spirit of Christians towards Moslems: Memorial to Henry Martyn,"
    M.W., 2 (1912), 225-229.
"The Present Situation," M.W., 3 (1913), 113-116.
"The Stumbling-Block of the Cross," M.W., 3 (1913), 147-158.
"The Clock, the Calendar and the Koran," M.W., 3 (1913), 262-274.
"The Evangelization of the Moslem World in This Generation," M.W., 4
    (1914), 113f.
"A New Statistical Survey," M.W., 4 (1914), 145-156.
"A United Front Over Against Islam," M.W., 4 (1914), 228f.
"After Five Years," M.W., 5 (1915), 337-339.
"The Call of India," M.W., 6 (1916), 1-3.
"Islam in South America," M.W., 6 (1916), 144ff.
"The Heart of our Message," M.W., 6 (1916), 225-227.
"The 'Akika Sacrifice," M.W., 6 (1916), 236-252.
"The Arab and the Turk," M.W., 6 (1916), 337-339.
"The Familiar Spirit or Qarina," M.W., 6 (1916), 360-374.
"Reinforcements," M.W., 7 (1917), 109-111.
"Jesus Christ in the Ihya of Al-Ghazali," M.W., 7 (1917), 144-158.
"Animism in Islam," M.W., 7 (1917), 245-255.
"Islam in China," M.W., 8 (1918), 1-3.
"A Chinese Moslem Primer," M.W., 8 (1918), 71-73.
"Animistic Elements in Moslem Prayer," M.W., 8 (1918), 355-375.
"The Printed Page," M.W., 8 (1918), 111-114.
"Supernational Because Supernatural," M.W., 9 (1919), 4-6.
"The Chasm," M.W., 9 (1919), 111-114.
"On Taking Hold of God," M.W., 9 (1919), 221-223.
"The Urgency of the Hour," M.W., 9 (1919), 331-335.

"Animism in the Creed and in the Use of the Book and the Rosary," M.W., 10
    (1920), 13-29.
"Islam--Its Worth and Its Failure," M.W., 10 (1920), 144-156.
"The Inadequacy of Statistics," M.W., 10 (1920), 217-219.
"The City of Cairo. According to the Census of 1917," M.W., 10 (1920),
    267-73.
"How is Reconciliation Possible?" M.W., 11 (1921), 111-114.
"The Sword or the Cross," M.W., 11 (1921), 329-331.
"The 'Illiterate' Prophet: Could Mohammed Read and Write?" M.W., 11 (1921),
    344-363.
"Vanquished yet Victorious," M.W., 12 (1922), 111-114.
"Where the Stones Cry Out," M.W., 12 (1922), 331-333.
"The So-Called Hadith Qudsi," M.W., 12 (1922), 263-275.
"The Road Makers," M.W., 13 (1923), 1-4.
"The Native Press of the Dutch East Indies," M.W., 13 (1923), 39-49.
"The Kerchief of Veronica," M.W., 13 (1923), 111-115.
"A New Census of the Moslem World," M.W., 13 (1923), 282-290.
"The Crown Rights of Christ," M.W., 13 (1923), 331-334.
"The Love that Will Not Let Go," M.W., 14 (1924), 331-333.
"The Law of Apostasy," M.W., 14 (1924), 373-391.
"Our Fifteenth Year," M.W., 15 (1925), 1-5.
"Islam in India," M.W., 15 (1925), 109-114.
"Islam in Africa," M.W., 15 (1925), 217-222.
"Islam in Capetown," M.W., 15 (1925), 327-333.
"Two Moslem Catechisms published at Capetown," M.W., 15 (1925), 349-360.
"Opportunity not Menace," M.W., 16 (1926), 111-115.
"The Undertow," M.W., 17 (1927), 111ff.
"Islam in South Eastern Europe," M.W., 17 (1927), 331-358.
"The Diversity of Islam in India," M.W., 18 (1928), 111-123.
"The Gospel of the Resurrection," M.W., 18 (1928), 221-226.

"Evangelism," M.W., 19 (1929), 111-114.
"The Use of Alms to Win Converts," M.W., 19 (1929), 141-150.

"The Unoccupied Areas," M.W., 20 (1930), 111-119.
"The Holy Spirit and Islam," M.W., 20 (1930), 221-225.
"After Twenty Years," M.W., 21 (1931), 1-3.
"The Sword of Mohammed and Ali," M.W., 21 (1931), 109-121.
"The Rosary in Islam," M.W., 21 (1931), 329-343.
"The Shiah Saints," M.W., 22 (1932), 111-115.
"Snouck Hurgronje's 'Mekka'," M.W., 22 (1932), 219-226.
"The Palladium of Islam," M.W., 23 (1933), 109-116.
"The Pulpit in Islam," M.W., 23 (1933), 217-229.
"The Fourth Religion of China," M.W., 24 (1934), 1-12.
"The Finality of Jesus Christ," M.W., 24 (1934), 109-114.
"Behold the Lamb of God," M.W., 24 (1934), 324-329.
"Da Costa's Hagar," M.W., 25 (1935), 109-114.
"A Chinese-Arabic Amulet," M.W., 25 (1935), 217-222.
"Islam in Ethiopia and Eritrea," M.W., 26 (1936), 5-15.
"Our Evangel and Islam," M.W., 26 (1936), 109-112.
"Tor Andrae's Mohammed," M.W., 26 (1936), 217-221.
"Surat Al-Ikhlas," M.W., 26 (1936), 325-328.
"The Worship of Adam by Angels," M.W., 27 (1937), 115-127.
"Herbert Udny Weitbrecht Stanton," M.W., 27 (1937), 325-328.
"With All Boldness," M.W., 28 (1938), 109-113.
"Islam a Sevenfold Problem," M.W., 28 (1938), 217-222.
"Broadcasting our Message," M.W., 29 (1939), 217-220.

"Veni, Sancte Spiritu," M.W., 30 (1940), 1-6.
"Islam in Madagascar: A Blind Spot," M.W. 30 (1940), 151-167.
"Prayer for the World of Islam," M.W., 30 (1940), 217-220.
"John Tackle," M.W., 30 (1940), 298.
"The Dynamic of Evangelism," M.W., 31 (1941), 109-115.
"Karl Gottlieb Pfander, 1841-1941," M.W., 31 (1941), 217-226.
"The Rose and Islam," M.W., 31 (1941), 360-370.
"James Rendel Harris on Al-Ghazali," M.W., 32 (1942), 51-54.
"Bringing the King Back," M.W., 33 (1943), 1.
"Ingrams' Peace in Hadhramaut," M.W., 33 (1943), 79-85.
"Islam in 'Arabia Deserta'," M.W., 33 (1943), 157-164.
"The Death of William Paton," M.W., 33 (1943), 238.
"Duncan Black MacDonald," M.W., 34 (1944), 1-6.
"The Clergy and Priesthood of Islam," M.W., 34 (1944), 17-39.
"The Doctrine of the Trinity," M.W., 35 (1945), 1-5.
"Good Friday, 1945," M.W., 35 (1945), 79-82.
"Atonement by Blood Sacrifice in Islam," M.W., 36 (1946), 189-192.
"The Allah of Islam and the God Revealed in Jesus Christ," M.W., 36 (1946),
    306-318.
"Al Haraimain: Mecca and Medina," M.W., 37 (1947), 7-15.
"Looking Backward and Looking from the Bridge," (Final Editorial)
    M.W., 37 (1947), 173-176.
"Francis of Assisi and Islam," M.W., 39 (1949), 247-251.

ASSORTED WORKS:

Zendings-Woorden, Missionary Words, New Brunswick, New Jersey, 1889.
The Message and the Man, New York, 1909.
Are More Foreign Missionaries Needed? New York, 1911.
A Working Library on Islam: Syllabus for Progressive Reading Courses, Cairo,
    1912.

"The Present Attitude of Educated Moslems Towards Jesus Christ and the
    Scriptures," I.R.M., 3 (1914), 696-707.
"A United Christendom and Islam," Constructive Quarterly, Sept., 1914,
    506-18.
"Kann Man von Leben Kraften im Islam Sprechen?" A.M.Z., 8 (1915), 337-345.
"Introduction," The Vital Forces of Christianity and Islam (London, 1915),
"The Horizon of the Moslem World," E.W., Oct., 1915, 401-408.
"Islam at Its Best," Constructive Quarterly, Dec., 1916, 823-842.
"The Present Attitude of Non-Christians in Egypt towards the Gospel,"
    Blessed Be Egypt, October, 1918.
"The War and Missions," C.M.R., Sept., 1919, 209-225.
"De Islam, zijn waarde en onwaarde," De Opwekker, 65 (1920), 278-289.
"Apostasy from Islam," E.W., April, 1921, 123-133.
"The Patience of God in Moslem Evangelisation...an Address," London, 1912.
"The British Empire and Islam," E.W., April, 1924, 108-124.
"A Survey of Islam in South Africa," I.R.M., 14 (1925), 560-571.
"Present-Day Journalism in the World of Islam," in The Moslem World Today,
    edited by J. R. Mott, London, 1925, pp. 123-154.
"Islam in Africa Today," World Dominion, Dec., 1926, 58-65.
"The Moslems of South-eastern Europe," I.R.M., 16 (1927), 495-510.
"Persia Faces the Future," M.R.W., Jan., 1927, 19-26.
"A United Christendom and Islam," The Review of the Churches (London),
    April, 1928, 233-243.
"The Mappillas of Malabar," Indian Standard (Allahabad), May, 1908, 105-
    115.
"Mohammedan Missionary Methods," Methodist Review (N.Y.), May-June, 1931,
    365-71.
"Calvinism and the World of Islam," Union Seminary Review (Richmond), July,
    1931, 357-366.
"Der Platz der Religionsgeschichte in der Theologie," E.M.M., 75 (1931),
    289ff., 334ff.
"Christ and the World of Islam," M.R.W., Jan., 1932, 34-37.
"Why is Arabia Still Neglected," M.R.W., Feb., 1932, 105-106.
"The Need of India's Moslems," Darkness and Light (London, July-Aug.,
    1932, 1-5.
"A Plea for Medical Missions to Moslems," The Edinburgh Medical Missionary
    Society Quarterly Paper, Nov., 1932, 171-173.
"Why Mohammedans Need the Gospel," M.R.W., Sept., 1933, 433-443.
"India--The Greatest Moslem Mission Field," M.R.W., May, 1935, 215-218.
"The Glory of the Impossible: The Evangelization of the Moslem World,"
    World Dominion (London), July, 1935, 292-298.
"Islam's Debt to the Bible," M.R.W., Sept., 1935, 405-407.
"Calvinism and Islam," The Calvin Forum (Grand Rapids), Jan. 1936.
"Signs of the Undertow of Islam," M.R.W., May 1938, 220-222.
"Islam and the War," Religious Digest (Grand Rapids), Oct. 1941, 1-9.
"The Allah of Islam and the God of Jesus Christ," Theology Today
    (Princeton), April, 1946, 64-77.

Notes

INTRODUCTION (p. 1)

1 Hendrik Kraemer has become known as the leading exponent of this view, cf. esp. The Christian Message in a Non-Christian World (London, 1938). Similar views have been held by Emmanuel Kellerhals, Der Islam. Seine Geschicte, Seine Lehre, Sein Wesen (Basel, 1945); J. Witte, Die Christus-botschaft und die Religionen, (Götingen, 1936); Harold Lindsell, "Fundamentals for a Philosophy of the Christian Mission," in The Theology of the Christian Mission edited by G. H. Anderson (London, 1961) and J. N. D. Anderson (ed.) The World's Religions (London, 1951).

2 The concept of fulfillment was best expressed by J. N. Farquhar in The Crown of Hinduism (Oxford, 1913) and was accepted to a lesser extent by such persons as Oldham, and E. S. Jones although it received sharp criticism from A. G. Hogg. It still receives recognition by E. C. Dewick, The Christian Attitude to Other Religions (Cambridge, 1953).

3 For several wide-ranging points of view cf. W. E. Hocking, Living Religions and a World Faith (London, 1940); E. L. Allen, Christianity Among the Religions (London, 1960); P. Tillich, Christianity and the Encounter of the World Religions (London, 1963); G. Parrinder, Comparative Religion (London, 1962); W. M. Watt, Truth in the Religions (Edinburgh, 1963) and articles by Edward Jurji and W. G. Oxtoby in Theology Today, October 1966.

4 W. C. Smith, The Meaning and End of Religion (New York, 1962-3); A. Toynbee, An Historian's Approach to Religion (London, 1956) and Christianity Among the Religions of the World (London, 1958).

5 E. C. Dewick, The Indwelling God(London, 1938) and The Gospel and Other Faiths (London, 1948); A. K. Cragg, The Call of the Minaret (New York, 1956), Sandals at the Mosque (New York, 1959); and Leroy S. Rouner, "Rethinking the Christian Mission in India Today," Religion in Life (October, 1966).

6 Arend Th. van Leeuwen, Christianity in World History (London, 1964); Paul Van Buren, The Secular Meaning of the Gospel (London, 1963); and The Christian Response to Asian Revolution by M. M. Thomas (London, 1966). One can also examine the works of Friedrich Gogarten, Dietrich Bonhoeffer, and Harvey Cox.

7 W. A. Bijlefeld, "Recent Theological Evaluation of the Christian-Muslim Encounter," Part II, I.R.M., 55 (1966), 430-441 and Part I in this periodical by Ian H. Douglas, pp. 418-429; Daud Rahbar, "Christian Apologetic to Muslims," I.R.M., 54 (1965), 353-359; R. Marston Speight, "Some Bases for a Christian Apologetic to Islam," I.R.M., 54 (1965), 193-205; R. Park Johnson, The Middle East Pilgrimage (New York, 1958) and "Renewal of the Christian Mission to Islam: Reflections on the Asmara Conference," I.R.M., 48 (1959), 438-444; J. Christy Wilson, The Christian Message to Islam (New York, 1950); Johannes Blauw, "The Witness of Christians to Men of Other Faiths," I.R.M., 52 (1963), 414-422, Gottes Werk in dieser Welt. Grundzüge einer biblischen Theologie der Mission (München, 1961) and The Missionary Nature of the Church: a Survey of the Biblical Theology of Mission (2nd edition, London, 1962); Donald A. McGavran, The Bridges of God: A Study in the Strategy of Missions (London, 1957) and How Churches Grow: The New Frontiers of Mission (London, 1959).

8 Ferdinand Hahn, Mission in the New Testament (Studies in Biblical Theology No. 47, London, 1965) is but one example of many recent comprehensive studies.

9 H. R. Mackintosh, Types of Modern Theology, Schleiermacher to Barth (London, 1964); Karl Barth, Rousseau to Ritschl (London, 1959); Alex. R. Vidler, 20th Century Defenders of the Faith (London, 1965); and Gustaf Wingren, Theology in Conflict (Edinburgh, 1958) are excellent introductions to this field.

10 The monumental work, A History of the Expansion of Christianity by K. S. Latourette, (7 vols., London, 1940) and monographs on particular countries provide the historical framework without which any discussion of the theory and practice of mission easily drifts into abstraction.

11 Donald McGavran, "Wrong Strategy: The Real Crisis in Missions," I.R.M., 54 (1965), 461.

12 Carl F. Hallencreutz, Kraemer Towards Tambaram: A Study in Hendrik Kraemer's Missionary Approach (Uppsala, 1966), p. 12.

CHAPTER I: THE FORMATION OF A PROTESTANT CONCEPT OF MISSION, 1500-1800 (p. 7)

1 Even as Muhammad has been called the East's answer to Alexander the Great, so Islam was Arabia's answer to the church's neglect, cf. Carl Brockelmann, History of the Islamic Peoples (trans. J. Carmichael and M. Perlmann, New York, 1960); Philip K. Hitti, History of the Arabs (London, 1937); Bernard Lewis, The Arabs in History (London, 1950); and G. Kirk, A Short History of the Middle East, from the Rise of Islam to Modern Times (London, 1948).

2 W. M. Watt, Muhammad at Mecca (Oxford, 1953), Muhammad at Medina (Oxford, 1956), Muhammad, Prophet and Statesman (London, 1961), Islam and the Integration of Society (London, 1961), "Economic and social aspects of the Origin of Islam," I.Q., 1 (1954), 90-103, and "Ideal Factors in the Origin of Islam," I.Q., 2(1955), 160-174. Also cf. Alfred Guillaume, The Life of Muhammad (Oxford, 1954); Arthur Jeffery, Islam: Muhammad and His Religion (New York, 1958); Tor Andrae, Mohammed: The Man and His Faith (trans. by Theophil Menzel, London, 1936); H. A. R. Gibb, Mohammedanism: an Historical Survey (London, 1953); and D. S. Margoliouth, The Early Development of Mohammedanism (London, 1914).

3 L. S. Browne, Eclipse of Christianity in Asia (Cambridge, 1933); W. Wilson Cash, Christendom and Islam: Their Contacts and Cultures Down the Centuries (London, 1937); and T. W. Arnold, The Preaching of Islam: A History of the Propagation of the Muslim Faith (Westminster, 1896).

4   R. Bell, The Origin of Islam in its Christian Environment (London, 1926); J. Windrow Sweetman, Islam and Christian Theology (2 vols., London, 1945-47); Loofty Levonian, Studies in the Relationship of Islam and Christianity (London, 1940); and John Bowman, "The Debt of Islam to Monophysite, Syrian Christianity," Nederlands Theologisch Tijdschrift (Wageningen), Feb. 1965, 177-201.

5   W. M. Watt, Islamic Philosophy and Theology (Edinburgh, 1963), The Faith and Practice of Al-Ghazali (London, 1953), and Muslim Intellectual: A Study of Al-Ghazali (Edinburgh, 1963).

6   A. S. Tritton, The Caliphs and Their Non-Moslem Subjects (Oxford, 1930); F. W. Hasluck, Christianity and Islam under the Sultans (2 vols., Oxford, 1929); G. E. Von Grunebaum, Medieval Islam (Chicago, 1946); Christopher Dawson, The Making of Modern Europe (London, 1932) and Medieval Essays (London, 1953), W. M. Watt and P. Cachia, Islamic Spain (Edinburgh, 1965); T. W. Arnold and Alfred Guillaume, The Legacy of Islam (Oxford, 1931); Steven Runciman, A History of the Crusades (3 vols., Cambridge, 1951-55); W. B. Stevenson, The Crusaders in the East (Cambridge, 1907); W. M. Baldwin and K. M. Setton (editors), A History of the Crusades (Philadelphia, 1955); A. S. Atiya, The Crusade in the Late Middle Ages (London, 1938); R. Grousset, Histoire des croisades et du régime franque à Jerusalem (3 vols., Paris, 1934-36); and William Miller, The Latins in the Levant (London, 1908).

7   Wilhelm Barthold, Turkestan Down to the Mongol Invasion (London, 1958) and Four Studies on the History of Central Asia (Leiden, 1956-58); H. H. Howarth, History of the Mongols (London, 1876-1927); R. Grousett, L'Empire des steppes (Paris, 1938) and L'Empire mongol (Paris, 1941); and Christopher Dawson, The Mongol Mission (London, 1955).

8   Norman Daniel, Islam and the West; Making of An Image (Edinburgh, 1960) and Harry G. Dorman, Toward Understanding Islam. Contemporary Apologetic of Islam and Missionary Policy (New York, 1948).

9   Erwin Graf, "Religiose and rechtliche Vorstellungen über Kriegsefangene in Islam and Christentum," W.I., 8 (1963), 89-139.

10   J. Schiltberger, The Bondage and Travels, 1396-1427 (ed. by K. F. Neumann, etc. London, 1879) or Reise in den Orient (ed. by A. J. Penzel, Munich, 1813).

11   J. A. B. Palmer, "Fr. Georgius de Hungaria, O.P., and the Tractatus de Moribus Condicionibus et Nequicia Turcoram," Bulletin of the John Rylands Library, 34 (1951-52), 44-68.

12   H. A. R. Gibb, "The Influence of Islamic Culture on Medieval Europe," Bulletin of John Rylands Library, 38 (1955-56), 82-98.

13   Well documented in Daniel, Islam and the West. One may question however Daniel's presupposition that there was an accepted "corpus" of materials re: Islam in Medieval Europe. While it is true that there was much repetition of earlier prejudice and polemics, there were also hopeful signs. For a more positive treatment of those aspects which foster Christian-Muslim dialogue cf. R. W. Southern, Western Views of Islam in the Middle Ages (Cambridge, Mass., 1962).

14   R. W. Southern, Western Views; M. W. Knowles, "Peter the Venerable," Bulletin of the John Rylands Library, 39 (1956-57), 132-145; James Kritzeck, Peter the Venerable and Islam (Princeton, 1964) and "Robert of Ketton's Translation of the Qur'an," I.Q., 2 (1955), 309-312; D. M. Dunlop, "A Christian Mission to Muslim Spain in the 11th Century," Al-Andalus, 17 (1952), 259-310; and Allan Cutler, "Who was the 'Monk of France' and when did He write?" Al-Andalus, 28 (1963), 249-270 and Catholic Missions to the Moslems to the End of the First Crusade (1099), (unpublished PhD. dissertation, University of Southern California, Los Angeles, 1963).

15 Berthold Altaner, Die Dominikanermissionen des 13 Jahrhunderts
(Habelschwert, Schlesien, 1924); Odulphus van der Vat, Die Anfaenge der
Franziskanermissionen (Werl in Westfallen, 1934); A. Graf,"Mohammedaner-
mission in Mittelalter," E.M.M., 1916, 58ff.; and M. A. Schmidt, "Thomas
von Aquino und Raymundus Lullus, zwei Grundtypèn missionarischen Denkens
im Mittelalter," E.M.M., 1953, 37ff. and "Thomas von Aquino und die
Mohammedaner-mission," E.M.M., 1955, 70ff.
16 Allison Peers, Ramon Lull (London, 1929); E. Kellerhals, Raymundus
Lullus, ein Ritter Jesu Christi (Basel, 1948) and S. M. Zwemer, Raymond
Lull, First Missionary to the Moslems (New York, 1902).
17 Dorman, Toward Understanding Islam, pp. 37ff.
18 The Opus Major of Roger Bacon (trans. by R. B. Burke, 2 vols.,
Philadelphia, 1928); Steward Easton, Roger Bacon (Oxford, 1952); and A. C.
Crombie, Robert Grosseteste and the Origin of Experimentation (Oxford, 1953).
19 Daniel, Islam and the West, pp. 50-52, 276-280, 381f., 400.
20 M. D. Knowles, "The Censured Opinions of Uthred of Bolden,"
Proceedings of the British Academy, 38 (1953), 315ff.
21 Southern, Western Views, pp. 72-83.
22 Ibid., pp. 85-104.
23 Ibid., and Nicholas Rescher, "Nicholas of Cusa on the Qur'an,"
M.W., 55 (1965), 195-202.
24 Gustav Warneck, Outline of a History of Protestant Missions (ed. by
George Robson, Edinburgh, 1901), pp. 8ff.; W. R. Hogg, "The Rise of
Protestant Missionary Concern, 1517-1914," in The Theology of Christian
Mission (ed. G. H. Anderson, London, 1961), pp. 95-111; and numerous Roman
Catholic histories.
25 Johannes Vanden Berg, Constrained by Jesus' Love: An Inquiry into
the Motives of the Missionary Awakening in Great Britain in the Period
Between 1696 and 1815 (Kampen, 1956), pp. 4ff. and "Calvin's Missionary
Message," Evangelical Quarterly, 22 (1950), 174-187; S. M. Zwemer, "Calvin-
ism and the Missionary Enterprise," Theology Today, 7 (1950), 206-216;
G. L. Plitt, Kurze Geschichte der lutherischen Mission (Erlangen, 1871);
W. Schlatter, "Kalvin und die Mission," E.M.M., 53 (1909), 48ff.: and Ernst
Pfisterer, "Der Missionsgedanke be Kalvin," A.M.Z., (March, 1934), 101ff.
26 As does Warneck, Outline, pp. 9ff. Compare with Vanden Berg,
Constrained, pp. 5ff.
27 Quoted in Warneck, Outline, p. 16. An excellent index to Luther's
statements regarding mission and spreading the Gospel may be found in
Eswald M. Plass, What Luther Says: An Anthology, 3 vols., (St. Louis,
Missouri, 1959), pp. 957ff. This provides a guide to D. Martin Luthers
Werke (Weimar Edition, 1883-1939). For example, Luther writes (March
1522) "This noble Word brings with it a great hunger and an insatiable
thirst, so that we could not be satisfied even though many thousands of
people believe on it; but we wish that no one should be without it."
(Weimar Edition 10, II, 54).
A hymn for mission success (based on Ps. 67) may be found in the Weimar
Edition 35, 418f.
28 Quoted in Warneck, Outline, p. 12.
29 Ibid., pp. 12f.
30 Ibid., p. 13.
31 This exposition of Mark 16:14ff. is followed by the metaphor
indicating that the Gospel's spread is like the waves in a pond caused by
a pebble. Ibid., p. 14.
32 Ibid., pp. 11f.; Weimar Edition 31, I, 228f.; or Pelikan, Jaroslav
(ed.), Luther's Works, (St. Louis, Missouri, 1958) vol 14, pp. 11ff.
33 Warneck, Outline, p. 11.
34 Ibid., p. 15.

35 For fuller treatment cf. E. Kellerhals, Der Islam, pp. 319ff.; G.
Simon, "Luther's Attitude toward Islam," M.W., 21 (1931), 257-62; C. U.
Wolf, "Luther and Mohammedanism," M.W., 31 (1941), 161-177; H. Barge,
"Luthers Stellung zum Islam," A.M.Z., 1961, 108ff.; Stephen A. Fischer-
Galati, Ottoman Imperialism and German Protestantism, 1521-55 (Cambridge,
Mass., 1959); F. Schlingensiepen, Luther's Doctrine of the Two Kingdoms
and his writings Against the Turks (unpublished dissertation, New College,
Edinburgh, 1953); and W. Holsten, Reformation und Mission (Archiv für
Reformationsgeschicte XIVL, 1953).
36 Weimar Edition, 30 II, 184, 189f., 207f.
37 R. C. Pfister, "Die Zurcher Koranausgabe von 1542/3," E.M.M., 1955,
37ff. Luther believed the best way to defeat Islam was to circulate the
Quran. Of it he says in comments on Genesis 17, "When that Mohammedan
Monstrosity, the Quran, is at its best, it is nothing but a sausage stuffed
with sentences mixed together in confusion from the Law and the Gospel.
For both Jewish and Mohammedan fanatics have picked from Scripture whatever
served their institutions and the flesh." Cf. Plass, E. M., What Luther
Says, p. 961 or Weimar Edition, 42, 603.
38 Luther frequently uses the Turks as a club on Rome. Cf. Bertram L.
Woolf, Reformation Writings of Martin Luther (2 vols., London, 1952-56),
I, pp. 140, 178, et passim. Also cf. Weimar Edition, 40 II, 275. At other
times he treats Islam as an apocalyptical sign of the approaching end of
the world. Cf. Southern, Western Views, pp. 40f.
39 Melanchthon took a harder polemical line with Muslims. Cf. Manfred
Kehler, Melanchthon und der Islam (Leipzig, 1938). Bucer stresses the motive
of compassion for the heathen and the desire to win their souls for Christ.
His emphasis on human piety as the work of God foreshadows pietist missions.
Cf. Vanden Berg, Constrained, pp. 7 and 10.
40 J. Pannier, "Calvin et les Tures," Revue Historique, 180 (1937),
268-286 and Calvin's Commentary of Daniel (Dan. 7:7f., 19f., 23f.).
41 Zwemer, "Calvinism and the Missionary Enterprise," pp. 210f.
42 Emil Brunner, Natural Theology: comprising "Nature and Grace"
and the reply "No" by...K. Barth (trans. by P. Franckel) London, 1946.
43 Ibid., pp. 206, 211; Vanden Berg, Constrained, pp. 7ff.; and G.
Baez-Camarge, "The Earliest Protestant Missionary Venture in Latin
America," Church History 21 (1952), 135-145.
44 Quoted in Zwemer, "Calvinism," p. 208.
45 Warneck, Outline, pp. 19f.
46 For example, the title page of the first Scottish Confession
presented to Parliament (1560) read: "And this glad tidings of the kingdom
shall be preached throughout the whole world for a witness to all nations;
and then shall the end come." Its concluding prayer petitioned: "Give
Thy servants strength to speak Thy word in boldness; and let all nations
attain to Thy true knowledge." Ibid., p. 20. The first Protestant missionary
to the Turks was a Reformed preacher, Wenzeslaus Budowitz of Budapest, a
Calvinist born in 1551. Cf. M.W., 17 (1927), 401ff.
47 For a fuller treatment of Saravia, cf. Warneck, Outline, pp. 20-22
and Vanden Berg, "Calvin's Missionary Message," pp. 182ff. Eramus also
deserves credit for his early ideas of missions to Muslims. Cf. Zwemer,
"Calvinism," p. 212 and George Smith, Short History of Christian Missions
(5th ed.), pp. 116-118.
48 Vanden Berg, "Calvin's Missionary Message," p. 186.
49 Vanden Berg, Constrained, pp. 11f.
50 Quoted in Warneck, Outline, p. 20. Also cf. Vanden Berg, Constrained,
p. 5.

51 Quoted in the superb work, "Were the Reformers Indifferent to Missions?" by D. H. W. Gensichen in History's Lessons for Tomorrow's Mission (W.S.C.F., Geneva, n.d.), 119-127, esp. pp. 121f. Also of interest: Wm. Clark, "The Conception of the Mission of the Church in Early Reformed Theology" with Special Reference to Calvin's Theology and Practice in Geneva (unpublished dissertation, New College, Edinburgh, 1928).

52 Latin and Greek translations of this Confession (1629-31) were followed by French and English editions, which aroused great interest in Europe. Wm. Rait published it in Aberdeen, Scotland under the title "A Vindication of the Reformed Religion" (1671).

53 G. A. Hadjiantoniou, Cyril Lucaris: His Life and Work (unpublished thesis, New College, Edinburgh, 1948), esp. pp. 103ff.; 162ff.; Gibb, H. A. R. and Bowen, H., Islamic Society and the West (London, 1950-51), I, 235ff.; Arnold, Preaching of Islam pp. 135ff.; and A. Pichler, Geschichte der Protestantismus in der orientalischen Kirche im 17 Jahrhundert oder Der Patriarch Cyrillus Lucaris und seine Zeit (Munich, 1862).

54 For a full treatment of the ferment under the Ottomans cf. Gibb and Bowen, Islamic Society and the West, pp. 78-244; Wilbur W. White, The Processes of Change in the Ottoman Empire (Chicago, 1937), and A. S. Tritton, The Caliphs and their Non-Moslem Subjects (Oxford, 1930).

55 Stephen Neill, A History of Christian Missions, pp. 142ff., 177ff., 204ff.; Latourette, Expansion of Christianity, II, 75-82; and Gibb and Bowen, Islamic Society and the West, pp. 244-251.

56 Neill, History of Christian Missions, pp. 220-231; Warneck, Outline, pp. 42ff.; Vanden Berg, Constrained, pp. 15ff.

57 Warneck, Outline, pp. 20ff. Vanden Berg, Constrained, pp. 16, 23f.; and Ruth Rouse and Stephen Neill, A History of the Ecumenical Movement, 1517-1948 (London, 1954), pp. 88ff.

58 Warneck, Outline, pp. 41ff., and Hogg, "Rise of Protestant Missionary Concern, 1517-1914," pp. 100ff.

59 Warneck, Outline, pp. 42ff., 62ff.; Karl Muller, 200 Jahre Brudermission (Herrnhut, 1931); and The Advance Guard, 200 Years of Moravian Mission, 1732-1932 (London, n.d.).

60 Warneck, Outline, pp. 47ff.; Rouse and Neill, History of the Ecumenical Movement, pp. 100ff.

61 Von Grunebaum, Medieval Islam, p. 48.

62 Daniel, Islam and the West, pp. 281-87; S. C. Chew, "Islam and England during the Renaissance," M.W., 31 (1941), 371-399 and The Crescent and the Rose (Oxford, 1937); Byron Smith, Islam in English Literature (Beirut, 1939); and Elie Salem, "The Elizabethian Image of Islam," Studia Islamica, 22 (1965), pp. 43-54.

63 H. Prideaux, The True Nature of Imposture fully display'd in the Life of Mahomet: with "A discourse annex'd for the Vindication of Christianity from this Charge. Offered to the Consideration of the Deists of the Present Age", (London, 1696-97, tenth edition, 1808). Deism or "natural religion" was best expressed by Tindal's Christianity as Old as the Creation (1730).

64 John Donne in his satire "Ignatius and His Conclave..." (1610) attacked Jesuits and Muslims alike making Mahomet and Pope Boniface II argue concerning the highest room in Hell. An attack on the Unitarians bore the title, Historical and Critical Reflections upon Mahometanism and Socianianism (1712). Also cf. Daniel, Islam and the West, p. 287.

65 Daniel, Islam and the West, pp. 289-299.

66 Dedication to William Duncombe by the Count of Boulainvilliers, The Life of Mahomet (trans. from French original of 1730, London, 1731).

67 M. Savary, Le Coran, traduit de l'arabe, accongagné de notes, et précédé d'un abregé de la vie d Mahomet (Paris, 1783) and Morale de Mahomet ou Recueil des plus pures maximes du Coran (Paris, 1784).

68 Le Fanatisme ou Mahomet Le Prophete (1741) and Essai sur les moeurs (1756).

69 The Decline and Fall of the Roman Empire (London, 1776-1788), chapters 38 and 50. Gibbon portrayed Muhammad "with the sword in one hand and the Koran in the other" and Islam as "the faith which is compounded on an eternal truth and a necessary fiction: that there is one God, and that Mohammed is the Prophet of God".

70 T. Carlyle, "The Hero as Prophet" in On Heroes (London, 1841).

71 This lecture reflects the ideas of Leibniz, Kant and Goethe. Cf. W. M. Watt, "Carlyle on Mohammed," Hibbert Journal, 55 (1954-55), 247-254. It may also be rooted in the essay, Of Heroic Virtue (1690) by a certain William Temple who appreciated Muhammad.

72 R. Hakluyt, The Principal Navigations, Voiages, Traffiques, and Discoveries of the English Nation (2 vols., London, 1599).

73 C. Angell, Travels (1617); F. Knight, A Relation of Seaven Yeares Slaverie under the Turkes of Argeire, suffered by an English Captive Merchant (London, 1640); and J. Harrison, The Tragicall Life and Death of Muley Adala Melek the late King of Barbrie (Delph, Netherlands, 1633).

74 Daniel considers Nau's sympathy for the partial truths of the Quran (Dialogus Pacificus) as a foreshadowing of A. K. Cragg's scholarly approach. Cf. Islam and the West, pp. 281ff.

75 J. Pitts, A True and Faithful Account of the Religion and Manners of the Mahometans (3rd ed., London, 1731); C. Niebuhr, Description of l'Arabie (Amsterdam, 1774); T. Hansen, Arabia Felix (English trans. of the report of the Danish Expedition of 1761-1767, New York, 1964); and Travels of Marcarius, Patriarch of Antioch as written by his Archdeacon Paul of Aleppo (trans. F. C. Belfour, 2 vols., London, 1829-36).

76 M. A. Hachicho, "English Travel Books about the Arab Near East in the Eighteenth Century," W.I., 9(1964), 1-206 and M. Anis, "British Travellers' impressions of Egypt in the late Eighteenth Century," Bulletin of the Faculty of Arts, Cairo University, 13, (1951), 9-37.

77 L. Twells, Theological Works of the Learned Dr. Pocock (includes "Life of Pocock", London, 1740) and J. H. Hottinger, Historia Orientalis (Zurich, 1651) and Smegna Orientalis (Heidelberg, 1658).

78 Christian Raue, "A Discourse concerning the Easterne Tongues" in A General Grammar (London, 1649) and Prima Tredecim partium Alcorani Arabico-Latini (Amsterdam, 1646).

79 For an example cf. Hadrian Reland, De religione Mohammedica (Utrecht, 1705) or the English version, Reland on the Mahometan Religion (London, 1712) and his tracts "Mahometan Religion" and "A Defence of the Mahometans" in Four Treatises Concerning the Doctrine, Discipline and Worship of the Mahometans (London, 1721(.

80 André du Ryer, L'Alcoran de Mahomet translaté d'arabe en francois (Paris, 1647) and the version by A. Ross, The Alcoran of Mahomet translated out of Arabique into French...and Newly Englished with the Life and Death of Mahomet and A Needful Caveat (London, 1649).

81 L. Maracci, Alcorani Textus Universus...His omnibus praemissus est Prodromus together with Refutatio Alcorani (Padua, 1698).

82 G. Sale, The Koran...to which is prefixed a Preliminary Discourse (London, 1734; revised edition by Wherry, London, 1882).

83 J. C. Schwartz, De Mohammed: Furto Sententiarum Scripturae Sacrae Liberunus (Leipzig, 1711) and J. Ehrhart, De illustrum ac obscurum scriptorum errorious praecipuis in Historia Mahometi eorumque causis dissertatio (Memmengen, 1831).

84 Bernard Lewis, British Contributions to Arabic Studies (London, 1941); W. M. Watt, "Scottish Islamic Studies: Retrospect and Prospect" (Inaugural Address, University of Edinburgh, 1965); and Daniel, Islam and the West, pp. 294-300.

85 For a fuller treatment of the awakenings cf. Warneck, Outline,
53-73; Vanden Berg, Constrained, pp. 66ff.; and K. S. Latourette, A History
of Christianity (London, n.d.), pp. 1001-1063, Expansion of Christianity,
IV, 78ff., and Christianity in a Revolutionary Age (New York, 1958), I,
189ff.

86 Webster's Collegiate Dictionary defines evangelical as: "pertaining
to or designating any school of Protestants which holds that the essence
of the gospel consists mainly in its doctrines of man's sinful condition
and the need of salvation, the revelation of God's grace in Christ, the
necessity of spiritual renovation, and participation in the experience of
spiritual renovation". The Oxford Shorter Dictionary adds: "applied to
those Protestants who hold that the essence of the Gospel consists in the
doctrine of salvation by faith in the atoning death of Christ, and deny the
saving efficacy of either good works or the sacraments (1791)".

87 Webster defines liberalism as: "a movement in contemporary Protestantism, emphasizing intellectual liberty and the spiritual and ethical
content of Christianity". The Oxford Shorter Dictionary notes that
whereas the term "liberal" originally referred to those "arts or sciences"
worthy of a free man, in the 16th and 17th centuries it meant "licentious".
In the 19th century it was revived to mean those "open to the reception of
new ideas or proposals of reform" and in theology applied to "those who
consider large parts of the traditional system of belief unessential".

88 To say they had a passion for souls is not to imply they neglected
education or social reform, e.g., cf. activities of Robert Raikes, John
Howard, Z. Macauly, W. Wilberforce and Hannah More.

89 Vanden Berg, Constrained, pp. 78-105.

90 For fuller coverage on Carey and the foundation and growth of the
societies cf. Warneck, Outline, pp. 74-144; George Smith, The Life of
William Carey (London, 1885); W. R. Hogg, Ecumenical Foundations (New York,
1952), pp. 5ff.; Vanden Berg, Constrained, pp. 106ff.; and J. P. Wheeler,
The Theological Justification of the Great Missionary Awakening of the Late
Eighteenth Century with Special Reference to William Carey (unpublished
dissertation, New College, Edinburgh, 1959).

91 Vanden Berg, Constrained by Jesus' Love, pp. 144-213, a superb
examination of nineteenth century mission motives; E.S.P. Heavenor, The
Eschatological Motive for World Mission in the New Testament (unpublished dissertation, New College, Edinburgh, 1962); Ross Kinsler, Love as
a Motive for Mission: an approach to the Biblical Theology of Mission
(unpublished dissertation, New College, Edinburgh, 1962); and H. Margull,
"The Awakening of Protestant Missions," in History's Lessons for Tomorrow's
Missions, pp. 142ff.

CHAPTER II: ANGLICAN AND REFORMED MISSIONS TO MUSLIMS IN INDIA, 1800-1910:
            A STUDY IN METHODS (p. 27)

1 Approximately one-quarter of the world's Muslim population (approximately one-fifth of the population of India) lived in nineteenth century
India.

2 Charles Grant's pamphlet, "Observations on the State of Society among
the Asiatic Subjects of Great Britain" influenced public opinion and the
work of the Church Missionary Society. Cf. Eugene Stock, The History of
the Church Missionary Society (4 vols., London, 1899-1916), I, 54f.

3 For fuller introduction cf. Latourette, Expansion of Christianity,
VI, 65ff.; Neill, History of Christian Missions, pp. 261ff.; Gustav Warneck,
Outline of a History of Protestant Missions from the Reformation to the
Present Time (Trans. George Robson, Edinburgh, 1901), pp. 213ff.; J. Richter,
Indische Missionsgeschichte (2. Aufl., Gutersloh, 1924); and G. B. Firth,
An Introduction to Indian Church History, (Madras, 1961).

4 Eugene Stock carefully documents the year of 1786 as the point when Wilberforce, Granville Sharp, David Brown, Charles Grant, William Carey and the Eclectic Society (seed of the C.M.S.) set into motion forces which not only produced the great Acts of Parliament but launched the modern mission-art movement, cf. Stock, History of C.M.S., I, 57f.

5 Even the proposals of Grant for evangelizing India followed the Dutch method of missions, i.e., government or company financed programs.

6 His pamphlet, Enquiry into the Obligations of Christians to use Means for the Conversion of the Heathen (1792) and his sermon on Isaiah 54:2-3 at Nottingham under the title, "Expect great things from God; attempt great things for God" (May, 1792) are stirring documents.

7 In addition to various translations of the Bible and grammars, Marshman wrote Thoughts on Propagating Christianity More Effectually among the Heathen (2nd ed., Edinburgh, 1827); "Hints relative to Native Schools, together with an Outline of an Institution for their Extension and Management" (1815); founded the newspaper, Mirror of News; and began the mission periodical, Friend of India (1818).

8 Neill, History of Christian Missions, p. 263.

9 John C. Marshman, The Life and Labors of Carey, Marshman and Ward the Serampore Missionaries (London, 1864); The Story of Serampore and its College (Serampore, 1961); and B. H. Bradley, Indian Missionary Directory and Memorial Volume (London, 1876) pp. 12ff.

10 In this study both apology and apologetics will be used in the broader sense of an appealing and reasonable defense and presentation of the Christian Gospel. Among nineteenth century evangelical missionaries it meant not only a defense but a communication of the Gospel. The Tokyo Conference of W.S.C.F. (1907) defined apologetics as the attempt to remove the hindrances to the acceptance of the Christian faith by means of a reasoned intellectual discussion of existing problems. Webster's New International Dictionary (2nd ed.) defines apology as "something said or written in defense or justification of what appears to others to be wrong or of what may be liable to disapprobation" and apologetics as "systematic argumentative discourse in defense esp. of the divine origin and authority of Christianity".

11 E. Chatterton, A History of the Church of England in India since the Early Days of the East India Company (London, 1924), pp. 109-113 and Memorial Sketches of the Rev. David Brown with a Selection of his Sermons, preached at Calcutta (London, 1816).

12 Memoir of the Expediency of an Ecclesiastical Establishment for British India. Also of interest are Claudius Buchanan, Christian Researches in Asia (London, 1812) and Hugh Pearson, Memoirs of the Life and Writings of the Rev. Claudius Buchanan, D.D. (Boston, 1818).

13 J. Sargent, The Life of the Rev. T. T. Thomason (New York, 1843).

14 Memoirs of the Right Rev. Daniel Corrie, LL.D., First Bishop of Madras. Compiled chiefly from his own Letters and Journals, by his Brothers (London, 1847).

15 Source materials include: Henry Martyn, Twenty Sermons (London, 1822) and Five Sermons never before published edited by G. T. Fox (London, 1862); Translations of Martyn's three Persian tracts by Samuel Lee, Controversial Tracts on Christianity and Mohammedanism (Cambridge, 1824); S. Wilberforce (editor) Journals and Letters of the Rev. Henry Martyn, B.D. (2 vols., London, 1837); the standard biography by John Sargent, Memoir of the Rev. Henry Martyn (London, 1820, 16th ed. 1848); the comprehensive biography by George Smith, Henry Martyn (London, 1892); and the popular account by Canstance E. Padwick, Henry Martyn, Confessor of the Faith (London, 1922). Good insight are found in Mrs. W. A. Stewart, "Henry Martyn and Serampore," and John Elder, "Henry Martyn in Iran," pages 5-22 and 23-33 respectively in The Bulletin of the Henry Martyn Institute of Islamic Studies, 57 (April, 1964).

16 Diary entries for July 22, 25, 1806 quoted in Smith, _Martyn_, p. 174.
17 Martyn and others considered the expansion of European culture as a
preparatory step to the spread of the Gospel. Cf. Smith, _Martyn_, p. 330.
This is not to be confused with a blind identification of Christianity and
Western civilization. They were aware that evangelization, the communication of the Gospel was in some way entangled in the surging tides of world
cultures. Compare this with the idea that cultural change, even revolution
and secularization may precede serious consideration of Christ's claims
regarding the ultimate issues of life in M. M. Thomas, _The Christian Response
to the Asian Revolution_ (London, 1966). Excellent background material may
be found in Martha Sherwood and Henry Sherwood, _The Life and Times of Mrs.
Sherwood (1775-1851)_. From _the Diaries of_ Captain _and_ Mrs. Sherwood,
edited by F. J. H. Darton (London, 1910).
18 Smith, _Martyn_, pp. 218ff.
19 _Ibid._, p. 225.
20 Sermons 19 and 20 in _Twenty Sermons_ (London, 1822), pp. 391ff.
21 _Five Sermons_ edited by G. T. Fox, pp. iv ff.
22 Smith, _Martyn_, pp. 240ff.
23 Cf. Wilberforce, _Journal...H. Martyn_, II, pp. 232f.
24 Smith, _Martyn_, p. 148.
25 Padwick, _Martyn_, p. 204.
26 Diary entried in June and July, 1811 quoted in Smith, _Martyn_, pp.
362ff.
27 _Ibid._, pp. 232f.
28 _Ibid._, pp. 233ff.
29 _Ibid._, pp. 229, _et passim._
30 _Ibid._, p. 379.
31 _Ibid._, pp. 363ff.
32 S. Lee in _Controversial Tracts on Christianity and Mohammedanism
Translated and Explained_ (Cambridge, 1824) includes the Tract of Mirza
Ibrahim defending Islam (pp. 1-39); an "Extract from the Tract of Aga Acber
on the Miracles of Mohammed" (pp. 40-69); the three tracts or "Replies"
of Martyn to Mirza (pp. 80-160); a later "Rejoinder of Mohammed Ruza of
Hamadam in Reply to Mr. Martyn" (pp. 161-450); and Lee's own contribution
to the continuing "controversy" (pp. 451-584). Summary usage of these
materials are found in William Muir, "The Mahommedan Controversy," _The
Calcutta Review_, 4 (1845), pp. 418-76 and George Smith, _Martyn_, pp. 400-
404. An examination of Martyn's three tracts is found in Appendix A.
33 Sargent, _Martyn_, pp. 158, 192.
34 Smith, _Martyn_, p. 217.
35 Diary entry of May 11, 1812, _Ibid._, pp. 461ff.
36 Entry of July 26, 1811, _Ibid._, p. 405.
37 Entry of August 29, 1811, _Ibid._, p. 409.
38 Entry of September 7-11, 1811, _Ibid._, p. 380.
39 Entries of September 12-15, 1811 and January 24, 1812, _Ibid._, pp.
402, 382.
40 Entry of September 20, 1811, _Ibid._, p. 413.
41 _Ibid._, p. 387.
42 For his struggles with C.M.S. cf. Stock, _History of C.M.S._, I, 187,
and Charles Le Bas, _The Life of the Right_ Rev. _Thomas Fanshaw Middleton,
D.D., Late Bishop of Calcutta_ (2 vols., London, 1831).
43 Heber wrote to Carey and Marshman: "Would to God, my honoured brethren, the time were arrived, when not only in heart and hope, but visibly,
we shall be one fold, as well as under one shepherd...if a reunion of our
churches could be effected, the harvest of the heathen would ere long be
reaped, and the work of the Lord would advance among them with a celerity
of which we now have no experience." in Neill, _History of Christian
Missions_, p. 268. Fuller accounts are in R. Heber, _Narrative of a Journey_

through the Upper Provinces of India, from Calcutta to Bombay, 1824-1825,
an Account of a Journey to Madras and the Southern Provinces, 1826, and
Letters Written from India (3 vols., London, 2nd edition 1828); The Life
of Reginald Heber, D.D., Lord Bishop of Calcutta, by his Widow (2 vols.,
London, 1830; condensation Boston, 1861); and George Smith, Bishop Heber
(London, 1895).
    44 Josiah Bateman, The Life of Daniel Wilson, D.D., Bishop of Calcutta
and Metropolitan in India (Boston, 1860) and Bishop Wilson's Journal,
Letters Addressed to his Family, during the first nine years of his
Episcopate, edited by his son, Daniel Wilson (London, 1863).
    45 Of the first 24 C.M.S. workers 17 were German and 7 English. Of
the latter, three were ordained and only one a graduate (William Jowett
who went to Malta). Cf. Stock, History of the C.M.S., I, 89ff.
    46 Ibid., I, 193ff.
    47 Ibid., I, 124f., 199f.
    48 Ibid., I, 99ff.
    49 At Krishnagar, Deerr baptised 30 in 1833 and 500 from ten villages
in 1838. Soon 55 villages were inquiring and by 1840 the adherents numbered over 3,000. Yet the mission hesitated. Stock offers these reasons
for the failure to act: "First, there were not native teachers enough,
and of good quality enough, to go in at once and lead the converted on to
a higher life. Secondly, it is clear that the German missionaries who
took charge...had not learned the importance of teaching the Native Church
its first lessons in self-support, self-administration, and self-extension.
...Scarcely any one at the time, at home or abroad had really grasped that
great principle; and in North India especially the patriarchal system that
suited the genius of the German brethren, making each missionary the
ma-bap (mother and father) of his people, was, kind as it seemed, a real
obstacle of the healthy independent growth of the Church. Then thirdly,
when the Society at home inspired by Henry Venn, adopted the principle
just indicated as its definite policy the missionaries were withdrawn
(or vacancies not supplied) too quickly; and the community that might in
its infancy have been taught to walk alone, when suddenly let go, stumbled
and fell." Stock, History of C.M.S., I, 316.
    50 Ibid., I, 293ff.
    51 "Sheikh Salih Abdul Masih," The Bulletin of the Henry Martyn
Institute of Islamic Studies, 53 (1964), pp. 3-4 and George Smith, Henry
Martyn, pp. 286f.
    52 Stock, History of C.M.S., I, 119ff., 251.
    53 Jerome Xavier, nephew of Francis Xavier of Goa followed the pattern
of Raymond Lull (Ars Major, etc.) at Adbar's Court in Agra (1580). A rela-
tive, P. Hieronymo Xavier wrote for the court two histories, Christi and
S. Petri and Jerome wrote in Persian for Emperor Jahangir (Akbar's suc-
cessor) A Mirror Showing the Truth (1609). Ahmed Ibn Zayn al-'Abidin, a
Persian Nobleman responded with The Divine Rays in Refutation of Christian
Error (1621). Phillip Gradagnoli of the College de propaganda fide in
Rome added a rejoinder Apologia pro Christiana Religione (1631) and L.
Maracci produced Alcorani Textus Universus (and Refutation) in 1698. The
Protestant works by Grotius, Pocock, and H. Martyn were the next steps.
Cf. Harry Dorman, Toward Understanding Islam (New York, 1948), pp. 37ff.
    54 It is interesting to note that this stress on miracles had dominated
the missionary work of the Nestorians and Jacobites in Central Asia. The
idea of rational evidences (cf. Grotius) was popular also in Europe. It
developed into a cold rationalism (proving the deity of Christ, etc.)
which prompted the reactionary liberal movement and a recovery of the
humanity of Christ later in the 19th century. When the pendulum had
shifted far to the left, Schweitzer and Barth triggered off a reversal in
its movement. Lee and Pfander stand in the middle of 19th century
rationalism.

55 S. Lee, Controversial Tracts on Christianity and Mohammedanism (London, 1824), pp. 4, 533ff., 474ff., 517ff.

56 Ibid., p. 466.

57 Ibid., pp. 511ff., 533, 537ff. Lee at times is severe with Muhammad: "Of him prophecy knows nothing, unless he be marked out as the anti-Christ, or as one of those pretenders who should almost deceive the elect. The religion recommended by Moses and Jesus, he confessedly opposed, laying down laws and precepts which they had reprobated. In appealing to the prophets, his blunders are those of ignorance; and, in charging the Scriptures with corruption he is guilty of palpable falsehood. His conduct in war is that of a man of the world, bloody and avaricious. As to the miracles related of him, they are either said to have been performed in private such for example, as his being saluted as a prophet by stocks and stones when he was a child; or are false such as his dividing the moon, causing the sun to stand still, etc...." (p. 566).

58 Ibid., appendix, pp. 124-138.

59 Ibid., pp. 548ff.

60 S. M. Zwemer, "Karl Gottlieb Pfander," M.W., 31 (1941), 223f. The episode at Constantinople will receive fuller treatment in chapter three.

61 Ibid., pp. 217-226. Julius Richter, a leader in developing a German apologetic to Muslims says of Pfander, "He fearlessly travelled through the Northwest as far as Baghdad, winning souls for Christ by his clear dialectic and his warm heart. (Of Mizan-al-Haqq)...In the first part he disposes of the foolish prejudices of Moslems against the Bible, above all, the utter unreasonableness of the talk about the corruption of the text of the Bible, a means of attack, which devised by Mohammed himself, has been reiterated again and again. (It is, he says)...the best Protestant work directed against Islam; it is still published and much read in Arabic, Turkish, Persian, Hindustani and English and is almost indispensable to every missionary among Mohammedans." J. Richter, A History of Protestant Missions in the Near East (New York, 1910), pp. 100f. Also cf. C. F. Eppler, Karl G. Pfander (Basel, 1888).

62 A fuller account of the debate and a list of Pfander's converts may be found in Stock, History of the C.M.S., II, 160-171, 562f.

63 The original MS is preserved in the archives of the Basel Mission. It was translated into Armenian (1829), Persian (1835), Hindustani (1853), Marathi (1865), Arabic (1865) and English (1867). The Persian text was revised by a liberal Persian Muslim and a mullah. For a summary examination of the English editions of R. H. Weakley (London, 1867, 134 pages) and St. Clair Tisdall (London, 1910, 370 pages) cf. Appendix B.

64 A Shiʿah Mujtahid of Lucknow found the four books of Pfander of such charm and merit, so far surpassing the composition of the Christian padres that he suspected they were written by a Persian. Cf. Wm. Muir, The Mohammedan Controversy (Edinburgh, 1897), p. 31.

65 Miftah-ul-Asrar, The Key of Mysteries was printed by 1844. A Persian edition with English summary (Agra, 1850) and an Urdu edition (London, 1862) are also available.

66 Wm. Muir, Mohammedan Controversy, pp. 27-30.

67 Pfander's rejoinder, The Solution of Difficulties was reprinted in a lengthy work (806 pages) by Sayyid Ali Hassan.

68 The title, Remarks on the Nature of Muhammadanism (Baptist Mission Press, Calcutta, 1840, 41 pages), has been inscribed as a correction over the printed title of "Traditions" by Pfander's own hand. This copy is located in Edinburgh University Library, #P. 291/a.

69 Ibid., pp. 40f.

70 Herbert Birks, The Life and Correspondence of Thomas Valpy French, First Bishop of Lahore (2 vols., London, 1895), I, 70.

71 William Muir, <u>The</u> <u>Life</u> <u>of</u> <u>Mahomet</u> <u>and</u> <u>the</u> <u>History</u> <u>of</u> <u>Islam</u> (4 vols.,
London, 1858 etc.), <u>The</u> <u>Coran</u>: <u>Its</u> <u>Composition</u> <u>and</u> <u>teaching</u>, <u>and</u> <u>the</u>
<u>testimony</u> <u>it</u> <u>bears</u> <u>to</u> <u>the</u> <u>Holy</u> <u>Scriptures</u> (London, 3rd ed., 1878) and many
more writings and translations.

72 Samuel Zwemer argues that there is a biblical, historical and contemporary basis for a Christian apology, cf. <u>M.W.</u>, 31 (1941), esp. pp.
224f. Bevan Jones in <u>The</u> <u>People</u> <u>of</u> <u>the</u> <u>Mosque</u> (pp. 238f.) fully acknowledges
Pfander's failings and sees his works as "a guide to something better".
Harry G. Dorman, missionary in Syria-Lebanon, contends that Pfander's method
stimulated the growth of both progressive and anti-Christian reform groups
within Islam and Hinduism, For him, it was a major accomplishment when
the polemical method ceased, cf. <u>Toward</u> <u>Understanding</u> <u>Islam</u>: <u>Contemporary</u>
<u>Apologetic</u> <u>of</u> <u>Islam</u> <u>and</u> <u>Missionary</u> <u>Policy</u> (New York, 1948), esp. pp.
114-131. Daud Rahbar, "Christian Apologetic to Muslims" and R. M. Speight,
"Some Bases for a Christian Apologetic to Islam" in <u>I.R.M.</u>, 54 (1965),
353ff. and 193ff. respectively state the case for and the method of a
contemporary apologetics.

73 Birks, <u>French</u>, I, 15-18. Also consider Eugene Stock, <u>An</u> <u>Heroic</u>
<u>Bishop</u>, <u>The</u> <u>Life-Story</u> <u>of</u> <u>French</u> <u>of</u> <u>Lahore</u> (London, 1913).

74 Birks, <u>French</u>, I, 201.

75 <u>Ibid</u>., I, 46.

76 <u>Ibid</u>., I, 62.

77 <u>Ibid</u>., I, 64ff.

78 <u>Ibid</u>., I, 66f., 78.

79 <u>Ibid</u>., I, 204. Minor discussions by Europeans did take place
however at Delhi in 1891 (Lefroy), Peshawar (Williams), and Amritsar in
1894.

80 <u>Ibid</u>., I, 57, 293.

81 <u>Ibid</u>., I, 73-81.

82 <u>Ibid</u>., I, 145ff.

83 <u>Ibid</u>., I, 258, II, 115f.

84 Cf. <u>ibid</u>., II, 56-58.

85 <u>Ibid</u>., II, 361f.

86 <u>Ibid</u>., II, 339-341, 363, 371ff.

87 Thomas P. Hughes of Peshawar dedicated his <u>Dictionary</u> <u>of</u> <u>Islam</u> (1885)
to Bishop French and J. D. MacBride, reader in Arabic at the University
of Oxford dedicated <u>The</u> <u>Mohammedan</u> <u>Religion</u> <u>Explained</u> (London, 1857) to
French in a three page open letter which is most reflective of the respect
French drew.

88 French's article written from Muscat, "Moslems in Arabia and North
Africa," <u>Indian</u> <u>Church</u> <u>Quarterly</u> <u>Review</u>, July, 1891.

89 Birks, <u>French</u>, II, 343ff.

90 <u>Ibid</u>., I, 35; II, 92.

91 <u>Ibid</u>., I, 37ff., 369.

92 <u>Ibid</u>., I, 20ff.

93 <u>Ibid</u>., I, 55f.

94 <u>Ibid</u>., I, 42f.

95 <u>Ibid</u>., I, 44f.

96 <u>Ibid</u>., I, 201.

97 <u>Ibid</u>., I, 324f.

98 The paper "Proposed Plan for a Training College of Native Evangelists, Pastors and Teachers for North-West India and the Punjab" (1866)
was read before seventy clergy and Henry Venn at Gloucester Deanery.
Quoted in Birks, <u>French</u>, I, 159ff.

99 Birks, <u>French</u>, I, 219, 246.

100 <u>Ibid</u>., I, 226, 256.

101 <u>Ibid</u>., I, 297, II, 115.

102 <u>Ibid</u>., I, 329ff., 381ff., 405.

103 Ibid., I, 39f. In the enthusiasm of the times there often was a
blurring of the interests of state and church, colonial expansion and
Christian mission in the minds of some. E.g., cf. C. K. Robinson, Missions
Urged Upon the State on Grounds Both of Duty and Policy: An Essay which
obtained the Maitland Prize in the year 1852 (London, 1853) and J. N.
Ogilvie, Our Empire's Debt to Missions (London, 1924).
104 Birks, French, I, 205ff., 250.
105 Ibid., I, 365, 369.
106 In 1888 the Punjab Mission News reported the Bishop had jurisdiction over 78 clergy (19 chaplains, 42 C.M.S., 6 S.P.G., 6 Cambridge Mission,
5 others); 8 lay missionaries; 37 lady Zenana missionaries; 19 Cambridge
and S.P.G. women missionaries; 3 sisters of St. Denys School at Murree;
28,700 European and Indian Christians; and an area populated by 23 million
Muslims, Hindus, and Sikhs. From 1877-86, thirteen new churches and the
Lahore Cathedral were opened. Cf. Ibid., I, 360f.
107 Ibid., I, 345, 405, et passim.
108 Ibid., I, 253, II, 137f.
109 Ibid., I, 233, 250ff.; II, 142.
110 Ibid., I, 252, et passim.
111 Ibid., I, 251.
112 Ibid., II, 143.
113 Cf. the biography by his adopted son, Henry Martyn Clark, M.D.,
Robert Clark of the Punjab: Pioneer and Missionary Statesman (London,
1907) and Robert Clark, Punjab and Sindh, Missions of the C.M.S., 1852-84
(London, 1885, revised edition, 1904).
114 Clark, Punjab and Sindh, p. 245.
115 H. M. Clark, Clark, p. 298.
116 Ibid., pp. 123, 118f.
117 Ibid., p. 190ff.
118 Ibid., pp. 278ff., 313, et passim.
119 Cf. Ibid., pp. 238, 246, 294.
120 Ibid., p. 243. Clark also backed T. P. Hughes' use of a Mughal
architecture in the midst of the city of Peshawar. Cf. F. E. Wilcox,
"Brief Resume of the origins of missions to Muslims in the Northwest Frontier Province (Pakistan)," M.W., 42 (1952), 100f.
121 Clark, Clark, p. 25.
122 Ibid., pp. 251, also cf. 278ff.
123 Ibid., pp. 242, 252f., 306, 324.
124 Ibid., p. 329.
125 Ibid., p. 305.
126 Ibid., p. 307.
127 Cf. Ibid., pp. 255ff., 306-309, 340.
128 For an excellent treatment of the growth of the Church, between
1851 and 1903 cf. the revised edition of R. Clark's book, Punjab and Sindh
(1904).
129 R. Maconachie, Rowland Bateman (London, 1917) and A. R. MacDuff,
The Utmost Bound of the Everlasting Hills or Memories of Christ's Frontier
Force in North-Western India (London, 1909).
130 Two converts, Waris and Datta (baptized 1874 and 1874) travelled
with Bateman to England. The former became a minister and the latter a
medical doctor (University of Edinburgh).
131 Maconachie, Bateman, pp. 127f., 173f.
132 The S.P.G. developed a considerable work force in India which by
1900 included 64 ordained men, 1938 Indian workers, 87 station, 30,349
communicants, 82,363 adherents. Cf. H. P. Beach, Statistics and Atlas of
Protestant Missions (New York, 1903), p. 25. The young Cambridge Brotherhood became related to their program. Other helpful sources include: C. F.
Pascoe, Two Hundred Years of the S.P.G. (London, 1901); C. F. Pascoe,

The Story of the Delhi Mission (Westminster, 1917); L. F. Henderson, The
Cambridge Mission to Delhi (London, 1931); F. F. Monk, A History of St.
Stephen's College, Delhi (Calcutta, 1935); F. F. Monk, Educational Policy
in India (Bombay, 1934); S. Bickersteth, The Life and Letters of Edward
Bickersteth (London, 1899) and Cecil H. Martin, Allnutt of Delhi, A
Memoir (London, 1922).

133 In 1897 the College had 54 Hindus, 7 Muslims, 9 Christians and in
1920: 130, 100 and 20 respectively. The School and its branches had an
even larger enrollment. Cf. Martin, Allnutt, pp. 75ff.

134 Ibid., pp. 79f.

135 Ibid., pp. 62f.

136 Ibid., pp. 38ff.

137 For example, examine the credit given to missions in the Report
of the Secretary of State and Council of India, "The Moral and Material
Process and Condition of India" to the House of Commons (1873). Quoted
in Clark, Punjab and Sindh, pp. 2ff.

138 "In probable connection with the Ebionites or anti-Paulinian
Christians, and under divine guidance Mahomed rejected the Essenic-
Buddhistic doctrines which Paul had applied to Jesus Christ..." Ernest
DeBunsen, Islam or True Christianity (London, 1889), p. 170.

139 Max Warren, The Missionary Movement from Britain in Modern History
(London, 1965) and G. A. Hood, "An Introductory Study of our Missionary
'Image', 1847-1965," The Journal of the Presbyterian Historical Society
of England, 13 (May, 1966), 78-97.

140 H. H. Montgomery, Life and Letters of George Alfred Lefroy
(London, 1920).

141 Montomery, Lefroy, pp. 67ff.

142 Ibid., pp. 76f.

143 Ibid., pp. 69f.

144 Ibid., pp. 73f.

145 Ibid., p. 90.

146 Ibid., p. 97.

147 "The Attempt to Estimate the Contribution of Great Races to the
Fulness of the Church of God," in Mankind and the Church written by seven
bishops and edited by H. H. Montgomery (London, 1907).

148 Montgomery, Lefroy, pp. 22f., 25, 42-45.

149 Ibid., pp. 19ff., 77.

150 Ibid., pp. 20, 90.

151 George Lefroy, Sweeps and Bridge, Being two sermons preached by
the Bishop of Lahore in Christ Church, Simla, August 13 and 20, 1905
(London, 1906) and Montgomery, Lefroy, pp. 130ff., 158ff.

152 Montgomery, Lefroy, pp. 174-178.

153 Methods of Missionary Work Among Moslems, (New York, 1906), pp.
225ff.

154 Stewart, "Henry Martyn and Serampore," p. 15.

155 Compare this to the C.M.S. Report of 1817 on the school at Kidder-
pore: "It is under the care of the missionaries, but is not likely to
alarm prejudice, as the schoolmaster is not a Christian." Once the idea
of educational evangelism had been accepted, however, many praised it as
the instrumentality by which Muslim, Hindu and other converts could be
drawn into the Church. Cf. Stock, History of C.M.S., I, 194-196.

156 For example cf. Grenville Ewing, "Defence of Missions from Christian
Societies to the Heathen World: A Sermon Preached before the Edinburgh
Missionary Society, February, 2, 1797," (Edinburgh, 1804) and D. Mackichan,
The Missionary Ideal in the Scottish Churches (London, 1927) pp. 68ff.
For a fine bibliography on Scottish missions cf. Elizabeth G. K. Hewat,
Vision and Achievement, 1796-1956: A History of the Foreign Missions of
the Churches United in the Church of Scotland (Edinburgh, 1960).

157 James Bryce, A Sketch of the State of British India: with a View of Pointing out the Best Means of Civilizing its inhabitants, and diffusing the Knowledge of Christianity throughout the Eastern World (Edinburch, 1810).

158 By 1827 there were some 80 small schools with some 3,000 pupils in Western India. Cf. Hewat, Vision and Achievement, p. 43. Two books by J. Murray Mitchell are of interest: Memoir of the Rev. Robert Nesbit, Missionary of the Free Church of Scotland (London, 1858) and In Western India, Recollections of My Early Missionary Life (Edinburgh, 1899).

159 Basic sources are the writings of Duff plus George Smith, The Life of Alexander Duff (2 vols, London, 1879); W. P. Duff, Memorials of Alexander Duff, D.D., (London, 1890); Lal Behari Day, Recollections of Alexander Duff, D.D., LL.D., and of the Mission College which He founded at Calcutta (London, 1879);   Thomas Smith, Alexander Duff, D.D., LL.D. (London, 1883); and Wm. Paton, Alexander Duff, Pioneer of Missionary Education (London, 1923).

160 G. Smith, Duff, II, 186.

161 Ibid., II, 239.

162 Paton, Duff, pp. 227f.

163 Some held that if Ram Mohun Roy, the Erasmus of India, had met Duff forty years earlier he would have become the Luther of India. Roy saw the Christian religion as a regenerative force and English as a doorway to Western learning and science. He founded the Brahmo Samaj which taught the worship of one supreme eternal God. It was he who urged Duff's first students to study the Bible: "Read and judge for yourselves. Not compulsion, but enlightened persuasion, which you may resist if you choose, constitues you yourselves judges of the contents of the book." Cf. G. Smith, Duff, I, 121ff., 219ff.; Paton, Duff, pp. 63ff.; Stock, History of the C.M.S., I, 305.

164 G. Smith, Duff, I, 109f.

165 Quoted in G. Smith, Duff, I, 108f.

166 Duff's attitude to other religions is suggested by his comments on Hinduism in India and India Missions: "It is nothing else than a stupendous superstructure raised upon this one grand central principle as its foundation-stone, namely; the principle of exclusive self-reliance, exclusive self-righteousness....all circulate forever around the grand central, but false and detestable principle that man, though fallen and sinful, may work out by his own unaided strength a title to the divine favour, a right to celestial rewards or to supreme beatitude" (p. 273). Or again "All your own learning we consider as teeming with error; all your religion as false; all your gods as monsters of wickedness. We have come hither, therefore to 'overturn, overturn, overturn,' the whole" (pp. 536f.). Although Duff expressed his love for the people of India, there was none to be lost on India's religions.

167 Quoted in Paton, Duff, p. 66. Also cf. India and India Missions, pp. 426ff.

168 The Church of Scotland College and Duff College (Free Church) were merged in 1908 to form the Scottish Churches College. By that date these institutions had reached thousands of students.

169 Examples of the caliber of these converts are: Mohesh Chunder Ghose (baptized August 28, 1832), Krishna Moham Banerjea (baptized Oct. 17, 1832, later C.M.S. teacher and Anglican minister), Gopinath Nuni (baptized Dec. 14, 1832, later Presbyterian minister), and Anundo Chund Mozumdar (baptized April 21, 1833). Other Muslim converts baptized by Duff and Ewart included Muhammad Bakar (December 1850), Ele Bua (early 1871), and Maulavi Abdulla (August, 1851). Cf. Julius Richter, A History of Missions in India, p. 184.

170 G. Smith, Duff, I, 280-83.

171 Day, Recollections, pp. 210ff., esp. 241f.

172 G. Smith, <u>Duff</u>, I, 454f., 476f.; II, 122f.

173 Quoted in <u>Ibid</u>., I, 145.

174 J. N. Farquhar, <u>Modern Religious Movements in India</u> (New York, 1915).

175 G. Smith, <u>Duff</u>, I, 251f.

176 <u>Ibid</u>., II, 61ff. and Paton, <u>Duff</u>, pp. 206f.

177 Stock, <u>History of the C.M.S.</u>, I, 304f. and Paton, <u>Duff</u>, pp. 59f.

178 Neill, <u>History of Christian Missions</u>, pp. 274f. and A. Mayhew, <u>The Education of India</u> (London, 1926) pp. 10ff.

179 G. Smith, <u>Duff</u>, II, 245.

180 Duff began the <u>Calcutta Christian Observer</u> and contributed to the <u>Friend of India</u> (edited by J. Marshman, 1835-1852, M. Townsend, 1852-1859, and George Smith, 1859-1875). He helped John Kaye start the <u>Calcutta Review</u> in 1844 and acted for a time as editor. His ideas are set forth in <u>India and India Missions</u> (Edinburgh, 1839); <u>Speech Before Assembly of the Church of Scotland, 1835, in Missionary Addresses</u> (Edinburgh, 1850); <u>Missions the Chief End of the Christian Church</u>...(Edinburgh, 1839); <u>Proposed Modes of extending the Foreign Mission Operations of the Free Church of Scotland, with an Appeal for Increase of Means and more fervent Prayer</u> (before the Assembly of 1865 and other addresses....) (Edinburgh, 1872); <u>Evangelistic Theology</u> (Edinburgh, 1868); and <u>The Indian Rebellion; its Causes and Results</u> (London, 1858) which contains some 25 letters to Dr. Tweedie on the Mutiny.

181 For example cf. Paton, <u>Duff</u>, pp. 213-215.

182 Cf. Wilson's <u>Exposure of the Hindoo Religion</u> (Bombay, ca. 1832); <u>A Second Exposure of the Hindoo Religion</u> (Bombay, 1834); <u>The Doctrine of Jehovah addressed to the Parsis: A Sermon preached on the occasion of the Baptism of two youths of that Tribe, May, 1839</u> (Edinburgh, 1847); and <u>The Parsi Religion: as Contained in the Zand-Avasta</u> (Bombay, 1843).

183 George Smith, <u>The Life of John Wilson</u> (London, 1878), pp. 113ff. Other information is found in John Wilson, <u>A Memoir of Mrs. Margaret Wilson</u> (Edinburgh, 1838).

184 John Wilson, <u>Narrative of a Missionary Journey in Gujerat and Cutch</u> (Bombay, 1838) and <u>The Darkness and the Dawn in India</u> (1853).

185 Robert Hunter, <u>History of the Missions of the Free Church of Scotland in India and Africa</u> (London, 1873), pp. 233, 260, 264.

186 For these educational principles and his attitude to culture, religions, cf. <u>The Evangelization of India</u> (Edinburgh, 1849); <u>Memoir on the Cave-Temples and Monasteries of Western India</u> (Bombay, 1850); <u>The Lands of the Bible Visited and Described</u> (2 vols., Edinburgh, 1847); <u>History of the Suppression of Infanticide in Western India</u> (Bombay, 1855); and his Grammar and Exercise books for Marathi. Also cf. Paton, <u>Duff</u>, pp. 210f.

187 George Smith, <u>Stephen Hislop, Pioneer Missionary and Naturalist in Central India from 1844 to 1863</u> (London, 1889) and Hewat, <u>Vision and Achievement</u> pp. 102-113. Also cf. T. W. Gardiner: <u>A House of Prayer for all Nations; The Nagpur Mission of the Church of Scotland, 1845-1945</u>; and <u>Hislop College; Diamond Jubilee, 1883-1945</u>.

188 John Braidwood, <u>True Yoke-Fellows in the Mission Field: The Life and Labours of the Rev. John Anderson and the Rev. Robert Johnston</u> (London, 1862), pp. 490, 525ff., 538ff., et passim.

189 Hewat, <u>Vision and Achievement</u>, p. 89f.

190 The Free Church and United Presbyterians (merged as the United Free Church, 1900) worked mainly in Rajputana (1860-) giving much attention to Christian medicine and service. Cf. <u>Our Church's Work in India: The Story of the Missions of the United Free Church of Scotland in Bengal, Santalia, Bombay, Rajputana, and Madras</u> (Edinburgh, n.d.) It is to be noted that with the further merger of the United Free Church and the Church of Scotland in 1929, the bulk of Scottish work in India came under one authority.

191 Basic sources include: J. F. W. Youngson, Forty Years of the
Punjab Mission of the Church of Scotland, 1855-1895 (Edinburgh, 1896); One
Hundred Years of Growth: A Brief History of the Work of the Church of
Scotland in the Punjab (Sialdot, 1957); H. F. L. Taylor, In the Land of
the Five Rivers; A Sketch of the Work of the Church of Scotland in the
Panjab (Edinburgh, 1906); Foreign Mission Committee Reports, 1901-1956,
Church of Scotland (General Assembly Reports); R. W. Weif, Foreign Missions
of the Church of Scotland (Edinburgh, 1900); and Hewat, Vision and
Achievement, pp. 115-126.
192 Youngson, Punjab Mission, pp. 78f.
193 Ibid., p. 218.
194 For fuller details cf. R. C. Thomas, "Annual Report, 1963-64," in
Murray College Magazine, April, 1964 and Hewat, Vision and Achievement,
pp. 124.
195 The literacy rate for 1963 was set at 19.2% according to Pakistan,
a Profile (Department of Films and Publication, Karachi, 1963).
196 Hewat, Vision and Achievement, pp. 116-119 and Youngson, Punjab
Mission, pp. 143ff.
197 For Taylor's plans of a presbytery cf. Youngson, Punjab Mission,
pp. 138f. For its actual development cf. pp. 170ff.
198 For this amazing growth cf. Ibid., pp. viii, 254ff., 290, and
Hewat, Vision and Achievement, p. 119.
199 Hewat, Vision and Achievement, pp. 121ff. and William Stewart, The
Church is There, in North India (Edinburgh, 1966). This united history
of the churches after 1904 will receive mention under the American
Presbyterians.
200 By 1912 the Congregationalists numbered 7,699 communicants and a
total membership of 13,972. These later became part of the United Churches
in North and South India. For resources on the early work of A.B.C.F.M.,
cf. Tufus Anderson, History of the Missions of the A.B.C.F.M. in India
(Boston, 1874); S. C. Barlett, Missions of the A.B.C.F.M. in India and
Ceylon (Boston, 1886); and W. E. Strong, The Story of the American Board
(Boston, 1910).
201 R. G. Wilder, Mission Schools in India of the A.B.C.F.M. (New
York, 1861), pp. 20-33.
202 Day, Recollections, pp. 118ff.
203 Ibid., pp. 138f.
204 Ibid., pp. 123-131.
205 Report of the General Missionary Conference, Allahabad, 1872-1873,
pp. 103-116.
206 World Missionary Conference, Edinburgh, 1910, Report of Commission
III, p. 443. Also cf. O. K. Chetty, William Miller (Madras, 1924) and
works by Miller, Indian Missions and How to View Them (Edinburgh, 1878),
Educational Agencies in India (Madras, 1893), and The Madras Christian
College. A Short Account of its History and Influence (Edinburgh, 1905).
207 Dr. D. Mackichan, Principal of Wilson College, Bombay in contrast
stressed that the conversion of pupils was the prime objective.
208 S. Radhakrishnan, East and West in Religion (London, 1933) and the
contrasting opinion of H. Kraemer.
209 W. B. Davis, A Study of Missionary Policy and Methods in Bengal
from 1793 to 1905 (unpublished thesis, New College, University of Edinburgh,
1942), pp. 170ff.
210 The Missionary Controversy (London, 1890), esp. pp. 1-14.
211 Ibid., pp. 83ff.
212 Farquhar edited three useful books: the Religious Quest of India,
the Religious Life of India, and the Heritage of India. His ideas on
fulfillment are found in The Crown of Hinduism (Oxford, 1913). Also cf.
Eric J. Sharpe, Not to Destroy but to Fulfil, the contribution of J. N.

Farquhar to Protestant Missionary Thought in India before 1914 (Uppsala, 1965) and a review of it by Duncan B. Forrester in The Indian Journal of Theology, 15 (1966), pp. 67-69. Sharpe examines the factors shaping this concept of fulfillment. Influential were: the change in Protestant theology and attitude towards other religions, the acceptance of the principle of evolution and historical criticism, the rise of the science of comparative religion under Max Müller, the renaissance of non-Christian religions, and the failure of Christian higher education to convert the upper classes. These prompted Farquhar to attempt a new approach.

213 Alfred G. Hogg's thoughts are found in Karma and Redemption (London, 1909), Christ's Message of the Kingdom (Edinburgh, 1911), Redemption from this World; or the Supernatural in Christianity (Edinburgh, 1922), The Challenge of the Temporal Process (Madras, 1934), and The Christian Message to the Hindu (Duff Lectures for 1945, London, 1947). A similar view is found in D. S. Carins, Christianity in the Modern World (2nd ed. London, 1907), "The Need for Apologists,"Student World, 4 (1911), 49ff., and "The Christian Message. A Comparison of Thought in 1910 and in 1928," I.R.M., 18 (1929), 321ff.

214 E. M. Wherry, Our Missions in India, 1834-1924 (Boston, 1926), pp. 88, 175f., 191ff., and William Wanless, An American Doctor at Work in India (New York, 1932). By 1900-1901, the Presbyterian Church, U.S.A. had 12 foreign doctors, 20 hospitals and dispensaries treating over 125,000 patients in India. Cf. Beach, Statistics and Atlas, p. 27.

215 For this dedicated phase of the work cf. John Jackson, Lepers, Thirty-One Years' Work Among Them: Being the History of the Mission to Lepers in India and the East, 1874-1905 (London, 1906) and Mary Reed, Missionary to Lepers (London, 11th edition, 1912); Lee S. Huizenga, Mary Reed of Chandag (Grand Rapids, Michigan, 1939); and E. Mackerchar, Miss Mary Reed of Chandag (London, n.d.).

216 J. M. Thoburn, The Christian Conquest of India (New York, 1906), p. 186.

217 It was the Letters on Missions by Swan, a missionary to Siberia, which had inspired Parker to go to China.

218 W. Burns Thomson, Reminiscences of Medical Missionary Work (London, 1895) and A Memoir of William Jackson Elmslie (London, 1881).

219 Youngson, Punjab Mission, pp. 125ff., 176ff., 273ff. and Hewat, Vision and Achievement, pp. 122ff.

220 J. Lowe, Medical Missions, their Place and Power (intro. by Sir. Wm. Muir, London, 1886), pp. 210ff. Also cf. the Quarterly Paper of the Edinburgh Medical Missionary Society; Lectures on Medical Missions (intro. by Professor William Alison, Edinburgh, 1849); David Brodie, The Healing Art: the Right Hand of the Church (Edinburgh, 1859); J. R. Williamson (University of Edinburgh), The Healing of the Nations: A Treatise on Medical Missions (London, 1899); R. Fletcher Moorshead, Appeal of Medical Missions (London, 1913); and H. T. Hodgkin, The Way of the Good Physcian (London, 1915).

221 Their adopted son, Henry Martyn Clark tells of those events which led him to become a medical missionary. Cf. Clark, pp. 238ff.

222 Quoted in Clark, Clark, p. 294.

223 Lowe, Medical Missions, pp. 39f., 57ff., 77, 182ff., 230, et passim, and Thomson, Memoir...Elmslie.

224 E. J. Neve, A Crusader in Kashmir (Biography of Arthur Neve, London, 1928), pp. 64-65. Also cf. Arthur Neve, Thirty Years in Kashmir (London, 1913) and Beyond the Pir Panjal (London, 1914).

225 Neve, Crusader, pp. 33f.

226 Ibid., p. 75.

227 Ibid., pp. 81ff.

228 Ibid., pp. 13ff.

229   Alice M. Pennell, _Pennell of the Afghan Frontier_ (London, 1914) pp. 183-187. Also of interest is T. L. Pennell, _Among the Wild Tribes on the Afghan Frontier_ (London, 1909).

230   A. Pennell, _Pennell_, pp. 111ff., 405ff. In 1897, seven converts were baptized. By 1901 there were 26 recognized Christians, by 1910, the total was 100.

231   _Ibid._, p. 397.

232   _Ibid._, pp. 398ff. For an account of the medical work and struggling church at Quetta (1900-) cf. Sir Henry Holland, _Frontier Doctor_ (London, 1958).

233   Beach, _Statistics and Atlas_, p. 25.

234   Cf. Annual Reports of the ZBMM and CHZMS and works such as A. R. Cavalier, _In Northern India. A Story of Mission Work in Zenanas, Hospitals, Schools, and Villages_ (London, n.d.); Thomas Carter, _Rose Harvey, Friend of the Leper_ (London, n.d.); Irene Barnes, _Behind the Pardah_ (CEZMS, London, 1898); E. M. Tonge, _Fanny Jane Butler, Pioneer Medical Missionary_ (London, n.d.); A. C. Wilson, _Irene Petrie, Missionary to Kashmir_ (London, 1901); and the works of Amy Carmichael, _Overweights of Joy_ (London, 1907), _Lotus Buds_ (London, 1910), _Gold Cord, The Story of Fellowship_ (London, 1932).

235   In 1889 there were 60 overseas medical missionaries in India, in 1914. Cf. Latourette, _Expansion of Christianity_, VI, 191.

236   For fuller background material cf. James S. Udy, _Attitudes with the Protestant Churches of the Occident towards the Propagation of Christianity in the Orient--An Historical Survey up to 1914_ (Doctoral Dissertation, Boston University, 1952).

237   By 1900-1901, there were 35 American societies and 34 British Societies. Cf. Beach, _Statistics and Atlas_, p. 25. By 1914, American personnel numbered about five-sixths of the British numbers. The largest bodies in India were in this order: Church of England, American Methodist Episcopal Church, American Baptist Missionary Society, Presbyterian Church, U.S.A. Cf. Latourette, _Expansion of Christianity_, VI, 165, 169.

238   For fuller treatment cf. A. C. Chaplain, _Our Gold Mine: Story of American Baptist Mission in India_ (Boston, 1879); Dana M. Albaugh, _Between the Two Centuries: A Study of Four Baptist Mission Fields: Assam, South India, Bengal Orissa, and South China_ (Philadelphia, 1935); Victor H. Sword, _Baptists in Assam, A Century of Missionary Service, 1836-1936_ (Chicago, 1935).

239   Wherry, _Our Missions,_ pp. 300f.

240   Excellent sources on the Methodist Episcopal work include: J. M. Thoburn, _My Missionary Apprenticeship_ (New York, 1887), _Light in the East_ (Evanston, 1894), _India and Malaysia_ (Cincinnati, 1896), and _The Christian Conquest of India_ (New York, 1906); F. F. Oldham, _Thoburn--Called of God_ (New York, 1918); W. Butler, _The Land of the Veda_ (New York, 1871) and _From Boston to Bareilly and Back_ (New York, 1886); Mrs. R. Hoskins, _Clara A Swain, M.D., First Medical Missionary to the Women of the Orient_ (Boston, 1912); M. H. Harper, _The Methodist Episcopal Church in India. A Study of Ecclesiastical Organization and Administration_ (doctoral dissertation at the University of Chicago, Lucknow, 1936); and F. B. Price (editor), _India Mission Jubilee of the Methodist Episcopal Church in Southern Asia_ (Calcutta 1907). The writings of Murray T. Titus on work with Muslims also deserve special attention.

241   In addition to the Annual Reports of the Board of Foreign Missions of the Presbyterian Church, U.S.A., the main sources are: John C. Lowrie, _Two Years in Upper India_ (New York, 1850) and _Travels in North India_ (Philadelphia, 1842); E. M. Wherry, _Our Missions in India, 1834-1924_ (Boston, 1926); Joseph Warren, _A Glance Backward at Fifteen Years of Missionary Life in North India_ (Philadelphia, 1856); R. Spear, _Presbyterian Foreign Missions_ (Philadelphia, 1902); Arthur J. Brown, _A History of the_

Foreign Missionary Work of the Presbyterian Church in the U.S.A. (New York, 1937); and *Historical Sketches of the India Missions of the Presbyterian Church in the U.S.A.* (Allahabad, 1886).

242 Lowrie, *Two Years in Upper India*, p. 131.

243 Lowrie, *Travels in North India*, p. 121.

244 Stations were founded at Ludhiana (1834), Allahabad, Saharanpur, Sabathu (1836), Fattehgarh (1838), Mainpuri (1843), Furrukhabad, Agra (1844), first station in the Punjab at Jalandhar (1846), Ambala (1848), Lahore (1849), Futtehpur (1852), Dehra (1853), Rawalpindi and Roorkee (1856), Peshawar (1857), Kapurthala (1859), Etawah (1863), Hoshyarpur (1867), Muzafarnaggar (1869), Ferozepur (1870), Kolhapur (adopted 1870), Gwalior (1875), etc. Cf. Badley, Directory of 1876, p. 129.

245 Wherry, *Our Missions*, p. 91.

246 *Ibid.*, pp. 45f.

247 *Ibid.*, pp. 217ff., 294ff. Also cf. J. C. R. Ewing, *A Prince of the Church. Being a Record of the Life of the Rev. Kali Charan Chatterjee* (Chicago, 1918).

248 Wherry, *Our Missions*, pp. 306ff.

249 Cf. *Ibid.*, pp. 40ff., 84ff.

250 *Ibid.*, pp. 268ff.

251 For examples of Wherry's work cf. *Zeinab the Panjabi* (New York, 1895), *The Muslim Controversy* (London, 1905), *Islam and Christianity in India and the Far East* (New York, 1907) esp. pp. 208ff. plus other works which he edited.

252 Wherry, *Our Missions*, pp. 127ff., 334f.

253 *Ibid.*, pp. 30ff.

254 By 1904-5, there were 179 day schools with 8,034 pupils and two higher institutions with 705 students. Cf. Thoburn, *Christian Conquest*, p. 271.

255 Wherry, *Our Missions*, p. 279.

256 *Ibid.*, pp. 131, 284ff.

257 *Ibid.*, pp. 88, 90, 153.

258 Beach, *Statistics and Atlas*, p. 24.

259 Latourette, *Expansion of Christianity*, VI, 164, and Wherry, *Our Missions*, pp. 311f., 328ff. Wherry indicates that by 1924 the Presbyterian Church in India included: 85,225 members, 801 organized churches, 33 stations, 151 sub-stations, 246 missionaries and 1,288 Indian ministers, teachers and other Christian workers.

260 Wherry, *Our Missions*, pp. 88ff.

261 *Ibid.*, pp. 195ff.

262 *Ibid.*, p. 267.

263 *Ibid.*, p. 262.

264 A letter of an Indian elder in Allahabad to the Secretary of the Board of Foreign Missions reflected the urgent need to bridge this gap. He correctly observed that reconciliation of church and mission was basic to effective witness. Cf. *Ibid.*, pp. 269-271.

265 A Plan for Cooperation was drawn up by the Conference at Saharanpur, U.P., March 30-April 2, 1921 under Rev. J. C. R. Ewing, Secretary of the India Council and adopted by all parties in 1924. *Ibid.*, pp. 321-27.

266 J. T. Maclagan, elder of the Church of Scotland and later Secretary of the Foreign Mission Committee proposed such a scheme in his pamphlet of 1863.

267 Wherry, *Our Missions*, pp. 250-261.

268 For fuller treatment cf. Andrew Gordon, *Our India Mission. A Thirty Years' History of the India Mission of the United Presbyterian Church of North America Together with Personal Reminiscences* (Philadelphia, 1888) and Wm. B. Anderson and Charles R. Watson, *Far North in India: A Survey of the Mission Field and Work of the United Presbyterian Church in the Punjab* (Philadelphia, 1909).

269 R. Rouse, "William Carey's 'Pleasing Dream'," I.R.M., 38 (1949), pp. 181-189.

270 Proceedings of the South India Missionary Conference held at Ootacamund, 1858 (Madras, 1858), pp. 339f.

271 Ibid., p. 311.

272 Report of the Punjab Missionary Conference held at Lahore, December and January, 1862-1863 (Lodiana, 1863), pp. 20ff.

273 Robert Bruce reveals he is not completely free of medieval polemics when he refers to Muhammad as "that father of lusts and teacher of lies." Ibid., p. 79.

274 Ibid., pp. 31-38, for discussion p. 39ff.

275 Ibid., pp. 46f.

276 Ibid., pp. 55ff., 96ff., 107ff., 268ff.

277 Ibid., pp. 159-172.

278 Ibid., pp. 299-308 followed by discussion pp. 308-317.

279 Report of the General Missionary Conference held at Allahabad, 1872-1873 (London, 1873), pp. 52ff.

280 Ibid., pp. 55ff.

281 Ibid., pp. 58ff.

282 Ibid., pp. 65ff.

283 Ibid., p. 77.

284 Ibid., pp. 92ff.

285 Ibid., pp. 207-373.

286 Ibid., pp. 300ff.

287 Ibid., pp. 313ff.

288 Ibid., pp. 349ff.

289 Report of the Second Decennial Missionary Conference held at Calcutta, 1882-1883 (Calcutta, 1883), pp. 111ff., 324ff.

290 Ibid., pp. 32-52.

291 Ibid., pp. 55ff., 85ff., 251ff.

292 Ibid., p. 229.

293 Ibid., p. 230.

294 Report of the Third Decennial Missionary Conference held at Bombay, 1892-1893 (2 vols., pages numbered consecutively, Bombay, 1893), pp. 258ff., 413ff., 814ff., 664ff.

295 Ibid., pp. 5ff., 96ff., 541ff., 637ff.

296 Cf. works such as T. W. Arnold, Preaching of Islam.

297 Cf. letter of Sir. Wm. Muir describing the legal battle to secure the rights of Muslim converts, Report...Bombay, pp. 73ff.

298 Report of the Fourth Decennial Indian Missionary Conference held in Madras, 1902 (London, n.d.), pp. 62ff.

299 Ibid., pp. 68ff.

300 Ibid., pp. 336ff.

301 Ibid., pp. 340ff., 347ff.

302 Cf. S. K. Datta, The Desire of India (Edinburgh, 1908).

303 Latourette, Expansion of Christianity, VI, 212. Also valuable for examining the growth of church and mission are: J. P. Jones (editor), The Year Book of Missions in India, Burma, and Ceylon, 1912 (India, 1912) and P. O. Philip, Report on a Survey of Indigenous Christian Efforts in India, Burma and Ceylon (Poona, 1928).

304 Cf. H. Kraemer, Christian Message, pp. 424f.; Neill, History of Christian Mission, pp. 256ff.; and Peter Beyerhaus, "The Three Selves Formula: Is it Built on Biblical Foundations," I.R.M., 53 (1964), pp. 393-407. Beyerhaus notes: "What conclusion can we reach, after weighing both the truth and the dangers contained in Anderson's and Venn's idea of self-supporting, self-governing and self-propagating church as the goal of missions? Firstly, it must be said that this formula can never be the one absolute goal of missions...The goal of missions is nothing less than

the proclamation of the Kingdom in the whole world, until Christ, the Lord of missions, returns. Secondly, although the formula once served as an excellent strategical challenge, we can hardly continue to use it, in view of the fact that it has already been found to lead to an attitude of self-sufficiency and jealously, incompatible with the ecumenical age in which we now live. The truth will not die with the formula. In the future, every church in the world will be asked to be faithful to the Church's threefold ministry of leiturgia, diakonia, and martyria. But we shall have to insist increasingly that this ministry should be fulfilled in accordance with Christ's will for the Church, 'ut omnes unum sint'."

305 Cf. Julius Richter, Indische Missionsgeschicte (Gütersloh, 2nd edition, 1924) esp. pp. 391-449; Latourette, Expansion of Christianity, VI, 189ff.; and Jones, Year Book...1912, pp. 344-355.

306 Latourette, Expansion of Christianity, VI, 206. For later attempts to understand the bearing of social units on mission cf. J. W. Pickett, Christian Mass Movements in India. A Study with Recommendations (Cincinnati, 1933) and the writings of D. A. MacGavran, How Churches Grow, etc.

CHAPTER III: REFORMED AND ANGLICAN MISSIONS TO MUSLIMS IN THE NEAR EAST,
              1800-1910 (p. 97)

1 For example cf. A. L. Tibawi, British Interests in Palestine, 1800-1910: A Study of Religious and Educational Enterprise (London, 1961).

2 W. R. Hogg, "Protestant Missions, 1864-1914," in History's Lessons for Tomorrow's Mission. Milestones in the History of Missionary Thinking (W.S.C.F., Geneva, n.a.) pp. 160f. For fuller treatment cf. Latourette, Expansion of Christianity, esp. vol VI; Max Warren, The Missionary Movement from Britian in Modern History (London, 1965); and J. van den Berg, Constrained by Jesus' Love: An Inquiry into the Motives of the Missionary Awakening in Great Britain in the Period between 1689 and 1815 (Kampen, 1956).

3 H. A. R. Gibb and H. Bowen, Islamic Society and the West, A Study of the Impact of Western Civilization on Moslem Culture in the Near East (vol. I, parts I & II, London, 1950-1957), pp. 19ff., 39ff., 201ff.

4 Bernard Lewis, "Some Reflections on the Decline of the Ottoman Empire," Studia Islamica, 9 (1958), 111-127.

5 Wilbur W. White, The Process of Change in the Ottoman Empire (Chicago, 1937), pp. 29f.

6 Lists of these territorial losses with dates are found in Erich Bethmann, Bridge of Islam, A Study of the Religious Forces of Islam and Christianity in the Near East (London, 1953), pp. 96f. and W. Miller, The Ottoman Empire and its Successors, 1801-1927 (Cambridge, 1936).

7 Alfred C. Wood, A History of the Levant Company (London, 1935); A. L. Horniker, "Anglo-French Rivalry in the Levant from 1583 to 1612," Journal of Modern History, 18 (1946), 289-305; H. G. Rawlinson, "Early trade between England and the Levant," Journal of Indian History, 2 (1922-23), 107-116; and William Roe Polk, The Opening of South Lebanon, 1788-1840. A Study of the Impact of the West on the Middle East (Cambridge, Mass., 1963).

8 Lewis, "Decline of the Ottoman Empire...," pp. 125ff.; Gibb and Bowen, Islamic Society and the West, pp. 200-234; and G. Jaschke, "The Moral Decline of the Ottoman Dynasty," W.I., 4 (1955), 10-14.

9 For an excellent discussion of the three eras experienced by the Ottoman millets, cf. Gibb and Bowen, Islamic Society and the West, pp. 224-295.

10 Julius Richter, A History of Protestant Missions in the Near East (London, 1910), pp. 89-103.

11 J. E. Hutton, "Moravian Missions in Moslem Lands," M.W., 14 (1925), 125-130; John Holmes, Historical Sketches of the Missions of the United Brethren up to 1817 (London, 1827); The Advance Guard: 200 Years of Moravian Missions, 1732-1932 (London, n.d.); and Periodical Accounts Relating to the Missions of the Church of the United Brethren (numerous volumes, London, 1790-).

12 Eli Smith and H. G. O. Dwight, Missionary Researches in Armenia (London, 1834), p. 196.

13 The Rev. John Dickson and his friend Melville collected a number of Turkish MSS now on deposit at New College Library, Edinburgh. Cf. John R. Walsh, "The Turkish Manuscripts in New College, Edinburgh," Oriens, 12 (1959), 171-189. Also cf. Hewat, Vision and Achievement, pp. 9f.

14 W. Glen, Journal of a Tour from Astrachan to Karass (Edinburgh, 1823).

15 Wurtemberg evangelicals anticipating the millennium and believing the area near the Caspian Sea to be the only safe region (an interpretation of the Apocalypse) settled in Georgia about 1817. Although nearly two-thirds of the 1500 families died enroute, seven colonies settled in Odessa and Georgia. Smith and Dwight found some 2,000 souls alive. While the Basel missionaries were distinct from these emigrants, they helped them establish congregations.

16 Smith and Dwight, Researches, pp. 166-205; Richter, Missions in the N.E., pp. 97-103; and of more novel interest, H. A. Zwick and J. G. Schill, Calmuc Tartary or a Journey from Sarepta to several Calmuc Hordes of the Astracan Government (May 26-August 21, 1823) on behalf of the Russian Bible Society (London, 1831).

17 It was an accepted fact in the Ottoman Empire that the farther you traveled from the capital, the more dependent you were on local authorities. In some cases this resulted in greater liberty and heterodoxy (e.g. Persia) and in other cases in greater fanaticism (e.g. Arabia, Sudan, etc.).

18 Gibb and Bowen found that a German, French, English and Italian bibliography for the Near East in the nineteenth century alone listed over 20,000 titles. It remained a formidable task to sort superficial travel-ogues, hearsay, etc. from reliable accounts. In addition there are quan-tities of Greek, Arabic and Turkish sources. A great mass of Ottoman records and chronicles remain largely unexamined and unpublished in Istanbul. Cf. Islamic Society and the West, pp. 1f.

19 For basic historical sources of the A.B.C.F.M., cf. Rufus Anderson, History of the Missions of the American Board of Commissioners for Foreign Missions to the Oriental Churches (2 vols., Boston, 1872); Joseph Tracy, History of the American Board of Commissioners for Foreign Missions (New York, 2nd ed., 1842) I, 32ff. For the life of Fisk also cf. Alvan Bond, Memoir of the Rev. Pliny Fisk (Edinburgh, 1828); James Gardner, Memoirs of Christ-ian Missionaries (Edinburgh, 1850); and H. W. Pierson (ed.), American Missionary Memorial (New York, 1853), pp. 245-262.

20 Anderson, Oriental Churches, I, 1.

21 Ibid., I, ix.

22 Ibid., I, 2f.

23 Ibid., I, 10.

24 Daniel O. Morton, Memoir of Rev. Levi Parsons, First Missionary to Palestine from the United States (Burlington, 1830); Anderson, Oriental Churches, I, 1-15; and H. H. Jessup, Fifty-Three Years in Syria (2 vols., New York, 1910) I, 32ff. For the life of Fisk also cf. Alvan Bond, Memoir of the Rev. Pliny Fisk (Edinburgh, 1828); James Gardner, Memoirs of Christ-ian Missionaries (Edinburgh, 1850); and H. W. Pierson (ed.), American Missionary Memorial (New York, 1853), pp. 245-262.

25 Temple served 23 years with the Board in the Near East. Cf. Life and Letters of Rev. Daniel Temple. By his son, Rev. Daniel H. Temple (Boston, 1855). Jonas King, had recently been appointed professor of

Oriental Languages at Amherst College and was studying Arabic in Paris
when he voluteered for his first term of three years. He later became
the key figure of the Mission in Greece and helped link its evangelical
community with New College, Edinburgh.

26 Researches in Armenia (London, 1834) by Eli Smith and H. G. O.
Dwight contains 24 letters covering various stages of the survey with full
descriptions of the land, people and customs of various Muslim, Armenian
and Nestorian groups; their beliefs, superstitions and practices as seen
through the eyes of American evangelicals in the 1830s.

27 Ibid., p. 457.
28 Ibid., pp. 340f.
29 Ibid., pp. 409f.
30 Ibid., pp. 461f.
31 Ibid., pp. 464f.
32 Ibid., pp. 465f.

33 Annual Report, 1842 (A.B.C.F.M., Boston, 1842) pp. 57-85. Similar
instructions were given to Cyrus Hamlin, cf. Missionary Herald, (Boston,
1839), 39-44.

34 Richter reports that in 1906 these areas contained about 2.5 million
Christians and nearly 10 million Muslims. Missions in the Near East, p.
105.

35 E. G. Prime, Forty Years in the Turkish Empire. Memoirs of Rev.
Wm. Goodell, D.D. (New York, 4th ed., 1877), pp. 170-172.

36 H. A. O. Dwight, Christianity Revived in the East; or A Narrative
of the Work of God Among the Armenians of Turkey (New York, 1850) or its
second edition Christianity in Turkey: A Narrative of the Protestant
Reformation in the Armenian Church (London, 1854), a prime source for this
period.

37 George Herrick, Christian and Mohammedan, A Plea for Bridging the
Chasm (New York/London, 1912).

38 This plan was originally developed by Mr. Bell in Madras and taken
to England where Joseph Lancaster (1778-1838) gave it wider fame and helped
its spread to India, Africa, N.E. and U.S.A. The system used conduct
monitors and teaching monitors drawn from the more advanced students. It
was thus possible for one teacher to control several hundred children, and
to establish many schools with limited finances.

39 The exact cause for the hierarchy's appeal to the Sultan to banish
or imprison the reformers is difficult to determine. Perhaps the Sultan
had been delayed by the Egyptian-Turkey War (1831-1841) in which he depended on European favors. Hostile Jesuits would have supported the idea.
Dwight accused American Episcopal Bishop Horatio Southgate of personally
advising Matteos to subdue the dissenters (Dwight, Christianity Revived,
pp. 211-13). The fairest and fullest treatment of the matter is found in
P. E. Shaw, American Contacts with the Eastern Churches, 1820-1870,
(Chicago, 1937). Cyrus Hamlin believed that the Patriarch was under
pressure from Russia to root out this new heresy of Protestantism and
democratic ideals-My Life and Times (Boston, 1893), pp. 284, 353f., 406ff.

40 Anderson, Oriental Churches, I, 386-426 and Dwight, Christianity
Revived, pp. 326-332.

41 Dwight, Christianity Revived, pp. 267ff. and Richter, Missions in
the Near East, pp. 113ff.

42 Dwight, Christianity Revived, pp. 259-263 and Leon Arpee, The
Armenian Awakening (Chicago, 1909).

43 By 1895 the Board had in Turkey-Armenia: 14 stations, 268 outstations, 46 ordained and educational, 1 medical, 63 lady missionaries
plus 42 wives (total 152). Nearly 800 Armenian workers included 90
pastors, 117 catechists, 529 teachers and 66 others. The 111 churches
listed 11,835 full members, 20,000 adherents and Sunday Schools enrolling

32,092 adults and 24,132 children or a total Protestant community of about 50,000 souls. Richter, Missions in the N. E., p. 134.

44 The Armenians were tormented by the wavering promises by Russia and Britain regarding the hope of recovering a homeland. When a few agitated for this (1894), Turkish authorities and Kurdish raiders were given adequate excuse for a blood bath. Even the seasoned Latourette writes, "Thereupon the Ottoman Government, in an endeavour to preserve its authority, connived at and even ordered extensive massacres. These were by Turks and Kurds and wrought great destruction among the Armenian communities"-Expansion of Christianity, VI, 47. Richter summarizes the tragedy: 88,243 Armenians killed including 10,000 Evangelicals; 175 Orthodox priests and 25 Evangelical ministers tortured and killed; 646 Christian villages and 55 priests yield to Islam under threat of death (of which only a few are given liberty to return to Christianity); 568 churches including 50 Protestant ones lost (of which 282 were turned into mosques); 500,000 Armenians in some 2,493 villages robbed; 100,000 widows and orphans left destitute to face the terrible hard winter (1895-96)-Missions in the N.E., pp. 143ff. For fuller documentation, cf. F. D. Greene, The Armenian Crisis and the Rule of The Turk (London, 1895); J. Rendel Harris, Letters from Armenia (New York, 1897); Edwin M. Bliss, Turkey and the Armenian Atrocities (Philadelphia, 1896); W. J. Wintle, Armenia and Its Sorrows (London, 1896); Krikor Behesnilian, Armenian Bondage and Carnage (London, 1903); The Treatment of Armenians in the Ottoman Empire; Documents presented to Viscount Grey ...and...the Houses of Parliament (London, 1916); and Hagop Chakakjian, Armenian Christology and Evangelization of Islam (Leiden, 1965), pp. 95-108.   Regardless of causes and moral judgements, it was a holocast of personal suffering, death and sorrow.

45 Copies of the texts of many of these documents are found in Anderson, Oriental Churches, II, 8ff., 32ff.; Prime, Memoirs of Wm. Goodell, pp. 480-89; and Dwight, Christianity Revived, pp. 267-290.

46 Anderson, Oriental Churches, II, 44f.

47 Communicants had increased by a third and adherents had almost doubled. In 1908, there were 130 churches, 15,748 communicants, 41,802 adherents, 92 pastors, 102 lay preachers, 728 teachers, 8 colleges, 41 boarding and high achools, 312 elementary schools with a total of 20,861 students. The American Board had 20 stations, 269 outstations, and 42 ordained, 12 medical and 68 lady missionaries. Richter, Missions in the N.E., p. 160.

48 Financial assistance came from the American Board and England via the Turkish Mission Aid Society founded in 1854 (later named The Bible Lands' Mission Aid Society). This Society was formed by C. G. Young and the Earl of Shaftesbury when H. G. O. Dwight asked "How can British Christians help the Missions in Turkey?" Its support of existing missions, native evangelists, church construction, literature and schools extended also to Syria, Persia, Palestine and Egypt. Cf. W. A. Essery, The Ascending Cross, Some Results of Missions in Bible Lands. Stories of help given through the Bible Lands Mission's Aid Society in Fifty Years, 1854-1904 (London, 1905).

49 Richter, Missions in the N.E., pp. 122f.

50 Dwight quoted by Anderson, Oriental Churches, II, 214f.

51 Ibid., II, 472, also 113ff., 249ff. and Richter, Missions in the N.E., pp. 134ff.

52 The Near East and American Philanthropy, A Survey...by Frank A. Ross, et al. (New York, 1929), p. 165.

53 James L. Barton, Daybreak in Turkey (Boston, 2nd ed., 1908), pp. 181-193.

54 Anderson, <u>Oriental</u> <u>Churches</u>, II, 443-457; <u>The</u> <u>Higher</u> <u>Educational</u> <u>Institutions</u> <u>of</u> <u>the</u> <u>American</u> <u>Board</u> (Boston, 1904); George E. White, <u>Charles</u> <u>C</u>. <u>Tracy</u>,...<u>First</u> <u>President</u> <u>of</u> <u>Anatolia</u> <u>College</u>, <u>Marsovan</u> <u>Turkey</u> (Boston, 1918) and <u>Advertising</u> <u>with</u> <u>Anatolia</u> <u>College</u> (Grinnell, Iowa, 1940).

55 Cyrus Hamlin, <u>My</u> <u>Life</u> <u>and</u> <u>Times</u> (Boston, 1893), p. 414. Also by Hamlin are <u>Among</u> <u>the</u> <u>Turks</u> (Boston, 1878) and "Fifty Years of Missionary Education in Turkey," (2nd in a set of six lectures for 1888-89, Grave's Lectures, Library of New Brunswick Seminary, New Jersey).

56 Christopher Robert, a New York merchant contributed some $400,000 before his death (1878).

57 Hamlin, <u>My</u> <u>Life</u> <u>and</u> <u>Times</u>, pp. 276ff., <u>et</u> <u>passim</u>.

58 In 1910, only 5% of the students were non-Christian. In 1872 there were prayers morning and evening, Bible study and Sunday worship. Anderson, <u>Oriental</u> <u>Churches</u>, II, 450ff.

59 G. Washburn, <u>Fifty</u> <u>Years</u> <u>in</u> Constantinople (Boston, 1909), esp. pp. 296ff. and Caleb F. Gates, <u>Not</u> <u>to</u> <u>Me</u> <u>Only</u> (Princeton, 1940), pp. 159ff.

60 Cf. Mary Mills Patrick, <u>Under</u> <u>Five</u> <u>Sultans</u> (New York, 1929) and <u>A</u> <u>Bosporus</u> <u>Adventure</u>. <u>Istanbul</u> (<u>Constantinople</u>) <u>Women's</u> <u>College</u>, <u>1871-</u> <u>1924</u> (Stanford, 1934) plus G. D. Jenkins, <u>An</u> <u>Educational</u> <u>Ambassador</u> <u>to</u> <u>the</u> <u>Near</u> <u>East</u> (Mary M. Patrick) (New York, 1925).

61 President Dwight J. Simpson in a letter to the author (Sept. 6, 1966) wrote: "As you will guess, after passage of more than 100 years, Robert College's nature has changed a great deal. We are now an entirely secular institution and indeed this is one of the requirements of Turkish Law that we have no religious content whatever. Missionary activity in any form is explicitly forbidden by Turkish Law and, of course, we fully comply."

62 Cf. Anderson, <u>Oriental</u> <u>Churches</u>, II, 489ff.; W. S. Tyler, <u>Memoir</u> <u>of</u> <u>Rev</u>. <u>Henry</u> <u>Lobdell</u>, <u>M.D.</u>, <u>Late</u> <u>Missionary</u> <u>of</u> <u>the</u> <u>American</u> Board at <u>Mosul</u> (Boston, 1859); George Herrick, <u>An</u> <u>Intense</u> <u>Life</u>. <u>A</u> <u>Sketch</u> <u>of</u> <u>the</u> <u>Life</u> <u>and</u> <u>Works</u> <u>of</u> <u>Rev</u>. <u>Andrew</u> <u>T</u>. <u>Pratt</u>, <u>M.D.</u>, <u>Missionary</u>...<u>in</u> <u>Turkey</u>, <u>1852-1872</u> (New York, n.d.); E. M. Dodd, <u>The</u> <u>Beloved</u> <u>Physician</u>. <u>An</u> <u>Intimate</u> <u>Life</u> <u>of</u> <u>the</u> <u>Wm</u>. <u>S</u>. <u>Dodd</u> (privately printed, 1931); Clarence D. Ussher, <u>An</u> <u>American</u> <u>Physician</u> <u>in</u> <u>Turkey</u> (Boston, 1917); and Alice Shepard Riggs, <u>Shepard</u> <u>of</u> <u>Aintab</u> (New York, 1920).

63 Richter, <u>Missions</u> <u>in</u> <u>the</u> <u>N.E.</u>, pp. 149ff. and Latourette, <u>Expansion</u> <u>of</u> <u>Christianity</u>, VI, 52.

64 Sources include: Richter, <u>Missions</u> <u>in</u> <u>the</u> <u>Near</u> East, 279ff.; <u>A</u> <u>Century</u> <u>of</u> <u>Mission</u> <u>Work</u> <u>in</u> <u>Iran</u> (Beirut, 1936); John Elder, <u>History</u> <u>of</u> <u>the</u> <u>American</u> <u>Presbyterian</u> <u>Mission</u> <u>to</u> <u>Iran</u>, <u>1834-1960</u> (Iran, n.d.); Aubrey R. Vine, <u>The</u> <u>Nestorian</u> <u>Churches</u>; <u>a</u> <u>concise</u> <u>history</u> <u>of</u> Nestorian Christianity <u>in</u> <u>Asia</u> <u>from</u> <u>the</u> <u>Persian</u> <u>Schism</u> <u>to</u> <u>the</u> <u>Modern</u> <u>Assyrians</u> (London, 1937); W. C. Ehrhardt, <u>The</u> <u>Oldest</u> <u>Christian</u> <u>People</u>; <u>a</u> <u>Brief</u> <u>Account</u> <u>of</u> <u>the</u> <u>History</u> <u>and</u> <u>Traditions</u> <u>of</u> <u>the</u> <u>Assyrian</u> <u>People</u> <u>and</u> <u>the</u> <u>Fateful</u> <u>History</u> <u>of</u> <u>the</u> <u>Nestorian</u> <u>Church</u> (New York, 1926); A. J. Maclean and W. H. Browne, <u>The</u> <u>Catholicos</u> <u>of</u> <u>the</u> <u>East</u> <u>and</u> <u>His</u> <u>People</u> (Nestorians) (London, 1892); and John Stewart, <u>Nestorian</u> <u>Missionary</u> <u>Enterprise</u>: <u>A</u> <u>Church</u> <u>on</u> <u>Fire</u> (foreward by Samuel M. Zwemer, Edinburgh, 1928).

65 The great culture and country of Iran (628,000 sq. miles) with its lofty plateaus and desert sands, its varied temperatures, races, and tongues stood between Ottoman Turkey, the frontier Kurds, Czarist Russia, the nomadic Afghans and the British presence in India and the Gulf. Anglo-Russian rivalry continued until 1922. By 1850, Russia gained extra-territoriality in the north and Britain in the south. The Shah ruled as an absolute monarch through a grand vizier and a chain of departments according to Shi'ite Law, but the government was notorious for corruption and oppressive taxation. The mujtahids, Muslim clergy, had control of

various legal aspects and were ever in a power struggle with the Shah.
Citizens and missionaries often knew not which authority to obey and
local figures (e.g. Kurds)   made their own law.

66 Lake Urumia or Oroomiah is 80 miles long and 30 miles wide. The
key city in the plain is today called Rezaieh. Perkins estimated there
were 30-40,000 Nestorians in the plains and 100,000 in the mountains, but
a more accurate tabulation was probably 25,000 and 50,000. Once the
largest and most favored Christian group in the Near East, they bore
various titles, e.g. Nestorian, Assyrian, Syrian, Chaldean, or Aramaeans.
The Nestorian Church separated from Rome after the Council of Chalcedon
(451) and experienced a golden era from the 4th to 13th centuries. Its
25 flourishing colleges produced the most learned doctors, scholars,
authors, from China to Palestine. The Nestorian Tablet in China and
reports of 200,000 converts in Central Asia reveal at least limited success. The Mongol invasions had a shattering effect upon them as millions
of Christians were massacred. One estimate claims that 9 million Christians in Iran and Mesopotamia died. The Nestorian Church never recovered
from this and by early 19th century numbered under 125,000 members.

67 Rome's charge of Nestorian heresy regarding Christ's nature
seemed unjust in that they held to the Nicene Creed, using it in their
liturgy. Anderson, Oriental Churches, I, 197.

68 Justin Perkins, A Residence of Eight Years in Persia Among the
Nestorian Christians (Andover, 1843), p. 9. Also cf. his work, Missionary Life in Persia (Boston, 1861) and Life of Rev. Justin Perkins, D.D.,
by H. M. Perkins (Chicago, 1887).

69 The Instructions given by Anderson are quoted in Perkins, Eight
Years, pp. 27-32. This is in line with Smith's report that a missionary
among the Nestorians would feel "he has found a prop upon which to rest
the lever that will overturn the whole system of Mohammedan delusion;
that he is lighting a fire which will shine upon the corruption of the
Persian on the one side, and upon the barbarities of the Kurd on the
other, until all shall come to be enlightened by its brightness; and
the triumph of faith will crown his labor of love." Quoted in R. E.
Speer and R. Carter, Report on India and Persia (New York, 1922), pp. 383f.

70 Dr. Stoddard's "A Grammar of the Modern Syriac Language," Journal
of the American Oriental Society, 5 (1853) became the base for Theodor
Neoldeke's Grammatik der Neusyrichen Sprach (Leipsic, 1868) and A. M.
MacLean's Grammar of the Dialects of the Vernacular Syriac (Cambridge,
1895) and Dictionary of the Dialects of Vernacular Syriac (Oxford, 1900).

71 Perkins, Eight Years, pp. 497ff.

72 By 1867-1877 there were 58 village schools with 1,023 pupils under
evangelical teachers in addition to the seminaries. Also cf. Wm. M.
Miller, How the Revivals Came to Persia (New York, 1933); D. F. Fiske,
The Cross and the Crown, or Faith working by Love as exemplified in the
Life of Fidelia Fiske (Boston, 1868); David T. Stoddard, Narrative of
the Revival of Religion among the Nestorians of Persia (Boston, 1848);
and Joseph P. Thompson, Memoir of Rev. David Tappan Stoddard, Missionary
to the Nestorians (New York, 1858).

73 Perkins, Eight Years, pp. 496f.

74 Ibid., p. 502.

75 Asahel Grant, The Nestorians; or The Lost Tribes (New York, 1845);
Thomas Laurie, Dr. Grant and the Mountain Nestorians (Boston, 1853);
Dwight W. Marsh, The Tennessean in Persia and Koordistan. Being the
Scenes and Incidents in the Life of Samuel Audley Rhea (Philadelphia,
1869) and Mary Jewett, Twenty-Five Years in Persia (Chicago, 1898). The
mission program of Nestorian evangelists in the mountains was supervised
by William Shedd and resulted in 16 congregations by 1863. Cf. Anderson,
Oriental Churches, II, 285 and Wm. A. Shedd, Islam and the Oriental
Churches, their Historical Relations (New York, 1908).

76 Anderson, _Oriental Churches_, I, 318ff. and Latourette, _Expansion of Christianity_, VI, 56.

77 Anderson, _Oriental Churches_, I, 212f. and Shaw, _American Contacts_, pp. 94ff.

78 Anderson, _Oriental Churches_, II, 317.

79 Elder, _Mission to Iran_, pp. 21ff.

80 Anderson, _Oriental Churches_ II, 320ff. and Presbyterians in Persia, below.

81 About one-fifth of Syria's population was Christian (Greek, Jacobite, Armenian, Maronite and Latin). By sheer determination and protective terrain they had resisted Muslim rule. Roman Catholic contacts continued after the Crusades through the Maronite College at Rome (founded by Pope Gregory XIII, 1584), the Capuchins (1627), Carmelites (1650), Lazarites (1784), the Oriental Seminary at Ghazir (1846) and Beirut (1874, later named St. Joseph University). Muslim sects such as the Druze tribes (linked to Fatmid Caliphs of Egypt) and the Nusairis (mixture of Christian-pagan-Shiᶜite beliefs) also tried to maintain their autonomy from Ottoman-Turkish overlords. Cf. Latourette, _Expansion of Christianity_, VI, 41ff.; Richter, _Missions in the Near East_, pp. 181ff.; James S. Dennis, _A Sketch of the Syrian Mission_ (New York, 1872); P. Hitti, _The Origins of the Druze People and Religion_ (New York, 1928); and A. H. Hourani, _Minorities in the Arab World_ (London, 1947) and _Syria and Lebanon: A Political Essay_ (London, 1946).

82 Anderson, _The Oriental Churches_, I, 236ff., 254ff.

83 _Ibid._, I, 261ff.

84 _Ibid._, I, 52-72; and Isaac Bird, _The Martyr of Lebanon_ (Boston, 1864).

85 F. E. H. Haines, _Jonas King, Missionary to Syria and Greece_ (New York, 1879) and Jessup, _Fifty-Five Years in Syria_, I, 38ff.

86 H. H. Jessup, _The Women of the Arabs_ (London, 1874).

87 Jessup, _Fifty-five Years_, I, 299f.; Anderson, _Oriental Churches_, II, 387ff.; Frederick J. Bliss, _The Reminiscences of Daniel Bliss_ (New York, 1920), pp. 162ff.; and S. B. L. Penrose, _That They May Have Life: the Story of the American University of Beirut, 1866-1941_ (New York, 1941), pp. 8ff.

88 Anderson, _Oriental Churches_, II, 387.

89 _Ibid._, I, 264ff.

90 _Ibid._, I, 362ff., II, 355ff.

91 Charter membership included three former Druzes, ten former Greek Orthodox, plus representatives of four other traditions.

92 _Ibid._, I, 368f.

93 Jessup, _Fifty-five Years_, I, 243, 346.

94 Anderson, _Oriental Churches_, II, 396.

95 By contrast American Board ventures in Mesopotamia (Iraq) were spasmodic. At Mosul (1841-44, 1849-) the only results were a small congregation and schools. In this inhospitable climate and population only medical work by David Nutting, Henry Lobdell, and Henri Haskell began to alter public opinion. See C. H. Wheeler, _Ten Years on the Euphrates or Primitive Missionary Policy Illustrated_ (Boston, 1868). It would be well into the twentieth century before evangelical Christianity would take root in Iraq.

96 Anderson, _Oriental Churches_, I, 173f., 367, II, 482f., 497 and Richter, _Missions in the Near East_, pp. 171ff.

97 Anderson, _Oriental Churches_, II, 479f.

98 _Ibid._, II, 483ff.

99 George Herrick was one of the few who concentrated in this area.
Cf. Christian and Mohammadan: A Plea for Bridging the Chasm (New York,
1912). Herrick, after serving fifty years in the Near East offers stinging
criticism of the British government's policy (as illustrated by Lord
Cromer) condoning injustices in Near Eastern lands simply because they hid
under religious cloaks. This so-called tolerance at the sacrifice of
Christian conviction and ethics may have been profitable for British
interests but it failed to reform the lands concerned, lost the respect
of these peoples, and created a climate detrimental to Christian mission
(pp. 73ff., 229ff.). Rejecting the rational-controversial approach, Herrick
develops what may be called a service-ethical approach. Muslims are to
be approached with the fruits of Christianity that are welcomed (e.g.
education, bible and literature, scientific healing and relief during
calamity). While acknowledging that J. Christy Wilson, Samuel Zwemer
and D. M. Thornton place the emphasis on God's revelation in Christ as a
Word to be proclaimed, Herrick develops a slightly variant approach.
Christianity is preferred over Islam because of the consequences for
man. Its superior ethics are demonstrable by a comparison of the two
systems (documented in their source books: N.T. and Quran), of the founders (Jesus and Mohammed) and of recent historical events. He hopes that
a reform wing of Islam (by historical research) will come to Christ. It
is the approach of the Christlike life, the Christian ethic that will win
men to Christ. Herrick was heavy on the humanitarian emphasis of
education, service, and philanthropy (pp. 220-245). But his view was
balanced by stress on the Bible as revelation (205ff.), the motive of love
(215) and the missionary as herald (247f.). In a sense, Herrick
represents a mediating theology.

100 Ibid., pp. 205f.
101 Ibid., p. 215.
102 Ibid., pp. 247f.
103 Ibid., pp. 220f. Also of interest: J. L. Barton, The Christian
Approach to Islam (Boston, 1918).
104 Latourette, Expansion of Christianity, VI, 62ff.; Barton, Daybreak
in Turkey (1908), p. 237; and Prime, Goodell, p. v.
105 F. J. Bliss, The Religions of Modern Syria and Palestine (New
York, 1912), pp. 313-335 and George Antonius, The Arab Awakening (London,
1939).
106 For example cf. Hagop A. Chakmakjian, Armenian Christology and
Evangelization of Islam. A Survey of the Relevance of the Christology of
the Armenian Apostolic Church to Armenian Relations with its Muslim
Environment (Leiden, 1965) and John Joseph, The Nestorians and their
Muslim Neighbors. A Study of Western Influence on their Relations
(Princeton, 1961).
107 At the time of the transfer there were four stations, 9 men and
9 women missionaries, Syrian workers included 1 pastor, 11 catechists and
34 teachers. There were 8 churches, 245 communicants, 31 schools with
1,184 pupils, 1 theological seminary at Abeih, 1 seminary for girls
(Beirut), 1 press and the independent Syrian Protestant College. Later
stations at Abeih (1873), Zahleh (1872) and Schuweir (formerly Scottish)
united as the Lebanon Station. Cf. Richter, Missions in the N.E., p. 212.
108 H. H. Jessup, The Mohammedan Missionary Problem (Philadelphia,
1879), pp. 107-138.
109 Jessup, Fifty-five Years, II, 436, 503ff. and Richter, Missions
in the N.E., p. 210.
110 Jessup, Fifty-five Years, II, 541, 555-59. Also cf. H. H. Jessup,
Kamil Abdul Messiah, a Syrian Convert from Islam to Christianity
(Philadelphia, 1898).
111 Jessup, Fifty-five Years, II, 565, 617.

112 _Ibid._, II, 606-633, 519, 813, 641.
113 _Ibid._, II, 433f., 549, 753 and Richter, _Missions in the N.E._, p. 215.
114 Jessup, _Fifty-five Years_, II, 673ff.
115 _Ibid._, II, 508ff. and Richter, _Missions in the N.E._, pp. 221,, 228.
116 Bethmann, _Bridge to Islam_, pp. 152f.
117 Cf. writings of James S. Dennis, _A Sketch of the Syrian Mission_ (New York, 1872); _Social Evils of the Non-Christian World_ (London, 1899); and _Christian Missions and Social Progress. A Sociological Study of Foreign Missions_ (Edinburgh, 1905/6).
118 Cf. Appendix C.
119 Jessup, _Fifty-five Years_, II, 521, 651, 802f.; R. E. Speer, _Presbyterian Foreign Missions_ (Philadelphia, 1902), p. 207, Latourette, _Expansion of Christianity_, VI, 45, and Richter, _Mission in the N.E._, p. 217.
120 For comparative statistics in 1876 and 1908: churches 10 and 34, ordained pastors 3 and 10, licensed preachers 13 and 31, teachers 96 and 174, contributions by Syrians $1,252 and $49, 536. For more details cf. Jessup, _Fifty-five Years_, II, 814.
121 _Ibid._, I, 353.
122 Observations gained by study of _Ibid._, I, 142, 348, II, 604f., _et passim_.
123 _Ibid._, II, 483ff.; Richter, _Missions in the N.E._, p. 224; and Addison, _Christian Approach_, pp. 133f.
124 E.g., cf. Abraham Mitrie Rihbany. _The Syrian Christ_ (Boston, 1916) and P. K. Hitti, _The Syrians in America_ (New York, 1924). Writings by Lootfy Levonian, A. H. Hourani, E. J. Jurji as well as P. Hitti demonstrate the ability of Syrian Christians.
125 Jessup, _The Mohammedan Missionary Problem_ (1879), pp. 14ff.
126 Jessup, _Fifty-five Years_, I, 146.
127 Addison, _Christian Approach_, p. 138.
128 Jessup, _Fifty-five Years_, II, 546ff.
129 _Report of the Edinburgh World Missionary Conference_, IX, 255.
130 For fuller treatment cf. _A Century of Mission Work in Iran, 1834-1934_ (Beirut, 1936); J. Elder, _History of the American Presbyterian Mission to Iran, 1834-1960_ (Iran, n.d.); R. E. Speer, _Missions and Politics in Asia_ (New York, 1897); W. A. Shedd, "Relation of the Protestant Missionary Effort to the Nestorian Chruch," _M.R.W._, 8 (1895), 741ff.; Samuel G. Wilson, "Conversion of the Nestorians of Persia to the Russian Church," _M.R.W._, 12 (1899), 745ff.; Mary L. Shedd, _The Measure of a Man, the Life of William Ambrose Shedd_ (New York, 1922); W. A. Shedd, _Islam and the Oriental Churches, their Historical Relations_ (Philadelphia, 1904); _Under the War Clouds in Urmia, West Persia, 1914-19_, (Preabyterian Board, New York, 1919); and _The Assyrian Tragedy_ (Annemasse, 1934).
131 England, Russia, Turkey and France had legations there in 1872. By 1885, Austria, U.S.A. and Germany would join the list. The population of 200,000 included 1,000 Armenians, 5,000 Jews, numerous Parsis, several hundred Europeans and a majority of Muslims.
132 James Bassett, Persia, _Land of the Imans, A Narrative of Travel and Residence, 1871-1885_ (London, 1887), pp. 328f.
133 The growth of an ex-patriate population after W.W. II resulted in the formation of the Community Church and Community School. By 1953, they called their own pastor and became largely independent of the Mission.
134 Quoted in R. E. Speer, _Presbyterian Foreign Missions_, pp. 225f.
135 James Bassett, Persia, _Eastern Mission_ (Philadelphia, 1890), p. 230.

136 Ibid., pp. 171f.
137 S. G. Wilson, Perisa, Western Mission (Philadelphia, 1896),
p. 189. Also of interest, Persian Life and Customs (2nd edition, London,
1865) and Mary Jewett, Twenty-five Years in Persia (Chicago, 1898).
138 Bassett, Persia, Eastern Mission, pp. 175ff., 213, and John
Elder, Mission to Iran, pp. 33ff.
139 By 1940, this congregation numbered 90 communicants and had
branches in three neighboring villages. Cf. Elder, Mission to Iran,
pp. 56ff. and A Century of Mission Work in Iran, pp. 13ff.
140 Quoted in A Century, p. 26.
141 Bassett, Persia, Eastern Mission, pp. 281ff.
142 Elder, Mission to Iran, pp. 60, 87; A Century, pp. 155ff.
143 Elder, Mission to Iran, p. 95.
144 Ibid., pp. 74ff., et passim; A Century, pp. 79-104, S. G. Wilson,
Persia, Western Mission, pp. 311ff.; and Richter, Missions in the N.E.,
p. 323.
145 Robert Speer, The Foreign Doctor. A Biography of Joseph Plumb
Cochran, M.D., of Persia (Chicago, 1911).
146 Issac M. Yonan, The Beloved Physician of Teheran (Nashville,
1934) and J. C. Wilson, The Christian Message to Islam (New York, 1950),
pp. 120-132. For fuller treatment of this program cf. A Century, pp.
40-73; Richter, Missions in the N.E., pp. 320f.
147 One of the finest discussions in this area is the consultation
on The Healing Ministry in the Mission of the Church, Tubingen, May 19-
25, 1964, Division of World Mission and Evangelism of the World Council
of Churches, Geneva.
148 R. E. Speer and Russel Carter, Report on India and Persia (New
York, 1922), pp. 340, 403ff.
149 A Century, pp. 14, 108f., 124; Elder, Mission to Iran, pp. 38f.,
90.
150 Cf. John Joseph, Nestorians and their Muslim Neighbors. A
Study of Western Influence on Their Relations (Princeton, 1961).
151 A Century, pp. 31ff.
152 Elder, Mission to Iran, p. 97.
153 Speer and Carter, Report (1922), p. 393.
154 Ibid., pp. 510-516 contains a Report by J. C. Wilson. Also see
his books, The Christian Message to Islam and Introducing Islam (New
York, 1950).
155 For fuller treatment cf. E. L. Butcher, The Story of the Church
in Egypt (2 vols., London, 1897); Alfred J. Butler, The Ancient Coptic
Churches of Egypt (2 vols., Oxford, 1884); W. S. Blackman, The Fellahin
of Upper Egypt, (London, n.d.); S. H. Leeder, Modern Sons of the
Pharaohs. A Study of the Manners and Customs of the Copts of Egypt
(London, ca. 1918); and Latourette, Expansion of Christianity, VI, 21ff.
156 Later they were joined by the revived C.M.S. Mission (1882), the
interdenominational Egypt General Mission (1898) and smaller Scottish,
German, Canadian, Dutch, Pentecostal, YMCA-YWCA groups.
157 Technically, work in 1854 was begun by the Associate Reformed
Church of the West which soon became part of the United Presbyterian
Church of North America (1858).
158 Lansing's work is described in his book, Egypt's Princes; a
Narrative of Missionary Labor in the Valley of the Nile (Philadelphia,
1864).
159 John Hogg, son of a frugal devout mining family of Penston (south
of Edinburgh) and graduate of the University of Edinburgh was teaching
at the Scottish Boys' School at Alexandria. When the scheme of a Protestant College for Egypt fell through, his close friendship with
Lansing and McCague led him to accept the new appointment. Cf. Rena

L. Hogg, A Master-Builder on the Nile, Being a Record of the Life and
Aims of John Hogg, D.D., Christian Missionary (New York, 1914).
   160 Andrew Watson, The American Mission in Egypt, 1854-1896
(Pittsburgh, 1898).
   161 Esp. cf. J. R. Alexander, The Sound of Marching, Bestir Thyself
(Cairo, 1928) and A Sketch of the Story of the Evangelical Church in
Egypt (Alexandria, 1930).
   162 Cf. C. R. Watson, Egypt and the Christian Crusade (Philadelphia,
1907), In the Valley of the Nile, A Survey of the Missionary Movement in
Egypt (New York, 1908), What is this Moslem World (London, 1937) and
Earl Elder, Vindicating a Vision, The Story of the American Mission in
Egypt, 1854-1954 (Philadelphia, 1958).
   163 A. Watson, American Mission, pp. 129ff.
   164 Hogg, Master-Builder, p. 87.
   165 C. R. Watson, In the Valley of the Nile, pp. 162ff.
   166 J. R. Alexander, A Sketch, pp. 32ff.
   167 Erich Bethmann, Bridge of Islam, p. 177.
   168 Of interest are: S. A. Morrison, Middle East Survey: the Political, Social and Religious Problems (London, 1954) and Religious Liberty
in the Near East (London, 1949); D. M. Finney, Tomorrow's Egypt (Pittsburgh, 1939), Charles Adams, Islam and Modernism in Egypt (London, 1933);
Arthur Weigall, A History of Events in Egypt from 1798-1914 (New York,
1915); J. M. Landau, Parliaments and Parties in Egypt (New York, 1954);
James Dunne, Religious and Political Trends in Modern Egypt (Washington,
D.C., 1950); and M. Rifast Bey, The Awakening of Modern Egypt (London,
1947).
   169 Hogg, Master-Builder, p. 93.
   170 Ibid.
   171 A. Watson, American Mission, p. 140.
   172 Hogg, Master-Builder, p. 86.
   173 Some of these experiences are recounted in Egypt's Princes by
Lansing.
   174 A. Watson, American Mission, pp. 212-224.
   175 J. R. Alexander, A Sketch, pp. 12-15.
   176 A. Watson, American Mission, pp. 253ff.
   177 C. R. Watson, In the Valley of the Nile, pp. 167ff.
   178 The comparative statistics drawn up by Andrew Watson for each
five year report between 1870 and 1897 tells the story most effectively.
By 1897, there were 47 missionaires (incl. 16 ordained, 3 doctors, etc.).
Cf. American Mission, pp. 279ff. The Church's statistics concerning
communicants and clergy would more than double by W.W. I. By W.W. II
the Evangelical Church would list 155 clergymen, 150 organized churches,
and 22,000 members.
   179 Stanley, "The Policy of the Christian Church in Egypt," Church
Missionary Review (June, 1922), 152.
   180 J. R. Alexander, A Sketch, pp. 49f., et passim.
   181 C. R. Watson, In the Valley of the Nile, pp. 183ff., and A. Watson, American Mission, pp. 443ff. For more recent studies cf. W. S.
Rycroft and M. M. Clemmer, A Factual Study of the Middle East (United
Presbyterian Church, U.S.A., New York, 1962); Addison, Christian Approach, pp. 156ff.; Educational Conference at Assiut, 1937 (Papers of the
Egypt Inter-Mission Council, n.p., 1937); J. Heyworth-Dunne, An Introduction to the History of Education in Modern Egypt (London, 1938); and
R. C. Sloan, Recent Educational Advances in Egypt (Washington D.C., 1946).
   182 A Watson, American Mission, pp. 458ff.
   183 Hogg, Master-Builder, pp. 197ff.
   184 Hogg had turned down appealing offers from the Beirut College, an
Australian college, and sacrificed family life and finances to build this

distinctive school. Cf. Ibid., p. 180.

185 C. R. Watson, In the Valley of the Nile, p. 184.

186 In contrast, the American University at Cairo, like its sister institutions in Beirut and Istanbul, soon drifted out of the sphere of Christian concern. Lacking Christian norms and church controls, its faculty
became more involved in educational technique and public service projects
than with presenting the Christian faith. Its first President, Charles R.
Watson, son of Andrew Watson and for a time secretary of the United Presbyterian Mission Board was certainly not lacking in dedication or hope for
this school. Cf. C. R. Watson, What is this Moslem World (London, 1937),
pp. 163f. But an example of how the faculty soon became preoccupied with
other things is evident in Harris Erdman's New Learning in Old Egypt,
(New York, 1932).

187 A. Watson, American Mission, pp. 243, 300, 394 and C. R. Watson,
In the Valley of the Nile, p. 186.

188 A. Watson, American Mission, pp. 305-311.

189 Lansing, Egypt's Princes, pp. 275ff.

190 Hogg, Master-Builder, pp. 236ff.

191 Ibid., p. 250

192 A. Watson, American Mission, p. 360.

193 Hogg, Master-Builder, p. 255.

194 C. R. Watson, In the Valley of the Nile, p. 225.

195 R. Young, Light in Lands of Darkness (London, 1883) pp. 19, 255ff.

196 Joseph Wolff, Researches and Missionary Labours among Jews, Mohammedans, and other Sects...(London, 1835) and W. T. Gidney, The History of
the London Society for Promoting Christianity Amongst the Jews, from 1809-
1908 (London, 1908). Wolff had been baptized in the Church of Rome and
trained at the College of the Propaganda Fide. Arriving in England (1819),
he joined the Church of England and studied theology under Charles Simeon
and Arabic under Samuel Lee at Cambridge before his wide travels in the
Near East with the L.J.S.

197 When the Congregation De Propaganda Fide had to cut back its
efforts, Dr. Cleardo Naudi, a Roman Catholic of Malta appreciative of
Protestant thought and Scripture work, invited C.M.S. to come. In a letter
to Pratt (June, 1811), he says: "It now devolves upon you to enter on this
labour of propagating the Christian Faith among Infidels and of confirming
it among the Ignorant." Stock, History of the C.M.S., I, 222f.

198 Ibid., I, 121.

199 Ibid., I, 224ff.

200 William Jowett, Christian Researches in the Mediterrean from 1815
to 1820 in Furtherance of the Objects of the C.M.S. (London, 1822), passim.

201 William Jowett, Christian Researches in Syria and the Holy Land in
1823 and 1824 in Furtherance of the Objects of the C.M.S. (London, 1825),
pp. 24ff.

202 Ibid., p. 382. These documents disclose that Tibawi's charges that
C.M.S. set out to divide the Eastern Churches by proselytism are un-
founded. Cf. A. L. Tibawi, British Interests in Palestine, 1800-1901, A
Study of Religious and Educational Enterprise (Oxford, 1961).

203 Tibawi, British Interests, pp. 31-37.

204 Ibid., p. 57.

205 Gobat (who studied Arabic and the Quran in Paris and under Lee at
Islington College) felt drawn to the Muslim world. While appreciative of
Anglican liturgy and government, his evangelical outlook and frankness
earned him the attack of those of Tractarian sympathies. His indefatigable
venture in Abyssinia (cf. S. Gobat, Journal of Three Years' Residence in
Abyssinia, London, 1834) was admired by evangelicals. After serving in
Palestine (e.g. the Druzes of Lebanon) and Malta, he received priest's
orders in the Church of England (1845) and then appointment as bishop.

Cf. Samuel Gobat, Bishop of Jerusalem, His Life and Work. A Biographical
Sketch Drawn Chiefly from His own Journals (London, 1884). The portion up
to 1846 is largely autobiographical and the remainder, biographical.
    206 Gobat...Life and Work, pp. 236f. Also see his Circular Letter of
1847 describing the readers, fledging schools, and conversions from Judaism. pp. 239ff.
    207 Ibid., pp. 263ff.
    208 Ibid., pp. 271ff.
    209 Stock, History of the C.M.S., II, 145ff.
    210 Cf. James Graham, Jerusalem, Its Missions, Schools, Convents...
under Bishop Gobat (London, 1858). The humanitarian schemes of Consul
Finn, Stirring Times, or Records from Jerusalem (London, 1878). The evangelical concept of conversion was offensive to many in the British church
and Gobat became a target for attack. Even Tibawi seems enslaved to the
"Ottoman mentality" that any transference of persons from one religious
community to another is evil and that social-religious ferment is a threat
to empire or nation. His failure to appreciate religious freedom within a
pluralistic society seriously handicaps his evaluation of Gobat and C.M.S.
Thus he is quick to label any activity as a form of imperialism. His
judgment of Gobat fails to measure up with those of the Archbishop of Canterbury and such creditable historians as Richter and Latourette. Cf.
British Interests in Palestine, pp. 90-121.
    211 C.M.S. had been reduced to three remnant stations at Syra, Smyrna
and Cairo staffed by four German clergy (Hildner, Wolters, Kruse, Lieder)
and a Polish layman (Charles Sandrecski). A tour by John Bowen and Sandrecski (1849-50) prompted C.M.S. to act.
    212 Stock, History of the C.M.S., II, 143f.
    213 Gobat...Life and Work, pp. 275-280. Matters were not helped when
members of the high schurch party wrote a protest against Gobat's proceedings, had it signed by a thousand Anglicans and sent to the Greek Patriarch. Then (1853), four Anglican Archbishops sent a counter declaration
supporting Gobat. Cf. Ibid., pp. 286-296.
    214 Tibawi, British Interests, pp. 108ff.
    215 Gobat...Life and Work, p. 328.
    216 Stock, History of the C.M.S., III, 116ff. and Gobat...Life and
Work, pp. 384ff.
    217 Stock, History of the C.M.S., III, 121.
    218 Cf. Anon, Joseph Barclay, D.D., LL.D., Third Anglican Bishop of
Jerusalem. A Missionary Biography (London, 1883) and W. H. Hechler, The
Jerusalem Bishopric (London, 1883).
    219 Cf. Correspondence Respecting the Protestant Bishopric at Jerusalem
Printed and Presented to both Houses of Parliament, London, July, 1887.
    220 E.g. favoring close relations with Orthodox clergy, vestments and
such liturgical practices as the eastward position, altar lights, a mixed
chalice, ablutions, the necessity of morning communions, cf. Stock, History
of C.M.S., III, 527.
    221 G.F.P. Blyth, The Primary Charge (London, 1890) and submitted to
the Guardian (Dec. 1890); G.F.P. Blyth, Facts and Correspondence (Canterbury, 1891); Reply of the C.M.S. to the Charges made by the Right Rev.
George F. P. Blyth, D.D., Bishop of the Church of England in Jerusalem and
the East, 1891 (marked confidential); G.F.P. Blyth, The Second Charge
(London, 1893); and G.F.P. Blyth, The Third Triennial Charge (London, 1896).
The account of this ongoing duel is covered by Stock, History of the C.M.S.,
III, 523ff. and Tibawi, British Interests, pp. 357ff.
    222 H. Danby, Studies in Eastern Church History: Relations between
Anglican and the Eastern Orthodox Churches (Jerusalem, 1922) and Why'Chris-
tian' Schools? (Jerusalem, 1936); and the Annual Reports and publication,
Bible Lands, of the "Jerusalem and the East Mission" (1889-).

223 Some Anglicans rejected the idea of conventional missions to Muslims.
Canon Isaac Taylor read a paper on Islam at the Wolverhampton Church Congress (1887) which caused a stir. His view was that Islam stood halfway between Judaism and Christianity and that it was best to help perfect Islam
rather than to replace it. "We shall never convert the Moslems but we may
possibly transform Islam into Christianity." Although his views were challenged for lack of substance, his opinion influenced many of those who saw
Christianity as "truth", "ideals", and "ethics" rather than as a unique
"revelation" of and "relationship" to God in Jesus Christ.
224 Richter, Missions in the N.E., p. 253.
225 Stock, History of the C.M.S., III, 517ff. and IV, 124-28. By 1914
there were 6 ordained and 7 lay men, 10 wives and 29 other women. Notice
that this means women outnumbered men 3 to 1.
226 Tibawi, British Interests, p. 165 and Richter, Missions in the
N.E., pp. 252f.
227 Tibawi, British Interests, pp. 176f. and Latourette, Expansion of
Christianity, VI, 36.
228 Mrs. James Bowen-Thompson, The Daughters of Syria (2nd ed. edited
by H. B. Tristram, London, 1872).
229 Stock, History of the C.M.S. IV, 126ff.
230 Richter, Missions in the N.E., pp. 256ff. Also of interest are
Ludwig Schneller, Vater Schneller, Ein Patriarch der Evangelischen Mission
im Heiligen Lands (Leipzig, 1898); W. P. Livingstone, A Galilee Doctor.
Being a Sketch of the Career of Dr. D. W. Torrance of Tiberias (New York,
n.d.); and F. J. Scrimgeour, Nazareth of Today (London, 1913).
231 Richter, Missions in the N.E., pp. 253f.
232 Ibid., p. 253 and Stock, History of the C.M.S., IV, 126.
233 Stock, History of the C.M.S., III, 529ff. and Tibawi, British
Interests, pp. 242-246.
234 Quoted in Richter, Missions in the N.E., p. 254.
235 John Hartley, Researches in Greece and the Levant (London, 2nd ed.,
1833). Hartley with affection for the hellenic people found Turkey "dismal
and dark" and "exposed to the righteous vengeance of God".
236 Stock, History of the C.M.S., II, 153ff.
237 F. J. Bliss, Religions of Modern Syria, p. 315.
238 Stock, History of the C.M.S., III, 114. For fuller insights into
this experience cf. Tibawi, British Interests, pp. 166f. and Samuel Zwemer
in M.W., 31 (1941), 221ff. Zwemer absolves Pfander of any blame for the
Porte's actions which resulted in at least 47 converts and inquirers being
condemned to the galleys.
239 Stock, History of the C.M.S., I, chapter 26; E. B. Pusey, Letter to
the Archbishop of Canterbury (London, 2nd ed., 1842); W. F. Ainsworth,
Travels and Researches in Asia Minor, Mesopotamia, Chaldea and Armenia (2
vols., London, 1842) and Travels in the Track of the Ten Thousand Greeks
(London, 1844); and G. P. Badger, Nestorians and their Rituals (London,
1843).
240 Literature coming from this period include E. L. Cutts, Christians
under the Crescent in Asia (London, 1877); A. Riley, Narrative of a Visit
to the Assyrian Christians in Kurdistan (London, 1884) and The Archbishop
of Canterbury's Mission to the Assyrian Christians (London, 1891); The
Catholicos of the East and His People by A. F. Maclean and W. H. Browne;
The Liturgy of the Apostles Adai and Mari by W. H. Browne; and Six Months
in a Syrian Monastery by O. H. Parry.
241 Fuller discussion found in Shaw, American Contacts, pp. 41ff.,
94ff.; Joseph, Nestorians and their Muslim Neighbors, passim; Richter,
Mission in the N.E., pp. 309ff., and J. A. Douglas, Relations of the Anglican Churches with the Eastern Churches (London, 1921).
242 For a most valuable study, cf. Shaw, American Contacts, pp. 157-

163, et passim.

243 Stock, History of the C.M.S., III, 125.

244 C. H. Stileman, The Subjects of the Shah (London, 1902) pp. 61ff.

245 Birks, French, II, 224; Mrs. Isabella L. Bird Bishop, Journeys in Persia and Kurdistan (2 vols., London, 1891); and A. H. Hume-Griffith, Behind the Veil in Persia and Turkish Arabia (London, 1909).

246 Napier Malcolm, Five Years in a Persian Town (New York, 1905).

247 C. H. Stileman, "Open Doors in Southern Persia," Intelligencer (1899), 498ff.; Stock, History of the C.M.S., III, 530; W. J. Thompson, "The Awakening of Persia," C.M. Review (March, 1920), 36-44; W. W. Cash, Persia, Old and New (London, 1929) A. Wilson, South West Persia (Oxford, 1941); and J. R. Richards, The Open Road in Persia (London, 1933).

248 J. Christy Wilson, Christian Message to Islam, pp. 134-160.

249 Tisdall's works include: The Sources of Islam (Persian original, English epitome by Sir. Wm. Muir, Edinburgh, 1901); The Religion of the Crescent, or Islam: Its Strength, Its Weakness, Its Origin, Its Influence (James Long Lectures, 189-92, London, 1895); India; Its History, Darkness and Dawn (London, 1901); and A Manual of the Leading Muhammadan Objections to Christianity (London, 1904). For a brief examination of the apologetic approach cf. Appendix D.

250 Clara C. Rice, Mary Bird, the Friend of the Persians (C.M.S. pamphlet, London, 1920), pp. 9f., and Mary Bird in Persia (London, 1916).

251 Malcolm, Five Years in a Persian Town, p. 255.

252 Cf. Addison, Christian Approach, pp. 299ff. for a fine discussion of the "Care of the Convert".

253 Cf. N. N. Hoare, Something New in Iran (London, 1937), pp. 40ff.; W. W. Cash, "The Anglican Church in Persia," M.W., 20 (1930), 45-49 and "Church Building in Persia," Church Overseas, October, 1928, 330-336.

254 Cf. Hassan Dehqani-Tafti, Design of My World (World Christian Books, London, 1959), a fascinating autobiography of his pilgrimage to faith in Christ. After mission schools, he attended Cambridge for theology before becoming deacon (1949) and later bishop. He feels a unique call to interpret to Muslims the Gospel of the love of God.

255 Quoted in R. Young, Light in Lands of Darkness, pp. 251f.

256 Ibid., p. 291. Also cf. C. R. Watson, In the Valley of the Nile, pp. 130ff.; M. Whately, Ragged Life in Egypt (London, 1863) and More About Ragged Life in Egypt (London, 1870); and E. J. Whately, The Life and Work of Mary Louisa Whately (London, n.d.).

257 Cf. article by W. W. Cash in C.M. Review, February, 1914.

258 Cf. Kyriakos Mikhail, Copts and Moslems under British Control. A Collection of Facts and a Resume of Authoritative Opinions on the Coptic Question (London, 1911) esp. pp. 19-30 and Stock, History of the C.M.S., IV, 105-107.

259 By 1914, there were 39 C.M.S workers in Egypt and Kartoum (5 clergy, 7 laymen including 5 doctors, 7 wives, and 20 other women). Stock, History of the C.M.S., IV, 111f.

260 W. H. T. Gairdner, D. M. Thornton, A Study in Missionary Ideals and Methods (London, 1908), p. 73.

261 Cf. Thornton's accounts in C. M. Review, August and October, 1907. Also cf. W. W. Cash, Christendom and Islam. Their Contacts and Cultures down the Centuries (London, 1937) and The Moslem World in Revolution (London, 1925).

262 Latourette, Expansion of Christianity, VI, 28.

263 Arabia proper covers about one million square miles with distances, e.g. Aqaba-Yemen (1,800 miles), Aden-Muscat (ca. 1,500), Muscat-Bahrain (500), Bahrain-Basrah (ca. 400) Kuwait-Jerusalem (ca. 900), which exhaust even the experienced traveler. Its harsh terrain of desert waste,

rocky wadis, plateaus and mountain ridges plus extremes of temperature take
an added toll in life.

264 For the best travel literature see the works of C. Niebuhr, Bruck-
hardt, Burton, Palgrave, and Doughty.

265 For more background cf. F. M. Hunter, An Account of the British
Settlement of Aden in Arabia (London, 1877).

266 S. M. Zwemer and J. Cantine, The Golden Milestone: Reminiscences
of Pioneer Days Fifty Years Ago in Arabia (New York, 1938), pp. 25f., 78ff.

267 J. Wolff, Travels and Adventures, pp. 496-512; A. A. Isaacs, Biography of the Rev. Henry Aaron Stern (London, 1886), pp. 101-138; and Latourette, Expansion of Christianity, VI, 59f.

268 "Gate of Arabia," in C.M. Intelligencer and The Christian (February,
1885), 13ff., and Stock, History of the C.M.S., III, 521ff.

269 Quoted in A. D. Mason and F. J. Barny, History of the Arabian
Mission (New York, 1926), pp. 67f.

270 Quoted in The Golden Milestone, p. 40.

271 Printed in the C.M. Intelligencer (July, 1891). Also cf. Stock,
History of the C.M.S., III, 116ff., 532ff., IV, 130f. and Birks, French,
II, 361ff.

272 Aden (about 80 sq. miles) and Aden protectorate (112 sq. miles),
bordered by the fertile Hadramaut, the waste Rubʿal Khāli (Empty Quarter)
and Yemen, had a small population which by W.W. II was under 50,000. Its
inhabitants came from Arabia, India, Africa and Europe. Aden came under
the British Indian government (1839) until it became a Crown Colony (1935),
under the Colonial Office, London. It was scheduled for full independence
in 1968.

273 Ion Keith-Falconer descended from two noble Scottish families prominent in the chivalry surrounding the Danish Invasion (1010), the founding
of Marischal College, Aberdeen (1593), Cromwell's rule (1657-) and the
Restoration (1677). He was born the 3rd son of the Eighth Earl of Kintore,
an active elder of the Free Church of Scotland. Cf. James Balfour Paul
(ed.), The Scots Peerage (Edinburgh, 1908), V. 240-255; James Robson, Ion
Keith-Falconer of Arabia (London, n.d.); and Robert Sinker, Memorials of
the Hon. Ion Keith-Falconer (London, 1888).

274 Sinker, Keith-Falconer, pp. 113ff.

275 The sanskrit original was reportedly a story of the Lion and the
Ox as told by Bidpai, chief of the Brahmins, but probably put into Persian,
Syriac and Arabic (ca. A.D. 570) for specific reasons. Arberry says:
"This repertory of animal fables is by no means the simple entertainment
it might at first be presumed to be. The stories are a shrewd and sometimes caustic commentary on political life under an absolute monarchy, and
it is not far fetched to suppose that the portraits presented are thinly
disguised cartoons of the entourage of the caliph himself. The animals
are made to deliver themselves of sententious wisdom matured through centuries of Sassanian rule,...It is one of the world's great classics." Cf.
A. J. Arberry, Aspects of Islamic Civilization (London, 1964), p. 74.

276 Sinker, Keith-Falconer, p. 164.

277 Haig's persuasiveness is seen in his article, "On Both Sides of the
Red Sea," C.M. Intelligencer (May, 1887), 282ff.

278 Sinker, Keith-Falconer, pp. 176-186.

279 Ibid., pp. 193-197.

280 Keith-Falconer was newly appointed Lord Almoner's Professor of
Arabic in the University of Cambridge. It was understood that he could
hold this historic chair by returning to give a minimum of one lecture
series annually, Cf. Ibid., pp. 217ff.

281 Ibid., p. 212.

282 The death of Keith-Falconer stirred Christian circles around the
world, but the work in Aden was never granted the means and personnel for

an extensive program which could reach out to the peoples of the Arabian
Peninsula. Incidently, the four hundred books of Keith-Falconer's library
were given to New College Library, Edinburgh.

283 W. Idris Jones, The Arab (Edinburgh, n.d.) pp. 52ff.

284 Affara, How I Found Christ (Church of Scotland Bookstore, Edinburgh, n.d.).

285 The Church is There: In Two Moslem Lands, South Arabia and West
Pakistan (Church of Scotland Overseas Council, Edinburgh, 1964); Hewat,
Vision and Achievement, pp. 285ff.; plus the Annual Reports of the Foreign
Mission Committee, Church of Scotland.

286 The Golden Milestone, Reminiscences of Pioneer Days Fifty Years Ago
in Arabia (S. M. Zwemer and J. Cantine (New York, 1839) is a mine of valuable information.

287 Gulian Lansing, Egypt's Princes (1864).

288 John G. Lansing, "The Origin and Plan of the Arabian Mission," The
Christian Intelligencer (August 28, 1889) reprinted in The Golden Milestone, pp. 148ff.

289 After Kamil's sudden death, authorities seized and buried his body
before an autopsy could be performed. Assassination by poison was the fate
of more than one convert from Islam. Zwemer wrote of him, "Ever since he
was here Kamil has been a faithful and at times a very bold confessor of
Christ and the Gospel. Around his dead body were many who witnessed to the
purity of his life and motives." Cf. Mason and Barny, Arabian Mission, p.
71 and H. H. Jessup, Kamil Abdul Messiah.

290 The Golden Milestone, chapters 3, 4, 5, 7.

291 These islands including about 250 square miles and at the time
about 50,000 persons (mainly Shi'ah Muslims) date their history back to the
times of Abraham and Alexander the Greek. Occupied by Portuguese (1507),
Persians (1602) and then the 'Utaybe Tribe from the Arab Mainland, they had
contact with the East India Company after 1820. They became a British protectorate in 1861.

292 The Golden Milestone, pp. 108ff. and J. C. Wilson, Apostle to
Islam, A Biography of Samuel M. Zwemer (Grand Rapids, 1952) pp. 53ff.

293 The Golden Milestone, chapters 6, 8, 11.

294 Muscat had attracted both Martyn and French. Its land varies from
the coastal Batina to the scorching desert empty quarter to Jabal Akhdar
(10,000 ft.). Its semi-tropical valleys produce oranges, bananas, coco-
nuts, etc. Oman's 82,000 square miles shelters an estimated million persons, a people mingling the blood of Arab, Indian, Baluchi, African, Persian and others. While these people have been long isolated, they were
admired by missionaries. Harold Storm wrote, "The most hospitable, friendly and responsible type of Arab in Arabia is to be found in the Oman
field." Cf. Whither Arabia? (London, 1938) p. 69. Paul Harrison noted:
"There seems more hope for future progress in Oman than in any other province of Arabia." Cf. The Arab at Home (New York, 1924), p. 104.

295 Cf. "Experiences in Muscat" by Cantine, The Golden Milestone,
chapter 12 and R. E. Speer, Missionary Principles and Practice (New York,
1902), pp. 462f.

296 Within seven years the Mission lost five adults and two children
by death including Peter Zwemer (d. 1898), George E. Stone (d. 1899), and
Harry J. Wiersum (d. 1901).

297 In 1923, the Reformed Church in America joined with the Presbyterian Church, U.S.A. to form the United Mission to Iraq. Basrah formed a
natural connecting link between this venture and the Arabian Mission. Unfortunately the question of religious liberty in Iraq as in Arabia went
unresolved. Cf. S. A. Morrison, Religious Liberty in the Near East
(London, 1949) and "Religious Liberty in Muslim Lands" in The Church and
the State, vol. IV. of the Reports on the Madras Conference (Madras, 1938).

298 Also cf. R. Kilgour, "The Bible in Arabia," in Whither Arabia? by
W. H. Storm, pp. 116f.
299 Cf. J. Beatty, "Desert Doctor," American Magazine. (October, 1938);
W. H. Storm, "Hadramaut -- Its Challenge," World Dominion (January 1937),
53ff.; L. P. Dame, "Four Months in Nejd," M.W., 14 (1924), 353ff., "From
Bahrain to Taif," M.W., 23 (1933), 164ff., "Objectives in Arabia," M.W., 20
(1930), 179ff.; and G. D. Van Peursem, "Methods of Evangelism in Arabia,"
M.W., II (1921), 267ff.
300 Storm, Wither Arabia?, p. 93.
301 Mason and Barny, Arabian Mission, p. 155.
302 Writings by Louis P. Dame and W. Harold Storm have already been
listed. Henry R. L. Worrall, Sharon and Marion Thoms, and Arthur K. Bennett were also capable spokesmen. Anglican C. S. G. Mylrea wrote "Arabia-
a Retrospect, 1912-22," C. M. Review (Dec. 1922), 269ff., "Kuweit, Arabia,"
M.W., 7 (1917), prepared, How to be Healthy in Hot Climates (New York,
1949), and My Arabian Days and Nights (New York, 1961). Paul W. Harrison,
famed for speech and pen, wrote: "The Arab Mind and the Gospel," M.W.,
12 (1922), 225ff., "The Gospel and the Bedowin," M.W., 4 (1914), 368ff.,
The Arab at Home (New York, 1924), Doctor in Arabia (New York, 1940),
The Light that Lighteth Every Man. Expositions in the Gospel of St. John
(Grand Rapids, 1958) plus a commentary on Romans. His wife, Anne M.
Harrison wrote: Pearls are Made (New York, 1958) and A Tool in His Hand
(New York, 1958)
303 Continuation Committee Conference in Asia, 1912-13 (New York,
1913), section 13, p. 354 and section 1, pp. 81, 356.
304 Cf. Dr. Bulme, Where Medical Missions Fail, quoted in H. T.
Hodgkin, The Way of the Good Physician (London, 1915), p. 106.
305 Quoted in Hodgkin, The Way, p. 105.
306 P. Harrison, The Arab at Home, pp. 290-294.
307 Edwin E. Calverly later became a professor at Hartford Theological
Seminary and an editor of The Muslim World. In addition to his scholarly
articles, he wrote: Worship in Islam (New York, 1925) and Islam: An
Introduction (New York, 1958).
308 The school enrolled 30 boys and 29 girls in 1910, 146 and 94 in
1914, and 200 and 100 in 1924. Cf. Mason and Barny, Arabian Mission, pp.
149ff., 187f. The new High School(1966) served a vital role in the
community.
309 John Van Ess, "Educating the Arab," M.W., 21 (1931), 380ff. Dr.
Van Ess also wrote Meet the Arab (New York, 1943); Living Issues (privately
printed in both Arabic and English, 1950) giving a fuller example of his
approach; several Arabic grammars; and "A Quarter Century in Arabia," M.W.,
19 (1929), 196ff. For chapters on Van Ess and Harrison cf. Jerome Beatty,
Americans All Over (New York, 1938) and Paul Geren, New Voices, Old
Worlds (New York, 1958).
310 Quoted in E. M. Dodd and R. W. Dodd, Mecca and Beyond (Boston,
1937), p. 60.
311 For more materials cf. Annual Reports and the periodical, Neglected
Arabia (1892-1948), Arabia Calling (1949-) of the Arabian Mission; The
Church Herald, official periodical of the Reformed Church in America, and
Dorothy Van Ess, History of the Arabian Mission, 1926-1957 (New York,
mimeographed).
312 Secularization (to be distinguished from secularism) may in some
cases be a preliminary stage in the arrival of the kingdom of God. Cf.
Charles Davis, God's Grace in History: A Discussion on the Christian's
attitude to the modern secular world (London, 1966); A. Th. van Leeuwen,
Christianity in World History, (trans. by H. H. Hoskins, London, 1964);
Harvey Cox, The Secular City (London, 1965); and M. M. Thomas, The Christian Response to the Asian Revolution (London, 1966).

313 W. H. Storm, Whither Arabia?, pp. 97-99.
314 Ibid., pp. 88ff. Helpful in this area of study are: Where in the
World? (London, 1965) and What in the World? (London, 1965) by Colin W.
Williams, an executive director of the N.C.C. (U.S.A.) and Chairman of the
Dept. of Studies in Evangelism (W.C.C.). Also cf. Johannes Blauw, "The
Biblical View of Man in His Religion," in The Theology of the Christian
Mission, G. H. Anderson (ed.), (London, 1961).
315 Latourette, Expansion of Christianity, VI, 62.
316 Latourette argues that while "influence upon individual lives and
upon a civilization" is a more difficult yardstick than geographic spread
or numerical accounts, it too is a valid indicator of advance or recession,
Cf. The Unquenchable Light (London, 1945), p. xi.
317 Richter, Missions in the Near East (1910), pp. 62-80.
318 Latourette's thesis is that the spread of Christianity over the
earth has come in four surging tidal waves. In this light, the growth of
Christian influence in the Near East is but one phase of the larger advancement. While acknowledging that each major wave of advance is followed
by a recession, the incoming tide results in new high water marks. For
this concept of the coming kingdom, cf. K. S. Latourette, The Unquenchable
Light, p. x and Anno Domini: Jesus, History, and God (New York, 1940).
319 Anderson insists that the drawing together of church and mission
has been forcing a reformulation of a theology of mission since 1900. Cf.
G. H. Anderson (ed.), The Theology of the Christian Mission (London, 1961),
pp. 3ff.

CHAPTER IV: MATURING ANGLICAN AND REFORMED APPROACHES BEFORE 1938:
            W. H. T. GAIRDNER AND S. M. ZWEMER (p. 184)

1 H. R. Mackintosh, Types of Modern Theology (London, 1964); K. Barth,
From Rousseau to Ritschl (London, 1959); Alec R. Vidler, 20th Century Defenders of the Faith (London, 1965); and K. Hartenstein, Was hat die Theologie Karl Barths der Mission zu sagen? (München, 1928).
2 Cf. W. B. Glover, Evangelical Nonconformists and Higher Criticism in
the Nineteenth Century (London, 1954).
3 F. M. Müller's views may be found in Chips from a German Workshop,
(4 vols., London, 1867-1875), Lectures on the Origins of Religion (London,
1882) and the introduction to his edition of Sacred Books of the East.
4 Eric F. Sharpe, Not to Destroy But to Fulfill, pp. 43ff.
5 The Student Volunteer Movement After Twenty-Five Years, 1886-1911
(New York, 1912); T. Tatlow, The Story of the Student Christian Movement in
Great Britain and Ireland (London, 1933); R. Rouse, The World's Student
Christian Federation (London, 1948), R. Rouse and S. C. Neill (editors), A
History of the Ecumenical Movement, 1517-1948, (London, 1954), W. R. Hogg,
Ecumenical Foundations. A History of the International Missionary Council
and its nineteenth-Century Background (New York, 1952); and the various
reports and periodicals of the SVM, WSCF, and IMC.
6 Sources include: Constance E. Padwick, Temple Gairdner of Cairo
(London, 1929); W. H. T. G. to His Friends. Some Letters and Informal
Writings of Canon W. H. Temple Gairdner of Cairo, 1873-1928 (ed. by his
wife, London, 1930); I. Smith, To Islam I Go (Eagle Book # 17, London, n.
d.); Alfred Nielsen, William Temple Gairdner (Copenhagen, 1932); H. A. R.
Gibb, "Canon W. H. T. Gairdner," B.S.O.A.S., 5 (1928), 207; and W. H. T.
Gairdner, D. M. Thornton, A Study in Missionary Ideals and Methods (London,
1908).
7 Padwick, Gairdner, pp. 3ff.
8 Ibid., pp. 17ff.
9 Quoted in Padwick, Gairdner, p. 39.

10 Ibid., p. 48
11 Gairdner's Studies in Prayer (1897), Helps to the Study of St.
John's Gospel (1898) and Helps to the Study of the Epistle to the Romans
(1899).
12 Padwick, Gairdner, pp. 62ff. and D. M. Thornton, pp. 34ff.
13 Padwick, Gairdner, p. 72.
14 "The Sources of Oriental Music," M.W., 6 (1916) and Oriental Hymn
Tunes: Egyptian and Syrian (London, 1930).
15 Padwick, Gairdner, p. 93.
16 Ibid., pp. 84f. and D. M. Thornton, p. 127
17 Padwick, Gairdner, p. 128.
18 D. M. Thornton, p. 80.
19 Padwick, Gairdner, p. 129.
20 D. M. Thornton, p. 113.
21 Ibid., pp. 274ff.
22 D. M. Thornton, p. 193.
23 Padwick, Gairdner, p. 145.
24 Ibid., pp. 139-142; D. M. Thornton, pp. 200ff.
25 Padwick, Gairdner, p. 139.
26 Quoted in Ibid., pp. 142f.
27 D. M. Thornton, p. 206.
28 For a selection of Gairdner's works cf. Appendix F.
29 Padwick, Gairdner, pp. 160ff.
30 Ibid., pp. 179f.
31 Ibid., pp. 193ff.
32 Padwick, Gairdner, pp. 196ff.
33 Ibid., p. 218
34 Ibid., p. 226
35 Ibid., p. 228
36 Ibid., pp. 231f.
37 Ibid., pp. 244f.
38 W.H.T.G. to his Friends, pp. 159-173.
39 Padwick, Gairdner, pp. 201f.
40 Ibid., pp. 280ff.
41 Ibid., pp. 263f.
42 Ibid., p. 302.
43 Ibid., p. 276.
44 Ibid., pp. 266f.
45 Gairdner, Edinburgh, 1910 (Edinburgh, 1910), p. 203.
46 Padwick, Gairdner, pp. 275f.
47 Ibid., pp. 276f.
48 Reprinted in M.W., 23 (1933), pp. 230f.
49 Cf. Appendix E.
50 Cf. Gairdner's Science and Faith in Whom? (1910) and D. Bonhoeffer,
Christology (trans. John Bowden, London, 1966), pp. 27ff.
51 Quoted in M.W. 23 (1933), p. 235.
52 Ibid., p. 238.
53 Ibid., p. 239.
54 Ibid., p. 248.
55 E.g. cf. "The Vital Forces of Christianity and Islam," (articles
reprinted from I.R.M. of 1912 in volume with same title, London, 1915),
pp. 11-44.
56 Cf. R. Allen, "Islam and Christianity in the Sudan," I.R.M., 9
(1920), 531-543; W. H. T. Gairdner, "Islam in Africa: The Sequel to a
Challenge," I.R.M., 13 (1924), 3-25; and Professor Westermann's earlier
article in I.R.M., 1 (1912).
57 Gairdner, "Islam in Africa," pp. 5f.
58 Ibid., pp. 6f.

59 It is interesting to note how the Communists in China used the
"Three Selves Movement" to isolate the national church. Bishop Stephen
Neill and Bishop A. R. Tucker of Uganda (1890-1908) fully agree with Gaird-
ner. Cf. Neill, History of Christian Missions, pp. 257-260. Also cf. P.
Beyerhaus, "The Three selves Formula," I.R.M., 53 (1964), 393ff.

60 The Student Volunteer Movement was founded in the U.S.A. by Robert
Wilder and others (1886) soon to be followed by the Y.M.C.A. and the
British College Christian Union. These gave birth to the World Student
Christian Federation (ca. 1895).

61 Even Dr. J. R. Mott at the Zeist Conference (1905) admitted that the
apologetical approach may be necessary to remove philosophical and scientific barriers for students prior to evangelism in some cases. It was at
this same time that J. N. Farquhar, the W.S.C.F. resource person on India,
developed his "fulfillment" concept in answer to scientific religion and
religious nationalism. Cf. Sharpe, Not to Destroy, pp. 228-271 and R.
Rouse, The World's Student Christian Federation (London, 1948), passim.

62 Cf. accounts in Egyptian Studies; Science and Faith in Whom?; and
reports in the Orient and Occident.

63 "Work Among the Educated Moslems in Cairo," by Gairdner in Methods
of Mission Work Among Moslems (New York, 1906), ch. 4.

64 Richter, Missions in the Near East, pp. 83-87.

65 W. H. T. G. to His Friends, pp. 124ff. Also cf. R. Voillaume, Seeds
of the Desert: The Legacy of Charles de Foucauld (English trans., London,
1955).

66 Cf. K. Cragg, Sandals at the Mosque: Christian Presence Amid Islam
(London, 1959), and Appendix G.

67 Egyptian Colloquial Arabic, A Conversation Grammar and Reader
(Cambridge, 1917; London, 1926); The Phonetics of Arabic (Oxford, 1925);
"The Arab Phoneticians on the Consonants and Vowels," M.W., 25 (1935), 242-
257; "A Modern Meter of Egyptian-Arabic Verse," American Journal of Semitic
Languages, 37 (1920-21), 230f.

68 "The Study of Islamics at Cairo," M.W., 12 (1922), 390ff.

69 M.W., 18 (1928), p. 226. Also cf. Gairdner's guest editorial,
"Signs of Progress--A Backward Look," M.W., 18 (1928), 1-5.

70 The Reproach of Islam (Edinburgh, 1909) was renamed The Rebuke of
Islam in its fifth and revised edition. This edition contains additions
but no significant alteration. The preface of 1920 explains the change in
title: "Islam was a perpetual reminder to Christendom of the latter's
failure truly to represent her Lord. For if she had done so, Mohammed
would have been a Christian. And the world by this time would have been
won for Christ. The Biblical sense of the word reproach escaped him--
namely a thing so unspeakably vile that its very existence is a shame."

71 Quoted in Padwick, Gairdner, p. 184.

72 Cf. preface of Reproach (1909).

73 Gairdner, Reproach (1909), p. 29.

74 Ibid., p. 104.

75 Ibid., pp. 77f.

76 At this point Gairdner is not far from Kraemer's distinction between man's religions and the Christian faith (1938). While Gairdner later
develops a sympathetic view of Islam (1928) which acknowledges fragments,
half-truths in Islam, he never repudiates this early criticism.

77 Gairdner, Reproach (1909), pp. 127ff. This identification of Islam
with the natural man and the world is reminiscent of Luther (later Kellerhals, Der Islam). In 1909, Gairdner saw little in Islam that resembled
the revelation   or work of God.

78 Gairdner, "The Way of a Mohammedan Mystic," M.W., 2 (1912), p. 180.

79 His reviews of Macdonald's three major books are found in M.W., 2
1912), 312-317.

80 Gairdner, "Professor Snouck Hurgronje's Mohammadanism," M.W., 7
(1917), 5-4. For favorable reviews of Henri Lammens, cf. M.W., 3 (1913),
432-434.
    81 Gairdner, Al-Ghazzāli's Mishkāt al-Anwār (The Niche for Lights, a
trans. with intro., Royal Asiatic Society, London, 1924).
    82 Ibid., cf. introduction.
    83 Cf. M.W., 7 (1917), 348.
    84 Gairdner, "Moslem Tradition and the Gospel Record. The Hadith and
the Injil," M.W., 5 (1915), pp. 349-379. Note how he avoids a frontal
attack on the Quran, or an unequal comparison of it with the Gospel. He
hopes Muslims will later apply historical criticism to the Quran on their
own.
    85 Ibid., pp. 349f.
    86 Gairdner holds the traditions were coined to meet the political,
social and philosophical needs of the Muslim community, agreeing with Goldziher (Mohammedanische Studien, II) re: the unscrupulous business of
tradition-falsification during the Umayyad and the first part of the
ʿAbbasid period. Cf. Ibid., p. 355.
    87 Harnack's four tests were: (1) early dating of written accounts;
(2) eye witness accounts; (3) cross check with contemporaries; and (4) the
trustworthiness of the recorder. This reminds one of Samuel Lee's appeal
to Locke's tests, "First, the conformity of anything with our own knowledge, observation and experiences. Secondly, the testimony of others,
vouching their observation and experience....In the testimony of others is
to be considered 1. the number of witnesses, 2. their integrity, 3. their
skill, 4. the design of the author (where it is a testimony out of a book
cited), 5. the consistency of the parts, and 6. contrary testimonies."
Cf. Controversial Tracts (1824), p. 466.
    88 Cf. Gairdner, "Moslem Tradition and the Gospel Record," pp. 363f.
    89 Ibid., pp. 378f.
    90 Gairdner, "Mohammed without Camouflage. Ecce Homo Arabicus," M.W.,
9 (1919), 25-57.
    91 Ibid., pp. 56f.
    92 "Present Day Movements in the Moslem World," M.W., 1 (1911), 74-77,
187-191, 435-443.
    93 Gairdner, "Islam under Christian Rule," Islam and Missions (Papers
of the Missionary Conference at Lucknow, New York, 1911), p. 205.
    94 W. H. T. G. to His Friends, pp. 96, 139-156 and the "Editorial:
Tempora Mutantur," M.W., 4 (1914), 1f. for his identification with the
national aspirations.
    95 Gairdner, Reproach, pp. 171f.
    96 Ibid., pp. 218ff.
    97 Ibid., pp. 335f.
    98 Gairdner, "The Doctrine of the Unity in Trinity," M.W., 1 (1911),
381-407; and M.W., 6 (1916), 28-41, 127-139.
    99 M.W., 6 (1916), 28ff.
    100 This article from I.R.M., 1 (1912) 44-61 is republished in a volume
of the same title: The Vital Forces of Christianity and Islam (London,
1915), pp. 11-44, esp. p. 32.
    101 Ibid., pp. 16-21.
    102 Ibid., pp. 26f
    103 Ibid., p. 38.
    104 Ibid., pp. 39-43.
    105 E. Kellerhals misunderstands Gairdner when he classifies him as one
of the comparative religions school which made works/ethics the measure of
truth in religion. While this thought was evident at Jerusalem (1928), it
is erroneous to so categorize Gairdner. Cf. Kellerhals Der Islam, p. 341.
    106 Farquhar has been treated superbly in E. J. Sharpe, Not to Destroy

But to fulfill (Uppsala, 1965).

107 Gairdner, Edinburgh, 1910, pp. 134, 137.

108 Report of Commission IV (Edinburgh Series, 1910), pp. 249-267.
Also D. S. Cairns, "The Need for Apologists," Student World, (1911), 49ff.,
The Faith that Rebels (London, 1928) and "The Christian Message. A Com-
parison of Thought in 1910 and in 1928," I.R.M., 18 (1929), 321f.; and A. G.
Hogg, Karma and Redemption (Madras, 1909), Christ's Message of the Kingdom
(Madras, 1911), Redemption from This World (Edinburgh, 1922), and The
Christian Message to the Hindu (London, 1947). Hogg's books provide a
sharp criticism of Farquhar's Crown of Hinduism (Oxford, 1913).

109 Padwick, Gairdner, p. 200 and Sharpe, Not to Destroy, pp. 110ff.,
et passim.

110 Sharpe, Not to Destroy, pp. 310f. For a fair assessment of Farquhar, cf. pp. 344-360.

111 Gairdner like Cairns, Hogg and Zwemer would acknowledge the dia-
bolical, the evil existing in non-Christian systems, which Christ certainly
does not fulfill in any revolutionary process. Instead he stands in
"judgement" of such. Gairdner is at this point closer to Zwemer who in the
crisis of the 1920s and 1930s stood convinced that Christ is more than the
"highest" or "best"; He is the "Final" Lord and Judge of all.

112 For example, Julius Richter and several others. Cf. Hallencreutz,
Kraemer towards Tambaram, pp. 171-177.

113 Ibid., pp. 180ff.

114 For fuller treatment of the Gairdner-Eddy paper, cf. Appendix E.

115 Gairdner, Edinburgh, 1910, p. vi.

116 The Edinburgh Conference followed the Madras pattern (1902) of
eight commissions with preparatory research and reports. It drew 1200
delegates from 160 Mission Boards or Societies.

117 Ibid., pp. 9f.

118 Ibid., p. 75.

119 Ibid., p. 120.

120 Ibid., pp. 148f.

121 Ibid., pp. 196ff.

122 Ibid., p. 241.

123 "The National Mission and Mohammedanism," M.W., 7 (1917), 343.

124 "Oriental Christian Communities and the Evangelization of the
Moslems," in The Moslem World Today ed. by J. R. Mott (London, 1925), pp.
279-287, esp. p. 282.

125 Ibid., pp. 282f.

126 "Introduction and Conclusion: The Missionary Significance of the
Last Ten Years. A Survey," I.R.M., 12 (1923), 4f.

127 Ibid., pp. 53f.

128 Cf. M.W., 14 (1924), 235-246 and its repetition in the Jerusalem
Paper (1928).

129 Ibid., p. 236.

130 Cf. "Values in Christianity," M.W., 18 (1928), 350f. Gairdner
felt that Zwemer's Arabic booklet, "The Way to the Heart of Moslems" was
in the right direction.

131 Quoted in M.W., 14 (1924), 235f. Also cf. J. Blauw, The Missionary Nature of the Church (London, 1962).

132 Quoted in W. M. Watt, Truth in the Religions (Edinburgh, 1963),
p. 64.

133 Ps. 145:13 (LXX) quoted in Reproach of Islam, pp. 336f.

134 For a consideration of the ongoing influence of Gairdner within
the Anglican Communion, cf. Appendix G.

135 The author is deeply indebted to J. Christy Wilson, Apostle to
Islam, A Biography of Samuel M. Zwemer (Grand Rapids, 1952) and William
M. Miller for vital source materials and comments.

136 For additional background regarding the Arabian Mission, see chapter three.

137 Wilson, Apostle to Islam, pp. 78ff.

138 Ibid., p. 83.

139 Cf. Appendix K. observing that a good portion of his articles on Islam fall in this period, 1912-1928.

140 "Editorial," M.W., I (1911), 1-4.

141 Ibid.

142 For example: James S. Dennis (Syria), W. H. T. Gairdner (Cairo), W. St. Clair Tisdall (Persia), Marshall Broomhall (China), H. U. Weitbrecht (India), E. M. Wherry (India) Johannes Lepsius (Deutsche Orient Mission, Potsdam Seminary), Julius Richter (Berlin), Friedrich Wurz (Basel Mission, editor of E.M.M.), D. B. Macdonald (Hartford), David S. Margoliouth (Oxford), A. J. Wensinck (Leiden), Alfred Guillaume (Durham), S. Khuda Bukhsh (Calcutta), Louis Massignon (Paris), H. Kraemer (Java), Murray T. Titus (Lucknow), et al.

143 Wilson, Apostle to Islam, pp. 186ff.

144 Ibid., pp. 181f.

145 Ibid., pp. 88ff.

146 Quoted in Ibid., pp. 85f.

147 Ibid., pp. 91f.

148 Ibid., pp. 84f.

149 Ibid., p. 92. Zwemer received the Doctor of Divinity from Hope College (1904) and Rutgers University (1919) and the LL.D. from Muskingum College (1918). For his explorations in Yemen, he was elected Fellow of the Royal Geographical Society in 1900.

150 His message on "The Fullness of Time in the Moslem World" at the Keswick Convention (July 21, 1915) moved a small group of people to prayer, including Annie Van Sommer. Becoming the "Fellowship of Faith for Muslims", this group still links together in partnership those concerned for the salvation of Muslims.

151 S. Eddy, Pathfinders of the World Missionary Crusade (New York, 1945), p. 245.

152 A study prepared in Cairo and edited by Zwemer released at this time.

153 Wilson, Apostle to Islam, pp. 97ff., 143ff.

154 Ibid., pp. 119-136.

155 Quoted in Ibid., p. 125.

156 Wilson considers these conferences the zenith of Zwemer's career. Ibid., p. 176. The Cairo reports were Mohammedan World Today (New York, 1906), Methods of Mission Work Among Moslems (private circulation only, New York, 1906) and women's work in Our Moslem Sisters (New York, 1907).

157 These same ideas are treated by E. Kellerhals in Der Islam (Basel, 1945).

158 The conference stimulated the forming of three Islamic Study Centers: the Newman School of Missions (Jerusalem), the Henry Martyn Institute (India), the School of Oriental Studies (Cairo); and the Missionaries to Moslems League (India). For reports cf. Islam and Missions (New York, 1911) and Daylight in the Harem (New York, 1912). The sympathetic spirit of the conference was not conveyed in "The Conquest of the Moslem World", a Roman Catholic review by Professor A. Le Chatelier in the Revue du Monde Musulman, 16 (1911).

159 Islam and Missions, pp. 41f.

160 K. S. Latourette, "Samuel M. Zwemer: A Centennial," The Church Herald (Grand Rapids), March 24, 1967, p. 15.

161 Cf. Appendix K and Wilson, Apostle to Islam, pp. 193ff.

162 E.g. cf. Arabia: The Cradle of Islam (1900), Islam, A Challenge to Faith (1907), The Unoccupied Mission Fields (1911), Mohammed or Christ

(1915), The Disintegration of Islam (1916), The Law of Apostasy in Islam (1923), and Across the World of Islam (1929).

163 E.g. cf. Christianity the Final Religion (1920), Thinking Missions with Christ (1934), The Solitary Throne (1937), Dynamic Christianity and the World Today (1939), Into All the World (1943), and Evangelism Today (1944).

164 E.g. cf. The Moslem Doctrine of God (1905), The Moslem Christ (1912), The Influence of Animism on Islam (1920), A Moslem Seeker After God, Life of Al-Ghazali (1921), Studies in Popular Islam (1939), and Heirs of the Prophets (1946). There is considerable overlapping between these works and the articles in the Moslem World.

165 Esp. cf. "The Nearest Way to the Moslem Heart" so appreciated by Temple Gairdner and the popular tract, "Do You Pray?"

166 E.g. cf., Raymond Lull (1902), The Glory of the Cross (1928), Taking Hold of God (1936), It is Hard to be a Christian (1937), The Glory of the Manger (1940), The Art of Listening to God (1940), The Glory of the Empty Tomb (1947), How Rich the Harvest (1948), and Sons of Adam (1951).

167 Zwemer, The Unoccupied Mission Fields of Africa and Asia, pp. viii ff.

168 Cf. Disintegration of Islam and Mohammed or Christ.

169 Cf. The Law of Apostasy.

170 "A United Front Over Against Islam," M.W., 4 (1914), 339.

171 He notes that "the guild of scholarship (incl. Jesuits) offers opportunities for religious fellowship, in which our very diversities lead to enrichment and do not tend to separation, but to mutual understanding." Cf. Mohammed or Christ, p. 48.

172 "...the Christian Church Catholic will be forced to work out her theology and creeds experientially in contact and conflict with unitarian, deistic Islam. In this respect the Mohammedan problem may possibly be as life from the dead to the Oriental Churches, when they face its real and spiritual issues and become conscious of the duty of evangelism. The doctrine of the Incarnation and of the Holy Spirit are not pieces of polished armoury to be kept on exhibition in proof of our orthodoxy but are vital to the very life of the Christian." Cf. Ibid., p. 48.

173 "A Factual Survey of the Moslem World" (1946), p. 28.

174 Ibid., p. 27.

175 Islam, A Challenge to Faith (1907), p. 224 and "Editorial", M.W., 7 (1917), 219ff.

176 Preface of Islam, A Challenge to Faith (1907), p. vii.

177 Preface to Arabia: The Cradle of Islam (1900), p. 5.

178 Ibid., p. 158

179 Ibid., pp. 168, 170.

180 Cf. Arabia, pp. 179ff., Islam, pp. 29ff.

181 In 1900, Zwemer accepted Koelle's estimate that Muhammad was a clever and ambitious enthusiast. Cf. Arabia, pp. 181f.

182 Cf. Islam (1907), pp. 42, 46.

183 Cf. Arabia (1900), pp. 189f.

184 Ibid., p. 179.

185 E.g. cf. James Dennis, Missions and Social Progress.

186 Cf. Islam, pp. 131f.

187 Cf. The Moslem Doctrine of God (1905), p. 109.

188 Ibid., p. 7.

189 Ibid., pp. 21f.

190 Cf. Arabia (1900), p. 175.

191 Cf. Moslem Doctrine of God, pp. 75ff., 93ff. Also cf. W. M. Watt, Free Will and Predestination in Early Islam (London, 1948).

192 Extracted from Moslem Doctrine of God, pp. 109f.

193 At this point Zwemer is following the 19th century pattern of

stressing the work of Christ. With the failure to find the "historical
Jesus" and the abuse of Jesus as the pinnacle of spirit or ideal, Zwemer
and others were forced to restate the bond between the person and work of
Christ (1920-1940).

194 Cf. The Moslem Christ (1912), p. 53. Goldziher in Muhammedanische
Studien, II, p. 268 holds that the Muslim traditions were contributed
largely by Christian converts to Islam. Cf. Ibid., pp. 13f.

195 Ibid., pp. 113ff.

196 At this point Zwemer agrees with Gairdner over against Farquhar.
How can Christianity ever be called the fulfillment of Islam? "How can
that which denies the whole essential and particular content of the message
be said to prepare for Him, or to be a half-way house to His Kingdom?"
Gairdner, Reproach of Islam (p. 141) quoted in Zwemer, Moslem Christ,
pp. 155ff.

197 Zwemer, Moslem Christ, pp. 157, 166.

198 Ibid., pp. 7, 173.

199 E.g. Jesus ('Isā), son of Mary, the Messīah (al-Masīh), the Word of
God (Kalimat Allāh), Spirit of God (Ruh Allāh) and prophet (Rasūl apostle/
messenger or Nabī prophet).

200 Cf. Unoccupied Mission Fields (1911), pp. 95, 123, 126, 153, et
passim.

201 Cf. Disintegration, pp. 9f.

202 Cf. Arend Th. van Leeuwen, Christianity in World History (London,
1964); M. M. Thomas, The Christian Response to Asian Revolution (London,
1966); and Charles Davis, God's Grace in History, The Maurice Lectures,
1966 (Fontana, London, 1966).

203 Cf. Disintegration, p. 64.

204 Ibid., p. 178.

205 Ibid., esp. pp. 69, 73, 94f.

206 Cf. Ibid., pp. 181ff. and Mohammed or Christ, esp. pp. 134f., 201ff.
Compare this with Oscar Cullmann, "Eschatology and Missions in the New
Testament," The Theology of the Christian Mission (ed. G. H. Anderson), pp.
42ff. The shock of World War I appears to have liberated many from the
myth that they could or must bring in the Kingdom.

207 "Dr. Zwemer's writings on Islam were based on first-hand research
in the Arabic sources and on first-hand investigation of Muslim beliefs and
practices. The results are true and real descriptions of Muslim life and
thought. His descriptions of popular Islam, dealing with wide-spread customs often not approved by Muslim religious leaders, since they were true,
have tended to start actions that will change conditions and make his descriptions of historical rather than social interest." Cf. E. E. Calverly,
Zwemer's obituary, M.W., 42 (1952), 157-59.

208 Cf. Our Moslem Sisters (1907) and Daylight in the Harem (1911)
edited with Annie Van Sommer which contain articles from Cairo and Lucknow
by such sensitive figures as Lilas Trotter. Zwemer's theme was that God's
promises to Hagar are fulfilled in Christ.

209 Cf. Childhood in the Moslem World (1915), an expanded and illustrated version of Zwemer's address to the World Conference of Sunday
School Association, Zurich, 1913.

210 A remarkable statistician, Zwemer published his first survey of the
Islamic world in The Missionary Review of the World (1898) which was followed by other surveys at Cairo (1906), Lucknow (1911) and in almost every
decade (cf. M.W.) until his final appeal in A Factual Survey of the Moslem
World with Maps and Statistical Tables (New York, 1946).

211 Cf. Appendix K.

212 Preview in the New York Times book section (July 4, 1920).

213 Influence of Animism, pp. vii-viii.

214 Studies included: (1) Islam and Animism, (2) Animism in the Creed

and the Use of the Rosary, (3) Animistic Elements in Moslem Prayer, (4) Hair, Finger-Nails and the Hand, (5) The 'Aqiqa Sacrifice, (6) The Familiar Spirit or Qarina, (7) Jinn, (8) Pagan Practices in Connection with the Pilgrimage, (9) Magic and Sorcery, (10) Amulets, Charms and Knots, (11) Tree, Stone and Serpent Worship, (12) The Zar: Exorcism of Demons.

    215   Including The Palladium of Islam (the Ka'aba); The Sword of Mohammed and 'Ali; The Clock, the Calender and the Koran; Translations of the Koran; The 'Illiterate' Prophet, The So-called 'Hadith Qudsi'; The Worship of Adam by Angels; etc. Across the World of Islam (1929) is largely a travelogue which lacks the scholarly tone of the 1920 and 1939 volumes.

    216   Studies in Popular Islam (1939), pp. vii ff.

    217   S. M. Zwemer, A Moslem Seeker After God: Showing Islam at its Best in the Life and Teaching of Al-Ghazali, Mystic and Theologian of the Eleventh Century (with Intro. by Dr. J. Rendel Harris, New York, 1920). Beginning with the earlier article by D. B. Macdonald (cf. "Life of Al-Ghazali," Journal of the American Oriental Society, vol. XX), Zwemer examines Al-Ghazali's environment, life, writings, ethics and understanding of Jesus.

    218   Ibid., pp. 12f., and M.W., 32 (1942), 51-54.

    219   Al-Ghazali (d. 1111 A.D.) in his Ibya' like Anselm (d. 1109 A.D.) in his Our Deus Homo? refuted the philosophers of the day in effort to establish a theology alive with mystical faith. For him religion was more than law or doctrine. It was the Soul's experience. The danger with infatuation with mathematics and philosophy which rest upon proofs is that one is tempted to miss the religious truth he cannot perceive. Neither ignoring nor rejecting the sciences, Al-Ghazali argues for the fact and experience of revelation. After passing from the traditional Islamic view backed by rational proofs (as professor of Nizamiyya College in Bagdad) through scepticism to sufi mysticism, he experienced a new consciousness of God (age of 38). In his next ten years of wandering, teaching and writing, he wedded the experience and enlightenment of mystic faith to traditional Sunni theology. Zwemer gives most attention to his major work, Ihya' 'ulūm ad-Dīn (The Revival of Religious Sciences).

    220   A Moslem Seeker After God, p. 181.

    221   Ibid., p. 218.

    222   Ibid., pp. 163-167.

    223   Ibid., pp. 253, 286-89.

    224   Quoted in Ibid., p. 294.

    225   Ibid., pp. 252, 294.

    226   Law of Apostasy (1924), p. 7.

    227   D. B. Macdonald, S. A. Morrison and J. N. D. Anderson have prepared fine studies of the question of Islamic jurisprudence and religious liberty.

    228   Ibid., p. 131.

    229   For a study of consensus,cf. Kenneth Cragg, Counsels in Contemporary Islam: Islamic Surveys III (Edinburgh, 1965).

    230   Heirs of the Prophets (1946), pp. 127ff.

    231   Arabia: the Cradle of Islam (1900), pp. 300ff.

    232   Moslem Doctrine of God (1905), passim.

    233   Islam, A Challenge to Faith (1907), pp. 209f.

    234   Ibid., p. 212.

    235   Ibid., pp. 243, 256.

    236   Cf. Unoccupied Fields (1911), pp. 153ff.

    237   Ibid., p. 181.

    238   The Moslem Christ (1912), p. 177.

    239   Ibid., pp. 181-185.

    240   Disintegration...(1915), pp. 184-186.

    241   These ideas about communicating the Gospel to religious man find fuller treatment in Johannes Blauw, "The Biblical View of Man in His Re-

ligion," The Theology of Christian Mission (ed. G. H. Anderson), pp. 31-41
and D. T. Niles, Upon the Earth, p. 235.
    242 Calverly, M.W., 42 (1952), 158.
    243 Cf. Zwemer and Macdonald in The Vital Forces of Christianity and
Islam (reprinted from I.R.M., London, 1915).
    244 Quoted in Zwemer, Mohammed or Christ?, p. 272.
    245 Ibid., p. 274.
    246 Ibid., pp. 273f.
    247 Ibid., p. 282. Zwemer's message to the world is represented by his
triology on the incarnation, crucifixion, and resurrection: The Glory of
the Cross (1928), The Glory of the Manger (1940), and The Glory of the
Empty Tomb (1947).
    248 M.W., 9 (1919), 111ff.
    249 At this point Zwemer foreshadowed the warnings of Willingen (1951)
that the church in its obligation in mission must never take the center
which only Christ and his cross can occupy. Cf. Wilhelm Andersen, "Further
Toward a Theology of Mission," in The Theology of the Christian Mission,
pp. 300-313.
    250 M.W., 11 (1921), 114.
    251 M.W., 18 (1928), 221ff.
    252 D. T. Niles, Upon the Earth, pp. 227ff.
    253 R. Allen, Missionary Methods: St. Paul's or Ours (London, 1912),
The Spontaneous Expansion of the Church and the Causes that Hinder it
(London, 1922), and with T. Cochrane, Missionary Survey (London, 1920).
    254 J. N. Farquhar, The Crown of Hinduism.
    255 A Schweitzer, Christianity and the Religions of the World (Lec-
tures at Selly Oak Colleges, Birmingham, 1922, trans. by J. Powers,
London, 1923).
    256 A. J. Toynbee, "Islam and Ourselves," Atlantic Monthly, 1930, pp.
114-121, and An Historian's Approach to Religion (Based on Gifford Lectures, 1952-53, London, 1956).
    257 Cf. B. Lucas, The Empire of Christ (London, 1908) and Our Task in
India (London, 1914).
    258 F. A. Ross, et. al., The Near East and American Philanthropy (New
York, 1929).
    259 J. R. Mott, "The Outlook in the Moslem World," I.R.M., 13 (1924),
321-339 and D. S. Cairns, "The Christian Message. A Comparison of Thought
in 1910 and 1928," I.R.M., 18 (1929), 321-331.
    260 John E. Merrill, "The Christian Approach to Moslems," I.R.M., 11
(1922), 551-60.
    261 H. S. Bliss, "The Modern Missionary," The Atlantic Monthly, May,
1920 reprinted in Penrose, That They May Have Light, pp. 178-196.
    262 Ibid.
    263 Ibid., p. 185.
    264 A. Jeffery, "The Presentation of Christianity to Moslems," I.R.M.,
13 (1924), 174ff.
    265 Compare with W. A. Visser't Hooft, No Other Name (Philadelphia,
1963) and H. Kraemer, Why Christianity of all Religions (Philadelphia,
1962).
    266 Zwemer, Christianity, the Final Religion (Grand Rapids, 1920), a
series of addresses made to Christian and Muslim audiences before 1920, pp.
3f.
    267 Ibid., p. 42.
    268 Cf. the writings of Karl Barth, Emil Brunner, E. Gogarten, E. Thur-
neysen, Karl Heim, Dietrich Bonhoeffer, noting that these begin about 1924
with the exception of Barth's Der Romerbrief (Bern, 1919).
    269 K. Barth's own pilgrimage from dialectical philosophy, to a theo-
logy of the Word to Christian dogmatics, to "Church Dogmatics" has been

capably documented by T. F. Torrance, _Karl Barth: An Introduction to His Early Theology, 1910-1931_ (London, 1962).

270 K. S. Latourette, _The Unquenchable Light_ (London, 1945), pp. 108f.

271 For one of the finest statements of these implications, cf. Karl Hartenstein, "The Theology of the Word and Missions," _I.R.M._, 20 (1931), 210-227. Cf. Appendix H.

272 _Harper's Magazine_, January, 1933.

273 Cf. Appendix I. This was neither the first nor last of Hocking's comments on missions. Cf. "Palestine--An Impasse?" _Atlantic Monthly_, July, 1930, 121-132; "The Ethical Basis Underlying the Legal Right of Religious Liberty as Applied to Foreign Missions," I.R.M., 20 (1931), 493-511; and _Living Religions and A World Faith_ (London, 1940).

274 Cf. their articles, _I.R.M._, 22 (1933), 153-173, 174-188, 313-324 respectively.

275 Cf. Latourette, _I.R.M._, 22 (1933), 158ff.

276 _Ibid._, p. 173.

277 Mackay, _I.R.M._, 22 (1933), 187f.

278 R. E. Speer, _The Finality of Jesus Christ_ (Stone Lectures, Princeton, 1933) and _Re-Thinking Missions Examined_ (New York, 1933).

279 J. F. Edwards, "_Re-Thinking Missions_" _An Answer from India_ (London, 1933).

280 Cf. _M.W._, 24 (1934), 109.

281 Cf. Zwemer, _Thinking Missions with Christ_ (London, 1934), p. 20.

282 From _Botschafter an Christi Statt_ as quoted in _Ibid._, p. 36.

283 Compare with above, p. 392.

284 _Ibid._, pp. 65ff.

285 Quoted in Ibid., pp. 133-135. The writings and work of Jans Christensen among the Muslims of North India, Alfred Nielsen of Damascus-Jerusalem, and Bengt Sundkler, Bishop of Tanzania show how these ideas were applied.

286 S. Zwemer, _The Origin of Religion_, based on the Smyth Lectures delivered at Columbia Theological Seminary, Decatur, Georgia, 1935 (London, 1935).

287 These ideas were developed by Wilhelm Schmidt, Professor at the University of Vienna in _Origin of the Idea of God_ and by Langdom of Oxford in _Semitic Mythology_. Andrew Lang's discovery of a high-god among primitives also helped shatter the evolutionary theory of the origin of religion. Cf. _Ibid._, p. 14.

288 _Ibid._, pp. 29, 40f.

289 _Ibid._, pp. 44f.

290 _Ibid._

291 _Ibid._, pp. 46ff.

292 Published as _The Solitary Throne_ (London, 1937).

293 Foreshadowing in a way Kraemer's running debate with President Radhakrisknan.

294 Quoted in _Ibid._, p. 28.

295 Cf. Appendix J.

296 These ideas are found in the _Report of the Near East Christian Council Inquiry on the Evangelization of Moslems_ (Beirut, 1938); H. H. Riggs, "Shall We Try Unbeaten Paths in Working for Moslems?" _M.W._, 31 (1941), 116-26; and reappears in A. Carleton, "A Bold Experiment in Muslim Christian Relationships" (a paper privately circulated, December 1965).

297 Cf. H. H. Riggs (chairman), "The Near East: Christian Council Enquiry," in _The Madras Series_ (London, 1939), vol. III, ch. 10, pp. 226-265.

298 Cf. the acceptance of the Delhi recommendations in "Findings of Tambaram," _The Madras Series_ (London, 1939), vol. III, ch. 17, pp. 407-444, esp. pp. 442f.

299 Hallencreutz also finds Kraemer's roots in Brede Kristensen, Chantepie de la Saussaye and J. W. Gunning. Cf. Kraemer Towards Tambaram, pp. 290f.

300 Ibid., pp. 141ff.

301 Zwemer's life-long friend and biographer, Dr. J. Christy Wilson writes: "I am certain that Hendrik Kraemer in his discussion of Islam in his Christian Message reflected the thinking of Samuel Zwemer on Islam. He wrote to many of us in different parts of the world and gathered the material for the volume....Kraemer and Zwemer were both conservative Dutchmen, as you know, and would very largely agree in their theology. Both were very strong in their Christology. Zwemer tended to the practical and Kraemer to the philosophical or theoretical approach. They would agree on discontinuity between Christianity and the non-Christian religions. Kraemer and Zwemer were both on our Princeton Institute of Theology Program." From a personal letter from Dr. Wilson to the author, January 13, 1967.

302 Cf. development of this idea by Johannes Blauw, "The Biblical View of Man in His Religion," The Theology of the Christian Mission, ed. G. H. Anderson (London, 1961), pp. 31-41.

303 Cf. S. M. Zwemer, "Broadcasting our Message," M.W., 29 (1939), 217-220 and "Veni, Sancte Spiritu," M.W., 30 (1940), 1-6.

304 Zwemer, Dynamic Christianity and the World Today (London, 1939), pp. 10f.

305 Cf. W. E. Hocking, Living Religions and a World Faith (London, 1940); H. H. Riggs, "Shall We Try Unbeaten Paths in Working for Moslems?" M.W., 31 (1941), 116-126; and S. M. Zwemer, "The Dynamic of Evangelism," M.W., 31 (1941), 109-115.

306 Cf. M.W., 31 (1941), pp. 113ff.

307 S. M. Zwemer, The Cross Above the Crescent: the validity, necessity and urgency of missions to Moslems (Grand Rapids, 1941), pp. 215f.

308 Ibid., pp. 246ff.

309 S. M. Zwemer, Evangelism Today; Message Not Method (New York, 1944), p. 7.

310 Ibid., p. 8

311 Introduction by Latourette to Apostle to Islam by J. C. Wilson, pp. 5f.

312 Quoted in Ibid., p. 205.

313 One is prone to agree with Latourette in that as "one attempts to summarize the course of Christianity thus far he becomes painfully aware of the imperfections and superficialities of the historian's craft. From the standpoint of the Christian affirmation the most important 'effects of Christianity on its environment' lie 'beyond history'. The environment with which Christianity deals is human lives and these, so Christians have always confidently declared, have only barely begun this side of what men call death and have their finest fruitage the other side of the grave.... Into that life 'beyond the river' the historian cannot reach....Yet, difficult though the task...is, there is in it much of exciting challenge. The story of which we...write is one in which we live and are participants.... Great issues are at stake, for us as individuals, for nations, for cultures, and for mankind and civilization as a whole. We are dealing with basic problems of human history. They have to do with the ultimate meaning of life." Expansion of Christianity, VII, pp. 1f.

ABBREVIATIONS

A.B.C.F.M.	American Board of Commissioners for Foreign Missions
A.J.S.L.L.	American Journal of Semitic Languages and Literature
A.M.Z.	Allgemeine Missions-Zeitschrift
B.S.O.A.S.	Bulletin of the School of Oriental and African Studies
C.E.Z.M.S.	Church of England Zenana Mission Society
C.M.I.	Church Missionary Intelligencer
C.M.R.	Church Missionary Review
C.M.S.	Church Missionary Society
C.S.M.	Church of Scotland Mission
E.M.	Die evangelischen Missionen
E.M.M.	Evangelisches Missions-Magazin
E.M.M.S.	Edinburgh Medical Missionary Society
E.M.Z.	Evangelische Missions-Zeitschrift
E.W.	The East and the West
I.C.	Islamic Culture
I.M.C.	International Missionary Council
I.Q.	Islamic Quarterly
I.R.M.	International Review of Missions
J.A.O.S.	Journal of the American Oriental Society
J.R.A.S.	Journal of the Royal Asiatic Society
L.M.S.	London Missionary Society
M.E.J.	Middle East Journal
M.R.W.	Missionary Review of the World
M.W.	Moslem World/Muslim World
O.B.	Occasional Bulletin (Missionary Research Library, N.Y.)
O.I.C.C.U.	Oxford Inter-Collegiate Christian Union
O.O.	Orient and Occident (Cairo)
S.C.M.	Student Christian Movement
S.I.	Studia Islamica
S.P.C.K.	Society for the Propagation of Christian Knowledge
S.P.G.	Society for the Propagation of the Gospel
S.V.M.	Student Volunteer Missionary Movement (in Britain "Union")
S.W.	Student World
W.C.C.	World Council of Churches
W.I.	Die Welt des Islams
W.S.C.F.	World Student Christian Federation
Y.M.C.A.	Young Men's Christian Association
Z.M.R.	Zeitschrift für Missionskunde und Religionswissenschaft
Z.M.	Zeitschrift für Missionswissenschaft

Names of other journals, organizations, etc., are either shortened or given in full.

Bibliography

Only those sources of a broader interest and application have been selected for the final bibliography. A number of works, both primary and secondary, which were used to a lesser extent are documented only in the notes or appendices.

Abdul Haqq, A., "The Quran and the Trinitarian Dogma," Bulletin of the Henry Martyn School of Islamic Studies, July-Sept., 1956, 3-13.

Addison, James Thayer, The Christian Approach to the Moslem, New York, 1942.

Ainslie, E., Charles Grant and British Rule in India, London, 1962.

Ainsworth, Wm. F., Travels and Researches in Asia Minor, Mesopotamia, Chaldea, and Armenia, 2 vols., London, 1842.

Alexander, J.R., The Sound of Marching: Bestir Thyself, Cairo, 1928.

_____, A Sketch of the Story of the Evangelical Church of Egypt, Alexand-1930.

Allen, E. L., Christianity Among the Religions, London, 1960.

Allen, Roland, Missionary Methods: St. Paul's or Ours, London, 1912.

_____, and Cochrane, T., Missionary Survey, as an Aid to Intelligent Co-operation in Foreign Missions, London, 1920.

_____, The Spontaneous Expansion of the Church and the Causes which Hinder It, London, 1922.

Andersen, Wilhelm, Towards a Theology of Mission, London, 1955.

_____, "Dr Kraemer's Contribution to the Understanding of the Nature of Revelation," I.R.M., 46 (1957), 361-371.

Anderson, Gerald H., The Theology of Missions, 1928-1958 (dissertation, microfilm, Boston University), Boston, 1960.

_____ (ed.), The Theology of Christian Mission, London, 1961.

Anderson, J.N.D. (ed.), The World's Religions, London, 1950, revised 1975.

Anderson, Rufus, History of the Missions of the A.B.C.F.M. to the Oriental Churches, 2 vols., Boston, 1872.

_____, History of the Missions of the A.B.C.F.M. in India, Boston, 1874.

Antonius, George, The Arab Awakening, London, 1939.

Arberry, A.J., and Landau, R. (editors), Islam Today, London, 1943.

Arberry, A.J., The Koran Interpreted, 2 vols., London, 1955.

Arnold, T.W., The Preaching of Islam, Oxford, 1896.

_____, The Caliphate, Oxford, 1924.

_____, and Guillaume, A. (editors), The Legacy of Islam, Oxford, 1931.

Arpee, Leon, The Armenian Awakening, Chicago, 1909.

Badley, B.H., Indian Missionary Directory and Memorial Volume, London, 1876.

Baly, Denis, Multitudes in the Valley: Church and Crisis in the Middle East, Greenwich, Conn., 1957.

Barth, Karl, Commentary on Romans (trans. by E.C. Hoskyns), London, 1933.

_____, The Word of God and the Word of Man (trans. D. Horton), London, 1928.

_____, From Rousseau to Ritschl, London, 1959.

_____, Church Dogmatics (Trans. of Die kirkliche Dogmatik, editors: G.W. Bromiley and T.F. Torrance), vols. I-IV, Edinburgh, 1956-1962, esp. III/2 and IV/3.

Bartlett, S.C., Missions of the A.B.C.F.M. in India and Ceylon, Boston, 1886.

Barton, J. L., Daybreak in Turkey, Boston, 1908.

_____, Christian Approach to Islam, Boston, 1918.

_____, Story of Near East Relief, New York, 1931.

Bassett, James, Persia, the Land of the Imams, A Narrative of Travel and Residence, 1871-1885, London, 1887.

_____, Persia, Eastern Mission, Philadelphia, 1890.

Bavinck, J.H., The Impact of Christianity on the Non-Christian World, Grand Rapids, 1949.

Beach, H. P., Geography and Atlas of Protestant Missions, 2 vols., New York, 1901-3.

_____, India and Christian Opportunity, New York, 1904.

_____, World Statistics of Christian Missions, New York, 1916.

Becker, C.H., Christianity and Islam (trans. H.J. Chaytor), London, 1909.

Bell, R., The Origin of Islam in Its Christian Environment, London, 1926.

Bethmann, Erich, Bridge to Islam: A Study of the Religious Forces of Islam and Christianity in the Near East, London, 1953.

Beyerhaus, Peter and Lefever, H., The Responsible Church and the Foreign Missions, London, 1964.

Bijlefeld, Willem A., "Recent Theological Evaluation of the Christian-Muslim Encounter" (Part II), I.R.M., 55 (1966), 430-441.

_____, "A Prophet and More Than a Prophet?" M.W. 59 (1969), 1-28.

_____, "Islamic Studies Within the Perspective of the History of Religions," M.W., 62 (1972), 1-11.

_____, "Introducing Islam: a Bibliographical Essay," M.W., 63 (1973), 171-184; 269-279.

_____, "Some Recent Contributions to Qur'anic Studies: Selected Publications in English, French, and German, 1964-1973," M.W., 64 (1974), 79-102, 172-179, 259-274.

Bird, Isaac, Bible Work in Bible Lands, Philadelphia, 1872.

_____, The Martyr of Lebanon, Boston, 1864.

Birks, Herbert, The Life and Correspondence of Thomas Valpy French, First Bishop of Lahore, 2 vols., London, 1895.

Blauw, Johannes, The Missionary Nature of the Church: A Survey of the Biblical Theology of Mission, London, 1962.

Bliss, Edwin M., Turkey and the Armenian Atrocities, Philadelphia, 1896.

_____, and Dwight, H.D. (editors), The Encyclopaedia of Missions, New York, 1904.

_____, The Missionary Enterprise: A Concise History of its Objects, Methods and Extension, New York, 1908.

Bliss, Frederick, The Religions of Modern Syria and Palestine, New York, 1912.

_____, The Reminiscences of Daniel Bliss, New York, 1920.

Boer, Harry, Pentecost and Mission, London, 1961.

Bonhoeffer, Dietrich, Christology, London, 1966.

Bouquet, A. C., The Christian Faith and Non-Christian Religions, Welwyn, 1958.

_____, Comparative Religion, Hammersmith, 1964.

Brockelmann, Carl, History of the Islamic Peoples (trans. J. Carmichael and M. Perlmann), New York, 1960.

Brown, A.J., One Hundred Years: A History of the Foreign Missionary Work of the Presbyterian Church, U.S.A., New York, 1937.

Brown, David, Christianity and Islam Series, London, 1967ff.

Browne, Laurence E., The Eclipse of Christianity in Asia, Cambridge, 1933.

_____, The Quickening Word: A Theological Answer to the Challenge of Islam (Hulsean Lectures, 1954), Cambridge, 1955.

_____, The Prophets of Islam, London, 1944.

Brunner, Emil, The Mediator (trans. O. Wyon), London, 1963.

_____, Natural Theology: comprising "Nature and Grace" and the reply, "No" by... K. Barth, (trans. P. Fraenkel), London, 1946.

_____, Eternal Hope, Lond, 1954.

_____, The Letter to the Romans, London, 1959.

Cairns, D. S., Christianity in the Modern World, London, 1907.

_____, "The Christian Message. A Comparison of Thought in 1910 and 1928," I.R.M., 18 (1929), 321-331.

Calverly, E. E., Worship in Islam, New York, 1925.

_____, Islam: An Introduction, Cairo, 1958.

Calvin, John, Institutes of the Christian Religion, 2 vols., Grand Rapids, 1957.

_____, Commentary on Daniel (trans. T. Myers), 2 vols., Edinburgh, 1852-53.

Cash, W. W., The Moslem World in Revolution, London, 1925.

_____, Persia, Old and New, London, 1929.

_____, Christendom and Islam: Their Contacts and Cultures Down the Centuries, London, 1937.

_____, The Missionary Church, London, 1939.

_____, A Century of Mission Work in Iran (Presbyterian, U.S.A.), Beirut, 1936.

Chakmakjian, Hagop, Armenian Christology and Evangelization of Islam, Leiden, 1965.

Chatterton, Eyre, A History of the Church of England in India since the Early Days of the East India Company, London, 1924.

Christiansen, Jens, The Practical Approach to Muslims, Mardan, Pakistan, 1952-53.

Clark, Henry Martyn, Robert Clark of the Punjab, Pioneer and Missionary Statesman, London, 1907.

Clark, Robert, Punjab and Sindh: The Missions of the C.M.S., 1852-84, London (revised edition), 1904.

Clark, Wm., The Conception of the Mission of the Church in Early Reformed Theology: With Special Reference to Calvin's Theology and Practice in Geneva (unpublished dissertation, New College), Edinburgh, 1928.

Cragg, A Kenneth, Islam in the 20th Century, the Relevance of Christian Theology and the Relation of the Christian Mission to its Problems (mimeographed dissertation), Oxford, 1950.

_____, The Call of the Minaret, New York, 1956.

_____, Sandals at the Mosque: Christian Presence Amid Islam, New York,1959.

_____, "Operation Reach" and "Emmaus Road" (Study Series under the auspices of the Near East Christian Council), Beirut, 1959 onwards.

_____, The Dome and the Rock, London, 1964.

_____, Counsels in Contemporary Islam (Islamic Surveys III) Edinburgh,1965.

_____, The House of Islam, Belmont, California, 1969.

_____, "The Christian Church and Islam Today," M.W., 42 (1952), 11ff., 112ff., 207ff., 277ff.

_____, "Persons, Situations, Books," M.W., 43 (1953), 197ff.

_____, "The Arab World and the Christian Debt," I.R.M., 42 (1953), 151-161.

_____, "Each Other's Face: Some Thoughts on Muslim-Christian Colloquy Today," M.W., 45 (1955), 172-182.

_____, "Hearing by the Word of God," I.R.M., 46 (1957), 241-251.

_____, "Introduction" to City of Wrong, A Friday in Jerusalem by M. Kamel Hussein, London, 1959.

Daniel, Norman, "The Development of the Christian Attitude to Islam," Dublin Review, 231 (1957), 289-312.

_____, Islam and the West: the Making of an Image, Edinburgh, 1960.

Davis, Charles, God's Grace in History (Maurice Lectures), London, 1966.

Davis, W. B., A Study of Missionary Policy and Methods in Bengal from 1793 to 1905 (unpublished dissertation, New College), Edinburgh, 1942.

Dawson, Christopher, The Making of Europe, London, 1937.

_____, Mediaeval Essays, London, 1953.

_____, The Mongol Mission, London, 1955.

Day, Lal Behari, Recollections of Alexander Duff, D.D., LL.D., and of the Mission College which He founded at Calcutta, London, 1879.

Dehqani-Tafti, Hassan, Design of My World, London, 1959.

Dennis, James, A Sketch of the Syrian Mission, New York, 1872.

_____, Foreign Missions After a Century, London, 1894.

_____, Christian Missions and Social Progress, New York, 1899.

Devannandan, P. D., Preparation for Dialogue, Bangalore, 1964.

Dewick, E. C., The Indwelling God, London, 1938.

_____, The Gospel and Other Faiths, London, 1948.

_____, The Christian Attitude to Other Religions (Hulsean Lectures, 1949), Cambridge, 1953.

Donaldson, Dwight, The Shi'te Religion: A History of Islam in Persia and Iraq, London, 1933.

_____, Studies in Muslim Ethics, London, 1953.

Dorman, Harry G., Toward Understanding Islam. Contemporary Apologetic of Islam and Missionary Policy, New York, 1948.

Duff, Alexander, India and India Mission, Edinburgh, 1839.

_____, Missions the Chief End of the Christian Church, Edinburgh, 1839.

_____, Proposed Modes of Extending the Foreign Mission Operations of the Free Church of Scotland, Edinburgh, 1865.

Duff, W. P. Memorials of Alexander Duff, London, 1890.

Dwight, H.G.O., Christianity Revived in the East; or A Narrative of the Work of God Among the Armenians of Turkey, New York, 1850.

Encyclopedia of Islam, The (editors, M.T. Houtsma, T.W. Arnold, et al.) 4 vols., Leiden, 1913-36; new edition, vol. I-., Leiden, 1960-.

Elder, Earl E., Vindicating a Vision: The Story of the American Mission in Egypt, 1854-1954, Philadelphia, 1958.

Elder, John, History of the American Presbyterian Mission to Iran, 1834-1960, Iran, n.d.

Farquhar, J. N., Christ and the Gospels, Calcutta, 1901.

_____, The Crown of Hinduism, Oxford, 1913.

_____, Modern Religious Movements in India, New York, 1915.

Field, Claud H.A., Mystics and Saints in Islam, London, 1910.

Finney, D. M., Tomorrow's Egypt, Pittsburgh, 1939.

Fortescue, A., The Uniate Eastern Churches (ed. George Smith), London, 1923.

_____, The Orthodox Eastern Church, London, 1907.

Foster, F.H., "Is Islam a Christian Heresy?" M.W., 22 (1932), 126-133.

Foster, John, Beginning from Jerusalem, Lond, 1956.

_____, To All Nations, London, 1960.

Gairdner, W. H. T., For a classified bibliography, see Appendix F.
Garlick, P.L., The Way of Partnership: With the C.M.S. in India, London, 1938.
_____, The Wholeness of Man: A Study in the History of Healing, London, 1943.
———' Man's Search for Health: A Study in the Inter-relation of Religion and Medicine, London, 1952.
Gaudefroy-Demombynes, Maurice, Muslim Institutions, London, 1950.
Gibb, H.A.R., The Arab Conquest in Central Asia, London, 1923.
_____, Arabic Literature: An Introduction, London, 1926.
_____, Whither Islam? A Survey of Modern Movements in the Moslem World, London, 1932.
_____, Modern Trends in Islam, Chicago, 1947.
_____, Mohammedanism: An Historical Survey, London (2nd ed.), 1953.
_____, An Interpretation of Islamic History, Lahore, 1957.
_____, and Bowen, H., Islamic Society and the West: A Study of the Impact of Western Civilization on Moslem Culture in the Near East, 2 vols., London, 1950-57.
Glover, W. B., Evangelical Nonconformists and Higher Criticism in the Nineteenth Century, London, 1954.
Gobat, Samuel, Journal of Three Years' Residence in Abyssinia, London, 1834.
_____, Samuel Gobat, Bishop of Jerusalem, His Life and Work: A Biographical Sketch Drawn Chiefly from his own Journals, London, 1884.
Goldsack, W., Christ in Islam: The Testimony of the Quran to Christ, London, 1905.
Goldziher, Ignaz, Muhammedanische Studien, 2 vols., Halle, 1889-1890.
_____, Vorlesungen über den Islam, Heidelberg, 1910.
Goodall, Norman (ed.), Missions Under the Cross (Addresses at Willingen), London, 1953.
_____, Christian Missions and Social Ferment, London, 1964.
Gordon, Andrew, Our India Mission. A Thirty Years' History of the India Mission of the United Presbyterian Church of North America Together with Personal Reminiscences, Philadelphia, 1888.
Grant, Asahel, The Nestorians; or, The Lost Tribes, New York, 1845.
Guillaume, Alfred, The Life of Muhammad, Oxford, 1954.
_____, The Traditions of Islam, London, 1924.
Hahn, Ernest, Jesus in Islam - A Christian View, Vaniyambadi, India, n.d.
Hahn, Ferdinand, Mission in the New Testament, London, 1965.
Hallencreutz, Carl F., Kraemer Towards Tambaram. A Study in Hendrik Kraemer's Missionary Approach, Uppsala, 1966.
Hamlin, Cyrus, Among the Turks, Boston, 1878.
_____, My Life and Times, Boston, 1893.
_____, "Fifty Years of Missionary Education in Turkey," (Graves Lectures at New Brunswick Theological Seminary, 1888-89), New Brunswick, N.J., 1889.
Hargreaves, A. R., "A Method of Presenting Jesus Christ to Moslems," M.W., 37 (1947), 255-265.
Harris, G. K., How to Lead Moslems to Christ, Philadelphia, 1947.
Harrison, Anne M., A Tool in His Hand, New York, 1958.
Harrison, Paul W., The Arab at Home, New York, 1924.
_____, Doctor in Arabia, New York, 1940.
_____, The Light that Lighteth Every Man. Expositions in the Gospel of St. John, Grand Rapids, 1958.
Hartenstein, Karl, Was hat die Theologie Karl Barths der Mission zu sagen? Munich, 1928.
_____, "The Theology of the Word and Missions," I.R.M., 20 (1931), 210-227.
_____, Die Mission als theologisches Problem, Berlin, 1933.
Hasluck, F.W., Christianity and Islam under the Sultans, 2 vols., Oxford,

1929.

Hawkes, J. W., "Fifty Years of Mission Work in Persia," M.W., 13 (1923), 236-241.

Heavenor, E.S.P., The Eschatological Motive for World Mission in the New Testament, (unpublished dissertation, New College), Edinburgh, 1962.

Henderson, Lilian F., The Cambridge Mission to Delhi. A Brief History, London, 1931.

Herrick, George F., Christian and Mohammedan: A Plea for Bridging the Chasm, New York, 1912.

Hewat, Elizabeth, Vision and Achievement, 1796-1956: A History of the Foreign Missions of the Churches United in the Church of Scotland, Edinburgh, 1960.

History's Lessons for Tomorrow's Mission: Milestones in the History of Missionary Thinking (W.S.C.F.), Geneva, n.d.

Historical Sketches of the India Missions of the Presbyterian Church in the U.S.A., Allahabad, 1886.

Hitti, Philip K., History of the Arabs, New York, (1937) 1964.

_____, History of Syria, London, 1951.

_____, Lebanon in History, London, 1957.

Hoare, J. N., Something New in Iran (C.M.S.), London, 1937.

Hocking, Wm. E., The Meaning of God in Human Experience. A Philosophic Study of Religion, New Haven, Conn., 1922.

_____, (chairman), Re-Thinking Missions: A Laymen's Inquiry after One Hundred Years, New York, 1932.

_____, Living Religion and a World Faith (Hibbert Lectures), London, 1940.

Hogg, A. G., Christ's Message of the Kingdom, Edinburgh, 1911.

_____, Redemption from this World; or the Supernatural in Christianity, Edinburgh, 1922.

_____, The Christian Message to the Hindu (Duff Lectures), London, 1947.

Hogg, Rena L., A Master-Builder on the Nile. Being a Record of the Life and Aims of John Hogg, D.D., Christian Missionary, New York, 1914.

Hogg, W. Richard, Ecumenical Foundations, New York, 1952.

_____, One World, One Mission, New York, 1960.

Holsten, Walter, Das Kerygma und der Mensch, Munich, 1953.

Hough, James, The Protestant Missions Vindicated, London, 1837.

Hughes, T. P., Dictionary of Islam, London, 1885.

Hunter, Robert, History of the Missions of the Free Church of Scotland in India and Africa, London, 1873.

Hurgronje, Snouck, Mohammedanism, New York, 1916.

Index Islamicus, 1906-1955 and Supplement, 1956-1960 compiled by J. D. Pearson, Cambridge, 1958-1962.

Ireland, P. W., (ed.) The Near East: Problems and Prospects, Chicago, 1942.

Jeffery, Arthur, "Eclecticism in Islam," M.W., 12 (1922), 230-247.

_____, "The Presentation of Christianity to Moslems," I.R.M., 13 (1924), 174-89.

_____, "A Collection of Anti-Christian Books and Pamphlets Found in Actual Use Among the Mohammedans of Cairo," M.W., 15 (1925), 26-37.

_____, "The Real Muhammad and the Ideal. A Study of One Phase of Modern Muslim Apologetic," I.R. M., 18 (1929), 390-400.

_____, The Foreign Vocabulary of the Qur'ān, Baroda, 1938.

_____, Islam: Muhammad and His Religion, New York, 1958.

Jessup, Henry H., The Mohammedan Missionary Problem, Philadelphia, 1879.

_____, The Greek Church and Protestant Missions, Beirut, 1891.

_____, Kamil Abdul Messiah, A Syrian Convert from Islam to Christianity, Philadelphia, 1898.

Johnson, R. Park, The Middle East Pilgrimage, New York, 1958.

_____, "Renewal of the Christian Mission to Islam: Reflections on the Asmara Conference," I.R.M., 48 (1959), 438-444.

Jones, E. Stanley, et al., The Christian Message for the World Today, London, 1934.

Jones, J. P., (ed.) The Year Book of Missions in India, Burma, and Ceylon, 1912, India, 1912.

Jones, L. Bevan, "Our Message to Muslims," M.W., 20 (1930), 331-336.

_____, The People of the Mosque, London, 1932.

_____, "Christ's Ambassador to the Muslim," M.W., 41 (1951), 80-81.

_____, Christianity Explained to Muslims: A Manual for Christian Workers, Calcutta, 1952.

Joseph, John, The Nestorians and their Muslim Neighbors. A study of Western Influence on their Relations, Princeton, 1961.

Jowett, Wm., Christian Researches in the Mediterranean from 1815 to 1820 (C.M.S.), London, 1822.

_____, Christian Researches in Syria and the Holy Land in 1823 and 1824 (C.M.S.), London, 1825.

Jurji, Edward J., The Great Religions of the Modern World, Princeton, 1947.

_____, The Christian Interpretation of Religion: Christianity in its Human and Creative Relationship with the World's Cultures and Other Faiths, New York, 1952.

_____, The Middle East: Its Religion and Culture, Philadelphia, 1956.

_____, The Phenomenology of Religion, Philadelphia, 1963.

_____, "Impact of Christianity upon the Middle East," Theology Today, 8 (1951), 55-69.

_____, "Religious Pluralism and World Community," Theology Today, 23 (1966), 346-362.

Kellerhals, E., Der Islam: Seine Geschichte, Seine Lehre, Sein Wesen, Basel, 1945.

_____, Raymundus Lullus, ein Ritter Jesu Christi, Basel, 1948.

Kinsler, F.R., Love as a Motive for Mission: An Approach to the Biblical Theology of Mission (unpublished dissertation, New College), Edinburgh, 1962.

Kirk, George, A Short History of the Middle East, from the Rise of Islam to Modern Times, London, 1948.

Koelle, S. W., Mohammed and Mohammedanism, Critically Considered, London, 1889.

Kraemer, Hendrik, The Christian Message in a Non-Christian World, London, 1938.

_____, Religion and the Christian Faith, Philadelphia, 1956.

_____, The Communication of the Christian Faith, London, 1957.

_____, From Mission Field to Independent Church, London, 1958.

_____, A Theology of the Laity, London, 1958.

_____, World Culture and World Religions: The Coming Dialogue, Philadelphia, 1960.

_____, Why Christianity of All Religions, Philadelphia, 1962.

_____, "Christianity and Secularism," I.R.M., 19 (1930), 195ff.

_____, "Islam in India Today," M.W., 21 (1931), 151-176.

_____, "A Modern Revindication of Islam," M.W., 29 (1939), 141-150.

_____, "Syncretism as a Religious and a Missionary Problem," I.R.M., 43 (1954), 253-273.

Lammens, Henri, Islam: Beliefs and Institutions (trans. E. D. Ross), London, 1929.

Lansing, Gulian, Egypt's Princes, a Narrative of Missionary Labor in the Valley of the Nile, Philadelphia, (2nd.ed.) 1864.

Latourette, Kenneth Scott, Missions Tomorrow, London, 1936.

_____, A Expansion of Christianity, 7 vols., London, 1938-1945.

_____, A History of Christianity, London, n.d.

_____, The Christian World Mission in Our Day, London, 1954.

_____, Christianity in a Revolutionary Age, 5 vols., New York, 1958.
Laurie, Thomas, Dr. Grant and the Mountain Nestorians, Boston, 1853.
_____, Science and Missions, Boston, 1882.
Lee, Samuel, Controversial Tracts on Christianity and Mohammedanism,
    Cambridge, 1824.
Lefroy, George A., Christ the Goal of India (Cambridge-Delhi Occasional
    Papers, No. 15), Cambridge, 1889.
_____, Sweeps and Bridge (Two Sermons), London, 1906.
Levonian, Lootfy, Moslem Mentality, London, 1928.
_____, Studies in the Relationship of Islam and Christianity, London, 1940.
_____, "The Criticism of Religion in Islam," I.R.M., 19 (1930), 87-97.
_____, "Fulfillment not Destruction," M.W., 21 (1931), 122ff.
_____, "Muslim Evangelization: A Psychological Study," I.R.M., 29 (1940),
    236-40.
_____, "Millet System in the Middle East," M.W., 42 (1952), 90-96.
Levy, R., The Social Structure of Islam, Cambridge, 1957.
Lewis, Bernard, British Contributions to Arabic Studies, London, 1941.
_____, The Arabs in History, London, 1958.
_____, The Emergence of Modern Turkey, London, 1961.
_____, Historians of the Middle East, London, 1962.
_____, The Middle East and the West, Bloomington, Indiana, 1964.
_____, "Some Reflections on the Decline of the Ottoman Empire," Studia
    Islamica, 9 (1958), 111-127.
Longrigg, S. H., Four Centuries of Modern Iraq, Oxford, 1925.
_____, Iraq, 1900-1950, London, 1953.
Lowe, John, Medical Missions, their Place and Power, London, 1886.
Lowrie, John C., Travels in North India, Philadelphia, 1842.
_____, Two Years in Upper India, New York, 1850.
Lucas, Bernard, Our Task in India. Shall We Proselyte Hindus or Evangelize
    India? London, 1914.
Macdonald, Duncan Black, Development of Muslim Theology, Jurisprudence and
    Constitutional Theory, London, 1903.
_____, The Religious Attitude and Life in Islam, Chicago, 1909.
_____, Aspects of Islam, New York, 1911.
_____, "The Vital Forces of Christianity and Islam," I.R.M., 2 (1913),
    657-73.
_____, "Whither Islam?" M.W. 23 (1933), 1-5.
Macdonald Presentation Volume, Princeton, 1933.
MacDuff, A. R., The Utmost Bound of the Everlasting Hills, or Memories of
    Christ's Frontier Force in North-Western India, London, 1902.
Mackay, John A., "The Theology of the Laymen's Foreign Missions Inquiry,"
    I.R.M., 22 (1933), 174-188.
Mackickan, D., "A Present-day Phase of Missionary Theology," I.R.M., 3
    (1914), 243ff.
_____, The Missionary Idea in the Scottish Churches, London, 1927.
MacLean, A. F. and Browne, Wm., The Catholicos of the East and His People,
    London, 1892.
MacNicol, Nicol, "Islam at the Madras Council," M.W., 29 (1939), 1-4.
Maconachie, James R., Rowland Bateman, Nineteenth Century Apostle, London,
    1917.
Malik, Charles H., "The Basic Issues of the Near East," Annuals, 258
    (1948), 1-7.
_____, "Near Eastern Witness to Christian Missions," Theology Today, 5
    (1949), 527-32.
_____, in The Prospects of Christianity throughout the World (editor, M. S.
    Bates), New York, 1964.
_____, "These Things I believe," Christianity Today, 10 (1966), 3-6.

Margoliouth, D. S., Mohammed and the Rise of Islam, London, 1905.
_____, Cairo, Jerusalem and Damascus, London, 1907.
_____, The Early Development of Mohammedanism (Hibbert Lectures), London, 1914.
_____, "Islam a Christian Heresy?" M.W., 23 (1933), 6-15.
Marshman, Joshua, Thoughts on Propagating Christianity more Effectually among the Heathen (2nd ed.), Edinburgh, 1827.
Martin, Cecil H., Allnutt of Delhi, A Memoir, London, 1922.
Martyn, Henry, Twenty Sermons, London, 1822.
_____, Journals and Letters (ed. S. Wilberforce), 2 vols., London, 1837.
_____, Five Sermons, London, 1862.
Mason, A.D. and Barny, F.J., History of the Arabian Mission, New York, 1926.
Massignon, Louis, "The Roman Catholic Church and Islam," M.W., 5 (1915), 129ff.
McClenahan, R.S., "The Evangelization of the Enlightened Moslem," I.R.M., 6 (1917), 534-545.
McGavran, Donald A., The Bridges of God: A Study in the Strategy of Missions, London, 1957.
_____, How Churches Grow, London, 1959.
_____ (ed.), Church Growth and Christian Mission, London, 1965.
_____, "Wrong Strategy: The Real Crisis in Missions," I.R.M., 54 (1965), 451-61.
Mckintosh, H.R., Types of Christian Theology, Schleiermacher to Barth, London, 1964.
McLeish, Alexander, The Frontier Peoples of India: A Missionary Survey, London, 1931.
_____, Objective and Method in Christian Expansion, London, 1952.
Memorial of Missionaries in Syria and Palestine, London, 1886.
Merrick, James L., The Life and Religion of Mohammed, Boston, 1850.
Merrill, J.E., "The Christian Approach to Moslems," I.R.M., 11 (1922), 551-60.
_____, "A Christian 'Word of Testimony' for Use with Muslims," Macdonald Presentation Volume, Princeton, 1933, 193ff.
Mez, A., The Renaissance of Islam (English trans.), London, 1937.
Miller, W., The Ottoman Empire and its Successors, 1801-1927, Cambridge, 1936.
Miller, Wm., Indian Missions and How to View Them, Edinburgh, 1878.
_____, Educational Agencies in India, Madras, 1893.
_____, The Madras Christian College, A Short Account of its History and Influence, Edinburgh, 1905.
Miller, William McElwee, "How the Revivals Came to Persia, M.R.W., 1933, 486ff.
_____, Telling the Good News, (mimeographed) Teheran, 1960.
_____, "A Man Sent from God Whose Name was Samuel," (Sunday School Times Booklet) Philadelphia, 1966.
_____, Ten Muslims Meet Christ, Grand Rapids, 1969.
_____, A Christian's Response to Islam, Philadelphia, 1976.
Monk, F.F., A History of St. Stephen's College, Delhi, Calcutta, 1935.
Montgomery, H.H., Life and Letters of George Alfred Lefroy, London, 1920.
_____ (ed.), Mankind and the Church, London, 1907.
Moorshead, R.F., The Way of the Doctor: A Study in Medical Missions, London, 1926.
Morgan, Kenneth (ed.), Islam, the Straight Path: Islam Interpreted by Muslims, New York, 1958.
Morrison, S.A., The Way of Partnership: With the C.M.S. in Egypt and Palestine. London, 1936.
_____, "Muslim Lands--Church and State," Madras Series, vol. VI, London, 1939.

_____, Religious Liberty in the Near East, London, 1949.

_____, Middle East Survey: the Political, Social, and Religious Problems, London, 1954.

Mott, John R., The Evangelization of the World in This Generation, London, 1903.

_____, "The Outlook in the Moslem World," I.R.M., 13 (1924), 321-339.

_____ (ed.), Evangelism for the World Today, New York, 1938.

Muir, Wm., Life of Mohammed (4 vols. 1858), Edinburgh, 1912.

_____, The Coran: Its Composition and Teaching, and the Testimony it bears to the Holy Scriptures, London, 1878.

_____, The Caliphate: Its Rise and Fall (1883, revised by T. H. Weir) Edinburgh, 1915.

_____, Mohammedan Controversy, Edinburgh, 1897.

Neill, Stephen, A History of the Ecumenical Movement, 1517-1948, London, 1954.

_____, Christian Faith and Other Faiths, London, 1961.

_____, A History of Christian Missions, Grand Rapids, 1964.

Neve, Arthur, Thirty Years in Kashmir, London, 1913.

Neve, Ernest F., Beyond the Pir Panjal, London, 1914.

_____, A Crusader in Kashmir (Arthur Neve), London, 1928.

Newbigin, J.E. Lesslie, The Household of God. Lectures on the Nature of the Church, London, 1953.

Nida, Eugene A., Customs, Culture and Christianity, London, 1954.

_____, Message and Mission: The Communication of the Christian Faith, New York, 1960.

Nielsen, Alfred, William Temple Gairdner, Copenhage, 1932.

_____, "Difficulties in Presenting the Gospel," M.W., 19 (1929), 41-46.

_____, "The Two Faces of Islam," I.R.M., 23 (1934), 345-366.

_____, "Islam in Palestine," M.W., 25 (1935), 257-263.

_____, "Can Islam be 'Modern'?" I.R.M., 44 (1955), 257-263.

Niles, D.T., Upon the Earth: The Mission of God and the Missionary Enterprise of the Churches, London, 1962.

Nöldeke, Theodor, Sketches from Eastern History, (English trans.) Edinburgh, 1892.

O'Leary, De Lacy, Islam at the Cross Roads, London, 1923.

Oldham, J.H., The World and the Gospel, London, 1916.

One Hundred Years of Growth: A Brief History of the Work of the Church of Scotland in the Punjab, Sialkot, 1957.

Orchard, R. K., Out of Every Nation: a Discussion of the Internationalizing of Missions (I.M.C. Research Pamphlet, No. 7), London, 1959.

_____, Missions in a Time of Testing, London, 1964.

_____, "Joint Action for Mission: Its Aim, Implications and Method," I.R.M., 54 (1965), 81-94.

Our Church's Work in India: The Story of the Missions of the United Free Church of Scotland in Bengal, Santalia, Bombay, Rajputana, and Madras, Edinburgh, n.d.

Padwick, C., Henry Martyn, Confessor of the Faith, New York, 1923.

_____, Temple Gairdner of Cairo, London, 1929.

Pannikkar, K.M., Asia and Western Dominance: A Survey of the Vasco Da Gama Epoch of Asian History, 1498-1945, London, 1953.

Parrinder, Geoffrey, Comparative Religion, London, 1962.

_____, What the World Religions Teach, London, 1963.

_____, Jesus in the Qur'an, London, 1965.

Pascoe, C. F., Two Hundred Years of the S.P.G., London, 1901.

_____, The Story of the Delhi Mission, London, 1917.

Paton, David M., Christian Missions and the Judgment of God, London, 1953.

Paton, Wm., Alexander Duff, Pioneer of Missionary Education, London, 1923.

_____, Jesus Christ and the World's Religions, London, 1928.

Pennell, Alice, _Pennell of the Afghan Frontiers_, London, 1914.

Pennell, T.L., _Among the Wild Tribes on the Afghan Frontier_, London, 1909.

Penrose, S.B.L., _That They May Have Light: The Story of the American University of Beirut, 1866-1941_, New York, 1941.

Perkins, H.M., _Life of Rev. Justin Perkins, D.D._, Chicago, 1887.

Perkins, Justin, _A Residence of Eight Years in Persia Among Nestorian Christians with Notices of the Muhammedans_, Andover, 1843.

Perry, Edmund F., _The Gospel in Dispute; the Relation of Christian Faith to Other Missionary Religions_, New York, 1958.

Pfander, Karl G., _Mizan-ul-Haqq (Balance of Truth_, trans. R. H. Weakley) London, 1867, (revised and enlarged by W. St. Clair Tisdall), London, 1910.

_____, _Remarks on the Nature of Muhammadanism_, Calcutta, 1840.

Pfannmüller, D. Gustav, _Handbuch Der Islam--Literatur_, Berlin, 1923.

Philip, P.O., _Report on a Survey of Indigenous Christian Efforts in India, Burma, and Ceylon_, Poona, 1928.

Pickett, J. W., _Christian Mass Movements in India. A Study with Recommendations_, Cincinnati, 1933.

Polk, William Roe, _The Opening of South Lebanon, 1788-1840. A Study of the Impact of the West on the Middle East_, Cambridge, Mass., 1963.

Prime, E.D.G., _Forty Years in the Turkish Empire; or, Memoirs of Rev. William Goodell, D.D._, (4th ed.) New York, 1877.

Rahbar, Daud, "Christian Apologetic to Muslims," _I.R.M._, 54 (1965), 353-359.

Report of the World Missionary Conference, Edinburgh, 1910, 9 vols., Edinburgh, 1910.

Report of the Continuation Committee Conferences in Asia, 1912-1913, (chairman, J. R. Mott), New York, 1912.

Report of the International Missionary Council, meeting at Jerusalem, March 24-April 8, 1928, 8 vols., London, 1928.

Reports of Conferences of Missionaries to Muslims:
Methods of Mission Work Among Moslems (Cairo, 1906), New York, 1906.
Mohammedan World Today (Cairo, 1906), New York, 1906.
Our Moslem Sisters (Cairo, 1906), New York, 1907.
Islam and Missions: Report of the Lucknow Conference, New York, 1911.
Daylight in the Harem (Lucknow, 1911), New York, 1912.
Conferences of Christian Workers Among Muslims, 1924, New York, 1924.

Report of the Commission on Christian Higher Education in India: An Enquiry into the Place of the Christian College in Modern India (Lindsay: chairman), London, 1931.

Report of the Consultation on The Healing Ministry in the Mission of the Church, Tubingen, May 19-25, 1964, Geneva, 1964.

Report of the Near East Christian Council Inquiry on the Evangelization of Moslems (H. H. Riggs, chairman), Beirut, 1938.

Re-Thinking Missions. A Laymen's Inquiry After One Hundred Years (By the Commission of Appraisal, W.E. Hocking, chairman), New York, 1932.

Re-Thinking Our Role as a College: Report of a Joint Consultation of the Christian Institute for the Study of Religion and Society and the Madras Christian College, Madras, 1964.

Richter, Julius, _A History of Protestant Missions in the Near East_, Edinburgh, 1910.

_____, _Indische Missionsgeschichte_, Gütersloh, 1924 (trans. S. H. Moore, London, n.d.).

_____, "The World-Wide Mission of Christianity," _M.W._, 2 (1912), 263-276.

_____, "The Missionary Crisis," _I.R.M._, 22 (1933), 313-324.

_____, "A Protestant View of Moslem Missions," _M.W._, 29 (1939), 114-119.

Riggs, H.H., "The Missionary Situation in Turkey," _I.R.M._, 27 (1938), 195-

200.

_____, "Shall We Try Unbeaten Paths in Working for Moslems?" M.W., 31 (1941), 116-126.

Robson, James, Christ in Islam, London, 1929.

_____, Ion Keith-Falconer in Arabia, London, n.d.

Ross, F.A., et al., The Near East and American Philanthropy, New York, 1929.

Rouse, R., The World's Student Christian Federation, London, 1948.

_____, and Neill, S. C. (editors), A History of the Ecumenical Movement, 1517-1948, London, 1954.

Rycroft, W. S., The Ecumenical Witness of the United Presbyterian Church, New York, 1966.

_____, and Clemmer, M. M., A Factual Study of the Middle East, New York, 1962.

Sadiq, E., "Man in Society According to Islam in the Light of Christianity," Bulletin of the Henry Martyn School of Islamic Studies, 1961, 36-48.

Sadiq, John W., "Plea for a Fresh Apprach to Muslims," National Christian Council Review (India), May, 1948, 213-219.

Sargent, John, Memoir of the Rev. Henry Martyn, London, 1819.

Scherer, G. H., Mediterranean Missions, 1808-1870, Beirut, n.d.

Schlatter, W., Geschichte der Basler Mission, 1815-1915, 3 vols, Basel, 1916.

Schlette, H. R., Towards a Theology of Religions (English Trans.), Freiburg, 1966.

Schuon, F., Understanding Islam (trans. D.M. Matheson), London, 1963.

Schweitzer, Albert, Christianity and the Religions of the World (trans. J. Powers), London, 1923.

Sell, Edward, The Faith of Islam, London, 1896.

_____, The Life of Muhammad, London, 1913.

Sharpe, E.J., Not to Destroy, but to Fulfill. The Contribution of J. N. Farquhar to Protestant Missionary Thought in India before 1914, Uppsala, 1965.

Shaw, P. E., American Contacts with Eastern Churches, 1820-1870, Chicago, 1937.

Shedd, Wm., Islam and the Oriental Churches, their Historical Relations, New York, 1908.

Sinker, Robert, Memorials of the Hon. Ion Keith-Falconer, London, 1888.

Smith, Eli and Dwight, H.G.P., Missionary Researches in Armenia, London, 1834.

Smith, I., To Islam I Go. Temple Gairdner of Cairo, London, 1939.

Smith George, The Life of John Wilson, London, 1878.

_____, The Life of Alexander Duff, London, 1879.

_____, Stephen Hislop, Pioneer Missionary and Naturalist in Central India from 1844 to 1863, London, 1889.

_____, Henry Martyn, New York, 1891.

Smith, M., Studies in Early Mysticism, London, 1931.

Smith, W, C., Modern Islam in India. A Social Analysis, London, 1946.

_____, Islam in Modern History, Princeton, 1957.

_____, "Comparative Religion: Whither--and Why?" in The History of Religions. Essays in Methodology (ed. M. Eliade and J.M. Kitagawa),

_____, The Meaning and End of Religion. A New Approach to the Religious Traditions of Mankind, New York, 1963.

Southern, R. W., Western Views of Islam in the Middle Ages, Cambridge, Mass., 1962.

Speer, Robert E., Missions and Politics in Asia, New York, 1897.

_____, Presbyterian Foreign Missions, Philadelphia, 1902.

_____, Missionary Principles and Practice: A Discussion of Christian
    Missions and Some Criticism upon Them, New York, 1902.
_____, Missions and Modern History, 2 vols., New York, 1904.
_____, Christianity and the Nations (Duff Lectures), New York, 1910.
_____, and Carter, R., Report on India and Persia, New York, 1922.
_____, "Re-Thinking Missions" Examined, New York, 1933.
_____, The Finality of Jesus Christ (Stone Lectures), Princeton, 1933.
Speight, R. Marston, "Some Bases for a Christian Apologetic to Islam,"
    I.R.M., 54 (1965), 193-205.
Spencer, H., Islam and the Gospel of God: A Comparison, Madras, 1956.
Stade, Robert, Ninety-Nine Names of God, Ibadan, 1970.
Stanton, H. U. Weitbrecht, The Teaching of the Qur'an, London, 1969.
Stewart, John, Nestorian Missionary Enterprise: A Church on Fire,
    Edinburgh, 1928.
Stobart, J.W.H., Islam and Its Founder, (S.P.C.K.) London, 1876.
Stock, Eugene, An Heroic Bishop, the Life-Story of French of Lahore,
    London, 1913.
_____, The History of the Church Missionary Society, 4 vols., London,
    1899-1916.
Storm, W.H., Wither Arabia? A Survey of Missionary Opportunity, London,
    1938.
Strong, E. B. and Warnshuis, A. L. (editors), Directory of Foreign
    Missions, New York, 1933.
Strong, Wm., The Story of the American Board, Boston, 1910.
The Student Volunteer Movement After Twenty-Five Years, 1886-1911, New
    York, 1912.
Sundkler, Bengt, The World of Mission, London, 1965.
Sweetman, J. Windrow, Islam and Christian Theology: A Study of the Inter-
    pretation of Theological Ideas in the Two Religions, Part I, 2 vols.,
    London, 1945-47.
Tabawi, A.L., British Interests in Palestine, 1800-1901: A Study of
    Religious and Educational Enterprise, London, 1861.
Takle, John, The Faith of the Crescent, Calcutta, 1913.
Tatlow, T., The Story of the Student Christian Movement of Great Britain
    and Ireland, London, 1933.
Taylor, H.F.L., In the Land of the Five Rivers: A Sketch of the Work of
    the Church of Scotland in the Punjab, Edinburgh, 1906.
Thayer, P.W. (ed.), Tensions in the Middle East (intro. by C. Malik)
    Baltimore, 1958.
Thoburn, James M., The Christian Conquest of India, New York, 1906.
Thomas, M.M., The Christian Response to Asian Revolution, London, 1966.
Thornton, D., "Eastern and Western Education in Cairo," E.W., July, 1906,
    278ff.
Tillich, Paul, Christianity and the Encounter of the World Religions,
    London, 1963.
Tisdall, W.St. Clair, The Religion of the Crescent or Islam: Its Origin,
    Its Influence (James Long Lectures, 1891-92), London,1895.
_____, India, Its History, Darkness and Dawn, London, 1901.
_____, The Sources of Islam (trans. Wm. Muir), Edinburgh, 1901.
_____, A Manual of the Leading Muhammadan Objections to Christianity,
    London, 1904.
Titus, Murray T., Indian Islam, London, 1930.
_____, The Young Moslem Looks at Life, New York, 1937.
_____, "Islam and the Kingdom of God" in Macdonald Presentation Volume,
    Princeton, 1933.
_____, "To My Muslim Friends," M.W., 41 (1951), 233ff.
Torrey, C. C., The Jewish Foundation of Islam, New York, 1933.

Toynbee, Arnold J., An Historian's Approach to Religion (based on the
    Gifford Lectures, 1952-1953), London, 1956.
_____, Christianity Among the Religions of the World, London, 1958.
Tracy, Joseph, History of the A.B.C.F.M., New York, 1842.
Trimingham, John Spencer, The Christian Approach to Islam in the Sudan,
    London, 1948.
_____, The Christian Church and Islam in West Africa, London, 1950.
_____, The Christian Church and Missions in Ethiopia, London, 1950.
_____, Islam in East Africa, Oxford, 1964.
Tritton, A.S., The Caliphs and their Non-Moslem Subjects, Oxford, 1930.
_____,Muslim Theology, London, 1947.
_____, Islam: Belief and Practices, London, 1957.
Tyler, M. W., The European Powers and the Near East, 1875-1908, Minnea-
    polis, 1925.
Udy, James S., Attitudes within the Protestant Churches of the Occident
    Towards the Propagation of Christianity in the Orient--An Historical
    Survey up to 1914 (doctoral dissertation, Boston University), Boston,
    1952.
Van den Berg, Johannes, Constrained by Jesus' Love, An Inquiry into the
    Motives of the Missionary Awakening in Great Britain in the Period
    Between 1698 and 1815, Kampen, 1956.
_____, "Calvin's Missionary Message: Some Remarks about the Relation
    between Calvinsim and Missions," Evangelical Quarterly, 22 (1950),
    174-187.
Van der Leeuw, Gerardus, Religion in Essence and Manifestation. A Study
    in Phenomenology, (trans. by J. E. Turner),London, 1938.
Van Ess, Dorothy, History of the Arabian Mission, 1926-1957, (mimeographed
    New York, n.d.
Van Ess, John, Meet the Arab, New York, 1943.
Van Leeuwen, Arend Th., Christianity in World History: the Meeting of the
    Faiths of East and West (trans. H.H. Hoskens), London, 1964.
Vaughn, James, The Trident, the Crescent and the Cross...Religious History
    of India, London, 1876.
Vine, A. R., The Nestorian Churches; A Concise History of Nestorian
    Christianity in Asia, London, 1937.
Visser't Hooft, W.A., No Other Name, Philadelphia, 1963.
Voillaume, R., Seeds of the Desert: The Legacy of Charles de Foucauld,
    London, 1955.
Von Grunebaum, Gustave E., Medieval Islam, Chicago, 1946.
_____ (ed.), Unity and Variety in Muslim Civilization, Chicago, 1955.
_____, Islam: Essays in the Nature and Growth of a Cultural Tradition, New
    York, 1961.
Wanless, Wm., An American Doctor at Work in India, New York, 1932.
Warneck, Gustav, Outline of a History of Protestant Missions (ed. George
    Robson), Edinburgh, 1901.
Warren, Max, The Christian Mission, London, 1951.
_____, The Missionary Movement from Britain in Modern History, London,
    1965.
Watson, Andrew, The American Mission in Egypt, 1854-1896, Pittsburgh,1898.
_____, "Our Only Gospel," M.W., 4 (1914), 69-72.
Watson, Charles R., Egypt and the Christian Crusade, Philadelphia, 1907.
_____, In the Valley of the Nile, A Survey of the Missionary Movement in
    Egypt, New York, 1908.
_____, What is This Moslem World, London, 1937.
_____, "Re-thinking Missions," I.R.M., 21 (1932), 106-118.
Watt, W. Montgomery, Free Will and Predestination in Early Islam, London,
    1948.

_____, Muhammad at Mecca, Oxford, 1953.
_____, The Faith and Practice of Al-Ghazali, London, 1953.
_____, Muhammad at Medina, Oxford, 1956.
_____, The Reality of God, London, 1957.
_____, The Cure for Human Troubles: A Statement of the Christian Message
   in Modern Terms, London, 1959.
_____, Islam and the Integration of Society, London, 9161.
_____, Islamic Philosophy and Theology, Edinburgh, 1962.
_____, Muslim Intellectual: A Study of Al-Ghazali, Edinburgh, 1963.
_____, Truth in the Religions: A Sociological and Psychological Approach,
   Edinburgh, 1963.
_____, "Islamic Theology and the Christian Theologian," Hibbert Journal,
   49 (1950-51), 242-248.
Weber, H.R., The Communication of the Gospel to Illiterates, London, 1957.
Webster, Douglas, The Continuing Missionary Task, London, 1962.
_____, Survey of the Training of the Ministry in the Middle East, Geneva,
   1962.
_____, Yes to Mission, London, 1966.
Weigall, Arthur, A History of Events in Egypt from 1798-1914, New York,
   1915.
Wheeler, John P., The Theological Justification of the Great Missionary
   Awakening of the Late Eighteenth Century with Special Reference to
   William Carey, (unpublished dissertation, New College) Edinburgh, 1959.
Wheeler, Wm. R., The Crisis Decade: A History of the Foreign Missionary
   Work of the Presbyterian Church in the U.S.A., 1937-1947, New York,
   1951.
_____, A Man Sent from God. The Biography of R.E. Speer, New York, 1956.
Weir, R. W., A History of Foreign Missions of the Church of Scotland,
   Edinburgh, 1900.
West, C.C. and Paton, D.M. (editors), Missionary Church in East and West,
   London, 1959.
Wherry, E. M., The Muslim Controversy, London, 1905.
_____, Islam and Christianity in India and the Far East, London, 1907.
_____, Our Missions in India, 1834-1924, Boston, 1926.
White, Wilbur W., The Process of Change in the Ottoman Empire, Chicago,
   1937.
Wilcox, F. E., "Brief Resume of the Origins of Missions to Muslims in the
   Northwest Frontier Province (Pakistan), M.W., 42 (1952), 97-103.
Wilder, R.G., Mission Schools in India of the A.B.C.F.M., New York, 1861.
Wilkinson, M., Sketches of Christianity in North India, London, 1844.
Wilson, John, Narrative of a Missionary Journey in Gujerat and Cutch,
   Bombay, 1838.
_____, The Evangelization of India, Edinburgh, 1849.
Wilson, J. Christy, The Christian Message to Islam, New York, 1950.
_____, Apostle to Islam: A Biography of Samuel M. Zwemer, Grand Rapids,
   1952.
Wilson, Samuel G., Persian Life and Custom, New York, 1895.
_____, Persia: Western Mission, Edinburgh, 1896.
_____, Modern Movements Among Moslems, New York, n.d.
Wolff, Joseph, Researches and Missionary Labours Among Jews, Mohammedans,
   and other Sects, London, 1835.
Wood, Alfred C., A History of the Levant Company, London, 1935.
Wortabet, John, Religion in the East, Beirut, 1860.
Wysham, Wm. N., "The Basic Hope for Religious Freedom in the World of
   Islam," M.W., 39 (1949), 91-96.
Youngson, John F.W., Forty Years of the Panjab Mission of the Church of
   Scotland, 1855-1895, Edinburgh, 1896.

Zaehner, R.C., _At Sundry Times: An Essay in the Comparison of Religions_,
    London, 1958.
_____, _The Convergent Spirit: Towards a Dialectics of Religion_, London,
    1963.
Zwemer, Samuel M., For a full bibliography, see Appendix K.

About the Author

Dr. Lyle Vander Werff is presently Professor of Religion at Northwestern College, Orange City, Iowa (51041). He first encountered the Muslim world while serving as a missionary with the Arabian Mission in Kuwait. The need for historical perspective on Christian-Muslim relations and for a workable pattern for fulfilling the Great Commission prompted studies in Islamics with Dr. Kenneth Cragg at Jerusalem, and later a doctoral program at New College (theology and mission) and the William Muir Institute (Islamics) at the University of Edinburgh. This volume represents research completed under the direction of professors W.M. Watt and A.C. Cheyne.

In addition to teaching world religions and Christian mission at Northwestern College, Dr. Vander Werff served as a visiting professor at Western Theological Seminary in Holland, Michigan, and at the United Theological College (Church of South India), Bangalore, South India, during 1974-75. A minister of the Reformed Church in America, he serves with the Theological Commission of that body and continues to research and write in the field of Christian mission.

BOOKS BY THE
WILLIAM CAREY LIBRARY

GENERAL

American Missions in Bicentennial Perspective edited by R. Pierce Beaver, $8.95 paper, 448 pp.

The Birth of Missions in America by Charles L. Chaney, $7.95 paper, 352 pp.

Education of Missionaries' Children: The Neglected Dimension of World Mission by D. Bruce Lockerbie, $1.95 paper, 76 pp.

The Holdeman People: The Church in Christ, Mennonite, 1859-1969 by Clarence Hiebert, $7.95 cloth, 688 pp.

On the Move with the Master: A Daily Devotional Guide on World Mission by Duain W. Vierow, $4.95 paper, 176 pp.

Social Action vs. Evangelism: An Essay on the Contemporary Crisis by William J. Richardson, $1.95x paper, 64 pp.

STRATEGY OF MISSION

Church Growth and Christian Mission by Donald A. McGavran, $4.95x paper, 256 pp.

Church Growth and Group Conversion by Donald A. McGavran et al., $2.45 paper, 128 pp.

Committed Communities: Fresh Streams for World Missions by Charles J. Mellis, $3.95 paper, 160 pp.

The Conciliar-Evangelical Debate: The Crucial Documents, 1964-1976 edited by Donald McGavran, $8.95 paper, 400 pp.

Crucial Dimensions in World Evangelization edited by Arthur F. Glasser et al., $7.95x paper, 480 pp.

Evangelical Missions Tomorrow edited by Wade T. Coggins and Edwin L. Frizen, Jr., $5.95 paper, 208 pp.

Everything You Need to Grow a Messianic Synagogue by Phillip E. Goble, $2.45 paper, 176 pp.

Here's How: Health Education by Extension by Ronald and Edith Seaton, $3.45 paper, 144 pp.

A Manual for Church Growth Surveys by Ebbie C. Smith, $3.95 paper, 144 pp.

Readings in Third World Missions: A Collection of Essential Documents edited by Marlin L. Nelson, $6.95x paper, 304 pp.

AREA AND CASE STUDIES

Aspects of Pacific Ethnohistory by Alan R. Tippett, $3.95 paper, 216 pp.

A Century of Growth: The Kachin Baptist Church of Burma by Herman Tegenfeldt, $9.95 cloth, 540 pp.

Church Growth in Burundi by Donald Hohensee, $4.95 paper, 160 pp.

Church Growth in Japan by Tetsunao Yamamori, $4.95 paper, 184 pp.

Church Planting in Uganda: A Comparative Study by Gailyn Van Rheenen, $4.95 paper, 192 pp.

Circle of Harmony: A Case Study in Popular Japanese Buddhism by Kenneth J. Dale, $4.95 paper, 238 pp.

The Deep-Sea Canoe: The Story of Third World Missionaries in the South Pacific by Alan R. Tippett, $3.45x paper, 144 pp.

Frontier Peoples of Central Nigeria and a Strategy for Outreach by Gerald O. Swank, $5.95 paper, 192 pp.

The Growth Crisis in the American Church: A Presbyterian Case Study by Foster H. Shannon, $4.95 paper, 176 pp.

The How and Why of Third World Missions: An Asian Case Study by Marlin L. Nelson, $6.95 paper, 256 pp.

I Will Build My Church: Ten Case Studies of Church Growth in Taiwan edited by Allen J. Swanson, $4.95 paper, 177 pp.

Indonesian Revival: Why Two Million Came to Christ by Avery T. Willis, Jr., $6.95 paper, 288 pp.

People Movements in the Punjab by Margaret and Frederick Stock, $8.95 paper, 388 pp.

Profile for Victory: New Proposals for Missions in Zambia by Max Ward Randall, $3.95 cloth, 224 pp.

The Protestant Movement in Bolivia by C. Peter Wagner, $3.95 paper, 264 pp.

Protestants in Modern Spain: The Struggle for Religious Pluralism by Dale G. Vought, $3.45 paper, 168 pp.

The Religious Dimension in Hispanic Los Angeles by Clifton L. Holland, $9.95 paper, 550 pp.

The Role of the Faith Mission: A Brazilian Case Study by Fred Edwards, $3.45 paper, 176 pp.

La Serpiente y la Paloma (La Iglesia Apostolica de la Fe en Jesuchristo de Mexico) by Manual J. Gaxiola, $2.95 paper, 194 pp.

Solomon Islands Christianity: A Study in Growth and Obstruction by Alan R. Tippett, $5.95x paper, 432 pp.

Taiwan: Mainline Versus Independent Church Growth by Allen J. Swanson, $3.95 paper, 300 pp.

Tonga Christianity by Stanford Shewmaker, $3.45 paper, 164 pp.

Toward Continuous Mission: Strategizing for the Evangelization of Bolivia by W. Douglas Smith, $4.95 paper, 208 pp.

Treasure Island: Church Growth Among Taiwan's Urban Minnan Chinese by Robert J. Bolton, $6.95 paper, 416 pp.

Understanding Latin Americans by Eugene A. Nida, $3.95 paper, 176 pp.

A Yankee Reformer in Chile: The Life and Works of David Trumbull by Irven Paul, $3.95 paper, 172 pp.

THEOLOGICAL EDUCATION BY EXTENSION

Principios del Crecimiento de la Iglesia by Wayne C. Weld and Donald A. McGavran, $3.95 paper, 448 pp.

Principles of Church Growth by Wayne C. Weld and Donald A. McGavran, $4.95x paper, 400 pp.

The World Directory of Theological Education by Extension by Wayne C. Weld, $5.95x paper, 416 pp., *1976 Supplement only*, $1.95x, 64 pp.

Writing for Theological Education by Extension by Lois McKinney, $1.45x paper, 64 pp.

APPLIED ANTHROPOLOGY

Becoming Bilingual: A Guide to Language Learning by Donald Larson and William A. Smalley, $5.95x paper, 426 pp.

Christopaganism or Indigenous Christianity? edited by Tetsunao Yamamori and Charles R. Taber, $5.95 paper, 242 pp.

The Church and Cultures: Applied Anthropology for the Religious Worker by Louis J. Luzbetak, $5.95x paper, 448 pp.

Culture and Human Values: Christian Intervention in Anthropological Perspective (writings of Jacob Loewen) edited by William A. Smalley, $5.95x paper, 466 pp.

Customs and Cultures: Anthropology for Christian Missions by Eugene A. Nida, $3.95 paper, 322 pp.

Manual of Articulatory Phonetics by William A. Smalley, $5.95x paper, 522 pp.

Message and Mission: The Communication of the Christian Faith by Eugene A. Nida, $3.95x paper, 254 pp.

Readings in Missionary Anthropology edited by William A. Smalley, $5.95x paper, 384 pp.

Tips on Taping: Language Recording in the Social Sciences by Wayne and Lonna Dickerson, $4.95x paper, 208 pp.

POPULARIZING MISSION

Defeat of the Bird God by C. Peter Wagner, $4.95 paper, 256 pp.

The Night Cometh: Two Wealthy Evangelicals Face the Nation by Rebecca J. Winter, $2.95 paper, 96 pp.

The Task Before Us (audiovisual) by the Navigators, $29.95, 137 slides

The 25 Unbelievable Years: 1945-1969 by Ralph D. Winter, $2.95 paper, 128 pp.

The Word-Carrying Giant: The Growth of the American Bible Society by Creighton Lacy, $5.95 paper, 320 pp.

World Handbook for the World Christian by Patrick J. St. G. Johnstone, $4.95 paper, 224 pp.

REFERENCE

An American Directory of Schools and Colleges Offering Missionary Courses edited by Glenn Schwartz, $5.95x paper, 266 pp.

Bibliography for Cross-Cultural Workers, edited by Alan R. Tippett, $4.95 paper, 256 pp.

Church Growth Bulletin, Second Consolidated Volume (Sept. 1969-July 1975) edited by Donald McGavran, $7.95x paper, 512 pp.

Evangelical Missions Quarterly Vols. 7-9, $8.95x cloth, 330 pp.

The Means of World Evangelization: Missiological Education at the Fuller School of World Mission edited by Alvin Martin, $9.95 paper, 544 pp.

Protestantism in Latin America: A Bibliographical Guide edited by John H. Sinclair, $8.95x paper, 448 pp.

The World Directory of Mission-Related Educational Institutions edited by Ted Ward and Raymond Buker, Sr., $19.95x cloth, 906 pp.